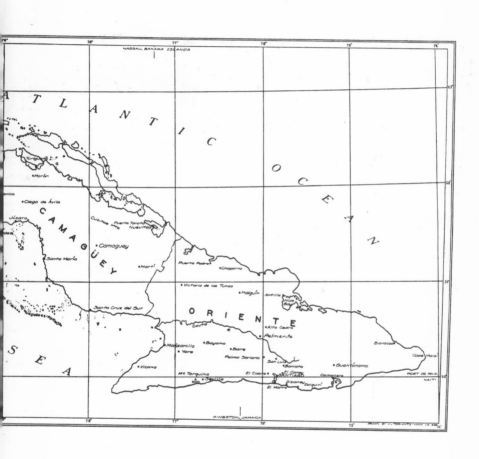

DATE DUE

OCT 0 7 2002		
NOV 1 8 2002		

#47-0108 Peel Off Pressure Sensitive

A HISTORY OF
THE CUBAN REPUBLIC

A STUDY IN HISPANIC
AMERICAN POLITICS

A HISTORY OF
THE CUBAN REPUBLIC

A Study in

HISPANIC AMERICAN POLITICS

BY

CHARLES E. CHAPMAN

1969

OCTAGON BOOKS

New York

Reprinted 1969
by special arrangement with The Macmillan Company

OCTAGON BOOKS
A DIVISION OF FARRAR, STRAUS & GIROUX, INC.
19 Union Square West
New York, N. Y. 10003

LIBRARY OF CONGRESS CATALOG CARD NUMBER: 75-96177

Printed in U.S.A. by
NOBLE OFFSET PRINTERS, INC.
NEW YORK 3, N. Y.

PREFACE

WHEN asked to write a one-volume history of Sicily the historian Freeman is said to have replied that he would do so provided he might first bring out a four-volume work, which he did. The writer could have wished that he might have engaged upon a similar detailed study of Cuban history before attempting the single volume presented here, for, brief as is the period covered by this survey, the amount of material available is beyond the capacity of any one individual to absorb quickly, and aids in monographic studies are all but entirely lacking. Each chapter might well have been written out to the extent of a volume, and then the task of synthesis into the shorter work would have been simple and sure. All things are relative, however, and three years of this writer's time were as much as he could spare. So he prepared his condensations as he went along, and offers his twenty-seven volumes in one at the first publication.

The task was not so hard as it might otherwise have been, because the student of Hispanic America "recognizes" Cuban history. The conclusion is soon irresistible that here is Hispanic America as one may have met with it in Argentina, Brazil, Chile, Mexico, Perú, or Venezuela,—each one different from the rest, but all possessing the underlying similarity of Hispanic traditions. That accounts for the sub-title of this volume, for in studying Cuban politics one finds the politics of all the countries to the south. One may never have set foot in Cuba, but if he has lived in Colombia, Costa Rica, Honduras, or elsewhere below the Rio Grande, the story will come home to him like an experience of his own. There might almost, indeed, be another sub-title, which could read: "A study in United States diplomacy." Here, certainly, there is something more than the Spanish War and the Platt Amendment. The man who is acquainted with the Caribbean world will meet with much that he has encountered already in the Dominican Republic, Haiti, Nicaragua, Panamá, or even Mexico.

This work aims to tell the whole truth, instead of a mere fraction. And admittedly, since this is a *political* history, the "whole truth" often may be disagreeable to those who would avoid straight speaking. For politics is one of the least amiable phases of the Hispanic heritage. It was bad enough in Cuba under Spain. One may well raise the question whether it has not been yet worse under the republic. A patriotic Cuban asked that question of himself in the presence of the writer, and answered sadly in the affirmative, for taxes are far higher now, with less service rendered,— almost to the point of no service at all. To be sure, there is plenty to criticize in the politics of all countries, but there are degrees of difference. It is doubtful if the most notorious political rings in the United States, for example, whether in national, state, or municipal affairs, have gone as far in bad practices as the usual government in Cuba, and certainly none of the presidential administrations in the north can even closely approximate the evils that developed in the rule of three out of the first four Cuban executives.

There are many who regard Hispanic character as hopeless, at least from the standpoint of government, and none more readily assert this than Hispanic Americans themselves. They feel that they are the victims of their inheritance. Foreigners may reach the same conclusion, to the accompaniment of unfavorable comparisons with other peoples. This writer admits the problem, but not the conclusion. There *is* a handicap of evil political traditions that the Cuban, like other Hispanic Americans, is obliged to overcome. There is the further handicap of a lack of political training. Cuba has had but the experience of a single generation in government. How does that compare with the centuries of practice in the background of Anglo-American life? Certainly there is an excuse for political evils, but is there anything which gives promise of something better? Most assuredly! Argentina, Chile, and Uruguay have their imperfections, but one cannot study their history without realizing that they have made remarkable political progress over a century of independence. People of Spanish blood have gone to non-Hispanic countries, and their children have grown up with the sterling qualities of the land of their adoption in equal degree with those who were descended from the native-born. The point is important, for it is a refutation of any notion that the Hispanic heritage on its evil side is changeless.

Cuba, far from being hopeless politically, is somewhat more promising than most of the republics of Hispanic America. To begin with, she is free from handicaps that hold many of the others back,—a disagreeable climate, difficulties of communication, distance from the best markets, or lack of wealth to apply to her social, political, economic, or intellectual needs. Furthermore, there is no such serious racial problem as some of the Hispanic American republics suffer from, no exaggerated militarism, and no unbearably overdeveloped individualism. Not to go into more detail, it may confidently be asserted that Cuba already has the elements within her own body politic that could make government attain to the level of decency that most other factors in Cuban life have already reached. Indeed, encouraging reports have come to hand that give reason to hope that the

initial steps may already have been taken since the inauguration of General Gerardo Machado as President on May 20,
1925. The administration of an honest and able President
must be the preliminary to a development of political rectitude. If Machado is such a man he may indeed fail, but,
even though failing, render a service to Cuba and make his
own name the greatest in the history of the republic. One
good President, however, is merely a detail in all that must
be accomplished. The people themselves must be trans-
formed, and bad traditions banished. This is possible, but
it takes years to accomplish it. At present there is no foundation in social unity to ensure the maintenance of respectable self-government. The Cubans will fight for their
country and die for it in a national emergency, but at other
times the bonds of family and self-interest surpass those of
the loyalties due the state.

This matter very deeply concerns the people of the United
States. The relations of this country with Cuba are possibly
more important than those with any other Hispanic American republic, not even excepting Mexico. Cuba far outranks
the others in the value of United States investment and
trade. Strategically, Cuba is the key to the United States
and to the greater part of the Western Hemisphere. These
things aside, however, the United States under the Platt
Amendment and Permanent Treaty has a special duty and
obligation toward Cuba. If affairs are not going satisfactorily there, it is at least open to question whether this
country is not in a measure to blame. From many stand-
points, therefore, the people of the United States cannot
afford to be ignorant of Cuban history.

The public has a right to know an author's relation to
his volume. In Shaw's *Fannie's first play,* one of the dra-
matic critics refused to express an opinion until he knew who

wrote the play, remarking that if it had a good author it was a good play, and if a poor author it was a poor one. Whatever the judgment may be about the present writer he has at least had an experience that should have given him a chance to learn something of Hispanic life in general and Cuba in particular. For eighteen years he has devoted himself continuously to Hispanic and Hispanic American history. During this time he lived nearly two years in Spain, a year in Chile, spent another six months in South America, and made a number of shorter trips which have enabled him to visit every country of Hispanic America except Paraguay. In 1916 and 1920 he made brief visits to Cuba. In 1924 he was there on two different occasions for a total of nearly half a year, gathering material for this volume and traveling through the island. The writer is not conscious of any bias, except such as may be imputed to him as an American. This, however, should have scant weight, as he is firmly convinced that what is best for Cuba is also best for the United States in the relations between the two countries. The idea of writing the volume developed from the importance of the subject, which seemed for the moment to be heightened by the conduct of the Zayas government during the somewhat hectic days of 1923. The writer believes that he is rendering Cuba a service by speaking out frankly, as a Cuban himself would. By so doing he hopes to contribute to an aroused public opinion that may in the future make the evils he describes impossible. If he hits hard, it is not because of malice, and if he has made mistakes, he sincerely regrets them.

When the writer began this volume he hoped to avoid the nuisance of excessive footnoting, which some regard as the hallmark of scholarship. Reasonably ample bibliographical notes appear at the end of most chapters, and the subject as a whole is discussed, the writer hopes adequately, in his

"Essay on authorities." It proved impossible, however, in a field so lacking in monographs to avoid making a number of citations within the chapters, although the amount of this type of *impedimenta* is cut down to moderate proportions. As matters are, the scholar will have no difficulty in finding his way, and the general public will not be annoyed.

The writer of this volume is solely responsible for the matter it contains. Nobody else is accountable for it in whole or in part, except as statements are attributed to different individuals through the medium of footnote citations or quoted paragraphs. A debt of gratitude is due, however, to a great many persons for help, but especially to Francisco de Paulo Coronado and Carlos Trelles, heads respectively of the National Library and the Library of the House of Representatives, both in Havana. These men and the members of their staffs very generously furnished the writer with every facility for carrying on his investigations. All students of Cuban history owe a great deal to Trelles, in particular, because of his important bibliographical work, without which this writer could not have finished his task.

CHARLES E. CHAPMAN

June 3, 1926.

CONTENTS

MAP

A HISTORY OF
THE CUBAN REPUBLIC

A STUDY IN HISPANIC
AMERICAN POLITICS

A
HISTORY OF THE CUBAN REPUBLIC

CHAPTER I

THE PEARL OF THE ANTILLES

JUST off the coast of Florida, about a hundred miles from Key West, lies the island republic of Cuba, the "Pearl of the Antilles." Reasons without number have combined to make this an attractive spot, but to the people of the United States the course of affairs in Cuba has come to possess an especially vital interest. The very nearness of this island to the Atlantic shores of the northern republic has been an important factor in the relations of the two countries. Cuba controls the Caribbean Sea, and so commands not only the approaches to Panamá but also a great part of the two American continents. In consequence a very close and peculiar political connection between the United States and Cuba has developed. Cuba has a guarantee of American protection, but must keep her house in order or be liable to an intervention of the United States. The possibility of such an intervention has in recent years been brought unpleasantly to the fore by political happenings in the island republic. There are many angles other than the political that attract the attention of Americans. Cuba is extraordinarily rich, the real "gold mine" of Hispanic America, though the "gold" comes indirectly through agriculture and commerce. American investment and trade in Cuba are phenomenal in amount, while other countries share in Cuban economic activities in only

1

a somewhat lesser degree. Socially, too, Americans and Cubans mingle more freely than most other peoples of different lands. Thousands of tourists from the United States enjoy the delights of Cuba in the winter, and in the summer there are other thousands of Cubans who visit the United States. Young men and young women of Cuba frequently enroll in American schools. In fine, the relations of the two countries are about as close as they can be without having the same flag. It is probable that there are many regions within American political boundaries that do not have such an intimate connection with the country of which they form a part as does the rich Caribbean isle.

Cuba is long and narrow, seven hundred and sixty miles in length from east to west, and some twenty-five to a hundred and twenty-five miles in width, with an area about the same as that of Pennsylvania. Short stretches of water separate it from Florida to the northwest and Haiti to the east, and through these passes the greater part of the traffic of the Caribbean Sea. Most of the island is comparatively level, but there are some mountains in the province of Pinar del Río in the extreme west, and the easternmost province, Oriente, is quite rugged in parts. The other four provinces are not so completely flattened out as popularly supposed. Mount Tarquino on the southern coast, not far from Santiago (the capital of Oriente), rises sheer up from the sea to an altitude of some eight thousand four hundred feet. Not only is Cuba the "Pearl of the Antilles," but it is also the "Isle of a Hundred Harbors." There are over thirteen hundred long islets, or "keys," off shore, and these form a bulwark for the numerous mainland ports along the two thousand miles of coast. Nature has been unusually kind to this tropical isle. It has a remarkable wealth in fruits, flowers, plants, and trees. On the other hand, animal life is limited. There are a great number and variety of birds, and plenty of serpents and insects. The island derives its principal wealth from the fertility of the soil. Cuba is by far the greatest sugar-producing country in the world, and most of the sugar consumed in the United States comes from Cuba. Tobacco is also an important crop, and Cuban tobacco is usually reputed to be the best in the world. Delicious fruits, though less important as an item of export, are raised in considerable quantities for local consumption.

An idea has developed outside of Cuba that the climate is good only from January to the end of March. But in point of fact, though south of the Tropic of Cancer, Cuba can hardly be said to have a tropical climate at all. The temperature in the eastern states of the United States is often higher than that of Cuba. The highest ever recorded at Havana was 98°, in August 1899, and the lowest was 47° in January 1901. The normal extremes in that city are from 60° to 92°, and the average temperature in the four hot months, June to September, is about 80°. The climate of the island as a whole has been described as "remarkably moderate and uniform, due to the influence of the prevailing winds, the equalizing effect of the surrounding ocean, and to the fact that the long axis of the island extends east and west." The ocean breezes as a rule are indeed quite moderate, but in the fall of the year there is sometimes a moment of anxiety over the possible danger from cyclones in the Caribbean. Cuba has a dry season from December to April, and rains from May to November. Despite a rainfall of from fifty to sixty inches a year, the island is often troubled from a scarcity of water, as it runs too quickly into the sea. But the engineering problems involved in overcoming this situation are by no means insuperable. Cuban health records make an even better showing than the climate. On the basis of the death rate, Cuba has ranked as high as second in the world, with a little over twelve deaths to the thousand. Australia alone has had a better mark. The normal rate in the United States is over fifteen. Cuba's standing in this particular is a recent development. Prior to the twentieth century the death rate was very high, due primarily to the ravages of yellow fever and malaria, but these diseases were stamped out during the American occupation of the island from 1898 to 1902. There has been some falling off in recent years from normal healthfulness, because of governmental laxity in matters of sanitation, but it would seem that the patient is too strong to be very seriously affected.

The population of the island, over three millions, is far greater in proportion to area than that of most Hispanic American republics. And yet it is remarkably lacking in density when one considers Cuba's extraordinary wealth. It is about sixty-five to the square mile. England has a rate approximately six times as much, and Belgium about nine times. The normal development of the republic, with a growing economic variety, should eventually permit of a much greater population,—possibly as many as fifteen millions. There are many negroes in Cuba, but fewer than is usually supposed by foreigners. It is said that less than thirty per cent are colored. There may be some "optimism" in this estimate, but it cannot be far from the truth. At any rate, the white population is gaining rapidly through immigration, for Cuba is one of the most favored lands among European peoples, especially Spaniards, who are in search of New World homes. Climate and economic productivity are not the only attractions Cuba has for the foreign visitor or home-seeker. It is a country with a highly developed civilization. The island is extraordinarily well equipped with railways built by private capital. Ordinary roads, however, due to the unsatisfactory workings of government, lag unnecessarily far behind, though much more numerous than in most other Hispanic American republics. There are hospitals and schools and the other accompaniments of up-to-date, modern life, although the political handicap is too often manifest. But government, the one weakness in Cuban armor, comes into the life of the average individual in a comparatively small degree. So life in Cuba, on the whole, offers a wide range of opportunity and delight.

The capital and largest city of the republic is Havana, with a population of 363,506, according to the latest census, that of 1919. Next in order are Santiago with 62,083, Camagüey, 41,909, Matanzas, 41,574, and Cienfuegos, 37,241. Eighteen other cities have populations of from ten to thirty thousand. Havana has an importance even out of proportion to its size, for, as in most Latin countries, the capital tends to absorb all currents of life in the land as a whole.[1] That too is almost the only city which tourists ever know. Thousands gather there in the winter to enjoy a warm clime and the exotic flavor of Cuban life. Though Havana is on a site that is very nearly level to the eye, it has an attractive approach from the sea. Some of the finest buildings and streets in the city are along the waterfront, and the surf beats high against the sea-wall which protects the driveway known popularly as the Malecón. At the eastern edge of the entrance to the bay is a promontory surmounted by an imposing castle. This is the Morro, a famous Spanish fortress of a bygone day, now used as a Cuban national military school and as a maritime signal station. Just beyond that is the

[1] If *Who's who in America* and *Cubans of to-day* may be considered as accurately representing the more distinguished persons in the United States and Cuba, it will be noticed that there is a wide geographical distribution in the northern republic, while in Cuba there are very few who do not reside in Havana. Cf. *infra*, p. 589.

more formidable and more gruesome, if less imposing, Cabañas fortress. The entrance to the bay is very narrow, seemingly not wider than a good throw from the boat's deck to either side. Inside, it broadens out, but is at no point very large. There seems to be an extraordinary activity in the port, due in part to the fact that many vessels anchor in the bay and discharge or load their cargo to the accompaniment of much Latin shouting and the comings and goings of numerous small craft. The western shore, on the side toward the city, is well lined with docks, and the visitor from the United States will come in about at the point where the "Maine" was sunk in 1898, and there, or just beyond, his boat will tie up.

There are virtually three Havanas. The "old" city goes west from the bay to the Parque Central and the broad avenue called the Prado, which runs out of it toward the ocean shore on the north. The "new" city is west of that. At some indeterminate point still farther west is the modern residential section for the wealthy and the moderately well-to-do. While everything about Havana will seem odd and strange to the American on his first trip abroad, the experienced traveler will recognize that it is really a conglomerate of Spanish and American influences. One will find much that is Spanish in the old city. To be sure, the greater business interests are located there, but off the main streets there is a typical Hispanic hodge-podge of warehouses, small shops, hotels, restaurants, crowded tenements, and an occasional wealthy home, with perhaps all varieties in a single block. Here too are the cathedral, fort, and the old *plaza,* or central square, that are among the surviving reminders of the Spanish past. Streets are so narrow that wheeled traffic is required to go but one way. They are paved with cobblestones. Sidewalks are rarely wider than the space required by one man. And yet there is a busy flow of pedestrians striving to make some progress while dodging the equally busy flow of automobiles. By far the best known streets in this section are those called popularly "Obispo" and "O'Reilly,"—"popularly," because these streets, in common with most others in Havana, have official names on the signboards that differ from those in common use. The presence of an "O'Reilly" in Havana is accounted for by the rule of a famous governor of that name during the eighteenth century. These two streets are teeming with life, noise, and action. They are occupied in the main by first-class retail shops, cafés, and restaurants. Shops open wide to the sidewalk, euphemistically so-called, and people eat, drink, bargain, and sit in the barber's chair to the unrestricted gaze of all. During hot weather many great awnings, or canopies, are put out, suspended high up and reaching across the street. These are often gaily decorated, and help give an impression of the whole as of a bazaar. But window displays, goods, and one-price methods are like those in the United States.

The Parque Central and the Prado form a boundary line between the old city and the new, but have a character all their own. They are the tourist centre *par excellence*. There, or in the immediate vicinity, are the more widely known large hotels and the high-priced restaurants with "American food" and copious "ex-American" drink. This region is also a centre for Cuban life, with imposing clubhouses, the principal theatres, and some locally patronized cafés. The Prado is a magnificent broad avenue, with a shaded parkway down the centre. This is crowded with strollers in the early evening hours, while the smooth roadways on either side are alive with automobiles. Indeed, the old *plaza* stroll of Spanish life has been wholly displaced by

the American machine. With it, too, has gone that delightful and perfectly proper custom in Hispanic lands of young
women glancing frankly at the young men. The Cuban
young woman has adopted the American manner, but in so
doing has gone farther than her neighbor to the north, for
she *never* "looks." Oddly enough, this is true even of the
women of the street. Other imitations, if such they are,
show a similar variance in degree. For example, powder and
paint have been adopted with rather too much "enthusiasm"
by Havana belles, who are, nevertheless, very pretty as one
sees them in the evening in their light but attractive attire.
At the end of the Prado, by the ocean front, just across from
the Morro, is a band-stand and consequent gathering-place
for the public on nights when the band plays. Thence proceeds another broad avenue, the Malecón, running west,
just back of the sea-wall. The sea often runs high along the
water-front, beating with great volumes of spray against the
wall. Sometimes the force of wind and wave carries the
water over the wall, putting the Malecón very nearly knee-
deep in water. Along this street, too, are a number of fine
residences.

In many respects the "new" city is much more Cuban, if
not exactly Spanish, than the old. There are great shopping
districts in the new city that the tourist rarely visits but the
Cuban frequents perhaps more often than Obispo and
O'Reilly. In the late afternoon Galiano (officially Italia)
and other streets going out of it toward the Parque Central
are thronged with shoppers and casual strollers, including
bevies of good-looking *señoritas*. Here lives a great part
of what might be called the middle-class population. And
here, as in outlying streets of the old city, are a number
of moderate-priced restaurants, serving good Spanish food
and wholesome Spanish wines at phenomenally low prices.

The old foreign resident in Havana and the traveler who is familiar with the Spanish tongue will usually prefer this section to the tourist-ridden centre.

The Vedado and other residence districts to the west are a twentieth century development and an outgrowth of American influences, for a well-to-do residence section, as such, is not at all typical of Hispanic life. It is a region of magnificent private homes, a convincing bit of testimony of the wealth and perhaps also the extravagance of the upper ranks of Cuban society. Foreign business men, too, quite generally live in this section. The exotic touch, to the American visitor, is in the character of the edifices, grounds, and streets. There is often a fantastic richness in architectural forms that is foreign to American taste, but not inappropriate in a warm country like Cuba. The grounds are more likely to be a riotous but luxurious confusion of plants and walks than given to grassy lawns. Often they are hidden from the public by high walls. The streets are lined with trees, but are usually quite wretched in other respects, perhaps deep-furrowed with the rains and utterly unkempt. Bare lots next to a princely palace may serve as dump-heaps. This is a seeming incongruity that is in fact rather typically Hispanic, and one looks behind it to find the responsibility therefor in the neglectful hand of government.

Havana is a city with "atmosphere." It perhaps resembles Mexico more than other Hispanic American cities on account of its blend of American and Hispanic influences. But it has more wealth, more activity, and more tourists by far than the Mexican capital. The American has an entering wedge in that he recognizes, though perhaps dimly, much that he has already known. Business blocks are after the American pattern. Big business itself is usually American-owned. The merchandise one buys comes mainly from the

United States. Sanitation and external cleanliness are more nearly in accord with American conditions than they are with their Spanish prototypes. And finally, in addition to the thousands of Americans in Havana, one will meet few Cubans who do not speak at least a little English. The very nearness of Cuba to the United States keeps the American from feeling that he has strayed utterly away from home. And yet, the Hispanic flavor of Cuban life is never lost. This gives tang and sparkle to the whole.

Though it covers a considerable area, Havana is a city of easy communications. There is an excellent, wide-reaching street-car service, with a five-cent fare. Ford motor cars are everywhere, and will carry one or two persons for twenty cents, with an increased tariff for longer rides. In the winter the tourist agencies have great automobiles for suburban trips. Havana has its "sights" for visitors, like any other city. One of the most curious is the cemetery (Cemeterio Colón), which is of interest because of certain peculiar customs to be observed there. Funeral processions may be very elaborate, with a gaudy, red and gold, horse-drawn hearse, around which are a number of liveried outriders. This is distinctly a part of the Spanish heritage of Cuban life. At one place in the cemetery is a huge pile of human bones. Enquiry develops the fact that it is the practice to *rent* graves, and when the family of the deceased fails to meet the recurring payments his bones are removed from the ground, to make room for a more profitable customer. The market in Havana is somewhat odorous, but interesting. There is an amazing variety of products, especially fruits, many of which are unknown to the foreigner, and there are also many different kinds of vegetables, fish, and other things for the human palate. Some of the customs, too, differ from those in vogue in the United States. For example if one wants chicken, he does not necessarily have to buy the whole bird, but may order a liver or a leg, or any part or portion he desires. Aside from visits to the cathedral and various government edifices, old and new, one may find interest in trips that yield something in modern Cuban life. One sees more in a cigar factory than the making of cigars. For example, there is the professional entertainer who reads newspapers or stories to the workmen at their toil. Out in the country one may visit a sugar estate. Across the bay the Morro and Cabañas, with its dungeons, are worth a visit. West of Vedado is the beach at Marianao, where the water is so buoyant that all who wish may float. In another part of Marianao is the Country Club, which has an excellent golf course. Across from the club-house is the Casino, famous for its entertainment in the winter season. More important than all of these places in themselves is the life of the people that one may encounter anywhere.

The old city and the shopping districts of the new are the animated part of Havana in the morning. In the hot midday hours there is comparative quiet everywhere. In the late afternoon and early evening the Parque Central and the Prado awake. Thousands of human beings put in an appearance there, and at night there are tens of thousands. From the noise, one gets the impression that they never go to bed, and indeed there is considerable activity up to as late as two in the morning. Those who are not riding or walking seat themselves in the wide-open cafés, and watch the passers-by or, more likely, engage in spirited discussions. Havana cafés are after the European fashion, unlike anything in the United States. One may use them as a club, or as a place in which to read the newspaper, staying as long as one likes, all for the price of a cup of coffee. One is not limited to coffee. Almost anything that is edible or potable is to be had. The American visitor in a burst of preliminary enthusiasm not infrequently orders beer, wine, the Cuban *daiquiri*, or other alcoholic beverages, but he has an opportunity to try many a concoction that he would not get at home, though quite within the law. Such, for example, is the delicious *piña*, or pineapple drink, served strained (*colada*) or not strained (*sin color*), as desired. The *ensalada*, made of fruits, soda-water, and pomegranate juice, is another. Drunkenness, it may be said in passing, is not a Cuban habit; the Cuban drinks in moderation, but rarely to excess. If a man is seen staggering along the street or in other ways making him self unpleasantly conspicuous, it is an odds-on bet that he comes from the prohibition country to the north.

Havana offers a variety of entertainment to the tourist, and has indulgent laws that permit him to squander his money in games of chance. The bull-fight ended with Spanish rule, and has not returned. So too, cock-fights and the government lottery came to an end, but they are now back in all their pristine glory. In the winter there is horse-racing at an excellent track within the limits of Marianao, west of Vedado. And the already-mentioned Casino has as its most conspicuous feature all those advantages that have made Monte Carlo famous. The numerous Spanish population of the city takes delight in *jai-alai*, or Basque ball, a remarkably skilful and beautiful game which is a sort of glorified tennis and hand-ball on a large scale. This game is played at night. Then too there are the scores of American "movies," with the same heroes and heroines one sees in the United States. In the daytime an American may enjoy his game of baseball, for the Cuban professional league has its season in the winter. And it is "real" baseball that is played. Teams of American major league ball-players have often met defeat at the hands of Cuban teams. Years ago the Cincinnati team of the National League signed two players who were regarded at the time as "freaks," simply because they were Cubans. These men were Marsans and Almeida. Both proved to be good players, and one of them, Marsans, was among the greatest outfielders of his day. Since that time Cuba has furnished almost as many players to American professional leagues as most American states.[2]

January, February, and March are the three great tourist months. They are indeed an ideal time from the standpoint of climate. One need have no fear, either, of insect pests, for mosquitoes and flies have all but disappeared from the Cuban capital since the automobile replaced the horse. But the presence of so many tourists is not without disadvantages for those who would glady dispense with the company of a few thousands of their fellow-countrymen. Hotel accommodations are sometimes insufficient to take care of the inflow. Profiteering at once makes itself felt, and the American-owned hostelries are no better on this score than the rest. The writer recalls a time in 1920 when some hotels were charging as much as twenty-five dollars a night, merely for a room, but a better housing situation is rapidly being developed. Petty profiteering at the expense of the notoriously simple-minded (from the standpoint of travel) American tourist is widespread, if not universal. Unless he has some knowledge of Spanish or of prices he may pay a few pennies extra for what he buys. During nine months of the year, however,—out of tourist season,—it is little or no handicap to be a citizen of the United States.

If there is one city outside of Havana that the tourist will probably visit it is likely to be Matanzas. One may make the journey in a little over two hours on either the United Railways or the Hershey Line, the latter an electric rail-

[2] Cf. *infra*, pp. 606-607, n. 26.

way. The name "Hershey" recalls a widely known American sweet chocolate, and rightly so, for it is to this same company that the railway belongs. A little less than half way to Matanzas the line passes through the Hershey sugar estates, winding in and about the grounds at the mill as if to give the passengers a better view. The scenery along this route is about as fine as any in Cuba, although the ingredients are simple enough: a rich green color,—with now and then a tree of blazing red,—the graceful royal palms, sugar fields, and a succession of valleys. The near-by hills that shut in the valleys give this trip a character that distinguishes it from the comparative level of other railway vistas in the island. The Hershey plant is typical of the larger American-owned mills of Cuba. Everything about the place is spic and span,—good mill, ball-field, neat cottages, and attractive grounds.

The ideal way to approach Matanzas is from the sea. There is an ample bay running east and west, with a wide opening to the north at the eastern end. Boats handle cargoes through the medium of lighters in the bay. The city lies in a semicircle at the western end, rising with the hills that surround the port. On the northern shore, beyond the Yumurí, are a number of large business plants of oil or molasses interests. Beyond the San Juan, on the southern shore, are some fine residences, also a hemp factory and the fields of henequen on which it depends. The city proper lies between the two rivers. In all three sections there is a wealth of trees and shrubbery which combine to produce an attractive setting. Next after Havana, Matanzas probably makes a better appearance than any other city in the island. The *plaza* is not large, but is well-shaded and pleasing to the eye. Here, too, something of old Spanish custom obtains, for the prettily dressed young women come out in the early evening to take the *plaza* stroll. There are two principal "sights" in Matanzas. One of them, the view of the Yumurí valley, the traveler on the Hershey Line will already have seen, though not from such a point of vantage as is afforded from the hills above Matanzas. It is pretty,—though perhaps not more so than a hundred other such valleys. Far more worth while are the caves of Bellamar at the opposite end of the city, beyond the henequen fields to the east. The *"mar"* (sea) in "Bellamar" is misleading, for the caves do not touch the sea at all, so far as anybody knows. They consist of a series of winding chambers, through which one may pass with reasonable facility, as there are well-made paths and electric lights to assist one on his way. A number of miles of the caves have already been explored, without reaching the end. The casual visitor, however, will probably be satisfied with considerably less than one mile. The main interest is in the curious natural forms that the shining white stalactites have taken. Scores of them have received names which recall something they are supposed to resemble. For example, there are the mantle of Columbus, the American eagle (with wings outstretched), the head of an elephant, and a plethora of figures that remind of church architecture or Catholic services.

A few tourists, especially those who enter Cuba at Antilla in northern Oriente, pay a visit to Santiago. Some others make the trip by train from Havana. En route the most frequent stop is Camagüey, where the traveler who has begun his journey on the English-controlled United Railways proceeds thenceforth by the American-owned Cuba Railway, though without change of cars if he is riding on the Pullman. The Hotel Camagüey, three minutes from the station, is in itself quite interesting and unique. It was formerly a Spanish cavalry barracks, but no unpleasant survivals of its former condition are apparent to the guest. What was once an enormous corral is now filled in with walks and gardens, around which are the quarters in a wide-reaching two-story edifice. This hotel is one of the great gathering-places for Americans in eastern Cuba, and a day does not pass but sees a throng of them in the bar-room shaking dice for cocoanut water, orangeade, Bacardí rum, cocktails, or beer. Many who are employed by the Cuba Railway reside in this city throughout the year, for Camagüey is the principal centre of that company's activities.

Camagüey is a city that differs not a little "from the brag." It is often described as a health resort, and that, no doubt, is what nature intended it to be, but man, in the person of the Cuban government, has allowed a condition to develop that can be anything but advantageous to the health of the inhabitants. In this connection it is to be borne in mind that it is the national government, not the local as in the United States, that finances most municipal needs. The dirt of Camagüey contrasts sadly with the comparative cleanliness of Havana and Matanzas. The streets are fairly wide, but are full of holes ranging from the moderate "chuck-hole" to cavernous openings several feet deep. They are full of dust or a varicolored mud, as the case may be, and there is an all-pervading, dead odor about the town. Things might be better if it were not that Camagüey is on a level site, and in consequence the rains cannot wash away the dirt. And yet Camagüey is a centre of wealth and the Cuban aristocracy. It is almost incongruous to see so many attractive people in such a dirty place. Dainty señoritas trip along the streets, seeking a relatively clean spot on which to plant their expensively shod feet. They are undeniably pretty, and dressed in fashionable materials. And yet, people who live in Camagüey, native or foreign, enjoy the city, despite its external drawbacks. On the principle that one should never "judge a book by its cover" it would seem that there is a great deal of happiness in Camagüey, owing to the delightful quality of the people.

A better place, perhaps, than Camagüey to get a real touch of Cuban life would be Sancti Spíritus, which has a population of 23,572. Sancti Spíritus, which is one of the oldest towns in Cuba, is not on the main line at all, but can be reached at the terminus of a branch which goes south from Ciego de Ávila, just before Camagüey. First impressions take in the dirty, narrow streets and somewhat primitive hotel arrangements, but there are the honesty and fair prices one encounters "off the beaten track" of tourist travel, and the people are delightful,—simple, kindly, courteous, and wholesome. As one young resident put it: "Everybody in town was good, until the railway came. Since then some bad people have come to the city, and a few good ones have gone away." Most of the people never leave Sancti Spíritus, however, but remain there, as did their fathers, grandfathers, and great-grandfathers before them. And why not? Everybody "knows everybody," they see one another daily in the ample *plaza*, and all are happy.

But Camagüey and Sancti Spíritus are not places for the ordinary tourist, who will usually see no more of the former than the twenty-five minute train stop will allow and will not take in the latter at all. He certainly will not have seen Cuba, however, unless he has visited Santiago. This is a city that is surpassed only by Havana in importance and historic interest, and it has some features that are in marked contrast to those one finds at the capital. It is a little over five hundred miles from Havana, a distance which the express train covers in approximately twenty-four hours. There is not a great deal that is striking in car-window scenery en route. It consists mainly of a level plain, dotted with royal palms and with miles and miles of sugar estates, interspersed with bits of pasture. The old-time forests, "murdered" to make way for sugar, have for the most part gone, though many stumps mark where they stood. Here and there, besides the palms, however, are other beautiful trees, standing alone. Among these is the *jobo* ("hobo"), which resembles a wide-spreading oak, symmetrically shaved off at the top. Another, of great beauty, but not so wide-spreading, is the *ceiba*, the so-called "national tree" of Cuba. This is very graceful, growing to a good average height, with a deep green, oak-like leafing. It is not until the province of Oriente is reached that one sees any mountains at all, and then they appear only in the dim distance until shortly before Santiago.

The human angle of the trip is perhaps more interesting than the scenery. Americans and well-to-do Cubans divide the Pullman, and are served rather meagre meals from the buffet at one end of the car. First-class coaches are used by whites and near-whites, and second-class almost wholly by negroes. There are few towns of considerable size along the way. The express train goes through Matanzas and Santa Clara during the night, passes Ciego de Ávila early in the morning, and reaches Camagüey just before noon. From Camagüey to Santiago there is nothing deserving the name of city. Most places are sad, neglected villages, reeking with mud or dust, inhabited mainly by negroes, whose homes are "shacks," thatch-roofed or covered with corrugated iron. Travel seems to be mainly on horseback, for the roads in this section are notoriously boggy and uneven trails. The whole day's ride convinces one, however, not only of the fertility of Cuba's soil, but also of its remarkable availability. Given good roads and a greater diversity of crops, and given, above all, a good government that renders a reasonable amount of service, then the country will support millions of inhabitants beyond those it now possesses.

The *plaza* in Santiago is typically Hispanic. Among the buildings that surround it are the cathedral, the municipal government building, two first-class hotels (the Casa Granda [*sic*] and the Venus), a three-story club house, and a number of shops. The *plaza* itself is a neat affair, covered with tiles, and has a few shade trees and a number of benches. One odd feature about the cathedral is that the part even with the *plaza* is rented out for shops; the church proper is up one story, entered from the side. Santiago is a mountainous city, rising along a sharp declivity from the water's edge. There are a few docks at the port, but many large-sized steamers handle their cargo out in the bay. Santiago is on the eastern shore. The quite distant opposite bank is a virgin green, and there are few habitations to the north. It helps make an attractive picture, as the bay is surrounded by high hills which almost deserve the name of mountains. Going up into the city and beyond it to the northeast one comes to the rich suburb of Vista Alegre, Santiago's Vedado. Here there are several hundred fine homes, not Spanish and not American, but with something of each style. Every place has a yard, usually fenced in with an iron grating. Some yards are planted to grass, and others have a profusion of flowers, while still others combine both features, often with a landscape garden effect. The houses have columned verandas, grated windows, tiled roofing, and at times a somewhat fanciful decoration. All are of one or two stories. The streets in Vista Alegre are excellent, in contradistinction to those of the rest of the city.

The main parts of Santiago, while much better than most cities of Spain and Spanish America, have certain defects.

There is a great deal of dust and dirt, streets are in need of repair, and there is an inadequate water supply. In all these matters Santiago is the victim of the government. It is the national government that is supposed to provide water for the streets, but it does nothing. So the streets of Santiago are sprinkled only when it rains. Fortunately, the sharp slope of the city causes much of the refuse to be washed down hill to the bay. For years, successive administrations have promised Santiago an aqueduct, but the matter never gets beyond an appropriation that is squandered in engineering plans. Some politician and his lay partner, the "engineer," divide the monies between them. It is conditions such as these that make one realize that Havana is not Cuba. On the contrary, one often hears in Oriente that Havana is a "parasite." As one man told the writer, with no little heat, Havana has a population about six times that of Santiago, but gets fifteen times as great an appropriation for sanitation. Moreover, it probably *does* get a larger percentage of its appropriation,—with less in proportion for the politicians. The streets of Santiago are wider than those of most Hispanic cities, but in other respects they follow type. Sidewalks are mere devices to keep one from being run over, by leaning against the housewall above the curb. They are from one to three feet in width. There are no yards, and blocks are solid, with buildings but one or two stories high.

There are two trips one ought to take while in Santiago, one up "Wood's Folly," and the other down the bay to the Morro. The first-named is a road built by General Leonard Wood while governor of Oriente in 1899. Almost without exception Cubans speak well of General Wood, but the building of this road was regarded at the time as unwise. Time has vindicated General Wood, however, in this as in almost everything else he did in Cuba. It is the best road in the vicinity of Santiago, even though it has gone a quarter of a century without much in the way of repairs, and it is one of the principal outlets to the north. The road is some nine or ten miles long to the top of a hill beyond Boniato. In 1899 when Wood built it the Cuban soldiers around Santiago were being maintained at considerable expense, without any work to do. He thought it would be better to keep them occupied, believed that the hill (which is about nine hundred feet high) might serve as a defensive point for Santiago, and felt that it would make a suitable acclimatization camp for the American soldiers. Today, the hill is perhaps the best place from which to get a view of Santiago and the surrounding country. From it one sees the city and the bay, but not the entrance to the bay. There are mountains all about, notably some high ones to the west. Looking east of the city one can easily reconstruct the American military campaign of 1898. At one place there is the cut in the range leading up from Siboney, where the American troops landed. From there they proceeded part way around the city along the eastern side to El Caney, which is not far beyond Vista Alegre. Near there is San Juan Hill, made famous by the charge of Roosevelt's "Rough Riders."

One must take a boat to go out to the Morro, for the old Spanish road which once approached it from Santiago has been allowed by the Cuban government to fall into decay. It is nearly an hour's ride by launch. On the way there are a number of islands, strewn with summer homes, many of them very rich,—evidence that some people in this section have money. The entrance to the bay is very narrow, only two hundred and twenty yards across, while the channel itself is but twenty-two feet wide. Two cannon on the shore, partly buried in the earth, mark the spot opposite which Hobson sank the "Merrimac." The Morro is one of the most fascinating structures of its kind in the world. It stands much higher than the one at Havana, on a steep ascent that lacks little of the perpendicular. It has not been kept up. So it is now a ruin, but is perhaps the more impressive for being so.

For all the historic and scenic interest of Santiago, one must turn to social factors for the most striking feature of a visit to that city. Most of the people in Santiago,—and in all Oriente for that matter,—are black, or partly black. In Havana the negro is said to possess political, but not social, equality. In Santiago he is more nearly on an equal social plane with the whites than in most parts of the world. It is not uncommon to see a white man and a negro arm in arm, or dining or drinking together on terms of perfect intimacy. The *plaza* stroll has become a colored function, with few if any young women of white race in attendance. Many negroes are well-to-do. There is a finely appointed negro club, just off the *plaza* from the Casa Granda. No white men are admitted and no negroes of "low degree." On one occasion, recently, when a member of the club brought a woman who had worked in a menial capacity to one of the social functions of the club, everybody else left! The gaming at this club is often for high stakes. It is said that as much as twenty-five thousand dollars has been called for, for the operations of a single night. Cuban negroes, indeed, are far superior in many ways to the members of their race in the United States. Except for the color of their skin, they do not look or act like the American negro. They dress quite as well and in as good taste as the whites. They are not loud or insolent, and they are not thick-featured. Some of the girls might even be called pretty. It is probable that they all have some Spanish blood in their veins, however black they may be. One wonders what is the basis of their well-being.

Many are employed in the sugar industry, but they are not among the mill-owners or rich planters. The only obvious source of their wealth provides yet another indictment of the government. The negroes dominate the vote in Oriente! So it is the practice to give well-paying sinecures, called *"botellas"* (bottles), to some negro who can deliver ten or a dozen votes. If the stories one hears on every hand can be believed, this is the mainspring of negro wealth in Oriente.

On the return from Santiago to Havana, one might well make a detour for a visit to the fifth city of the republic, Cienfuegos, the population of which is 37,241. One changes cars at Santa Clara, capital of the province of the same name, and has ample time for a stroll through that small, not altogether "comfortable," but interestingly typical city of the "neglected" kind. Cienfuegos is an important port, but is a place the average tourist never sees. It has a particularly neat business centre, one of the best in Cuba, with good streets and a *plaza,* enormous in size and filled with attractive gardens, that has no equal in the island. Streets in outlying districts are as full of holes and unkempt, however, as those in the business district are smooth and clean. The life of Cienfuegos is chiefly to be seen on the Avenida (Avenue) de Independencia, which runs through the city, with a parkway down the centre, and continues straight ahead several miles along the bay to the land's end at La Punta (The Point). The bay is of great size, and appears as if it were entirely surrounded by land, with the entrance not visible from the city, but it has no particular scenic charm, since there are no mountains in the background. In the early evening hours the parkway of the avenue is crowded with young people taking the typical Hispanic American stroll. They seem to prefer the avenue and its closer contacts to the greater space and elegance of the *plaza,* but move to the latter whenever there is a band concert. One sees much in Cienfuegos that reminds him of Matanzas on the one hand or Santiago on the other, but in the walk along Independencia their differences would seem to have merged, for whites and negroes equally take part. One wonders whether this is a transition stage toward an eventual appropriation of this custom by the colored people. Old residents of Cienfuegos will tell you, like those of Camagüey and Sancti Spíritus, that they like the city, and in this instance the casual tourist can more readily see why they should.

There is a great deal more that the visitor to Cuba ought to see, but when he has gone as far as the writer has carried him he will know best what to choose. Much in Cuban economic life deserves more extensive study, such as the sugar and tobacco industries and the railways. Investigations bearing upon sanitation or education will reward those who are interested in either. One ought not to leave the island without improving the easily obtained opportunity of associating with Cubans, who will almost certainly possess those delightful qualities for which Hispanic peoples are famous and perhaps also be able to speak with the Anglo-Saxon visitor in his own language. Finally, one may wish to know why in the midst of such excellence the government appears to be so unsatisfactory. That will necessitate his making some study of Cuban history. Perhaps also that will provide a clue for an understanding of the political regeneration Cuba must undergo if it is to become the model Hispanic American republic that its resources and the calibre of its people should entitle it to be.[3]

[3] Much of the social and economic data touched briefly here is given in more ample detail in chapters XXV and XXVI.

CHAPTER II

THE OLD RÉGIME, TO 1895

On October 28, 1492, Columbus discovered Cuba. Just where he first touched the coast has never been determined, though every considerable port from Baracoa to Nuevitas has been suggested for the honor. Nineteen years later, in 1511, Diego Velázquez landed in the extreme east at Baracoa, and founded the first Spanish settlement in Cuba. Within a comparatively short time thereafter he effected a conquest of the island, and by 1515 there were no fewer than seven Spanish towns, including Havana (though not at its present site) and Santiago, which date respectively from 1514 and 1515. For a few years Cuba was a flourishing colony, but suffered on account of the expeditions of Cortés, De Soto, and others to Mexico and Florida, which gravely diminished the resources of the island in man-power and wealth. From that time forward for many years the history of Cuba was in most respects that of the typical Spanish colony. Cuba had the same autocratic political, economic, social, and ecclesiastical system that other colonies had, with the same bickerings of the different representatives of the king. The Indians were killed off or died at such a rapid rate that negroes began to be imported at least as early as 1523 to serve as laborers in the mines and fields. Particularly noteworthy in the early years, owing to Cuba's strategic position with reference to Spain's mainland colonies, was the matter of international relationships. Realizing that her empire in America would be imperiled if she lost Cuba, Spain put forth all her strength

25

to retain the "Pearl of the Antilles." Yet, French, English, and Dutch pirates caused serious embarrassment by their activities in Cuban waters in the sixteenth and seventeenth centuries. Smuggling made its appearance at the same time, continuing in the eighteenth century and becoming the principal basis of the island's wealth.

Absolutism and centralization were the two key-words of Spanish colonial government. The captain-general of Cuba, a royal appointee, virtually had in his hands all functions of government, and exercised them for the island as a whole and also within local units. Other machinery limited his powers to some extent, but rarely proved an insuperable barrier, for any great length of time, to his own predominance in Cuban affairs, subject to the orders of the king. Even the administration of the church, save in matters of faith, was controlled by this official as vice-patron of the king, to whom the popes had granted special powers in America. The economic life of the island was restricted in many ways. Only such products could be raised as would not compete with those of Spain. All commerce was required to be carried on with Spain alone, and then only with a single Spanish port. Spaniards, too, were given first place in the social life of the island. The merest Spanish clerk was the social superior of the wealthiest creoles, as the native-born whites were called. This became most unpleasantly apparent when the young women of Cuba married Spaniards instead of Cubans, if the chance offered, thereby improving their social station. In fine, Spain governed Cuba wholly for the benefit of Spain and Spaniards. Cuba, "the ever faithful isle," was perhaps more patient under these restraints than other parts of the empire, but it is not surprising that a feeling of discontent made its appearance that grew in intensity until the final outburst at the close of the nineteenth century.

Undue trade restrictions, arbitrary and unscientific methods of taxation, and the virtual exclusion of Cubans from government are the three most frequently mentioned causes of Cuban discontent in the nineteenth century. During the reign of the great Charles III (1759-1788) the Spanish government made some concessions to Cuba in the direction of freedom of trade. Far more important, however, was the actual, though illegal, freedom the island enjoyed in the frequently recurring periods of war between Spain and England. At such times Spain was unable to enforce the usual laws of trade, owing to British control of the sea. In 1801 Spain opened Cuba to world commerce, but withdrew this freedom in 1809. Trade with other lands continued in despite of law, however. Making a virtue of necessity, Spain adopted a new policy in 1818, permitting foreign trade, subject to heavy export and import taxes and to certain discriminations in favor of Spain. The Cubans were far from satisfied with the change, however. The system operated harshly at times and was usually inconvenient. In particular there was a growing demand for greater freedom of trade with the United States, the island's best customer. Eventually, in 1891, a reciprocity treaty was made with the United States, but in 1894 it was withdrawn, and the special advantages in favor of Spain were restored. This was one of the immediate causes of the revolution of 1895.

It is probable that the denunciations of Spain on account of the amount and burdensome nature of the taxes have been overdrawn, but their arbitrary and unscientific character can hardly be denied. For example, the laws for the taxation of real estate were not unjust and the rate not excessive, but there was very unequal application of the laws in fact. Favoritism and bribery were notoriously important considerations in assessing valuations. The number and variety of taxes were another cause for complaint. With its eye on easily collectible revenues the government made a point of taxing necessities in every conceivable way. Thus, the right of slaughtering was sold by the government, but there were also taxes on each animal slaughtered and on dressed meat. There were taxes on fuel, building material, farm produce, and on horses used either for pleasure or in transportation service. License fees had to be paid to the government by lawyers, doctors, brokers, carpenters, shoemakers, and masons. There were taxes on theatres, concerts, balls, cockfights, and other forms of amusement. And there were stamp taxes on legal documents. In all of these cases the application was more objectionable than the taxes themselves. The arbitrary whim of an official and wholesale corruption, even to the point of threatening taxation in order to elicit bribes, were the real determining factors. And yet it is probable that the fundamental dissatisfaction of the Cubans was because they objected to paying any taxes at all that were imposed by Spaniards and not by themselves.

There were some Cubans who held political office under Spanish rule, but almost invariably they were in a subordinate capacity. The captain-general, or (as he eventually came to be called) governor-general, was a Spaniard, and he appointed, or at least dominated, the other officials. Even after provincial and municipal governments were provided for in the nineteenth century, there was no real diminution in his control of local units. The office of captain-general, with its many perquisites, legal or otherwise, was a very lucrative post. A few years usually sufficed to make the incumbent wealthy, and it became the practice to change this officer frequently, as if to give some new individual a chance for the rich returns the position afforded. There were 136 captain-generals in all. Between 1859 and 1898 there were thirty-eight, an average of more than one a year. This also meant frequent changes of subordinates and a consequent upsetting of administrative stability. Political office for the sake of the office-holder, with scant thought of its place as a position of trust on behalf of the public, was the firmly imbedded tradition of Spanish rule. The desire for political office is almost "epidemic" among Hispanic peoples, and the Cubans were no exception to the rule. To be sure, they had ample cause for complaint. In any event the time came when they wanted the jobs for themselves.

The evils of Spanish rule that have just been recited were only a few out of many. No doubt a far stronger case on this score could be made. It is not necessary to accuse Spain of cruelty or crime, however, or even to insist too much on her lack of forethought or incompetence. The revolution was bound to come, whatever the nature of Spain's rule. At best, Spain might have retained a shadowy title to Cuba by an early grant of such virtual independence as Canada, South Africa, Australia, and New Zealand now enjoy, but even this is doubtful. A comparatively weak country like Spain could not offer the same prestige, protection, and economic advantage that the relation to England gives to the self-governing colonies of the British Empire. The revolution came because Cuba had outgrown the Spanish connection. Despite all the evils that may be cited against Spain in her government of Cuba, that country is deserving of more sympathy than blame. Spain did the best she could, according to her lights. The most severe charge that can be brought against her is not that she committed misdeeds that forced the Cubans to rebel, but that she transmitted to the Cubans themselves some of the worst evils in her own political life, evils that Spain would gladly have overcome if she could have done so. In particular, she passed on to Cuba, as to all Spanish America, the already mentioned unfortunate tradition that political office is for the private advantage of the office-holder.

As early as the closing years of the sixteenth century the creoles had begun to consider themselves Cubans rather than Spaniards, although there was as yet no thought of a separation from Spain. On occasion they could express a vigorous dissent, however. One such instance occurred as early as 1717. There was a proposal at that time to establish a tobacco monopoly. A number of Cubans disapproved of the plan, and some five hundred of them rose in arms. They went so far as to capture Jesús del Monte in the outskirts of Havana, but were at length persuaded to retire to their homes. Twice again, in 1721 and 1723, there were tobacco revolts, but they were checked before they became serious. In 1762 a British expedition captured Havana. The next year the city was restored to Spain, but the brief English occupation proved to be of the utmost importance in the history of Cuba. There was a fleeting moment of freedom of trade, revealing to the world for the first time and to the Cubans themselves the wealth of the island when not hampered by restrictions. It served also to bring to Cuban attention the course of world affairs, overcoming to some extent the narrow provincialism which had formerly limited their intellectual horizon. From this time forward the revolutionary doctrines of the French philosophers had some meaning for the Cuban people. They took a lively interest in the progress of the American Revolution and keenly followed the events of the French Revolution at the close of the century. When the Spanish American Wars of Independence began on the mainland in 1810 the Cubans had the issue of separation from Spain squarely presented to them, but they were not yet ready to sever the ties that bound them to Spain.

A number of reasons account for this. Ever since the English occupation Cuba had been treated, on the whole, quite liberally by Spain, and had been favored by a number of worthy governors during the reign of Charles III. And where the law fell a little short of Cuban desires in matters of trade, the exigencies of the times had, nevertheless, permitted of commercial relationships that the law did not sanction. So, as gauged by the ideas of the period, the Cubans did not have a serious grievance. And yet they probably would have joined their Spanish American brothers if it were not that Cuba is an island. A rebellion in Cuba had far less chance of success than on the mainland. As the strategic key to Spain's possessions in the New World, too, Cuba was more strongly held than the other colonies, and the Spanish navy could prevent the island from receiving any substantial help. As the wars continued, other drawbacks developed. Some of the ideas of the revolutionists did not appeal to large bodies of the Cuban people. In particular, they hesitated before Bolívar's pronouncement for freedom of the slaves. This was due only in part to the character of Cuban economic life, depending as it did on a large and cheap labor supply. In addition, the Cubans had almost before their eyes the gruesome scenes that had attended the winning of independence in the black republic of Haiti to the east. There the whites had been killed off by the negroes or forced to flee, and many of the exiles had taken up their residence in Cuba. There were too many negroes in Cuba for the people to be willing to risk emancipation. According to the census of 1817, for example, in a total of about 688,000 inhabitants there were over 250,000 slaves and more than 115,000 free colored persons. Taken together, they represented more than half of the population.

Throughout the war period, however, there were many Cubans who sympathized with the revolutionists and hoped to bring about a separation from Spain. Most of them were not in favor of Cuban independence, but wished to cast in their lot with Colombia, Mexico, or the United States. A number of secret societies were formed that favored a revolt. Of these, the most famous was an organization whose principal activity was in the year 1823, known as the "Soles de Bolívar," or, to give it its full name, "Soles y Rayos de Bolívar" (literally, "Suns and Rays of Bolívar"). There were now growing causes of grievance, too. Ferdinand VII (1808-1833) had begun to restore some of the worst features of the old colonial system, and the officials sent to Cuba in recent years had been notoriously unscrupulous. So at length the Cubans felt that the time had come to declare themselves, and a revolt was planned for August 16, 1823. But the Spanish authorities had kept well informed through their spies in the different organizations, and when the day came, most of the leaders were arrested, while others saved themselves only by fleeing from the island. Every possible means was taken to break up the secret societies. Members, when caught, were thrown into prison or executed. Temporarily, the authorities were fairly successful. On the other hand, the desire for separation from Spain was never again to die away in Cuba. The secret organizations continued to exist, despite the watchfulness of Spanish officials, and outside the island an active propaganda against Spain was carried on unceasingly by those who had been driven from their homes.

The bitterness of Cubans against Spain was greatly increased by the severity of the rule of General Miguel Tacón

(1834-1838), one of the most famous captain-generals Cuba ever had. Tacón is the man who planned and started the Prado in Havana, among a number of notable public works. Many stories have attached themselves to his name. On one occasion, it is said, he sat in judgment over a wealthy but profligate count, who had abducted a charming young woman of the people. Being informed of the matter by the betrothed of the young woman, a man of humble circumstances, Tacón gave a decision in favor of the count, and had him married to the girl on the spot. The count was ordered to return to his plantation without his bride, and while on his way he was killed by an emissary sent for that purpose by Tacón. Thus was the young woman enabled presently to get a husband of her choice, together with the estates of the man who would have taken her against her will.

In 1836 a successful liberalist revolution in Spain restored the Constitution of 1812, which provided, among other things, for Cuban representation in the Spanish Cortes. A certain General Lorenzo commanded the eastern department of Cuba at this time, and he immediately proclaimed the Constitution and called for an election of deputies, all this without consulting Tacón. Tacón was furious when he heard of it. He himself was an ultra-conservative monarchist, and paid no attention to the new order in Spain. By a royal decree of 1825 the captain-general had been empowered to set aside any instructions from Spain, if it seemed to him to the best interests of Cuba to do so. Tacón proposed to take advantage of this decree to prevent the Constitution of 1812 from having its normal force in Cuba. Meanwhile, he proceeded against Lorenzo, and met with success when that officer went to Spain to press his side of the case. Tacón came down with a heavy hand on those who had supported Lorenzo. Scores of men of the most distinguished creole families were imprisoned or banished. Even the soldiers, who had done no more than obey Lorenzo's orders, were punished by sentences to hard labor. And when the Cuban deputies reached Spain the Cortes refused to seat them, declaring that the Constitution did not apply to Cuba, which was governed by special laws. Thus was Tacón sustained, and the Cubans supplied with a new grievance. It was brought home to them that Spanish liberalism was no more liberal with respect to Cuba than the most reactionary conservatism. Tacón, in Cuba, became even more severe in repressing opposition to his government. "I am here," he is reported as saying, "not to promote the interests of the people of Cuba, but to serve my master, the king." [1] This service he interpreted as best performed through a restoration of the old political rigors of the Spanish colonial system.

Tacón's very success was probably of doubtful advantage to Spain. Certainly it did not prevent the Cubans from plotting an uprising, and it did arouse a bitterness and desire for vengeance that made for greater constancy in the eventual patriot cause. In the United States there were a number of Cuban *juntas,* or committees, and Cuban newspapers that advocated revolt against Spain. Many Cubans in the United States and in Cuba itself were in favor of an annexation of the island to the United States. An annexation party (Partido Anexionista) was formed in 1848; a prominent society, the Club Habanero, took the same stand in that year; a Cuban annexationist paper, La Verdad, was published in New York from 1848 to 1853; and the Cuban Council (Consejo Cubano) in New York declared for annexation in 1849. In the early 50's there were a number of annexationist or-

[1] As usually written, Tacón is alleged to have said, as stated here, that he was in Cuba to serve his master "the king." During the period of his rule, however, Spain was governed by the queen-mother on behalf of her daughter, Isabella II.

ganizations, such as the Order of the Solitary Star, the Cuban Junta of New York, and the Junta of Havana, and El Cubano and El Filibustero were two Cuban papers published in New York that favored annexation. Some few who would have preferred independence regarded annexation as the only practicable means of escape from Spain. Among these was José Antonio Saco, the distinguished historian of slavery, one of the greatest men the island has produced. Saco wrote in 1837:

"I have always wished that Cuba might be only for the Cubans, but, now that perhaps that cannot be, we have no other recourse than to throw ourselves into the arms of the United States. That is the idea that it is best to diffuse and inculcate in the minds of all."

Out of this idea there developed the next serious effort against Spain, in the López conspiracies and expeditions of 1848-1851.

Narciso López, the leader in this movement, was a native of Venezuela who had risen to the rank of general in the Spanish army on account of his services to the mother country in the Wars of Independence in Venezuela and against the Carlists at a later time in Spain. He had taken up his residence in Cuba, however, married there, and become devoted to the island and the interests of the Cuban people. A man of liberalist tendencies, he at length resolved to promote a revolt against the arbitrary Spanish rule. An independent Cuba he did not wish, as he feared it might become a negro republic after the Haitian pattern. But free Cuba, like free Texas, might offer itself to the United States and be accepted. That was what López desired. The day for the revolt was set for June 24, 1848. Meanwhile, López had gained assurances of aid from many Americans, especially men of the southern states, who offered to provide him with arms and ammunition. Owing to the vigilance of both the

American and Spanish authorities, however, it was impossible to get the supplies to Cuba on time. The plot was discovered, and López had to make a hasty departure from the country in order to escape capture. Arrived in the United States, López found a favorable atmosphere for the revival of his plans. So he proceeded to organize an expedition. He offered the command in turn to Jefferson Davis, Robert E. Lee, and Governor Quitman of Mississippi. It is worthy of note that each gave the matter serious consideration, though declining in the end. So López himself took charge. Late in the spring of 1850 he set sail for Cuba, with a force of nearly six hundred men, mostly Americans from the trans-Allegheny west, among whom were several officers who had taken part in the Mexican War.

A landing was made at Cárdenas, east of Matanzas, but it proved necessary to fight a spirited battle with the Spanish garrison. López won, displaying great courage himself, but he lost more than sixty men. This would not have been serious if the Cubans had risen back of him as López expected them to do. Many of them sympathized with the undertaking, but doubted of its success. The tradition of Spanish power was as yet too strong for the Cubans to risk the wager of battle. And annexation to the United States did not constitute so strong an appeal to Cuban patriotism as would a cry for that independence which even the creole followers of López were not ready to espouse. So, when word came that a Spanish army was approaching from Matanzas, López reëmbarked his forces. He himself would have liked to try another landing, but his companions persuaded him to put back for Key West.

López had failed, but he was greeted in the United States like a conquering hero. It proved impossible for the government to get a jury that would convict him or his companions.

Urged to organize a fresh expedition, he set about to do so. Everything was in readiness in April 1851, but the matter was brought to the attention of the United States authorities, who prevented the López party from sailing. Many of his followers felt, indeed, that there should be some assurances that the Cubans would rise, before another landing in the island should be attempted. Leaders in Cuba were advised of this opinion, and they replied that they would start a revolution between July 1 and 4. This was almost too early, for López was in no position to send aid by that time, owing to the recent interference with his plans by the United States government. Nevertheless, the uprising did take place as promised. Under the leadership of Joaquín de Agüero the cry for Cuban liberty was raised in the public square at Puerto Príncipe (as Camagüey was then called), on July 3, 1851. Only fifteen of an expected four hundred patriots put in an appearance on this occasion, and they were routed by Spanish forces. But next day at a near-by town Agüero was more successful. Several hundred gathered there to listen to the reading of a declaration of independence. Presently they were attacked by Spanish troops, but drove them away. Two days later the Spaniards were again defeated when they made an assault on the patriot positions at Guanamaquilla. Hopes of ultimate victory now ran high among the Cubans, and the most optimistic messages were sent off to López in the United States. Immediately thereafter Agüero made the fatal mistake of dividing his forces into six bands of about a hundred each. The Spaniards then caught them and beat them in detail. Agüero met death on the scaffold, and others of his companions were shot.

Encouraged by the early messages he had received, López now prepared a second descent upon the island, discrediting the rumors of Agüero's later defeats. Early in August, with a force of four hundred men, most of whom were Americans, López set sail. Just before starting, he was induced by information he received from Cuba to make his landing in Pinar del Río, west of Havana, instead of in the east in the section where the recent uprising had taken place. This was the first of a series of mistakes that were to prove disastrous to the expedition. A landing was made near Bahía Honda, some fifty miles west of Havana, but there were no Cuban patriots to greet them. Dividing his forces, López began a fruitless and pitiful search for the expected, but non-existent Cuban supporters. One portion of his command, under Colonel William S. Crittenden, was captured and taken to Havana. On August 16 fifty-two members of this party, Crittenden among them, were shot! López himself met with one discouragement after another, and presently was taken prisoner, along with the other survivors of the expedition. Sent to the scaffold, López met death bravely, as he had lived. "My death will not change the destinies of Cuba," he said from the platform, just before he was executed. He was right. Cuba had need of a courageous example before it could take up arms with any hope of success. López had served that purpose.

For a while, following the defeat and death of López, it seemed as if the Cuban cause were hopeless. The New York Times on October 18, 1851, gave its opinion that the charges of Spanish oppression in Cuba must have been exaggerated, since hardly any Cubans had risen in arms. There was great discontent in fact, however, and the López movement had served as a spur to bring this out more clearly. Cubans and Spaniards refused to associate with one another. There were private collisions in which occasionally some lives were lost. A number of students who were outspoken in their expressions against Spain were seized and executed. Nothing could have been calculated to stir up Cuban hostility more than this incident. Indeed, it has never been forgotten, and the names of the boys who were put to death are now commemorated in a fine monument near the foot of the Prado in Havana. So at length Cuban feeling was at the fever point, and it was certain that a fresh uprising would not lack supporters.

These were years of a strong liberalistic movement in Spain, accompanied by the establishment of the principle of constitutional government. At length, in 1868, Isabella II (1833-1868) was dethroned, and a liberal monarchy set up under Amadeo, a prince of the House of Savoy. Meanwhile, a strong republican party had developed, and upon the resignation of Amadeo in 1873 Spain became a republic. The experiment was unsuccessful, and in 1874 the Bourbons were restored, in the person of Alfonso XII (1874-1885), but on the basis of a limited monarchy. The course of events in Spain could not fail to have their repercussions in Cuba. In 1865, for example, an organization of prominent Cubans demanded a constitutional, home-rule government, with freedom of the press, the right of petition, and the right of Cubans to hold office in Cuba and be represented in the Spanish Cortes. Nothing came of these demands. Clearly Spain did not intend to give Cuba a share in the liberal provisions that were granted in the peninsula. Feeling in Cuba was more intense now than formerly, because by this time the majority opinion was in favor of Cuban independence, instead of annexation to the United States. As early as 1848, Saco had come out for independence, opposing now the idea he had once favored of joining the northern republic.

"I would like to see Cuba not only rich, illustrious, moral, and powerful, but also Cuban and not Anglo-American," he said. "Cuba, our adored Cuba, will one day be Cuba."[1]

[1] It is said that Saco later changed is no longer any hope for Cuba exhis mind, remarking in 1866, "There cept in annexation."

Two years earlier he had made a strange prediction. He asserted that the acute tyranny of Spain would eventually compel the Cubans to revolt. Havana and the west would not join the patriots in this war, and would even help the Spaniards, while in the east there would be devastations and assassinations in the name of war. The Cubans would fail the first, second, and perhaps the third time, he said, but finally would get outside help and win. Saco foresaw almost exactly what was to happen. The López expeditions may be counted as the first Cuban effort, although they did not get far enough to come within Saco's general description of the wars. The Cubans were now ready for a second trial of arms.

On October 10, 1868, at the plantation of Yara in Oriente a group of men declared the independence of Cuba from Spain. That marked the beginning of the terrible Ten Years' War. Under the leadership of Carlos Manuel de Céspedes a provisional government for a Republic of Cuba was formed. Even yet, many still hoped for annexation to the United States. In 1869 Céspedes suggested to the Cuban agent in New York that he should ask the Washington government for annexation, and he himself wrote to President Grant to the same purpose. Later that same year, prominent members of the Cuban Assembly of Representatives came out for this idea. Meanwhile, however, it was necessary to consider the immediate needs of the war with Spain. One of the first acts of the new government was to declare for an emancipation of the slaves. Unquestionably one of the moving causes of this decision was a desire to obtain the services of colored men in the patriot armies. And in fact they did make up a large proportion of the soldiery. On April 10, 1869, a Constitution for the new republic was drawn up, and Céspedes became president. This government was of necessity self-constituted and roving, having many vicissitudes which need not be followed here. Céspedes was succeeded in the presidency by Salvador Cisneros (who, as a member of the Assembly, had favored annexation), Francisco Aguilera, Tomás Estrada Palma (later, first president of the republic after the winning of independence), and several others with a somewhat shadowy claim to the honor. But the real story of this period of Cuban history concerns the warfare in the field.

When the revolution of Yara was proclaimed, the patriot forces consisted of just 147 men, with not enough arms for a weapon apiece. But the army grew literally over night, and amounted to twenty-six thousand by the close of 1868. This was a great change from the days of López. Spain had far greater resources, however, both in men and equipment. So the Cubans began a guerrilla warfare which, while it won for them few substantial advantages, was very difficult to suppress. There was no centre of operations, no territory definitely under patriot control, and, as Saco had predicted, it was a war of destruction and murder, hardly touching the west, then the richest part of Cuba, at all. Indeed, the commerce of western Cuba actually increased in amount over former years. Santa Clara, Camagüey, and Oriente were in a continual turmoil, however. Life and property, especially in the rural districts, were never safe, whatever one's opinions might be. Early in the war the Spanish authorities in Oriente ordered the people to remain at their homes, on penalty of death for any man found absent without an excuse. Unoccupied habitations were to be burned, while those which were occupied were to fly a white flag. Women not living in their own homes were to go to one or other of two specified towns. The patriots replied by burning the estates of Spanish sympathizers. These actions of the contending parties were typical of the ruthless character of the war.

Eventually, Máximo Gómez, a native of the Dominican Republic, came to the fore as the principal patriot leader. His achievements at this time were to win for him the supreme command also in the final conflict of the century between Spain and Cuba. He gained a number of brilliant victories, but in 1875 was badly beaten at Puerto Príncipe (Camagüey), and this marked the turning-point of the war. It dragged on, another three years, but degenerated into something like banditry, with a motley throng of many races and varying colors making up the patriot forces. Most of the creole soldiers had by this time been killed, captured, or driven into exile, while a number, convinced of the hopelessness of the cause, had withdrawn from the struggle, accepting Spanish terms. In 1877 Martínez Campos, one of the ablest Spaniards of those times, became captain-general, and in 1878 persuaded the Cuban leaders to lay down their arms. By the Treaty of Zanjón, arranged by Martínez Campos and Gómez, peace was declared, Spain promising a political amnesty, the emancipation of the slaves who had fought in the Cuban cause, and various governmental reforms. Several Cuban leaders refused to recognize this treaty, and continued their operations. Among these were Calixto García, already a famous soldier and one of the Cuban presidents in the closing months of the war, and Antonio Maceo, an able mulatto, who was to become the greatest military leader in Cuban history. García was accompanied by the distinguished poet and patriot José Martí. All three of these men were to win their principal fame in the next Spanish war. There was some fighting to the close of the year 1880, an outbreak in 1885, and at all times a great lack of security. After 1880, however, the Cuban forces were more outlaws than patriots. And yet the Treaty of Zanjón was little more than a truce. The Cubans had by this time determined on independence, and irrespective of the fulfilment or non-fulfilment of the treaty they were certain to strike again at a favorable moment. The years from 1878 to 1895 were virtually, therefore, merely a period of preparation for the next war.

The Ten Years' War had cost some two hundred thousand lives and seven hundred million dollars in property loss, ending in defeat for the Cubans. Several matters had played a noteworthy part in bringing about the result. The Cubans themselves were as yet by no means in agreement over the desirability of a separation from Spain, let alone independence. Perhaps the strongest element in the Spanish armies during the war were the bodies of "Volunteers," as the resident soldiery fighting on the Spanish side were called. They played a part paralleling that of the Tories of the American Revolution, but were a comparatively more powerful group in Cuba than were the Tories of the United States. Another factor of note was the failure of the Cubans to get that outside help which Saco had prophesied would be essential if they were to win. A great deal of assistance was received from citizens of the United States, but the American government held back, as will be told in the next chapter.

Nevertheless, as Saco also foresaw, the Ten Years' War had been a necessary preliminary to the winning of independence. The Cubans needed to prove to themselves that they could cope with the military power of Spain. And they needed traditions of heroism and self-sacrifice as a foundation upon which to rear a structure of patriotism that would embrace all elements of Cuban citizenry. These things the Ten Years' War had accomplished. When the next conflict came the Cubans, far from being overawed by the might of Spain, were confident of victory, and the sons of the Volunteers of the previous war were, most of them, on the patriot side. They had learned that before all else they were Cubans, and no hardships or privations were too great for them to endure for love of country. And this time the great northern republic did not hold back for long, but came into the war, to decide the issue.[3]

[3] The best work on the beginnings of Spanish Cuba is Wright, Irene Aloha, *The early history of Cuba, 1492-1586*, New York, 1916. Johnson, *The history of Cuba*, v. I-III, was most prominently used for the rest of the chapter, but a number of valuable items were obtained from Trelles, *Biblioteca histórica cubana*, II, 142-176. Taylor, Charles Belden, *Spanish colonial institutions of Cuba in the nineteenth century* (M. A. thesis, 1925; Ms. in the Library of the University of California), is a useful study of the period it covers.

CHAPTER III

THE UNITED STATES AND CUBA, TO 1895

Few regions of the world have been more continuously a matter of concern to the government and people of the United States than the island of Cuba. Among the many causes for this interest, that of the strategic importance of the island in American affairs is deserving of first place. The seal of the republic represents Cuba in the form of a key to the Americas, stretching out from Florida on the one hand to Yucatán on the other. This has been expressed in a recent article as follows:

"Cuba, lying at important crossroads of Caribbean and Gulf trade routes, commands the only two entrances to the Gulf of Mexico and one of the chief passages to the Caribbean Sea . . . Thus it is in a position to bottle up the Gulf ports of the United States and to jeopard that nation's control of interoceanic canal routes. Furthermore, its many large and easily defensible harbors could serve as unexcelled bases for enemy ships engaged in blockading the ports or hampering the commerce of the United States." [1]

The precise reasons for American interest in the strategic position of Cuba have changed from time to time, but the importance of the geographic position and character of the island has continued, whatever the new conditions. Other considerations making for close relations between the United States and Cuba have been set forth in the same article, as follows:

[1] Whittlesey, D S, *Geographic factors in the relations of the United States and Cuba*, in *Geographical re-* *view*, v. XII, pp. 241-256, at 241; Apr., 1922.

"To commerce the proximity of island to continent is of basic import, for the short and cheap carriage between Cuban ports and those of the southern and eastern coasts of North America has helped to make the United States Cuba's best customer and one of the countries from which it buys most heavily. The climatic contrasts between the two domains, in conjunction with their proximity, have had further far-reaching results. Cuba, lying in the path of warm rainy trade winds, produces as its agricultural staples sugar and tobacco, besides cacao and tropical fruits and nuts. These find a ready and constant market in the United States, which in turn can supply Cuba with cereals, meat products, and fabricated goods. Furthermore, the predominance of large-scale agriculture in Cuba opens an outlet near home for capital of American investors who wish to keep an eye on their projects. Finally, the fact that Cuban agriculture is chiefly of the plantation type resulted in the use of negro slaves, and the island was entangled for years in the perplexing slavery issue of the continent. More recently the mild Cuban winters have attracted pleasure seekers from the rigorous climate of northern United States, and Cubans in turn have spent their summers in the northern Appalachians."[2]

Long before the United States came into being with the Declaration of Independence in 1776, Cuba had inevitably been a prominent factor in the international rivalries of European powers in the Americas. Many a project was devised in England for filching the island from Spanish control, but Spain clung tenaciously to Cuba, realizing how the rest of her empire depended on it. English interest, meanwhile, passed on to the American colonies, which were fully aware of the importance of Cuba in their affairs. A Mr. Hamilton proposed the conquest of the island by English colonial troops in 1739, saying:

"If the Crown of England could become possessed of the Island of Cuba, that Key of all America, no man of knowledge can denye but that Great Britain, in that case must become possessed of the whole Trade of the Spanish Empire; and if the simple Privilege of trading with these People, upon very high terms, is now become one of the greatest Prizes contended for by all the Powers in Europe, sure England will not neglect

[2] Whittlesey, D S, *Geographic view*, v. XII, pp. 241-256, at 241-242; *factors in the relations of the United* Apr., 1922. *States and Cuba*, in *Geographical re-*

any opportunity which is offer'd of acquiring such a possession as must Infallibly Secure that whole Invaliable trade to its Subjects alone." [2]

During the Seven Years' War, Governor Pownall of Massachusetts suggested an attack on Cuba, and when Lord Albemarle took Havana in 1762 there were a number of colonial troops in his army. Both Spain and France insisted upon the return of Cuba to the former in 1763, declaring that peace would be of no avail without it. This may have been a bit of good fortune eventually for the United States. As one writer has put it,

"If England had held it during the American Revolution it would doubtless have delayed the success of the American colonies. It was there that many of the fleets which harmed England found a harbor. If England had held Cuba after 1783, the United States boundary might have been limited to the Mississippi."

In the years following the winning of American independence there was a great migration across the Alleghenies from the Atlantic states. The newly-founded western settlements had no outlet for their goods to compare with that of water transportation down the Mississippi to New Orleans and thence through the Gulf of Mexico. The acquisition of New Orleans at the time of the Louisiana purchase in 1803 served to relieve the situation only in part, for the west was still at the mercy of any power that might hold Florida or Cuba. As early as 1807 Jefferson remarked that in case of a war with Spain, Cuba might "add itself to our confederation." The invasion of Spain by Napoleon in 1808 caused no little anxiety in the United States on account of possible complications in Spanish America. Gallatin wrote Jefferson that he was

[2] This quotation and others in this chapter for which no citation is given are from the Callahan volume (cf. n. 10), of which this chapter is in the main a summary.

afraid England might now try to get Cuba, saying its possession by either France or England would be a "drawback" to the United States. "I shall sincerely lament Cuba falling into any hands but those of its present owners," he added. With these views Jefferson was in entire agreement. The western attitude about Cuba was squarely presented in a letter to the Secretary of State, dated December 10, 1810, by Governor Claiborne of Louisiana.

"There is nothing I so much desire," said Claiborne, "as to see the flag of my Country reared on the Moro Castle. Cuba is the real mouth of the Mississippi, and the nation possessing it, can at any time command the trade of the Western States. Give us Cuba and the American Union is placed beyond the reach of change."[4]

Jefferson was among the earliest and most enthusiastic proponents of the acquisition of Cuba by the United States. Late in 1808 he was visited by a Cuban deputation which came to urge the annexation of the island to the northern republic, now that Spain seemed to have passed over to Napoleon. Jefferson took no action, but just before he went out of office in 1809 is alleged to have said, "We must have the Floridas and Cuba." In later years he wrote many letters to Madison and Monroe, pointing out the importance of Cuba to the United States. In a letter of 1809 to Madison, for example, he suggested that Napoleon might be willing to give Cuba to the United States to keep this country from interfering with French plans elsewhere in Hispanic America.

"That would be a price," said Jefferson, "and I would immediately erect a column on the southernmost limit of Cuba, and inscribe on it a *ne plus ultra* as to us in that direction."

The same wish was often expressed by leading American statesmen of the next fifty years. It was not so much that

[4] Cited in Pérez, Luis Marino, Re- association, *Publications*, v. X, pp. lations with Cuba, in Southern history 203-214, at 203; July, 1906.

they desired Cuba for itself, as that they were afraid some European power, as Madison put it, "might make a fulcrum of that position against the commerce and security of the United States."

The purchase of Florida in 1819, following the earlier acquisition of West Florida, added to the peace of mind of the western states, but made the Cuban question all the more acute, as the only surviving problem of its kind. For several years before 1819 there had been frequent rumors that Spain might cede Cuba to England. A large body of English public opinion favored such a settlement, and when it was evident that the United States was to get Florida this element almost insisted that England take steps at once to acquire Cuba. During July and August 1820 the London Morning Chronicle ran a series of articles by Mr. J. Freeman Rattenbury, discussing the Florida purchase. According to him this added vast strength to the United States, which needed no longer to fear a secession of the trans-Allegheny country, and it constituted a grave danger to British interests in the West Indies. He suggested that Spain should turn over Cuba to England as an indemnity for the harm the latter had suffered by the transfer of Florida to the American republic. England must now have Havana as a "depot of thunder" to awe the United States, and if Spain would not cede Cuba, then as a matter of self-defence England should take it by force. "The apologists for the seizure of the fleet at Copenhagen could not want an excuse for this equally necessary violence," he added.[5] The London Times took the same view. Referring to the proposed cession of Cuba to England as an offset to the acquisition of Florida, a writer in

[5] This is a reference to the British seizure of the Danish fleet in 1807 without a declaration of war. This was done to prevent its falling into the hands of Napoleon.

the Times insisted that "The two transactions are necessary parts of the same whole, and must be, if possible, put out of hand together." The much desired Cuban "compensation" to England was not obtained, however. Whatever other considerations may have held back the British authorities at this time, they well knew that they would meet with vigorous resistance by the United States.

For the next quarter of a century the United States was constantly disturbed, nevertheless, by a fear that England or France might get Cuba. There were rumors that England would give Gibraltar and cash for Cuba, that Spain would turn over Cuba as security for a loan from England, that the British and French fleets appearing from time to time in Cuban waters (ostensibly to check piracy or, in the case of English ships, the slave trade) were to be utilized in fact to seize the island, or that the Spanish Bourbons might cede it to the Bourbons of France in return for military or financial assistance. On at least one occasion Spain really was ready to cede Cuba to France. Hard pressed for funds with which to carry on the Carlist War, the queen regent, Cristina, planned to sell Cuba, Porto Rico, and the Philippines in 1836. The agreement had been made, and was ready for signature, when the *bourgeois* French monarch, Louis Philippe, haggled for a slight reduction in price. Pushing the contract across the table he said that the reduction would have to be made, or the contract might as well be thrown in the fire. Thereupon the Spanish envoy, who was personally opposed to the cession, crumpled up the document and threw it into the fire! Thus narrowly did the United States escape a controversy over the Monroe Doctrine idea.

The United States was unceasingly vigilant to oppose any such contingency. Indeed, its concern over Cuba had been one of the principal factors leading to the enunciation of the Monroe Doctrine. John Quincy Adams, the author of that famous document, expressed his views about Cuba in a letter he wrote on April 28, 1823, to our minister in Spain.

"Cuba," he said, "almost in sight of our shores, from a multitude of considerations, has become an object of transcendent importance to the commercial and political interests of our Union. Its commanding position, with reference to the Gulf of Mexico and the West India seas; the character of its population; its situation midway between our southern coast and the island of St. Domingo; its safe and capacious harbor of the Havana, fronting a long line of our shores destitute of the same advantage; the nature of its productions and of its wants, furnishing the supplies and needing the returns of a commerce immensely profitable and mutually beneficial,—give it an importance in the sum of our national interests with which that of no other foreign territory can be compared, and little inferior to that which binds the different members of this Union together. Such, indeed, are, between the interests of that island and of this country, the geographical, commercial, moral, and political relations, formed by nature, gathering, in the process of time, and even now verging to maturity, that, in looking forward to the probable course of events, for the short period of half a century, it is scarcely possible to resist the conviction that the annexation of Cuba to our federal republic will be indispensable to the continuance and integrity of the Union itself. It is obvious, however, that for this event we are not yet prepared. Numerous and formidable objections to the extension of our territorial dominions beyond sea, present themselves to the first contemplation of the subject; obstacles to the system of policy by which alone that result can be compassed and maintained, are to be foreseen and surmounted, both from at home and abroad; but there are laws of political, as well as of physical gravitation; and if an apple, severed by the tempest from its native tree, cannot choose but fall to the ground, Cuba, forcibly disjoined from its own unnatural connexion with Spain, and incapable of self-support, can gravitate only towards the North American Union, which, by the same law of nature, cannot cast her off from its bosom." [6]

In the same year Jefferson wrote:

"I have ever looked on Cuba as the most interesting addition which could ever be made to our system of States . . . Her addition to our

[6] U. S., House, Exec. Doc., 32d   121, pp. 6-7.
Cong., 1st Sess. (1851-1852), Doc. No.

confederacy is exactly what is wanting to advance our power as a nation to the point of its utmost interest."

On the whole, however, the United States was satisfied to see Cuba remain in the possession of Spain, a country that was too weak to threaten the United States. A long line of American Secretaries of State kept England and France constantly apprised of the fact that the United States would resist an acquisition of Cuba by either of them, and advised the Spanish authorities that they could count on the full support of the American military and naval forces to prevent a forced cession to another European country.

Realizing the attitude of the American government, England and France adopted a similar policy concerning Cuba. Both wanted it if ever a propitious moment should favor them, but in the meantime preferred Spain's retention of the island to an acquisition by either of the other two powers involved. According to a writer in the London Courier in 1825, Cuba was the

"Turkey of trans-Atlantic politics, tottering to its fall, and kept from falling only by the struggles of those who contend for the right of catching her in her descent."

The British government, however, seems eventually to have become convinced that there was slight hope of an annexation to England. Cuban sentiment rejected the idea because with England the island could be no more than a colony and because of England's stand in favor of the emancipation of slaves; many in England itself drew back on account of slavery, since it would cost heavily to bring about abolition through purchase of the negroes from their owners; and finally there was the determined adherence of the United States to the Monroe Doctrine as an obstacle in England's path. So British statesmen for a while tried to persuade the

American and French governments to join with them in a
self-denying ordinance, guaranteeing the island to Spain.
France usually rejected these suggestions, but in any event
the United States would at no time have agreed to them.
Quite aside from the "no entangling alliance" principle, there
were few American statesmen who did not believe but that
Cuba would some day be a part of the United States, and
they were unwilling to bind the country indefinitely. As
John Quincy Adams put it in 1823, the United States had
no intention of playing a game of "grab," but the Cubans
might some day wish to "exercise their primitive rights,"
and seek admission to the Union, while it was certain that
they would not seek annexation to England. Therefore an
agreement with England meant only a pledge as against
the United States.

The Spanish American Wars of Independence introduced
a further complication. Apart from the question of independence, there was the added factor of Cuba's serving as a
base for Spanish attacks against the rebellious colonies.
Several times in the later years of the war, plans were set
on foot to revolutionize the island or to send expeditions
from Colombia or Mexico to overwhelm the Spanish forces
there. In each case France, England, and the United States
opposed the idea. France, as a close ally of the Spanish Bourbons, was against it on every score. England and the United
States objected primarily because they feared that a Colom-
bian or Mexican occupation could not be permanent, wherefore Cuba might fall into other hands. In particular, England feared the United States, and the United States feared
England, though each had some fear of France. The Washington authorities were also alarmed at the prospect of abolition in Cuba, because of the effect it might have on the
southern states. The American people were enthusiastically

in sympathy with the patriot cause in the mainland parts of Spanish America, but Cuba occupied a special position calling for a different point of view. Indeed, it was the Cuban question that caused the United States to delay in sending delegates to Bolívar's Panamá Congress of 1826. When at length they were allowed to start, they received instructions that were opposed to the separation of Cuba from Spain. As already pointed out, Cuban opinion itself was not at that time in favor of independence. Many wanted a separation from Spain, but desired to join with Colombia, Mexico, or the United States. Probably most of this element favored annexation to the American republic. Cuban agents visited Washington to urge the idea, and it was discussed in Cabinet meetings. Some Americans wished to "take the goods the gods provide us," John C. Calhoun among them, but the wisdom of Adams prevailed in this instance as in so many others. He was unwilling to risk British opposition, for if England went to war about the matter her fleet would enable her to get Cuba for herself, at least for many years. The best policy was to let Spain keep the island until the United States could get in, without risk of losing it.

The annexation of Texas in 1845 and the further annexations resulting from the Mexican War, 1846-1848, gave rise to a new attitude in the United States with respect to Cuban affairs. For a little over a decade, down to the outbreak of the Civil War, the American people were in the grip of "manifest destiny." There was no longer any great fear of England or France, and southward expansion had its advocates in all sections of the country. Cuba, primarily because of its strategic position, was particularly desired. The Mississippi valley was not quite so much at the mercy of a strong power in control of Cuba as formerly, for direct communications with the east by way of the Great Lakes and the canals, but especially through the medium of railroads, were rapidly being developed. A large part of western commerce still made its way through the gulf, past Cuba, however. But the question of trans-isthmian routes to the Pacific Ocean, especially to the newly-won golden California, had come prominently to the fore. Cuba now occupied the same position with respect to the far west and Pacific coast that it had held earlier to the Mississippi valley. On this score a report by a naval expert, Lieutenant Dahlgren, is interesting:

"The true and only key, however, to the defense of these shores, and to the immense interest there collected, is the Havana. The island to which it belongs enters its western extreme in the Gulf, leaving but two passages for vessels, so narrow as to be commanded with the greatest facility; these are the great thoroughfares of trade and the mail steamers from New Orleans to California and New York. Hence, if the use of the Havana be even at the disposal of an enemy while in the hands of a neutral Power, each and all of these interests could be with difficulty defended, even by a superior naval force, and never guaranteed against severe losses. While from it, as a United States port, a squadron of moderate size would cover the southeast and Gulf coasts, protect the foreign and inshore traders, and secure the lines from New York or New Orleans to the Pacific States by way of the Isthmus, its occupation would necessarily be the object of every expedition, military or naval, preliminary to any attempt on the southern trade or territory." [1]

Already, too, plans were being broached for a canal in Central America or Panamá, to which Cuba would have just as important a relation as it did to California. These years, therefore, were filled with projects for the acquisition of Cuba, ranging from filibustering expeditions to proposals for a purchase of the island. Presently, another factor made itself felt that may have decided the issue against an American acquisition of Cuba: the slavery dispute in the United States. The southern states began to regard "manifest des-

[1] U. S., Cong. Globe, 35th Cong., 2d Sess. (1858-1859), Part I, p. 453.

tiny" as a medium for slavery extension, through which they might build up their political strength against the onslaughts of the abolitionists. Cuba was ideally suited to their purposes, not only because of its close connection with the United States, but also because it was one of the few remaining regions where slavery existed. It was not long, therefore, before the early enthusiasm of the north dwindled away, until at length all desire for the annexation of Cuba had passed.

James K. Polk, frank exponent of American expansion, was not satisfied with the acquisitions of what had once been Mexican territory. He distinctly wished to add the annexation of Cuba to his list of achievements. There was hardly any concealment of his desire. Vice-President Dallas publicly toasted "the annexation of Cuba" in 1845, and a resolution was introduced in the Senate, late that same year, for the President to open negotiations for the purchase of the island. Polk was not willing to compromise the honor of the government, however, and when asked to lend his support to a proposed Cuban revolution in favor of annexation, he replied, as he sets forth in his diary,

"That if Cuba was ever obtained by the U. S. it must be by amicable purchase, and that as the President of the U. S. I could give no countenance to such a step, and could not wink at such a movement." [8]

Polk also drew back before a parallel opportunity to acquire Yucatán, the great peninsula that juts out from southern Mexico toward Cuba. That vast territory had for some years been an unwilling member of the Mexican federation. It drew out from 1829 to 1832, and did so again in 1841, but was overcome in 1843. In 1846 Yucatán again resumed her independence, taking no part in the war between Mexico and

[8] Polk, James Knox, *Diary* (4 vols., Chicago. 1910), III, 476-477.

the United States. On the contrary, in the spring of 1848 the Yucatán authorities asked Polk's government to annex their territory to the United States, hoping in that way to protect the country from Mexico on the one hand and the British in Belize on the other. Some of the people of Yucatán had considered an annexation to England, but Polk was unwilling to see a transfer of the territory to any other power, though not disposed to favor the Yucatán offer to come under the American flag.

"From its vicinity to Cuba, the Capes of Florida, to New Orleans, and indeed to our whole southwestern coast, it would be dangerous to our peace and security if it should become the colony of any foreign nation," he said.

Neither Polk nor his successors would lend any encouragement to López or other promoters of violence in getting Cuba, but Polk did take steps, as soon as the Mexican war was over, to secure Cuba by purchase. British activities in Central America were one of the reasons for his desire for an immediate acquisition of Cuba, and he also feared that England still had designs on the island. This was pointed out by Secretary of State James J. Buchanan, June 17, 1848, in a long letter to Mr. Saunders, the American minister to Spain. Minister Saunders soon became convinced, however, that no Spanish government could survive a sale of Cuba to the United States. The Spanish Minister of State told him that "he believed it to be the feeling of the country, that sooner than see the island transferred to any power, they would prefer to see it sunk in the ocean." Defeated in the elections of 1848, the Democrats were succeeded in 1849 by the less imperialistic Whig administrations of Taylor (1849-1850) and Fillmore (1850-1853). Taylor might have been ready to take over Cuba, but was not willing to go even to the length of suggesting a purchase, holding that any such pro-

posal must come *from* Spain. Fillmore, however, was doubtful whether the acquisition of Cuba would be desirable at that
time. It was during these administrations that the principal
efforts of López were made, but no moment could have been
chosen when the help or the connivance of the United States
in aid of filibustering expeditions was less likely to be obtained.

The Democrats returned to power in 1853, and remained in the saddle until 1861. Pierce (1853-1857) and
Buchanan (1857-1861) were willing to go to lengths that
might have been successful if employed at an earlier time by
Polk, before the anti-slavery movement had gained full
headway in the north. Pierce announced in his inaugural
address that he would "not be controlled by any timid fore-
bodings of evil from expansion," adding that "the acquisition
of certain possessions not within our jurisdiction" might become "eminently important for our protection, if not in the
future essential for the preservation of the rights of commerce and the peace of the world." Diplomatic posts abroad
were filled primarily with a view to the Cuban question.
Buchanan, Mason, and Soulé were sent respectively to England, France, and Spain. Soulé's appointment was not calculated to please Spain, for he had publicly favored the
López expeditions, and was known to prefer the "Texas
game" as a method of acquiring Cuba rather than a purchase. He was received, however, though heartily disapproved by the higher Spanish officials and the press. It was
not long before an incident occurred in Cuba which gave him
a chance to exert pressure on the Spanish government.

There had been much cause for irritation in American
relations with Cuba. Aside from the legal restrictions on
American trade, the manner of enforcing the laws gave rise
to much annoyance. Whenever a complaint was made at

Havana, the captain-general was in the habit of denying his right to handle diplomatic business, referring the American government to the Spanish minister in Washington or the State Department in Spain. Officials in Spain or the minister in the United States would then refer to one another or set on foot an enquiry of the captain-general. As a result there were exasperating delays and perhaps an evasion of the issues involved. The most striking instance of this kind was the "Black Warrior" affair of 1854. The "Black Warrior" plied between Mobile and New York, stopping at Havana for passengers and mail. The law required a manifest of the cargo in such cases, but as it was a mere formality it had never been asked for. The "Black Warrior" had a cargo of cotton, but the captain, following the usual custom, made no mention of it to the officials of the port. He was advised presently that the cargo would be confiscated because he had failed to comply with the law. Asking permission to correct the manifest, he was refused, and abandoned the ship with his officers and crew when the Spaniards came on board to unload the cotton.

The above incident took place on February 28, 1854. Instructions were at once forwarded to Soulé to demand satisfaction of the Spanish government. A somewhat acrimonious correspondence between Soulé and the Spanish Minister of State followed, during which Soulé all but threatened war. Meanwhile, the Spanish government made haste to settle with the owners of the "Black Warrior," leaving the United States with scant cause for complaint. President Pierce seemed willing for a time to go to war, but something occurred in another quarter to assure the opposition of the north to the project. This was the Kansas-Nebraska legislation of 1853-1854. It is probable that the victory of the slavery-extensionists in this issue was the principal stumbling-block in the way of an acquisition of Cuba, whether by purchase or by force, because of the now insistent opposition of the north. The southern extremists were eager to bring about annexation by filibustering expeditions, but neither Pierce nor his secretary of State, Marcy, would countenance that. Instead they proposed to use the vast body of American claims against Spain, including the "Black Warrior" case, as a lever to bring about a voluntary cession of the island. In this connection Soulé was instructed to confer with Buchanan and Mason. This brought on the somewhat celebrated Ostend Manifesto.

The three American diplomats met at Ostend, Belgium, in October 1854, and exchanged views. Soulé had prepared an elaborate document, and with this as a basis Buchanan wrote the manifesto, which all three signed. It was in the form of a report to Secretary Marcy, but gained its title of "manifesto" because it was given out for publication. It began by urging the purchase of Cuba for not exceeding $120,000,-000, going on to recite the advantages both to Spain and the United States. To the United States, however, its "immediate acquisition" was of "paramount importance," and any delay in getting it would be "exceedingly dangerous to the United States." Taking up the question of a possible Spanish refusal to sell, the authors of the document made the following bold suggestion of policy, based on the principle that "Self-preservation is the first law of nature, with States as well as with individuals":

"After we shall have offered Spain a price for Cuba far beyond its present value, and this shall have been refused, it will then be time to consider the question, does Cuba, in the possession of Spain, seriously endanger our internal peace and the existence of our cherished Union? Should this question be answered in the affirmative, then, by every law, human and divine, we shall be justified in wresting it from Spain if we possess the power."

Though met with ridicule or denunciation in both Europe and the United States, the Ostend Manifesto did not in fact represent the attitude of the administration. It is now regarded as a clever political trick of Buchanan's to secure the Democratic nomination for the presidency,—a trick that worked. Marcy wrote Soulé repelling the suggestion that Cuba was necessary at that time to the self-preservation of the United States, and to a friend in New York he expressed his opinion in a letter of April 15, 1855, as follows:

"I am entirely opposed to getting up a war for the purpose of seizing Cuba . . . The robber doctrine, I abhor. If carried out it would degrade us in our own estimation and disgrace us in the eyes of the civilized world . . . Cuba would be a very desirable possession, if it came to us in the right way, but we cannot afford to get it by robbery or theft."[9]

The Ostend Manifesto made Buchanan acceptable to the south, and he secured the Democratic nomination in 1856. The Democratic platform had a strong plank in favor of the acquisition of Cuba, while the newly-founded Republican party stigmatized the Ostend Manifesto as "the highwayman's plea." In his speech accepting the nomination Buchanan said that if he could settle the slavery question, "and then add Cuba to the Union," he would be "willing to give up the ghost," and let the Vice-President succeed him.

Buchanan won the election, but met with as little success in his efforts to acquire Cuba as in settling the slavery question in the United States. "Expansion is in the future the policy of our country, and only cowards fear and oppose it," he said on one occasion in 1858, but the "cowards" were too much for the "brave" Buchanan. A bill was introduced in the Senate in 1859 appropriating thirty millions, designed as a first payment, to facilitate the acquisition of Cuba as a

[9] Quoted in Moore, John Bassett, in *Forum*, v. XXI, pp. 288-300, at *The question of Cuban belligerency*, 300; May, 1896.

state in the American Union at a price of not more than $120,000,000. But the bill never got to a vote. Once again a convention year, 1860, rolled around, and again the annexation plank appeared in the Democratic platform. This time, however, the Republicans won, and the election of Lincoln was followed by the great American Civil War, during which the long-fought Cuban question was very nearly eclipsed from view.

Spain showed a tendency to favor the Confederacy during the Civil War, granting rights of belligerency only sixty-six days after the firing on Fort Sumter, but the battle of Gettysburg ended any prospect there might have been for her to extend effective aid. The north felt the lack of a naval base in the West Indies, which the experts claimed would have enabled her to bring the war to an end much sooner. For this purpose, however, any one of a number of places other than Cuban ports might later have been obtained, but the United States came out of the war with such power that there was no immediate prospect of a conflict with a foreign country. Indeed, a chance to acquire portions of the Danish West Indies (since bought in entirety) was allowed to pass. Furthermore, many of the issues that had made for the American policy of an annexation of Cuba no longer existed. Slavery had been abolished in the United States, and a slave-holding Cuba was now certainly not desired. Some few might have wished to acquire Cuba in order to abolish slavery, but this argument was not very insistently put forward. Direct communication with the trans-Allegheny west had long since developed on a considerable scale, and a few years after the war a railway to the Pacific coast was completed. By the Clayton-Bulwer Treaty of 1850, too, the United States was assured of participation with England in the building and use of an isthmian canal.

All of these things made the possession of Cuba by the United States less necessary than before. In Cuba a new state of affairs now existed. A strong pro-Spanish party wanted to keep conditions as they were, with slavery as the cornerstone of Cuban institutions, while the Cuban party leaned toward abolition, but favored independence rather than annexation to the United States. American concern about Cuba therefore entered a comparatively unimportant phase. The United States urged Spain to take steps looking toward emancipation, which was eventually accomplished, but met with little success in her efforts to promote American commerce with Cuba or to get Spain to establish a more liberal system of government. The Ten Years' War, commencing in 1868, inaugurated an active diplomatic era, though divorced from desires of annexation or fears of England or France. The two latter powers, indeed, might no longer have interposed serious objections to an American acquisition of Cuba, so greatly had the situation changed.

As was to be expected, the American people sympathized with the Cuban patriots in the Ten Years' War, very ardently at first, but less enthusiastically as the conflict dragged out almost interminably and degenerated in character. Only at infrequent intervals was there anything approaching a desire for war with Spain. As for the United States government, it was faithful to its international duties toward Spain, and was quite effective in preventing the despatch of help from American ports to the Cuban insurgents. To be sure, some boats escaped with shipments of supplies and occasional small parties of recruits, and large numbers of Cubans who were engaged in an active propaganda against Spain resided in the United States. Most of the war (1868-1878) was coincident with the administration of President Grant (1869-1877), whose personal sympathies were in favor of the Cubans, though he gave them no material help. On one occasion, in 1869, he signed a proclamation recognizing Cuban belligerency, an act which would have been of inestimable value to the insurrectionists, but Mr. Fish, the Secretary of State, who disapproved of it, held up the document. Grant was grateful when he learned that it had not been issued, for by that time he realized that his action had been premature. Thereafter he repeatedly opposed an accord of the rights of belligerency. For example, he pointed out in his message of June 13, 1870, that such a grant must depend on conditions showing a probability of success. The Cubans held no seaports or considerable towns, had no established seat of government, and no commerce or manufactures. There was therefore no war in the international sense, however severe the fighting might be.

The patience of the American administration was strained to the breaking-point at times by Spanish practices. In 1869 the Spanish captain-general authorized the capture of any vessel on the high seas, whatever the flag, if it were carrying aid to the insurgents, and ordered that persons found on such boats should be executed as pirates. The United States denied Spain's right to take such action except in time of war, intimating that a continuance of the practice would be considered as a Spanish declaration of a state of war in Cuba, which meant that the insurrectionists could have the rights of belligerents. This brought about a quick modification of the decree, not however before several American vessels had been seized. The fighting in Cuba was carried on in a most barbarous fashion by both sides, in course of which grave damage and loss of life were inflicted upon Americans. No protests could be made to the unrecognized Cubans, although they lost a great deal of the world's sympathies by their manner of conducting the war, but there were frequent representations made to Spain, both on account of her inability to end the devastating conflict, and because of the direct acts of her own soldiery or officials. In 1869 two Americans were captured with an insurgent force, and were put to death after barely the shadow of a trial. That same year the Cubans began a general destruction of property, especially sugar estates, which entailed no small loss to American interests. The Spaniards retaliated by confiscating the estates of those suspected as Cuban sympathizers, and much American-owned property was seized. The most flagrant disregard of American sentiment came up, however, in connection with notorious "Virginius" affair.

The "Virginius" was a former American vessel that had been purchased by Cuban sympathizers for use in conveying war supplies. In 1873 this boat, while flying the American flag, was captured either on the high seas or else in British waters off Jamaica, and was taken into Santiago. There, after a mockery of a trial, the captain of the "Virginius" and fifty-one others, largely Americans or Englishmen, were shot. Ninety-three more probably owed their lives to Sir Lambton Lorraine of the British man-o'war "Niobe." "Shoot another Englishman or American," Lorraine informed the Spanish commander, "and the 'Niobe' will bombard the city." The executions stopped! This barbarous affair was deprecated everywhere, and caused great indignation and excitement in the United States. For a time there was a clamor for war. General Sickles, the American representative in Spain, was instructed to demand the punishment of General Burriel (the Spanish commander responsible for the outrage), indemnities to the families of the deceased, and a salute to the American flag. Failing satisfaction, he was to ask for his passports. The Spanish government announced its willingness to accede to the first two of these demands, but objected to the third, on grounds that the "Virginius" had no right to fly the American flag, since it was in fact owned by citizens of Cuba. General Sickles pressed the American claims vigorously, but did not receive the full support of the government. Spain had just become a republic, and had been recognized as such by the United States; so there was no wish to embarrass her too greatly with American claims. The Attorney General of the United States upheld Spain on the question of the flag. The salute was therefore dispensed with. Eventually, after a year of pressure, Spain paid an indemnity of eighty thousand dollars for the heirs of the Americans who had been executed, but General Burriel, far from being punished, as Spain had promised, was promoted! Meanwhile, General Sickles had resigned. The authorities at Washington had not disapproved of his conduct, but he himself had disapproved of the government's vacillation "between extreme demands at the outset and large concessions to Spain in the end."

Early in the war the United States offered her mediation in the conflict, being moved to that end by the serious damage occasioned to American interests, as well as by the dictates of humanity. In 1869 the United States proposed the following terms as the basis for American mediation: an acknowledgment of Cuban independence by Spain; in return therefor, payment of an indemnity to Spain by Cuba; the abolition of slavery in Cuba; and an armistice, pending negotiations. The first of these provisions was the principal stumbling-block. Spanish statesmen were often able to contemplate the idea of Cuban independence, and General Prim while he was virtual dictator in Spain distinctly favored it, but they invariably insisted that Spanish honor would not permit of this while the insurgents were still in the field; if they would lay down their arms, Spain might consent to independence, provided a majority of the Cubans wanted it. This, however, was an impossible condition, as there was no likelihood of persuading the Cubans to trust in Spanish promises. The negotiations over mediation were continued a while, but as no real progress was made they were presently withdrawn.

Spanish public opinion was at no time in favor of Cuban independence. Fear of reprisals against Spaniards, as well as concern over the national honor, influenced them in their opposition. Curiously enough, however, there were moments when many Spaniards would have agreed to a transfer of Cuba to the United States, in return for an indemnity and commercial advantages. In 1870, for example, several Spanish newspapers, most of them republican, advocated the cession, asserting that it could be done without loss of honor, as the insurrection was nearly suppressed. In this way, they argued, Spain might obtain a much-needed sum of money, and be relieved of the burden of managing Cuban affairs. To the American who is accustomed to the somewhat wearisome charges against the United States of an "all-grabbing" imperialism, one further assertion of these Spanish journals is interesting. They referred to a traditional American policy *against* the acquisition of colonies, citing the frequent American refusals to take the Sandwich (Hawaiian) Islands and the neglect to annex the Dominican Republic or the Danish island of St. Thomas when they were offered to the United States. The Spanish proponents of a sale were afraid that the growing indifference of the United States to annexations of territory might later make it impossible to sell Cuba to the American republic.

Offers of mediation had failed, but still the war dragged on, though the Spanish government ever insisted that it was "about to end." Domestic troubles in the peninsula, however, kept Spain from exerting her full force in Cuba. So the United States, unwilling to suffer a prolongation of a state of affairs so harmful to American interests, began at length to consider an intervention. Having no intention of annexing Cuba, the Washington authorities hit upon a device that for a moment seemed likely to jeopardize that cornerstone of American foreign policy, the Monroe Doctrine. Late in 1875 Secretary Fish wrote to the American ministers at six of the European capitals, reciting the American grievances and suggesting the necessity for United States intervention unless Spain could be persuaded to end the war. The European powers were requested to urge Spain to stop it, thus avoiding the contemplated American action. This closely approximated an association for the settlement of an American problem, and when the House called on Fish for his department files he seems to have realized that he had made a mistake, for he suppressed some of the papers, denying that any "correspondence" had taken place, though admitting that he had sought the moral backing of Europe. The answers received were in any event none too favorable. The support of England was especially hoped for, but Lord Derby, who certainly understood that something more than silent approval was desired, told the American minister that the British government was not ready to bring pressure to bear upon Spain, and so did not wish to act unless Spain were willing. The answers of the other powers were even less satisfactory, and Spain herself thoroughly opposed the idea.

Secretary Fish next applied directly to Spain. Without going so far as to threaten intervention, he suggested, early in 1876, a better observance by Spain of treaty relations, the establishment of a more liberal and less corrupt government in Cuba, the gradual emancipation of the slaves, and an improvement of commercial facilities, together with a removal of the obstructions that hampered trade with the United States. The Spanish authorities agreed to all of these suggestions, though insisting that some time would be necessary to put them into effect. As now it did seem in fact as if the war were "about to end," the United States was virtually estopped from taking any further steps looking to an intervention. The Carlist wars in Spain had just been concluded, and the Bourbons firmly reëstablished on the throne. So it was possible to send considerable bodies of troops to Cuba. The fighting continued nearly two years more, but in 1878, as already related, an agreement was reached between the contending parties in the Peace of Zanjón.

For a few years the main problem in the relations of Spain and the United States was the fulfilment of Spanish promises. At the very outset of the Ten Years' War, in 1869, Spain had agreed to bring about an emancipation of the slaves in Cuba. During the war she was unable to do much on this score, however, as the insurgents had taken a stand for abolition, while the pro-Spanish element, on whom Spain had to depend in carrying on the war, was opposed to it. A law of 1870 provided for gradual emancipation over a long period of years, but this act was virtually thrown into the discard. Eventually Spain decided that there could be no emancipation while the insurrection continued. Even after the close of the war, abolition was for a time a football of Spanish politics, but in 1881 a law for gradual emancipation was again passed, and by 1886 slavery in Cuba came altogether to an end. Thus one of the promises made both to the United States and to the Cuban chieftains at Zanjón was fulfilled.

Another Spanish promise, to introduce good government in Cuba, one feature of which was to be Cuban representation in the Spanish Cortes, was also tardily fulfilled, but more in appearance than in fact. The constitutional rights of Spaniards were extended to Cubans, but there was an inconsistent definition, in 1878, of the powers of the Spanish governor-general. He was to have all the authority of a captain-general of other days. So the old evils went on. Offices were held by Spaniards as before, the governor-general named the representatives to the Cortes, and the former corrupt and unscientific methods in taxation and judicial procedure were continued. The debt occasioned by the Ten Years' War was saddled upon Cuba. Just before 1895, for example, it is said that but $746,000 out of twenty-six millions in taxes were employed on internal improvements. The remainder went to the Spanish army and administration and to payments on the debt. From about 1880, therefore, an autonomist, or home rule, movement developed in Cuba. Many who despaired of the possibility of a separation from Spain regarded this as the only solution for Cuban ills. Beyond the growth of a strong autonomist party, nothing was accomplished, for Spain was slow, as usual, to meet the wishes of her colonists. Naturally, therefore, many Cubans began to consider a fresh attempt to gain independence. The Ten Years' War had taught Spain nothing.

Americans and Cubans both were concerned over the restrictive Spanish commercial policy and the annoying methods of enforcing trade regulations. Seventy-five per cent of Cuba's exports went to the United States, and were paid for mostly in cash, because the Spanish tariff laws hindered the purchase of American goods. In sixteen years, 1876 to 1891 inclusive, the United States bought Cuban products to the extent of some $924,000,000 worth, and sold an amount valued only at about $189,000,000, leaving a balance of trade against the United States that was in fact quite as unfavorable to the Cubans as it was to the American merchants. It was cheaper to ship flour from the Mississippi valley to Spain, paying a duty there, and thence back to Cuba, than it was to send it direct to Havana. There were similar burdensome duties on other articles that had to be imported into Cuba, such as butter, lard, boots, and calicoes, to mention only a few. Even such American goods as were shipped in were always subject to exactions by grafting Spanish officials. Heavy penalties were inflicted for mere verbal inaccuracies or failure to observe trivial requirements. In 1881, for example, an American cattle vessel, which normally would have paid $14.90, was taxed $387.40, because it had some lumber on board. An agreement was made in 1884 removing some of the restrictions on American commerce, but President Cleveland had to protest, in 1886, that the treaty was not being observed. A reciprocity arrangement was made in that year, but in 1890 Spain suddenly increased the duties on American goods. The United States then offered Spain a more than usually broad reciprocity treaty, and there was a considerable Cuban agitation in favor of it. So the Spanish government yielded, and the new schedules were adopted in 1891. American commerce with Cuba took an immediate jump. In 1894 the volume of trade was $105,000,000, as against seventy-six millions in 1880. In that same year, however, the treaty was withdrawn.

Unsatisfactory commercial relations, such as those just mentioned, together with a continuance of the old evils in Cuba and the tardiness of Spain in settling American claims, caused some Americans and many Cubans to wonder whether annexation to the United States might not, after all, be the most desirable outcome of the Cuban problem. John Sherman visited Cuba in 1887, and was impressed by what he considered to be the deplorable conditions there. The inhabitants were, almost to a man, in favor of annexation, he said, but he felt that they were not ready for self-government, and was opposed to annexation. That same year the Englishman Froude visited the West Indies, spending some time in Cuba.

"The opinion of Cuba was and is that America is the residuary legatee of all the islands, Spanish and English," he said, "and that she will be forced to take charge of them in the end, whether she likes or not . . . If I were a West Indian, I should feel that under the Stars and Stripes I should be safer than I was at present from political experimenting."

Under President Cleveland (1885-1889) there was a momentary return of the traditional Democratic desire for the annexation of Cuba. Some overtures for a purchase were made to Spain, but were rejected. The next administration took the opposite stand, however, and in this it probably reflected American opinion more accurately than its predecessor had, because of the strong social objection to incorporating Cuba, with its motley and ill-prepared population, into the American Union. The United States wished for an end to the bad situation in Cuba, but hoped for some way out of it other than by annexation.

It was now time for Cuba to settle matters in her own fashion. On February 24, 1895, the revolution began. Spanish authorities looked on it as little more than a riot. One officer said that he did not like the prospect of chasing mountain goats. In fact, however, the *"grito,"* or cry, of '95 was to be the death-knell of Spanish rule in the island.[10]

[10] The principal work on this subject is Callahan, *Cuba and international relations,* Baltimore, 1899. This is an exceedingly meritorious study. There is an excellent chapter entitled *The diplomacy of the United States in regard to Cuba* in Latané, John Holladay, *The United States and Latin America* (New York. 1920), 83-143.

CHAPTER IV

THE CUBAN WAR OF INDEPENDENCE, 1895-1898

WHY did the last war for Cuban independence commence when it did? It is customary to recite a long list of causes, all of which may, indeed, have had their share of weight. There were the oft-given promises of reform, but a continuance of old evils. The world panic of 1893 may in a sense be said to have "caused" the outbreak of war. The price of sugar fell, and, as always happens in such an event in Cuba, it was followed by acute economic distress. The people looked to the government for help, but, as one writer has put it, they might as well have looked "at the moon." It is doubtful whether the authorities could have provided any noteworthy assistance, but they seemed to have taken the opposite course in 1894, when they cancelled the reciprocity treaty with the United States. But to say that the panic of 1893 or the various specific grievances of the Cubans were the vital factor in the background of independence would be like insisting that the murder of Sarajevo caused the World War of 1914. Indeed, it is all too easy to overemphasize the harshness of Spain. Veteran residents of Cuba in the foreign colony usually speak favorably of the days before '95. The following is a sample comment by an American who lived in Cuba in the early '90s:

"The Spanish period was an Acadia. Don't you believe the stories of Spanish oppression. Furthermore, the Spaniards were the ones who paid the taxes, as they were the principal element in business."

73

This may be an exaggeration in the opposite direction, but in point of fact it is not necessary to belabor Spain in connection with the outbreak of 1895. The war came because a great many Cubans wanted independence irrespective of the character of Spanish rule. The only way Spain could have prevented it would have been by a free grant of complete home rule at the least, and probably of independence. The war started at the precise time it did, because of the organizing genius of José Martí, famed Cuban patriot and poet, the hero and martyr of the revolution.

Cuban opinion was not more than usually hostile to Spain in the years just prior to 1895, despite the discontent over economic and political affairs. Possibly the majority among the educated classes would have been satisfied with autonomy for the island, though there were widely differing views as to the form it should take. In 1895 the Spanish government enacted a Cuban home rule law which may very well have been a sincere attempt to meet the Cubans part way. It was provided that the island was to be ruled by the governor-general (still to be appointed by the king) in conjunction with an insular Council, all of whose members were to be Cuban inhabitants, half of them appointed by the crown, and the other half elected by the Cuban people. Obviously this left control in the hands of the king, but it was only with difficulty that the Spanish loyalists in Cuba would consent to even this much of the home rule principle. The law was passed in February 1895, but never went into effect, for in that same month the revolution began. After all, the law of 1895 was merely an incident of no particular importance, for the revolution had really "begun" at least as far back as 1868. The defeat in the Ten Years' War and the failure of subsequent uprisings represented a mere interruption of the program in the minds of the leaders of the movement. They were waiting for a favorable opportunity to strike again. Certainly this was true of men like José Martí and Tomás Estrada Palma, who were the moving spirits in the background of the revolt.

Martí, though a mere youth, had been deported by the Spaniards as a dangerous revolutionary at the outbreak of the Ten Years' War. Returning to Cuba after the war, he was again arrested, following several anti-Spanish addresses, and was sent to a Spanish prison. He escaped, and made his way to the United States, where he devoted himself henceforth to the cause of Cuban freedom. Estrada Palma had been taken prisoner by the Spaniards at the time when he was President of the revolutionary government in the Ten Years' War, and had been immured in a Spanish prison until after the treaty of Zanjón. Refusing to accept the amnesty of the Spanish authorities, he went to the United States, and became the principal of a boys' school at Central Valley, New York. In 1892 Martí reorganized the Cuban Junta in New York City, with Estrada Palma as its president. Other clubs were formed subordinate to this in various parts of the world, but especially in Florida, where a great many Cubans were congregated. There were sixty-one such clubs at Key West and fifteen at Tampa. Funds were solicited for the cause, especially from Cubans in the United States, many of whom contributed a tenth of all their earnings. Much money was also given by Americans. Beyond question, the enthusiasm, spirit, and magnetic personality of Martí were the chief factor in the success of the Junta. He traveled about the United States and the Caribbean countries inspiring veterans of the previous war to lend their support to a new enterprise and gathering funds. All seemed to be in readiness in 1894, but the United States government seized the three vessels that the Junta had equipped. A little while later the revolution was formally launched with the *"grito"* of Baire, near Santiago, on February 24, 1895.

Martí himself had proceeded to the Dominican Republic to enlist Máximo Gómez, Cuban *generalissimo* of the previous war. On April 11 these two men, with a few companions, landed in eastern Cuba. It was not intended that Martí should remain in the island, as he could render much greater service in foreign countries, but it seems that the intrepid leader wanted at least a taste of fire, before resuming his diplomatic tasks. So far, the revolt had made only moderate progress. There had been outbreaks in several provinces, but they had gathered headway only in Oriente. Another of the famous veterans of the past war had taken the field in the person of that daring and capable mulatto, Antonio Maceo, who had proclaimed a provisional government, with Estrada Palma as President, Gómez commander-in-chief of the army, and Martí diplomatic agent abroad. Satisfied that a reasonably good beginning had been made, Martí left Gómez in May, and went south with an escort of fifty men, hoping to get to Jamaica and from there to the United States. A guide betrayed him to the Spaniards, who ambushed Martí's party and killed them to a man. Thus perished the acknowledged Father of Cuban Independence. It seemed at the time like an irreparable loss, but it may well have been a fortunate, if lamentable, accident,—fortunate, because it gave the revolution the stimulant of a hero and a martyr,—fortunate possibly for the later republic and for Martí's own fame, since it prevented him from risking his reputation in the whirlpool of partisan politics, leaving him as perhaps the one figure of the Independence era, concerning whom all Cubans can unite in expressions of love and praise. And in the meantime the work he could have done was capably performed by Estrada Palma and his aides in New York. Martí's real task, that of organizing and inspiring the revolution, was already accomplished.

And yet, at the time of Martí's death an unbiased observer would hardly have conceded the Cubans much prospect of success. With some thirty-three thousand soldiers already in the island, Spain might easily, as in fact she did, send two hundred thousand more. The Cubans could not muster nearly so many. Indeed, they probably did not have more than twenty-five thousand men in the field at any one time during the war. Their total enrollment for the entire three-year conflict, including those who were killed and those who served but a part of the time, with perhaps also a great many names that did not belong on the list at all or that represented only a very slight military service, was 53,774. In other respects, as well, the resources of Spain were far superior, while the Cubans themselves were by no means unanimous for independence, though the revolutionary current was stronger than before. The unthinking masses, responding only to their feelings, were desirous of independence, and so too most of the professional class, although there were many of this group who hesitated to cast in their lot with the revolution, as they did not feel confident of Cuban success. Conservative families were as a rule opposed to the movement, but the younger men among them, including the sons of the autonomists or of the loyalists of other days, tended to look with favor upon the patriot cause. Furthermore, there were as yet no racial or other partisan questions to disturb the internal unity of the movement. On the other hand, the merchants and the clergy, both of which groups were made up very largely of Spaniards, were unalterably opposed to independence, and property-holders in general (including the proprietors of the sugar and tobacco estates) leaned rather to Spain, or at least to autonomy, than to the revolution.

Spain failed to make proper use of the advantage she possessed, however. Her military strategy was almost unbelievably bad, based on principles of defensive warfare rather than the attack, which the circumstances seemed to call for. An attempt was made to occupy and hold all prominent cities, while numerous fortified posts in the rural districts also received a considerable quota of troops. In particular, the Spaniards expended vast sums and great effort in long lines of entrenchments, called *trochas,* the entire width of the island, from north to south. In consequence, the Spanish army was scattered, and failed to get the benefit of its great preponderance in numbers. So the Cubans were allowed to choose their own time and place in which to fight. Furthermore, the Spanish army of nearly two hundred thousand men was made up almost wholly of infantry, though cavalry would have been a far more useful medium for coping with the guerrilla warfare of the insurrectionists under the tropical sun of Cuba. A well-known American military expert has held that the very size of the Spanish army was a handicap, as there were so many soldiers that they got in one another's way, raised up grave problems in the matter of supplies, and put an unnecessary strain on Spain's financial resources. According to him, an army of sixty thousand men, of whom twenty-five thousand should have been cavalry, might have suppressed the insurrection in less than a year, if Spain had taken the aggressive and had possessed a single general worthy of the name. In addition to her military errors, Spain made political mistakes that drove large numbers of Cubans into the ranks of the patriots. The ultra-conservative Spanish party brought discredit on the autonomists and other proponents of liberal reforms by calling attention to features of their program that resembled the tenets of the revolutionaries. It became necessary for each individual to decide whether to be wholly for one side or wholly for the other, and many chose therefore to fight against Spain rather than for her; indeed, many were virtually forced into the arms of the insurrectionists in order to save their lives. Harsh measures of the Spanish authorities accounted for still further accessions to the insurgent forces.

Spanish policy and Spanish leadership were bad, but the fighting itself was desperate, as the soldiers on both sides were amply endowed with courage. The war was less than two months old when Spain's "greatest general" became the governor and commander-in-chief in the island. This was Martínez Campos, the victor in the Ten Years' War and a man of tremendous prestige as the "king maker" who had restored the Bourbons to the throne and very nearly dominated Spanish politics ever since. Martínez Campos began his work by building *trochas* to confine the Cuban operations to Oriente, and promised to end the insurrection in a hurry. To his chagrin, however, Gómez and Maceo broke through his fortified lines almost as they pleased, and other bands of insurgents rose up behind them. Indeed, it may be said that the arrival of Martínez Campos marked the turning-point in the war, but in favor of the Cubans, not against them.

The Cubans had more than held their own in Oriente against the Spanish captain-general, but in the fall of 1895 they started upon the most spectacular campaign of the war. The plan was to carry the struggle to every province of the country, instead of leaving the east to bear the whole burden of the conflict. So Gómez broke through the *trocha* into Camagüey, and was presently followed by Maceo. Then came a series of startlingly brilliant operations that took the patriots through Camagüey, Santa Clara, Matanzas, Havana, and Pinar del Río, with the hardest fighting of the war going on almost within gunshot of the capital. Gómez and Maceo rarely counted more than ten thousand men in their commands, while the Spanish forces vastly outnumbered them. Nevertheless, in scores of pitched battles, the Spaniards were defeated. Gómez showed great military abilities in his conduct of affairs, but the skill and courage of Maceo were so astonishingly remarkable as to capture the attention of the entire world. He seemed to range at will between the provinces of Havana and Pinar del Río, breaking into one or the other, despite *trochas* and Spanish armies. His once great prestige utterly lost, Martínez Campos was recalled to Spain in January 1896, but Cuban victories, especially of the spectacular Maceo, continued to be the order of the day. In December, however, the great mulatto leader was killed in battle, and from that time forward the balance began to swing toward Spain.

From the very first, the war had been one of destruction on a great scale, like its predecessor, the Ten Years' War. Gómez declared that if the Spaniards would not give up Cuba, then he would make it worthless to them. That might induce them to leave, he said, since they were in the island only for what they could get out of it. In keeping with this policy, he issued two orders in 1895 to the effect that nobody was to engage in any commerce with towns in Spanish possession or raise any sugar, since these things would in fact redound to the advantage of Spain. Laborers, too, were forbidden to work in sugar factories. The penalties for infractions of these orders was destruction of one's property and death. Indeed, the desire to make these commands operative in all parts of Cuba was one of the primary reasons for the invasion of the west. This was no mere threat, either, but was enforced, at great cost to the offenders. Other properties, too, that might be of aid to the Spaniards were put to the torch. The Spaniards were not behindhand with severe measures in furtherance of their own cause. It must be said for Martínez Campos that he followed a comparatively mild and conciliatory course, but his successor, General Valeriano Weyler, was a man of different stamp, with a record for cruelty in the Ten Years' War. He proceeded to confirm and increase his former reputation until he attained to very nearly world-wide notoriety as "Butcher" Weyler. The keynote of his methods was his so-called *reconcentrado* (reconcentration) policy. All Cubans (men, women, and children) were ordered to move into garrisoned Spanish towns or concentration camps, and no civilian was to go into the rural districts without a passport. The penalty of death and forfeiture of one's property was imposed for failure to observe these orders. The real effect was that Weyler met Gómez more than half way in a process of starving out the island. People crowded into the cities or camps, where there was nothing for them to do and no provisions supplied to keep them alive. So they died by the thousands. It is said that fifty-two thousand perished in the province of Havana alone. Indeed, what with the reciprocal policies of Gómez and Weyler there was very little destructible property left standing, while misery and distress were general.

If Cuba could have been removed from the current of the world's news, Weyler might have succeeded in overwhelming the insurrection in course of time. But he had not taken into account how he was creating sympathy for the Cuban cause in other countries, especially in the United States. Even so, he might have won, if his generalship in the field had been equal to his harsh treatment of non-combatants. The tide had, indeed, turned toward Spain since the death of Maceo, but the patriots were still fighting grimly. Gómez in Camagüey and Calixto García (another famous veteran of the previous war) in Oriente were able to make a showing, though the conflict died down in the west. Meanwhile, public opinion against Spain rose to such a pitch in the United States as to make Spanish retention of the island as unacceptable to the vast body of the American people as to the Cubans themselves. Demands for intervention in the name of humanity were being made, long before President McKinley finally issued the call. So Weyler, too, failed, and late in the year 1897 he was recalled to Spain. The last chapter in Cuba's struggle for separation from Spain was now about to be written, and the "outside help" which Saco foresaw would decide the issue was on the verge of bringing itself to bear.

The real Cuban political leader after the death of Martí was Tomás Estrada Palma, at the head of the Cuban Junta in New York. There was, indeed, a somewhat shadowy patriot government in Cuba. The Cuban Assembly, composed of delegates from the Cuban army, elected Bartolomé Masó, an insurgent leader in Oriente, as President in May 1895, with Estrada Palma as delegate-at-large to the United States and other countries. Independence was formally declared on July 15, and in September a constitution for the self-styled Republic of Cuba was drawn up. This provided for a Council of six members, with all the functions of government in its hands. The President of this body was Salvador Cisneros, former Marquis of Santa Lucía (a title he had sacrificed when he joined the Cuban forces in the Ten Years' War), and Masó was Vice-President. Later Masó became President. Practically, however, this organization was a mere instrument of Gómez, the commander in the field. It maintained headquarters for a time in the Cubitas Mountains in northern Camagüey, signing its *pronunciamentos* from there, which led certain political humorists in the United States to refer to it as a "government in the woods." Estrada Palma in New York had a more important work to do. Funds were collected by him, and expended for war material and recruits for the Cuban army. Expedition after expedition was sent away to Cuba. Many others were prevented from sailing, because of the vigilance of United States officials, who were faithfully endeavoring to enforce the neutrality laws, however little their heart may have been in the task. Still others ran afoul of some vessel of the Spanish navy. Enough got through to destination, however, to bring invaluable aid to the patriots. Quite as important a work was done, too, in disseminating propaganda on behalf of Cuba and in representing the patriots before the United States government. No man could have handled these delicate matters any better than Estrada Palma, who commanded respect for his unimpeachable integrity as well as for his ability and unselfish love of the Cuban cause.

As the year 1897 drew to a close, prospects of Cuban success were none too flattering in the island itself. Weyler had indeed left Cuba, and had been succeeded, November 1, 1897, by General Ramón Blanco, a man of more humane impulses than his predecessor. On orders from the Spanish government, which was desirous of placating the United States and thus avoiding intervention, he announced a program of reform, including the abolition of Weyler's *reconcentrado* policy and the establishment of Cuban home rule, with most of the functions of government in the hands of an elected legislature. Nevertheless, despite the liberal sound of the law for Cuban autonomy, it was stated that "the supreme government of the colony shall be exercised by a governor-general," to be appointed by the crown. This was much the same language as that employed for the British government of Canada, but nobody expected that the phrase would be interpreted in the same way. It was improbable that Spain meant to give any really great measure of home rule to the Cubans. In any event, the law came too late to affect the course of affairs. Spain's sun had set. Meanwhile, the warfare went on in desultory fashion into the year 1898, without anything of consequence being done.

The law for the autonomist government went into effect on January 1, 1898, and an executive council was appointed, but the new régime had by no means a rosy path. The Autonomists and the Reformists (a Spanish group) accepted it, but the die-hard Spaniards in the Constitutional Unionist party were uncompromising in their opposition. They organized demonstrations against Blanco and home rule, and even against the United States and the Americans in Cuba. The American consul-general became alarmed, and requested that a war-vessel be sent to Havana to protect American citizens in case of an emergency. A former American consul-general advised against it, fearing that some untoward incident might develop out of the hostility of Spaniards in Cuba to the United States. Nevertheless, orders were given for the "Maine" to proceed to Havana, and in due time she came to anchor in the harbor of the Cuban capital. Some days later, on February 15, 1898, the "Maine" was mysteriously blown up. While never definitely proved just how it happened, the evidence seemed to point to an explosion from the outside, possibly the act of some over-wrought Spanish sympathizer. From this time forward, there was no possible way of stemming American insistence that Spanish rule in Cuba must end.

The blowing-up of the "Maine" is by no means to be considered the cause of the United States entry into the war. One must look much farther back than that. The traditional interest of the northern republic in Cuba's fate has already been reviewed. The government at Washington could not be indifferent to the course of affairs in the island. Naturally, popular opinion in the United States favored the Cubans, but with only a faint idea at first of any American participation in the conflict. American sympathy began to be reflected presently in various resolutions that were proposed in Congress,—for an enquiry into conditions in Cuba,—for a recognition of belligerency,—for intervention,—and even for recognition of Cuban independence. At length, in April 1896, Congress passed a resolution recognizing Cuban belligerency and proposing a tender of American good offices on the basis of independence for the island, but leaving it to the President's decision whether the resolution should be carried into effect. President Cleveland felt that there was as yet no basis in international law for a recognition even of belligerency, but began negotiations with Spain for the enactment of reforms which might satisfy the Cubans. Estrada Palma let it be known, however, that the Cubans were not interested in anything short of independence.

As the United States elections approached in the fall of 1896 the Cuban question had reached a stage where it could not be disregarded. By this time there was an overwhelming popular sympathy for *"Cuba libre"* (free Cuba). With a strategic advantage in their hands, as the party out of power, the Republicans put a plank in their platform stating that since Spain had "lost control of Cuba" and was "unable to protect the property or lives of resident American citizens," the government of the United States "should actively use its influence and good offices to restore peace and give independence to the Island." The Democratic platform extended "sympathy" to the Cubans in their struggle for independence. Cleveland devoted a long paragraph to Cuban affairs in his annual message of December 1896. After mentioning a number of reasons for American concern, including the nearness of Cuba to the United States, an American investment of from thirty to fifty millions in the island, and a volume of trade that had reached $103,000,000 in 1893 and ninety-six millions in 1894, he went on as follows:

"When the inability of Spain to deal successfully with the insurrection has become manifest, and it is demonstrated that her sovereignty is extinct in Cuba for all purposes of its rightful existence, and when a hopeless struggle for its reëstablishment has degenerated into a strife which means nothing more than the useless sacrifice of human life and the utter destruction of the very subject-matter of the conflict, a situation will be presented in which our obligations to the sovereignty of Spain will be superseded by higher obligations, which we can hardly hesitate to recognize and discharge."

Weyler's harsh policies occupied the attention of the press during 1897, and animosity toward Spain and sympathy for the insurgents were at fever heat. Considerable sums of money were collected by the Red Cross for the relief of victims of the *reconcentrado* policy. In his first annual message, in December 1897, President McKinley had this to say of Weyler's system:

"It was not civilized warfare; it was extermination. The only peace it could beget was that of the wilderness and the grave."

Going on, the President remarked that the "near future will demonstrate" whether the United States should take action concerning Cuban affairs, holding that it must work out in a recognition of belligerency or independence, or in an intervention against both sides, or in favor of one side against the other.

"I speak not of forcible annexation," he added, "for that cannot be thought of. That, by our code of morality, would be criminal aggression."

Events now moved rapidly. Popular opinion in the United States called for action, but McKinley held back. The "Maine" was despatched to Havana in January 1898, as already stated. Shortly afterward, on February 9, 1898, it came to light that the Spanish minister, Dupuy de Lome, had written a letter to a friend in which he used insulting language about McKinley, calling him a "would-be-politician who tries to leave a door open behind him while keeping on good terms with the jingoes of his party." Though a private communication, this letter had in some way reached the hands of the Secretary of State. Dupuy de Lome hastened to resign in order to forestall his recall, but the uproar over this incident was out of all proportion to its merits. It had by no means died down, when on the 15th of the same month the "Maine" was destroyed with a loss of 264 men of its crew. Only those who lived through those times can realize the tremendous outburst of excitement that swept the United States when news of this event was received. Whatever the truth may have been, the American people held Spain responsible, either directly or by culpable neglect, for this disaster. In the writer's opinion there was no moment in the United States during the recent World War when enthusiasm for the cause approached the furore of '98. People nearly went out of their heads in a wave of patriotic feeling that was mingled with a call for vengeance against Spain. "Remember the Maine" speeches and "Remember the Maine" buttons were the order of the day. And loud were the complaints because McKinley "couldn't be kicked into a fight."

McKinley held out for a time in the face of the clamor for war, trying to adjust the situation. Eventually, on March 27, he issued what amounted to an ultimatum, demanding that Spain consent to an armistice until October 1st (to permit of negotiations for peace), revoke the *reconcentrado* policy (still in operation, despite Blanco's announced intention of abolishing it) and institute relief measures for those in the camps, and permit the United States to be final arbiter in case Spain and the Cubans should not have reached an agreement by October 1st. It will be observed that no reference was made to a recognition of Cuban independence. Spain virtually rejected these demands when she replied, March 31, with a counter-proposition. She agreed to end the *reconcentrado* system, but suggested arbitration to fix responsibility for the destruction of the "Maine,"—an utter impossibility in the existing state of American opinion. The idea of an armistice was opposed until such time as the new autonomist legislature, which was to meet on May 4, could arrange for that and also an honorable peace, "it being understood that the powers reserved by the constitution to the central government are not lessened and diminished." This seemed to be only another example of the familiar dodging of Spanish politicians. So, despairing of any settlement that would be acceptable to the Cubans and the American people, McKinley decided to submit the question to Congress. That meant war!

The President's message to Congress was all ready, when on April 10 new proposals were received from Spain, who announced an armistice and a willingness to grant Cuba the same sort of self-government that Canada enjoyed, though still insisting on arbitration of the "Maine" affair. Much point has been made of this Spanish message by those who have wished to find fault with the United States or the McKinley administration. It has been said that it amounted to an acceptance of the March 27 note and that McKinley, nevertheless, suppressed it, thus bringing on a war that might have been avoided. A meeting of foreign ministers at Washington on April 14 went so far as to hold that it met the demands of the message of March 27. It would seem, however, that any fair consideration of the situation would not sustain the charges against McKinley. The meeting of the foreign ministers represented a German maneuver, growing naturally out of the world politics of that day, a factor that need not be explained here. The amnesty proclamation was limited as announced by General Blanco in Cuba, who stated that it was to continue at the pleasure of the Spanish authorities; in any event, it was rejected by the Cubans, who replied, through Máximo Gómez, that Spain must consent to evacuate the island before they would accept an armistice. And, certainly, McKinley did not suppress the Spanish note, for he mentioned it in his message to Congress, though briefly, in a few lines added to the message as already prepared. Furthermore, quite aside from the legal principle that a counter-offer is equivalent to a rejection, this would not have been acceptable as an answer to the American note of March 27; the note of April 10 failed to meet the American proposals in several particulars, and in its insistence on the "Maine" arbitration injected an issue that could not possibly be allowed. The truth of the matter was, that war was inevitable. The marvel is that McKinley had been able to hold it off so long.

McKinley's message to Congress was submitted on April 11. In it he reviewed events in Cuba, and reached the conclusion that intervention was justified, but specifically declared that a recognition of independence was inexpedient. Then came the heart of the message in the following terms:

"The long trial has proved that the object for which Spain has waged the war cannot be attained. The fire of insurrection may flame or may smoulder with varying seasons, but it has not been and it is plain it cannot be extinguished by present methods. The only hope of relief and repose from a condition which can no longer be endured is the enforced pacification of Cuba. In the name of humanity, in the name of civilization, in behalf of endangered American interests which give us the right and the duty to speak and to act, the war in Cuba must stop. In view of these facts and of these considerations, I ask the Congress to authorize and empower the President to take measures to secure a full and final termination of hostilities between the government of Spain and the people of Cuba, and to secure in the island the establishment of a stable government, capable of maintaining order and observing its international obligations, insuring peace and tranquillity and the security of its citizens as well as our own, and to use the military and naval forces of the United States as may be necessary for these purposes . . . The issue is now with Congress. It is a solemn responsibility. I have exhausted every effort to relieve the intolerable condition of affairs which is at our doors. Prepared to execute every obligation imposed upon me by the Constitution and the law, I await your action."

The key-word in this stirring message was the one which called for an end to the war in the name of "humanity." The term was received with something like derision in European countries, which were then engaged in one of the greatest eras of expansion that the world has ever known. It was "obvious" to most of the world that the McKinley message was a mere excuse for the conquest of the island. Anyone familiar with American interest in Cuba throughout the nineteenth century will, of course, recognize that the United States had a very substantial concern over the island that well-informed members of the executive branch of the government could not fail to take into account. Nevertheless, Americans in general, including their representatives in Congress, had little knowledge of the importance of Cuba to the United States, and the appeal in the name of "humanity" in fact represented the overwhelming sentiment of the American people. This was reflected in the action of Congress in the famous Joint Resolution of April 20, which empowered the President to use the army and navy to bring about a relinquishment of Spanish authority in Cuba. The Senate at first wished to go beyond the recommendations of McKinley by recognizing the Cuban republic, but, when the House refused to concur (as a result of the personal intervention of the President, who "in effect compelled the omission from the resolution"),[1] the following oddly worded paragraph was nevertheless retained:

"That the people of the island of Cuba are and of right ought to be independent."

A further expression of American disinterestedness was added in the shape of the Teller Amendment, as follows:

"That the United States hereby disclaims any disposition or intention to exercise sovereignty, jurisdiction, or control over said island except for the pacification thereof, and asserts its determination, when that is accomplished, to leave the government and control of the island to its people."

It will be necessary to revert to these paragraphs later, in connection with the establishment of the republic.

The passing of the Joint Resolution amounted to a declaration of war, and hostilities commenced soon afterward. The powers of continental Europe were for a time disposed to lend at least moral support to Spain, but England came out strongly for the United States. That ended Spain's only remaining hope of escape from the dilemma. And yet, though Spain's expulsion from the island was now virtually sure, there was strangely little enthusiasm in Cuba. Gómez wished that no American troops might be landed there, unless perhaps some artillery, of which he was greatly in need. He did desire help in the form of shipments of ammunition

---

[1] See statement of John Bassett Moore, quoted *infra*, pp. 643-645.

and the prevention of supplies from reaching the Spaniards. No doubt, the Cubans wanted the credit of winning their own independence, but they also almost certainly believed that an American intervention would mean a transfer of Spanish sovereignty to the United States. The language of the Joint Resolution, for all that it seemed to promise, was not reassuring, for it had been the habit of various European powers during the previous quarter of a century to make sounding phrases the preliminary of a conquest. And what reason was there to expect any other course of action from the United States? There was no idea of resisting the great northern republic, but there was little wholehearted support of the American campaign. This attitude continued, even after the American forces were landed in Cuba, and was a source of no little surprise to the invaders, who expected to be received with open arms.

This is not the place for the details of the war. On May 1st Admiral Dewey won a fine naval victory at Manila Bay, and this was followed by an American occupation of the Philippines. Later on in May the major part of the Spanish fleet was blockaded in the Bay of Santiago, Cuba, and toward the end of June an American army was landed near that city. It is worth noting, with an eye to later events in the era of the republic, that Theodore Roosevelt played a prominent part in this campaign as second in command of the "Rough Riders" regiment, an organization recruited by Roosevelt himself and made up largely of western cowboys. Another man who was destined to fill a great place in Cuban history was at the head of this regiment, Roosevelt's friend, Colonel Leonard Wood. Other matters of greater import from the standpoint of the war, as such, may here be passed by. The Spanish fleet attempted to run the blockade on July 3, but was utterly destroyed. Two weeks later, on

July 17, the Spanish army in Santiago surrendered.[2]   Meanwhile, too, the American forces had entered Porto Rico, and presently they conquered that island.

Spain was now ready for peace, and on July 26 sent an enquiry to the United States through the French government to find out upon what conditions the war might be brought to an end. The President replied, naming the following terms as a preliminary to negotiations for peace:

1. The "relinquishment" by Spain of all claim of sovereignty over or title to Cuba, and her immediate evacuation of the island.

2. In lieu of indemnity, a cession to the United States by Spain of "Porto Rico and other islands now under the sovereignty of Spain in the West Indies, and also the cession of an island in the Ladrones."

3. The retention of Manila by the United States until it should be determined in the treaty of peace what disposition was to be made of the Philippines.

Spain accepted these terms, rather unwillingly, and they were presently embodied in more ample form in the protocol of August 10. The provisions of the protocol virtually repeated the paragraphs just recited, except that more ample provision for the evacuation of Spain's possessions in the West Indies was made in a new article. Article five of the protocol concerned the appointment of peace commissioners, and article six called for an armistice immediately following the signing of the protocol. The document was signed on August 12.

On October 1st, five commissioners from each country met at Paris, to draw up a definitive treaty of peace. There

[2] It is a temptation to tell more about the Santiago campaign, especially from the standpoint of American participants therein, many of whom have since taken up their residence in Cuba. They pretty generally take much of the glamor away from the story.

were several controversial points, but the work was carried on so expeditiously that everything was ready by December 10. Of particular interest was the discussion over the meaning and effect of Spain's "relinquishment" of Cuba. In the earlier negotiations the Spanish minister of State had written a communication (presently forwarded to the American Secretary of State) that Spain was ready to accept "absolute independence, or independence under an American protectorate, or annexation to the United States, preferring annexation, because this would guarantee better the security of the lives and property of Spaniards who resided or had estates there." The answer of Secretary Day set forth that the United States did not share Spain's apprehensions over Cuban independence, but in the disturbed condition of the island felt that it might need aid, which the American government was disposed to give. The Spanish commissioners in Paris must have felt that this left the question open, for they endeavored to get the United States to annex Cuba, but the American commissioners were unwilling to entertain any such proposition.[3] This drew forth the following eulogy from Luis Estévez Romero, the later first Cuban Vice-President:

"It should be said very emphatically in honor of the American commissioners that few times in political history has there been a grander inflexibility, rejecting all insinuations, all advances, all offers of the Spanish commissioners for the United States to keep Cuba. The honor of their nation forbade it."[4]

It was decided that the United States should for the time being act as a trustee of the island, and take responsibility "for the protection of life and property." Another clause of the treaty provided that on the termination of American

[3] See statement of John Bassett Moore, quoted *infra*, pp. 643-645.   [4] Quoted in Martínez Ortiz, I, 112.

occupancy the United States was to "advise any government established in the island to assume the same obligations." One of the most difficult matters was the question of the Cuban debt, which had been incurred by Spain very largely as a result of the war in Cuba. Spain wanted Cuba to take over at least a portion of this debt, but the American commissioners were adamant in refusing to saddle it upon them. So Spain had no recourse but to yield. Among non-Cuban features of the treaty were the acquisition of Porto Rico, Guam, and the Philippines by the United States; a payment of twenty million dollars was made for the Philippines. Ratifications came later, and the treaty was proclaimed on April 11, 1899, the anniversary of McKinley's message of the year before.

Cuba's separation from Spain was now accomplished, but independence was yet to be attained. That was to be a question of the fulfilment of its pledges by the great republic of the north.[5]

[5] The materials for a study of the war of 1895-1898 are, of course, vast in amount. Trelles, *Biblioteca*, I, 404-478, and II, 1-86, has several hundred items on this period alone. In addition, there are quantities of documents in United States government publications, as also, no doubt, in those of Spain and other European countries, to say nothing of papers still existing in manuscript form only. For a rapid survey, Johnson, IV, 1-117, and Latané, John Holladay. *The United States and Latin America.* (New York. 1920), 125-136, are worthy of note, and Robinson, Albert Gardner, *Cuba and the Intervention*, 2 ed. (New York. 1910), 31-49, 66-83, is particularly helpful. Among a number of interesting accounts by American eyewitnesses are volumes of Frederick Funston (later a distinguished soldier in the American army), Richard Harding Davis, Grover Flint, George Clarke Musgrave, and Charles Melville Pepper. For the American military campaign, perhaps the best work is Sargent, Herbert Howland, *The campaign of Santiago de Cuba*, 3 vols., Chicago, 1907.

CHAPTER V

THE UNITED STATES MILITARY GOVERNMENT, 1898-1902

DURING the closing months of 1898 Spanish rule in Cuba still existed legally, but the only effective work being done was in Oriente, where General Leonard Wood (recently promoted from a colonelcy) was in charge as the representative of the American military occupation. There he had already begun to "make things hum," showing extraordinary energy and efficiency. Conditions in Oriente were very bad. People were dying by the thousands from disease; there was little or no work to do, and starvation was adding its quota to the toll of the dead; sanitation was in an indescribably wretched state; and local government in its various forms—administration, justice, education,—had virtually ceased to function. General Wood's earliest measures were in the nature of what might be called "first aid." He took care of the sick, and fed the starving; made the city of Santiago more habitable; reëstablished the municipal governments and the courts; started a program of public works, especially the building of roads, in part in order to give employment to men out of work; and he saw to it that people of the rural districts were supplied with tools and food and sent back to their farms. Presently he was able to stamp out epidemics of smallpox and yellow fever, to found schools, and put local government on a firmer basis, reinforced by his organization of a body of rural guards. In fine, by the close of the year, the territory under his jurisdiction was, as one of his most bitter critics has admitted, "orderly, peaceable, and self-sustaining." The exceptional character of his achievements in Oriente made General Wood a national figure in his own country as well as renowned in Cuba. In the language of Theodore Roosevelt, he had proved himself a "model administrator." It was certain that his services would be called upon again.[1]

General Blanco did not remain to the end of Spanish rule, but turned over his command to General Adolfo Jiménez Castellanos, who formally surrendered the government to the American military governor, General John R. Brooke, on January 1, 1899. It was not possible by that date to repatriate all the Spanish troops in the island, but by February the evacuation was complete. In the last few months of their occupation the Spanish authorities, naturally, paid very little heed to problems of administration, and many officials took an interest only in salvaging what they could for themselves, after which they deserted their posts and returned to Spain. Referring to the condition in which they left public buildings one writer has said:

"They looted and gutted them of everything that could be removed. They destroyed the plumbing and lighting fixtures. They broke or choked up the drains. They left every place in an indescribably filthy condition. There was nothing in all their record in Cuba more unbecoming than their manner of leaving it."[2]

The general situation in Cuba at the outset of American rule was about as bad as it could be, except in Oriente, where Wood's measures had already made themselves felt. The rest of the island was in much the same state as that in Oriente had been in the summer of 1898, except that affairs were even worse off in western Cuba, owing to the greater

[1] For a vigorous brief account of Wood's services in Oriente, see Roosevelt, Theodore, *General Leonard Wood: a model American military* *administrator,* in *Outlook,* v. LXI, pp. 19-23; Jan. 7, 1899.
[2] Johnson, IV, 133.

severity of the war in that section. Famine and disease were everywhere. Children wandered about like wild animals, without parents or homes. Referring to the sufferings of the people in the cities, a Cuban writer, Martínez Ortiz, has drawn a gruesome picture:

"Those poor people, without any help, had exhausted their resources, and put hands to any kind of food. The most unclean and repugnant animals were devoured with delight, and were hunted for with frenzied zeal. Roots, branches, and herbs were also utilized. Women and hungry children looked in the mangers of the horses in the forces of cavalry encamped in the streets, to find the abandoned grains amidst the dirt in order to eat them raw, and seeds and cuttings of fruits were also gathered as precious discoveries. Frequently, despite the efforts of the police to stop them, they bore away pieces of the remains of animals that had died of contagious diseases. Those unfortunate human beings, thus left to themselves, were the relics of what had once been the country people brought into the concentration camps by General Weyler."[3]

Steps were at once taken by the United States government to alleviate the distress. A method of food distribution was established that proved very effective. It is said that in Havana alone there were twenty thousand people dependent on this bounty to save them from starvation. Nor was this all. There was an utter lack of sanitation. Whole streets were so choked with filth as to be almost impassable, and there was "no public building . . . in a fit state for use." For example, over twelve hundred cubic yards of rubbish were removed from the custom-house alone. The work of cleaning up streets and buildings was undertaken at once, and good results were quickly obtained. The situation in the custom-house may also serve as an illustration of the disorganization in governmental affairs. The records had been either removed or destroyed, and there was not a stick of furniture in the place. By a personal appeal to his Spanish

[3] Martínez Ortiz, I, 15.

predecessor the United States official in charge managed to get a chair and desk for himself. The personnel was made up of a few Spaniards, but was altogether inadequate, as most of those formerly stationed there had left or resigned. So too with the post-office, in which not so much as a cent of money or a single stamp was found. Naturally, the treasury was bare, but, fortunately, there was scarcely anything owing by the state, thanks to the insistence of the United States that Spain herself should be responsible for the Cuban debt. There was an issue of about two million dollars in Cuban insurgent bonds, and, rather more important, the promises that had been made to pay the soldiers for their services in the war.

Out in the rural districts matters were just as bad. Cuba's whole life depends upon agriculture, especially the raising of sugar, but both local and world conditions militated against the economic prospects of the island at the time. Sugar is not a crop that will take care of itself, but requires an expensive equipment in the way of machinery, domestic animals, and labor. Most of the sugar-mills had been destroyed, however, and hunger and the vicissitudes of the war had caused a virtual disappearance of beasts of burden. And just then, too, European countries were paying subsidies to promote the beet-sugar industry, and the United States had raised up a tariff wall for the same purpose.

Such was the state of affairs when the United States military government began its work. It was under instructions to prepare the people of Cuba for self-government, bring about conditions which would make the founding of a republic possible, and establish them in such a sound manner as to ensure an orderly and successful maintenance of Cuban rule. The United States assumed "military" control, but not in the sense in which the word had been employed under

Spain. Nearly all the officials—ninety-seven per cent, it has been stated,—were Cubans, who were given important tasks to perform and not a little responsibility. One of the principal criticisms of General Brooke was that his "Cuban appointees made a tool of their chief," in consequence of which it was often said that the "American governor reigns, but the Cuban Secretaries govern." A kindly critic, such as Martínez Ortiz is entitled to be called, has written that "he was even of a somewhat better stamp, perhaps, than was fitting for a man in such a high post in that difficult and exceptional situation." On one occasion, indeed, when there was some talk in the United States of replacing the military government with civilian rule, there was an uproar in Cuba until assurances were received that no such change would be made.

One of the greatest difficulties that the military government was to encounter was that of the inevitable friction between alien rulers and a nation which had fought for independence and wanted to have its expected benefits bestowed upon it at once. Perhaps no two peoples ever get on together in complete friendliness under such conditions, for differences of language and habits are sure to cause misunderstandings, even when other circumstances do not contribute to the same end. The average American of that day expected the Cuban to be grateful to the United States for the aid given in defeating Spain, to say nothing of the "glorious opportunity" of coming in contact with American institutions. But the Cubans, as so often happens in the case of a people experiencing their first taste of freedom from absolute rule, tended toward radicalism, and forgot any gratitude they might have had in their impatience over the delay in their attainment of independence. If they knew of Cuba's importance in the foreign relations of the United States, they did not care about it, except as it might have served to make them suspicious of the northern republic. And, finally, if the provincialism and lack of experience of the American people in anything like colonial affairs are added to the unpreparedness of the Cubans for political life, it is not surprising that an already difficult situation was rendered yet more perplexing. It will be necessary to refer again to the attitude of the Cuban revolutionaries toward the United States, but it should be borne in mind in the meantime, as a factor in the background of the achievements of the intervention.

General Brooke was at the head of Cuban affairs during almost all of 1899, until succeeded by General Wood in December. It fell to his lot to take the initial steps in resolving the chaotic conditions in the island and reconstructing the governmental machinery. By the month of June the most pressing of the relief work in the shape of supplying food and medicine to the stricken people was well in hand. The Cubans were entitled to praise in this connection, for many of them went back to their farms, and met the situation as best they could, helping one another, too, so that a crop might be raised. Often a single plow served a number of farms, and for lack of horses or mules the men harnessed themselves to it, to draw it, at least after a fashion, through the soil.

One of the most troublesome problems in the first year of the occupation was the handling of the Cuban military forces. They were still under arms, and not inclined to disband until they should receive pay for their services during the war. Gómez had suggested that sixty millions might be given to the men, to cover their pay and also the losses they had suffered. The plan of division showed a rather wide disparity between the amounts to be given to privates on the one hand and generals on the other. The former were to get from six to seven hundred dollars, and the latter from seven to twelve thousand! The United States authorities pointed out that this would necessitate a large loan, greater than the existing resources of Cuba could stand, and might therefore prolong the American occupation indefinitely. It was essential to the success of the intervention to bring about the disbandment of the Cuban forces; so the United States offered a free gift of three million dollars, out of the surplus remaining over from the amount Congress had appropriated for the war; it was suggested that this might be distributed in equal portions to the men who could prove their service and would turn in their arms. Gómez at first resisted the plan for demobilizing the army, as he had been inclined to keep it until the United States should relinquish the island to the Cubans themselves, but he was at length persuaded to accept the American project.

The lesser officers were furious when they heard of what Gómez had done. They had maintained their Assembly of delegates of the Cuban army since early in the war, but this had begun to make its voice heard only in the days since the fighting had stopped. At this time the Assembly was in the control of three men who represented a current of opposition to the United States. Two of these, Manuel Sanguily and Juan Gualberto Gómez (a negro), were noted orators, while the third, Fernando Freyre de Andrade, was a man of great personal and family prestige. Under the influence of these three men the Assembly came out uncompromisingly for the bonus as originally proposed. There was a great deal of excitement, and, no doubt, some little trepidation in Washington lest the Cubans might "fly off the handle" into revolution, but the Assembly itself saved the situation by its own exaggerated acts. In a burst of emotion it deposed Máximo Gómez as commander-in-chief. This turned the sober-minded citizenry against the Assembly, for the old general was one of the great heroes of the war. Realizing that they had made a mistake, the leaders of the Assembly made an effort to get the authorities in Washington to change their views about the bonus, but were unsuccessful. So the Assembly met for the last time on April 4, and dissolved itself. Meanwhile, the demotion of Gómez had not been recognized by the United States, and had been disavowed in a meeting of Cuban generals. Negotiations for the distribution of the three million dollars were continued with Gómez, and presently an agreement was reached to pay each soldier who had been in service prior to the end of hostilities the sum of seventy-five dollars. Thereupon, the Cuban army grew suddenly from about thirty thousand to forty-eight thousand men, but an investigation of the records reduced the number to 33,930, each of whom surrendered his arms, received his money, and went his way. With the Cuban army disbanded, the military government was able to proceed more surely to the accomplishment of its objects.

One of the important tasks was the reconstruction of governmental machinery. The military governor, supported by his Cuban Secretaries, was the supreme authority, and under him were other American generals at the head of affairs in the provinces. These were later replaced by Cuban governors. The extension of General Wood's system of rural guards in Oriente to all parts of the island was a helpful supplement in the maintenance of order. Incidentally, too, this gave employment to a great many former soldiers of the Cuban army. It was particularly necessary to set up governments in the municipalities, as a beginning in training the people to handle their own affairs. Pending elections, to be held later, a number of Cuban officials were put into office, with more power than their predecessors had possessed under the centralized system of Spain. Other steps were also taken to develop municipal government, but more particularly during the rule of General Wood, at which point they may better be taken up.

Some of the other achievements of General Brooke's administration may be summed up briefly. There was an immediate need of revenue; so the custom-house was put in working order, and new taxes, notably excises on liquors, were introduced. By the end of the year the government could show revenues of fifteen and a half million dollars, which was quite satisfactory, as expenditures were two millions less. But the balance of trade still ran heavily against the island. The taking of a census was deemed essential to an understanding of the problems the government had to face; so this was done in the fall of 1899. The results, while not so bad in some respects as had been anticipated, were none too flattering. In a population of a little over a million and a half, approximately two-thirds were white, and only about one-third of negro or mixed race, together with a small number of Chinese. Nearly twelve per cent of the people were of illegitimate birth, due largely to the habit of forming unions without the expense of a marriage ceremony. No fewer than sixty-six per cent were illiterate, which led Elihu Root, the United States Secretary of War, to say that

"If sixty-six per cent of the people were to continue illiterate, the permanence of free constitutional government could hardly be expected, and a definite ascertainment of the facts emphasizes the urgent necessity for popular education." [4]

Naturally, therefore, something was done to establish popular education, but not a great deal was accomplished before the end of the year. Encouragement of foreign capital might

[4] *Extract from the report of the Secretary of War for 1900,* quoted in   Root, 193.

have proved helpful to bring the island out of the grip of economic depression, but it was politically desirable that there should be no hint of exploitation by American promoters. So in 1899 a bill passed Congress, called the Foraker Law, to the effect that no franchises should be granted during the United States occupation. A number of other policies also had their beginning under General Brooke, but were carried so much farther by his successor that they may more appropriately be dealt with in connection with the next administration.

On December 13, 1899, President McKinley appointed General Wood to succeed General Brooke as head of the United States military government in Cuba, and ten days later the last-named departed from the island. His administration was to be somewhat overshadowed by the achievements of General Wood, but was nevertheless praiseworthy. As La Discusión said in its issue of December 15, 1899,

"It may be asserted that the honesty of the present government is so conspicuous that nobody has dared to think that influence could be acquired over its members through use of money." [5]

This is a fair sample of the comments that have been made about his government. As Martínez Ortiz has put it,

"It is enough for the fame of General Brooke to say, with entire truth, that no act of his merited censure." [6]

General Wood, who had already won his spurs as an administrator by his work in Oriente, now took charge. The writer just quoted above has this to say of the new governor:

"Still a young man, he was barely approaching thirty-nine years of age. He was tall of stature, likeable in appearance, and Herculean of complexion. When he shook hands he pressed the hand of the other man

[5] Quoted in Martínez Ortiz, I, 96.
[6] Ibid., I, 98.

so hard that it hurt. A finished example of a very strong people, there shone forth in his face a certain boldness and confidence in his own strength. One divined, on seeing him, that there was no situation, however difficult it might be, capable of making him lose his absolute self-command." [7]

General Wood was, indeed, of a somewhat different stamp from his likeable and rather easy-going, if also able, predecessor. He was a veritable human dynamo, moving surely and swiftly from one task to another. A tireless worker, he took his rest "doing gymnastic exercises or playing some game calling for rapidity of movement and muscular force." If Brooke allowed his Secretaries to dominate him, Wood "essayed autocracy," so his most bitter opponent says, and "made tools of his Cuban appointees," but yet it has to be admitted that he "met with notable success in his effort." Indeed, the very attacks of his enemies are one of the best sources of information to show the extraordinary greatness of his record. At present one hears only praise when General Wood's name is mentioned, but he had plenty of enemies, or at least plenty of criticism, at the time. Through it all, he was imperturbable and composed, not deviating an iota from the line of conduct he had marked out for himself.

General Wood was instructed to prepare Cuba as rapidly as possible for an independent republican government and, meanwhile, to arrange for an efficient administration of justice and a good school system. The President left him to work out the details. Wood went to work with his customary energy, and saw to it that the holders of government jobs put in the full time at their tasks, which was something new in Cuban experience.[8] He then proceeded with his series of

[7] Martínez Ortiz, I, 99.

[8] A popular bit of doggerel, poking fun at Wood's ordinance, ran as follows: "Don't stop to take a drink; don't expectorate; don't scratch yourself or smoke; arrive at work very early, and go away almost at night. There is no time for luncheon or anything but to write . . . Whoever wishes a government job for himself is one who wishes to die."

reforms. Naturally, many of these were going on at the same time, but they reached at least a reasonably successful stage one after another. Indeed, one of the characteristics of the Wood government was that something new was happening all the time, with each fresh action obviously a step nearer independence. There is high authority to the effect that this was one of the important factors in keeping the country in order at all, as suspicion of American policy was given scant opportunity to develop. It will, however, be more convenient to take up General Wood's activities according to subject-matter, abandoning strict chronology.

One of the objects of the government was the reorganization of the department of justice. There was a prevailing American notion that the Spanish laws were bad and ought to be changed, but Wood had been forewarned that the trouble was not so much in the law as in its administration. And indeed, broadly speaking, the law itself (which was the same as that of Spain, with a *habeas corpus* act, bill of rights, and other worthy features) was good enough, though outworn in many particulars and not altogether applicable under the new conditions growing out of the separation from Spain. The governor realized that this law was far better for the Cubans than any unfamiliar United States innovation could be, and left it undisturbed, in the main, except for a body of constructive legislation to fit the changed situation.[9] There was a vast reform of judicial practices, however. General Brooke had already established a judicial hierarchy, with a Supreme Court at the top, six provincial superior courts (*audiencias*), and courts of first instance and municipal courts, together with a police court (after the United States pattern) in Havana. General Wood made improvements in

[9] For some comment on this phase of General Wood's work, see p. 515, n. 10.

the entire organization, and extended the system of police courts to all parts of the island. Many evils had existed under Spain. Judges performed their work at their own homes, and their clerks at theirs, perhaps in another part of the city. There were no fixed salaries, but merely fees growing out of litigation. Consequently, judicial service became little more than a matter of commerce in fees. If there were no fee, there would be no business. There was no thought of moral wrong about it. As one of the United States officials in Cuba put it, "It was difficult to say what official was free from it." It had become a *tradition,* which "has left its effect on these people," and it "will probably take some years to completely change the wrong ideas with which many office-holders seem to have become imbued."

General Wood's reform of the judiciary came to a head with his order of December 31, 1900. In this he decreed that judges and other court officers should be put on salary, and fees abolished. Buildings were to be provided for the handling of judicial cases, doing away with the former haphazard practices, and the various court positions subordinate to the judge were to be awarded as a result of competitive examinations. Much attention was given to the police courts, to relieve the higher courts of the volume of lesser business and avoid the law's delays. Another American innovation was the provision of lawyers for the poor. The careful preparation and keeping of records were insisted upon, and stenographers began to be employed for the first time. An attempt was made to introduce the jury system, but this proved a failure. Hispanic peoples everywhere show little willingness to pass judgment on one another, especially in cases involving human weakness. Furthermore, it was difficult to get juries, as professional men were exempt, and the percentage of illiteracy was so high that not many others were available.

So juries were abandoned, and tribunals of three, five, or seven judges substituted, to pass on both law and fact. As part of this same general reform a great deal was accomplished for the betterment of prisons. When taken over by the military government they were in a state that was nothing less than monstrously bad. Prisoners were herded in together, young and old, of both sexes, in the midst of utter filth. Many had been put in prison years before, and forgotten, without ever having been brought to trial. Some six hundred were released at once, either because the evidence of criminality was not sufficient or because they had already been in prison long enough. Later, others were pardoned, until about a thousand in all had been given their freedom. Regular prison inspections were instituted, and prisoners were segregated according to their crimes, while cleanliness, elementary education, and the ideal of a prison sentence as a means of reform (rather than merely as a punishment) were introduced.

By the end of the intervention the Department of Justice had gained "respect and confidence" and was "honest and highly efficient," according to General Wood. On the other hand, an American critic of General Wood denies that the governor had established "confidence" in the courts, and insists that the Department of Justice was no better at the end of the military government than at the beginning. This was unquestionably an exaggeration, though, as a Cuban writer puts it, "a long road has been traveled since then, and even yet it is not possible to say that the judicial branch is swimming in rosewater." It may fairly be said that the situation was satisfactory while General Wood was in control and that many of his reforms were of permanent utility, but he could not change traditions,—not in two years and a half; so corruption and inefficiency were again to make their presence felt in the later and present-day administration of justice.[10]

From the very first, steps were taken to make ready for an eventual independent Cuban government, but these may be treated more conveniently in the next chapter. Something may be said here, however, about political developments in the municipalities. General Brooke had installed governments in the 138 municipalities of Cuba, but it could not be said that they were a flattering success. It has been asserted that the newly appointed Cuban officials took some seventy per cent of the revenues for themselves, thus proving that colonial traditions still lived. General Wood introduced a much more sweeping reform. Under Spain the municipalities had enjoyed no autonomy in fact, but had been managed from Havana. The authorities at the capital, too, had paid officials out of the general treasury. With the natural Anglo-Saxon feeling that local government is the foundation-rock of democratic institutions General Wood issued an order, in 1901, to the effect that municipalities must henceforth pay their own officials and police. That necessitated local taxes and, therefore, a reassessment of values in the whole country. All Hispanic peoples hate direct taxation, and the Cubans were no exception. There was plenty of criticism, but the governor went ahead with his plan. As part of the work, fifty-six unnecessary municipalities were suppressed. In this connection it must be borne in mind that the term "municipality" in Cuba is more nearly equivalent to "county," as used in English, than it is to "city" or "town." [11]

[10] For a discussion of current evils, see chapter XXII.

[11] As it is customary for a Cuban municipality to have the same name as its principal city, the statistics of population are often confusing to an American. Thus the municipality might have several times the population of the city.

By the end of the United States military rule the municipalities were not, indeed, self-supporting like an American city, for the public schools, hospitals, and sanitation work were being taken care of by the general government, but they were paying all other expenses. Naturally, there was a great deal of local corruption and incompetence, and General Wood frequently intervened in such cases, especially in Havana. At any rate, the new system was a considerable advance over what had existed before, and has been retained by the republic in all its essentials. However much corruption and inefficiency may have developed in recent years, a local government organization was turned over to Cuba that was in good working order at the time.

One of the chief interests of the United States in Cuban affairs was in the development of a good school system. This and sanitation were, perhaps, the objects of General Wood's greatest activities, and the two of them were responsible for a considerable proportion of the government's expenditures. As for education, there was everything to do, with little foundation to build upon. There had been a public school law under Spain, but the system was one in name only. About all there was of real education was what might be obtained in private schools. There were some public schools, but they were conducted in a way that was "corrupt and inefficient." Teaching positions were a matter of traffic. There were few or no school-houses, and pupils, if any, went to the house of the school-teacher, if he had one and was at home! A school law was first enacted just at the end of General Brooke's administration, on December 6, 1899. This had been drawn up by an American named Alexis E. Frye, whom Brooke had appointed Superintendent of Schools, and provided for the opening of primary and grammar schools by December 11, or as soon thereafter as possible.

No complaint could be made of Mr. Frye's work on the score of activity. He had already founded some six hundred schools in the few days before General Wood's induction into office, and continued thereafter at such an amazing rate that he had mustered a total of 3313 before the new governor called a halt. The trouble was, that there had been rather too great a desire to make a record for numbers, and too little thoroughness in getting the schools ready for actual work. One might wonder how, in any event, Mr. Frye had been able to establish so many, but an understanding of Hispanic character will make this clear. Among Hispanic peoples,—and certainly this was the case in Cuba,—it is customary to look upon the government as powerful, rich, and alien, wherefore anything that can be obtained from it is just so much clear profit. So the Cubans were enthusiastic for schools, because the government was paying for them (though, according to this law, the local government), and they meant jobs for teachers, rents for buildings, and sales of school furniture. It was necessary to discard a great many of the schools founded by Mr. Frye, but enough more were established, this time on a more substantial basis, to bring the total about to the maximum previously obtained.

A new school law, prepared by Lieutenant Mathew E. Hanna of the governor's staff, was put into effect in 1900. Lieutenant Hanna had once taught school in Ohio, and so used the school law of that state as the basis for his work. It was provided, however, that the general government should support the schools, as they had proved to be a plaything of local politics during the brief tenure of the 1899 law. The system was expensive, taking nearly a fourth of the revenues (approximately four millions in seventeen for the first year of operation). The unit cost per pupil at the outset was about $26.50, compared with $22.50 for the

United States as a whole. It is well to bear in mind, however, that the cost in many states was far higher, but the average was pulled down by a low rate in the southern states, some of which expended only about $8.60. The initial cost of equipment was necessarily a heavy item, and it was deemed wise to pay good salaries, so as to attract the best elements in Cuba. The teachers were Cubans. Americans were not used, so as to avoid the all too easily kindled suspicions of a possible "Americanization" program. Besides, it was important to train Cubans, as they would have to be relied on when United States control should be withdrawn. A great impetus to the teaching profession was given when Harvard University, of which General Wood was an alumnus, extended an invitation for a number of Cuban teachers to spend the summer of 1900 at the northern institution. Nearly fifteen hundred teachers availed themselves of this opportunity, of whom nine hundred were women. All their expenses were paid, and the whole affair was a great success. The following year two hundred more Cuban teachers spent the summer at Harvard. Higher education was provided for, through the medium of the already existing University of Havana and six high schools, or *institutos,* one for each province. The University at that time had ninety-six professors and 406 students, and its equipment was scanty and "almost worthless." The professors were doing "little or nothing"; so nearly all were dismissed. The new professors were required to win their posts by competitive examinations, and up-to-date scientific apparatus was installed in the different departments. It remained, for the time being, a typical Hispanic American university, giving degrees in medicine, law, engineering, and arts and architecture. A normal school, a school for orphans, a correctional school for boys, and another for girls were also founded. Private schools still continued, but were required to submit to government supervision.

The immediate result of the educational reforms was very gratifying. There was an enrollment of 256,000 in the schools. After the first enthusiasm, however, this fell off to about 160,000, with an average attendance of 125,000, or seventy-eight per cent. The educational gain over the past was in any event very great, and many of General Wood's reforms have since been retained, even though there has been a falling off in administrative fervor concerning education in recent years.[12]

Rivaling education in the amount of attention it received and surpassing every phase of the military government's work on the score of positive achievement was the matter of sanitation. This was a subject in which General Wood had a peculiar interest, for he himself had taken a degree in medicine at Harvard, and had entered upon his military career as an army surgeon. The authorities at Washington were also deeply concerned, in part because of the national habit of cleanliness, but also because the southern parts of the United States were in constant danger from epidemics having their origin in Cuba, especially the terrible yellow fever. Martínez Ortiz sums up the problem the intervention government had to face, as follows:

"Nobody had occupied himself with public hygiene for many years back. During the War of Independence the lack of observance of sanitary rules reached its height. The island had managed to attain to a universal reputation for unhealthfulness, and yellow fever had obtained letters of naturalization in its ports. It was a constant threat to foreigners, and its annual victims were counted in many thousands. The cities, dirty beyond all exaggeration, were equal in that respect to those of the Turks. In Havana itself La Punta and all the littoral of San Lázaro, where the picturesque walk and the elegant buildings of

[12] Cf. *infra*, pp. 592-596.

the Avenida del Golfo beautify it, were converted into an immense dung-hill, infected and bad-smelling. In private houses, with very few exceptions, even in those of well-to-do or wealthy families, there were black, open wells, without any protection, that filled the air with malarial poisons and stench." [13]

The early tasks in the way of sanitation were comparatively simple. The cities were cleaned up. More than that was necessary, however, in order to combat sickness, especially yellow fever. Cuba was overrun with this, and the precise cause of it was not known, but it was believed to be a filth disease. An epidemic broke out in Santiago while General Wood was governor of Oriente in 1899. He thereupon plunged into a campaign of cleaning, burning, and disinfecting, put the inhabitants under martial law, and segregated those showing symptoms of the fever. That worked at Santiago, and the epidemic stopped, but the same measures would not have been practical in so large a city as Havana. In 1900 Havana was caught in the grip of a yellow fever attack, much to the surprise of the authorities, for the city had just been cleaned up and was perhaps cleaner than most cities of the United States. It seemed obvious to General Wood, therefore, that the accepted views as to the origin of yellow fever were wrong. So he appointed a commission, headed by Dr. Walter Reed, to enquire into the matter.

There was living in Cuba at this time a physician named Dr. Charles John Finlay, Cuban-born (1833), of English parents, who some years before had advanced the theory that yellow fever was transmitted by the bite of the *stegomyia* mosquito. At the request of Dr. Reed, General Wood resolved to give Finlay's idea a trial, and commenced a series of experiments that was to produce remarkable results. As a preliminary, two American doctors, Dr. James Carroll and

[13] Martínez Ortiz, I, 23-24.

Dr. Jesse W. Lazear, allowed themselves to be bitten by mosquitoes that had previously gorged themselves on the blood of yellow fever patients. Dr. Carroll caught the disease in a severe form, but eventually recovered. Dr. Lazear, much to his own disappointment, did not contract it, and so *caused himself to be bitten again.* This time the experiment was a "success," for Dr. Lazear got the yellow fever and died! Too much praise cannot be accorded to Carroll and Lazear, and, as for Lazear, if ever a man deserved a martyr's crown, he did.

Further experiments were now made on a larger scale, with a number of men volunteering for the purpose. Two rooms were prepared, under identical conditions so far as the air and other things were concerned, except that mosquitoes infected with yellow fever were in one room, while they were excluded from the other. The man in the room with the mosquitoes caught the fever, but the other did not. A number of men were put into another room in which matters were as bad as possible, except that there were no mosquitoes; the air was foul, and the clothing and other effects employed by the men were taken from yellow fever patients who had died. But not one of them got sick. Yet other ingenious tests were made, until at length it was possible to announce that yellow fever was transmitted by the bite of the female of the species of the *stegomyia* mosquito. This must have bitten someone infected with yellow fever, during the first three days of the attack, and at least twelve more days would have to have elapsed before it could pass the disease on to another!

If the intervention had accomplished nothing else, this one discovery would have made it worth while. Its value to the world was incalculable, as it made it possible for the first time to combat yellow fever with some prospect of success. As for Cuba, a war on mosquitoes began at once. Incidentally, too, this contributed to check malaria which had also ravaged the island, as this disease was already known to be transmitted by the bite of mosquitoes. Their breeding-places in stagnant pools were attacked with gasoline, which proved effective. In his report of 1901 the sanitation officer claimed that the number of mosquitoes in the island at the end of the year was not more than a tenth of what it had been at the start. One may wonder how the mosquito "census" was taken, but in point of fact yellow fever had been stamped out in Cuba. This achievement, together with other measures contributing to the same general result, presently converted Cuba from a pest-hole into one of the most healthful countries in the world. At the end of the United States occupation in Cuba a comparison of the figures for death from disease in the American army showed 20.26 per cent in the Pacific islands, 4.83 per cent in the United States, and only 1.67 per cent in Cuba. Furthermore, the idea of sanitation was inculcated in the minds of Cubans, and, though the government in recent years has at times shown a reprehensible lack of attention to this matter, there has been no relapse to anything approaching the bad situation existing prior to 1900. Incidentally, the officer in charge of the sanitation campaign was a certain Major William Crawford Gorgas, presently to win fame in the same connection in the building of the Panamá Canal and in aid to various stricken regions of Hispanic America.

Not so spectacular as the war against disease, General Wood's achievements in the domain of public works were noteworthy. Much that he did was in connection with education and the health program. For example, hospitals and charities were put upon an up-to-date basis. Under Spain the intent had been humane, but the management bad.

Necessary equipment was lacking, and unhygienic practices were prevalent. All this was changed. Roads and bridges were built, an extensive and efficient telephone and telegraph service was developed, the customs service was most capably handled under the management of Colonel Tasker Howard Bliss. The post-office was made to function in first-class fashion. Indeed, with the expenditures on sanitation included, more money was put out for public works than on any other branch of the service. This has led one writer to make the following observations:

"Despite the complaints of American critics that too much money was spent on schools in proportion to other things, therefore, it appears that much less was spent on them than on public works. Perhaps such complaints would have been less numerous and less bitter if General Wood had been willing or able to give profitable contracts and franchises to American speculators." [14]

There was one instance of graft on a large scale by Americans in the post-office, involving some of the higher officials of that institution, including the director, Mr. Estes G. Rathbone, who has been described as

"a person who was much 'set up' and full of importance, given to 'throwing the house through the window' in receptions and banquets. He was very well connected in his own country, and had a close friendship with various of the most well-known chieftains of the Republican party, then in power." [15]

Hardly anybody in Cuba imagined for a moment that punishment could overtake a man so strongly entrenched as Mr. Rathbone and his associates, but General Wood intervened personally in the matter, overcame a most formidable opposition, and secured a conviction of the delinquents. The manner in which this affair was handled more than made up for the crime itself, so far as its effect on Cuban

[14] Johnson, IV, 168.   [15] Martínez Ortiz, I, 130.

opinion was concerned. The barest understanding of Hispanic life will make it clear in any event, as Martínez Ortiz
has said, that "in Cuba itself the case never raised a dust
comparable to that produced in the United States." But
there was one after-effect that ought to be borne in mind.
This is expressed by the same Cuban writer as follows:

"The friends of these men never forgave Mr. Wood for his inflexibility
in the affair. As often as they could oppose him they did so furiously,
and despite his great influence they tried to put obstacles in the way of
his advancement and fame." [16]

Among innumerable other acts of the governor was his disposition of a difficult church question. The Roman Catholic
faith is virtually the only religion with any standing in Cuba
and all other Hispanic countries, but there is almost invariably a bitter opposition to the church as an institution (apart
from its beliefs) that Americans who have not lived in one
of the southern republics find hard to understand. In Cuba
there was a special local reason for hostility, as churchmen
had pretty generally espoused the cause of Spain. Three
issues were raised in attacks on the church, after the war
was over. There were proposals for confiscation of church
property, the secularization of cemeteries, and the replace-
ment of church marriages by a civil function. Left to themselves, there is no telling how far the Cubans might have
gone, and it was fortunate for the church that an American
who was not a Catholic had the decision in the matter. The
church was allowed to keep its estates and retain its control
over cemeteries already in its possession, without being sub-

[16] *Ibid.*, I, 131. The writer has in
his possession a number of statements
from veteran residents of Cuba to the
same effect. For example, the following is quite typical: "The objections
to General Wood were chiefly on the
part of grafters and those who wanted
improper concessions they couldn't
get. Some Cubans were suspicious
of him as an agent of the United
States, but admired him personally."

jected to hostile regulation. Under General Brooke the Cuban Secretaries did put through some measures against the church,—for example, the civil marriage decree. Up to that time church marriages alone were legal, and it was customary to charge rather high fees for the service. General Brooke was prevailed upon to enact a law establishing civil marriage for a fee of one dollar and making it the only binding ceremony. , The church fought this law, and it was changed in 1900 by General Wood, who decreed that a church marriage (by any lawful sect) or a civil marriage should be equally valid. As an illustration of the Cuban attitude toward this law it is interesting to note that eighty municipalities, out of the then 107 existing, were opposed to the change from the law of General Brooke, and so also were all but one of the judges of the Supreme Court, the majority of the judges in courts of first instance, and three of the six Cuban governors of the provinces.

It is on the score of the economic situation that General Wood's critics have endeavored to make the most capital against him, trying to give the impression that the lack of prosperity at this time was due to his administration. It would seem that the complaints were hardly justified. In the first place, Cuba was in the midst of a serious economic depression, due to the ills that had befallen her in the war and to the position of sugar in the world's markets. In the second place, a great deal *was* done in order to assist the island to get back on a satisfactory business basis. One critic has pointed out, however, that only a little over a million dollars was applied to agriculture, industry, and commerce, out of a total expenditure of fifty-five millions for the whole period of the intervention, while justice and instruction (mainly education) received eleven millions, and sanitation nine. Nevertheless, without counting amounts devoted to the two last-named services, various sums were spent that must have been of great assistance to business, such, for example, as the nearly six millions for public works and five for the rural guards. And certainly it is open to question whether direct paternalistic aid to agriculture is advisable. Anyway, it was a matter of choice with the monies available, and it is quite generally admitted by the Cubans themselves that General Wood, following instructions from Washington, chose well. The burden of proof would still seem to be on his opponents.

It is impossible to be precise about the condition of commerce and industry under Spain, for "no reliance" can be placed "on even official reports," and Spanish "methods" were "nothing other than well-organized corruption," a bargain between importers and the custom-house officials, high and low. Coffee, which was supposed to pay $12.15 per hundred kilograms, would be entered as corn, paying $2.40, and sheet copper at $14 would come in as sheet iron at $2.90, or pianos might enter as organs, at half the rate. There were similar frauds in exports, on which duties were also collected. An honest administration might have produced a far greater yield. For example, exports of the fiscal year 1893-1894 were officially about a hundred million, and imports sixty, with revenues of twelve millions, while a much smaller volume of trade under the United States military government, with exports ranging from forty-nine to sixty-six millions and imports from sixty-seven to seventy-four, yielded an average of seventeen millions in revenues. Under American rule Cuba was at first too poor to make much profit out of commerce, but there was a "better condition" each year, as the arch-critic admits, despite an unfavorable sugar situation. The sugar crop had fallen from an average of about a million tons in the early nineties to some three hundred thousand in the fiscal year 1897-1898.[17]   Imports were heavy, as stocks of merchandise had been depleted during the war. A provisional tariff, prepared just prior to the official close of Spanish rule, went into effect on December 13, 1898, but was succeeded by a more carefully worked out schedule of duties in a decree of June 15, 1900.   There was some criticism because certain United States products were favored, though others were unable to compete with European goods. Despite an increase in rates against the former group at a later time, after the republic was established, the proportion of Cuban trade with the United States was not then so great as it has since become.   Cuba imported from the United States approximately $109,000,000 worth of goods out of a total of $224,000,000, or less than fifty per cent, and exported $135,000,000 in $179,000,000, or over seventy-five per cent, making a total volume of trade of some sixty per cent.   The government's revenues were almost wholly derived from customs duties.   In a total of some fifty-seven millions for the whole period of United States rule, less than five millions were obtained from other sources.   Incidentally, as already pointed out, all but about two millions of the revenues were spent.   The tariff was designed to produce just about the amount needed.   There was no desire to pile up a surplus.   Possibly the authorities realized that it would be politically dangerous, as was later amply to be proved during the first presidential administration of the republic.

Among the acts designed to help the business situation may be mentioned the decrees to assist debtors.   The island was mortgaged up to approximately three-fourths its value, and there was a general inability to pay, during the early

[17] Compare this with the four to   times.
five million tons a year of recent

years of the intervention. In consequence both Brooke and Wood issued mortgage decrees, which carried payments over to 1901. A number of other debts, after due investigation, were cancelled. It is worthy of note, too, as in some measure reflecting the security of conditions during the intervention, that there was not a single financial failure in the entire period, despite the fact that a large proportion of business was in the hands of the then hated Spaniards. A still further example of indirect economic aid was in the encouragement of railway building. At the close of Spanish rule there were 1135 miles of public lines and 965 that were privately owned, the latter mainly by sugar companies operating between their plantations and ports also owned by themselves. Most of the railways were English-controlled, and nine-tenths of the entire system was in the west. To develop the eastern provinces, since become the great sugar mart of the island, a new line was built during General Wood's administration. This was the Cuba Railway, running from Santa Clara to Santiago. There was some difficulty in aiding this enterprise, because of the Foraker Law against concessions, but it was held that it did not apply, since the company had not taken a Cuban charter, but was incorporated in the state of New Jersey. So the company was allowed to purchase a strip of land 450 miles long and thirty meters wide. The permission was more easily given than taken advantage of. Owners made extortionate demands for their property, and newspapers and politicians attacked the project, many of them hoping "to be paid for their silence or approval." The aid of government was necessary if the road was to be built at all; so on February 7, 1902, General Wood issued a decree concerning railways, in which he applied the eminent domain principle of Anglo-American law, allowing land to be "denounced" and taken by public service companies, on payment of an adjudged fair price. As a result, half of Cuba, previously of scant value, was "opened to settlement and to productive cultivation." [18]   General Wood's critics claim that his assistance to the Cuba Railway was in violation of the Foraker Law, though admitting the benefit derived by the island. Certainly no "subservience to Wall Street" cry could be raised in connection with his later railway law of April 28, 1902, however. In this, rates were fixed at a much lower tariff than had been collected before. For example, where passengers had been charged from seven to twelve cents a mile, the fare was reduced to four and a third to six cents. Other rates were in proportion to these, designed to give a reasonable, but not excessive, profit. The railways protested, but to no avail, and even the critics aver that this was a "good law."

One more phase of the military government's work has yet to be discussed,—that involved in the instructions to prepare Cuba as rapidly as possible for an independent republican government. This is so important that it merits separate treatment.[19]

[18] For something further about the building of the Cuba Railway, see *infra*, pp. 617-618.

[19] Few periods of recent United States history have more ample materials upon them and are more worthy of monographic study than that of the military government in Cuba from 1898 to 1902. Trelles, *Biblioteca*, II, 87-99, for example, cites 128 items, mainly, but not wholly, of Cuban and American origin. Of special note are the reports of the two governors, Brooke and Wood, that of the former in a single volume (Brooke, John Rutter, *Civil report*, Washington, 1900), but supplemented by individual reports of the different military governors of the provinces, and that of General Wood in no fewer than thirty-three great tomes (Wood,

Leonard, *Civil report, 1899-1900,* 12 vols., Havana, 1901; *Civil report . . . 1901,* 15 vols., Havana, 1902; *Civil report . . . 1902,* 6 vols., Havana, 1903).

Of secondary accounts the best, perhaps, is that of the Cuban historian, Martínez Ortiz, which is neither hyper-laudatory nor afflicted with any observable bias, in addition to which it makes use of much worthwhile contemporary material and has a Cuban atmosphere not apparent in works by American writers. A close rival to the work of Martínez Ortiz is that of Albert Robinson, already cited (*supra*, p. 95, n. 5). In many particulars this is even more detailed, and, despite the author's hostility to General Wood, there are few volumes in which the great achievements of that official stand forth more clearly. The criticisms in this work are so obviously unfair or, in the light of subsequent events, so inaccurate that they fail to make the impression that was intended. Robinson visited Cuba during this period as the representative of the New York *Evening Post,* then managed by Oswald Garrison Villard, since widely known as an editor of *The Nation.* Villard was a virulent opponent of the United States policy in Cuba and a personal enemy of General Wood. Furthermore, Robinson was closely associated, while in Cuba, with the Rathbone coterie, and he makes a weak attempt to defend that official in his book. Nevertheless, it is not hard to separate the "wheat" from the "chaff," and Robinson's volume is deserving of commendation. Without adding anything of special account, Johnson, IV, 133-254, has an interesting story of this period. Among numerous articles, one by General Wood himself (*The military government of Cuba,* in *American academy of political science, Annals,* v. XXI, pp. 153-182, Mar., 1903) is specially worthy of note.

CHAPTER VI

THE ESTABLISHMENT OF THE REPUBLIC

ONE must go far back from the period of the United States military rule for an understanding of the American attitude concerning the establishment of a republic in Cuba. The essential factor to bear in mind is that of the vital importance of the island to the United States strategically. Early dreams of annexation had passed away, and in the popular mind, reflected also in the halls of Congress, Cuba meant no more than, for example, Venezuela. The administrative branch of the government, however, whatever party might be in control, soon became aware of the fact that Cuba held out that "speck of war" for us that Jefferson had once feared. Annexation to the United States was no longer necessary or desirable, provided American interests might be conserved. That proviso, however, was an unavoidable necessity of American policy. McKinley realized this, and kept Congress from committing the United States too quickly to Cuban independence. In his message to Congress of April 11 the President made no reference to a Cuban "government," but spoke of the war between "Spain and the Cuban people," for the insurrectionists had not as yet been recognized even as belligerents.

Naturally, the American administration's attitude was not received with whole-hearted enthusiasm by the Cubans in the field. They were quite as little aware of the inevitable position of Cuba in American policy as were the rank and file of people in the United States, and, furthermore, they had endured terrible hardships on behalf of independence, and saw no reason why they should not have it at once. Any thought about their own political inexperience very probably did not occur to many of them, and if it had it would have been rejected as a reflection on those who had risked their lives to win freedom from Spain. So there was some friction between Cubans and Americans, even before the war was over. It seemed to the former that the American officials in Cuba acted as if the Cubans were merely a side-issue in the war. Not much attention was paid to the provisional government of the insurrectionists, or even to Gómez or their other military leaders. Calixto García, who had participated in the operations around Santiago, was not invited to be present at the ceremonies attending the surrender of that city, and General Wood was appointed governor of Oriente without previously consulting the Cuban revolutionary authorities. A sensitive people like the Cubans could not fail to be unfavorably impressed by treatment such as this. Naturally, there was no thought, at least for the time being, of resisting the United States occupation. The Assembly of the Cuban army met in November 1898, and set up a special committee to look out for Cuban interests during the period of American control. The provisional government was thereupon dissolved, but it was decided that the army, with Gómez as commander-in-chief, should be retained.

Something has already been said about the Cuban suspicion of American intentions, despite the virtual promise of independence contained in the Joint Resolution of April 20, 1898. Any number of incidents contributed to this, in addition to the fact that annexation in that ultra-imperialistic age was the normally to be expected thing on the part of a country with such a chance as the United States had. Indeed, the altruistic fervor of early '98 was no longer manifest in the United States in nearly the same degree. People in the street and those in high places were known to subscribe to the doctrine that "the flag, once raised, must never come down." The Washington administration did not swerve from its plans for Cuban independence, but the Cubans could hardly be expected to know that or to put much faith in official pronouncements, however strong. The Cuban leaders accepted the American military government, because there was nothing else they could do, but there was not a little friction, right from the start. Early in 1899 General Calixto García died. Ranking with Gómez and Maceo as one of the three greatest military figures of the Cuban wars, it was natural that his funeral should be a grand and solemn affair. It was held in Havana in February, and was attended by thousands of people. It had been arranged that the Assembly of the Cuban army should march in the procession just behind the American authorities, but when General Brooke's carriage appeared it was observed that he was followed by his staff and some of his military escort. Thereupon the members of the Assembly, under the leadership of Fernando Freyre de Andrade, withdrew, and were followed by many other Cubans in the line. Indeed, it was necessary for the American soldiers to do the honors at the interment of the old Cuban hero, as the Cubans who had been designated for that purpose refused.

The scandal of the García funeral had its counterpart in numerous other incidents, all of which were indicative of a certain lack of cordiality or confidence on the part of the Cubans toward the American trusteeship. Something has already been said about the relations of General Brooke with the Cuban Assembly. This body claimed that it was the only legal government in Cuba, and wanted an immediate withdrawal of the United States authorities. It was not supported by conservative opinion in Cuba, however, and when it deposed Gómez on account of his attitude over the bonus issue it lost all standing, as already related, and dissolved itself. It was clear, nevertheless, that steps must constantly be taken in order to allay the all too ready suspicions of many of the Cubans. So one of the early acts of of General Wood was to decree a law of elections, promulgated in April 1900. Several political parties had already been formed, but up to this time they had had no real life. As already pointed out, there was, at best, only a half-hearted hope that the United States would fulfil her pledges, and, besides, there were no issues. Now, however, the parties attained to a new-born vigor, and in casting about for an issue hit upon the duration and character of the American occupation. One of General Wood's cabinet officers, General Ríus Rivera, went so far as to publish a letter advocating the immediate recognition of Cuban independence, on the basis of the Joint Resolution, rejecting the Treaty of Paris. General Wood reminded Ríus Rivera that it was not proper for his Secretaries to unbosom themselves on certain subjects without first consulting him, whereupon Ríus Rivera resigned. Another incident of similar type, serving in the same manner to stir up Cuban opinion over the independence issue, occurred later that year when the French government at first declined to allow the Cuban flag to be raised over the building which was to house the Cuban exhibit. This action was taken on the ground that it would be an affront to Spain, as it would be tantamount to a recognition of a new nation. The United States government took occasion once again to announce that it proposed to fulfil its promise to make Cuba independent, and persuaded the French authorities to permit of the raising of the flag. So, for the moment, the restless elements among the Cuban patriots were warm in their praise of the United States, putting by their suspicions until another day.

General Wood had called an informal meeting of notables, prior to the enactment of his election law, to get their views, at the same time submitting a plan prepared by Cuban officials under his direction. The majority favored a most sweepingly democratic law as regards grant of the suffrage, but the governor adopted the opinions of the minority, which accorded with his own. It was provided that all native-born Cuban men who were at least twenty-one years old might vote, if they could read and write, or had $250 worth of property, or had served in the Cuban army during the war. The secret ballot and other familiar American features were also called for in the new law. The first trial of the law was set for the municipal elections to be held in June 1900. Among numerous parties in the field, three were especially prominent. Two were immediate independence parties, differing only in leadership and locality, though one of them, the Nationalists of Havana, professed to favor a centralized republic, while the Republicans of Santa Clara came out for states' rights. The former were supposed to represent the friends of Máximo Gómez, while the latter were charged with being affiliated with his enemies in the now defunct Cuban Assembly. The leader of the Republicans was a man who now comes prominently to the fore for the first time, General José Miguel Gómez, a veteran of the two wars and civil governor of Santa Clara. The third party, the Union Democratic of Havana, represented something quite different from the other two, worthy of special note as indicative of the fact that not all Cuban society was impatient for immediate independence. Many of the members of this group were one-time Autonomists, men who had been the leading spirits among the Cubans in the interval between the two wars, but who had lost caste for seeking home rule under Spain instead of independence. Their feeling was accurately expressed in the following comment of El Nuevo País, which represented the Autonomist element:

"Cuba is not well prepared for absolute independence. It is necessary to establish the government of this country in a way to bring about the preservation of order and peace through conservative and evolutionary processes." [1]

This was the quite generally held idea of the conservative classes, who made up the bulk of the Union Democratic party. Some of them, perhaps, hoped for annexation to the United States, or at least an American protectorate, but the charges that were quite freely bandied about to the effect that the whole party stood for these things were probably not warranted. At any rate there was great bitterness against this group on the part of the more radical Cuban elements, —so much so, that the Union Democratic party presently withdrew, expressing its disapproval of the election laws and alleging corrupt practices on the part of its opponents.

The elections were held on June 16, 1900, and were peaceful enough. There were some claims of fraud, but, on the whole, the result was probably reasonably fair. The Republicans elected every one of their candidates in Santa Clara and Matanzas, but lost to the Nationalists in Havana. Elsewhere regional tickets prevailed. Despite the subsequent somewhat improper conduct of the municipal governments that were elected, it was felt that an acceptable beginning had been made. The election was hardly "cold," when General Wood announced a fresh step in the direction of independence. Acting on orders from Washington, General Wood issued an order, on July 25, 1900, for the election of

[1] Quoted in Martínez Ortiz, I, 115.

delegates "to frame and adopt a Constitution for the people of Cuba, and, as a part thereof, to provide for and agree with the Government of the United States upon the relations to exist between that Government and the Government of Cuba." Robinson is probably right in saying the call was issued in part to check the reiterated Cuban suspicions of the United States. He also says that the date of the order was timed so as to keep the Cuban issue out of the American presidential campaign of 1900. Whether or not this is true, it certainly must be considered probable; Republicans and Democrats alike in the past quarter of a century have frequently subordinated national policies relating to Cuba and other lands to the political situation in the United States. In the present instance, however, the action of the Washington authorities was in accord with what had been determined upon from the moment of the American entry into the war with Spain in 1898.

Naturally, the requirement for determining upon the nature of relations with the United States "as a part" of their own Constitution did not escape the notice of the Cuban politicians, and many of them announced that they and their parties would have nothing to do with the election of delegates. Before election day, on September 15, 1900, they had changed their minds, however, having in the meantime received assurances that the terms of the order would be modified. Thirty-one delegates were elected, apportioned among the provinces according to population, with Havana getting eight, Santa Clara and Oriente seven apiece, Matanzas four, Pinar del Río three, and Camagüey two. All the delegates but one were members of the more radical revolutionary elements, the men who were prominent in the Nationalist and Republican ranks. Among their numbers were men who were to be outstanding figures in the presently to be formed republic, such, for example, as Gonzalo de Quesada, General Emilio Núñez, Manuel Sanguily, Alfredo Zayas, Domingo Méndez Capote, José Miguel Gómez, and Juan Gualberto Gómez. The Convention met for the first time in Havana on November 5, 1900, on which occasion General Wood read an order setting forth that the "first" duty of the delegates was to "frame and adopt a Constitution," and then "formulate what, in your opinion, ought to be the relations between Cuba and the United States." Afterwards, "the Government of the United States will doubtless take such action on its part as shall lead to a final and authoritative agreement between the people of the two countries to the promotion of their common interests."

Without paying much attention to the matter of relations with the United States, the Convention went to work to prepare a Constitution for Cuba, being left to its own devices by General Wood, who made no attempt to intervene in its deliberations. While no serious differences developed as to the main features of the document, there were a number of disputes over what seem to have been comparatively unimportant items. A phrase in the preamble about "invoking the favor of God" raised quite a storm. Salvador Cisneros, the much-esteemed one-time Marquis of Santa Lucía and a former revolutionary President of Cuba, now seventy-five years old, proposed to strike it out. Sanguily supported him, asserting however that it was a matter of no importance one way or the other. Following an impassioned appeal for it by an eighty year old delegate named Pedro Llorente, the phrase was allowed to stand. In like manner there was an animated debate over the paragraph concerning religious worship. It was decided to do away with the Spanish system of a state-supported church and permit of freedom for all sects. These two matters are interesting as an illustration of a certain aggressive attitude against the church that is so common in Hispanic America. Furthermore, by definitely pronouncing for a separation of church and state the Cubans rid themselves of an issue that has disturbed the politics of many of their sister republics to the south. The most bitterly fought paragraph of the Constitution grew out of a matter which proved to have no importance at all. This was the one concerning the qualifications for the presidency, and it turned on the eligibility of Máximo Gómez, who, as already observed, was a native of the Dominican Republic. The issue was whether the chief magistracy should be restricted to native-born Cubans only or whether the article should be framed in such a way as to admit of an election of Gómez. On this issue the pro-Gómez Nationalists and anti-Gómez Republicans clashed. In the end a clause was put in (now obsolete) that a naturalized citizen who had served ten years in Cuba's wars might be eligible. Later, when the time came for a presidential election, the old general declined to allow his name to be put in nomination. Possibly the most notable of the other contested points before the Convention was the paragraph concerning qualifications for voting. On account of the great number of illiterates and not too highly civilized negroes in Cuba, some were in favor of restricting the suffrage, but the majority were not even willing to adopt the limitations that had been imposed by General Wood in the elections of 1900. So, except for insane persons and those civilly dead, universal manhood suffrage was decided upon.

The Constitution was declared ready, and was signed by the delegates on February 21, 1901. It was received without great enthusiasm, for many felt that the United States would not accept it. Conservative elements outside the Convention were not ready for a severance of the connection with the United States, and many, doubtless, still hoped for annexation. But the Washington authorities interposed no objections to the document as it stood. Elihu Root, then Secretary of War and therefore in charge of matters relating to the military government in Cuba, remarked of it in his annual report for 1901,

"I do not fully agree with the wisdom of some of the provisions of this constitution; but it provides for a republican form of government; it was adopted after long and patient consideration and discussion; it represents the views of the delegates elected by the people of Cuba; and it contains no features which would justify the assertion that a government organized under it will not be one to which the United States may properly transfer the obligations for the protection of life and property under international law, assumed in the Treaty of Paris."

Nevertheless, the United States was not satisfied merely "to prepare Cuba for self-government." The Washington authorities were interested also in the matter of "relations" between Cuba and the United States, and the solution of this problem was, it has been stated,

"To require from the Cubans guarantees for the conduct of their government and to prevent the island from falling into the hands of any other nation so that the United States would not be placed in a worse position than before by reason of turning Spain out of the island. This was accomplished by including in the Cuban constitution and in the legislation of the United States and in a treaty between the United States and Cuba the provisions known as the Platt Amendment." [2]

For convenience, the terms of this famous document may well be set forth here:

"*Provided further*, That in fulfillment of the declaration contained in the joint resolution approved April twentieth, eighteen hundred and ninety-eight, entitled 'For the recognition of the independence of the people of Cuba, demanding that the Government of Spain relinquish

[2] Comment of the editors of Root, *Elihu, The military and colonial policy of the United States*, 185. Other quoted paragraphs given in this chapter without citation may also be found in that volume.

its authority and government in the island of Cuba, and withdraw its land and naval forces from Cuba and Cuban waters, and directing the President of the United States to use the land and naval forces of the United States to carry these resolutions into effect,' the President is hereby authorized to 'leave the government and control of the island of Cuba to its people' so soon as a government shall have been established in said island under a constitution which, either as a part thereof or in an ordinance appended thereto, shall define the future relations of the United States with Cuba, substantially as follows:

I. That the government of Cuba shall never enter into any treaty or other compact with any foreign power or powers which will impair or tend to impair the independence of Cuba, nor in any manner authorize or permit any foreign power or powers to obtain by colonization or for military or naval purposes or otherwise, lodgment in or control over any portion of said island.

II. That said government shall not assume or contract any public debt, to pay the interest upon which, and to make reasonable sinking fund provision for the ultimate discharge of which the ordinary revenues of the island, after defraying the current expenses of government, shall be inadequate.

III. That the government of Cuba consents that the United States may exercise the right to intervene for the preservation of Cuban independence, the maintenance of a government adequate for the protection of life, property, and individual liberty, and for discharging the obligations with respect to Cuba imposed by the Treaty of Paris on the United States, now to be assumed and undertaken by the government of Cuba.

IV. That all acts of the United States in Cuba during its military occupancy thereof are ratified and validated, and all lawful rights acquired thereunder shall be maintained and protected.

V. That the government of Cuba will execute, and, as far as necessary, extend, the plans already devised or other plans to be mutually agreed upon, for the sanitation of the cities of the island, to the end that a recurrence of epidemic and infectious diseases may be prevented, thereby assuring protection to the people and commerce of Cuba, as well as to the commerce of the southern ports of the United States and the people residing therein.

VI. That the Isle of Pines shall be omitted from the proposed constitutional boundaries of Cuba, the title thereto being left to future adjustment by treaty.

VII. That to enable the United States to maintain the independence of Cuba, and to protect the people thereof, as well as for its own defense, the government of Cuba will sell or lease to the United States lands necessary for coaling or naval stations at certain specified points, to be agreed upon with the President of the United States.

VIII. That by way of further assurance the government of Cuba will embody the foregoing provisions in a permanent treaty with the United States."

It was not until after a bitter struggle of several months that the Convention at length accepted these conditions. The Convention did not consider the matter of relations until after the Constitution had been completed, and then showed an utter unwillingness to provide anything in line with the inevitable requirements of the United States. What the nature of these would be was already known, for Secretary Root had despatched a long communication on this score to General Wood on February 9, 1901, which had been communicated to members of the Convention immediately upon its arrival in Havana, on February 15. After reciting the self-imposed duty assumed by the United States under the Joint Resolution of April 20, 1898, and the obligations toward Spain derived from the Treaty of Paris to provide for "protection of life and property" during the American occupation and upon its termination to "advise any government established in the island to assume the same obligations," Mr. Root discussed the kind of government that should be set up in Cuba, and then went on to make the following important comment on the score of relations:

"It seems to me that no one familiar with the traditional and established policy of this country in respect to Cuba can find cause for doubt as to our remaining duty. It would be hard to find any single statement of public policy which has been so often officially declared by so great an array of distinguished Americans authorized to speak for the Government of the United States, as the proposition stated, in varying but always uncompromising and unmistakable terms, that the United States would not under any circumstances permit any foreign power other than Spain to acquire possession of the island of Cuba.

Jefferson and Monroe and John Quincy Adams and Jackson and Van Buren and Grant and Clay and Webster and Buchanan and Everett have all agreed in regarding this as essential to the interests and the protection of the United States. The United States has, and will always have, the most vital interest in the preservation of the independence which she has secured for Cuba, and in preserving the people of that island from the domination and control of any foreign power whatever. The preservation of that independence by a country so small as Cuba, so incapable, as she must always be, to contend by force against the great powers of the world, must depend upon her strict performance of international obligations, upon her giving due protection to the lives and property of the citizens of all other countries within her borders, and upon her never contracting any public debt which in the hands of the citizens of foreign powers shall constitute an obligation she is unable to meet. The United States has, therefore, not merely a moral obligation arising from her destruction of Spanish authority in Cuba and the obligations of the Treaty of Paris for the establishment of a stable and adequate government in Cuba, but it has a substantial interest in the maintenance of such a government.

We are placed in a position where, for our own protection, we have, by reason of expelling Spain from Cuba, become the guarantors of Cuban independence and the guarantors of a stable and orderly government protecting life and property in that island. Fortunately the condition which we deem essential for our own interests is the condition for which Cuba has been struggling, and which the duty we have assumed toward Cuba on Cuban grounds and for Cuban interests requires. It would be a most lame and impotent conclusion if, after all the expenditure of blood and treasure by the people of the United States for the freedom of Cuba and by the people of Cuba for the same object, we should, through the constitution of the new government, by inadvertence or otherwise, be placed in a worse condition in regard to our own vital interests than we were while Spain was in possession, and the people of Cuba should be deprived of that protection and aid from the United States which is necessary to the maintenance of their independence."

Mr. Root then recited five provisions which the United States felt that "the people of Cuba should desire to have incorporated in her fundamental law." Though in somewhat different phraseology, they were virtually the same as articles one, two, three, four, and seven of the eventual Platt Amendment.

Opinion about these provisions was divided in Cuba. The Convention did not like them, especially the articles about intervention and naval stations for the United States. But Conservative elements would have preferred even more. The recommendations had been made by Secretary Root, however, with full information of the situation. Not only had he and General Wood kept in touch by correspondence, but they had also gone over matters in conversations they had had on visits of Root to Havana and Wood to Washington. Indeed, the Secretary's suggestions had been foreshadowed in President McKinley's annual message of December 5, 1899, in which he said:

"This nation has assumed before the world a grave responsibility for the future good government of Cuba . . . The new Cuba yet to arise from the ashes of the past must needs be bound to us by ties of singular intimacy and strength if its enduring welfare is to be assured. Whether those ties shall be organic or conventional, the destinies of Cuba are in some rightful form and manner irrevocably linked with our own."

General Wood's reply of February 19, 1901, to Root's long communication of the 9th intimated that there was "no serious objection to any of the conditions excepting the Fifth,"—the one about naval stations. There was some disapproval of the intervention article, but the governor had informed the Cuban political leaders that this "could not be modified as it embodied the obligations which the United States had assumed under the . . . treaty." Continuing, General Wood said:

"In my opinion the demands are liberal, equitable and just and should be insisted on throughout. It is very probable that we shall have to exercise directly the intervention provided for under the Third Article and it is certain that we should, were it not known in Cuba that in case of lack of stability and failure to observe the provisions imposed by the Treaty of Paris the United States would promptly intervene. Such knowledge will probably act as a check on the government to come. In reference to the Naval Stations: the objection to this seems to be a matter principally of sentiment combined with a certain amount of selfishness. Among the elements now dominating in the politics of the island there is little or no gratitude for what has been done by the United States. Among the bulk of the people there is a feeling of appreciation and gratitude."

The governor then went on to make a strong argument in favor of requiring the Cubans to maintain a good state of sanitation, which accounts for the eventual inclusion of article five in the already cited Platt Amendment.[3]

Presently, the opposition of the political class to the Root proposals became much more active than General Wood seems to have anticipated. At least one writer claims the members of the Convention and their adherents were encouraged in this attitude by "the factional enemies of the President in the United States," some of whom were false to their Cuban friends in that they entertained a "deliberate and malignant hope of precipitating an armed conflict between the two countries which would result in the conquest and forcible annexation of Cuba." [4]   At any rate, the Convention seemed willing to consider a modified acceptance of the first and fourth articles suggested by Mr. Root, but was clearly opposed to all the others.   Meanwhile, there was no change in the attitude of the Washington authorities.   Senator Orville Hitchcock Platt, chairman of the important Foreign Relations Committee, remarked that Cuba was free to adopt any Constitution she liked, but the United States had guaranteed a stable government in the island, and a Constitution was not in itself a sufficient guarantee.

[3] Letter quoted in full in 186-187. The argument on sanitation

[4] Root, is quoted *infra*, p. 645. Johnson, IV: 200; 202.

So the committee began preparing a measure about relations which included not only the five suggestions of Mr. Root and the one by General Wood, but also the other two articles numbered six and eight. An interesting explanation of the probable reason for including article six, which left sovereignty over the Isle of Pines in doubt, has been made by Gonzalo de Quesada, who was a member of the Convention and later Cuban minister to the United States. According to him, it grew out of the Cuban opposition to the Root proposals, especially the naval stations article. On this account some believed "that the Isle of Pines could be made the basis of defence for American interests in the Caribbean Sea, or that, if the Isle of Pines was found unsuitable—as it was afterwards shown to be—for coaling and naval purposes, it could be made the basis of negotiation for the acquisition of other sites." [5] As for article eight, that was to provide a form of insurance against a Cuban removal of the other seven proposed articles from the Constitution.

The Platt Amendment, named for Senator Platt,—though many have suggested that it might more appropriately have been called the "Root Amendment,"—was an "amendment," not on account of its eventual place in the Cuban Constitution, but because it was an addition to the army appropriation bill before the United States Congress,—to the army bill, as Cuba was being administered by the War Department. It was submitted to the Senate on February 25, 1901, passed that body on the 27th, and passed the House on March 1st. Opinion in the United States about it was very much divided, and not wholly on straight party lines. To many it seemed at first sight like breaking faith, and the manner in which the bill had been put through, as a "rider"

[5] Quesada, Gonzalo de, *Cuba's claims to the Isle of Pines*, in *North American review*, v. CXC, pp. 594-604; Nov., 1909.

to an appropriation bill, with little discussion, was also criticized.

In Cuba, conservative elements accepted the Amendment, but the politicians boiled over for a while in a perfect furor of opposition. The Convention rejected it by a vote of twenty-four to two, and then sent a committee to Washington to negotiate about the matter. Meanwhile, Mr. Root had endeavored to calm Cuban opinion by a statement to the effect that no limitation of the new republic's independence was intended. Writing to Wood on April 3, 1901, he said:

"You are authorized to state officially that in the view of the President the intervention described in the third clause of the Platt Amendment is not synonymous with intermeddling or interference with the affairs of the Cuban government, but the formal action of the Government of the United States, based upon just and substantial grounds, for the preservation of Cuban independence, and the maintenance of a government adequate for the protection of life, property, and individual liberty, and adequate for discharging the obligations with respect to Cuba imposed by the Treaty of Paris on the United States."

Similar assurances were also given to the committee the Convention had sent to Washington. These men were told that there would be no use made of intervention except in case of foreign or domestic disturbance, and that Cuba would have entire control of her own affairs, foreign as well as domestic, at other times. Some intimations were offered to them that Cuba might get a favorable commercial treaty after the Platt Amendment should have been accepted, though the bill would have to pass Congress. And meanwhile, until the American proposals should be adopted, the military government would go on. So on May 28, 1901, the Convention accepted the Platt Amendment by a vote of fifteen to fourteen, but added an interpretation of its own to the document. The authorities in Washington came back

with a statement that the acceptance must be without qualifications. So on June 12, 1901, by a vote of sixteen to eleven,
with four members absent, the Convention adopted the
Amendment. In due time it was added as an "appendix" to
the Constitution, together with the Permanent Treaty embodying the first seven articles of the Amendment.[6]

It now remained for a Cuban government to be elected
which could take over control of the island's affairs. General Wood issued an order for the holding of a presidential
election on December 31, 1901. Meanwhile, municipal elections had again been held in which "the issue" was the Platt
Amendment. There were a number of frauds committed.
In Cienfuegos the anti-Platt Amendment candidate for the
post of *alcalde,* or mayor, made such strong representations to
the effect that his victorious opponent had stolen the election that General Wood sent one of his officers to investigate. It was expected that the winner would be sustained,
as it was believed that the governor was favorable to him,
but the decision went to the other man. This might have
been taken as fairly conclusive evidence that the United
States authorities would not try to impose their own prefer-
ences on the voters of Cuba. It seems that it was as yet
difficult for the Cubans to believe it, however, as the same
suspicious attitude was present in the ensuing national elections. The Nationalists would have been glad to back
Máximo Gómez as their candidate for the presidency, and
he might very probably have won the election, despite the
bitter hostility to him of some of the other political groups.
But Gómez did a thing that has few parallels in Hispanic
American history. He declined to run. "Men of war, for
war," he said, "and those of peace, for peace." Besides, he

[6] For a discussion of the meaning   see *infra,* pp. 638-647.
and reach of the Platt Amendment,

felt that he could render greater service to the country outside the presidency and partisan politics than in them, helping out with his counsel. With Gómez out of the reckoning the two leading candidates were Tomás Estrada Palma and Bartolomé Masó, both of whom had played prominent parts in the two Cuban wars. Estrada Palma had won the respect of everybody by his conduct as Cuban delegate abroad, during the revolution of '95-'98. He had been a most meticulously honest, careful, and capable administrator of the funds that came to his hands, and by the austerity of his private life and his seriousness of purpose had made an excellent impression on leading Americans in furthering the Cuban cause. Masó was of the likeable Hispanic type, but his rather excessive generosity toward his friends and a certain decline in mental powers somewhat unfitted him for the post to which he aspired.[7] Furthermore, he displayed great lack of tact by coming out in a public onslaught on the already adopted Platt Amendment.

It has often been said that Masó was the favorite of the majority of the Cuban electorate, but Martínez Ortiz has shown almost conclusively that such was not the case.[8] In the first place, Estrada Palma's own record was sufficient to attract many votes. In addition, he had the support of Máximo Gómez, the most popular man in Cuba, and, if that were not enough, the backing of the Nationalist and Republican parties, the two most powerful political groups in the island, to say nothing of the good will of the great northern republic,—an important consideration in Hispanic lands, which have an inherent respect for authority. Gómez paid a visit to Estrada Palma in the United States before coming out publicly in his favor. Asked to state his views on Cuban affairs, Estrada Palma wrote a long letter in which he pro-

[7] Martínez Ortiz, I, 314.   [8] *Ibid.*, I, 316-338.

claimed the need for economy in the new government, for an advantageous commercial treaty with the United States, and for pay of the army of the revolution, though without putting too heavy burdens on the treasury. On the score of the Platt Amendment "issue" he asserted that that document should be interpreted "in the most favorable manner to the interests of Cuba and her sovereignty and independence,"—a vague phrase, but at least more tactful than the outburst of Masó against the famous appendix. After a little more negotiation the leaders of the two principal parties announced themselves as satisfied, and signed a campaign paper in his favor which they published to the country. It is interesting to note the names of some of the signers, especially of those who were to be prominent in later years, including several who afterward turned on the man whom they now were backing for the presidency. José Miguel Gómez and Alfredo Zayas were among them. Other names attached included those of Máximo Gómez, Domingo Méndez Capote, Manuel Sanguily, Emilio Núñez, Ricardo Dolz, Martín Morúa Delgado, and Gonzalo de Quesada.

In October, Masó came to Havana, and published his own program. This was a very different thing from that of Estrada Palma,—inevitably so, no doubt, since Masó had to seek adherents in various quarters in order to counteract the powerful support that had gathered to the standard of Estrada Palma. He made promises to elements that had been to some extent neglected by the other parties,—to the Spaniards, the old Autonomists, and the negroes. Presently he objected to the constitution of the Central Board of Scrutiny, which contained Nationalists and Republicans, but no partisans of Masó. Neither General Wood nor the Washington authorities would make any change in the Board (which, indeed, had been created prior to the announcement of Masó's candidacy), although they assured him that the election would be handled impartially. Not satisfied with this, Masó and his friends announced that they would refuse to go to the polls. So, naturally, Estrada Palma had a walk-over. Nevertheless, the vote was large, though General Wood later remarked that the conservative elements took too little interest in the election, and therefore had very slight representation in congressmen and other officials of the new government.

The work of the intervention was now very nearly done. The first congress of the republic was called together on May 5, 1902, to give its official approval of the candidates that had been declared elected. The following May 20 at noon was set for the formal raising of the Cuban flag. Meanwhile, Estrada Palma had come to Cuba from New York, going first to his old home at Bayamo in Oriente. From there he made a veritable triumphal progress, to the accompaniment of dinners, speeches, and balls, across the island to Havana. On the night of May 19 pandemonium broke loose in Havana. Fireworks were set off, and people exhibited their enthusiasm to the full over the dawning of independence on the morrow. An impressive ceremony took place at noon of the 20th, and when it was over the Cuban flag was run up on the Palace. Immediately thereafter it was unfurled also on the Morro,—as significant to the Cubans as the fall of the Bastille had been to the French. Then, indeed, there was excitement, noise, and a perfect frenzy of patriotic ecstasy. Amidst it all, General Wood went off to a vessel that was waiting to carry him to the United States.

The intervention was over. It had accomplished much. Some issues, such as the question of tariff concessions to Cuba, ownership of the Isle of Pines, and the selection of naval bases for the United States, were yet to be settled. But these were details. Taken by and large, had the military government been a success? According to overwhelming opinion, both then and since, it was. Naturally, there was friction at the time, growing out of the suspicion felt by the more radical elements of Cuban society toward the United States. On the other hand, the conservative classes, including the Spaniards, would have preferred annexation, or at least an American protectorate, although they were afraid to express themselves too strongly, as prevailing opinion was contrary. No less competent an observer than the distinguished English statesman James Bryce expressed that view.[9] Still others in Cuba are said to have wished temporary independence as a step toward eventual annexation as a state. Writing at a much later time, at the close of the United States intervention of 1906-1909, but with the work of 1899-1902 perhaps even more prominently in mind, another well-known Englishman, Sir Harry Johnston, remarked that

"The impartial traveller cannot but feel sincere admiration for the results of American intervention in Cuba. Nowhere has the work of the Anglo-Saxon been better done or with happier results." In fine, all had been "carried out quietly, unostentatiously, honestly, and in a manner to attract and conciliate the Cuban people. It has been an achievement in the best 'Anglo-Saxon' style."[10]

Martínez Ortiz devotes an entire chapter to an appreciation of the work of General Wood.

"Very rarely will history offer twenty-four months of administration more fruitful than his," he said. ". . . If the government of General Wood was very notable from an administrative point of view, from a political point of view it was even more remarkable. It may be said

[9] Bryce, James, *Some reflections on the state of Cuba,* in *North American review,* v. CLXXIV, pp. 445-456, at 450-451; Apr., 1902.
[10] Johnston, *Sir* Harry, *An English-*   *man's impressions of American rule in Cuba,* in *McClure's,* v. XXXIII, pp. 496-504, at 496 and 497; Sept., 1909.

that Cuba owes to him the constitution of its government in the form
in which it was established,—a form which permits it to go on strengthening itself . . . Beyond a doubt the permanent relations between Cuba
and the United States were prepared in the first place by Secretary Elihu
Root, but without the very effective aid of Mr. Wood things might
have taken a quite different course . . . He maintained himself relatively
aloof from intimate association with Cubans, but was accustomed
to do justice to the personal qualities of prominent and virtuous sons
of the country. Neither favors nor gifts had any place with him;
nobody dared propose to him an unclean piece of business or any sort
of participation of doubtful honesty in any affair whatever. His own
wealth did not increase a single penny while he managed the millions
of the treasury . . . Friends and adversaries, high and low, those who
were satisfied and those who complained, all joined at the conclusion of
his rule in this assertion: 'he was an honorable man!' " [11]

Even such a carping critic as Albert Robinson says it was

"beyond question that . . . the United States left in Cuba an immeasurably better and surer foundation for a Cuban Republic than any
upon which the Cubans could have built had they succeeded, without
American aid, in expelling the Government of Spain." [12]

If this is so, it is impossible to withhold a great share of the
credit from General Wood. The Cubans, not even the comparatively hostile members of the political class, do not withhold that credit. One often hears the remark in Cuba that
if the people might elect the man they wanted for the presidency they would choose Leonard Wood. In fine, his reputation as one of the greatest, or possibly the greatest, of the
rulers the island ever had is so secure that presentation of
evidence to this effect would be a mere work of supereroga-
tion.

One question is often raised, however. Did the United
States get out too soon? There were many in the northern
republic, as well as in Cuba, who thought that the United

[11] Martínez Ortiz, I, 387-397.   *and the intervention,* 2 ed. (New
[12] Robinson, Albert Gardner, *Cuba*   York. 1910), 346.

States ought not to have gone out at all. Still others,—for example, Richard Olney, Secretary of State in Cleveland's second administration,—felt that Congress ought not to have promised in the Joint Resolution to give independence to Cuba, pointing out that its action was taken with undue haste, on the crest of a wave of sentimentality; nevertheless, although the "declaration of intention was not a contract,"[13] it was usually held to be a morally binding obligation.[14] Similar expressions of opinion were, and still are, frequently offered in Cuba that the United States got out too soon. The writer has a number of statements to this effect from veteran residents of Cuba, including Spaniards, Englishmen, and Americans as well as Cubans. The following, from a Cuban, is typical of the group:

"The only unfortunate feature of General Wood's administration was that it came to an end too soon. Against the advice of Wood himself[15] and that of many prominent Cubans, President Roosevelt resolved to get out before the American presidential campaign of 1902. He wished to avoid the issue of imperialism as applied to the relations of the United States with Cuba. Many Cubans have since felt that the United States should have remained at least twenty-five years longer. The chief difficulty was that it was necessary to give full political rights to the ignorant negroes, as they had made up a large part of the patriot armies and therefore could not be refused equal treatment with others. If another generation could have passed, a situation more in keeping with Cuba's peculiar needs might have been developed,—perhaps like that in the southern states of the United States,—and the Cuban people in general would have been much better prepared for government. In this way many of the political evils from which the island now suffers could have been avoided."

Somewhat the same idea was expressed by another person, but in the form of a criticism of General Wood:

[13] Comment of the editors in Root, 185.

[14] For an interesting contemporary discussion of these points of view, see Wellman, Walter, *The Cuban republic—limited,* in *American review of reviews,* v. XXII, pp. 708-712; Dec., 1900.

[15] The writer has seen no direct evidence that Wood gave any such advice, and doubts his giving it.

"The military government of Cuba should have been administered in such a way as to prepare the people for *early self-government.* Did Wood leave the people any better prepared to administer republican government than he found them? Did he not, in fact, by precept and example teach them autocratic rather than democratic government? He had no Congress to restrain him, he dominated the judiciary by force of character, and he accomplished his results primarily by such methods, making little effort to elicit the coöperation of the people. The result was that the ground was not prepared by him for institutional government, but rather he employed the autocratic government which had preceded and was to follow him. All else about Wood's record was good, and speaks for itself."

The writer agrees with the assertions in this statement, but differs as to the advisability of following another course. In the intervention of 1906-1909 the method suggested was to be tried, with disastrous results in loss of prestige for the American authorities and no counterbalancing advantageous effect on Cuban political practices. The truth is, an autocratic government alone could have been for the moment successful, for it was the only one which the Cubans could understand. In two years and a half it was no more possible to impart to them any real conception of democratic, republican institutions than it would be to teach a wildcat to be the playmate of a child. One has but to study the experiences of the other southern republics over a century of independence to realize that Hispanic political evils of an anti-republican character are too deep-seated to be uprooted by anything but a long and painful process of correction.

There is another point of view, less often voiced, but worthy of consideration. Would the militant Cuban political group have endured a longer occupation without an uprising? A prominent American statesman of those times once remarked to the writer that he hardly ever glanced at his morning paper but that he expected to see a headline that the Cubans had "taken to the woods." A Cuban revolution could have been put down, but not without difficulty, and almost surely it would have involved annexation of the island to the United States, or at least an indefinitely prolonged occupation. The American government was eager to fulfil its pledges. The Cubans were not yet ideally equipped for self-government,—far from it! But they had been carried along, from one step to another, just about as far as they would stand American tutelage without resisting it. So it was that

"On May 20, 1902, the world saw the unwonted spectacle of a country living up to its solemn promise and turning over a coveted possession to the inhabitants thereof in pursuance of a solemnly declared purpose, the hauling down of the American flag, the symbol of sovereignty during the occupation, and the unenforced, voluntary evacuation of Cuba Libre by the American troops." [16]

[16] Comment of the editors in Root, 185. The Root volume and the works cited at the close of the preceding chapter, especially Wood's reports and the writings of Martínez Ortiz and Robinson, are useful here. Note-worthy among Cuban contributions to Platt Amendment literature are the volumes by López Hidalgo and Machado, used more particularly in chapter XXVII.

CHAPTER VII

THE BEST YEARS OF THE REPUBLIC: ESTRADA PALMA, 1902-1905

THE United States government took over Cuba in 1898-1899 at a time of terrible distress. It left the island, as General Wood put it, "a going concern." Furthermore, the country was in the hands of perhaps the best man that could be found, the new President, Tomás Estrada Palma. There is hardly an incident of Cuban history since 1902 that is not matter of controversy, but if there is anything on which there is even an approach to a general agreement, it is that Estrada Palma was honest and incorruptible. Despite the fierceness of party feeling in Cuba, his political opponents have rarely attempted to impugn the motives of Estrada Palma himself, though alleging that he was mistaken in his policies or else deceived by his friends. Born at Bayamo, Oriente, July 9, 1835, he was nearly sixty-seven years of age when he became President. Many assert that he was too old, and some go so far as to say he had reached the point of senility,—a charge that is extravagant to the point of being silly. Omitting the obviously absurd characterizations, the following are typical of statements obtained by the writer from opponents of Estrada Palma:

(1) "Estrada Palma was honest, and would have made an excellent President of the United States, but he was too good for the Cubans."

(2) "Estrada Palma was a fine, honest, old man. The main trouble with him was that he was too old. It was easy, therefore, for the crooked politicians to 'put something over' on him. He was innocent

of any wrong-doing himself, but could not prevent his subordinates from indulging in improper political practices."

(3) "Estrada Palma was a very *good* man, but a dreamer who trusted everybody and could not believe that other people were not as unselfish as himself."

(4) "Estrada Palma was a man who had never seen a thousand dollars in his life until he became President, and he had lived away from Cuba for so long that he was really not Cuban. So he economized and built up a vast balance in the treasury, which was not the right thing to do in Cuba."

On the other hand, those who praise Estrada Palma wholeheartedly are legion. The following comments are representative:

(1) "He had the lofty virtue of North American Presidents and of many Presidents in South America. His has been the only such case in our republican life. His life was exemplary. Virtue was his norm, and honor his guide . . . Whenever people talk of the governors we have had, one hears this exclamation: 'Don Tomás has been the only good President.' "[1]

(2) "Cuba's first president, Don Tomás Estrada Palma, was a simple, unaffected, democratic gentleman, too unsophisticated, possibly, for the task before him. During the early part of his term in office he traveled from his home to the executive offices in street cars, discussing affairs of state and mundane matters with such of his fellow-travelers as cared to address him."[2]

Martínez Ortiz says Estrada Palma was stubborn and obstinate, but despite a certain obvious lack of approval of the new President he has drawn an attractively intimate picture of him.

"Affable and courteous, he was in the habit of saying little, but of having his way. However many wished to 'measure swords' with him, he vanquished them. Escobar says he always had ready a slight cough, which attacked him at opportune moments when it was best not to say anything, and with the affectionate phrase 'Sonny,'[3] which was habitual in fact almost untranslatable, having a friendly but not undignified quality for which there seem to be no words in English.

[1] Pérez, 4.
[2] *Cuba, an American ward again?*, in *Independent*, v. CXIII, pp. 35-38, at 35; July 19, 1924.
[3] *"Hijito,"* literally "little son," but

with him, he overcame the opposition of the ablest men. 'This man seems like rubber,' Sanguily exclaimed on a certain occasion, 'for when one thinks he has put his fist in him up to the elbow, why, not at all, for when one draws it away he remains as he was before.' Small in stature, but erect and firm, he carried his years very well, and they were already running on seventy. A slight '*tic*' frequently obliged him to close one eye. This and the ruddy color of his face gave his features a certain mixture of firmness and kindliness which inspired respect. By way of complement he had a white moustache that fell toward the corners of his mouth and white hair that was always carefully combed." [4]

In fine, Estrada Palma was little, but honest, earnest, and capable. He did not have the traits that appealed to the Cuban masses, and was personally known to few people on the island, but he was in every sense of the word a respectable figure. It had not been necessary for him to affiliate with any party in order to win the presidency, and he was not involved in the compromises that would have handicapped almost any other man in that office. Furthermore, his own prestige, on account of his lifetime services to the cause of independence and his known rectitude of character, was enhanced by the support Máximo Gómez had given him, and even the reputedly benevolent attitude of the United States was more a help than a hindrance, because of the innate Cuban reverence for authority and power.

On May 26, 1902, the President delivered his first message to Congress. After some preliminary remarks, in which, among other things, he paid his respects to Presidents McKinley and Roosevelt and spoke of the "gratitude" which Cubans owed the United States, he proceeded to make some admirable recommendations for legislation, mainly in the direction of enacting the supplementary laws called for by the Constitution. He laid great stress on furtherance of education, "for in reality the problem of Cuba's future lies

[4] Martínez Ortiz, I, 313-314.

with the school." The keynote of the message was the need for economy, avoiding every extravagance. On this score, though recognizing the justice of the claims for pay by the soldiers of the War of Independence, he felt that an early settlement could not be made. He also omitted any recommendation for a permanent army, beyond strengthening the rural guards. "Public tranquillity and security rest on the discipline of the country itself," he asserted.[5]   Indeed, he is said to have remarked that Cuba should never have an army, because military life had been the curse of most of the revolution-ridden Hispanic American republics. This was to prove something of a mistake. And it also showed too great confidence in the stability of the Cuban people.

Estrada Palma was especially successful in his handling of relations with the United States. There were several issues left over from the period of the military government. One of these was the question of tariff concessions to Cuba, which had virtually been promised by President McKinley. Both McKinley and Roosevelt (who succeeded to the presidency after the murder of the former in 1901) did what they could to get the American Congress to pass the necessary legislation, and they were backed by such men as Elihu Root, Senator Orville H. Platt, and General Wood. General Wood, while still in Cuba, encouraged the holding of demonstrations in favor of a reduction of the United States tariff. Roosevelt and Root publicly asserted that there was a moral obligation involved, and insisted also that it was good political policy to set up an economically strong Cuba. The matter came before Congress in 1901, but met with powerful opposition, owing to the objections, so it is said, of the beet sugar interests in the United States. Public opinion was in favor of generous treatment of Cuba, and therefore Congress

[5] *Mensajes presidenciales,* I, 5-8.

tried to dodge the issue, through delay or the proposal of inadequate measures. After adjournments without action in July 1902 and March 1903, Roosevelt called the Senate in extra session to pass upon a treaty he had made. The Senate ratified the treaty, but inserted an unusual provision that it was not to have any effect until both houses of Congress approved it. The President then called Congress as a whole in extra session, and the House passed the bill, but the Senate allowed the session to expire without taking action! The regular session was then at hand, and the bill finally passed in December 1903. It called for a twenty per cent reduction in duties by both countries on a number of products, including Cuban sugar and tobacco, but gave an even higher reduction on certain American products. There were some complaints at what seemed the extra favors accorded the United States, but, as Martínez Ortiz points out, they served merely to balance the difference in the volume of trade between the two countries.[6]   In any event the slow and grudging response of Congress to the demands of the situation was unfortunate. To be sure, an anti-United States element in Cuba, including men like Manuel Sanguily and Alfredo Zayas, had on political grounds opposed any kind of a commercial treaty with the United States, despite the obvious economic advantages to Cuba, but they were in a decided minority.

The matter of the naval bases in Cuba for the United States was also settled in its main particulars during the Estrada Palma administration. In November 1902 the United States government suggested the cession of the bays of Guantánamo, Cienfuegos, Bahía Honda, and Nipe. Estrada Palma was successful, however, in cutting down this demand, with the result that the treaty of 1903 included stations only in the bays of Guantánamo and Bahía Honda,

[6] Martínez Ortiz, II, 419-428.

and those not as an outright cession, but on a rental basis, for such time as the United States might need them. Later, the United States gave up its rights at Bahía Honda for increased advantages in the bay of Guantánamo. This was by the treaty of December 27, 1912. The United States now has virtually complete control over a tract of land at Caimanera on the above-named bay.

Estrada Palma was also measurably successful in his negotiations over one other surviving issue,—that involved in article six of the Platt Amendment, concerning title to the Isle of Pines. Whatever may have been the underlying reason for including this provision in that document, the legal basis for any United States claim grew out of article two of the treaty with Spain. Article one had dealt with Spain's relinquishment of sovereignty over Cuba. The main feature of article two was the "cession to the United States . . . of the Island of Porto Rico and other islands now under the sovereignty of Spain in the West Indies." The question to determine was whether the Isle of Pines should be regarded as included in the "other islands" mentioned in the Spanish Treaty. The Isle of Pines, which has an area of some eighty-four square miles, is about fifty miles south of western Cuba. It had always been administered as part of the province of Havana, and General Wood made no provision for any American management when he turned over the government to Estrada Palma. The normal interpretation of the article in the treaty of Paris would have been to apply it to the islands around Porto Rico. But several complications developed. The possibility of the inclusion of this clause in the Platt Amendment as a means of pressure to bring about a grant of the coaling stations has already been alluded to. It may also have been believed that the island could serve as a strategic base, pending the transfer of more suitable ports in Cuba itself. Perhaps the main factor holding up the treaty developed, however, from one of those oddities of history that can never be foreseen. Some real estate companies induced a number of Americans to settle in the island, playing up the fact that it was "under the American flag," as well as enjoying those advantages of a tropical isle that real estate fancy could so readily depict. In a very short time the whole island was virtually in American hands, though the majority of the inhabitants were Cubans of the laboring class. According to the census of 1919 there were 4288 persons there, of whom 3275 were Cubans or Spaniards and 953 of "other and unknown citizenship,"—almost wholly Americans. These people wanted the island to be considered part of the United States, and were always able to find champions of their cause.

On July 16, 1903, the representatives of Cuba and the United States signed a treaty in which the latter gave up sovereignty over the Isle of Pines to the former. This treaty was not ratified within the time that had been prescribed; so a new treaty was signed on March 2, 1904, without any limitations as to date of ratification. It was specifically stated that the "relinquishment" was "in consideration of the grants of coaling and naval stations" already made by Cuba to the United States. The Senate failed to ratify it. In April 1907, in a case involving payment of customs duties, the Supreme Court of the United States held that the island was at least *de facto* Cuban territory, since the United States had never taken possession. Yet, on a vote in the Senate in 1908 the treaty was rejected. Repeated attempts were made to revive it, always with the backing of the various Presidents of the United States. President Coolidge's administration was especially active on this score, and early in 1925 was successful in its endeavor to procure a ratification of the treaty. Though this act of justice toward Cuba was reprehensibly long delayed, it must be said that the Isle of Pines, all along, had been administered as a part of Cuba.[7]

In his handling of the domestic situation Estrada Palma was to prove less successful, in the end, than he had been in dealings with the United States, but his failure was due primarily to the shortcomings of his people. It is perhaps true that he would have made a better chief executive as President of the United States than it was possible for him to be as President of Cuba. To be sure, his judgment as to certain of his administrative policies may have been open to question, but his main difficulty was in getting effective coöperation from the flock of politicians with whom he was obliged to work. This was a time when the economic outlook was still very dark. The military government had left little over half a million in the treasury.[8] The sugar industry

[7] As Cuba's national pride has been very much aroused over the Isle of Pines question, there is a vast literature upon it. Most of the items are listed in Trelles, *Biblioteca* II: 94; 102-103; 208-209. A number of other pamphlets made their appearance too late for inclusion in the Trelles bibliography. One such is the following: *The title of the republic of Cuba to the isle of Pines,* Washington, 1924. For an interesting article to the same effect, see: Ortiz, Fernando, *Cuba's title to the isle of Pines,* in *Cuba review,* v. XXIII, pp. 14-20; Dec., 1924. This article quotes a letter of Elihu Root, then Secretary of State, to the president of the American club of the Isle of Pines on November 27, 1905, wholly in accord with the Cuban contention. According to Mr. Root, the island "is not and never has been territory of the United States. This is the view with which President Roosevelt authorized the pending treaty . . . Nor would a rejection of the pending treaty put an end to the control of Cuba over the Island. A treaty directly contrary to the one now pending would be necessary to do that." This has been the stand of recent American statesmen, and notably of Secretary of State Hughes in the latest phases of the negotiations. Secretary Root's letter appears in full in U. S., 59th Cong., 1st sess. (1905-1906), ser. no. 4913, Senate Docs. no. 205, p. 11. This document, 277 pages long, contains a mass of material on the subject. For a brief summary of the whole question the following items, both by the well-known internationalist James Brown Scott, are noteworthy: *The isle of Pines,* in *American journal of international law,* v. XVII, pp. 100-104, Jan., 1923; and *The isle of Pines and the solidarity of Pan-America,* in *Advocate of peace,* v. LXXXVII, pp. 228-232, Apr., 1925.

[8] Really $539,984.99. In a message to Congress of November 3, 1902, Estrada Palma referred to a communication of June 27 to the House, in which he explained the difference between the sum he calculated and the $689,191.02 in the report of General Wood. *Mensajes presidenciales,* I, 16.

and agriculture in general were in the doldrums, harassed by competition with the subsidized beet sugar interests abroad, by the failure of the United States to grant the much needed reciprocity treaty, and by the continued prostration of the Cuban fields that had been devastated in the war. Yet Congress showed scant disposition to pass any laws except those that gave a political or pecuniary advantage to members of the governing class. There was considerable criticism of Congress because its first activities were devoted to procuring good salaries for office-holders, without any prior discussion of the revenue-producing possibilities of the republic. It seemed too indicative of the old colonial spirit.[9] The same thing appeared in the haste with which the politicians proceeded to enact a bonus bill for the Army of Liberation, as the veterans of '95-'98 were called. The United States authorities had insisted on heading this off during the military occupation, and Estrada Palma was lukewarm, but no Cuban government could have avoided this bill. It went through on the basis of a dollar for each day of service to privates, which was little enough, but with an extravagant sum for officers, running well into the thousands for those of higher rank. The obvious lack of a broad culture in the majority of the members of elective bodies was also a disturbing factor. The president of the House, Pelayo García, once remarked to Martínez Ortiz that he hoped the next Congress would contain better material. The latter replied with a prediction that, bad as this Congress was, it would be many years before Cuba had a better. Unhappily the prediction came true. Cuba has never had a good Congress, but, if "least bad" is equivalent to "best," then this first legislative assembly of the republic is entitled to the last-given superlative. At any rate, it met regularly

[9] Barbarrosa, 14-18, and *passim*.

and accomplished something, though falling far short of what the times demanded.

Under the heading "Progress of Cuba (1902 to 1905)" Carlos Trelles has described Estrada Palma's government as follows:

"Public instruction continued to be developed vigorously. The number of schools, teachers, and children in attendance was almost the same as in the epoch of his predecessor, General Wood, and a fourth part of the budget went on being devoted to popular instruction. It was his motto, inspired by the vivid example of the United States, that the republic ought to have more teachers than soldiers; and the former principal of the Central Valley school demonstrated from the heights of power the great love he felt for public education and the instruction of his people. Due to the brilliant results obtained by the Cuban sanitation department the figure for mortality fell away to thirteen or fourteen to the thousand. Our President surpassed the intervention governors in the construction of roads, for they built ninety-eight kilometres (from 1899 to 1901) and he 328. He continued, like them, to foment white immigration, which began to increase in his epoch . . . But the first of our Presidents (first in time and in quality) distinguished himself most as an honest and economical administrator of the national revenues. He governed with a budget of eighteen million dollars, out of which he realized acts of great prowess, managing to save twenty-six million dollars.[10] This amount and something more he planned to devote to paying off the loan of thirty-five millions which had been negotiated in order to pay the Army of Liberation. At the time he took charge of the government there was the sum of $689,000[11] in the treasury, and he saved, as I said before, twenty-six millions . . . It may almost be said, and this by way of the highest praise, that he surpassed his two predecessors, who were two model governors and honorable in the fullest sense of the word."[12]

This is high praise, though followed by Trelles with a condemnation of Estrada Palma in connection with the elections of 1905. It is perhaps in one particular too high praise.

[10] As is pointed out later, this amount was by no means all surplus, however.

[11] Cf. *supra*, n. 8.

[12] Trelles, *El progreso (1902 a 1905) y el retroceso (1906 a 1922) de la república de Cuba*, 6-7.

Don Tomás may have saved *too much*. It is quite generally asserted that the real cause of the revolution of 1906 was the desire of the politicians to get at the millions in the treasury. Furthermore, the surplus was more apparent than real, as it was later found that obligations under the floating debt of the republic would have more than swallowed the whole of it, leaving a deficit. Either it was bad policy to accumulate those millions, or else it was bad policy not to spend them, at least for debts already accrued. The mistake, if such it was, was an honest one, however.

The keynote in Estrada Palma's domestic policy was economy. This, coupled with honest administration and a favorable turn in the general economic situation, helped him to bring Cuba out of distress into remarkable prosperity. In a message of November 3, 1902, at the opening of the second session of Congress, he was able to point out no inconsiderable achievement already. A great deal had been done in the building of roads, bridges, docks, lighthouses, and government buildings, together with repairs on previously existing public works and some dredging.[13] This story was repeated on a greater scale in each succeeding message of the President at the beginning of a legislative session, each April and November. In every case the items of work were clearly set forth, with the amounts expended upon them.[14] On November 3, 1902, the President also sent in his first budget estimate to Congress. It called for a little less than fifteen million dollars, with receipts estimated at seventeen millions and a half. Discounting expenses involved in new governmental machinery, this asked for six million dollars less than had been required during the last year of the intervention government.[15] In point of fact, however, it proved necessary

[13] *Mensajes presidenciales*, I, 15-17.   [15] For the budget message, see
[14] Each of these messages is to be   *Mensajes presidenciales*, I, 17-22.
found in *Mensajes presidenciales*, I.

to spend some $16,700,000, by far the smallest expenditure for a single year in the history of the republic, and rivalled only by Estrada Palma's second year, when about $20,400,000 was spent. The first year of the Estrada Palma government was hardly a prosperous one, however. The evils already described were as yet too powerful to be overcome, and there was a great deal of criticism and pessimism over the agricultural outlook for the republic.[16] It had even been impossible at the outset to negotiate a small loan of four million dollars to aid agriculture. By the close of 1903, however, the credit of the country was already so well established that negotiations were well on their way for the loan of thirty-five millions, with which to pay half of the debt which it had been decided was owing to the soldiers of the Army of Liberation. The law providing for this loan was passed in February 1903, and was modified by another of January 1904. In the following February a contract for the loan was signed with the New York house of Speyer and Company.

Perhaps the most noteworthy thing about the bonus law was that a group of politicians and their associates took advantage of the situation to make a great profit for themselves. Some officials high up in the government so manipulated the payments as to delay them or else make the soldiers feel that they were never going to get them, in consequence of which they sold their certificates at a discount that ran as high as fifty or sixty per cent.[17] Estrada Palma himself asserted that 26,103 soldiers, or approximately fifty per cent, sold out at an enormous sacrifice.[18] In addition, a number of men were listed as veterans who had never served in the field; the length of service of others was made to appear

[16] For example, in most of the thirty-eight articles in the *primera parte* (first part) of Barbarrosa, 11-68.

[17] Barbarrosa, 51.

[18] Message to Congress of Nov. 7, 1904, in *Mensajes presidenciales*, I, 108.

greater than it was, so that the amount due, on the *per diem* allowance basis, would be larger; the rank of many was entered as superior to that to which they had attained, for the same purpose of inflating the bonus check; and not a few imaginary names were placed upon the rolls. One man who was sent to prison for his part in these practices was later to become vice-president of the Cuban House of Representatives during the presidency of Zayas.

Estrada Palma would have preferred to pay the army out of savings from surplus revenues, but had been obliged on account of political pressure to consent to an earlier settlement through the agency of the loan. With the loan become a fact, however, he was eager to pay it off as soon as possible, and accentuated his endeavors to create a surplus for this purpose. A law of January 1904, for example, had authorized the President to increase customs duties, from a minimum of fifteen to a maximum of thirty per cent. Estrada Palma proceeded to make collections at the maximum rate, and continued to do so, though receipts were far outrunning expenditures. Meanwhile, too, other factors contributed to the prosperity of the government and the country as a whole. The commercial treaty with the United States was producing beneficial effects; European countries were beginning to drop their subsidies to beet sugar interests; the Cuban sugar crop of 1903-1904 rose to 850,000 tons, as against 636,000 in the previous year, and better prices were obtained for it; the shortage of domestic animals was already made up; a number of minor industries, notably the manufacture of beer, gathered a great impulse as a result of the higher tariff on foreign goods; foreigners began to be attracted to the island, and to invest their capital there; immigration, mostly of Spaniards, increased from less than ten thousand in 1902 to more than fifteen thousand in 1903, twenty-five thousand in 1904, and forty thousand in 1905; the balance of trade in this period greatly favored Cuba; and the money put in circulation through the Speyer loan stimulated business. By October 31, 1904, there were nearly ten millions in the treasury, of which some $6,700,000 was surplus over and above the monies of the loan. In April 1906 the amount in the treasury had reached approximately twenty-five million, of which over nineteen either belonged to the loan or was affected by special laws, leaving five and three quarters millions clear. Certainly there seemed to have been an amazing advance from the small sums of early republican finance. Nevertheless, as already pointed out, the surplus was presently to disappear, and the accumulation, anyway, was of doubtful advisability. However that may be, the twenty-five millions were *there* and in good hands.

The national treasury was by no means the only institution to profit from the economic success of the Estrada Palma administration. Each new budget raised the amounts devoted to directly beneficial expenditures of the government. For example, the budget of 1902 gave less than three millions to public works, while that of 1905 called for nearly five millions and a half. Expenditures themselves were now larger, reaching some twenty-six millions a year,[19] but receipts were running above thirty millions. There was a quite general well-being in the country. Cubans began to indulge themselves in luxuries that heretofore had been denied them. In Havana, especially, new homes went up as if by magic, and lands in the Vedado district which had gone begging in 1902 at a dollar a meter were selling at seven

[19] Estrada Palma spent nearly eighty-nine millions in his last two years, but thirty-five of it was the Speyer loan for the bonus to the soldiers. Guiral Moreno, Mario, *Nuestros problemas políticos, económicos* *y sociales,* in *Cuba contemporánea,* v. V, pp. 401-424, at 416-417; Aug., 1914. Guiral Moreno does not make clear whether the $11,250,000 domestic loan was also included in his estimate of expenditures.

or eight in 1905. The provinces, too, had recovered from the war, and Camagüey and Oriente were for the first time becoming centres of colossal sugar enterprises. Interest rates had fallen to ordinary levels, as compared with the usury of earlier days. There had been no backsliding, either, in attention to problems of health. Incidentally, at least one item of government expenditure had been cut to the very bone. The monies allotted to the "presidency," including twenty-five thousand dollars as the salary of the President, were $85,700 in 1902, but this sum was reduced until it reached $62,390 in the budget of 1905,—an amount so small that certain latter-day Presidents of Cuba would have despised themselves for taking such a mere bagatelle, even under the heading of *"gastos de representación,"* or expenses growing out of the social obligations of the office, an item, by the way, that rarely appeared, and then only for comparatively small amounts, during the rule of Estrada Palma.[20]

In fine, from the standpoint of honest government and good times there would seem to have been no more auspicious moment than that in which Cuba found herself in 1905. The future, too, held out much promise. Far from having the mere "avarice" of a miser in piling up a surplus, "Don Tomás" (as Estrada Palma is usually called) was on the point of embarking upon a much enlarged program of public works, together with improving the credit of the country through a reduction of the debt. He proposed to put in sanitary tunnels in Havana and provide that city with the paving it needed, paying the bill in cash obtained from surplus revenues, thus saving the country from a loan estimated at sixteen millions and a half. The extension and beautifying of the Malecón boulevard at Havana and engineering works to overcome the dangers from the floods of the Roque were

[20] Cf. pp: 278; 464-465.

other projects of his. On one occasion he bought up a million dollars' worth of Cuban domestic bonds, a portion of an issue of $11,250,000 which had been brought out in supplement to the Speyer loan, to provide a further part payment of the debt to the army. Political opponents brought all manner of charges against him because he kept these bonds alive, though depositing them in the treasury,—but when the same people came into power under President Gómez the bonds were reissued to the public! [21] Not least among other favorable indications in 1905 was the decision of the United States to build the Panamá Canal, which would inevitably put Cuba along the course of a vast world trade. All was well,—*except that the defects of Cuban character had not yet had time to cure themselves!* Beneath the pleasing exterior of Cuban affairs there was an ominous current that boded ill for the republic. This found its principal opportunity for manifestation in the sphere of politics.

Economical as was Don Tomás, he could not avoid many evils to which all governments are subject and for which there was a particularly fertile field in Cuba. There were far more government employes than were necessary,[22] and the old instinct for political plunder was very much alive. Frauds were discovered in the custom-house at Santiago. Some officials lived in an unbecoming luxury; one of them, it is said, managed to pay a debt of seventeen thousand dollars out of "savings" from a salary of seven thousand a year over a period of fifteen months, and that too without denying him-

[21] *Tomás Estrada Palma: para la historia*, in *Cuba*, Nov. 4, 1909, and ¡*La "avaricia" de don Tomás!*, in *Discusión*, Feb. 11, 1911. Both quoted (with amplifications in footnotes) in Velasco, respectively at 11-24 and 77-79.

[22] Barbarrosa says that there were seventy thousand job-holders in 1903, and four or five hundred thousand other Cubans who wanted these positions. Fifteen thousand of the government posts were nothing but sinecures. In a later article he speaks of forty or fifty thousand employes as "so many useless wheels of the administrative machine." Barbarrosa: 32; 43; 53.

self or his family any of the good things of life. Provincial and municipal governments were notoriously inefficient and corrupt; the President was obliged to intervene to check some of their improper attempts to raise funds for themselves through absurd taxes. And congressional activities left much to be desired. It seemed to many that affairs were too reminiscent of colonial days. As one writer said, in making a comparison between revolutionary Cuba and the republic,

"Between the past and the present there is an immense difference. The former represented the sacrifice of everything on the altar of the ideal; the latter, the shame of the country at the mercy of egoism. The former, the love of Cuba; the latter, the philosophy of the stomach." [25]

By comparison with later times the evils were as a molehill to a mountain, but they were important as a symptom of Cuban political character and as a forerunner of darker days.

Congress early showed a disposition to protect members of the political coterie from punishment for crime. In 1903 Mariano Corona, a representative from Oriente, murdered an opponent, whereupon Congress passed an act to save him, on the basis of the constitutional paragraph concerning congressional immunity. Despite the President's veto the bill became a law.[24] Shortly afterward, the President was again obliged to make use of the veto. Senator Morúa Delgado,— a mulatto, by the way,—introduced an act for the reëstablishment of the lottery, discarded since Spanish days. The bill was rushed through on a surprise vote, but Estrada Palma had ready a surprise of his own, for he vetoed it in a notable message (prepared beforehand) on the very day he received it, January 6, 1904. In course of a long argument against the lottery as an institution, he cited a number of well-

[23] Article of Joaquín Aramburu, quoted in Barbarrosa, 62-63. See also ibid: 32; 36; 46-51.

[24] For further consideration of this bill, see pp. 512-515.

known men of different countries against it, and among others quoted Senator Morúa himself, who had referred to it in 1891 as "social gangrene." Concluding, he said:

"Last year, already, a law was on the point of being authorized for the creation of public pits for cock-fights, a cruel, semi-barbarous, and demoralizing spectacle. If the lottery should now become established as a speculation of the state, we might be able to say that an insurmountable wall has been raised to separate the nation of which we dreamed in the revolutionary epoch from that which really exists and which appears to be inclined to retrograde in the direction of the former metropolis."

This message raised up a furor in Congress. Naturally, Senator Morúa felt aggrieved. Senator Manuel Sanguily also turned against the President in all his eloquence.[25] But the veto was sustained.

In February 1904 the first elections under the republic were held. The two principal parties reorganized themselves for this event, with the idea of winning at all costs. Under the leadership of Senator Ricardo Dolz of Havana and General José Miguel Gómez, governor of Santa Clara, the Republicans took on a somewhat conservative tendency under the name Conservative Republican party. The Nationals also appeared under a new name, that of the National Liberal party. There were no real issues in the campaign,—only difference of leadership,—though the terms "Conservative" and "Liberal" were supposed to represent the political tendencies of the two groups. The National Liberals had as their chief plank "the abrogation of the Platt Amendment!" This gave them good fuel for speeches. The word "Liberal" and the supposed favor of General Máximo Gómez were other advantages they possessed. Meanwhile, Estrada Palma inclined toward the Conservative Republicans, though without

[25] Sanguily, II, 395-411.

giving them any undue aid.   The elections, in the language of Emilio Terry, Secretary of Agriculture at the outset of Estrada Palma's rule, were "a farce represented with less shame than in the times of the colony." Each side proceeding to win wherever possible by means of what was called "*el copo*,"—a fraudulent device to deprive the minority of its due representation.[26]   There was not even a pretence of doing otherwise.   The day of the elections passed off with reasonably good order, but each party worked the *copo*, especially in Havana and Oriente, where the National Liberals held sway, and in Santa Clara and Matanzas, which were Conservative Republican territory.   Specific irregularities were charged by each party as against the other.   In Pinar del Río two provincial electoral boards functioned independently.   In Camagüey the votes of twenty-three voting districts (*colegios*) were not examined at all, and those of seventeen others were annulled.   Senator Juan Gualberto Gómez, of the National Liberal group, obtained many more votes in Oriente than had actually been cast.   On the returns for the whole country, however, it seemed that the Conservative Republicans had won.   Their opponents were by no means ready to concede the victory, however.

When Congress opened in April 1904 the National Liberals resorted to a device which has since become almost the norm of Cuban parlimentary procedure.   The deputies of their party absented themselves from meetings of the House, and thus kept that body from gaining a quorum, as the presence of two-thirds of the members was required by the

[26] The noun "*copo*" comes from the verb "*copar*," a military term signifying to cut off the retreat of an enemy. In politics the "*copo*" is applicable only where the law calls for representation of minorities, as is the case in Cuba.   By means of the "*copo*" the majority not only elects its own candidates but also elects others as if of the minority, thus falsely gaining unanimous representation instead of the proportion accorded by law to a majority party.

Constitution. Since the president of the House was a member of the National Liberal group, there seemed no way to overcome the difficulty by compelling the attendance of absent members. For months the deadlock continued, despite the impatience of the country. In particular, the veterans were clamoring for legislation to enable them to get their bonus, of which some details had still to be arranged. As neither party wished to offend this powerful electoral element, a temporary solution was reached whereby the House was constituted, for bonus purposes only, with the half of its membership that had remained over from the previous election, together with such new members as were veterans,— this, despite the fact that the credentials of the latter had not been duly approved and that many of them were quite likely never to receive them, because of frauds in connection with their election. With the bonus bills out of the way the deadlock was resumed. Finally, in September, an ingenious, if also somewhat questionable, solution was reached through a device called the "Quorum Dolz,"—the suggestion of Senator Dolz a month before. The constitutional requirement meant that two-thirds of the members must be present for the *beginning* of a legislative term, he contended, and that thereafter regular meetings might be held, with or without two-thirds of the membership. Over the protests of the National Liberals this view was adopted for the time being, and as two-thirds of the members had been present for the bonus legislation, Congress for a brief time resumed its sessions, until the recess in October. Clearly the country had gained very little from this Congress! And the whole affair was an evil political augury for the future.

Meanwhile, Estrada Palma had lost not a little of the political support with which he had begun his administration. Martínez Ortiz ascribes this to his habit of considering those who did not agree with him or yield to his superior position as his enemies. At any rate, it was impossible in the fiercely partisan atmosphere of Cuba to keep on good terms with everybody, especially in view of the pressure for jobs and the desires of "higher-ups" to "administer" the many millions that Don Tomás had saved. A number of men aspired to succeed him in the presidency. Most insistent of these was General José Miguel Gómez, who held the province of Santa Clara in his hand. Alfredo Zayas, Domingo Méndez Capote, and General Emilio Núñez (then governor of Havana) were others that hoped some day to reach that eminence. The last-named was reputed to have the favor of General Máximo Gómez, who had become somewhat cool in his relations with Estrada Palma and was in any event opposed to plans for his reëlection. Possibly the old commander-in-chief was disappointed because the President had shown no disposition to seek his advice about the problems of the country.

As the year 1904 drew to a close, plans were in the making for the presidential elections of 1905. As the Conservative Republicans had made no headway in Oriente, it was decided to form a new party, to be called the Moderates. Dolz and Méndez Capote of Havana were the leaders in this project. They were suspected of being lukewarm over the presidential aspirations of José Miguel Gómez, and so their political breathren of Santa Clara were cautions about committing themselves to the movement. Dolz and Méndez Capote suggested that the new party should be organized on the basis of equality of representation for each province, expecting in this way to dominate it. The backers of José Miguel insisted on representation according to the number of members in Congress, which would have given them the whip-hand. Over this supposed issue the party split,—

though the real underlying issue was the candidacy of Gómez. The Conservative Republicans of Havana went through with their plan, and formed the Moderate Party. The Conservative Republicans of Santa Clara turned to the National Liberals, yielding their former attitude about representation in return for an assurance of backing for Gómez, and presently the new Liberal Party emerged as a result of the fusion of these two previously hostile factions. A prime mover in this arrangement was Alfredo Zayas, who became president of the party. General Núñez was not willing to postpone his own aspirations to those of José Miguel Gómez, and so retained the old name Nationalist for a following of his own, hoping that his power as governor of the province of Havana and the support of Máximo Gómez might pull him through. On June 17, 1905, however, Máximo Gómez died at Havana,—a great loss to the country, for in the troublesome days that were to come Gómez was the only man in Cuba who might have had influence enough to bring about an adjustment. As for Núñez, it killed his chances for victory. So presently he veered over to the side of the Moderates.

In due time the Liberals nominated José Miguel Gómez for the presidency and Zayas for Vice-President. The Moderates felt that they would be strongest if they could go to the polls in their first campaign with Estrada Palma as a candidate for reëlection. While he had never been the type of man to attract the rabble, he had the respect of the country, and his achievements as President could not be gainsaid. Business men in particular were enthusiastic over him. But Estrada Palma hesitated to run. Many writers assert, Martínez Ortiz among them, that he was really eager for reëlection, mindful of the fact that most of the great Presidents of the United States had served two terms, but for some time, certainly, Estrada Palma was seriously in doubt. As one Cuban gentleman whose assertions merit consideration said to the writer:

"Estrada Palma was persuaded to run for reëlection by his followers, who convinced him that his successors would spend the millions he had accumulated. At first he did not intend to, and gave out an interview to that effect, but recalled it before it was published. The point was, that he hoped to save enough out of receipts to take up the thirty-five million dollar loan, and then keep the bonds in the treasury, while continuing to collect the same amounts of revenues to employ on education and public works. His followers persuaded him,—and it was probably true,—that his successor would not retain his policy, but would get his hands on the funds in the treasury for the use of himself and his partisans."

This is very likely an accurate estimate of the situation. It seemed as if the interests of the country had not yet been sufficiently far advanced to risk a government in the control of the average run of Cuban politicians. Gradually, therefore, Don Tomás turned towards an acceptance of a nomination by the Moderates. Disappointed over his inability to get much-desired legislation from Congress, he had for some time tended more and more to abandon his earlier neutrality between the parties, in hopes of getting a working majority, and presently, in February 1905, he affiliated himself with the Moderates. This carried with it a certain admission of duty to help that party, within proper limits, in the forthcoming election. Eventually that was to involve Don Tomás in countenancing measures that were far beyond anything he had contemplated. At length, he agreed to run for the presidency, and though not formally notified of his nomination until September 11, 1905, the issue was fairly joined by the early spring of that same year. Nobody could have foretold it at the time, but it

meant that the "best years" in the first quarter century of
the republic had already gone their way.[27]

[27] The work of Martínez Ortiz (v.
II) remains the best that has yet
been published for this period.
Though a Liberal and a partisan of
José Miguel Gómez and not in sympathy with Estrada Palma, Martínez
Ortiz has, nevertheless, written an account which is remarkably fair. It is
also the only attempt at a complete
history of these years thus far made.
All other works touch this era merely
at odd points. A number of the volumes bearing primarily on the subject of the next two chapters are also
useful to some extent here. The Estrada Palma administration is still in
need of a monograph, however, which
shall avail itself of the *Memorias,* the
Diarios de sesiones, and the *Mensajes presidenciales,* as well as newspapers and other contemporary evidences.

CHAPTER VIII

THE REËLECTION OF ESTRADA PALMA

WHAT caused the Revolution of August, as the uprising of 1906 is called? While that conflict was at its height Barbarrosa wrote as follows:

"Two impotent factions are at war in Cuba: the constituted power and the armed revolution. In the background there is nothing more than the interests of parties, ambitions for jobs. The conquest of the twenty millions of the treasury!" [1]

The evidence to the same effect is so overwhelming in amount that it can hardly be doubted that political and financial considerations far outweighed principles.[2] Back of that, however, was the fact that the Cubans were as yet unprepared for self-government, and had something of the turbulence of Hispanic American character, with a none too highly developed understanding of the consequences of their acts. Fortunately, they had an exceptionally good man as their first President, and the excellence of his government postponed domestic strife for more than four years.

In a sense, however, Estrada Palma was a victim of his own "excess" of goodness, in that he could not believe that other people might be swayed by motives so much more sordid than his own, and therefore took no steps to handle

[1] Barbarrosa, 65.
[2] The writer has any number of statements of the same character from persons who lived through those times. For example: "The revolution of 1906 broke out primarily because there was a surplus in the treasury, and the politicians felt that they had a better use for it than employing it on Cuba's debts." In this instance the word "better" was used somewhat satirically.

a possible outbreak of civil war. His public documents are replete with expressions of confidence in the "orderliness" and "good sense" of the Cuban people,—at the very moment that a casual observer might have been more impressed by an opposite tendency. In his message to Congress of November 3, 1902, he said that "the most complete order has reigned," attributing it to Cuban patriotism and love of peace. Referring to the somewhat notorious elections of 1904, he remarked, on April 4 of that year, that there was no disorder, despite political agitation and the fact that there were 658 electoral complaints to the courts. Such was the "good judgment of the Cuban people" and "their obedience to the laws," however, that there was no violence. The Cuban "love of order" in connection with the unchanging "tranquility" of the times, and "the sentiment which generally prevails already among our compatriots of respect for the law and love of our institutions" found their place in messages of November 7, 1904, and April 3, 1905. Even the excitement and violence of the electoral period in 1905, while causing the President several moments of doubt, seemingly failed to shake his belief in "the good sense of the Cuban people," which was able to rise superior to "party jealousies," as he put it in his message of November 6, 1905. As late as April 2, 1906, Estrada Palma was impressed by the "cry of indignation" against those who had attacked the barracks of the rural guard at Guanabacoa, asserting it proved that nobody in Cuba could "promote disturbances of a serious character such as may put our institutions in danger." [3] Not until the revolution of August 1906 did the rude awakening come. An extraordinary session of Congress was called "on account of the serious disturbance of the public order," and in his message of September 14 the Presi-

[3] *Mensajes presidenciales*, I: 15; 73; 105; 125; 139; 155.

dent was under the sad necessity of admitting that "it throws doubt on the seriousness of our institutions," raising up "a lack of confidence in our capacity for self-government" and "putting the independence of the country in danger."[4]

Even before the events in connection with the election of 1905 there were a number of violent disturbances, some of them directed against the government. One of the earliest incidents of this character was the general strike in the capital in November 1902. It began with a walk-out of laborers in some of the tobacco factories. Not realizing the full implications of their acts and intent on gaining popularity, the *alcalde,* or mayor, of Havana and the national Secretary of Government openly encouraged the strikers, and were backed up in their attitude by a number of the newspapers. Presently there were conflicts between the men on strike and those of other factories who had not gone out. The police arrested some of the strikers most prominent in these incidents, whereupon the mayor dismissed the chief of police and was sustained in his action by the Secretary of Government. This so lowered the prestige of the police and increased that of the strikers that the whole affair soon took on alarming proportions. A general strike was declared for November 24. The strikers decreed that business activity of every sort should stop for that day. This was serious, and the Secretary of Government now found it necessary to call in the rural guards to assist the police in maintaining order. On the 24th there were numerous exciting incidents. Hordes of laborers filled the streets. The street railway company, a foreign enterprise, attempted to run its cars, but was forced to desist. There were a number of encounters between the laborers and the police, in which several were killed and many more wounded. At length

[4] *Ibid.,* I, 175.

the government got the situation in hand, but not without difficulty. The offending mayor and the Secretary of Government lost their posts, and the chief of police was restored to his position. So the matter ended,—but it had revealed the dynamite in Cuban character.

The earliest of the attempts directed against the government was a plot at Guanabacoa, early in July 1903. This was nipped in the bud,[5] but on the 14th of that month there was a seemingly insignificant uprising at Vicana, near Manzanillo. Four men got possession of some arms, and tried to raise a following on an "immediate pay of the army" platform. The rural guards gave scant chance for this movement to get under way, for they captured one of the would-be revolutionists on the 26th and killed the other three next day.[6] A somewhat more serious affair was an outbreak at Sevilla, near Santiago, on September 13 of the same year. The plan was to raise a band of four or five hundred men, and hold up the President during his visit in that section, exacting from him assurances of an immediate payment of the debt to the Army of Liberation. Some sixty or seventy men got together for this purpose, but by September 22 all had been captured or dispersed by the rural guards, acting in conjunction with the governor of Oriente. Estrada Palma said that the veterans were not behind this move and that it caused a "cry of indignation" in all the island, besides which it was lacking in any just basis, as the government had done a great deal toward getting pay for the army.[7] While the rebels of Sevilla were still out, there was an attempt to blow up the President's train near Palmarito.[8] Such incidents as these were to take place with increasing

[5] Velasco, 18, n. 19.
[6] Ibid.; also Mensajes presidenciales, I, 55-56.
[7] Mensajes presidenciales, I, 55.
[8] Velasco, 19, n. 23.

frequency after the inauguration of the electoral campaign of 1905.

And yet Estrada Palma was not altogether deceived in his people. His messages abound in remarks about the necessity of raising the social level of Cuba. He was disturbed, too, by the fall in attendance at school, noting that it was due in many cases to the "censurable desire of the parents or guardians to utilize the children in their own service."[9] And even when he praised his Cuban people, he also took occasion to lecture them about good citizenship, just as if he were still the teacher of Central Valley, talking to his pupils. In an interview of September 4, 1905 (and, indeed, on other occasions), he made his oft-quoted remark: "In Cuba we have a republic, but there are no citizens."[10] One wonders whether the laudatory comments of the presidential messages did not represent, in part at least, a hope of the schoolmaster that he might persuade the Cubans to believe in themselves and thus help them really to become as good as he told them they were. On the other hand, there is the convincing evidence that he did not create an army and was caught wholly unprepared for civil war when it came. He had relied on good government and prosperity as his safeguards, backed up by the connection with the United States, being perhaps "overconfident as respects the 'self-acting' character of the Platt amendment."[11]

As already stated, Estrada Palma formally affiliated himself with the Moderates in February 1905. From that time forward he was besieged with requests by leaders of the party to take active steps to assist in winning the election.

[9] *Mensajes presidenciales*, I, 155, and, indeed, in various messages.

[10] *Espigando: Sesión de espiritismo*, in *Prensa*, Feb. 8, 1910, quoted in Velasco, 34.

[11] *Cuba in factional eruption*, in American review of reviews, v. XXXIV, pp. 387-393, at 389; Oct., 1906.

In particular, they wanted him to appoint a new Cabinet, to be made up of men who were better adapted for an election campaign than were those then in office, in that they could be expected to check the illegal practices of the opposition (the idea which appealed to Estrada Palma) or perhaps indulge in some illegalities of their own, to win at any cost (the firm intention of some of the Moderates). It was a logical thing to do, involving no necessary impropriety. But the President hesitated. Members of the existing Cabinet offered him their resignations on February 2, 1905. At length, he consented to accept them, and on March 6 he did so. The great mistake of Estrada Palma was, not that he changed the Cabinet, but that, on advice of the Moderates, he appointed unsuitable men. This was particularly true of the principal figure in the new Cabinet, General Fernando Freyre de Andrade. This individual was, indeed, "a man of courage and intellectual and physical activity," but of an uncompromising and violent temperament, as he had shown himself to be while a leader of the Cuban Assembly in the early days of the United States military occupation. Freyre was Secretary of Government. Next after him in prominence was the new Secretary of Public Works, General Rafael Montalvo. Taken as a whole the new Secretaries were soon referred to as the "Fighting Cabinet" (*Gabinete de Combate*), a term which they later explained on the ground that they were veterans of the War of Independence, but which was generally understood at the time as having a present and future application, with reference to the elections. The Liberals insisted it meant that the Moderates were determined, by hook or crook, to win. That interpretation was probably correct.

It was the opinion of William Howard Taft and Robert Bacon, who were presently to serve as the *dei ex machina* to bring an end to civil war, that Estrada Palma would in all probability have been elected if no improper steps had been taken. Their view is reinforced by that of the Cuban historian Martínez Ortiz, who was a member of the Liberal opposition in the exciting days of 1905-1906. The Moderates were resolved to take no chance of failure, however. Freyre, whose department had control of the police and rural guards, the supervision of municipalities, and the conduct of the elections, was to be the principal instrument in winning the victory. The other Secretaries were to help out, especially through pressure brought to bear on the personnel subject to their orders,—an important factor in a centralized state like that of Cuba, where family influence, too, had a remarkably wide reach.

Freyre and his companions made use of machinery and took advantage of acts for which the men who were now Liberals were at least in part responsible. The existing electoral law was based on that established by General Wood, but it had been converted into a notoriously bad instrument through an amendment which placed control of the elections largely in the hands of the *alcaldes,* or mayors, of towns. The new law of December 25, 1903, called for two elections, at the first of which the electoral boards for the main election were to be chosen. These boards were to handle the registration, and also act as judges of the election and count the votes. The preliminary election in each voting district was to be in charge of a delegate appointed by the mayor, who might therefore, if he were so minded and had sufficient force, dominate the whole affair. The author of the amendment to General Wood's law was none other than Alfredo Zayas. Estrada Palma repeatedly asked Congress for a new election law, notably in his messages to Congress of April 4, 1904, and April 3, 1905, but despite the fact that it had given rise, as the President put it, to "many abuses, acts of injustice, and frauds, and, what is even worse, that the law should remain unfulfilled in part in the province of Pinar del Río," Congress did nothing.[12] In like manner Estrada Palma, in message after message, asked Congress to enact the supplementary legislation called for by the Constitution for a judiciary law (to provide, among other things, for a regular method of attaining to judicial positions and to promotion, and to guarantee judges against removability)[13] and for a law making municipal governments elective, but Congress took no action on these requests, either. As a result, judges continued to be subordinate to the executive, appointable and removable at will, while there had been no municipal elections since the departure of General Wood; municipal officials were therefore held to be within the purview of the old Spanish law, which placed removals and appointments unappealably in the hands of the executive. Even the constitutional provision calling for the representation of minorities had been given no effect, though the President had called the attention of Congress to the need of legislation on this score. General Freyre now proposed to take advantage of these defects and omissions in the laws.

In the elections of 1905 not only a President and Vice-President were to be chosen, but also half the Senate and half the House and the six provincial governors. José Miguel Gómez and Zayas were soon nominated as the Liberal standard-bearers, and presently Estrada Palma and Méndez Capote were put up for the Moderates. Among the earliest moves of the Fighting Cabinet was the wholesale dismissal

[12] *Mensajes presidenciales,* I: 73-74; 126-127. The reference to Pinar del Río bears upon the two provincial electoral boards, each of which claimed the right to function, but neither of which was recognized by the government.
[13] *Ibid.,* I, 127.

of government employes not addicted to the Moderate cause. Their places were filled with political partisans, who brought with them the value of their family influence.[14] Even school-teachers were not exempt from the rule requiring service to the party in power. But this was not enough. The key to victory lay in controlling the local governments. So just prior to the first elections in September, Freyre as Secretary of Government dismissed the local officials in some twenty or more municipalities. All of the men involved happened to be Liberals, while Moderates were appointed in their place. It is true that formal charges of incorrect adminis-tration were brought against the officials who were ousted, and it is probably true that the charges in most cases were well founded, but since only Liberal mayors were affected and the things complained of had happened in some in-stances several years before, the whole move was obviously political. Most of the removals took place in the provinces of Santa Clara, Havana, and Pinar del Río, too, where the Liberals had their strongest following. These acts stirred up an extraordinary amount of bitterness, and turned public sentiment against the Moderates, for to people in the country the local mayors and councillors were almost more important than the President. Liberal leaders protested to Estrada Palma, and he was able to convince them, according to Martínez Ortiz, that many of these steps had been taken without his knowledge or without any realization on his part of the purely political motives behind them. One might wonder at this, since the accusations were trumpeted forth in the Liberal press, but the newspapers of Cuba make such a habit of exaggerated statement that one could be pardoned for not believing them. In any event the President did not

[14] Cf. pp: 319-320; 403; 565-566.

succeed in quelling the electoral enthusiasms of his all too zealous Fighting Cabinet.

The Moderates were not alone to blame. The violence of the Liberals justified the Moderates to some extent in preparing to meet them. The island ran riot with incendiary speechmaking on the part of the Liberals. In Congress they not only lashed the government with their oratory, but also prevented a quorum in the House, so that the budget could not be passed. When the President thereupon issued a decree putting into effect the previous estimates until Congress should resolve the matter, they freely reminded him of the fate of Charles I of England and of President Balmaceda of Chile. Talk of revolution in case the Liberals should be "robbed" of victory—and defeat was taken as the equivalent of robbery—was everywhere in the air. The Liberal candidate himself gave voice to this threat on more than one occasion. The Liberals had organizations, too, certainly in Santa Clara and possibly in Pinar del Río, that were prepared to use force in gaining votes. On April 14, 1905, six congressmen stole a file of papers which formed the basis of charges that had been brought against some of the councillors of the *ayuntamiento,* or municipal council, of Havana. They published an open letter proclaiming their act, and defending it on the grounds of their profound conviction that the Fighting Cabinet was riding roughshod over the laws. A little later, on July 22, 1905, the local government building at San Antonio de las Vueltas was burned by Liberals in course of a riot. Obviously there was need for some display of the iron hand on the part of the government, even if it had not gone beyond the bounds of propriety. The turbulence was not all on one side, but on both.

As the day for the preliminary elections, September 23,

approached, acts of violence followed one after another until there was something like a reign of terror. The government was prepared to use the police and the rural guards, ostensibly to keep order and prevent electoral frauds, but really to hinder the Liberals, many of whom were arrested. The most shocking incident took place at Cienfuegos, which was the principal fighting ground in Santa Clara, the most bitterly contested of the six provinces. Representative Enrique Villuendas, who was the principal Liberal leader in that city, had publicly charged the Moderates with all manner of crimes in and near Cienfuegos, including a number of shootings and the pardon of two murderers, one of whom had been added to the police force of Cienfuegos and the other to the rural guards! On September 22 he sent a letter to Gómez in which he asserted that there were plots against his life. A few hours later he was dead. Reams of paper have been covered in writings on this incident, with the idea of fixing responsibility for it on the Moderates or the Liberals, as the case may be. It seems that a meeting of Liberal leaders had been called that day in Villuendas's room at the Hotel Suiza, to see whether they should send their followers out "to be killed" at the election next day. The gathering was interrupted by a visit of the police, under Chief Illance, who had come with an authorization to search for arms and bombs. Exactly what followed cannot be stated with certainty, but when it was over both Villuendas and Illance had been killed, besides two others, while several persons were wounded. The whole country was stirred up over the incident. The Moderates were impressed by the murder of the chief of police in course of an authorized search,[15] while the Liberals looked on the death of Villuendas

[15] For example, see message of Estrada Palma to Congress, Nov. 6, 1905, in *Mensajes presidenciales*, I, 139.

as a case of deliberate assassination and raised up the young congressman to the category of a martyr to their cause.[16]

It will be observed that nothing has been said of issues in this campaign. That is because there were none worthy of the name. The Liberals, as the party out of power, did indeed declare for the immediate abrogation of the Platt Amendment, while the Moderates, with the disadvantage of being the government party, could do no more than advocate eventual abrogation,[17] but, obviously, this was nothing but the familiar loud-noise "issue" of Hispanic American politics, with its appeal to patriotism through an arraignment of the United States. The nearest thing to a real issue was the record of the government. On this score, in an interview of September 4, 1905, Estrada Palma is quoted as making the following statement about his platform:

"What better or more eloquent platform can there be than deeds themselves? The past is a guarantee and sure pledge of the future." [18]

The President then went on to tell of the financial achievements of the administration, and of the prosperity of the country. The Liberals could not well meet Estrada Palma on this ground, as the assertions of the President were, certainly in the main, true. So it may safely be said that there were "no issues worthy of the name." It was a battle of personalities,—and of violence.

The day of the preliminary elections, September 23, 1905, was filled with political "electricity," and it was evident from the first that a Moderate victory, by force if neces-

[16] The most ample and most violent discussion of this incident is to be found in Collazo, *Cuba intervenida,* 29-84.

[17] Brownell, Atherton, *The Cuban republic on trial,* in *American review of reviews,* v. XXXIV, pp. 424-430, at 426; Oct., 1906.

[18] España, Gabriel Ricardo, *Con el jefe del estado: oyendo a Estrada Palma,* in *Discusión,* Sept. 5, 1905, quoted in Velasco, 34-35.

sary, had been provided for in advance. So the Liberal leaders called off their followers shortly after noon. Naturally, the Moderates were overwhelmingly successful. In many districts their candidates got more votes than there were inhabitants. The electoral boards that had been chosen then proceeded to draw up the lists of voters for the final election, to be held on December 1st. They were so zealous in the performance of their duties that they made up a total registry of 432,313 voters, of whom at least 150,000 were mere fraudulent names. Their action was denounced even by La Discusión, a leading Moderate journal, which pointed out that the list of voters added up to approximately a third of the population of the republic, "a monstrosity, the paternity of which should be denied by its various perpetrators, because it gives them the title of idiots." In the same article La Discusión expressed its views as follows:

"The election leaders have shown such little brains in conducting their schemes that they have made themselves ridiculous and foolish. The schemes referred to were nothing more than to gain a victory at all hazard, which could have been gained without going beyond the limits of probability." [19]

Freyre himself, when questioned later by Taft about the surplus 150,000 names, admitted that it was "possibly true" that they were fraudulent, adding that it was "impossible to hold an election in Cuba without fraud," and suggesting that the extra names were put on the lists by Moderate registrars "merely out of a spirit of mischief" when they heard that the Liberals were not going to register or to vote. Of course, the Moderates had a walk-over in the elections of December 1st. The Liberals did not go to the polls, and all Moderate candidates were elected.

[19] Quoted in Taft and Bacon, Re- (1906-1907), ser. no. 5105, House port, in U. S., 59th Cong., 2d sess. Docs., 500.

The Liberals had not withdrawn with any idea of yielding the plums of office. Their abstention from voting was a familiar Hispanic American maneuver indicative of an intention to organize a revolution, and it was so understood in Cuba. Months before the end of 1905 plots were being formed, and there were several minor outbreaks. Between November 21 and 27 there were armed uprisings in the province of Havana at Alquízar, La Salud, and Batabanó, and at San Juan and Martínez in Pinar del Río. These moves were premature. Many who had intended to join in them "thought better of it" when the moment came. So the government, by a slight show of force and an offer to forgive the insurrectionists, was able to restore order. A little later, however, on the night of February 24-25, 1906, a band of thirty or more broke into the barracks of the rural guards at Guanabacoa (a considerable town in the outskirts of Havana), killed two of the guards and wounded several others, and made away with a number of horses and a quantity of arms. They expected that their audacious act would be the forerunner of an insurrection, but the country did not rise. The band was scattered, and most of the men were captured and the stolen properties recovered. Estrada Palma described the participants in this affair as "men of a very low stamp, mostly illiterates,"[20] but back of them were a number of prominent Liberals, as also in the other outbreaks that had taken place. In this particular instance Senator Morúa Delgado was probably the instigator.

Meanwhile, plots to overthrow the Moderates were being formed, even though the methods to be employed were as yet uncertain. Some Liberals favored an intervention by the United States as the guarantor of new elections. Among

[20] Message to Congress of Apr. 2, 1906, in *Mensajes presidenciales,* I, 155.

these was the Liberal candidate himself, José Miguel Gómez, who made a visit to the United States shortly after the elections of September 1905. There he gave out interviews censuring the government of Estrada Palma in bitter fashion. Under date of October 4, while in New York, Gómez said in this connection:

"The United States has a direct responsibility concerning what is going on in Cuba. Estrada Palma can continue at the head of the government only by telling the people that in case of disorder or revolution the United States will immediately send troops to chastise the insurrectionists and sustain his power. The United States is under the duty of putting an end to this situation, which, if it continues any longer, will oblige us to go to the government of Roosevelt with a petition for it to do so. If the United States would intervene and insist that the presidential elections should be held honestly, it would prove that eighty per cent of the Cuban people were Liberal." [21]

Again, on October 6, Gómez expressed himself as follows:

"In my judgment the moment has arrived for the United States and Cuba to give an authentic interpretation to the Platt Amendment. That interpretation ought to be literal or broad. In the latter case the United States ought to assume a completely passive attitude, so long as the rights that foreigners enjoy in Cuba are respected. As a man of peace, if the decision were left to me, I would prefer the first solution, the literal interpretation, although I have always besought for my country the most absolute sovereignty in exercising the normal functions of the national life." [22]

Diario de la Marina, in its edition of October 7, remarked that Gómez was "in favor of having the government of the United States mingle in the contests of Cuban parties as an arbiter," and El Mundo observed, on the same day, that he had stated that it was "the duty of the United States to intervene." The events of the following year were to prove,

[21] *Declaraciones del general J. M. Gómez*, in *Diario de la marina*, Oct. 4, 1905, quoted in Velasco, 89-90.

[22] *Más declaraciones de José Miguel Gómez*, in *Diario de la marina*, Oct. 7, 1905, quoted in Velasco, 27.

however, that the United States had no desire to take any such step if it could possibly be avoided.

Congress met in April 1906, and one of its first duties was to pass upon the elections of 1905. The Liberals still had a number of senators and representatives, as only half of the membership of Congress had been affected by the elections. These left-over Liberals protested against the validity of the elections, but the Moderates stood firm. On one occasion the Liberal representatives, who had been outvoted on a measure impugning the elections, left the chamber in a body. As they were going out, one of them, General Faustino Guerra, exclaimed: "There is nothing for us to do here; we must seek justice somewhere else." The implication was clear. And the man who made the remark, better known by his nickname as "Pino" Guerra, was to strike the first blow on behalf of the revolution. On May 20, 1906, Estrada Palma took the oath of office for his second term. If the Liberals had hoped for some favorable turn in affairs up to this point, the way now seemed closed, except by revolution. The leading men of the party came together, therefore, and signed a formal revolutionary pact. One of the signers was José Miguel Gómez. He had long since returned from the United States, announcing that he had been employed by a group of capitalists to establish a great sugar-mill. Presently, however, for reasons (possibly political) that are not exactly clear, he was asked to resign this position. So he entered into the plan for the revolution, and "was the soul of this movement." [23]   Alfredo Zayas was another signer. A Central Revolutionary Committee was established, and the work of preparation began.

The plan was to effect a *coup d'état,* by seizing the police-

[23] Lozano Casado, 13.

stations of Havana at a given hour and at the same time attacking the palace to get possession of the person of the President. In like manner the Vice-President was also to be taken. It was hoped that the business would be finished in a few hours, without any complications of civil war or intervention. It was a project that had only a scant chance of success. As Martínez Ortiz has said:

"To none of the conspirators was it unknown that in speed of action lay the only possibility of not losing the game and occasioning a foreign intervention." [24]

This is worthy of note, because it has been the habit of Liberal writers to charge the Moderates with having been "traitors" for eventually bringing in the United States. The truth is, that on this score both sides were tarred with the same brush. Failure of the plot meant almost certain civil war, and would draw in the United States. In a letter of September 27, 1905, to the president of the Liberal party, renouncing his candidacy, Gómez himself had remarked that "armed strife would inevitably bring foreign intervention." [25] And, indeed, intervention under the Platt Amendment was just what he had wanted in October 1905, as already stated. Later, some other leaders also came out openly in favor of an American intervention for the supervision of new elections; for example, "Pino" Guerra and Ernesto Asbert, important chieftains in the provinces of Pinar del Río and Havana. [26] And Zayas certainly accepted the intervention when it came. In a letter of September 26, 1906, to Taft and Bacon he said:

"The Government of Cuba having granted to the United States the right of intervention in accordance with Clause III of the Constitutional

[24] Martínez Ortiz, II, 608.   560.
[25] Quoted in Martínez Ortiz, II,   [26] Velasco, 26-27, n. 35.

Appendix, it would seem but natural that the exercise of this right should not be hindered or resisted by the Government of Cuba." [27]

The project of the conspirators needed secrecy as much as speed. It also required considerable forces and ample funds for arms and other uses. The men might have been obtained, but secrecy, where so many were in the plot, was impossible, and the financial resources of the revolution were too slender to permit of rapid action. The government was quite aware of the plans, and kept close watch over Gómez and most of the other leaders. The revolution was in the air. Indeed, it was almost shouted from the housetops, and few precautions were taken to keep the authorities from knowing what was going on. Estrada Palma himself was none too well informed. As Martínez Ortiz puts it, "Many rumors of the revolutionary proposals were not accustomed to reach the President, just as formerly those referring to complaints for illegal acts did not do so." He confided in the honesty of his government, the millions in the treasury, and the general prosperity. He also had great hopes of the new Congress, which might be expected to be amenable to party discipline and to put through some much-needed legislation. It was at this time, too, that he began a series of public works, in which he was assisted by some really laudable acts of Congress. And whether it occurred to *him* or not, it appeared to be in the minds of other Moderate leaders that the United States would provide the force required to subdue any revolutionary outbreak. That at least was the deduction of Taft and Bacon a little later in 1906.

The much heralded "secret" of the *coup d'état* never got a chance for trial. Instead, the spark of revolution touched

[27] Quoted in Taft and Bacon, *Report,* in *Op. cit.,* 514.

powder, and on August 16 "Pino" Guerra raised the standard of revolt in Pinar del Río. Little else could have been expected, but the Liberal leaders had been willing to take that chance, and, indeed, a more serious one still. As Martínez Ortiz has said:

"Perhaps the greatest error of the directors of the uprising was in not taking sufficiently into account how dangerous it was, for the future tranquility of the country and for the security of its institutions and its nationality, to offer to the multitude that objective lesson: the facility with which it was possible to overthrow a government which was without sufficient force to guard property from depredations and make the weight of its authority quickly felt." [28]

[28] Martínez Ortiz, II, 622. For general comment on authorities for this chapter, see note at the end of chapter IX.

CHAPTER IX

THE REVOLUTION OF AUGUST

THE war was on! "Pino" Guerra was already under arms. Gómez's principal panegyrist censures the redoubtable "Pino" for starting the conflict, saying that the former Liberal candidate never intended to have a civil war,[1] but, as already pointed out, no serious attention need be paid to this assertion. It is probable, however, that Guerra acted on his own initiative, or else on orders of General Carlos García Vélez, titular head of the movement in the province of Havana, and not by command of his immediate chief in Pinar del Río, Colonel Manuel Lazo, or of Gómez or Zayas, in charge of the campaign as a whole. Alarmed by the "Pino" Guerra revolt, the government acted swiftly. On August 19 orders were issued for the arrest of the leaders. General José Monteagudo (revolutionary commander for the province of Santa Clara), General Castillo Duany and Juan Gualberto Gómez (the leaders for Oriente), and José Miguel Gómez himself were seized in course of the next day or two, and taken to Havana. Zayas went into hiding in the capital. A number of the less prominent conspirators either were not caught in the first place or else escaped, and presently they appeared in the field. Colonel Ernesto Asbert and General Enrique Loinaz del Castillo raised bands in the province of Havana. Eduardo Guzmán, Orestes Ferrara, and others put themselves at the head of columns in Santa

[1] Lozano Casado, 14.

195

Clara. Camagüey and Oriente participated only slightly in the uprising, while in the loyal province of Mantazas there was virtually no revolutionary activity at all.

In the other three provinces, however, the campaign gathered a momentum that was surprising to the leaders of the movement themselves. To be sure, the government had lost standing in the election, and had scant military resources at its command, but those "who thought themselves to be familiar with the conditions of Cuba" had "regarded the government as established on the firmest basis." The American minister, Mr. Edwin V. Morgan (a man of unusual ability in the American foreign service), had so little anticipated such an event that he was at this very time on his vacation in the United States. Taft and Bacon ascribed the success of the outbreak in part to a "natural tendency to insurrection," growing out of "a long history of insurrection in Cuba," though they were also impressed by the loss of moral force by the existing government. This was accentuated, they pointed out, by the fact that property in the island was owned mainly by foreigners or by Cubans who had no connection with politics. The politicians of both parties were a group apart, lacking the stabilizing influence of a property-holding class. This made it easy for any insurrection to rob the government of active support among conservative elements, as the insurrectionists, however weak they might be in numbers, had an unlimited capacity for destruction, especially since most of Cuba's wealth was in such highly inflammable property as sugar estates.[2] Martínez Ortiz, too, despite his condemnation of the government, freely admits that the rank and file of the revolutionists were "illiterates without landed property, desirous

[2] Taft and Bacon, *Report*, in U. S.,   no. 5105, House Docs., 456. 59th Cong., 2d sess. (1906-1907), ser.

of adventure and novelty," for whom "all causes were good
if they gave an opportunity to 'do the August.' " [3]

Aside from the police, who could not be trusted, as many
of them were in sympathy with the revolution, the government had only some six hundred artillerymen and three
thousand rural guards with which to combat its enemy,
and as the rural guards were distributed in small detachments throughout the island they were not in a position
to render much help. Steps were taken to raise an emergency
force of militia, but the recruits obtained were insufficient
both in numbers and in quality. Furthermore, the overwhelming sentiment of the country, even that of Havana,
favored the insurrectionists. Eventually there were some
eight or ten thousand rebels in the province of Havana,
and almost from the very first they threatened the capital
itself. There were six or eight thousand more in Santa
Clara, besides other scattering bands throughout the country.
They were ill-equipped and lacking in resources, but surpassed the government troops in strength. Living on the
country, they had respected foreign property in the main,
though there was no telling how long their leaders could
keep them in hand. Indeed, it was a question whether some
of the lesser leaders themselves would refrain from gathering in the spoil. There were several "battles," with scant
loss of life, in most of which the government was defeated.
It was thus far more a "war of bulletins than bullets," as a
New York Sun reporter described it, but there was a general
feeling of insecurity and a fear of what might easily happen. Business came to a standstill,—so much so that the
problem of subsistence in the capital was serious. In other

[3] Martínez Ortiz, II, 622. To "do
the August" is a Spanish idiom, growing out of the fact that August is the
time when the wheat crop is gathered
in Spain. Thus one "does the August" who brings his plans to a head
in a way to make a profit for himself.

words, things were in a state of crisis. Something had to
be done,—and quickly!

The veterans of the War of Independence had retained
their organization intact, and they now authorized some
of their leaders to take steps to effect a compromise between the two parties. The Constitutionalists, as the revolutionary leaders styled themselves, wanted the elections of
1905 thrown out. That was their basic idea, although they
also wanted a redress of various wrongs, such as those having
to do with the dismissals of municipal officials and other
government employes. At the opposite pole was the
government, standing on its dignity as the constituted authority and refusing to yield under the pressure of revolution.
Chief among the representatives of the veterans was General
Mario Menocal,[4] a comparatively young man who had made
an excellent record, not only as a soldier, but also as an
engineer and as the organizer and manager of the great
sugar estate of Chaparra. He had an interview with Estrada
Palma on September 4, and suggested that all officials elected
in 1905 should resign, except the President and Vice-President, and that Estrada Palma should take it upon himself
to see that proper electoral and municipal laws should be
enacted and that the officials unjustly ousted should be restored to their posts. Without committing himself the
President for the moment seemed favorable. Four days later,
however, he rejected the proposals, root and branch. Nothing could be done until the insurrectionists should lay down
their arms, he said. Indeed, from this time forward he
could not conceal a feeling of impatience with reference to

[4] Strictly speaking, Menocal's name
should be rendered Mario García
Menocal, but as the gentleman himself prefers to be known by his
mother's name (Menocal) and to use
the father's name (García) only as a
kind of "middle name," it is no doubt
proper to let him have his own way
about it.

Menocal and his companions, who, he felt, should have ranged themselves on his side from the first. Liberal pamphleteers insist that Estrada Palma had "flirted" with Menocal at the outset, merely to gain time for another maneuver that he had in mind,—that of United States intervention under the Platt Amendment.[5] Indeed, the President and his advisers had decided that no other course than that was left to them. To compromise with the revolution would destroy the dignity and moral force of the government, opening the way to future revolutions. To resist meant certain defeat, for even at that moment Havana was at the mercy of the insurrectionists. It seems probable, too, that Estrada Palma expected the United States government to stand behind him.

For a time, with the American minister away on vacation, the United States was inadequately represented in Havana. The young secretary temporarily in charge of the legation was hardly of the calibre to handle the situation. On one occasion he caused a body of marines to be landed in Havana, with Estrada Palma's consent. Next day they were back on shipboard,—by order of President Roosevelt! On another occasion, so it is said, he sent a cablegram to Washington saying "Revolution spreading. Everything quiet." This was too much for President Roosevelt! He got in touch with the American consul-general, Mr. Frank Maximilian Steinhart, and told him to handle affairs, pending Morgan's return. Steinhart was a man of outstanding ability. Born in Germany, he came to the United States as a young man, and for sixteen years was a soldier in the regular army, rising from the ranks to positions calling for executive ability in clerical branches of the service. He was transferred to Cuba at the beginning of the United

[5] For example, see Collazo, 113.

States military occupation, and was chief clerk of the government to the end of United States rule. Remaining thereafter in Cuba, he served as United States consul-general from 1903 to 1907. At the time of the revolution of 1906 he was already one of the best-known men in the island, acquainted with leading Cubans and thoroughly familiar with the conditions and customs of the country. From this time forward, down to the present day, Steinhart was to be reputed the right-hand man of every United States minister to Cuba, and was to acquire for himself a vast fortune in his business ventures in the country.

On September 8, 1906, Steinhart telegraphed to the State Department in Washington, as follows:

> "*Absolutely confidential.* Secretary of State, Cuba, has requested me, in name of President Palma, to ask President Roosevelt send immediately two vessels; one to Habana, other to Cienfuegos; they must come at once. Government forces are unable to quell rebellion. The Government is unable to protect life and property. President Palma will convene Congress next Friday, and Congress will ask for our forcible intervention. It must be kept secret and confidential that Palma asked for vessels. No one here except President, Secretary of State, and myself know about it. Very anxiously awaiting reply."[6]

Two days later he sent another message:

> "President here worried because no reply received my message, and asks war vessels be sent immediately."[7]

The same day Acting Secretary of State Bacon, in the absence of Secretary Root (then in South America), replied to him that two ships were being sent, but remarked that "The President directs me to state that perhaps you do not yourself appreciate the reluctance with which this country would intervene,"[8] following this up with a letter of the 11th, saying that President Roosevelt believed "actual, im-

[6] Quoted in Taft and Bacon, *Report,* in *Op. cit.,* 444-445.   [7] *Ibid.,* 445.   [8] *Ibid.,* 445.

mediate intervention to be out of the question." [9] On succeeding days Steinhart sent more and more urgent messages. On the 12th he transmitted a memorandum to him by the Cuban Secretary of State to the effect that the government was unable to withstand the revolutionists, also saying

"President Estrada Palma asks for American intervention and begs that President Roosevelt send to Habana with the greatest secrecy and rapidity 2000 or 3000 men." [10]

In his cablegram of the 13th Steinhart said

"President Palma, the Republic of Cuba, through me officially asks for American intervention because he can not prevent rebels from entering cities and burning property." [11]

He further stated that Estrada Palma was resolved to resign and turn over the government to the representative whom the President of the United States might designate. Next day he cabled that Estrada Palma, the Vice-President, and all the Secretaries proposed to resign, which would mean a condition of anarchy, as there would be no legally constituted power that could convoke Congress. [12]

The United States was indeed unwilling to intervene. Secretary Root was just completing a tour of South America in an attempt to allay the suspicions of the southern republics about the supposed imperialistic designs of the great republic of the north, and political considerations in the United States, with a congressional election at hand, made it desirable to avoid giving the slightest foundation for any criticism on this score. Furthermore, it had long ago been decided in Washington that the interests of the United States were best served by the existence of an independent

[9] *Ibid.,* 445.
[10] *Ibid.,* 446.
[11] *Ibid.,* 446.
[12] *Ibid.,* 446-447.

republic of Cuba. Yet Steinhart's messages made it apparent that something must be done. So as a first step, Roosevelt sent an open letter on September 14 to Gonzalo de Quesada, the Cuban minister to Washington. In it he urged the Cubans to sink their differences, and announced his intention of sending his Secretary of War, William Howard Taft, and the Assistant Secretary of State, Robert Bacon, to Havana to aid the Cubans in reaching a peaceful solution. Among other things he also said:

"Whoever is responsible for armed revolt and outrage, whoever is responsible in any way for the condition of affairs that now obtain, is an enemy of Cuba . . . For there is just one way in which Cuban independence can be jeoparded, and that is for the Cuban people to show their inability to continue in their path of peaceful and orderly progress . . . Our intervention in Cuban affairs will only come if Cuba herself shows that she has fallen into the insurrectionary habit, that she lacks the self-restraint necessary to secure peaceful self-government, and that her contending factions have plunged the country into anarchy." [13]

This letter, which was at once given out for publication, created an excellent impression both in Cuba and in the United States, and probably saved the revolution from entering a dangerously destructive stage. The insurrectionist chiefs were getting impatient over the failure in the efforts that were being made to effect a compromise. As Guzmán, one of their leaders, had said:

"If there is no satisfactory arrangement soon, I shall proceed to the destruction of the railways and even of foreign properties." [14]

Now, both sides were disposed to wait. The government issued a decree suspending military operations throughout the republic. Several of the opposition generals took similar action, and the others at least engaged in no activities of major consequence. The representatives of the veterans

---

[13] Quoted in *Ibid.*, 491-492.   [14] Martínez Ortiz, II, 635.

made one last effort to effect a compromise before the arrival of the American commissioners, but they accomplished very little. Some, but not all, political prisoners were released, and Zayas was given permission to come out of hiding to act on behalf of the revolutionists. On the other hand, the government insisted that it could not treat with rebels in arms. And the insurrectionists, self-styled "Constitutionalists," would not lay down their arms without an annulment of the 1905 elections,—for which course, incidentally, there was no warrant in the Constitution. There was not a little disappointment over the unwillingness of the two parties to come together, but it was "too good to be true" that they should have done so, as Enrique José Varona, the most respected thinker in Cuba, pointed out in El Fígaro on September 23. As Varona put it,

"I have already said what is the attitude of the parties, which are *joint authors* of this dishonorable convulsion. They are concerned with nothing more than to make the best capital of the moment, at the cost of the country, destined beforehand to fill the rôle of a propitiatory victim. But what with greatest reason ought to cause us indignation is to see that they talk only of the good of the country, the honor of the country, the liberty of the country, and those who speak in this manner are loosing upon the country that greatest calamity of the many that afflict the miserable human species, war." [15]

Taft and Bacon, accompanied by the American minister, reached Havana on September 19. They were the last hope for a solution of the problem without formal intervention. Anyone acquainted with Hispanic American character in general and the Cuban situation in particular might have felt safe in predicting that they were foredoomed to failure. Nobody could complain, however, of any lack of industry or effort on their part to bring about an adjust-

[15] Quoted in Martínez Ortiz, II, 675-677. For something further about Varona, see *infra*, pp. 633-634.

ment of affairs, though many have questioned the decision they reached. Taft was the virtual head of the mission, and was generally recognized as such. Speaking of Bacon, Martínez Ortiz comments upon his "reserve" and "discretion" and the fact that "he did not let his thoughts appear," noting also that "one hardly ever heard a word from him, except when he was answering some question of Mr. Taft." Taft, on the other hand, was "loquacious," and had "a perpetual smile," besides which he had an enormous prestige as a leader in American national life. The very morning of their arrival the two commissioners paid a visit to the President, and were much impressed by their conversation with him. Estrada Palma acquainted them with the main features of the situation, and suggested that they confer with Méndez Capote and Zayas, as representatives of the Moderates and Liberals respectively. The rest of the conversation was described in the report of Taft and Bacon as follows:

"This was in substance all of the conversation, except a long and interesting statement which the President made of his efforts to teach his people the knowledge of self-government which by twenty years of residence in the United States he had acquired from association with the American people, of his successful handling of the finances of the Cuban Government, of the economy of expenditure in his administration, of the encouragement he had given to the investment of foreign capital, and of the consequent prosperity which had come to Cuba during the four years of his incumbency as President. He manifested an intense interest in the large balance which there was in the treasury, and the greatest regret that that balance was likely to be much reduced by the extravagance of expenditures required in the efforts made and making to suppress the insurrection. He said that he had insisted upon the maintenance of all the guaranties of civil liberty under the constitution, and had declined to suspend them until the insurrection had proceeded to a point where it could not be avoided; that for six months he had been made aware of the plotting which was going on against the government, but that so great was the prosperity and the comfort of the people, and so successful had his government been in arts of peace, he declined to take rigorous steps against the conspirators, for he had not supposed that such an insurrection as had occurred was possible. He deplored what he regarded as a lack of gratitude and patriotism on the part of those who were supporting the insurrection, and gave us a number of instances tending to show that the leaders of the insurrection were moved only by the basest of purposes—by a pecuniary greed and for office. His demeanor was dignified and earnest, the evidences of his sorrow were touching, and what he said made a deep impression on us." [16]

Taft and Bacon accepted the invitation of Minister Morgan to reside at his home in Marianao, nine miles from the centre of Havana. This gave them something of a neutral position, as Marianao was in possession of the government, while there were insurgent posts across a bridge about a thousand yards from the Morgan home. They now proceeded at a phenomenal rate of activity to interview everybody who might throw light on what had happened in Cuba or suggest to them what course should be followed. They frequently communicated with Méndez Capote and Zayas, as also with men who were, or had been, Secretaries in Estrada Palma's Cabinet. They talked with congressmen, revolutionary generals, the representatives of the veterans associations, bankers, merchants, manufacturers, planters, and, indeed, men of prominence in all branches of life in the island, including foreigners as well as Cubans. Consul-General Steinhart was of the greatest assistance to them, as he "was better acquainted with conditions and public men than any other American whom we could have consulted." Several other Americans were in constant attendance upon the two commissioners, and gave them invaluable aid. Inevitably Taft and Bacon reached one conclusion early in the enquiry: that the procedure of the government in connection with the elections of 1905 had been fraudulent. The

[16] Taft and Bacon, *Report,* in *Op. cit.,* 449.

testimony of Freyre himself, already mentioned, was conclusive on this score.

Any American will readily understand the enormous influence this fact was bound to have on the commissioners, and there was perhaps nobody in Cuba who expected them to believe that the election had been honest. There were a great many people, however, who thought they would in any event back the government. The commissioners themselves would have preferred to do that, as is clearly apparent from the correspondence between Taft and Roosevelt. For example, in a long cablegram of September 21 Taft said:

"If the present government could maintain itself, or if it had a moral support or following which would be useful in case of intervention, Bacon and I would be strongly in favor of supporting it as the regular and constitutional government, because the election was held under forms of law and has been acted upon and recognized as valid, but the actual state of affairs is such that we would be fighting the whole Cuban people in effect by intervening to maintain this government." [17]

So, presently, it was perhaps natural that Taft and Bacon reached practically the same conclusion that Menocal had, before them. As early as September 21 the Moderates had formally agreed to accept the arbitration of the American commissioners, provided the insurrectionists should first lay down their arms, and Méndez Capote had given assurances that all the issues in dispute could be adjusted if only the dignity of the government might be conserved by its not being required to treat with armed rebels. Zayas was also empowered by the Liberal party, by the Central Revolutionary Committee, and (after a somewhat spectacularly arranged meeting at Marianao) by the insurrectionist generals themselves to act on behalf of the opposition.

[17] Quoted in *Ibid.*, 469-471, at 470.

Zayas consented to the Taft and Bacon suggestions, essentially like those of Menocal,—for the resignation of all officials elected in 1905 except the President and Vice-President, for the needed electoral, municipal, and judiciary laws and a civil service law covering government employes in general, and for a specified date in the near future for new elections,—but felt that he was not authorized to consider the matter of a prior laying down of arms by the Constitutionalist forces, although he did make a futile enquiry of the generals as to whether they would accept any such arrangement. So Taft came to the conclusion, influenced no doubt by his findings concerning the elections, that the government should waive this point, and continued the negotiations thenceforth on the basis of the compromise proposals themselves, without reference to the arms question. That meant that his mission as one of arbitration was over almost as soon as it began, for Estrada Palma and the Moderates were adamant on that score.

Matters now moved swiftly. The *seeming* changes in the situation were, as Taft almost daily described them, "kaleidoscopic." In fact, *nothing* changed! The issue was sure: intervention or civil war. Consistently with the stand they had taken, Taft and Bacon did what they could. Roosevelt in the United States rendered them great assistance, despite his distance from the controversy. At times, indeed, it seems as if his judgment of events were better than that of his emissaries in the field; at least that is an impression one is likely to get from a reading of his correspondence with Taft. On one occasion he said:

"It is undoubtedly a very evil thing that the revolutionists should be encouraged and the dreadful example afforded the island of success in remedying wrongs by violence and treason to the Government . . . I do not have much hope that with the example before them of such success in an insurrection the people who grow discontented with the new government will refrain from insurrection and disturbance some time in the future." [18]

On another occasion when Taft was inclined to reject a solution which some of the Cuban leaders had proposed, because it lacked any constitutional basis, Roosevelt came back quite characteristically:

"Upon my word, I do not see that with Cuba in the position it is we need bother our heads much about the exact way in which the Cubans observe or do not observe so much of their own constitution as does not concern us . . . I do not care in the least for the fact that such an agreement is not constitutional." [19]

None of the devices that were tried had any real chance of success, however. So the story may be quickly passed in review.

The commissioners first announced their suggestions for a compromise, minus the disarming of the insurrectionists factor, on September 24. As already mentioned, Zayas accepted it, though disliking some features; by this time he was ready to follow Taft and Bacon almost to any length, for their stand concerning the elections and the arms question had generally been accepted as a great Liberal victory, for which Zayas might hope to claim much of the credit. Taft himself recognized the existence of this opinion, as he pointed out in a cablegram to Roosevelt on the 26th, though he failed to see where it was justified. Méndez Capote and Estrada Palma, both of whom the commissioners talked with on the 24th, were of the opinion that the compromise was a mere temporary expedient that would not last more than a few months. By some accounts the meeting with Estrada Palma was rather stormy. At any

[18] Quoted in *Ibid.,* 478.   [19] Quoted in *Ibid.,* 480-481.

rate, the President "declined to assist in or accept the compromise, as offensive to his personal dignity and honor, and announced his intention irrevocable to send his resignation to Congress."[20] Taft and Bacon in a long communication of the same date begged him to reconsider; a telegram from Roosevelt of the 25th (corrected in some parts by the commissioners) also urged him to accept the compromise or to propose some other; but Estrada Palma could not be moved. In replies of the 25th and 26th respectively Estrada Palma reiterated his irrevocable decision to resign. Taft's messages about this time began to exhibit great impatience with Estrada Palma and the Moderates, and Martínez Ortiz remarks that he even lost his smile. He was convinced that the Moderates preferred intervention to the plan he had suggested, and was surprised and chagrined that they should do so. The Moderates held a meeting on the 25th, and rejected the compromise, and so, naturally, the Liberals formally accepted it on the 26th. The Moderates were now planning, as Taft called it, to "scuttle" the government, through the resignation of all executive officials and the dissolution of Congress without electing a successor, thereby forcing a provisional government. Even the Liberals generally favored intervention, too, Taft declared, "because they can earn their victory in the holding of new elections." Both sides were eager to have it appear, however, that the other party had caused the intervention. There were some Moderates and Liberals who were still eager to avoid that outcome, however, and there were various impossible proposals, such, for example, as that Menocal, Sanguily, or Zayas be put in as temporary President, with or without due congressional authorization. At a meeting of leading Moderates on the 27th some excited individuals went so

[20] Taft to Roosevelt, Sept. 26, 1906, in *Ibid.*, 475-477, at 476.

far as to propose forcing the intervention of England or Germany through the simple device of destroying the property of subjects of those countries. Fortunately, nothing came of these suggestions.

Congress assembled on September 28. The Liberals had held a preliminary meeting to decide whether they should attend. Fearful lest the government might put up a Moderate to succeed Estrada Palma, Zayas at first opposed having the Liberals present themselves, but the contrary opinion of Sanguily prevailed. The President offered the resignations of his Secretaries and then his own, while Méndez Capote also resigned the vice-presidency. A motion was passed asking the President to reconsider, but it was a foregone conclusion that he would not do so. The session was then suspended until nine that night. Following Estrada Palma's expected refusal to reconsider, there was a meeting of the Moderates to determine whether they should go to Congress again to solve the presidential succession, or remain away and thus break the quorum. Finally, by a vote of twenty to sixteen they decided to remain away. Liberal writers make a great point of this, holding that it established their case, that the Moderates caused the intervention, but one would have to be simple-minded to consider these charges seriously. The Moderates wanted intervention, yes, but so also did the Liberals, though as clever politicians they did not object to making as much capital as they could. They had won a victory, but wanted to clinch it for the future.

Congress did not meet again, and there was nobody to convoke it. So Cuba was without a government. In consequence, on September 29, 1906, Taft published a proclamation (previously submitted by cablegram to President Roosevelt) taking over control on behalf of the United States. Following is the proclamation:

"PROCLAMATION

To the people of Cuba:

The failure of Congress to act on the irrevocable resignation of the President of the Republic of Cuba, or to elect a successor, leaves this country without a government at a time when great disorder prevails, and requires that, pursuant to a request of President Palma, the necessary steps be taken in the name and by the authority of the President of the United States to restore order, protect life and property in the Island of Cuba and islands and keys adjacent thereto, and for this purpose, to establish therein a provisional government.

The provisional government hereby established by direction and in the name of the President of the United States will be maintained only long enough to restore order and peace and public confidence, and then to hold such elections as may be necessary to determine those persons upon whom the permanent government of the Republic should be devolved.

In so far as is consistent with the nature of a provisional government established under the authority of the United States, this will be a Cuban government, conforming, as far as may be, to the constitution of Cuba. The Cuban flag will be hoisted as usual over the Government buildings of the island. All the executive departments and the provincial and municipal governments, including that of the city of Habana, will continue to be administered as under the Cuban Republic. The courts will continue to administer justice, and all laws not in their nature inapplicable by reason of the temporary and emergent character of the government will be in force.

President Roosevelt has been most anxious to bring about peace under the constitutional government of Cuba, and has made every endeavor to avoid the present step. Longer delay, however, would be dangerous.

In view of the resignation of the cabinet, until further notice the heads of all departments of the central Government will report to me for instructions, including Major-General Alejandro Rodriguez, in command of the Rural Guard and other regular government forces, and General Carlos Roloff, treasurer of Cuba.

Until further notice, the civil governors and alcaldes will also report to me for instructions.

1 ask all citizens and residents of Cuba to assist in the work of restoring order, tranquillity [*sic*], and public confidence.

WM. H. TAFT,
Secretary of War of the United States,
Provisional Governor of Cuba." [21]

"Was the war just?" Martínez Ortiz asks, and answers his own question by saying "Surely not." Whatever his errors in the realm of politics, Don Tomás had been a good administrator, and had given the country a great prestige abroad. The Liberals were willing to risk a civil war, with its attendant destruction and possible loss of independence, to put Gómez in his place, not because Gómez was likely to prove a better President, which was improbable, but simply because they wanted him. "The mistake of Don Tomás was in delivering himself body and soul to the Fighting Cabinet and not knowing how to restrain it." Even the incorrect political action of the Moderates had its explanation, if not an excuse, and that is well expressed in the already oft-quoted report of Taft and Bacon, as follows:

"The truth seems to be that General [Freyre de] Andrade and those who sympathized with him in the plan which he pursued had become convinced that the universal-suffrage clause of the constitution and the holding of elections according to the constitution and the law, with the Cuban electorate in its present condition of ignorance, would produce such instability in the government as to prevent the growth and the development of the country on the prosperous lines which had been realized under President Palma, and that it was necessary in the best interests of Cuba to secure for him a solid support in both Houses of Congress in order that the proper policies might be followed. The difficulty which they did not fully realize in adopting such a plan was the necessity for a strong force to suppress the resistance and insurrection which those who were to be deprived of the right to take part in the government might find it possible to initiate." [22]

[21] Quoted in Taft and Bacon, *Report*, in *Op. cit.*, 486.   [22] *Ibid.*, 455.

The revolution showed that the Moderate leaders had judged their people aright, even if they had not taken proper precautions, possibly because they placed too much reliance on United States help under the Platt Amendment. For example, the Liberals of Santa Clara, the backbone of the conspiracy, were fighting not so much for Cuba as for José Miguel Gómez and themselves. They had once been Moderates, but broke with that party over an issue that they yielded without discussion in forming the union with the National Liberals, who consented to the nomination of Gómez. The revolutionists in the field were made up of the least stable elements in Cuban society, who had gone to the war as if to a picnic, without the slightest idea of the ruin and misery that might follow, and not least of all to themselves. Not only did they live on the country like robber bands, but they also appropriated horses for themselves and even took possession of the funds in some municipal treasuries as spoils of war, being encouraged in these acts by their own generals. With some exceptions the generals themselves, as well as their soldiery, were enough to induce horror in Mr. Taft. On one occasion Roosevelt was a little worried lest the resignation of the regular government might make it necessary under the Platt Amendment to substitute the hitherto insurrectionary party. Taft commented on that, on September 26, in this fashion:

"The even remote possibility suggested in your telegram of last night, that under any possible hypothesis the Platt amendment may require the present insurrectionary force to be treated as a government *de facto* makes me shiver at the consequences. It is not a government with any of its characteristics, but only an undisciplined horde of men under partisan leaders. The movement is large and formidable and commands the sympathy of a majority of the people of Cuba, but they are the poorer classes and the uneducated. The Liberal party, which is back of the movement, has men of ability and substance in it, but they are not titular leaders of the insurgent forces in whom such a government *de facto* must vest if in anybody." [23]

Again, remarking on the failure to agree upon a Cuban provisional government, in anticipation of the resignation of Estrada Palma, he said, on September 28:

"I am confident the provisional government . . . would probably have involved immediate appointment of insurgent generals to office, a circumstance most grave in itself." [24]

In fine, as to the question about the revolution of 1906 that most interests Cuban publicists, the determination as to which side was wrong, the writer would conclude that both were. He would be inclined to sympathize with the underlying motive of Moderate leaders, but to condemn them for stupidity. As for the Liberals, barring considerations of technical correctness in political maneuvering, there is little or nothing to say in their favor.

A much more interesting question is the judgment on the Taft mission. Martínez Ortiz says "The American commissioners proceeded in the only way they could," and he approves all they did. Many others are not so sure. One thing certainly was accomplished by the sending of the mission, and that was the stopping of the civil war before it reached a ruinous stage. That was the only success that could be claimed, but it was a great one. As for the compromise they suggested, the following is the calm view of Estrada Palma, written on October 10, 1906, in a private letter to a friend, but published in the press of Cuba the following November:

"The course of making a pact with the insurgents in arms was the worst which could be considered. Even supposing that the different rebel leaders and the directors and instigators of the movement arrived at an

[23] Quoted in *Ibid.*, 475-477, at 477.   [24] Quoted in *Ibid.*, 481.

understanding among themselves and that they agreed with the Government upon the fundamental bases for terms of settlement, the secondary problems which would afterwards arise would be so many and so difficult to decide, in view of the weakened if not lost moral force of the legitimate authorities and in the absence of other authority that might settle differences, these problems would, I repeat, be so many and so difficult that they would cause the country to remain for many months in constant agitation with results as pernicious as war itself. From the moment the Government treated with the rebels it placed itself on an inclined plan of interminable concessions, initiating an era of successive insurrections, and putting the stability of future governments on a frail basis. I could never consent to be an accomplice in such evil in exchange for being permitted to continue to occupy the Presidential chair of the Republic . . . When I saw the insurrection take serious proportions my soul was overcome with profound disenchantment, contemplating the patient and glorious work of four years overthrown; and I irrevocably resolved to resign the Presidency, to abandon completely public life and to seek, in the bosom of my family, the certain refuge against so many deceptions. But before carrying out this intention, so grateful to my desires, it was absolutely necessary to make a last sacrifice on the altar of my country. It was not possible that I leave the Government in criminal hands; in the hands of those who had dealt a fatal blow to the credit of the Republic and the good name of the Cuban people. The conscience of a superior duty, one of those duties which cause the heart to bleed and give rise to unpopularity and hate, imposed upon me as the only measure of salvation, the necessity of acquainting the Washington Government with the true situation of the country, and with the lack of means of my Government to give protection to property, and to say that I considered that an occasion had arisen for the United States to make use of the right granted them by the Platt Amendment. I did so, consulting few people, since it was not a time to expose myself to contradiction in order to seek partners in this responsibility, but to assume the responsability [sic] entirely, with the firmness of a legitimate conviction and the courage which always accompanies acts inspired in the most sterling patriotism . . . I have never feared to admit, nor am I afraid to say aloud, that a political dependence which assures us the fecund boons of liberty is a hundred times preferable for our beloved Cuba to a sovereign and independent republic discredited and made miserable by the baneful action of periodic civil wars." [25]

[25] Quoted in Republic of Cuba, Report of provisional administration from October 13th, 1906 to December 1st, 1907, pp. 12-15, at 13, 14, and 15.

A little nearer the event was a brilliant essay by Enrique José Varona, published September 30.

"There has occurred in Cuba . . . precisely the contrary of what it was reasonable to expect," said Varona . . . "The government of the United States, acting through the illustrious delegates of its distinguished President, after a very rapid investigation has sanctioned the complaints of the insurrectionists of Cuba . . . and has proposed them as the basis for an agreement to the government *de jure* of this republic. In a word, the government of the United States has exacted of the government of Cuba . . . that it abdicate before an armed insurrection."

Varona then went on in a calm and unimpassioned way to account for this unexpected event, and decided that the Cubans themselves were authors of their own misfortunes, primarily because they had given too much attention to politics and too little to a development by Cubans of the economic possibilities of the island. In consequence, Cuba was "a factory governed by Cubans and exploited by foreign capital." The one thing capital wanted was peace, for the protection of its investments; it was not interested in arguments about right and wrong. The insurrectionists had discovered the Cuban "heel of Achilles" in their ability to destroy foreign property. The avoidance of any such contingency was the real basis for the decision of the American commissioners.[26]

It cannot be denied that there was not a little warrant for this point of view. Roosevelt and Taft were certainly much concerned, and properly so, over the protection of foreign property. There was a moment when charges were being bandied about in the American press that business interests had provoked the outbreak, with the idea of forcing intervention and possibly annexation. Roosevelt directed Taft to enquire into that. There was no basis for these

[26] Varona, Enrique José, *El talón de Aquiles*, in *Fígaro*, v. XXII, p. 490;   Sept. 30, 1906.

charges, however. Foreign capitalists would indeed have
preferred American control, but the immediate certainty of
ruin in an insurrection found no palliative in the roseate
prospect of the general good under an American government
of the future,—after their particular properties had been
destroyed. That is equally as true today as it undoubtedly
was in 1906. Once the revolt began, business men wanted
intervention as soon as possible, but were afraid to speak
in a loud voice, as their estates were at the mercy of the
contending factions. In this connection it should be borne
in mind that American business men in Cuba by no means
occupied a position by themselves. As Martínez Ortiz points
out, it is almost certain that European insistence would have
compelled American intervention sooner or later, for the
interests of Europeans were imperilled, equally with those
of Americans; so the United States would either have been
obliged to drop the Monroe Doctrine to let Europe come
in, or else go in herself. It would be interesting to know
just how much pressure was brought to bear, especially
by England and Germany. Certainly Secretary of State
Root referred very pointedly to this factor in a conversation with General Ríus Rivera in the fall of 1906, and
President Roosevelt's annual message on December 4 remarked that the representatives of foreign countries might
have asked their governments for an armed intervention
if the United States had not taken it upon herself to act.
It should be remembered, too, that this was before the
World War, when the relative position of the United States
was very different from what it has since become; the
United States was not nearly so free to do as she pleased
in 1906 as she might be today.

The foreigners, whether American or European, were not
alone in desiring intervention. It is probable that most

wealthy Cubans at that time and very likely the small merchants and regular business employes would have preferred, above everything else, annexation to the United States. That was not true of the politicians, as a rule, but Taft several times spoke of the Moderates,—many of them certainly,—as eager for annexation. With respect to them he may have been deceived, through an imperfect understanding of Hispanic character. More likely what they really wanted was to keep their opponents from victory at all costs. Even at the sacrifice of their country? Yes, in Hispanic America. There is a Spanish refrain which runs as follows:

> "En España con gusto quedamos ciegos,
> Si le saltan un ojo al compañero."

Freely rendered, this might be translated "In Spain we gladly become blind, if we can get one eye of our opponent." There is a lot of Hispanic character in that, and it applies in Cuba,—and to Liberals, Moderates, or any group. As for the masses, they hardly knew what they did stand for, and did not comprehend it if they did. They were instinctively for free Cuba, but they were also for Gómez, for insurrection, for anything! They could not grasp consequences. They could only *feel*.

To sum up, the more stable elements in Cuban society, both native and foreign, objected first of all to the outbreak of the war. Once it began, they hoped that the United States would stand by the existing order, strengthening the hands of the Estrada Palma administration, and they still criticize Taft and Bacon for not doing so.[27] When that

---

[27] There were many contemporary articles in Cuban, American, and European periodicals to this effect. For a somewhat violent Cuban criticism, see Barbarrosa, 88. The writer also has a number of statements from men who continue to hold that opinion.

procedure was not taken, they wanted intervention, and many would have preferred to have it permanent. Under the same circumstances today, the United States would almost certainly uphold the *de jure* government, as was done by Wilson in 1917 and by Coolidge in 1924, because it has been discovered that that is the simplest way to avoid complications, while serving also to check civil war. Whether such a course is morally right is not the question here; on that score the writer has some doubt. But in 1906 the problem of Cuban insurrection, under the republic, was unfamiliar. Indeed, the United States was just experimenting with a new Caribbean policy growing out of the building of the Panamá Canal. It was a normal and an honest thing to do to send the Taft mission. And, once on the ground, it was difficult for the commissioners to take any other position than they did. If the enquiry had never begun, the United States might have supported a guilty government, as she did in 1917 and 1924, but not after she had taken cognizance of wrongs. It is sometimes said that the circumstances were different in 1906, because the Cuban government formally invited intervention, which later governments did not do. That is true, but the fact is overlooked that the invitation was *not accepted*. Every effort was made to keep the Taft mission from having the appearance of an intervention. Taft himself said that Roosevelt "ignored" Estrada Palma's request.[28] When the intervention came, with the proclamation of September 29, it came, not as a result of official request, but because there was no Cuban government at all. The defect, if any, was cured by the general acceptance with which the sending of the commissioners and the declaration of the interven-

[28] Taft to Roosevelt, Sept. 28, 1906,   483.
in Taft and Bacon, *Report,* in *Op. cit.,*

tion were received by all factions in Cuba. In fine, the Taft mission ended the civil war. It did not do anything else,—except to provide a valuable lesson for the future.

One other matter remains to be discussed. What became of Estrada Palma? Is it true that he had "compromised his fame"? The writer thinks not, and is inclined to regard him as greater in adversity than even at the height of his power. Don Tomás went to his downfall, without rancor or recriminations. He praised the Taft proclamation of September 29, and said it was the only possible solution under the circumstances. When he prepared to leave the palace and go to Matanzas, Taft offered him a battleship, which Estrada Palma declined in a simple and gracious note. It was not in keeping with the modesty or dignity of this man that he should have accepted any such conveyance. On October 2 he and his family took the train for Matanzas. A little over four years earlier he had come to Havana amidst the plaudits of the nation. Now he left with hardly anybody to bid him good-bye. Estrada Palma did not complain. There was no bitterness in this man. There was none in his already quoted letter of October 10. In fact, in all his life one finds nothing that was mean or unlovely to detract from the beautiful and unselfish idealism of his character. Early in the Ten Years' War his mother was captured by some Spanish soldiery who treated her in such a brutal and inhuman manner as to cause her death. Shortly afterward, the Cuban force to which Estrada Palma belonged captured some Spanish volunteers. They were about to be put to death, when Estrada Palma interceded for them. Reminded of the barbarous way in which the Spaniards had treated his mother, he replied:

"The memory of my mother is too sacred for me to stain it with a sentiment of vengeance." [29]

There was nothing of the "eye for an eye"—or even "two eyes for one"—in that! Indeed, Estrada Palma always carried around with him, to the moment of his death, a handkerchief of his mother's that was bound around her head at the time the body was discovered. He regarded it as a sacred relic.[30] It was this same Estrada Palma who accepted a loss of all his property after the Ten Years' War, rather than sacrifice his principles. As he put it himself,

"Presently came the Revolution of Yara, and all my property was embargoed, I being the only Cuban whose estates were not returned by the Spaniards, for they exacted from me as a condition precedent that I should adhere to the pact of Zanjón or return to the island, and I was never disposed to accept such terms, for it seemed to me lacking in decorum that I who had been taken prisoner while President of our revolutionary government should for material reasons submit myself again to the government of Spain." [31]

On the other hand, once he began to earn a little money as proprietor of the Central Valley School, he mortgaged his house at that place in order to contribute to the funds for the revolution of 1895.[32]

Estrada Palma's stay in Matanzas was comparatively short. Soon he took his way back to the old home at Bayamo in Oriente, for with the winning of independence his estates had been restored to him. There he lived in the utmost poverty, but uncomplaining still. The following excerpts are from letters he wrote to a friend, Jorge Alfredo Belt,

[29] Cruz, Carlos Maria de la, *Hechos históricos de la vida de don Tomás Estrada Palma,* in Velasco, 107-119, at 109-110.
[30] *Tomás Estrada Palma: para la historia,* in *Cuba,* Nov. 4, 1909, quoted

in Velasco, 11-24, at 12.
[31] Estrada Palma to Jorge Alfredo Belt, July 5, 1908, quoted in Cruz, *Op. cit.,* in Velasco, 107-119, at 113-114.
[32] Cruz, *Op. cit.,* in Velasco, 107-119, at 117.

who had been his private secretary during all his presidency. In one of these, dated August 29, 1907, after explaining his failure to finish a letter to Belt that he had begun before, he went on:

"In truth the conditions to which I see my family submitted are so hard and my economic problem is so serious that I need to employ all the effort of a strong will in order not to give up in the struggle I am obliged to sustain with the difficulties of an unfavorable situation, which, without my being able to foresee it, was awaiting me in the last years of my life . . . It will be enough to tell you that I have seen with anxiety that the only funds on which I have been able to count were diminishing rapidly, those proceeding from the sale of my house at Central Valley, for as there is no demand for cattle, I have had to put hands on that money in order to perform work and labor of an unavoidable character at this estate, which has been so long uncared for." [33]

Again, on September 1, 1907:

"For my part, if it were not for the fears which my pecuniary problem occasion me and my seeing my wife and children deprived even of those simple comforts of a modest position, I assure you that I would consider all the aspirations of my life realized." [34]

And this, most touching of all, on October 3, 1907:

"When I see my wife obliged to get up very early to prepare the coffee for the family, . . . when I see my daughters doing all the interior work of the house, including that of sweeping and washing the floors, when I consider that Cubans of a very modest position support their children in schools inside or outside the island and that for me it is not possible to do so, since I have to keep my two youngest boys at my side, for lack of means with which to send them to get a professional education, however modest it may be,—when I contemplate all this I ask myself: what crime have I committed, or what is the sin, in punishment of which, despite my having worked all my life, I find myself at the end of it, when the weight of years is bending my body upon the sepulchre, I find myself, I say, in such a precarious and difficult situation?" [35]

[33] Quoted in Velasco, 47-48.
[34] Ibid., 48.
[35] Quoted in Ibid., 50. In this connection it must be borne in mind that in Cuba it is unusual for families of even modest circumstances not to have servants to do menial labor, for the cost of house service is extraordinarily little.

There are more letters of the same sort. But the above are enough. On November 4, 1908, at 11.45 at night, Tomás Estrada Palma died at Santiago. On the 6th as his body was about to be covered with earth Colonel Rafael Manduley del Río, governor of Oriente, pronounced these words:

"The man whom we leave here, like every human being, had defects and virtues; like every human being, he made mistakes. But his defects and mistakes were as nothing compared with those virtues which he demonstrated as a loving son, faithful husband, affectionate father, and exemplary citizen. If he was a model in his private life, he was a model also in his honored public life; that is the mirror in which all Cubans ought to look, those that hear me and all the generations of those to come." [36]

Though it is a pity to say it, Estrada Palma died just in time,—only a few months before the end of the American provisional government. Governor Magoon forthwith issued a decree, on November 7, 1908, granting a pension of five thousand dollars a year to his widow and fifty dollars a month to each of his minor children (two daughters and two sons) until they should reach their majority.[37] It is more than doubtful whether the dire straits in which his family found itself would have been relieved if the Liberal government that went into office the following January had then been in power. Indeed, Liberal vindictiveness against Estrada Palma for a time pursued him with relentless fury, seeming all the more ignoble by comparison with the gentle virtues of the fallen Don Tomás. Just prior to his death hostile politicians were encouraging squatters to settle upon his lands, to despoil him of what he had.[38] Even toward the dead they showed their spite. The first issue of stamps of

[36] Quoted in Tomás Estrada Palma: para la historia, in Cuba, Nov. 4, 1909, in Velasco, 11-24, at 20-21.
[37] Decree in Velasco, 87.
[38] Estrada Palma to Jorge Alfredo Belt, July 5, 1908, quoted in Honrando al caído: palabras de Estrada Palma, in Discusión, Nov. 4, 1910, in Velasco, 43-54, at 50-51.

the Gómez era, 1909-1913, bore no effigy of Don Tomás.[39] The oil portrait of the former President was taken down and put in a corner, though in 1911 Sanguily, then in the Cabinet, had the grace to restore it to its place.[40] Perhaps the most striking incident of this sort took place on the first anniversary of Estrada Palma's death. On November 4, 1909, a group of students went to the palace to request President Gómez to fly the flag at half mast, out of respect for Estrada Palma. They failed to see the President, but did have some conversation with Orestes Ferrara. Ferrara is a man of whom much good may be said, but not always. This was one of the times when he did not show at his best, reviling the first President before those who had come to do him honor. Thereupon, the students of the high school (*instituto*) and university went on strike, absenting themselves from classes out of protest against the words of Ferrara. On the 8th Ferrara withdrew them, and the students went back to work.[41]

One writer has said that Don Tomás just missed being the Washington of his country. But did he? Cuba today has not yet progressed far enough to appreciate a man of Estrada Palma's stamp. If the republic is to last, however, it must have more men after the model of this fine figure, worthy to stand beside the great men of all countries in all times. If Cuba lives, Estrada Palma may yet be acclaimed her Washington,—or her Estrada Palma, which is quite enough.[42]

[39] Velasco, 39-41, 95-97, quoting newspaper items of *Prensa*, Mar. 12, 1910, and *Cuba*, Sept. 27 and Sept. 28, 1909.

[40] Velasco, 44, n. 51.

[41] Velasco, 25-30, quoting newspaper items in *Prensa*, Nov. 7 and Nov. 9, 1909.

[42] As usually happens in the case of events that attract widespread attention, especially where some element of controversy is involved, there is a vast literature on the subject of the elections of 1905 and their sequel, the revolution of 1906. Naturally, the invaluable Trelles is replete with

items. Perhaps no one thing is quite satisfactory, however. By all odds the best and fullest account, despite a not too marked Liberal leaning, is the already oft-cited Martínez Ortiz (v. II). Easily next in rank is the Taft and Bacon *Report* concerning their findings and experiences in Cuba in 1906. One of the best features of the *Report* is its inclusion of the correspondence of the commissioners and other useful contemporary evidences. It is at least mildly hostile to Estrada Palma and the Moderates, presumably because the commissioners' advice to them was not taken. It also omitted "a few sentences containing expressions of opinion regarding persons and things which it is not wise or prudent at this time . . . to make public." The correspondence between Roosevelt and Taft has an interest all its own, reflecting the different temperaments of those two gentlemen, quite apart from Cuban history. Velasco, *Estrada Palma,* was exceedingly useful on isolated phases of Es-

trada Palma's career, and is quite well done on the score of technique, making a good showing of authorities. Barbarrosa, *El proceso de la república,* is useful, but inclined to endless objection and extravagance. This confines itself mainly to the problems of Cuban agriculture. Collazo, *Cuba intervenida,* is a Liberal pamphlet, containing several essays on this period, to explain why the intervention came. It is so violent and extreme that it is more interesting as a study in Cuban political psychology than as a basis for the epoch of which it treats. There is an abundance of articles in American periodicals for the events of 1905-1906, but few of them are particularly useful, except as a reflection of American opinion. Several Cuban articles, however, are somewhat more important. Naturally, the public documents of Cuba and the United States have much worthwhile material. These years still need further study.

CHAPTER X

THE MAGOON ADMINISTRATION, 1906-1909

THE republic did not cease to exist with the publication of Taft's proclamation of September 29, 1906. That document made it clear that the country was to have a Cuban government, under the Cuban flag, though temporarily in the hands of the United States. The action of the United States met with very nearly unanimous approval; it was obvious that it had been undertaken, not in response to the much vaunted "Yankee imperialism," but unwillingly, and it promised a respite from strife and insecurity. If there were criticisms, they were for the failure to back the Estrada Palma government, or else because the United States would not take over a more thoroughgoing control than she proposed to do under the terms of the Taft proclamation. On this score the following from a Spanish journal, El País of Madrid, is interesting:

"As Spaniards we smart from the wounds once inflicted on us by the Yankees . . . Now, however, their intervention in the case of Cuba seems worthy of applause. If Cuba be annexed to the United States as an autonomous State peace will be safeguarded there and progress guaranteed." [1]

This accurately represented the sentiments of the thousands of Spaniards in Cuba, who were pro-United States, not from any love of the northern republic, but because they wanted peace for the sake of business. Others of the property-owning, tax-paying class, whether Cubans or foreigners, felt

[1] Quoted in *How intervention was brought about*, in *American review of reviews*, v. XXXIV, pp. 530-532, at 531; Nov., 1906.

the same way, though not disposed to give public expression of their views, from fear of violence when, or if, the United States should withdraw.[2]   Even the politicians were not unhappy over the turn of affairs, for it had not cost the country its independence and was believed to be the best way out of a bad situation.   The Liberals felt that they could make capital out of it by charging it to the Moderates, while the latter were "always in favor of intervention . . . though they had sought to escape responsibility for it." [3]

For the time being, Taft acted as governor, and busied himself in solving the more immediate problems connected with the reëstablishment of order.   Two thousand United States marines were landed at once, and stationed most of them at Camp Columbia, seven miles west of the centre of Havana.   A little later, 5600 men under General James Franklin Bell disembarked at the capital, and were distributed to various parts of the island.   It was the plan to employ them "as a background to give confidence," using the rural guards for the suppression of disorder.   The most pressing thing Taft had to settle concerned disarming and disbanding the insurrectionist forces and the no less difficult task of discharging the national militia, which in some instances was "even more unruly and less disciplined than the insurgents."   For the latter, the revolutionary committee agreed that they should lay down their arms, restore any property they had taken, and return to their homes, on the understanding that the United States provisional government would carry out the settlement that Taft and Bacon had suggesed, in so far as it might now be applicable under the changed conditions.   The disarming program was

[2] Cf. Weightman, Richard Coxe, Cuba's American governor, in American review of reviews, v. XXXIV. pp. 556-559, at 559; Nov., 1906.

[3] Taft and Bacon, Report, in U. S., 59th Cong., 2d sess. (1906-1907), ser. no. 5105, House Docs., 465.

"a ticklish business," but was well in hand in the course of two weeks. Only one serious hitch developed, and that had to do with the surrender of the "property which was taken by them for military purposes," or, as Taft said, "substantially only the horses."

Even the most prominent leaders of the insurrectionists had sanctioned the appropriation of horses wherever they might be found. When it came to restoring them, the authorities ran into the difficulty of proving ownership, as well as the very evident desire of the possessors to retain them for themselves. So it was decided to let each man in the insurgent forces take his horse back home, with a certificate describing the animal and showing his right to keep it until the owner should establish his claim. The certificates, however, were allowed to read in Spanish as if title were vested in the temporary holders, and the men of the Constitutionalist forces so understood them. Taft claimed that General Frederick Funston, one of his aides, was responsible for this mistake, though adding with somewhat less enthusiasm that he himself was "to blame for not exercising closer supervision." It was decided that the men should keep the horses, leaving owners to get damages from the government. This may have been the only practicable solution, but it certainly had very little to commend it. It has been considered as putting the stamp of official approval on an orgy of horse-stealing. Martínez Ortiz says that "many young men of good society" afterward went prancing around on fine steeds which they had taken from some poor farmers who had not joined the government forces in the conflict or had perhaps even voted the Liberal ticket. As for Funston, he was immediately relieved, and it was believed by many that it was because of his handling of this affair. Still others describe the whole incident as indicative of a too great inclination on the part of Taft himself to appease the revolutionists. At any rate, whether necessary or not, it avoided one pregnant possibility of trouble.

Taft released all political prisoners on the day of his proclamation, and followed this up a few days later with an amnesty for crimes committed in connection with the revolt. The Liberals had wished to exclude those responsible for the death of Villuendas, and the Moderates could not forgive the Liberals implicated in the attack on the rural guards at Guanabacoa, but Taft made no exceptions. Still another pressing matter came up over the distribution of political patronage. The insurrectionist leaders wanted Taft to put Moderates out of office and replace them with Liberals, but they were advised "that it was not the intention of the provisional government to oust faithful public servants to make places for Liberals," but were assured that Liberals would be preferred whenever vacancies occurred, "until an equality was restored" in the number of jobs held.

With the principal features of the immediate settlement now out of the way, Taft was called back to Washington. Meanwhile, a new governor had been selected in the person of Charles Edward Magoon. Several names were proposed, and in Cuba it was hoped that General Wood might be designated, but Martínez Ortiz says that Taft swung the balance in favor of Magoon. Magoon arrived on October 9, and on the 13th formally took over the government, issuing a proclamation in which he announced that he would strictly adhere to the policy of Secretary Taft, bringing about "the restoration of the ordinary agencies and methods of government under the . . . Cuban Constitution" as soon as might be practicable. A further assurance that Magoon would follow the course that Taft had laid down was provided in that he was made subject to the United States Secretary of War, an office that Taft continued to hold, although affairs in Cuba were to be conducted as for a civil rather than a military government.

Magoon was to rule Cuba until the end of the intervention, in January 1909. No man in the history of the republic has been so universally condemned. The following is a sample comment of a type one frequently finds in Cuban writings:

> "Magoon is a magnificent example of Yankee honor: gross in type, rude of manners, of a profound ambition, avid of constant rapines. He falls like a buzzard on the treasury of Cuba and devours it. He falls like a hurricane of administrative immorality upon everything and infects it all; he is a Jew who fondles gold like a sweetheart." [4]

This is obviously more a reflection on the author—and indeed on the Cuban people who read such "stuff," since the above is by no means unique—than it is on Magoon. A similar characterization, with slightly more point and a touch of rough humor, is the following in an item entitled "Portrait of Mr. Magoon":

> *"Intellectually:* a star without light. As an orator, ordinary; as a lawyer, the only suit he knew how to win in Cuba, with the assistance of politicians in Washington, was that of the millions of Estrada Palma accumulated in the treasury.
> *Morally:* a man of wax. Pliant and amiable with all. Nevertheless, he was an astute diplomat and a waster of the money of the republic. Sober and simple in his habits, at times he liked tobacco and champagne.
> *Physically:* a merchant of Broadway, New York. Tall and fat, with a massive abdomen. Small eyes, a pleasant smile, and a round face like a California apple.
> The favorite pleasures of Mr. Magoon while he filled the post of provisional governor of Cuba were a good table for his friends, drives in an automobile in the morning, and a shower-bath at night." [5]

Even the more serious-minded Cuban writers attack Ma-

[4] Lozano Casado, 17. There was worse the farther it went. still more to this statement, and it got   [5] Barbarrosa, 88-89

goon. Varona says it was Magoon "who began to write
the annals of the dilapidations of the Cuban treasury."[6]
Trelles condemns him without reserve,[7] and Martínez Ortiz
weighs him in the balance and finds him wanting, though
with that fairness so characteristic of him he gives praise
for some of the achievements of the Magoon administration
and says that Magoon may not have taken a single cent for
himself from the public funds.[8] A still more serious thing
is that the charges have gotten into the Cuban school-books,
and are being taught as part and parcel of the "patriotism"
ordinarily inflicted on the infant mind in all countries. One
such item is the following:

"The government of Mr. Magoon was very wasteful. He not only
expended the whole public income each year, but he also spent twelve
million dollars which he found in the treasury that had been economized
by Don Tomás. Mr. Magoon was prodigal with pardons, and although
he attended to the development of public works these were often not
completed in due form. The administration of Mr. Magoon left a bad
memory and a bad example in the country."[9]

This is in a book in which but twelve pages are devoted to
the period of the republic and in which the somewhat notorious grafting of the Gómez era (1909-1913) gets but a line
of gentle censure, as an addendum to much praise, and other
Cuban administrations are treated in laudatory fashion, with
the "soft pedal" on criticism.[10] Similar statements are made,
not only by other Cubans, but also by Americans and foreigners in general. But the surprising thing is that upon

[6] Varona, Enrique José, *Discurso
leído . . . la noche del 22 de diciembre de 1921,* in *Academia nacional de
artes y letras,* v. VI, pp. 239-246, at
240.
[7] For example, in Trelles, Carlos
Manuel, *El progreso (1902 a 1905) y
el retroceso (1906 a 1922) de la república de Cuba,* 8-9.
[8] Martínez Ortiz, II, 847-857.

[9] Guerra y Sánchez, *Historia ele-
mental de Cuba,* 243-244.
[10] Incidentally, the Cuban school-
children who read this book are
taught that the Platt Amendment was
"contrary to what had been agreed
upon in the Joint Resolution of the
Congress of the United States of
April 19, 1898." *Ibid.,* 239.

investigation the charges are not borne out by the facts. Like all governments, that of Magoon had its critics who may have been right in questioning its policies, but two things come out for the student who will look beneath the surface: Magoon was *an honest man;* and as provisional governor of Cuba he merely reflected Secretary Taft, whose honesty, certainly, will not be impugned by anybody of ordinary mental balance.

The evidence in proof of Magoon's honesty is too bulky a file for insertion here, but the main facts may be set forth briefly.   Charles E. Magoon was born in 1861 in Steele County, Minnesota.   His family was like a million others in middle-class American life,—sound and wholesome, but in modest circumstances financially.   Magoon, however, attended the University of Nebraska, and presently became a lawyer at Lincoln, the capital of that state.   In conjunction with a Mr. J. W. McDonald he engaged extensively in real estate transactions, and accumulated a fortune of approximately a hundred thousand dollars.   Magoon was primarily a law student, interested more in legal abstractions than in the direct practice of his profession, however.   So in 1899 he accepted a somewhat obscure position as a law clerk in one of the subordinate divisions of the War Department in Washington.   His knowledge of law soon attracted the attention of Elihu Root, then Secretary of War, who put him to work reconciling the emergencies of the United States military rule in Cuba with the Spanish legal system there. He handled the same problem in connection with the Philippines, and published his findings in 1902 in a bulky volume entitled *Report on the law of civil government in territory subject to military occupation by the military forces of the United States.*   His success in these tasks seemed to fit him for employment in United States relations with Hispanic

American peoples, and consequently he was appointed governor of the Panamá Canal Zone in 1905. In 1906 he was about to be sent to the Philippines as legal aide of the American governor, when the Cuban situation arose. Magoon seemed to be just the man that was required. It was expected at the time that some purely legal questions had to be solved, such as those of the proposed electoral and municipal laws, after which there would be an early withdrawal of United States rule. Perhaps no man in America was better acquainted with Cuban law at this time than Charles E. Magoon.

Magoon's private fortune must still have been about the same as it was when he left Lincoln. In 1904 he made a will, in which he left property worth approximately a hundred thousand dollars. As governor of Cuba he was painstakingly, almost picayunishly, honest in his handling of all funds for his personal use. On a salary of $1400 a month, he saved about ten thousand dollars for the twenty-seven months of his stay. He also bought two hundred shares of Havana Electric Railway common stock, then selling at about fifteen, but since become a valuable property. That was all he ever acquired in Cuba, and every penny was legitimate. In all the thousands of charges against Magoon, not one has ever been proved; indeed, the writer has yet to run across a *single specific charge* of dishonest action on the part of Magoon. After his departure from Cuba, Magoon lived until his death in Washington. Cuban writers point to the fact that he was never again employed in the United States service, making much of Taft's failure to give him an official post when he became President in 1909. While it is true in a certain sense that Taft "abandoned" Magoon, it was not for the reasons ascribed. He had not been attached to any regular organization, such as the army or the diplomatic corps; so there was no reason to employ him unless his services were desired. On the other hand, there was a very good reason for not employing him, in that his health had become impaired. He had become very stout, and was no longer fit for much active effort. So he lived in Washington in the most simple and inexpensive way. Indeed, far from enjoying any ill-gotten spoil from his career as governor of Cuba, he did not have enough income to live on. He felt that he could not resume the practice of law, but received substantial help from an old-time friend, Robert J. Flick of Kansas City, Missouri, whom Magoon and his mother had taken in hand as a youth and given a start to which Flick ascribed whatever he had "grown to be." When Magoon died in 1920, he left an estate of $86,595.04,—or less than he had when he went to Cuba.

The writer has numerous statements contributing to the defence of Magoon's name, a number of them from men of established reputation such as General Pershing, General Crowder, and (as a representative Cuban who can speak from first-hand knowledge) Manuel Landa, the last-named Acting Head of the Department of Justice during Magoon's rule and now President of the Civil Section of the *Audiencia* (or Superior Court) of Havana. Other equally well known men have contributed statements, but do not care to appear in a controversy, while still others who lack outstanding fame have, nevertheless, given important evidence. It may be well to leave this topic with a brief quotation from a letter of General Pershing, written in a burst of indignation when he was informed that a certain "professor" was "attacking" the name of Charles E. Magoon.[11] In this connection it

[11] The "professor" was at that time in the midst of the anti-Magoon current, and had just received what seemed to be some very damaging evidence, later disproved.

should be borne in mind that Pershing and Magoon grew
up together, and were something like "chums" during all
their life, keeping up an intimate correspondence. General
Pershing's letter follows:

"I am horrified at what you say with reference to these insinuations
about Magoon . . . I suppose I knew Charlie about as well as did any
of his friends, and I know as well as I know anything that he was as
honest as the day is long. So far as his having a fortune upon retirement
from the Governorship is concerned, he accumulated whatever he had,
long before he went to Cuba, and as I remember it before he came to
Washington. He was always thrifty and dealt to a certain extent in
real estate, and I know that on one occasion he made something between
$80,000 and $100,000 on one deal with a friend of his who is
now dead. So all of this is unfair, unjust and untrue . . . The whole
thing makes me very furious, as I know of no man who was a more
sincere friend and patriot, or more devoted to the service of his country
than was Governor Magoon, and I do not believe that he was ever
capable of doing a dishonest thing." [12]

The fact that Magoon was honest does not mean necessarily
that he was a great man or that the provisional government
is to be defended on every score. Nevertheless, it *was* responsible for a very considerable achievement, and its shortcomings were due more to policies in Washington than to any
fault of Magoon, though it is also probably true that the
combination of Elihu Root and Leonard Wood would have
been more successful. The story of Taft's abandoning Magoon on account of the latter's bad record is the more un-
reasonable because Taft as Secretary of War was about as
much the real governor of Cuba as was Magoon. Magoon
was not a natural leader and administrator like Wood; he
was, rather, the hard-working clerk who tries faithfully to
execute superior orders, without much initiative of his own.
Magoon and Taft were in constant communication, not only
by correspondence, but also through three trips of Magoon

[12] Pershing to Crowder, Sept. 16,
1924. General Pershing later offered
to prepare a more formal and detailed
statement, but the obviously genuine
character of the above, written without thought of publication (for which
consent was later secured), appeals
to the writer as more suitable here.

to Washington and one visit of Taft in Havana. If there was anything radically the matter with Magoon's administration Taft did not have to wait until 1909 to find it out.

The program of the provisional government was that which Taft had devised before he left Cuba in 1906. It was a good program, but two things prevented it from working out to the best advantage. In the first place, it was not possible in the short period of rule of the intervention authorities to overcome evils that were so deep-rooted as to be traditional. And in the second place, it is probable that too mild and ingratiating a policy was pursued. Why this course was taken, if the assumption that it was is correct, cannot be asserted positively. The obvious defence would be that it was advisable, to smooth over the differences that had developed from the revolution of 1906. It will be recognized by most Hispanic American students, however, that it was, perhaps, not the best calculated to produce an enduring achievement in Cuba. Cubans, like many Hispanic American peoples, respect and respond to authority much more certainly than they do to soft-handed kindliness.[13]

The main tenet in the program of the provisional government was that of holding an honest election and turning the island back to its people as soon as possible. This involved much else. As Taft and Bacon said in their report to President Roosevelt:

"We thought that it would be wise to have a commission, consisting of an equal number of Moderates and Liberals, with at least one American on it, to prepare needed laws on the subject of municipalities, elections, independence of the judiciary, and the classified civil service, according to the merit system, so that these laws might be enforced and adopted by Congress, as a matter of course and of previous agreement after they had been settled by the commission." [14]

[13] For an interesting statement suggesting that the Taft-Bacon compromise and the policy of the Magoon government were based on Taft's aspirations for the presidency, see Wright, 181-185, 191-192.

[14] Taft and Bacon, *Report*, in *Op. cit.*, 461.

This was virtually the platform of the Magoon government, lying in the background of the establishment of the Advisory Law Commission, which was responsible for much of the best work of this period. Unfortunately, however, other conditions would not stand still and wait for the Commission to complete its labors. Cuba had to be ruled in the meantime, and a great variety of economic and administrative problems dealt with, if not solved. It may be well to take up some of these first.

It is the habit of Cuban writers to tell of the twelve million or the thirteen million or the twenty-five or twenty-six million that Don Tomás had saved, and then go on to say that Magoon swallowed that sum, whatever it was, and all the revenues, increased expenditures unnecessarily, and left an enormous deficit.[15] On the assumption of the government by Taft there was in fact something less than fourteen millions in the treasury,[16] but, of this, more than four million was already pledged for specific purposes, and all of the rest was affected by legislation of the Cuban Congress calling for some $350,000 more than the entire fund. The acts of Congress were mostly for much needed public works, for which, it later proved, the amounts appropriated were entirely inadequate. For example, a number of roads and bridges were authorized at an estimated cost of $20,286,500, but the appropriation was only $4,879,609. In other words, there was an actual deficit of considerable proportions, not a surplus, in the Cuban treasury when the provisional government began, and it seemed at the outset as if this might be vastly increased through an expected falling off in revenues and an unavoidable jump in expenditures. One item that

[15] For example, in Barbarrosa, 71-87. Curiously enough, however, in one ordinarily so unbridled in his comment, Barbarrosa several times admits of the possibility that Magoon himself did not take any graft.
[16] Variously stated as $13,625,539.65, $13,775,186.44, and $13,848,747.16.

had to come out of the funds of the provisional government was the settlement of the bill for the revolution of 1906. This was estimated as of October 31, 1907, with most of the amounts already known, as $8,634,116.64,—substantially what it eventually proved to be. This was after a very considerable paring down of claims.[17] In addition to claims for damages, some of the other items in this bill were the following: an increase in the rural guards from a complement of 3020 men to 5305, subsequently reduced, but only to 5170 at the earnest solicitation of Cuban leaders, and later raised to 5243; a small increase in the artillery force which alone constituted the regular army; cost of the more or less useless Estrada Palma militia (over two million and a half); and various kinds of military equipment. This failed to account for a number of items in the indirect cost of the revolution. It did not include the transportation and maintenance of the Army of Cuban Pacification, as the American forces in Cuba were called. The mere rental of quarters had passed $850,000 by October 1, 1908. Another item was the additional cost involved in a bi-lingual government, requiring an expensive American officialdom and numerous translators. All in all, it is probable that Cuba paid at least ten million dollars to overthrow the Estrada Palma government, which would have retired anyway some four months later than the intervention came to an end.

The expense growing out of the revolution was by no means the only extraordinary item that the Magoon government had to pay. There were a number of prior claims that had accrued in earlier years, but for which Congress had

[17] For example, 15,027 claims for damage inflicted by the insurgent forces were reduced from the $3,803,-385.55 asked for to $1,389,827.39. Included in this were 6,557 claims on account of horses and mules carried off by the insurgents. The total asked was $653,027.20, with $296,508.84 allowed.

made no appropriation, such, for example, as mail-carrying contracts aggregating more than two hundred thousand dollars. A somewhat larger sum went into the purchase of certain properties from the church. These had been confiscated by the Spanish government in 1842, and utilized for administrative purposes,—for the custom-house at Havana, the Havana institute (or high school), and other public uses. The church put in a claim for these properties during the United States military rule which was allowed, but gave options for their sale to the government. The Cuban Congress did not act on the options, despite the recommendations of Estrada Palma, but continued to occupy the properties. These were bought by the Magoon administration for approximately a million and three-quarters. Cuban writers denounce this as a virtual gift to the church, and certainly it is improbable that any Cuban government would have paid for them,—such is the hostility to the church,— but the debt was an honest one. It may have been paid with a too generous sense of fairness, but even that is doubtful. Among other extraordinary expenses were the following considerable sums: an item of nearly four hundred thousand dollars that had been voted by the Cuban Congress for certain needs of the provinces; nearly five hundred thousand in the preparation of a census; and six hundred and fifty thousand in connection with the elections for a Cuban government.

And still this was not all. In October 1905 yellow fever reappeared in Cuba, and due to the unsanitary condition of the cities and towns and ineffective health administration of the local authorities it became a serious problem by the opening of the Magoon era. It was decided to have the national government take entire charge of sanitation, which involved an outlay of more than a million dollars extra a year, as well as another million for the special work of extirpating the disease. By February 1908 yellow fever had again been banished from the island. An unforeseen and expensive disaster turned up in the shape of unusually heavy rains in October 1906, culminating in a cyclone on the 17th. It caused a vast amount of damage to crops and forests and also in the cities, involving a loss of millions. Batabanó was swept by a tidal wave. The schooner "Elvira" was thrown high and dry on the reefs of the Malecón at Havana. This also cost the government considerable sums in the work of relief and repair, though the indirect expense to the country was greater. Meanwhile, business conditions were very unfavorable. The revolution had impaired Cuba's credit, resulting in a call for payment of private indebtedness which was accentuated by the financial stringency developing from the world panic of 1907. This made it hard to finance the Cuban crops, though the Magoon government eased over the situation by lending five million dollars to Cuban banks out of sums in the treasury. During these years, too, the agricultural situation itself was bad. Despite the damage from rain and cyclone the sugar crop of 1906 was heavy, but the price was low. In 1907 there was a drought and a small crop, though at a good price. The 1908 crop promised well, but the Gómez administration was to reap the benefit from that. The tobacco crop of 1907 did not "cure" rapidly, and was of poorer quality than usual. It reached the market just as the panic began, and therefore could not be sold. Conditions in 1908 were again excellent for tobacco,—but for Gómez, not Magoon.

Added to the above difficulties was the unpleasant aspect of labor questions. The dry season, from November through April, is the time when sugar is being harvested and there is plenty of work for everybody. In the rainy season, May through October, there is little to do in the sugar fields, and then jobs are hard to find. The bad crop situation made this a more than usually difficult period to handle. Magoon's public works program responded in part to the necessity of occupying what would have otherwise been a large idle class. Trouble came, too, from those who did have jobs, but were not satisfied with them. The propensity of the Cuban laborer to go on strike had frequent illustration in these years. The cigar-makers started the ball a-rolling in February 1907, with a demand for a ten per cent increase in wages. It was not until August that the issue was settled, in favor of the strikers. Then other strikes followed, galore. There were strikes of railway employes, masons and others of the building trades, stevedores, cart-drivers, waiters, and cooks. Naturally, these affairs were bad for business, to say nothing of the violence connected with them. Spanish governments of the past had handled strikes in military fashion, taking the side of the employers, but it will be readily understood that no American government would be likely to do that. For one thing, there was the American labor vote to consider! On the other hand, the requests of Cuban labor leaders for deportation of strike-breakers were denied. Among yet other bad business conditions that the Magoon government had to face was a paralysis in the cattle industry. By the close of 1908 the difficulties had been corrected, and a prosperous season was in sight.

In view of the foregoing it is not surprising that expenditures were more considerable than under the economical Don Tomás. Cuban critics make a great point of this, but under the circumstances the increase was not great. For the three year period from July 1, 1906, to June 30, 1909, including the exciting and expensive last months of Don Tomás and nearly half a year of José Miguel, a total of about $121,000,000 was expended, or an average of about forty millions a year, as against an average of about twenty-six millions in the two fiscal years preceding July 1, 1906.[18] This was not a bad showing in comparison with the Estrada Palma era, and it was much better than the average of any later administration. Furthermore, the sums expended paid for a great deal more than the things that have been mentioned already, plus the ordinary running expenses of government. In addition, Magoon embarked upon a program of public works that was admittedly greater than any which had been undertaken before, though criticized on the score of imperfections in the works themselves.

Unquestionably there was a need for improvement in the means of communication, especially through the building of roads, and also for other forms of public works. Railway mileage was not great enough to take care of traffic, and freights were high; the heavy rains made any roads but good ones an expensive medium of communication; many crops, especially in the case of tobacco (which found a favorable growing-place in the pockets of hills), were difficult of access, except by roads; there were only 610 kilometres of roads in the island,[19] whereas the near-by island of Jamaica, one-fifth the size of Cuba, had 10,113 kilometres; there were at least forty good ports in the island, but only six were serviceable for ocean-going vessels, and all needed dredging or other improvements; many new public buildings were required, while old ones called for repairs; other aids were also much wanted. Furthermore, in addition to giving employment for constructing these things, it was hoped that they would promote trade and commerce and tend to pre-

[18] The figures given here are taken from Guiral Moreno, Mario, *Nuestros problemas políticos, económicos y sociales,* in *Cuba contemporánea,* v. V, pp. 401-424, at 416-417; Aug., 1914.

[19] Of these, 256 were built under Spain, and the remainder by the United States military government or by Estrada Palma.

serve public tranquillity. Indeed, without the roads the country might be tied up any time by a railway strike, a contingency that threatened the tobacco crop of 1907 for a time.

A great many difficulties had to be overcome through lack of proper equipment and personnel, but by August 1907 the work was started. A little over a year later, on September 30, 1908, Magoon was able to report that 570 kilometres of road had been completed (including 120 bridges), while 395 kilometres more were under construction, of which 195 would be finished, making a total of 765, by the end of the intervention and the remainder by the end of the fiscal year on June 30, 1909. Altogether, the provisional government had by September 30, 1908, expended $13,361,406.70 on roads and bridges, or 55.35 per cent of the entire amount devoted to public works, and another $1,109,282.38, or 4.63 per cent, on harbors, and $378,032.14, or 1.58 per cent, for lighthouses and buoys. Not to go into detail on other matters, Magoon increased the roads of Cuba 124.6 per cent above what they were when he took charge, or 158 per cent if those left to be completed in the first few months of the Gómez régime may be included. The value of his work may be illustrated by the case of a road which tapped the territory of seven sugar estates in Matanzas. The cost of getting sugar to port was reduced in this instance from ninety cents a bag to fifty. Among other expenditures under the heading of public works were $4,415,468.05 for sanitation, $2,033,724.81 for the construction, improvement, or repair of 156 government buildings, and $1,464,041.95 for water supply and drainage. In addition to smaller sums for other purposes expended by the Department of Public Works, some of the lesser matters were taken care of by other departments,—for example, work on hospitals, jails, and rural guard barracks in the Department of Government. Much of the work was of the sort that would be done by local governments in the United States, but that was not possible on the existing basis of municipal revenues in Cuba. It is worthy of note, too, that most of the public works undertaken were in response to legislation by Congress in the time of Estrada Palma. For example, of the $22,958,659.36 expended in the Department of Public Works, no less than eighty-eight per cent was based on congressional appropriations or on authorizations for services for which inadequate sums were provided, leaving only $1,660,506.41 worth due wholly to the initiative of the provisional government.

Cuban writers admit the volume of Magoon's achievements in the realm of public works, but make numerous charges tending to detract from any credit to him on account of them. None of these are precise enough to merit attention, except that the works, more especially the roads, were extravagantly but poorly constructed, and did not last. In the absence of any better precise evidence concerning these charges the following statement made to the writer by an American who built one of the roads may be worth noting:

"The handling of road-building was in charge of Colonel W. M. Black, who was absolutely honest. The trouble with the roads was that too great an attempt was made to make a record for mileage. So, only certain portions of the roads were really very good. The rest was left for President Gómez to finish, but Gómez wished to make a record on his own account, with the result that Magoon's roads were allowed to go to rack and ruin. The newspapers charged vast corruption at that time in connection with these roads, but I know personally that the charges were untrue."

Magoon himself recognized that the roads would not last unless kept in repair, and he established what he intended to be a permanent force for attending to the work. In Cuba, however, "roads" is a word used like "patriotism" in many countries as a purely political device. Unfortunately it is to the advantage of a politician for his predecessor's roads to be bad and for those built by himself to make a showing in mileage and at least temporary serviceability. Magoon's roads may have been good or they may have been poor, but in either case they were doomed. Politics, plus heavy rains and the narrow-tired, two-wheeled Cuban cart, were sure sooner or later to account for them.

Obviously, since the Magoon government began with a deficit it was necessary to pay for a large part of expenditures out of revenues. Fortunately, and contrary to expectation, receipts from the custom-house were greater than ever down to February 1908, when the current set in the other way. The large sugar crop of 1907 and the stimulus of the public works program (through import of equipment and the free spending of amounts earned in wages) were helpful factors, as also was the considerable amount of travel to the island in these years. The financial misfortunes of 1907, however, when coupled with the political deterrent of a formal announcement of the intended withdrawal by the United States not later than February 1909, at length overcame the prosperity of the custom-house. Nevertheless, by December 1, 1908, all works were paid for to November 1, 1908, and expenditures for the remaining months were ordered curtailed. In his message to Congress of April 5, 1909, President Gómez said that he found $2,809,479.08 in the treasury, with obligations amounting to $11,920,824.54, leaving a deficit of $9,111,-345.46. Not all of this was chargeable to the provisional government. There was one item of $1,613,019 on credits granted by previous governments.[20] Assuming that these figures are correct and that the other debts had been incurred by the Magoon régime, it would mean a debit of some

[20] *Mensajes presidenciales*, I, 201.

seven millions and a half for which it was responsible, which is a long way from the vast amounts usually tossed off lightly by critics of Magoon as the deficit from his rule.[21] Furthermore, it compared very favorably with the situation that confronted the provisional government at the outset. An expert accounting of the books of the Estrada Palma and the Magoon administrations might even show that the latter *saved* something, for the actual deficit with which it began may well have been greater than the one it left. In any event, the Magoon deficit meant little or nothing, for every barometer of business life pointed clearly to an era of prosperity under José Miguel. And in the background of that prosperity when it arrived were the achievements of the Magoon government, which overcame a series of financial ills that in consequence were spared to the next administration.[22]

[21] Barbarrosa says in one place that the deficit would perhaps be "seventy-two million" and in another "nearly seventy." Barbarrosa: 77; 84.

[22] For authorities on this chapter, see comment at the end of chapter XI

CHAPTER XI

THE RESTORATION OF CUBAN GOVERNMENT

THE criticisms of the Magoon government on financial matters have very little foundation in fact. Its handling of political questions may in some particulars be less worthy of approval, but in certain of them it deserves unstinted praise. Especially is this so in the field of legislation. The great body of Cuban law consisted of provisions enacted for the Spanish peninsula, subsequently extended to Cuba, and there modified by royal orders or by orders of the military government of the United States or laws of the Cuban Congress. Most of it was monarchical in type and directly contrary to the spirit of the excessively liberal Cuban Constitution. The Cuban Congress, however, was too little informed about legislative matters and too busy with political discussions to enact the supplementary laws that were needed to give the Constitution its full effect.[1] This failure of Congress was one of the important causes in the background of the revolution of 1906, and it had to be remedied in certain particulars before the government could be turned back to the Cuban people. It was impossible to do the work through the medium of the Cuban Congress, as Taft and Bacon had gone on record to the effect that the rights of membership of those elected in 1905 had been vitiated by fraud, and had

[1] For a general discussion of this subject, see chapter XXI. An admirable statement of the legislative problem of the Magoon government is Crowder, Enoch Herbert, *Report of department of state and justice*, in Republic of Cuba, *Report of provisional administration from October 13th, 1906 to December 1st, 1907*, pp. 119-139.

247

made the resignation of these men one of the tenets in their peace compromise. That left but half a Congress,—not enough for the legal quorum of two-thirds. So it was decided that the provisional government should dispense with Congress. On December 3, 1906, Governor Magoon formally vacated the places of the congressmen elected in 1905, and took over responsibility for legislation himself. On December 24, 1906, Magoon appointed a body called the Advisory Law Commission to make the necessary studies on legislative matters. It consisted of nine Cubans and three Americans, with Colonel Enoch Herbert Crowder as the presiding officer.[2] The achievements of the Commission were due primarily to Colonel Crowder, whose record as an indefatigable worker is now well known. This was the man who was later to raise the American army for the World War and who has since become United States ambassador to Cuba. From this time forward he was to play in important part in the affairs of the republic. The Commission was charged with the duty of preparing five laws suggested by Taft and Bacon, concerning elections, provinces, municipalities, the judiciary, and the civil service, but it later proved necessary to enact yet others.

Both the municipal and the provincial law of Cuba were based on Spanish laws of 1878, with subsequent modifications which made no substantial change. As a result, a great deal of confusion developed, for, while the Constitution provided for a most broad local self-government, the Spanish law gave a supervisory control, amounting to centralization, to the general authorities in Havana. Since Congress had enacted no satisfactory legislation, the inconsistent Spanish

[2] Best known among the Cuban members were Alfredo Zayas and Juan Gualberto Gómez, the latter being secretary of the commission. The other two Americans were Judge Otto Schoenrich and Major Blanton C. Winship.

law prevailed over the Constitution, and had been made use of by the Estrada Palma administration.   One of the difficulties over the municipal law came up in connection with taxation.   The municipalities lacked resources to enable them to carry on functions ordinarily exercised by local governments in the United States.   This was remedied to some extent by opening up new avenues of income.   On the other hand, the excessively broad local autonomy that might have been interpreted as granted by the Constitution was limited by prescribing the exact forms of taxation which were to be regarded as not in conflict with the tax system of the national government, with which the Constitution forbade the municipalities to interfere.   The municipal law was promulgated on May 29, 1908, and put in force on October 1st by a decree of September 21.   In this instance, as also in the case of other laws, the Commission first published the document to the country, afterward making some revisions in response to criticisms and suggestions.   As a supplement to the municipal law it was deemed necessary to prepare two other laws.   These two, the municipal tax law and the municipal accounting law, were duly drafted, therefore, and put into effect also as of October 1st by decrees of September 21.

The provincial law was a more difficult problem, for the provincial government of the Constitution was really an anomaly of Cuban life.   There had been provinces under Spain, but merely as administrative subdivisions of the central government.   Furthermore, the municipalities answered all the needs of local government, for they took in not only the towns but also the surrounding country, much like an American county.   So with the national government on the one side and the municipalities on the other, there was little for the provincial governments to do.   They voted appropriations for minor public works and a few scholarships, but with the single exception of the province of Havana (where the difference was very slight) more was expended on provincial salaries than on public works; for example, the total budget of 1906-1907 for Pinar del Río was $46,320, of which $31,280 went in personnel, $5,000 in public works, and the rest on scholarships! But the provincial governments were in the Constitution; so about all the new law could do was to cut down the excessive number of employes and reduce the pay of provincial councillors to a *per diem* allowance. This law also was promulgated on September 21, 1908, to go into effect October 1st.

In preparing a judiciary law the Commission found that it was so involved with other laws of the republic that there was not time enough during the term of the intervention to do much more than try to protect the courts from interference by the executive. The judicial system was based on a Spanish law of 1891, which made the courts subordinate to the governor-general, while the Constitution made them independent. As Congress had neglected to legislate on the matter, the republican government had followed the Spanish law. Local affairs were involved, for the Constitution had provided that disputes between municipalities or provinces and the executive should be settled in the courts, but the executive had overawed the judges. The new law endeavored to correct this situation, and also provided for the intervention of the Supreme Court in appointments to lesser judicial bodies above the rank of municipal court. Revisions of the civil code, criminal code, code of civil procedure, code of criminal procedure, and commercial code (based on Spanish laws of 1889, 1879, 1885, 1889, and 1886) could not be completed, as experience in Porto Rico and the Philippines had shown that many years would be needed for the work, but some study of the subject was undertaken, and Colonel

Crowder recommended that the reëstablishment of the republic should be under "adequate guarantees that this work . . . shall be prosecuted to as speedy a conclusion as is possible."[3] Minus these desirable adjuncts, the judiciary law was promulgated prior to the end of the intervention, on January 27, 1909.

Among other important laws that were enacted, growing out of the work of the Commission, was a civil service law after the pattern of the one in the United States.[4] A great many laws were still needed, but the Commission had no time to prepare them.[5] The immense amount of labor that went into the work of the Commission has been barely more than hinted at here. And unfortunately the careful provisions of the laws it made had later to be administered by men to whom laws and the Constitution were as nothing "among friends," in consequence of which the evils they were designed to correct continued as before. It was worth something, however, to get the laws on the books.

The most important work of the Commission was considered to be the preparation of an election law, under which elections could be held as a preliminary to bringing the intervention to an end. A law was drafted which aimed to meet the various improper practices that had developed, as well as to put into effect the provisions of the Constitution. Comment on the law need not be given here.[6] It was ready by December 30, 1907, but was first published for criticism, and

[3] Crowder, *Op. cit.,* in Republic of Cuba, *Op. cit.,* 139. These laws, however, have yet to be enacted. Cf. *infra,* pp. 515-520.

[4] For a list of the laws of this period in supplement to the Constitution that still survive, see *infra,* pp. 516-517. Other laws dating back to Spanish times, but redrafted by the Commission and not put into effect or since changed fundamentally were a law of the executive power, a law of armed forces, a drainage and irrigation law, a telephone law, a notarial law, a mortgage law, and a game law. Other laws of the Magoon era are listed in Republic of Cuba, *Report of provisional administration from December 1st, 1907 to December 1st, 1908,* pp. 99-101.

[5] See *infra,* p. 517.

[6] It is considered *infra* at pp. 568-574.

later promulgated on April 1, 1908. Following a trial of the law in the provincial and municipal elections of August 1st, it was modified and promulgated anew on September 11. One of its main features was a careful registration of voters. This involved the taking of a census in order to find out who were entitled to vote. Under the direction of Victor Hugo Olmstead, an American, the census was taken between September 30 and November 14, 1907. The work was very well done, and by February 1908 the results were ready. It appeared that there were 419,342 voters in a population of 2,048,980, but efforts of party managers later raised the list of voters to 466,745,—a rather high percentage, but one which seems not to have occasioned any criticism. The secondary results of the census were, of course, interesting. Population had increased some thirty per cent from the 1,572,845 of the census of 1899 to 2,048,980. There were 1,074,882 males to 974,098 females; 1,428,176 whites to 620,804 people of color; 725,894 at least ten years old who were literate (which meant little more than that they could sign their names), against 643,615 who were not, but a majority of those eligible to vote were in the latter group! Among 228,741 foreign-born, 185,393 were Spaniards, 11,217 Chinese, and 6713 Americans.

The expectation at the outset was that the intervention would be a brief affair,—just long enough for elections to be held to put a Cuban government in control. It was at first believed that the elections might take place on January 1, 1907, but the date was advanced by general agreement to May 1907, to ensure tranquility until the sugar crop could be harvested, and later still further advanced, owing to the immense amount of preliminary work that had to be done. The failure to see how prolonged the intervention would be may have given rise to some of the practices for which the Magoon government has been most criticized.   It has been charged in particular with having been too indulgent with the politicians, especially in the giving of jobs and the grant of pardons.[7]   The Liberals had made a great pretence of fighting for principles, not for jobs, but they gave neither Taft nor Magoon much peace in their efforts to get the plums of office.   They appointed a committee, dominated by the revolutionary generals, to indicate whom they wished to be named.[8]   Later this committee was reconstituted so as to be made up equally of the three principal parties which took the field for the 1908 elections, and its suggestions were taken by the Magoon government.   When posts were open, the committee decided what party should get the appointment, leaving the party selected to name the man.   Frank Steinhart, whose "information and experience were especially helpful in handling political matters," acted as chairman of this committee, and, indeed, as Magoon's right hand man in kindred questions.

This would have been very well, but it is quite generally asserted that Magoon gave a number of soft jobs for purely political purposes, in order to keep turbulent spirits from stirring up trouble.   While it is difficult to get precise evidence on this score, it is more than probable that the post of secretary of the Advisory Law Commission, given to Juan Gualberto Gómez, was such a position, and it is quite likely that there were others.   It was a policy that may have seemed

[7] For example, in Barbarrosa, 83. Various other charges are too little backed up by evidence or too trivial to merit extended comment.   One such concerned permits to foreigners to practice pharmacy. See Barbarrosa, 76, and Republic of Cuba, *Report of provisional administration from December 1st, 1907 to December 1st, 1908*, pp. 94-96.

[8] The names of the Liberal committee read almost like a catalogue of the generals of the war. "Pino" Guerra was president; Eduardo Guzmán vice-president; Ernesto Asbert secretary; and Alfredo Zayas, José Miguel Gómez, Juan Gualberto Gómez, Tomás Recio, Demetrio Castillo Duany, José Monteagudo, and Carlos García Vélez were the others.

for the moment best calculated to keep the peace, but it was a great mistake; it gave the Cubans a handle that they were not slow to grasp, and in recent years they have been prone to excuse existing corruption on the ground that Magoon introduced the *"botella,"* as these appointments are called.[9] The claim is of course absurd, in that the *botella* under other names had probably been employed almost from the day the Spaniards set foot in Cuba. The United States authorities should have realized, however, that the Hispanic American memory of any American administrative impropriety is long and almost gloating. It would be interesting to know if Secretary Taft was cognizant of these appointments. If he were not, it must have been because he turned a deaf ear toward Havana, for they were denounced noisily in Cuba. On the score of the government's prodigality in this respect Martínez Ortiz says:

"The government . . . opened its hands and let loose the purse-strings without any consideration whatever. It had no other idea than that of pleasing the 'Committee on Petitions,' great provider of jobs. Mr. Magoon did not know how to say 'No'; he always answered 'Amen,' and signed the papers . . . The governor defended himself from his critics by saying he was doing nothing but accede to the requests of the great Cuban politicians. He washed his hands of the matter; he could not stop to be proper when those who were most interested were desirous of throwing the house through the window." [10]

From this it appears that the "great Cuban politicians" provided the initial impulse for these bad practices, but that does not excuse the provisional government. It is somewhat amusing, though, that the crimes of the said great politicians have been forgotten, while those imputed to Magoon go on forever.

On the score of pardons, too, it is probable that there was

[9] The word *botella*, or bottle, is used on the analogy of the nursing-bottle, with rich milk for the political baby. [10] Martínez Ortiz, II, 853.

some justice in the criticisms against Magoon. It would seem that he granted an excessive number, again yielding too easily to the importunings of politicians. There was some excuse in the disorder of the times (though political crimes were pretty well taken care of through the medium of amnesties) and especially in the severity of the Spanish law, which gave a trial judge no option for leniency in imposing sentence, if technical guilt were established. Thus, the executive in Cuba acted as a kind of final court of appeal, rather than as in the United States, where the pardon is in some sense a derogation of law, instead of a recognized part of legal procedure. Magoon pointed out that General Wood and Estrada Palma also granted a great number of pardons, but confused amnesties with pardons, and did not take into account the special circumstances (already described) attending the jail-delivery in the era of General Wood. As for Estrada Palma he issued but very few individual pardons, though a number of delinquents were freed by amnesty bills.[11] The number issued by Magoon is not clear. Magoon said there were 1110 pardons in 5183 petitions that had been acted upon up to September 30, 1908, but presumably included in this calculation those who were amnestied.[12] Trelles claims he gave 1140 pardons, mostly for common crimes.[13] And Fernando Ortiz says Estrada Palma pardoned an average of six a month, to forty-six for Magoon.[14] It is all too probable that the Magoon government, possibly on instructions from Washington, was, not corruptly, but mistakenly, pursuing the too gentle policy with which it has so often been accused.

[11] See *infra*, pp. 538-539.
[12] Republic of Cuba, *Report of provisional administration from December 1st, 1907 to December 1st, 1908*, pp. 87-94.
[13] Trelles, *El progreso (1902 a 1905) y el retroceso (1906 a 1922) de la república de Cuba*, 9.
[14] Ortiz, 15.

When these things are said, all else must be placed on the credit side of the Magoon government's account. Even its enemies acknowledge that it maintained order and gave the country two honest elections.[15]   In the background of this accomplishment was the American Army of Cuban Pacification, commanded in turn by generals James Franklin Bell, Theodore Jonathan Wint, and Thomas Henry Barry. After the departure of the marines, whom Taft had caused to be landed before the regular army came, the American forces ranged in numbers from 5300 to six thousand men, stationed at many different posts in the island. They were not called upon to do any fighting, but were a moral force tending to check possible major disturbances. The principal work in the suppression of banditry and political conspiracies was left to the rural guards. The increase in the numbers of this body has already been alluded to. It was also necessary to restore its prestige, which had been damaged by its use as a political agency in 1905. An effort was made to confine its activities to the rural districts, leaving the local police to handle disorder in the towns. By 1908 the credit of the guards was so thoroughly reëstablished that their conduct was praised by all parties. Provision was also made for a permanent army, separate from the rural guards, in a law of armed forces, prepared by the Advisory Law Commission. It was felt that a military establishment might be good insurance against an outbreak such as had occurred in 1906. The appointment of a commander-in-chief for the army was one that was considered too delicate for the incoming Cuban government to solve, as there were too many generals with an eye on the job. So one of the last acts of the Magoon government was to take this responsibility upon itself. "Pino" Guerra was selected, and José Monteagudo was

[15] For example, Barbarrosa: 81; 83.

named to head the rural guards. Somewhat earlier, in May 1908, "Pino" Guerra was given a trip to the United States and France to witness army maneuvers. Possibly the provisional government thought it was much safer, for the time being, for this gentleman to get his military education outside of Cuba rather than in it.

The rural guards did not lack work to do, though at all times able to cope with whatever situation arose. There were several minor outbreaks which endeavored to dignify themselves with the name of revolution. One such occurred late in 1906 near Rancho Veloz, province of Santa Clara. An uneasy spirit named Arturo Mendoza started another in Santa Clara early in 1907, and Urbano Guerra went out in Oriente in October of that year. These disturbances were all easily taken care of. Seemingly more serious for a time was a conspiracy headed by the self-styled "General" Mazó Parra, aided by Lara Miret, Juan Ducasse, and other "generals." Mazó was a notorious revolutionist in the Caribbean world. He had fought on the patriot side for a while in the Cuban war of '95-'98, and then deserted to the Spaniards. General Wood and Estrada Palma denied him admittance when he sought to return to Cuba, but he was allowed to land in the island during the summer of 1907. Straightway he organized a plot, with wide ramifications, for the overthrow of the provisional government, planning on the destruction of foreign properties and the killing of Americans as a first step in the uprising. The Magoon government kept in touch with the movement, and arrested the conspirators on September 26, the day before the time set for the insurrection. In addition to the above-named affairs there were a number of marauding bands to attend to, but the rural guards did their work so well that banditry had virtually ceased to exist by the end of the intervention.

Cuban public men were less concerned over the economic, legislative, or administrative reforms of the Magoon government than over the question of the political succession. A new party situation had developed. The Moderates met on November 3, 1906, and formally dissolved their organization. An attempt was then made to form a party on the basis of a reform of the Constitution in the direction of conservatism. At first the movement broke down, because it was recognized that no party could hope to win an election on such a platform, even though intelligent men recognized the desirability of the changes proposed. Meanwhile, from the very beginning of the intervention there was trouble in the Liberal camp. The Liberals had gone into the Revolution of August on the basis of leaving presidential candidacies for later decision, which seemed to imply that the Gómez nomination was at least subject to change. The majority of the Liberal leaders now proposed to drop Gómez, hinting that he had been captured somewhat too easily in 1906, and at the same time praising Zayas, whom they put forward for the presidency, claiming that he had won a victory for the Liberals in his handling of the negotiations with the American commissioners. Gómez still had his partisans, and they belittled the "victory" of Zayas which had been followed by intervention. The quarrel became bitter, and occasioned much embarassment to the provisional government in its endeavor to award political jobs to Liberals. Right at the start of Magoon's rule it seemed impossible to get either faction to consent to appointees for Cabinet Secretaries who belonged to the other group. On this account, at Taft's suggestion, Magoon made the chief clerks of departments acting heads, with an American adviser who was virtually in charge. Later it was necessary to appoint Americans as temporary governors of the provinces, for the Cuban politicians could not agree on candidates among themselves. And there was a lot of bickering over the lesser jobs, for Gómez would not recognize the nominees of the original, Zayas-controlled Liberal committee. It was on this account that the committee was later reconstituted.

This dissension among the Liberals caused a revival of hope among conservative elements for the founding of a new party, and in this they were encouraged by Magoon. Cuban writers insist that the United States authorities wanted to see a Liberal victory in the elections, as in some manner justifying the stand taken by Taft and Bacon, but a split in the Liberal party afforded no prospect for self-congratulation, and so the government hoped for a conservative opposition that might force the Liberals to come together. At any rate, there were fresh meetings of men of conservative leanings, and by early summer of 1907 the Conservative party was formally launched. It insisted it had no connection with the old Moderate party, and, of course, it had a platform, which included the proposed constitutional changes, though leaving them for an indefinite future. In point of fact, however, it was clearly understood that the election was to be fought on the basis of personalities, not principles. As Magoon put it,

"There was no discussion of platforms or of differences of principles but the campaign was based entirely on the records of the parties and the personality of the candidates. There being no political issues as understood in the United States, the political speaker is confined to the personal merits of his candidate and lack of merit of the candidate of the opposition; in order to enthuse his auditors he appeals to their patriotism, invokes the spirits of Martí, Máximo Gómez, Maceo and other names dear to the Cuban people and declares that he preserves in his mind and heart the spirit that actuated them." [16]

[16] Republic of Cuba, *Report of provisional administration from December 1st, 1907 to December 1st, 1908,* p. 67. This, together with "bombastic utterances" against the United States, may be taken as the norm of Cuban political speeches, both in 1908 and ever since.

On April 8, 1907, Secretary Taft visited Havana for a two-day stay, and took occasion to give a decision on the election date question. All parties agreed that the originally suggested early dates would be impracticable, and were not only willing, but eager, to have the intervention continue until such preliminary matters as the census and the municipal and electoral laws were satisfactorily resolved. This speaks volumes for their confidence in President Roosevelt and the United States! Taft decided that there should be two elections, one for municipal and provincial officials, and the other for those of the national government. Neither was set definitely, but it was understood that the first would be held as soon as practicable, presumably in 1908, and the second soon afterward. A gentle warning was given that they must be conducted peacefully, if the intervention were to end at all. The same admonition had already appeared in public statements of Roosevelt and Root, and was repeated by the former in his annual message of 1907. By the spring of 1908 there were three principal parties in the field, the two Liberal groups and the Conservatives. The followers of Gómez, known popularly as "Miguelistas," called themselves the "Historic Liberals," claiming that the election of 1905 was no election and that therefore Gómez was still the true Liberal candidate. The Zayas supporters, or "Zayistas," retained the name "Liberals," on the basis of the lapse of the Gómez candidacy and the superior claims of Zayas. Each group made formal nominations. The Conservatives preferred to await the result of the local elections before putting a presidential ticket in the field. There were yet other parties, but none was important at this time. One of them was later to attain to great prominence, the so-called Independent Party of Color, formed in 1907 by Evaristo Estenoz, a negro who had been an insurrectionist general in the uprising of 1906. Leading colored men, such, for example, as Senator Morúa Delgado, denounced this party, pointing out that it might mean a race war and that foreign interests would never consent to the existence of another black republic in the Caribbean. So the negroes had nothing to gain by it.

Eventually the local elections were set for August 1, 1908, and the national elections for November 14. As the former approached, the two Liberal groups demanded that the provincial governors be relieved of their posts, lest they act unfairly in favor of the Conservatives. These governors had been elected in 1905, but had been left in office, together with the councillors elected at the same time, so that the provincial governments could be kept up on some sort of legal basis. In the spring of 1908 the term of office of half of the councillors, those elected in February 1904, expired, leaving only the half elected in the fall of 1905. So it was decided to ask for the resignations of these councillors and the different governors. Accordingly, they were relieved, and, as already mentioned, succeeded by American army officers, who seem to have given entire satisfaction. The elections of August 1st passed off without disagreeable incident, —except that the Zayistas suffered a grievous disillusionment. They ran a poor third. The Conservatives won the governorship of three provinces, to two for the Miguelistas, and one for the Zayistas, while each party got respectively twenty-eight, thirty-five, and eighteen mayors, with one going independent. Altogether, sixty per cent of the vote was cast, and it was clear that the two Liberal groups, if united, would have had a vast majority over the Conservatives. The men chosen at this election went into office on October 1st, at which time the new municipal and provincial laws were put into effect. The municipal officials were the first that had been elected since 1901, for the failure of Congress to enact a municipal law had left no legal basis for an election during the Estrada Palma era.

The elections of August 1st were recognized as fair, and accepted by all parties. It was now clear, however, that a divided Liberal party could not win. So an arrangement was made whereby Gómez was to become the joint candidate of the two groups for the presidency and Zayas for the vice-presidency. Each group maintained its own organization, but agreed on a distribution of offices. The Conservatives could not believe that the fusion would carry all members of the two parties, and now entered the final campaign with enthusiasm, formally nominating General Menocal and Rafael Montoro on August 24 as their standard-bearers. Menocal has already made his appearance in these pages. Montoro had been an Autonomist and Spanish sympathizer in the nineties, but was a man of recognized ability and prestige. Again there was an exciting campaign, fairly conducted, and this time the united Liberals won. They elected, not only Gómez and Zayas, but also all twenty-four senators, and fifty-one representatives as against thirty-two, on a vote of 201,199 to 130,256. In all, seventy-one per cent of the vote was cast. The best of order prevailed, and leaders of the defeated party congratulated their opponents on the victory. The holding of these elections had entailed an enormous amount of labor, what with instruction in the new law, preparation of election equipment, and the maintenance of order. Colonel Crowder, as acting head of the Central Electoral Board, had everything in charge, and, as Magoon put it, a large share of the success of the two elections was due to his indefatigable energy. Magoon was very enthusiastic over the whole affair, but Martínez Ortiz points out that the elections proved nothing, as they were under

American supervision. And in point of fact it is probable that Cuba has never had such well conducted elections, either before or since. It was generally admitted that they were in all respects correct. Martínez Ortiz says the United States authorities hoped Gómez would win, but did nothing to incline the balance in his favor,[17] and that, undoubtedly, should be the verdict of history.

It was time to wind up the accounts of the intervention. There were many who regretted that it had to end at all. Magoon commented in his 1907 report on the discussions going on advocating annexation to the United States, and wondered if there might be some way to stop this talk. "Doubtless the desire to be brought under the jurisdiction and direction of the Government of the United States continues to prevail among the large alien contingent and a small number of Cubans who own property and fear a recurrence of disorder," he said.[18] Martínez Ortiz remarks the existence of this feeling as a result of the various uprisings of 1907, which caused some people to lose faith in the future.[19] And an article in Lippincott's for January 1908, signed "An English Resident," urged the United States to keep the island, saying that "sooner or later" the Cubans would have to be governed "from Washington." [20] The distinguished American journalist Henry Watterson was representative of another group that doubted Cuban ability at self-government, but felt that the Cubans ought to have their chance to try it.[21]

[17] Martínez Ortiz, II, 807.
[18] Republic of Cuba, *Report of provisional administration from October 13th, 1906 to December 1st, 1907*, pp. 34-35.
[19] Martínez Ortiz, II, 798.
[20] *The problem of Cuba*, in *Lippincott's monthly magazine*, v. LXXXI, pp. 142-144; Jan., 1908.

[21] In explaining his lack of confidence in their political character, Watterson first spoke favorably of some of the Cuban leaders, and then went on as follows about the people lower down: "But, the riff-raff; Lord, the riff-raff; injin, nigger, beggar-man, thief, — 'both m o n g r e l, puppy, whelp and hound, and cur of

The problem of the prosperous alien class, which lacked confidence in the republic, was indeed considered by the provisional government. At one time it thought of imposing Cuban citizenship on all foreign residents in a blanket act. This raised a storm of protest from Cuban and foreigner alike. The foreigners did not wish to lose their right to the protection of their home governments or to be injected into island politics, and as for the Spaniards both they and the Cubans felt that not time enough had passed to allay the bitterness of the War of Independence era. Both elements also protested when it was proposed to give foreigners the vote, without citizenship. In this connection it was pointed out that foreigners were in the majority among those of voting age in many cities, including Havana itself. A compromise was arranged whereby they might stand for election to municipal councils, though not permitted to vote.

There was never any doubt about the intention of the United States to withdraw from Cuba, whatever some of the residents of the island might have desired. Taft had at one time assumed that it would be fifteen months from the time of the completion of the census before the United States would get out, which would have brought the end of the intervention in April 1909. But Roosevelt, desirous, no doubt, of winding up this affair during his own term (which expired in March 1909), gave orders early in 1908 that Cuba should be turned over to her own officials not later than February 1, 1909, but sooner if possible. Eventually the date was set for January 28, 1909, the anniversary of the birth of Martí. On January 2, 1909, Magoon issued a call for the newly elected Congress to meet on the 13th. As part

low degree' . . . When the pie is cut, when the offices are filled, what of the rejected ones? Will each turn conspirator?" Watterson, Henry, *Again* '*Cuba libre,*' in Havana *Post,* Jan. 29, 1909. Most assuredly there was something more than doggerel in these lines!

of his decree he enacted laws tending to prevent the old quorum-breaking evil.[22]   This part of his message was not very well received, and many congressmen said they would later make short work of it, which they did.   In the absence of any congressmen except the half of the Senate (elected in 1903) whose terms expired in April 1910, a full number of senators and representatives had been chosen, instead of the usual half.   To bring the situation into accord with the Constitution, the representatives drew lots for the two and four year terms, and senators were elected for periods ending in 1913 and 1917, with the latter not taking their seats until the "lame ducks," or "senators of the reserve," as they were called in Cuba, should vacate them in 1910.   The two houses organized with Morúa Delgado, a "reserve" senator, as president of the Senate for the time being, and the brilliant Italian-born Orestes Ferrara as president of the House.

The day of withdrawal, January 28, 1909, passed off with the normally to be expected ceremonial and enthusiasm. Some of the declarations of Magoon's final message are all that need be noted here.   He pointed out that the President of the United States understood that article two of the Permanent Treaty prohibited Cuba from assuming or contracting any public debt in excess of that already existing, without the approval of the United States, and in this connection he stated that it was the final and conclusive resolution of the provisional government that all claims of the Army of Liberation had been satisfied by legislation already enacted and no fresh indebtedness on this score would be recognized.   Thus, one raid on the treasury was settled, and as the Magoon pronouncement had all the force of a condition precedent to a restoration of Cuban government the famous appendix to the Constitution was just so much the more reinforced.   That

[22] For the terms of this section of the decree, see *infra*, p. 512.

same day, Magoon departed from Cuba on a United States cruiser. He left amidst—for the moment—much plaudits. The city of Havana made him an "adopted son," and newspapers praised him—for the moment! Later, the chorus started a different tune, and nobody tried to drown it out. So it gathered momentum, and became an established hymn of scorn, if not of hate. Watterson said that the Magoon government, though benevolent, seemed oppressive to the Cubans, who would have preferred to be ruled by Spain rather than by the United States. This was probably true. What the Cubans really objected to was, not the shortcomings of Magoon, real or alleged, but the fact that he was an American, embodying the methods and spirit of American rule. A Spaniard might have committed twice as many errors and a Cuban ten times as many, without getting half the criticism; there would have been plenty at the time, but it would have been forgotten ten years later. Only a man like General Wood, with a Root-Wood policy, could weather the storm. So the charges against Magoon are primarily a medium for the expression of a racial emotion. José Miguel Gómez was actually to commit the various crimes imputed to Magoon, and José Miguel is now a national hero, while Magoon remains anathema.

In point of fact Magoon rendered excellent service, subject to the limitations in political policy that have already been mentioned. As Watterson put it,

"Magoon, the Magician, is the proper name for him. His work here has been far-reaching. It has been all-embracing. It has caused two blades of grass to grow where but one had grown before." He found Cuba "clouded by the smoke of burning property and military campfires. He leaves it echoing with the hum of industrial activity and overspread by the aroma of nearly one hundred mills grinding day and night." [23]

[23] Watterson, *Op. cit.*

It could hardly have been otherwise, for Magoon had as his aides a number of men who have since proved themselves in yet larger fields of activity. Two of these demand special mention, Frank Steinhart and Colonel Crowder. Common gossip always associates the name of Steinhart with the supposed iniquities of the Magoon administration. The writer has often heard Magoon referred to as "Frank Steinhart's office boy." Charges are also made that Steinhart owed his later financial success as the head of the Havana Electric Railway Light and Power Company to valuable franchises improperly given to him by Magoon. This charge may easily be disposed of. The one franchise acquired by Steinhart during the Magoon era was for an extension of the street railway system. This was awarded only after study and favorable recommendation by Colonel Crowder,—and anybody who questions the integrity of Enoch H. Crowder is not going to get very far! Steinhart was, not "the boss," but a big help to Magoon, who in his two annual reports warmly expressed his appreciation of Steinhart's services. Steinhart's knowledge of the customs, people, and personages of the country was of invaluable assistance. To be sure, he was associated with the system employed in awarding patronage, but he did not inaugurate that policy, and probably Magoon did not, either. His practical aid to Magoon was certainly one of the prime factors in the maintenance of order under the provisional government.

In the case of Colonel Crowder there has never been any question about the disinterestedness of the services he rendered. As Martínez Ortiz says of him in connection with what he did on the Advisory Law Commission:

"He was a tireless worker, always at the anvil. He did not rest, day or night. Well earned were the eulogies which were given in his honor.

All the other members of that body did their duty. But Colonel Crowder was its soul,—its driving will." [24]

Crowder was not only president of the Commission. As supervisor of the Department of State and Justice he was also virtual head of this important branch, and he was the legal adviser of the other departments, besides having the management of the successful elections of 1908. Magoon's reports several times singled him out for special and enthusiastic praise. And, indeed, Crowder failed—if he failed at all—only in that he may have placed too high a rating on Cuban political capacity. His legislation, with ordinarily honest administration, should have been waterproof, but later experience was to show that it wasn't. The basis is still there for good government, however, when, or if, it comes, and Crowder's manifold other services to Cuba, both in the Magoon era and since 1919, entitle him to the respect and the gratitude (which he may not get) of the Cuban people.

Martínez Ortiz, who made no such thoroughgoing study of this period as he did of the Wood and Estrada Palma years, aims as usual to be fair in his estimate of the Magoon régime, praising it for its taking the census, the legislation of the Advisory Law Commission, its maintenance of order, the correct handling of the elections, and its achievements in the realm of public works. He condemns it for extravagance and the job-giving and pardon evils. Sydney Brooks, writing from the standpoint of an observer, but not an investigator, says of the Magoon rule: "Its sole merit as a Government was that it kept the peace." [25] That is a bit ungenerous, but undoubtedly it is the really greatest thing that can be said of it from the standpoint of history.

[24] Martínez Ortiz, II, 849.
[25] Brooks, Sydney, *Cuba,* in *Fort-* *nightly review,* v. XCIV, pp. 796-806, at 802; Nov., 1910.

It tried to do more, and succeeded for the time being, but it could not make its Cuban successors maintain its roads and bridges or give effect to its laws. It kept the peace, and turned back the government to the Cuban people on a working basis. That is perhaps its epitaph. And for that much at least, it deserves credit.[26]

[26] By all odds the most important source for the period of the provisional government are the two *Report* volumes of Governor Magoon, of 1907 and 1908. They contain a wealth of data on all phases of the intervention. Martínez Ortiz (v. II) is less noteworthy for this period than for the earlier years of his work. He seems to be hurrying to a finish, and is interested only in the Cuban political succession. Subject to that limitation his treatment has the same high qualities of judicial-minded fairness that is so conspicuous of it elsewhere. The Taft and Bacon *Report,* used so extensively in chapter IX, has a direct bearing on the beginnings of the intervention, and is an always important factor in the background. This is a favorite period for treatment in periodical articles, some of which have interesting material, though few or none embody any real investigation. A good monograph might well be written on the provisional government.

CHAPTER XII

THE MOST TYPICALLY CUBAN PRESIDENT: GÓMEZ, 1909-1913

IF THERE might be an honest vote in Cuba to determine who had been the most popular President, José Miguel Gómez would assuredly get first place. This would not be because of any particularly great achievements of his administration, and most certainly it would not be on account of its integrity, a characteristic that very few of the Gómez supporters themselves would claim for it. Gómez is popular though his improprieties are well known and quite generally admitted. One explanation of this is that he more nearly resembled the typically likeable Cuban than any of the other men who have attained to the presidency. And, furthermore, though his faults would have made him an impossible figure in the higher political ranks of the United States, he had virtues, too. Whatever may be said against him, there is also much that is in his favor.

Born in the important and thoroughly Cuban old town of Sancti Spíritus on July 6, 1858, and member of an old Cuban family, Gómez received the equivalent of a high school education, and then, in 1875, joined the insurrectionists in the Ten Years' War. He also went out in the minor uprising of 1879, and became a lieutenant-colonel. From 1879 to 1895 he remained in Sancti Spíritus, occupied with the affairs of his father's estate. On the outbreak of war in 1895 he put himself at the head of the Sancti Spíritus brigade in the patriot army and rose rapidly until he be-

came a major-general. It does not appear that he played
an outstandingly prominent part in the conflict. At any
rate, his services were confined to his native province of
Santa Clara, in which he became a virtual political chief,
as well as a military leader of some renown. He surrounded
himself with a number of brilliant young men, who were
later to be among the most prominent backers of his aspirations for the presidency and to become leaders in the Liberal
party,—men like Orestes Ferrara, Gerardo Machado, Carlos
Mendieta, and José Monteagudo. After the war Gómez
was a prominent—but not *too* prominent—member of the
Cuban Assembly, and presently became civil governor of
Santa Clara under the United States military administration.
He was also a member—somewhat in the background—of
the Constitutional Convention, and was elected governor of
Santa Clara under the republic. There he built up his
political fences to such effect that almost the entire province
was in the Republican party he founded there. Hints are
not lacking as to some departure from "the proprieties"
while Gómez held this post. One well-known Cuban publicist accuses him of organizing a gang of bullies to win
elections for him by force, and hints that people mysteriously disappeared if they stood in Gómez's way and
that cattle also were appropriated to repair the Gómez
fortunes.[1] He was quite often looked upon as a provincial
cacique of the familiar Hispanic American type, and the
favorite epithet applied to him in the presidential elections
of 1908 was that of "tyrant," based on the record imputed
to him as ruler of Santa Clara. His connection with Cuban
affairs from the time of his entry into the lists for the presidency in Estrada Palma's time has already been told.
Opinions differ as to his manifestation of merit, or lack of it,

[1] Vasconcelos, 11.

in those years. One of his later political sayings was that "to provoke revolutions is to commit the worst crime and the greatest infamy," [2] but he seems to have had different views in 1906. To be sure, his own part in that affair was not very spectacular, and at least one writer says he "let himself be caught," though "later gathering in the fruits of victory" for himself.[3]

All accounts seem to agree that Gómez was an extraordinarily likeable person,—a *simpático* in the fullest sense of that delightful Spanish word. Martínez Ortiz, a Gómez supporter, describes him as follows, having reference to his Santa Clara days:

"General Gómez had the complexion of a robust man, attractive features, a friendly manner in conversation, and a character that was affectionate at the same time that it was energetic. Whoever had dealings with him found it difficult to resist him, for he possessed in the highest degree the gift of winning good-will. Just a few words from him gained what the long arguments of others would not have attained. Without conspicuous knowledge, he was endowed with a most sagacious talent and an exact perception with which to measure the intelligence and understanding of others. He assimilated what he heard, with marvellous facility, and was accustomed to follow the opinion of the majority, but not without imposing his own in many cases, though always by indirect and gentle means. Of simple habits and likes, he kept his house open at all hours, and was accustomed to pass the hours of rest in familiar conversation or in games for pleasure and recreation, amidst the discussions of those who were playing cards and the jokes of the spectators, who never failed to be there, back of the table." [4]

Much to the same effect was the pronouncement of another friend, Gualberto Hernández:

"General Gómez . . . is neither a tribune nor a publicist, nor can he be said to have a clear comprehension of the great social problems that stir the world. But on the other hand he possesses an enormous force:

[2] Quoted in Pardo Suárez, 124.   [4] Martínez Ortiz, II, 410.
[3] Pérez, 7.

an intuition as to means and formulae and an exact, precise understanding of men."[5]

Naturally, Gómez's eulogistic biographer, Lozano Casado, has many good things to say of his idol. "He possesses the miracle of smiles," he said, and quoted other prominent men who made remarks of the same tenor. For example, Ernesto Asbert spoke of his "courteous manner" and his "irresistible attraction". Even Zayas, his perennial rival, had remarked on his "great political brain", and called him a "model for tolerance of spirit". Juan Gualberto Gómez was quoted by Lozano as follows:

"He is a man of clear understanding and powerful suggestion. Moreover he has a broad, tolerant, magnificent spirit, very well tempered for meandering through the labyrinth of the politicians, without mistaking the way. He is what may be called a great leader of crowds."[6]

These statements are indeed representative of what people say of Gómez in private conversation, but they almost invariably refer to him, too, as a "ruined planter" before he became President and as having utilized his high office to build up a great fortune for himself through the medium of graft. The same men may also claim that he indulged in graft as governor of Santa Clara before he became President, but it is certain that he built up no great fortune there. Nearly all, however, will admit that he did not take everything for himself after he became President, but accomplished much good for the country. The following are sample statements of men who were neither partisans nor opponents of Gómez:

(1) "Both Gómez and his wife were simple country folk, and Gómez has always been very popular in Cuba. And he did a lot of good. The

[5] Hernández, Gualberto, *Anepígrafo*,   [6] Lozano Casado, 7-15.
in Lozano Casado, 4.

two pieces of graft for which he was most criticized were useful undertakings: the exchange of the water-front lot for the Villanueva lands within the city, and the Ports Company bill."

(2) "Each ruler of the past three (Gómez, Menocal, and Zayas) has been worse than the one before. That is why Gómez now seems like a saint. He was a poor man when he entered the presidency, and wealthy when he left it. But he accomplished a lot. And he never spent more than forty-eight millions a year." [7]

One thing certainly may be said concerning Gómez in his administration of the republic. He was lucky! It is customary in all lands to ascribe good times or bad to the government, whether the government in fact has much to do with the situation or not. This is more than usually absurd in Cuba, where prosperity or depression depends primarily on the amount of the sugar crop and the price it brings,—something that is to a considerable extent independent of governmental action. Gómez went into the presidency at a most favorable moment, and did not have a single bad year economically. To be sure, there were occasional uncertainties of weather and the usual cyclones each year, though none of outstanding import. [8] On the other hand, labor disputes were not nearly so prominent as they had been in the Magoon era, and crop and revenue conditions were generally good. Nowhere is this more clearly brought out than in Gómez's various messages to Congress at the opening of a legislative session. [9] The nearest thing to a political policy that Gómez had was to give the country an administration that would be favorable to business. As

[7] There is one statement about Gómez that might present him in a peculiarly distasteful light in certain parts of the United States. That is, that though of a good family he had a strain of negro blood in him. Cf. Wright, 94; also, The insurrection in Cuba, in Outlook, v. CI, p. 238, June 1, 1912. Most people who knew Gómez deny this, however, and the writer is convinced that it is not true.

[8] For references to cyclones, see Mensajes presidenciales, I: 273; 304; 310.

[9] For example, see Mensajes presidenciales, I: 227; 253; 273; 319; 343.

he himself once said, "In my program of government I put economic interests above every other public question," [10] an assertion that he repeated in various messages. Undoubtedly he did encourage business, assisted by a number of really worthy men who at one time or another were in his Cabinet or in Congress. And, as set forth in one of the statements quoted above, even the measures involving graft had also some possibility in them of benefit to the republic. On the other hand, it was not nearly as economical a government as its much criticized predecessor, though almost a model by comparison with later years. At the beginning of Gómez's rule his private secretary gave out that it was the plan to effect great economies in public expenses and not resort to any loans.[11] Some savings were now and then effected in one direction, but they were more than offset by extravagances in another, and the promise to seek no loans was not fulfilled.[12]

One considerable increase in expenditures came about through an addition to the budget for the army. Gómez was resolved that nobody should do to him what he himself had done to Estrada Palma. The Magoon government had passed a law for a permanent army, but left it to the incoming Cuban administration to work out the details and organize the forces. This was one of the first things with which Gómez concerned himself. In a long message of February 25, 1909, he asked for a large appropriation for the new army, and in numerous later messages called for legislation to build it up to a yet more formidable state. Eventually it consisted of about five thousand men, in three

[10] Message to Congress, Nov. 1, 1909, in *Mensajes presidenciales,* I, 227.
[11] Declarations of José Lorenzo Castellanos to a representative of the New York *Journal,* quoted in Barbarrosa, 95.
[12] For repeated criticisms of Gómez on this score, see Barbarrosa, 95 *et seq., passim.*

regiments of infantry, a considerable body of artillery, and a regiment of cavalry, together with the rural guards, which were presently incorporated into the permanent army. There were also various auxiliary units, including a military academy at the Morro Castle across from Havana and even a small navy.[13] Even though in all likelihood a Cuban army would be used only against other Cubans, this measure of Gómez was no doubt wise, as an anchor to windward in times of disorder. Even the navy proved its value in course of the race war of 1912.[14] It was too much to expect that there should not be some improprieties in certain features of military and naval administration, however. For example, quite apart from charges of extravagance, there were criticisms on account of the excessive number of officers [15] and for the introduction of what was deemed to be a bad precedent in a liberal retirement and pension system,— notably liberal for those in the higher grades.[16] Furthermore, so it is charged, great care was taken to see that the army, from general to private, should be made up of Gómez Liberals.[17]

The only loan contracted by the Gómez administration was for the sum of sixteen millions and a half. This had been authorized by the Magoon government for sanitary tunneling in Havana and Cienfuegos and for paving the streets of the first-named city and construction of an aqueduct for the latter. This had first been planned by Estrada Palma, who proposed to pay for the work out of surplus revenues, but the sudden end of his government had de-

[13] Among numerous Gómez messages on military and naval affairs, see *Mensajes presidenciales*, I: 184-190; 261-263; 313; 313-314; 333; 366-373; and extensive paragraphs in each message at the opening of a session of Congress.
[14] *Mensajes presidenciales*, I, 386.
[15] González Lanuza, 615-616.
[16] Barbarrosa, 114-115.
[17] Pérez, 8.

layed the project. Gómez early announced that he would set aside a portion of the revenues for the purpose, without resorting to a loan,[18] but it was only a few weeks later when the loan was contracted with the New York house of Speyer and Company, in June, at a discount of twelve per cent, though with a coupon rate of only four and a half per cent, yielding a little more than fourteen millions and a half. This sum was presently expended, and Gómez reported in 1912 that some thirteen millions more would be needed to finish the work! He therefore asked for authority to negotiate another loan,[19] but his term came to an end before any action was taken.

The extravagance of the Gómez government in providing political plums made itself manifest in numerous ways. The diplomatic service was unnecessarily expanded. This was criticized by an individual whose opinions in this period are more than usually entitled to weight, José González Lanuza, at that time a representative in Congress.[20] González Lanuza, though a member of the Conservative opposition, was a man of such high character and disinterestedness that he rose above party considerations in his discussion of events. Some others were less kindly in their comments. For example, Barbarrosa said that the Cuban diplomat was appointed "only in order that he may wear his uniform at court functions".[21] He might also have remarked on the important work he did in drawing his pay! In like manner administrative jobs in Cuba were multiplied. It is said that Gómez had posts for all his intimate friends, who were popularly called his *"cuneros,"* or "foundlings",[22] a

[18] Message of Apr. 5, 1909, in *Mensajes presidenciales*, I, 195-210, at 202.
[19] Messages of Apr. 12 and June 28, 1912, in *Mensajes presidenciales*, I: 352-353; 363.
[20] González Lanuza, 625-626.
[21] Barbarrosa, 123.
[22] Pérez, 8.

term in Cuban political slang which meant that a man had no relation by birth or residence to the region in which he aspired to office, owing his candidacy solely to the support of the political machine. Of course, too, places had to be given to a legion of henchmen in payment of political promises.[23]

The budget of the presidency jumped enormously over what it had been in the time of Estrada Palma. As compared with the $62,390 allotted in 1905, Gómez got $148,120 in the budget of 1910-1911. A comparison of some of the items of expense is interesting. Personal service in the palace cost $7,740 under Estrada Palma, and $14,620 under Gómez; the secretariat increased in cost from $11,950 to $56,700; the item for "various" expenses rose from $600 to $15,000,— quite "various", it would seem; and there were other items that had not appeared in Estrada Palma's time, entered as "unforeseen expenses" $12,000, and "secret expenses" $25,-000.[24] Presumably these amounts included the expenditures for the rich furnishings that were introduced into the palace, but probably *not* the cost of Gómez's fishing excursions and trips to Cayo Cristo, which he made in a coast-guard vessel of the Cuban navy.[25] But this was not all. Later the President received $105,000 for "secret expenses", and ran through this sum in less than six months, and there was a deficit of $26,000 in the expenditures of his secretariat.[26]

It must not be imagined because of these evils (and more yet to be related) that the Gómez government is to

[23] Barbarrosa, 101. Barbarrosa also noted that an exceptional number of positions had been given to a horde of suspiciously well dressed women "in order to prove that we are more gallant than the Yankees." Barbarrosa, 119.

[24] Barbarrosa, 130. Barbarrosa makes numerous charges, possibly in an exaggerated vein, as to just how these sums were employed. Barbarrosa, 93 *et seq., passim.*
[25] *Ibid.,* 100.
[26] *Ibid.,* 113.

be unqualifiedly condemned. Indeed, its shortcomings were to be multiplied many times over by the administrations that succeeded it. The great evil of it was that it put the bad Spanish traditions again in the saddle, and so opened the way to a recurrence of the old corrupt political practices, despite a great deal of good that it accomplished. Nor was Gómez alone responsible. He had an all too ready following in other branches of Cuban government, national, provincial, and municipal. Even if absolutely faultless himself he probably would have failed to hold the politicians in check, just as Estrada Palma had. So he might be excused altogether but for one thing: in Cuba one may expect so little from other governmental agencies, save for a few upright men here and there, that the President is almost the only hope for a beginning in ways of political rectitude.[27] Aside from their bad acts in association with the executive, there were numerous peccadillos of other bodies on their own account. Quite apart from graft, congressmen managed to procure for themselves the equivalent of sixty dollars a day, what with salary and "extraordinary expenses", for a period of some eighty days of work,[28]—provided they in fact turned up for the sessions. Far worse, because of the utter uselessness of these agencies in themselves, were the extravagances of provincial councils.[29] And one might run through the other branches of government and find the same conditions.

Each of the four Gómez budgets was considerably larger than any of those of his predecessors, but expenditures far outran budgets, in an effort to keep up with receipts. Including the product of the 1909 Speyer loan, the latter averaged about forty-six millions a year for the entire

[27] See chapters XXI-XXIV, in which the comparative worthlessness of other political agencies is amply described.

[28] Barbarrosa, 116.

[29] Ibid: 98; 172.

Gómez term. Expenditures were almost exactly the same.[30] Evidently José Miguel had no idea of piling up a surplus to tempt the revolutionaries. In his various budget messages he was at great pains to explain why larger sums were needed than had been required by Magoon, calling attention to new governmental services that had been established, but these state papers have only a certain academic interest, for uses were speedily found for any revenues that turned up over and above budgetary requirements.[31] The wealth in receipts,—mainly through customs duties, as before,— was in one sense an index of the prosperity of these years, but it has been characterized as more a manifestation of governmental good fortune than of the economic well-being of the people.[32] Nevertheless, some of the acts of the Gómez administration must have had permanently beneficial effects and others were at least temporarily helpful. A great deal was done for the betterment of communications. If Gómez let the roads of his predecessors go to ruin, he did build a number himself,—although most of them have in their turn been allowed to revert to a useless state.[33] Of more enduring value was the assistance given to railway-building projects. Right at the outset of his administration, he took steps in this direction. In his message to Congress of April 5, 1909, he censured Estrada Palma for not building railways when he had money in the treasury and a law of July 5, 1906, which would have enabled him to proceed. As for himself,

[30] Guiral Moreno, Mario, *Nuestros problemas políticos, económicos y sociales*, in *Cuba contemporánea*, v. V, pp. 401-424, at 416-417; Aug., 1914.

[31] There are three budget messages in *Mensajes presidenciales*, I: 214-217; 237-241; 284-285. These do not show forth the detail as to proposed expenditures.

[32] Barbarrosa, 106. See also *infra*, pp: 626; 630-633.

[33] Numerous Gómez messages deal in some detail with road-building. See especially *Mensajes presidenciales*, I: 203-204; 233; 241; 265; also opening messages of a session. The item at page 265 concerns the proposed building of the central highway from end to end of the island, a project which has always been one of the resounding "phrases" of the politicians of the republic.

"relying on the support of Congress and, above all, the aid of Divine Providence", he proposed to build the first of the lines formerly authorized,—one running from Martí on the Cuba Railway in western Oriente, south to Manzanillo, and thence east to rejoin the main line at San Luis, north of Santiago. For this purpose he offered the Cuba Railway six thousand dollars a kilometre to build the line. In due time it was finished, adding greatly to the capital resources of the republic. Gómez also interested himself in the building of other lines included in the law of 1906, and suggested some new ones, such, for example, as a railway from Nuevitas to Caibarién. Many kilometres of track were laid in Gómez's time and others in ensuing years in accord with the plans he made.[34]

The following may be named as among the other beneficial economic acts of the Gómez administration: the suspension or reduction of the duties on the export of sugar and other Cuban products; the lowering of duties on machinery for agriculture and railways; aid in the development of a Cuban manufacture of such things as soap, shoes, paper, food products, and beer by raising the duties; the encouragement of immigration; and legislation favoring the building of long-distance telephone lines, which formerly had been restricted by a Spanish law of 1890 to a length of ten miles. About some other acts of Gómez there are two opinions as to whether any particular benefit was derived from them. There was considerable legislation and large appropriations for the building of an aqueduct to supply Santiago with water,—something that has yet to be done in a really satis-

[34] The announcement of the contract for the Manzanillo branch was in the message of Apr. 5, 1909, in *Mensajes presidenciales*, I, 195-210, at 197. There are frequent other references to railway-building in the *Mensajes presidenciales*. See especially in I, at 227-228.

factory way. And there was not a little expended on public buildings, improvement of cities, and port works.[35]

Very few of the other measures of the government can honestly be characterized as helpful to the republic. Now and then, there was a gesture as of conferring some benefit upon labor. Some homes for laborers were built in a suburb of Havana. Gómez sent a message to Congress recommending the founding of a popular university for laborers.[36] His most famous connection with labor legislation, however, was his veto of a law requiring employers to ensure their workmen against accident, a measure which he had at first favored.[37] Apparently the real idea back of this bill was to provide an opportunity for graft, under the guise of a benefit to labor. The point was, that the law required the insurance company to be a Cuban corporation then in existence. El Siglo, a Conservative daily, charged that Gómez had intended to control the Cuban company that was to get the contract, "but, hearing the protests of the country, he preferred to reject the law, knowing that he was casting aside an opportunity to make a comfortable profit."[38] In a sense this is somewhat to his credit, at least in comparison with his successors, who would not have given much heed to public opinion.

Whatever may be said against Gómez on the score of bad legislation is chargeable in equal or perhaps greater degree against Congress. As already stated, there were a number of worthy men in Congress, but that body had deteriorated even from the none too highly recommendable quality of the earlier Congresses of the republic,—not nearly approaching, however, the depths that have more recently been

[35] Naturally the Gómez sections of the *Mensajes presidenciales* and the *Memorias* abound in references to these achievements.

[36] Dec. 11, 1911, in *Mensajes presidenciales*, I, 334.

[37] Aug. 28, 1912, in *Ibid.*, I, 374.

[38] Quoted in Lozano Casado, 35.

reached. Gómez several times recommended the enactment of laws that were still needed to supplement the Constitution,[39] but if this was a really serious request it at least got little or no attention from Congress. Congress was interested in other things,—in political maneuvers and in matters where there was some tangible advantage for congressmen. The first four laws of the restored Cuban republic that were discussed in the House are indicative of the character of Congress. One was a political spoils act which "deprived mayors (alcaldes) of their proper and legitimate functions."[40] Another restored cock-fighting.[41] A third was a notorious amnesty bill. And the fourth was the even more notorious lottery law. The two last-named are so important in the history of the republic that they have been reserved for special treatment elsewhere, along with yet other amnesties and another lottery law of the Gómez period,[42] but something may be said here of the cock-fighting bill.

Restoration of the cock-fight was almost in the nature of a Gómez campaign pledge. This had been a traditional "sport", if such it may be called, during the Spanish period, especially in the rural districts, where it was so highly favored that it was very nearly the end and aim of all existence. Naturally, it was repugnant to the American authorities of the military government, and General Wood outlawed it. It had no chance of getting back under Estrada Palma or Magoon, but with Gómez it was different. Prior

---

[39] Notably in his message of Apr. 4, 1910, in *Mensajes presidenciales*, I, 253-257, at 254. See also message of Apr. 3, 1911, in *Ibid.*, I, 303-311, at 303.

[40] Speech of Santiago Cancio Bello on Feb. 20, 1909, in República de Cuba, Cámara de Representantes, *Diario de sesiones*, for Feb. 19-20, 1909. Cancio Bello said this was the first law promulgated by the Gómez administration. Cf. n. 41.

[41] The Conservative daily, *Discusión*, named this as the first law of the new republic. Article quoted in Havana *Post*, Feb. 9, 1909. Cf. n. 40. The *Discusión* item refers merely to the presentation of the bill, for it did not become a law until the following July.

[42] In chapters XXII-XXIII.

to the elections of 1908 there were popular manifestations on behalf of a restoration of this favorite pastime, whereupon the Gómez campaign managers hit upon a plan to take advantage of this sentiment, without coming out openly, however, in advocacy of the cock-fight. At the suggestion of General Monteagudo they adopted as their party emblem a rooster on a plow. Professedly this was a symbol for "vigilance and work", but the masses understood it as a promise of their old sport. Undoubtedly it gained thousands of votes for the Liberal candidate. Magoon was hardly out of sight when the bill was introduced. It was taken up in the House on February 1, 1909. The opposition was unavailing, and on July 3 the bill became a law. Its principal paragraph was brief and to the point: "All dispositions which are opposed to cock-fights are derogated".[43]

A number of other bills belonging in a similar category were promptly introduced. In hopes that it might be accepted as a substitute for the more barbarous cock-fight, General Wood had authorized the playing of jai-alai, a beautiful Spanish game, which had the same gambling features, however, as the sport whose place it took.[44] In Gómez's time the concession ran out, and it came up for renewal. Jai-alai had, indeed, won a place for itself, but only in Havana, with its great Spanish population, where alone it was possible to get an adequate financial return that would justify the considerable expenditure required in erecting a suitable edifice. The jai-alai matter appeared in a so-called "tourist" bill, on the basis of providing attractions for visitors from the United States. Liberals like Martínez Ortiz and Conservatives of the stamp of González Lanuza were op-

[43] República de Cuba, *Colección legislativa*, v. XXVII. pp. 5-6.

[44] For a description of this game, see *infra*, p. 606, n. 25.

posed to it,[45] but the majority, including men of both parties, were in favor of it. As it eventually passed Congress it proposed to authorize both jai-alai and horse-racing, with betting allowed, for a period of thirty years. Apparently some graft was involved, as no provision was made for auctioning off these valuable rights. There was an outcry against the bill that went beyond the walls of Congress, and so Gómez vetoed it.[46] Under a later administration, however, both games were to find their way into the capital. Even a bull-fight bill appeared early on the calendar of Congress, but that game had never gained a great foothold in Cuba, and it was beaten when it came to a vote. A project for a Cuban Monte Carlo got a little farther on the way, passing the House in 1910, but it met with so much criticism that it was rejected in the Senate.[47] In more recent years, however, it has come into being in the famous Casino of Marianao (near Havana), to say nothing of the numerous "clubs" maintained by politicians. In opposing the cock-fight bill, González Lanuza made a keen estimate of the meaning of this type of legislation.

"Today," he said, "we have voted the totality of the project which authorizes cock-fights. Tomorrow we shall vote a project for the authorization of the national lottery. The bulls are on the point of coming out of the pen . . . And so, distinctly, we are reviving a past against which our fathers rose and against which we ourselves also rose . . . So it appears that our national conscience is declaring that the social state befitting this people was that which we formerly had, save for one difference: that then we did not hold public office." [48]

In yet one other even more reprehensible form the Gómez era "distinctly revived the past", and that was, as already

[45] For a speech of the Conservative representative, see González Lanuza, 853-855.
[46] Message to the House, Mar. 6, 1913, in *Mensajes presidenciales*, I, 380.
[47] Article on *Cuba*, in *New international year book . . . for the year 1910*, pp. 196-197, at 197.
[48] González Lanuza, 865-866.

stated, in bringing back the old tradition that government existed for the benefit of the office-holders, who must be expected to miss no reasonably good opportunity to improve their own fortunes at the expense of the state. This reached out into all branches of the service, and perhaps was at its worst, because without redeeming feature, in the case of those in the lower ranks of the legislative field, who made little more than a moderately good living out of it, since the chance to do better by themselves was not afforded. Scores of instances of graft by congressmen, provincial or municipal councillors, judges, and minor administrative officials might be given in a detailed story of the period. Here, however, there is space only for a comparatively brief treatment, and it is best, therefore, to take this up in connection with the man who profited the most, even though he might have taken more than he did and though he advocated few measures that did not also have in them some possibility of advantage to the country itself. That man was President Gómez.

Gómez gained a great fortune out of the presidency. Vasconcelos called him "the ruined planter who made himself a millionaire from night to morning, and not by the sweat of his brow".[49] A recent article in an American periodical has the following to say about Gómez and graft:

"It may be that General Gomez personally was benefited more than the government from these transactions . . . General Gomez entered the presidency as a poor man. He owned a farm in Santa Clara Province so covered with mortgages that if disposed of at forced sale he would have been left penniless. While President his salary was $25,000 a year. Nevertheless, when he left office in 1912 [sic] he constructed a white stone palace on the Prado at a cost in excess of twenty-five thousand dollars, and found investments in mines or sugar estates for about eight millions more. His business acumen displayed itself late, but was

[49] Vasconcelos, 18.

efficacious during the time he was chief executive. When reduced to private life it became somewhat atrophied, and he died three years ago in New York practically a pauper again." [50]

Any number of references to the same effect might be given.[51] Even the friends of Gómez rarely, if ever, go to the pains of denying that he profited from his office, and not infrequently they admit it. In his foreword to the Lozano Casado eulogy of Gómez, Gualberto Hernández applauded Gómez for the graft that had allowed a number of Cubans to build shining white, new homes in Jesús del Monte, a suburb of Havana.[52] It is of a piece with Cuban psychology that he did not seem to realize that the benefits which Gómez had conferred on these few individuals had been paid for at the expense of the mass of other less fortunate Cubans. At the end of his term El Mundo came out with a detailed and flattering summary of Gómez's achievements, but then went on as follows:

> "While all this will appear on the 'Credit' side of the governmental account of General Gómez, on the 'Passive,' or 'Debit,' side they will speak vaguely of certain measures or acts of his administrative conduct, consisting mainly in sanctioning laws voted by Congress in spite of the opposition of a part of public opinion,—measures or acts which it censured, but which (because of their littleness and insignificance), though they might have been worthy of vituperation, would not obscure and will not diminish the brilliance and value of the important items of the 'Active' account." [53]

[50] *Cuba, an American ward again?*, in *Independent*, v. CXIII, pp. 35-38, at 35; July 19, 1924. The price of the palace on the Prado was given as two hundred and fifty thousand in the original manuscript of this article (which the writer saw). Evidently there was a misprint from the "$250,000" of the manuscript.

[51] For example, note the imputation of graft contained in the writings of such respectable figures as Varona (*De la colonia a la república*, 247) and Trelles (*El progreso . . . y el*

retroceso . . . de la república de Cuba, 10). Naturally, Barbarrosa overflows with references on this score, and there are numerous other contemporary writings of the same tenor. Among these may be mentioned the following article by a prominent Liberal politician of those days: Loinaz del Castillo, Enrique, *El pillaje nacional*, in *Mundo*, Nov. 26, 1909.

[52] Hernández, Gualberto, *Anepígrafo*, in Lozano Casado, 3-5.

[53] Quoted in Lozano Casado, 85.

One of the most remarkable estimates of Gómez appears in a volume entitled *Tiburón* (Shark), employing the nickname most commonly applied to José Miguel. This was written by Lieutenant-Colonel Avelino Sanjenís, who was private secretary to the President during virtually his entire term. The American reader will not sympathize greatly with the main point of Sanjenís,—apparently that he had been badly used because Gómez "did not give me even the most meagre crumb of bread in that splendid banquet of four succulent years", in consequence of which Sanjenís lost money, rather than made it,—but the book is all the more valuable in that the author mentions graft only incidentally. He aims to stay by his thesis, resisting any inclination to "satisfy the voracity of the public" through giving "an inexhaustible wealth of data" which he possessed on the scandals of Gómez's administration.[54] Nevertheless, stray references constantly creep into the account. Some of these are worth quoting. For example:

"The characteristic thing about General Gómez, as everybody knows, is his selfishness. Deaf to the requests of friends, avid of wealth, obstinate and tenacious in acquiring it, he employed all means, including the sacrifice of his most intimate associates, to improvise a fortune."[55]

And again:

"From the ostentation and opulence manifested by General Gómez since the termination of his presidential functions the public has gathered how enormous is the fortune of the hero of Arroyo Blanco, calculated by those who know about it as some eight millions of dollars."

Sanjenís went on to tell of Gómez's "splendid voyage of pleasure" in Europe, the building of his palace along the Prado, the stocking of his cattle-farms with valuable animals, his purchases of costly works of art, and the "oriental pomp" in which the whole family lived.[56]

[54] Sanjenís: 12; 215-216.　　　　[56] *Ibid.*, 198-199.
[55] *Ibid.*, 12.

The financial advantages that come of being a President of Cuba were well illustrated in the case of certain business deals that Gómez entered into in association with Sanjenís, though it would appear that these particular deals were unprofitable. Gómez was allowed to subscribe to the stock of one company at eighty per cent of par. In another company he got some shares free and others at twenty-five per cent of par. In both instances others were being required to pay the full face value of the shares.[57] If there may have been a semblance of legitimacy in transactions of this character, there certainly was none in scores of others where Gómez and his associates profited at the expense of the country. There is not space enough here to give details about any but the most famous instances of graft in the Gómez era, but some of the other improprieties charged against the administration—quite probably with injustice in some instances—may at least be named. Following is a catalogue of acts in which graft is said to have been involved: the purchase of vessels for the national navy; the loan bill; certain dredging projects (in addition to those of the Ports Company); the construction of the railway from Júcaro to Morón; the monopolization of the collectorships and other operations in connection with the national lottery; the fraudulent introduction of foreign cattle for stocking Gómez's own estates, making him the richest cattleman in the country; the construction of the presidential palace; the rental of buildings for public service; auctions for arms, cannon, horses, and other materials of the army; the Territorial Bank project; sales of old iron; the telephone company concession; the auctions for road-building and other projects; the construction of Havana Bridge; the pro-

[57] *Ibid:* 157; 164.

ject for renting the Vento aqueduct; the Jicotea aqueduct contract; the Columbia Camp affair; the sewage and paving of Havana contracts; and innumerable other concessions, subventions, contracts, and pardons.[58]

The first of the major graft bills in the history of the republic, and one of the two most notorious deals of the Gómez administration, was the exchange of the Arsenal lands for those of Villanueva, both in Havana. The Arsenal lands, 109,474 square meters in extent (according to the statement of the President), lay along Havana harbor, and were the property of the government, while the Villanueva tract, of 43,418 square meters, belonged to the United Railways, an English company, and was almost in the centre of the city, along the southward extension of the Prado. There were some rumors about an exchange of these properties from the outset of Gómez's presidency, and by the middle of April 1909 the main features of the project were given out to the public. On the 19th of that month Gómez directed a somewhat flowery message to Congress about it, pointing out how his plan would be a long step in the direction of beautifying the capital and inviting Congress to join with him "in a great work which will be an imperishable and glorious memorial of my presidential period". According to him it was an exceptionally favorable deal for the republic, as the Villanueva lands had a "much greater value" than those of the Arsenal district, besides which the English company had agreed to spend not less than a

[58] Most of these are alluded to in Sanjenís, 145-147. See also Barbarrosa: 112; 116. According to Trelles, "In the matter of pardons President Gómez left Mr. Magoon far behind, for he granted eighteen hundred of them." Trelles, *Op. cit.*, 10. In a similar category were the amnesties of this period. See chapter XXII. One amnesty bill, passed in March 1913, was so objectionably broad in its terms that United States Secretary of State Bryan protested against it, whereupon Gómez vetoed it. Trelles, *Biblioteca*, II, 116.

million and a half in building five docks for the government and an incinerator to dispose of the refuse of the capital. The railway would then remove its terminal station from Villanueva, and the government would erect a number of beautiful public buildings at a total cost of some six millions and a half. Among these were to be a presidential palace, a congressional building, and edifices for the departments of state, justice, government, and public instruction, besides several lesser works. The message concluded with an expression of Gómez's "enthusiasm for the project".[59]

The vastness of the plan was enough to stir the imagination, and for a moment it was received with almost as much "enthusiasm" as that which Gómez professed. Very quickly, however, people began to look beyond outward seeming and to feel that it was startling primarily on account of the stupendous amount of graft involved.[60] Barbarrosa ridiculed Gómez's remarks about the profitable character of the deal. As he put it, somewhat sarcastically: "The Arsenal is worth very little. Villanueva, much. Cuba gains a few millions, therefore, thanks to English innocence." Previously he had charged, however, that the Arsenal was worth several millions more than Cuba got for it.[61] One estimate in a conservative American publication held that the Arsenal was worth four millions more than Villanueva, and calculated its area as far larger proportionately than

[59] In *Mensajes presidenciales*, I, 211-213.

[60] For example, the editorials in the Havana *Post* from Apr. 15 to Apr. 29, 1909, are an interesting illustration. In the article of the 15th it seemed as if the greatness of the project had quite taken the editor's breath away. On the 23d an editorial gave its stamp of approval to the deal. By the 28th the editor was doubtful. And on the 29th, in a "Villanueva not needed" article, it was pointed out that there was no necessity for giving up the valuable Arsenal lands for Villanueva, as the government owned other suitable tracts where the desired public buildings might be erected.

[61] Barbarrosa, 114-115.

would appear from the figures given above. Indeed, the transaction was so notorious that the United States government is said to have expressed its disapproval.[62] Gómez and Congress were not to be turned aside, however, though the bill did not become a law until July 20, 1910. It was substantially in the same terms as the President had suggested.[63] From the standpoint of results obtained by the government no deal of the Gómez era was a more complete failure than this famous exchange. The ragged skeletons of some of his proposed public buildings for "beautifying" the city were erected, and then the work stopped. So Villenueva remains to this day an eye-sore in the centre of the city, rather than a place of beauty,—all too "imperishable," and a "memorial" to something very different from the "glory" of the genial but nimble-fingered José Miguel. And yet, apart from the graft, the deal was not such a bad one. It was a good thing to get the railway a little away from the centre of the city and to beautify the Villanueva district in the way Gómez had planned. José Miguel cannot be blamed for the failure to finish the work. That is an episode of the era of his successor, Menocal. Menocal several times asked Congress for funds to complete the construction, but without success. There are those who claim, however, that these requests were not sincere and that Menocal himself prevented the completion of the task, as a *political* argument against his predecessor in office.

[62] Articles on *Cuba,* in *New international year book . . . for the year 1910,* pp. 196-197, at 197, and *Ibid . . . for the year 1911,* pp. 205-206, at 206.

[63] In República de Cuba, *Colección legislativa,* v. XXIX, pp. 421-424. One of the paragraphs of the law called for a formal valuation of the two tracts, for which purpose Gómez appointed four experts on behalf of the government. Apparently they caught the spirit of the deal, for they put in a bill for their services of $29,800 apiece, or a total of $119,200! This was a bit too much for Gómez, who sent a message to Congress about it. Message of Feb. 3, 1911, in *Mensajes presidenciales,* I, 296.

The other of the two most widely heralded scandals of the Gómez era was the celebrated Ports Company concession for dredging a number of the harbors of Cuba. As this attained to most of its peculiar fame through the action taken by the Menocal administration, it is perhaps best to discuss it there. It remains to deal with the political aspects of the Gómez era, which merit a chapter to themselves. First, however, something may be said here on the more intimate aspects of the President's life—all of it from the biography of Lozano Casado.

"In all my life," Gomez once remarked, "I have been jovial in spirit, with a smile on my lips." This was in part, it would seem, the result of deliberate design, for in telling of his manner of receiving visitors he speaks of causing a smile to light up his face. "I study men", he said, "as others study books". That, he remarked, was fundamental to government. As President he ruled according to conditions as they were in Cuba, and not in pursuance of a general plan that an Englishman might have considered right. As a good politician he kept in touch with those things that such a man needed to know. While at breakfast he read, not only the insults or eulogies of the local press concerning himself, but also and more particularly what people in the provinces were saying. And the last thing he did at night was to make entries on a chart which enabled him to keep informed daily of the changes in the population of the island. At times Gómez displayed remarkable cleverness in turning the intended thrust of an opponent back on the man who gave it,—though one wonders whether it might not have been Ferrara who provided him with the language. One such occasion came up in connection with Ricardo Dolz, who had been an influential figure in Estrada Palma's time and was accused by the

Liberals of being partially responsible for the United States intervention of 1906. Dolz wrote a letter about the veteranist question,[64] saying that if he were President he would solve it inside of forty-eight hours. This letter, dated November 29, 1911, was published. Two days later Gómez wrote to Dolz, and also gave out his communication to the press. In the guise of politeness, but with an admirable touch of irony, Gómez invited Dolz to come and tell him what to do, and on no account to wait until he should become President, implying that the delay might then be permanent. He wound up by saying that Dolz might have more energy than he, but he preferred the kind of reflection which might save the republic instead of delivering it to the foreigner. An even more amusing communication was one he wrote to a man who has since become President, General Gerardo Machado, at the time the latter withdrew from Gómez's Cabinet in protest over the reëlectionist plans of the President.[65] Machado's letter, dated April 23, 1912, was long and flowery, in somewhat too beauteous a form, seemingly intended for the general public more than for Gómez. And, indeed, it was at once given out to the press. The following is an excerpt from the President's reply of the 25th, written in the intimacy of the second person singular:

"People who, like you and I, are not writers or accustomed to offer our prose to the public are apt to fall into the temptation of making ours what others write for us, and on reading and re-reading it we soon find the conception of another so charming and sensational that we wind up by thinking it our own. Notwithstanding this, I shall take as yours the things you say to me . . . Up to yesterday everything was going along admirably in the republic according to the official reports you gave me on the 23d, and on the following day our people have suffered such

[64] See *infra*, pp. 306-308.
[65] The political bearings of this correspondence are discussed *infra*, at pp. 313-314.

a complete change and the social order has been so modified that a horrible catastrophe appears to threaten us. What has happened to produce so violent a transformation? I know of nothing other than your resignation from the Cabinet."

As Gómez told it himself, he was in the habit of getting up at six o'clock in the morning. After a visit to the palace barber, he went through some exercises, took a shower bath, and had a light breakfast at half past seven of fruit and coffee. It was at this time that he looked over the newspapers, afterward reading a book until nine. At nine he went to his office, looked over his correspondence, answered some letters and gave directions how to answer the others, and received his Secretaries and the various individuals who had been granted an audience. Between visits he wrote his own daily impressions, which, however, he never intended to publish. At twelve o'clock he took his *almuerzo*, or heavy breakfast, as the Hispanic noon meal is called, and afterwards slept for an hour. Then he glanced at the afternoon papers and played billiards, a game that he very much enjoyed, and later read books until six. At that hour he dressed for the evening and received private visits until dinner-time, which was usually at eight. Dinner over, he played *tresillo*, a game of cards (involving gambling and requiring much skill), in which he regarded himself as quite expert. Then, after his already mentioned excursion into demography, he retired. His occasional fishing trips to Cayo Cristo have already been mentioned. He also acquired a fine country estate which he called "Finca América", to which he retired from time to time. According to his opponents, who dubbed this place "the palace of the thousand and one nights", he lived there in oriental splendor, but Lozano Casado insists that there was no ostentation there of any sort.

Such was the life of José Miguel Gómez, one of the most attractive, if also by no means the best, of the figures in the history of the Cuban republic.[66]

[66] For this account of Gómez's daily life, see Lozano Casado, especially at pp. 36-41, 45-59, and 90-95. See note at the end of the next chapter for a discussion of materials in general concerning Gómez's presidency.

CHAPTER XIII

POLITICAL HAPPENINGS OF THE GÓMEZ ERA

THE principal question about which everything political revolved in the Gómez period was whether José Miguel would seek reëlection in 1912. If one could have relied upon his public statements there was no reason to believe that he would. He had agreed to support Zayas in 1912 at the time when the two branches of the Liberal party joined together for the elections of 1908,[1] and in the platform which he published to the country in September 22 of that year he spoke against reëlection.[2] In a statement of January 28, 1911, he said:

"I wish to have the honor of being the first who is opposed to his own reëlection; I wish to give that example to my people. That is what I understand to be prudent, foreseeing, and patriotic."[3]

And in a public letter of April 25, 1912, to General Machado he again remarked that he was not a candidate.[4]

This was one of those instances, however, where all the world knew that a "changed situation" would arise to make him become a candidate, in case he could conveniently arrange it. Anyway, he allowed his friends to support him for the nomination, and the Zayas wing of the party broke away from him because of the moral certainty that Gómez

[1] Though not published at the time, this agreement was a matter of common knowledge. Later, Gómez himself openly admitted it. Gómez, *Manifiesto* (Public declaration) to the

Liberals in December 1912, quoted in Lozano Casado, 73-75, at 75.
[2] Martínez Ortiz, II, 808.
[3] Quoted in Trelles, *Biblioteca*, II, 112.
[4] Quoted in Lozano Casado, 54.

297

intended to run for a second term. It is true, too, that there were moments of something mildly like persecution of Zayas followers, and it is said that the United States government warned Gómez not to seek reëlection.[5] Even after that, it is claimed, he persisted, and assertions are made that the revolutionary tendencies during his administration had more than a little encouragement from the President, who hoped that the "necessities" of the situation might require him to reside in the palace for another four years. The evidence of Gómez partisans to the same effect,—at least in private conversation,—is also so overwhelming in amount that it may be considered a fact that the President's anti-reëlection promises meant nothing at all. This fits in with the political happenings of the period.

Surely there was little cordiality or team-work between Gómez and Zayas during the former's presidency. Gómez lived up to the pact of 1908 in appointing four Zayas partisans to his Cabinet and several more to other high posts, but there were some protests over the distribution of the lesser jobs.[6] Gómez supporters rarely, if ever, had a good word for Zayas,[7] and the President himself expressed a very unfavorable opinion of his rival, admitting his own opposition to him in 1912, despite earlier promises to support him, for the "situation had changed."[8] The most famous incident illustrating Gómez's "disapproval" of Zayas partisans came up in connection with the outstanding figure of the

[5] Kennedy, W   M, *The revolution in Cuba,* in *Living age,* v. CCLXXVI, pp. 463-468, at 467-468; Feb. 22, 1913. Also, Vasconcelos, 13-14.

[6] On the very first day of Gómez's term it is said that Zayas protested against some of the dismissals from office that the President had already announced. See Havana *Post,* Jan. 28, 1909.

[7] Lozano calls him an "apostate," and refers to his "Machiavellism" and his "diabolical machinations." Lozano Casado, 18.

[8] Gómez to Ferrara, July 15, 1912, quoted in Lozano Casado, 68, and Gómez, *Manifiesto,* also in Lozano Casado, 73-75, at 75.

Revolution of August, General "Pino" Guerra, now become commander-in-chief of the Cuban army. "Pino" was known to be a Zayas follower, and the affair was complicated by the fact that General Monteagudo, who was perhaps nearer to Gómez than any other man, wanted the headship of the army for himself. For the time being, Monteagudo commanded the rural guards, which were maintained as a separate body. Personally, "Pino" and Gómez were very good friends, and the former often went to the palace to have a game of cards or billiards with his chief. On the night of October 22, 1910, as he was leaving the palace after the usual friendly game, he was attacked and fired upon by some assassins, who had been hired for this purpose, so it is said, by Gómez himself. The intended victim was not killed, but was wounded in the leg. Shortly afterward he resigned his command, and, as already related, was succeeded by General Monteagudo, under whom the rural guards were added to the regular forces.

It is impossible to prove Gómez's connection with this incident, but it was one of those things that everybody knew and admitted. The following is a statement made to the writer by a Gómez partisan,—one of several that might be given:

"Gómez was afraid that 'Pino,' as head of the army, might influence the elections or even start a revolution in favor of Zayas. He therefore tried to get rid of him decently by offering him a rich mission to Europe. But 'Pino' refused to go. So something else happened! The names of those who attempted to kill 'Pino' were perfectly well known. The case against them was not 'proved,' however, although everybody knew it was true and that Gómez was back of it."

Naturally, Gómez expressed great "indignation", and an "absolute confidence" that the guilty would be punished,[9]

[9] Message to Congress of Nov. 7, 1910, in *Mensajes presidenciales*, I, 273-283, at 274.

but the only man who ever suffered on account of this crime was "Pino" Guerra himself. This incident, which is almost incomprehensible to the Anglo-Saxon mind, has had many parallels in Hispanic American lands, and seems not to have detracted from the eventual popularity of Gómez, though it hurt him at the time. Indeed, no less a person than Guerra himself later deserted Zayas and became a follower of Gómez![10]

This was not the only instance of executive violence in this period. It has been charged that there were also plots to assassinate a number of other opponents of Gómez,[11] and one other case attained to a fame that even surpassed that of the Guerra affair. That was the shooting of Manuel Lavastida. Lavastida had been a captain in the rural guards until ousted on February 1, 1909, presumably on account of political opinions he had held in the campaign of 1908. Thereupon, according to Gómez, he began to conspire against the government, influencing a number of the men he had formerly commanded to follow him in his designs. He was arrested at Placetas, Santa Clara, on the night of March 15-16, but was shot and killed the following night when he attempted to escape,—according to the government account. Meanwhile, on the 16th, Sergeant Francisco Cortés of the rural guards and seven others, all of them connected with the Lavastida plots, were reported to have gone out in an insurrection at Taguayabón, Santa Clara. General Monteaguado immediately directed a pursuit, and the men were taken prisoners on the 18th. They denied any attempt at revolution, saying that they had run away because they had been informed that they were going to be killed.

[10] Pérez, 7.
[11] Several men are named in this connection in Sanjenís, 145, and some others in Barbarrosa, 112.

The Lavastida affair, otherwise Taguayabón revolt, caused a furor in the country. A great body of the public inclined to the view that Lavastida had been deliberately murdered. The Havana Post remarked that it savored of Díaz, the celebrated Mexican dictator.[12]   And the passage of years has not changed people's opinions. Even so unimpulsive a writer as Carlos Trelles has said that Lavastida was killed "by order of the government."[13]   The uproar over the event was so great that the men who had been responsible for the death of Lavastida were tried by court-martial, but were exonerated two weeks later. At the same time, Cortés and his companions were put on trial, and condemned to death. There was some expectation that Gómez might commute the sentence, but the President's message to Congress of April 5 made it clear that the men could hope for nothing from him. He said that Cortés had joined Lavastida because he had not been promoted to a captaincy to which he aspired, though he was "utterly without culture and even lacking in good manners." The sequel was told to the writer by a man of recognized authority in the following terms:

"After Cortés and his companions had been condemned to death, a decision was rendered by the *Audiencia*[14] of Santa Clara in June 1909 setting them free, on the ground that they had done nothing but 'take to the woods' because they were afraid they were going to be killed. One judge dissented on a minor point, holding that they were guilty of carrying arms, contrary to law, and therefore ought to be fined. Gómez was furious, because this made the decision of the military tribunal, which had practically been dictated by him, appear ridiculous. He did indeed let the men off, but took revenge on the judges. The judiciary law of the Magoon era, providing (among other things) for the irremovability of judges, was to go into effect the following month. So Gómez took advantage of the opportunity that was still open to him as a matter of law, and removed all of the judges, except the one who had voted for a

[12] Editorial of March 18.
[13] Trelles, *Biblioteca*, II, 113.

[14] That is, the highest provincial court.

fine, and he was transferred to another province. Several of these judges have since attained to eminence, however, as members of the Supreme Court." [15]

Gómez's action in the Guerra and Lavastida affairs was the sort of thing that many had expected of him when they characterized him as a "tyrant" at the time of the electoral campaign of 1908. On that occasion he had felt it necessary to disarm suspicion by announcing in his platform that if he were elected "the executive would have to maintain itself within the limits that the Constitution and the laws have fixed for that power." [16] Once in office, however, he showed the normal Hispanic American tendency to dominate all branches of the government,[17] though at no time remotely approaching the extremes of some of the petty tyrants of the Caribbean mainland. To be sure, Gómez was merely following tradition in acting as he did, and nobody has better expressed the habit of the Cuban people of looking to the executive for everything than has Gómez himself.[18] For this same reason the President was also the principal target of the critics, who rightly or wrongly assailed him with all the facile vindictiveness that Cuban writers have at their command. Gómez has often been praised for his patience in the face of these attacks, but there were times when he actively resented them.[19] This manifested itself especially in his relations with the press and the law courts.

In February 1910 the editors of La Prensa and El Gordo

[15] Gómez gives a detailed account of the Lavastida affair in his message to Congress of Apr. 5, 1909, in *Mensajes presidenciales*, I, 195-210, at 196-197. The newspapers were filled with comment for a month or more, and several pamphlets of Leandro González Alcorta (cited in Trelles, *Biblioteca*, II, 113) were published denouncing the action of the government.

[16] Quoted in Martínez Ortiz, II, 807.

[17] Note on this score Varona, *A los Conservadores*, one of *Siete circulares: 1910 a 1913*, in *De la colonia a la república*, 247-250.

[18] Message to Congress of Nov. 1, 1909, in *Mensajes presidenciales*, I, 227-236, at 227.

[19] Gómez frequently alluded to these criticisms in his messages. For example, see *Mensajes presidenciales*, I: 227; 254; 255; 304; 401.

were put in prison on account of articles that had appeared in their papers, and just prior to that time the editors of El Comercio, La Política Cómica, and Verdad y Justicia (of Regla) were fined. The editor of Cuba was cited for trial, but refused to appear on the ground that as a congressman he was immune from arrest. In most of the other instances, too, the offending articles had been written by congressmen, and under current interpretations of the law the editors should not have been held liable. Gómez went so far as to attempt to influence the law courts to render decisions that would allow him to wreak vengeance on his critics,[20]—this in addition to his many appointments of judges "who make public profession of their political faith and boast of the most perfect submission to their party and those who govern in its name." [21] To assist him in his battle with the newspapers Gómez had a "law of national defence" introduced in Congress, signed by Ferrara and others of his partisans, on January 31, 1910, the object of which was to muzzle the press. Every newspaper in Havana except El Triunfo, the government organ, protested against the bill, and presently it was withdrawn.[22] There may very well be some sympathy for Gómez in his procedure in this matter, for the excesses of the Cuban newspapers, hiding behind congressional immunity, are notorious.[23] Later, when he could do so with a show of grace, since his term was then coming to an end, Gómez sent a message to Congress suggesting that some limitations be set to this privilege, referring particularly to its abuse in the slanders of the press.[24] It is not likely that he expected any action from Congress, however, and certainly none was taken.

[20] Velasco, 32-33, n. 42-43.
[21] Varona, *Op. cit.*, 248-249.
[22] Velasco, 31, n. 41.
[23] Cf. Varona, *Op. cit.*, 248.
[24] Message of Feb. 10, 1913, in *Mensajes presidenciales*, I, 401.

One of the earliest political problems of the President was to bring about a fusion of the two Liberal groups that had for a time fought each other in the campaign of 1908. The arrangement between them on the eve of the presidential elections amounted simply to an agreement to give government jobs in equal proportions to each faction, but otherwise each was to maintain its own organization. Gómez was eager for a union of the two groups so that there might be harmony between the legislative and executive branches of the government. So in February 1909 he called a meeting of the two wings of the party, at which time the differences between them were ironed out,—though more in outward seeming than in fact. Gómez formally announced the restoration of the single party organization in his message to Congress of April 5, 1909.[25] It was generally understood that one of the most important articles of the agreement was that Zayas was to be the party's candidate in the elections of 1912.

Meanwhile the incoming administration had pounced on the spoils of victory like a buzzard on its prey. Thousands of men were thrown out of office, to make room for the favorites of the winning party. This procedure caused not a little misgiving in neutral and non-political quarters. As Barbarrosa expressed it, "The idea of putting new people in the place of honest functionaries who have been rendering good service would not occur to any serious government which wished to introduce a plan of economies."[26] Naturally, the Conservatives protested, both for political reasons and because so many of their own partisans had been swept out of office by the flood of new appointments. La Discusión came out early in February 1909 in a bitter ar-

[25] In *Mensajes presidenciales*, I, 195-210, at 196.   [26] Barbarrosa, 96.

raignment of the administration on this and other scores. No enquiry had been made as to the merit or length of service of public employes prior to the removals, it asserted, and the handling of government business,—for example, in the custom-house,—had been considerably disturbed as a result of the numerous dismissals. It also charged that civilians had been appointed to the army and that Gómez partisans had been jumped over the heads of others, while some of the appointments to the higher positions in the military bureaucracy were obviously political in character.[27] Even the Zayistas protested at first against the separation of some of the office-holders from their places.[28]

It was only to be expected, in a country where the government job is so important a factor in the general scheme of life, that there should have been considerable dissatisfaction among those who had lost their posts and also among the thousands of others whose self-styled "just aspirations" had not been gratified. And in Hispanic countries political dissatisfaction quite easily translates itself into violence and revolution. The Gómez administration had its full share of these experiences. The Lavastida affair has already been mentioned. On July 25, 1910, General Vicente Miniet went out on what he probably intended to be a combined Conservative and veteranist revolution against the party in power, though his act was condemned by La Discusión and leading Conservatives and veterans. Miniet had but a handful of followers,—perhaps about seven,—and was captured at an estate in El Caney, near Santiago, two days later. Curiously enough his captor, a certain Lieutenant Castillo, had been wounded and taken prisoner at precisely the same place when he went out in the uprising of 1903.[29] Another

[27] Quoted in Havana *Post,* Feb. 9, 1909.

[28] Havana *Post,* Feb. 1, 1909.

[29] This account was taken from the files of *Discusión* for July 1910.

affair of the same sort took place when on July 3, 1911, General Guillermo Acevedo attempted to get up a revolution in the province of Havana. This met with no more success than the Miniet uprising had. Rather more serious was a movement launched in August of that year by the veterans' association, under the leadership of General Emilio Núñez.[30]

The veteranist movement arose in part out of a sincere desire to rid the country of the evils that had developed under the Gómez administration, but it was interwoven from the first with political considerations that soon came to be perhaps the principal element involved. General Núñez, ever an influential figure in military circles, had not by any means put aside his aspirations for the presidency, and very likely hoped to attain to his ambition through the aid of the veterans. In a circular of September 5, 1911, the National Council of Veterans declared among other things that "neither traitors nor guerrillas" ought to be allowed to rule the destinies of the state, hitting at office-holders who had been Spanish sympathizers at the time of the War of Independence. This was followed by open threats that unless these men retired from office they would be hanged, and any judges who allowed indictments therefor would be hanged also. Neither General Núñez nor the National Council of Veterans authorized these violent pronouncements, but by their silence or vague answers to direct queries they virtually gave them countenance. At length the whole country was

[30] Another so-called revolutionary attempt was the "Conspiracy of the trunk" of September 1910. A trunk was discovered filled with arms, and the impression was allowed to go out that they had been collected in connection with a proposed revolution against Gómez. Later, so it is said, it was found that the trunk had been filled with old muskets by a Gómez official. The idea was, to make it appear that Gómez was so watchful and so capable in the face of revolution and conspiracy that he was the one real man for the presidency in the coming election of 1912. The "great trunk mystery" became one of the jokes of Cuban public life. Kennedy, W   M, *The revolution in Cuba,* in *Living age,* v. CCLXXVI, pp. 463-468, at 467; Feb. 22, 1913.

in an uproar, and it seemed as if another revolution might occur. At this point the United States took a hand in the game. On January 17, 1912, Secretary of State Knox sent a note to the government of Cuba, saying that the situation caused the United States "grave concern," intimating that the laws should not be "defied" (in the way threatened by the veteranists), and remarking that Cuba ought to prevent any development which might compel the United States government "to consider what measures it must take." This, clearly enough, was a threat of intervention. There was an initial splutter of fury when this communication was published in Cuba, and General Núñez is said to have declared that the veterans would "fight to the death" against any interference by the United States. Calmer views at length prevailed, for the politicians feared that the United States might never get out of the island if she came in again. So in March 1912 the veterans' organization reached an agreement with the government whereby the campaign against office-holders was dropped and the veterans consented to act merely as a beneficial association for their own members and to aid the authorities as supplementary guardians of the peace.

The veteranist movement did not fail altogether in its program. A number of officials did fall on account of it, including two Cabinet members. Many of the government officials against whom the veterans objected were civil service appointees, but Congress was prevailed upon to pass a measure suspending the civil service law for eighteen months, —so it would not protect these men. Furthermore, army officers openly attended the veteranist meetings, despite a law forbidding them to take part in political affairs. It must not be thought, however, that all the veterans were solidly behind the Núñez movement. Many opposed it from the first, on account of its violence and because they recognized the political maneuver involved, while others went no farther than to desire the suggested reforms. Nevertheless, it is more than probable that there would have been a civil war, if it had not been for the action of the United States.[31]

Gómez avoided a revolution in connection with the veteranist movement, but was not so successful in what seemed likely at one time to prove a far more dangerous affair. This was the famous race war of 1912. Reference has already been made to the formation of the Independent Party of Color in 1907. The leaders of this group, Evaristo Estenoz (founder of the party) and Pedro Ivonet felt that not enough political favors were being accorded colored men, in view of their services. To be sure, they had contributed very materially in the war against Spain and in the Liberal victory over the Conservatives. Negro leaders asserted that they had furnished eighty-five per cent of the soldiers in the war of '95-'98,[32] and it has been claimed that they constituted seventy-five per cent of the voters.[33] These estimates are surely too high, as approximately two Cubans in every three are white, but certainly the negroes had provided a majority of the Army of Liberation and most of them voted with the Liberal party. Furthermore, the Liberal politicians had been very generous with their promises to negroes in 1908, but short on fulfillment in 1909. At the same time, as no less a person than Enrique José

[31] Naturally, the newspapers carried columns each day about the veteranist campaign. Trelles, *Biblioteca,* II, 115, cites a number of other items, including the two following: Secades, Manuel, *La justicia en Cuba,* 2 vols., Habana, 1912-1914; and Suárez Vera, Luis, *General Emilio Núñez,* Habana, 1915. Other mention worthy of note includes: Sanjenís, 282-309; *A warning note to Cuba,* in *Independent,* v. LXXII, pp. 170-171, Jan. 25, 1912; and Forbes-Lindsay, Charles Harcourt Ainslie, *Curbing Cuba,* in *Independent,* v. LXXII, pp. 185-186, Jan. 25, 1912.

[32] *The insurrection in Cuba,* in *Outlook,* v. CI, p. 238; June 1, 1912.

[33] Wigdil, Walter, *Addition without division = revolution,* in *Independent,* v. LXXII, pp. 1352-1356, at 1352; June 20, 1912.

Varona later pointed out, the negroes had no great cause for complaint. In a country where they were a minority of the population and possessed but a scant fraction of the national wealth and culture, they had received equal rights with white men, and the fact that they had fought for Cuba did not necessarily entitle them to government positions, as aptitudes for the tasks of peace were different from those of war.[34] But Estenoz and Ivonet were not dealing in abstractions. They had *political jobs* in mind, and felt that they knew how to get them. Gómez was none too well pleased with the formation of this party, and referred to the "evil" in Hispanic countries of the "third party and even other groups" in his message of April 5, 1909, though without alluding specifically to the negro organization. Estenoz and his companions continued their work, however, and in such a manner as to stir up a veritable race question. On this account they were arrested and put on trial in April 1910, and in the following month the so-called Morúa Law was passed forbidding the formation of any political party on lines of race or color. The author of the bill was none other than Senator Morúa Delgado, himself a colored man and at one time president of the Senate, though more recently taken into the Cabinet as Secretary of Agriculture.[35]

For two years following the enactment of the Morúa Law, the Estenoz-Ivonet movement was so intermingled with other political issues that it is difficult to state with certainty just what was going on. The two leaders were released from prison, and allowed to continue the work of organizing their party. Many writers insist that Gómez was now using

[34] Varona, Enrique José, *A los Conservadores*, one of *Siete circulares: 1910 a 1913*, in *De la colonia a la república*, 250-252, at 251.

[35] Morúa died the same month in which the bill that bore his name became a law.

Estenoz to further his own pretensions to a second term; for example, Vasconcelos (a bitter opponent of Gómez, but a Liberal of the Zayista group) says that while the press was crying out against the colored party movement, Gómez not only protected Estenoz, but also "gave checks and passage-money in Pullmans to the agents and orators of Estenocism." Indeed, Vasconcelos goes so far as to say that Gómez fomented the race question to further his reëlection plans, promising villas and castles to Estenoz, and he asserts that the war-cry of the negroes when eventually they rose in revolt was "Down with the Morúa Law!" to be sure, but with that, "Long live the reëlection!" Then when Gómez's original plans seemed likely to fail he plotted with Estenoz and Ivonet (who frequently visited him at the government palace) to simulate a revolution, so that Gómez could get the credit of putting it down and use it as a lever to raise himself once more to the presidential chair.[36]   A similar statement was made by a foreign writer,[37] but another writer, presumably a naturalized Cuban citizen with pro-Gómez leanings, insisted that the Conservatives were responsible for the release of Estenoz in the first place, though admitting that the defeat of the colored uprising would "compel" Gómez's candidacy and "assure his reëlection." [38]

If the outbreak was intended only as a political maneuver, it got away from its organizers and became a revolt of serious proportions. It began on May 20, 1912, the tenth anniversary of the republic, but was soon well in hand everywhere except in Oriente, especially in the section running from the neighborhood of Guantánamo to San Luis. The

[36] Vasconcelos, 11-14.
[37] Kennedy, W   M, The revolution in Cuba, in Living age, v. CCLXXVI, pp. 463-468, at 467; Feb. 22, 1913. Even Varona gives a hint to the same effect. Varona, Op. cit., 252. Cf. supra, n. 30.
[38] The political situation in Cuba, in American review of reviews, v. XLVI, pp. 45-48, at 48; July, 1912.

whole island was alarmed, however,[39] and these fears presently communicated themselves to the government of the United States. On May 25, 1912, the American minister delivered a note to the Cuban Secretary of State announcing certain United States naval dispositions in Cuban waters and saying that if the Cuban government should be unable, or should fail, to protect the lives and property of American citizens that American troops would be landed to take care of them. The note went on to insist that "this ought not to be considered as an intervention." Gómez himself cabled that same day directly to President Taft in protest, pointing out (as in all common-sense it was true) that such an action would in fact be an intervention, and suggesting that it be taken only following a previous agreement with Cuba, so as not to render a blow at the prestige of the latter. He also asserted that no damage had yet been done to foreign estates, and expressed his conviction that he could continue to prevent it. Taft replied that he was pleased with the energetic measures of Gómez, but repeated the purport of the earlier note when he said that any precautionary acts of the United States would not in any way represent an "intervention." A later United States note of the 29th would not agree to make a prior arrangement with the Cuban government before effecting a landing, and, indeed, a body of marines was put on shore at Daiquirí, near Santiago, on the 31st. Just previously Gómez, making a virtue of necessity, had given his "consent," though it can hardly be said that it was asked. The American forces remained on Cuban soil for several weeks, affording protection to foreign-owned mines and sugar estates.[40]

[39] For example, Sanjenís tells how he raised a "Local Guard" of thirty-five hundred volunteers to protect the capital and allay the feeling of panic that possessed the white people of that city. Sanjenís, 148-154.

[40] The correspondence cited here appears in Gómez's message to Congress of May 31, 1912, in *Mensajes presidenciales*, I, 360-363.

The really serious stage of the revolt came a few days after this. According to Vasconcelos it would appear that one of the lesser leaders of the negro soldiery was not in the secret of the Gómez-Estenoz plot. This man, Isidoro Santos Carrera, attacked and burned the La Maya sugar-mill on June 2. That alarmed General Monteagudo, who was in charge of operations in Oriente, and he thereupon suspended constitutional guarantees on the 4th. The original plan, according to Vasconcelos, was for negro demonstrations in the vicinity of sugar estates, but no shooting; then Gómez was to offer an amnesty to those who would lay down their arms, and quickly "pacify" the country.[41] However true or false this charge may be, Gómez certainly proceeded with vigor, following the La Maya affair; indeed, there was nothing else to do, for now he had a real civil war on his hands. On June 3 Gómez asked Congress for the right to declare martial law in all the national territory or any part thereof,[42] and this was granted by a law of June 5,—though Monteagudo had anticipated the law the day before. On the 6th Gómez issued a proclamation denouncing the "ferocious savagery" of the rebels and promising to make short work of them.[43] Unquestionably the country was solidly behind him. Menocal, the Conservative candidate of 1908, offered the government a thousand cavalrymen,—an offer which was not accepted; [44] leading negroes were on the government side; [45] and business interests, of course, were of the same mind. For a few days there was some severe fighting, for there were about four thousand well-armed negroes in the field. It was necessary for Monteagudo to defeat them in battle, but this was done. Afterwards he had to deal with

[41] Vasconcelos, 15-18.
[42] In *Mensajes presidenciales*, I, 363.
[43] Vasconcelos, 19-22.
[44] *Ibid.*, 9-10.

[45] For example, note the speech of Cuesta Rendón, a colored representative in Congress, quoted in González Lanuza, 890-891.

separate small bands, until the death of the rebel leaders broke the back of the revolt. By July 18 the last body of rebels had been cut to pieces or taken. In all, the revolution cost the lives of some three thousand colored persons.[46] In due time an amnesty bill was passed, covering offences in connection with the uprising,[47] and the affair, as such, was buried. Incidentally, it may be noted, however, that political jobs for negroes have since been granted rather lavishly, though not those involving any high degree of responsibility, beyond the duty of adding up their pay and collecting it and of delivering a number of votes to a party chief.[48]

Whatever Gómez may have had in mind in connection with the race conflict, it did not lead to his renomination for the presidency. The pact with the Miguelistas of the Liberal party was viewed with suspicion and doubt by the Zayistas almost from the first. As early as the elections of 1910 there was something approaching an open split,[49] and as the time came nearer for the political conventions of 1912 there developed a violent controversy between them. Gómez was "not a candidate," but newspapers and political friends were working for his nomination tooth and nail. In April 1912 General Machado wrote an open letter resigning from the Cabinet, on the ground that the President's hatred "for a man" (meaning Zayas, though not naming him) was precipitating Cuba toward an intervention, just as Estrada Palma's hatred of Gómez had done (as Machado put it) in 1906. He also referred to "the secret" that everybody knew,

[46] Trelles, *Biblioteca*, II, 116.
[47] See *infra*, pp: 531; 533.
[48] Cf, *supra*, pp. 22-23.
[49] Incidentally, there were the usual queer and meaningless, though vote-catching, platforms in the congressional electoral campaign of 1910.

Among the planks advocated by different Liberals were those calling for the prohibition of religious orders, the prevention of foreigners from acquiring land, and the abolition of the Platt Amendment!

that Gómez was after reëlection, as Estrada Palma had been before him, and he intimated that Gómez should do what Estrada Palma did not, that is, resign.[50] Naturally, Gómez did not resign, but continued to work under cover for the nomination. He had as an opponent the cleverest politician that Cuba has yet produced, however, and when the party convention was held on May 15 Zayas came out of it with the Liberal nomination.

The nomination of Zayas was not taken with a good grace in the Gómez camp. Possibly Gómez still hoped, for a time, to retain the presidency as a result of the situation that developed immediately afterward in connection with the race war. Nevertheless, he dropped his pretensions eventually, whether or not because of alleged objections on the part of the United States cannot be stated with certainty. He and his followers did not accept Zayas, however. Governor Asbert of Havana, once a Zayas supporter, but more recently a close favorite of Gómez, now refused to support the Liberal candidate at the polls, and threw his influence to the Conservative nominee. Some Liberal papers attacked Zayas. La Lucha called him the "candidate of defeat," and said that he stood for "dissolution, ruin, and rout." This paper was one of several still clamoring for the election of Gómez. Gómez himself later published a letter of his to Ferrara, dated July 15, in which he asserted that Liberal union or victory was impossible in the face of the nomination of Zayas, as many Liberals felt that they were serving both the country and the party by working against him, for the government would lack "authority, respectability, and force" in his hands. On this account Gómez held that the Liberals ought still to reject his candidacy and nominate a new standard-bearer. Otherwise, like Bryan in the United

[50] Quoted in Lozano Casado, 50-53.

States, Zayas would carry his party down to defeat.[51]   Meanwhile the Conservatives had renominated General Menocal. They had the advantage of party solidarity, which the Liberals lacked,[52] and were able to get Asbert lined up on their side, thus assuring their victory in the normally Liberal great province of Havana.   The smaller province of Pinar del Río was safely Conservative.   It was therefore necessary to win one other large province (Santa Clara or Oriente) or the other two small ones (Matanzas and Camagüey).   The eventual decision was to make the effort in Oriente.

It is usually asserted that the elections of November 1912 were fair in every respect,[53] but there are many who do not admit that this was so.[54]   One distinguished Cuban, whose name would carry weight if it might be mentioned, described the whole electoral situation to the writer as follows:

"Gómez wanted to be reëlected, but would not come out in the open and say so, pretending that he favored Asbert. But Zayas manipulated things so that he got the Liberal nomination. Then Gómez aided Menocal. It developed that it was necessary to win Oriente in order to defeat Zayas, and there Gómez had Monteagudo and the rural guards employ all the usual electoral arts of military intimidation and the like in order to swing the balance for Menocal. Everywhere else the elections were fair."

Gómez asserted, after the election, that he had done what he could, within proper limits, to help Zayas (though it is exceedingly doubtful if Zayas himself knew it!), but the

[51] The election situation is discussed in detail from the Gómez standpoint in Lozano Casado, 66-89.

[52] In one of his circulars to the Conservatives, Varona called upon the party to take advantage of the "fractionalism" and "excessive personalism" of their opponents by presenting a solid front themselves. Varona, A nuestros correligionarios, one of Siete circulares: 1910 a 1913,

in De la colonia a la república, 241-243, at 241.

[53] For example, Trelles says: "Manuel Sanguily directed the elections of the first of November 1912 with the greatest impartiality." Trelles, Biblioteca, II, 117. Sanguily was Secretary of Government at the time.

[54] Cf. item in Havana Post quoted infra, p. 567.

statement just quoted represents the general opinion with regard to his action. This is what Pérez says:

"Yielding, so they say, to the pressure of General Monteagudo, who enjoyed an enormous prestige in the army, he had the unfortunate idea of turning traitor to his party, delivering the presidency of the republic to Mario García Menocal." [55]

It is probable, however, that the elections themselves were substantially correct, although the government may very well have been ready to use force in case it should have appeared to be necessary. As matters were, Menocal won, and the Conservatives even carried Congress, though by the narrowest of margins.[56] Once the issue was settled, Gómez was loud in his protestations of impartiality in the elections [57] and of his own non-reëlectionist ideas. On this score he said "I glory in having been the first ruler in Latin America who has established such a patriotic precedent," [58] and in his *manifiesto,* or public statement, of December 1912 to the Liberals he repeated that he had not been a candidate, personally favoring Asbert.[59] These remarks need not be considered very seriously, however, from the standpoint of what he had really wished to do.

On May 20, 1913, Gómez's term came to an end. As that date approached, various summaries of his achievements in office were published in the newspapers, mainly laudatory, in which many things were claimed for him. Yet, to one who can look at Cuban affairs from the outside, it would seem that the main significance of his administration lay in the fact that it marked a restoration of traditionalist tendencies, with the single exception that Cubans had taken the place

[55] Pérez, 7. Elsewhere, in referring to the election of Menocal, Pérez says that Monteagudo "raised him to power in 1912." Pérez, 11.

[56] Pardo Suárez, 119.

[57] For example, in his message of Nov. 4, 1912, to Congress, in *Mensajes presidenciales,* I, 380-393, at 381.

[58] Quoted in Lozano Casado, 94.

[59] Quoted in *Ibid.,* 73-75, at 75.

of Spaniards. Estrada Palma had tried to hold back the current, and it burst over him. Gómez swam with it. A president like Gómez in a country with more wholesome political traditions would deserve unqualified condemnation, but in Cuba it is a question whether, on the whole, he does not more nearly merit praise. He could not have prevented bad political practices, even if he had desired to do so, for he had to rely upon a horde of self-seekers whose idea of "patriotism" was to gather in the fruits of office for themselves. As for Gómez, he never went quite so far in improprieties as it would have been possible for him to go. He gave some heed to public opinion. And he did not reëlect himself President, as he most certainly could have done if he had been willing to make use of the violent methods that were classic in Hispanic America. As one writer has said:

"All his faults he redeemed with a single gesture: he did not aspire to power through the employment of power, descending the steps of the palace after having delivered his authority to his opponent of the previous electoral period." [60]

And, to be sure, if Cuba could for a time have had rulers who were no worse than José Miguel there might have been a more rapid evolution toward a better political state.[61]

[60] Pérez, 9.

[61] There is nothing remotely approaching a Martínez Ortiz for the Gómez era or, indeed, for succeeding administrations. Aside from comparatively brief pamphlets or articles, there is not a single work that deals in detail with this period as a whole, not even as part of a larger work. Lozano Casado is concerned with the personality of José Miguel, but is useful, though by no means safe, on some other phases of the period. The same thing may be said for Sanjenís, who was primarily interested in airing his own grievance against the President. A number of pamphlet-eers contribute incidentally to the story, here and there. Some of their works have been cited in this and the preceding chapter, but several more are noted in Trelles, *Biblioteca,* II, 112-117. So this period, even more than those before it, is in need of an exhaustive study making critical use of government documents, newspapers, and other contemporary evidences. Rowland, Donald Winslow, *The Cuban race war of 1912* (M. A. thesis, 1926; Ms. in the Library of the University of California), is a meritorious study of one phase of this period.

CHAPTER XIV

MENOCAL BEGINS, 1913-1916

THERE was great rejoicing by the best elements in Cuba when, on May 20, 1913, General Mario García Menocal, the successful candidate of the Conservative party, took over the presidency of the republic. At last, they thought, Cuba was to have the correct and efficient government of which the workers for independence had dreamed. For the Conservatives seemed to stand for the ideals of González Lanuza and Enrique José Varona, men of proven integrity and worth. Then too there was Menocal himself, rated the highest in his party. Respected as he was in Cuba, Menocal was even more admired by the foreign writers who celebrated his advent to power. He "stands . . . apart from and above the ordinary run of Cuban politicians," said Sydney Brooks, well-known English publicist, who then went on to compare him to Woodrow Wilson, the President of the United States. He was "the most distinguished and experienced man of affairs in the island," said Brooks, adding that of all the Cubans he was "the best man they possessed." Indeed, continued Brooks, it was unusual to find his type in Cuba, and even more so for him to have succeeded in politics. He was not a self-seeker, and not even accused of aspiring to the presidency in order to make money out of it, but was really disinterested and altruistic in his views, thinking of the welfare of the land and not of the manipulation of political jobs and loot-yielding concessions. Once he made up his mind, however, he was tenacious of his views, for he was "endowed

318

with a decisive and energetic temperament." Furthermore, he chose as his ministers men of first-rate quality, with the result that a healthier atmosphere had become apparent in Cuban politics.[1]

This characterization was merely representative of what foreigners in general and many Cubans thought, and, despite later "variations from type," was very likely what Menocal himself intended to be. Even at the outset of his second term some foreigners were still speaking favorably of him. For example, George Marvin, an American writer, said of him that he was "more of an American than . . . a Cuban," intending the remark as praise. He was open, frank, a good listener, and absolutely honest. He had "extraordinary administrative ability," which he had displayed in war, business, and in the presidency, in which last-named office he worked "twelve hours a day." This writer pointed out, however, that Menocal had one grave defect: he was typically Cuban (and one might add Hispanic American) in being a strong family man, "which is really at the root of most Cuban political troubles." [2]

Marvin's remarks on the score of the Menocal defect are worthy of somewhat more extended comment. Cuban wives, said Marvin, were the recipients of an oft-repeated, ardent devotion from their husbands, who might tell them "twenty times a day" how much they loved them,—and then tell the same story twenty more times to some woman around the corner. Nevertheless, the affection for the former was real, and extended far beyond wife and children, taking in relatives of various degrees as members of "the family." There

[1] Brooks, Sydney, *Cuba and its president,* in *Living age,* v. CCLXXXI, pp. 497-499, May 23, 1914; *Some impressions of Cuba,* in *North American review,* v. CXCIX, pp. 734-745, at 745, May, 1914.

[2] Marvin, George, *Keeping Cuba libre,* in *World's work,* v. XXXIV, pp. 553-567, at 564-565; Sept., 1917.

were some fifteen or twenty persons in one branch of the Menocal family who all lived in the same house, having little to do with anybody else, except others of the enlarged family group. And family loyalty makes its way into politics. An American military attaché once caught a relative of Menocal in the act of "embezzlements," but Menocal would not punish the man, though he did transfer him to another post. Thus, said Marvin, "loyalty to friends and kindred is actually a hampering influence in the public life of Cuba," and it was that sort of thing which made the Platt Amendment necessary, even in the background of such an otherwise fine man as Menocal.[3]

The name of Menocal has already appeared many times in these pages. He had, indeed, had a distinguished career. Born at Jagüey Grande, Matanzas, in 1866, he was taken two years later to the United States, to which country his father emigrated when forced to leave Cuba at the time of the Ten Years' War. Menocal spent much of his boyhood on a plantation in Mexico, but was educated in the United States, attending the Maryland College of Agriculture and eventually obtaining a degree in engineering at Cornell in 1888. He then went to work at his profession, at first for several years in Nicaragua in connection with the canal projects of that day, but presently he appeared in Cuba, and was there at the outbreak of the war in 1895. He enlisted forthwith as a private, but rose quickly until at length he attained to the rank of major-general. Few men saw more active service than he. He fought under Máximo Gómez, Maceo, and Calixto García, the greatest generals of the war, but his crowning glory came with the battle of Victoria de

[3] Marvin, *Op. cit.*, at 565.

las Tunas while at the head of a division of Calixto García's
army in 1897. On this occasion

"he made such skillful disposition of men and guns that competent
witnesses have said that the conduct of this battle stands out in the
entire record of the Revolution as the one combat in. which the Cuban
forces were disposed and directed in accordance with the principles of
military science. Not only did General Menocal direct the operations
in pursuance of a well-considered plan but he is said to have led his
soldiers in the assault with intrepid courage." [4]

Under the United States military government Menocal was
for a time chief of police of Havana and then inspector of
light-houses, but resigned in 1899 in order to accept an opening with the Cuban American Sugar Company. For that
company he set up the Chaparra sugar plantation, which
became under his management the largest estate of its kind
in the world. His success as a business man was unques-
tioned. Laboring men as well as great corporations had confidence in him. As one man (who was by no means pro-
Menocal) told the writer, he would "go right out in the fields
with his workmen and share their conditions." Furthermore,
as a sportsman and gentleman, in addition to being a hero
of the war against Spain, he was quite popular generally
among Cubans.[5] Some were a little hesitant about him as
a candidate for the presidency, however, because of his long
life in the United States and his close relations with American business enterprises. In the campaign of 1908, for example, the Liberals accused him of being an annexationist.[6]
Nevertheless, few men could have been found who gave
greater promise of success than Menocal did at the inception
of his presidency in 1913.

[4] *Cubans of to-day*, 4.
[5] Brooks, Sydney, *Cuba and its president*, in *Living age*, v. CCLXXXI,
pp. 497-499, at 497; May 23, 1914.
[6] Martínez Ortiz, II, 820.

But that was in 1913. For several years following the end of his second term in 1921 no man was ever more universally condemned. Indeed, the current began to turn against him from the time he decided to run for reëlection in 1916. One of the most noteworthy characterizations of the President's conduct appeared in an open letter directed to him by Juan José de la Maza y Artola early in 1917. Maza was also a Conservative, but had opposed the reëlection of Menocal, and espoused the cause of the Liberal candidate against him. He called upon Menocal to acknowledge his defeat in the elections of 1916:

"Never in America," he said, "has a citizen been exalted to the first magistracy of his people with more enthusiasm on the part of his own partisans and more respect among foreigners and even his opponents than you were in being raised to the presidency of our republic. In addition to all the honors and glory which you had legitimately acquired in the brilliant course of your history as an eminent patriot and exemplary citizen, you had the merit of having been proposed by a party which had distinguished itself by its vigorous and constant campaigns in favor of morality and economy in our administration and which as a solid guarantee of its seriousness and efficiency was offering the clean reputation of the illustrious men of high station who were directing it, by whose wise and honored counsels all thought that you would always be inspired . . . Your first steps . . . manifested clearly the honesty of your intentions . . . But why did you not persevere in that line of conduct? . . . Why did you not fortify yourself with the counsels of the illustrious and honored chiefs of the Conservative party . . . instead of . . . abandoning yourself to the intrigues of those among your friends . . . who, avid of advancement, ended by making you believe that you could not maintain yourself in the government without changing your course in radical fashion and compounding with what they were wont to call . . . the impurities of reality? . . . There were those who one day brought it about that you should employ bribery to assure measures that were fitting for the public good, utilizing only the collectorships, the distribution of which you could make, according to the law, at your pleasure.[7] And when they saw how satisfied you were with the efficacy

[7] For a discussion of the collectorships in connection with the evils of the Cuban lottery, see *infra*, pp. 554-557.

of the system they later got you to dispose profusely of the margin in the rent of the lottery for the same or other objects, not now so elevated, and recently from the other funds of the public treasury, even from those expressly devoted to specific expenditures, for purposes of very doubtful propriety . . . It is true, and to the sound part of our people it is perfectly clear, that these filtrations are not employed to increase your own patrimony. But, on the other hand, people see with increasing alarm that at your side there are rapidly being raised up not a few fortunes . . . And such is the state of mind that this alarm has created . . . that people do not hesitate to say . . . that instead of that mad prodigality with the public funds it is preferable, at the cost of the state, to enrich its own chief and a limited number of its functionaries, as this would be more economical for the nation and less compromising for our future." [8]

Of unqualified denunciations of Menocal in connection with graft, bad administration, election-stealing, and dictatorial methods there is enough to fill volumes. For the present, however, it will be sufficient to mention the summing-up which one Cuban writer has made of him as recently as 1924:

"He lacked the perception which the other Presidents have had, to gain the esteem of his people. In disposing of the funds of a nation it is necessary to respect liberties, even though it may be by debasing consciences, as Zayas has done." [9]

The election of Menocal in 1912 was accepted quietly in Cuba, and Gómez gave over his power on May 20, 1913. The new government had made promises of reform and achievement which it very probably hoped to fulfil. According to Carlos Martí and other Menocal panegyrists it proceeded to do so in ample measure, bringing prosperity to the country and accumulating good works, to the accompaniment of correct administration, in a way deserving of eulogies from the start. These assertions are not altogether

[8] Quoted in Cabrera, 357-367, at 359-362. Cf. infra, pp: 347-348; 350-   351; 358-360.
[9] Pérez, 14.

borne out by the facts. The difficulties in such a program were none too easy to resolve. Prosperity at length did come, but not with a rush. The last few months of the Gómez era were a period of depression on account of the low price of sugar, Cuba's chief product, and bad conditions affecting the tobacco crop. This situation continued into 1914, at which time it was aggravated by the outbreak of the World War. The immediate effect of that was to upset all the normal workings of Cuban commerce, although it seemed clear from the first that it must eventually have a beneficial effect on the price of sugar. Both the 1913-1914 and 1914-1915 crops were poor, though the product was already bringing an appreciably higher figure in 1915. Tobacco, however, did not enjoy a single good year during all Menocal's first term. In addition to bad weather, it suffered virtual outlawry in European markets, where it was regarded as a luxury that did not contribute to the winning of the war. Meanwhile, prices for goods imported into Cuba were rapidly going up, weighing heavily on the working classes. Menocal tried to tide over affairs in the dark period from 1913 to 1915 by inaugurating a program of public works, but there he was balked by Congress, which would not make the necessary appropriations. And at this time Menocal was still disposed to give some heed to constitutional limitations on his power. By 1916, however, there seemed not to be a cloud on the economic horizon. The sugar crop of 1915-1916 amounted to more than three million tons, which was by far the greatest in the history of the country, and it was sold at very high prices. The next year it was half a million larger still. The overflow from the good fortune in the sugar business found its way into other lines. Foreign capital was attracted, and many Cuban planters preferred to sell their estates "at prices which have fully satisfied the sellers and left the buyers content." Indeed, never had Cuba known such "astonishing prosperity," and even "the most powerful nations had enjoyed it but few times in equal measure." [10]

The prosperity of the government itself, depending as it did on custom-house collections, followed the same course as that of the general business of the country. Gómez had left only a million and a half in the treasury, together with so many unpaid debts as to constitute a substantial deficit. This was without taking into account the numerous bills carelessly "tossed off" by Congress and the President authorizing projects without assigning the expense to any particular funds, but upon which no work had yet been done. In this respect the Menocal government was no improvement on its predecessor. Whatever money came to hand was expended in one way or another, without much attention to budgets. Indeed, only once in Menocal's first term, for the year 1914-1915, did Congress so much as trouble itself to authorize the budget. The commerce of Cuba was approximately 302 millions in 1913-1914, 344 in 1914-1915, 474 in 1915-1916, and 604 in 1916-1917, with balances in favor of exports of some thirty-eight, eighty-six, 130 and 108 millions respectively. Most of this was with the United States, in which respect Cuba already far outranked any other Hispanic American country. Indeed, Cuba was importing from the United States more than the A B C countries (Argentina, Brazil, and Chile) combined and also more than the other fifteen republics of the Western Hemisphere, or, in other words, considerably more than a third of all United States exports to Hispanic America. And yet the other countries

[10] The President's messages to Congress, especially the long semi-annual messages at the opening of a session, contain abundant data on this subject. See *Mensajes presidenciales*, I, especially at pages: 459; 466; 505; 525; 529-530; 537; 544; 573; 579; 609; 617; 653; 658; 703; 709.

of Hispanic America outranked Cuba thirty times over in the sum total of their population. No country in the world had so great a *per capita* trade as Cuba. Nevertheless, the revenues were at first not equal to the necessities of the government,—so much so that Menocal once deemed it necessary to effect economies, even to the extent of exacting a rebate of from five to ten per cent on the salaries of public employes receiving over nine hundred dollars a year.[11] Presently, however, the treasury became more prosperous. Receipts and expenditures were approximately forty-one, thirty-seven, forty-six, and fifty-two millions in the four years from 1913 to 1917.[12]

Current revenues, much or little, did not suffice for all the needs of the state. One of the most urgent matters was for the completion of the Havana-Cienfuegos sanitary tunneling and paving contract on which the work had been started by Gómez. As already stated, Gómez had tried unsuccessfully to get Congress to authorize an additional loan of thirteen millions when the original monies devoted to this project were exhausted. Menocal took up this question at once, for, indeed, a considerable sum was due on work already completed and not paid for. In order to keep things going, Gómez had taken it upon himself to effect a short-term loan of a million and a half, and Menocal borrowed yet another million. The latter now called on Congress for authority to borrow fifteen millions, of which ten were to complete work under the old contract, together with some extensions that had been provided for by law, and the other five divided equally between reimbursement of the two millions and a half of the short-term loans and other old debts. Meno-

---

[11] Message to Congress, Aug. 22, 1914, in *Mensajes presidenciales*, I, 529-530.   [12] These figures are taken from Trelles, *Biblioteca*, II, 127.

cal had a majority in favor of the bill, but for months the Liberals prevented a vote through the familiar no quorum device. In October 1913 the President called a special session of Congress to act upon this matter, but again there was no quorum. At length, in the following December, the bill passed, but for ten millions instead of fifteen. Early in 1914 the loan was effected with the New York house of J. P. Morgan and Company, in an issue to mature in 1949, with a five per cent coupon rate. In addition there was one short-term domestic loan during Menocal's first presidency for five millions in 1915, to relieve the needs of the treasury. This made the total domestic debt some fifteen or sixteen millions at that time.[13]

Despite the general prosperity which eventually developed toward the close of Menocal's first term, the President found it difficult to do anything substantial in the way of positive achievements. Funds were lacking at the outset, and costs were too heavy later on. Furthermore, not very much could be accomplished without the consent of Congress, and that body was none too easy to handle. Time and again, measures were recommended, without any action being taken. Eventually, it would seem, Menocal "found a way," adapting himself to the corrupt practices of the Gómez era, while still later he hit upon the yet more convenient method of acting on his own initiative in the typical fashion of the Hispanic American dictator, but these executive shortcomings were not nearly so much to the fore in his first administration as in his second.

In spite of all obstacles, if Menocal's eulogists are allowed to tell the story, especially Carlos Martí, a great deal was accomplished by the President during his first administra-

[13] Loans were a frequent subject for discussion in the President's messages to Congress. See, for example, *Men-* *sajes presidenciales,* I: 453-454; 459; 465; 483-485; 546; 581; 709.

tion. In the first place, he "made the country more prosperous than it ever had been before." Never had there been so many individual fortunes in Cuba. He was solicitous for the welfare of labor, too, as witness a decree of 1915 for compulsory workmen's insurance, his successful mediation in various labor disputes, and his patronage of a national labor congress. He created a Cuban money system. He achieved great things on behalf of education and public health. He vastly aided agriculture, especially the sugar industry. One of his acts in this connection was a decree of 1915 permitting sugar brokers to quote their commodity in American money and in cents per pound, instead of, as formerly, in Spanish weights and money. Another measure was his encouragement of Spanish immigration as a much needed addition to the supply of labor. He did all he could to advance the pastoral industry, as, for example, by his patronage of the cattle exposition of 1914. He even promoted a baby show! He was responsible for the completion of a vast number of public works, such as the building of schools, hospitals, roads, bridges, municipal improvements, water-works, post-offices, wireless stations, and monuments. Many of Menocal's "achievements," however, were things that he merely recommended to Congress, without anything ever being done. Others were things that he was "going to do," such as the erection of the "Maine" monument "of Hellenic beauty" (but not done until 1925), the building of the great central highway (still in the legislative, conversational, and *spending* stage), the completion of the architectural plan of the University of Havana (not done yet), and the solution of Cuba's serious problem over distribution of its water-supply (not even very far along in the "spending stage" as yet).

The documents emanating from the presidency itself reveal more of the obstacles that Menocal met with than do the works of his eulogists. This appears, not only in the messages of the President, but also and more strikingly in the annual *Memorias* volumes containing the reports of the different departments of the administration. The report of the Secretary of Public Works for the year 1916-1917 may serve as an illustration. In that year there were fourteen laws carrying a total appropriation of $948,000 for roads and nine more in the sum of $1,128,000 for other public works. The Secretary pointed out that his department had encountered many difficulties. The effects of the economic crisis of 1913-1914 were still felt; prices of material had increased; and it was hard to get the needed labor supply. Many works had had to be stopped and contracts rescinded for lack of funds. The advance in the cost of both materials and labor had been excessive; for instance, coal had formerly been obtainable at four and a half to five dollars a ton, but now cost twenty or thirty. The revolution of 1917 paralyzed work, and caused destruction of much government property, besides which the insurrectionists in the eastern provinces appropriated large amounts of the national funds. The solution of water-supply problems for Havana and Santiago waited only for a grant of money by Congress, as the preliminary studies had been made. Much road work had been done, though at heavy expense. Great attention had been given to repair of roads, as they deteriorated rapidly. Altogether, the department had expended a little more than ten million dollars during the year.[14] Even Martí took occasion to defend Menocal for *not* building nine hundred schools that had been authorized by Congress, pointing out that this apparently liberal legislation had assigned no funds for the purpose.

[14] *Memoria de la administración ... entre el 1° de julio de 1916 y el*   *30 de junio de 1917*, pp. 219-405.

In point of fact, Menocal did very little on the score of what has been claimed for him, as will be shown more specifically in summing up about him at the end of his second administration. His reform of the money system, however, is worthy of special mention. United States money had served as the sole legal basis for the country, but in practice Spanish and French coins also circulated, and the cumbersome factor of determining exchange rates entered into most transactions. By the law of 1914, which went into effect the following year, a Cuban monetary system was established on a parity with that of the United States, with United States money also passing as legal tender. The value of this measure to business was incalculable.[15] A number of Menocal's other "meritorious" acts would seem, on the whole, to belong rather in the field of political maneuvers than in that of beneficial administration. He had been elected in 1912 as a result of the split in the Liberal party, and probably deemed it necessary to build up Conservative strength in order to win and retain a more thoroughgoing control over the government. Many of his political innuendoes, ungenerous though it may appear to some, were directed at the man to whom in great measure he owed his election, his Liberal predecessor in office.

In one of his first messages he asked Congress to omit the twenty-five thousand a year for secret expenses that had been awarded to Gómez, characterizing it as unnecessary and improper. He also asked for the derogation of a law of the preceding March 15 which had provided rich jobs for a number of "provincial inspectors of sanitation." These appointments were useless and wasteful.[16] The suppression

---

[15] Of interest on this subject are Menocal's messages to Congress of May 9, 1914, and Nov. 1, 1915, in *Mensajes presidenciales*, I, 525-526, at 526, and 609-636, at 618-619.

[16] Message to Congress of May 26, 1913, in *Ibid.*, I, 437.

of similar posts in the diplomatic service was also recommended by him.[17]   When it seemed likely that Congress might not only do away with the secret expense allowance of the President but also reduce that of the Department of Government to twenty-five thousand dollars, Menocal saw matters in a new light. He pointed out that previous budgets had allowed that department from fifty to seventy-five thousand a year, and something like $530,000 had been spent in fact during the four years of Gómez's rule, and therefore he asked that seventy-five thousand a year should now be assigned.[18] And as for *botellas,* or "soft jobs," it will appear that he gave rather more than his share of them, before he stepped down from power.

Some of Menocal's other messages had as high a moral tone as those which had emanated from Tomás Estrada Palma, but they carried no "punch" when it came to achievement. He asked Congress to abolish the lottery,[19] but when a year and a half later, on December 4, 1915, he issued a decree for an examination of the accounts of the nation, he exempted those of the lottery. As Trelles has said, "Comments are superfluous." [20]   In 1915 he vetoed a bill to grant a thirty year concession for horse-racing and jai-alai,[21] but both of these sports later established themselves in Cuba while Menocal was still in power. He also called for legislation on the prostitution evil,[22] and vetoed an objectionable amnesty bill,[23] but did not achieve what in outward seeming it appeared that he wanted in either case.

[17] Message to Congress of May 27, 1913, in *Ibid.,* I, 437-438, at 438.
[18] Message to Congress of June 18, 1913, in *Ibid.,* I, 438-439.
[19] Message to Congress of March 10, 1914, in *Ibid.,* I, 495-496.
[20] Trelles, *El progreso (1902 a 1905) y el retroceso (1906 a 1922) de la república de Cuba,* 23.
[21] Message to Congress of June 9, 1915, in *Mensajes presidenciales,* I, 602-603.
[22] Message to Congress of May 26, 1916, in *Ibid.,* I, 689-690.
[23] Cf. *infra,* pp. 531-532.

In his first long message to Congress, on November 3, 1913, Menocal availed himself of his opportunity to criticize the administration of his Liberal predecessor. For example, in telling of the unsatisfactory state in which he found the Department of Public Works he expressed himself as follows:

"On several occasions I ordered the suspension of various works in the different provinces, some because their contracts covered a larger sum than the credit approved for their execution, and others because they were being carried on with funds assigned by illegal transfers, the suppression of which left a deficit in their accounts. In the majority of cases in the works undertaken by the previous administration there has been inverted in general expenses and personnel a larger amount than on the works themselves, for which reason it exceeded the credit approved. This is why the works cannot be continued. The temporary personnel in all of them was consuming the greater part of the credit assigned, and the same thing has happened in budgetary credits for roads and bridges, betterments in rivers and ports, sanitation of the city of Havana, betterment of the water-supply of the same, and other allotments for works and services of great importance, which in good part, for the reason given, have not been attended to."[24]

The most resounding instance of Menocal's making political capital out of the shortcomings of the preceding administration, however, occurred in conection with the Ports Company affair, one of the major grafting measures of the Gómez administration. This story is told usually in connection with the presidency of José Miguel, but it attained to its greatest fame through Menocal's cancellation of the contract, and for various reasons, including the ultimate disposition of the affair, it belongs more properly to the era of Menocal.[25]

The thing that made this affair a particularly good medium

[24] Menocal to Congress, in *Mensajes presidenciales*, I, 459-474, at 467.

[25] The writer has in his possession a bulky file of papers on this subject, many of them from confidential sources. Problems of space make it necessary, however, to give a comparatively brief summary of the case, with citations merely to some of the documents that have appeared in print.

for political propaganda was that the Ports Company eventually developed into a foreign-owned corporation, but the plan was conceived by Cubans who got the graft for themselves. A number of prominent Liberals (who have since continued to hold a high place in political councils in Cuba) are said to have been involved in the formulation of the project. It had its basis in the fact that the ports of Cuba were in need of dredging and other improvements. The government was already collecting twenty-five cents a ton on all imports, for this purpose, but this was being expended mostly in salaries to engineers, who were supposed to be drawing up plans. The promoters of the new scheme hoped to get a concession from the Cuban government. If they expected to obtain it without undertaking the port improvements they were disillusioned when they consulted Gómez. He acted characteristically. He was willing to have the thing go through, but insisted that the work should be done. Thereupon the promoters approached an American engineer who had been a successful contractor for several years in Cuba, a certain Tillinghast L'Hommedieu Huston.[26] As head of the Huston Contracting Company he agreed to undertake the job. A resident of long standing in Cuba, Huston cannot have been surprised at the obvious likelihood that there was graft in the deal, but his company was called upon merely to do the work, without any necessary connection with the seamy side of the affair. The organizers of the project were not greatly interested in the port works as such, but were decidedly in a hurry to get the concession settled. On this score the following story, told to the writer by an engineer who was consulted about improvements at one of the ports, is quite illuminating:

[26] Colonel "Tilly" Huston is now former part owner of the New York well known in the United States as a American League Baseball Club.

"I received a wire from ———— asking me to tell him next morning how much it would cost to dredge the port. I replied that it was impossible to say. Aside from making off-hand estimates of prices and materials, I could not tell what condition the bay was in,—how much dirt would need to be taken out,—whether there was any rock,—and twenty other things. He wired back for me to make the estimate anyway and put it high enough to take care of any possibility. So I sent in the estimate."

With Congress and the President now willing, there was one further preliminary step before the deal should go through. Since Gómez required the improvements themselves to be made, it was necessary to finance them. So the promoters consulted the general manager of the Trust Company of Cuba, a former partner of Huston and a stockholder in the Huston Contracting Company, Mr. Norman H. Davis.[27] Davis suggested the formation of a stock company and an issue of bonds on the credit of the company's contract with Cuba. He agreed for the Trust Company to handle the bond issue. It is said that a preliminary enquiry was made of the American minister whether the United States would have any objection to the concession, and it was not until assurances were received from him that the Trust Company consented to act. The Ports Company was organized, with Carlos Miguel de Céspedes (reputed "master mind" of the whole affair) as general manager. Huston was induced to serve as president until some other reputable American engineer could be secured to take over the direction of the work. In 1912 this man was found in the person of Captain Eugene Klapp. Meanwhile, the financial structure of the company had long since been arranged. There was to be an authorized capital of ten million dollars in stock

[27] Mr. Davis later became financial adviser of the Secretary of the Treasury of the United States and a confidant of President Wilson. He is now president of the Woodrow Wilson Foundation.

and ten million more in bonds. The promoters took their profit in stock, and presently got clear of the affair by selling out. Bonds in an amount of seven million dollars were issued, of which six million were taken in England.

The Ports Company bill became a law on February 20, 1911.[28] The company was to dredge and improve the harbor of Havana and a number of other named ports, completing the work in six years. In return, it was to get approximately seventy-five cents a ton on all goods imported through these ports into Cuba for the next thirty years.[29] Work began in earnest in March 1911. On the score of what the company did in improving the harbors of Cuba there has never been any noteworthy criticism. The company gave its best effort in this direction, and something of value was accomplished. In the summer of 1911 an enquiry on the part of the representatives of the English bondholders brought out the fact that the United States government did not approve of the concession, despite what the American minister may have told Mr. Davis. The State Department criticized it as onerous to Cuba and possibly in conflict with the Platt Amendment. In consequence negotiations were entered into, as a result of which an agreement was reached for a reduction in the profits of the company. Furthermore, a method of arbitration was provided to ascertain the damages Cuba should pay in case she at any time chose to do away with the concession to the Ports Company. This action was taken with the consent and virtual participation of the United States, and embodied in Gómez's decree of May 12, 1913.

Affairs were at this stage when Menocal came into power a few days later. On June 18, 1913, without consulting the

[28] This law may be found in *Colección legislativa*, v. XXXI, pp. 12-16.
[29] There were various alterations in the contract at different times, but the above is substantially what it came to.

United States, which had been a party to the matter, Menocal issued a decree cancelling the agreement of May 12. On August 4 he went a step farther, giving out a remarkable and misleading decree in which he cancelled all rights of the Ports Company, on the ground that it was never a legal concessionary. The argument was that the company had not complied with certain technicalities required by the Cuban corporation law, such, for example, as a provision that all of the stock should be subscribed for and twenty-five per cent paid in. In consequence, the contract with the republic was not valid, according to Menocal, since the Ports Company was never a corporate entity capable in law of making an agreement. Instructions were given, therefore, to make no more payments to the company, although the work and the collections were to be continued by the government. There were some other interesting features of this document. While the impression was inescapable that the making of this contract had been an act of impropriety on the part of the previous administration, there were no specific charges against Cubans connected with the deal, but it was put in a yet worse light as an affair between a foreign organization and the Cuban state. The history of Huston and Davis was recited in such a way as to cause them to appear like two "carpet-baggers" preying upon the republic. Some startling allegations were made concerning swift changes in the stock ownership of the company. On January 21, 1911, Huston was declared to be the owner of five per cent of the stock, with ninety-five per cent in the hands of a Cuban named Moragas. But on March 4 Huston had nine hundred shares, then valued at ninety thousand dollars, in a total of a thousand. All nine hundred had been given to him for services. When the capital was increased to ten millions in common stock the company agreed to pay Huston ten thousand dollars a share for his former hundred dollar par value stock and in addition $825,000 in the company's bonds, but Huston and his associates were to give the company fifteen per cent of their stock. Whether these assertions were true or false and whatever may have been the meaning back of these strange figures, it certainly seemed as if "Huston and his associates," presumably Americans, were getting an astounding amount of graft. It was also represented that the company was deriving an unexpectedly great profit, having collected $2,990,000 in twenty-seven months, instead of an originally estimated $580,000.[30]

There were a number of substantial omissions in Menocal's account. In point of fact the company took in over three million dollars on its tonnage allowance, but spent over nine millions on dredging and other expenses, leaving a difference of over six millions against the company. And even if there may have been a technical defect in the original incorporation of the Ports Company, that had been cured by subsequent action of the government and the law courts, and even in a decree of Menocal ratifying its existence as a company, to say nothing of the rights in equity that it had acquired. Menocal's action was therefore a blow at Cuban credit, as the government had given its virtual guarantee to the bondholders by its contract with the Ports Company.[31]

Menocal was sustained by Congress and also by the Supreme Court, which upheld the President's decree of August 4, 1913. In all other respects the provisions of the contract were continued, with the Department of Public Works replacing the Ports Company. In fact, however, the work of dredging stopped, although the tax was regularly collected. Owners of the stock and bonds of the Ports Company, mean-

[30] For the decree of Aug. 4, 1913, 574-606.
see *Colección legislativa*, v. XLI, pp.   [31] Roig, *passim*.

while, had enlisted the support of the United States. Whatever of impropriety there may have been in the early stages of the affair these people, mostly Englishmen, were in the position of innocent purchasers for value who had bought their securities on the basis of Cuban credit. The United States adopted that view, and made strong representations to Cuba, holding that Cuba's failure to give compensation for the company's claims amounted to a violation of article three of the Platt Amendment. Menocal eventually consented to the demands of the United States, and in a message to Congress of January 21, 1916, recommended action to indemnify the "so-called" Ports Company, although only as a matter of "grace and equity," [32] and on July 24, 1917, a law was passed authorizing the President to settle with the Ports Company, though without recognizing its legal existence, and also to continue the work of dredging.[33] So presently matters with the Ports Company were arranged. As for the ports themselves, nothing of great consequence has been done since the Ports Company stopped its work, although the tax has continued to be collected.

The above is only part of the story. Why was there such an uproar over the affair, and why did Menocal take his action in the first place? There are any number of answers to these questions. It is said, for example, that the Céspedes group had some rivals for the dredging privilege who were vociferously disappointed when they failed to get their share of the easy profit. It seems, too, that certain prominent newspapers were at first paid large sums monthly to support the deal, but Captain Klapp stopped that when he took charge of the company's affairs. Thereupon these journals turned their batteries on the company. More trouble de-

[32] In *Mensajes presidenciales*, I, 641-642.   [33] In the *Gaceta*, July 26, 1917.

veloped because the Ports Company refused to contribute to the Conservative campaign fund, when solicited by individuals who had since taken high place in the government. Menocal himself is said to have been angered because Puerto Padre, a port of the Cuban American Sugar Company (in which Menocal was heavily interested), was not included in the dredging project. He later added Puerto Padre, by decree. Some say that a new group of Cuban politicians in the Menocal era hoped to carry through the plan on its original basis by first getting rid of the Ports Company, though the whole affair caused such a scandal that it proved to be impossible, at least for the time, to arrange the deal. Probably the most prominent, and certainly the most recognizable, cause for Menocal's action, however, is the political capital he was able to make out of the affair. For the time being, too, it worked. If there could have been a fair election between Menocal and Gómez in August 1913 the former would have won, "hands down."

Menocal's first administration was not lacking in evils of the usual order in the political life of Cuba, but these were not nearly so prominent as they were in his second administration, at which point they may more conveniently be taken up. These earlier years reflected one other current in Cuban life, however, that must needs be included here. During the first three years of Menocal's presidency, though a state of good order was the general rule, there were a few of the minor outbreaks so characteristic of Cuban life. For example, there was some momentary excitement in November 1913 when a mulatto named Crescencio García started a revolt in the province of Santa Clara, but the affair was handled quickly and effectively by the rural guards. There were violent labor strikes, too, on several occasions. But the incident which most strikingly represented the turbulence and lack of discipline in Cuban character, as also not a few political evils, took place when the chief of police of Havana was murdered in broad daylight by three men who were outstanding figures in the nation's affairs, including Governor Ernesto Asbert, a leading aspirant for the presidency. Asbert had been a colonel in the War of Independence, a prominent leader in the revolution of 1906, and governor and virtual political boss of the province of Havana since 1908. A very attractive man personally, not unlike José Miguel Gómez in his typically Cuban and likeable traits, he had also made an excellent record as governor of Havana. The part he played in the election of Menocal, when he threw his Liberal following to the Conservative candidate, has already been recorded. He was generally regarded as presidential timber, and, indeed, had been favored by many for the Liberal nomination in 1912.

The victim in the Asbert affair was General Armando de la Riva, a man not indeed without faults, but of a type that is all too rare in Cuba. He took an active part in the War of Independence, serving under Calixto García, and rose to the rank of brigadier-general, being the youngest general of the war. A soldier in every sense of the word, he was employed in 1908 in the organization of the permanent army, and in the following year became chief of police of Havana. According to many accounts he proved himself to be the best chief the city had ever had, rendering a conspicuous service at the time the city was flooded during the cyclone of 1910; on that occasion he personally saved a number of people by carrying them through the water on his own broad shoulders until they were out of danger. After less than a year, however, the politicians were able to effect his removal as chief of police, because of his war on gambling. Later, he was reappointed to the same position. Riva was a splendid figure, powerful, athletic, and commanding, and a man of character,—one of those, according to United States Secretary of State Bryan, who are "capable of sacrificing themselves for the honor and good of the community and of dying in fulfilment of duty." Furthermore, there was nothing of the grafter about him; he seemed not to care for money. Morally, he was perhaps like many others of his race,[34] and he has been accused of having a violent temperament and too uncompromising a nature for a Cuban ambient. These charges, however, are from a Cuban angle; to others he does not appear to have been too severe in his standards for the performance of duty.

It seems that Asbert, though usually reputed an honest governor, was one of a number of politicians who were conducting gambling clubs and resented Riva's campaign against them. Both Asbert and Julián Betancourt, a representative in Congress, had places on the Prado, the principal avenue of the city. The day before the shooting affray Riva said to a reporter that he had no quarrel with gambling that was done discreetly in private clubs, but it was being carried on notoriously. One man at the Julián Betancourt club was told that the police would be killed if they tried to interfere with the games there, as the place was frequented by important politicians. Riva said that he could not allow that.

"I well know the consideration that is due the politicians," he was quoted as saying, "and I am sufficiently a discreet man to respect their circles and even their games when these are conducted properly and discreetly."

This does not sound like the uncompromising man Riva is

[34] At the time of the shooting affray he was accompanied by two children, both said to be his sons, one legitimate, the other not.

said to have been. He had given notice, however, that the gambling in the two clubs on the Prado must stop.

On July 7, 1913, Riva was passing Asbert's place, when he saw a negro employe take out a revolver. So he went up to the man, and demanded the gun, and when the negro could show no permit except one that had expired had him arrested for illegally carrying a weapon. As the negro was being taken to the lock-up, he happened to meet Asbert, who was in a carriage with Representative Eugenio Arias of Matanzas and Senator Vidal Morales of Camagüey. There was an excited colloquy with the policeman, after which the three men drove away. Almost immediately afterward they met Riva, who was driving up the Prado, accompanied by his two sons, both of them children. There was a dispute, in course of which Arias, a violent man, twice punched Riva, and when the latter hit back Arias drew his revolver and started firing. Riva jumped from his carriage, —in part, so it appears, to get the children out of the area of the firing,—but Arias shot him before he reached the ground. Riva made his way to the sidewalk, and got behind a column in front of number 84 Prado, where he was joined by a captain of police, who returned the fire of Riva's opponents. By this time Asbert and Vidal Morales were also firing, though it is said humorously that the latter shot only "at the man in the moon." Riva, hit twice, was mortally wounded, and was taken to a hospital, where he died next day.

The affair occurred at 6:30 P. M., the hour before dinner, at the most crowded part of the Prado when "all the world" was out. Two persons besides Riva were wounded, and the wonder is there were no more. The three men gave themselves up, and Arias confessed his guilt, while the other two maintained that they were innocent. The incident aroused a perfect furor of excitement in the country. Asbert had his defenders, however. El Mundo asserted that Riva had been persecuting Asbert for political reasons, at the instigation of the Secretary of Government, asking why Riva pursued gambling at the Betancourt and Asbert clubs and let it go unpunished elsewhere. This argument is even yet maintained by the friends of Asbert, who claim that Menocal, although still in alliance with the Asbertist Liberals, was making plans to annihilate Asbert politically, as he was no longer needed by Menocal and was troublesome on account of his ambition for the presidency. Riva, however, was a Liberal, and it is at least doubtful that he was lending himself to any such Conservative project. Nobody denies that he was certainly enforcing the law as against Asbert. El Triunfo ascribed the affair to "assaults of the police" on the two clubs, and said this would not have happened under Gómez,—which was rather a left-handed compliment for José Miguel! La Lucha, in an interesting article defending Asbert, said that the incident was a reflection of Cuban social and political conditions. It asked the public not to condemn Asbert out of hand. "It is enough that we have to struggle against our sad destiny." The Riva murder did not pass unnoticed in Washington. There must have been some preliminary enquiry, for in a note of July 11, 1913, the United States *chargé d'affaires* expressed the satisfaction of his government that Menocal had evinced a determination to bring the perpetrators of this crime to justice. Menocal was assured of the "vigorous support" of the United States in his efforts on behalf of the maintenance of order and fulfilment of the laws.

Menocal *did* act, though not until after the receipt of this note, whether or not there may have been any relation between that and the steps he took. He suspended Asbert from his governorship by a decree of July 12, and on the 14th called the Senate in extraordinary session. A little later he summoned an extra session of Congress as a whole, sending a message on July 24 asking Congress to take up the question of congressional immunity, which had been raised in connection with the participation of Arias and Vidal Morales in the affair.[35] Congress was no more willing to discuss this much cherished privilege of its members than it had been under Gómez, and it was impossible to get a quorum. The sequel is concerned mainly with the efforts made to clear Asbert and the others, and is taken up in a later chapter dealing with amnesties.[36] There might have been no difficulty in the first place, but for the objections of the United States. Secretary Bryan is once said to have sent a note to the effect that to allow veterans like Asbert to commit murder was not consistent with Cuba's obligation to the United States to maintain a government that was adequate to protect life and property. On this account two amnesty bills were held up, and it was not until a bill went through which virtually excluded Arias but included Asbert that the United States government waived its objections. As for Vidal Morales, no great point had ever been made about him. Cuban opinion, too, has quite generally excused Asbert. It is admitted that he fired on Riva, but it is claimed that he did so after Arias had already mortally wounded that officer and consequently that his shooting should hardly be considered against him, as the issue was already settled. However that may be, the excessive disposition to leniency in Cuba in the aftermath of crime, together with the high regard in which Asbert was held by many Cubans, is explanation enough of the indulgent attitude toward the for-

[35] In *Mensajes presidenciales*, I, 449-450.   [36] See *infra*, pp. 531-533.

mer governor of Havana.   As for Asbert, it virtually killed his own chances in politics, although he still retained some influence on behalf of others.   The incident may also have had a bearing on the break that presently developed between the Asbertist Liberals and the Conservatives.   This in turn was a very nearly decisive factor in the events leading to the election of 1916 and its sequel, the revolution of February 1917.[37]

[37] The early years of the Menocal administration are lacking in any monographic work of even moderately respectable calibre. Martí covers the most ground, but is a eulogist pure and simple. The sections in Johnson about Menocal belong in a similar category, and are also lacking in precision and atmosphere. *Los sucesos del Prado* is a detailed and valuable account of the Asbert affair, and has been the principal basis of the story given here. Several other brief pamphlets on this and other questions are also mentioned in Trelles. But government documents, newspapers, and magazine articles (both Cuban and American), together with the accounts of living witnesses, must still be the principal resort of the investigator.

CHAPTER XV

THE ELECTIONS OF 1916

THE turning-point in Menocal's career came when he decided to run for a second term in the presidency. Reëlection in the United States is accepted as a matter of course when a man has made a good record in his first term, but in Hispanic America, possibly because of the insistent demand for a redistribution of the jobs, it is regarded as a dangerous evil.

"In no republic of the American continent," said José Manuel Cortina, "has the presidential reëlection brought anything but revolution, dictatorship, and corruption in all branches of the administration."

Cortina was thinking merely of Hispanic America in his use of the term "American continent." His remarks certainly describe what took place in Cuba under Menocal.[1] Even more significant were the words of Menocal himself in a letter of October 1912 to General Enrique Loinaz del Castillo:

"The effort of the President to bring about his own nomination for the post while he is still holding it will be taken . . . as an indication, in countries of our race, of a certain dangerous spirit of partiality in whomsoever may conceive this aspiration . . . The principle of non-reëlection is the firmest support of peace."[2]

Menocal had made a one-term preëlection promise, and, indeed, Dolz says it was hard to get him to run the first time, as also for a second term.[3] He at first backed General Emilio Núñez to succeed him, but later accepted the nomination for

[1] Quoted in Pardo Suárez, 168.   118. Also in Cabrera, 37, n. 1.
[2] Quoted in Trelles, *Biblioteca*, II,   [3] Dolz, 6.

himself. This factor in the political situation was not very prominent in the first two years and a half of Menocal's administration, however. For a little while his government managed at least moderately well, even in its relations with Congress, due to the alliance of the Asbertist Liberals and the Conservatives. But Menocal's stand in the Riva affair, unavoidable though it was, caused something of a break between the two groups, and in 1914, for political reasons, the *entente* between them was formally dissolved. Furthermore, in the biennial elections of that same year the Conservatives lost their majority in the House.[4] Mention has already been made of Menocal's difficulties from this time forward in getting needed legislation from Congress. It is probable that this factor turned his mind toward reëlection, as it did also to the employment of other evil methods in Cuban politics for the attainment of his ends. He was urged by leading politicians to stand for renomination, on the ground that he was the only man in the party strong enough to unite all factions and give hopes of success in the ensuing campaign for the presidency.[5]

During 1915 the name most commonly heard as candidate for the Conservative nomination was that of General Núñez, then Secretary of Agriculture, but toward the close of that year rumors were already in circulation that Menocal would run. These were not received with favor by some of the

[4] The elections of 1914 reflected the normal evils of Cuban functions of this sort, except that there seems to have been no noteworthy executive pressure. Menocal called attention to the frauds that had been committed, in a message to Congress of Dec. 14, 1914. The voting lists, made up in the time of Magoon, were now utterly untrustworthy. A great many persons did not vote in 1914, but it would appear from the count that everybody had done so. In some towns the voters were forty-six to forty-nine per cent of the entire population, an impossible figure. Menocal asked Congress to authorize a new census as the basis for a correct voting list. *Mensajes presidenciales,* I, 559-560. Congress, it may be mentioned, took no action on this message. See chapter XXIV for a further discussion of general election evils.

[5] Dolz, 6.

best men in the party,—by Enrique José Varona, among others. Varona had more and more been drawing away from active participation in Conservative councils. As early as 1913 he had remonstrated against the use of the spoils system, and had resigned his presidency of the party because his views did not appear to agree with those of the other leaders.[6] Other notable opponents of reëlection were José Antonio González Lanuza, Wifredo Fernández (then a representative and also editor of El Comercio), General Fernando Freyre de Andrade (then mayor of Havana), Senator Juan José de la Maza y Artola, and General Núñez, although the last-named eventually accepted the idea and battled as hard as anybody to win the election. The action of Freyre is especially interesting, as it represented a complete change of front from the days of 1906. Menocal adherents endeavor to discount his attitude, however, by saying that Freyre had hoped to receive the Conservative nomination himself.[7] The most vigorous of Menocal's opponents in his own party, however, was Maza.

Whatever may have inspired Freyre's opposition to Menocal, there was another veteran of 1906 who most certainly acted consistently with his stand of ten years before. This was Ricardo Dolz, successor to Varona as president of the Conservative party and virtual manager of Menocal's campaign. The party "assembly," or convention, was held on January 16, 1916. The following is the story of that affair, as told to the writer by a distinguished Cuban who has never been a politician:

"The opposition to Menocal was so great that he could not have won the nomination except by unfair methods. It was declared that all

[6] See on this score *A mis correligionarios*, the seventh of *Siete circulares: 1910 a 1913*, in Varona, *De la colonia a la república*, 254-256, and *Manifiesto de 1913: a mis correligionarios*, in *Ibid.*, 263-266.

[7] Merino and Ibarzábal, 20.

Conservative Secretaries or ex-Secretaries of government departments were members of the assembly *ex-officio*, but this device was not sufficient to give Menocal a majority. So all Secretaries under the old Moderate régime were also admitted, although it had been formally stated at the time when the Conservative party was founded that it was in no sense a revival of the Moderates, but was a new party. Even so, Menocal still lacked a majority, but the vote of the delegates was incorrectly counted, and one of the Menocal adherents stuffed the ballots in his pocket and left the room. So Menocal won. Núñez accepted the nomination for the vice-presidency, however, on a promise of support for the presidency in 1920."

This may be exaggerated, but one hears it on every hand in Cuba. There is a similar statement by Raimundo Cabrera,[8] and it is probably a fair approximation of the truth. According to the count, indeed, Menocal's victory was by a comfortable margin, ninety-two to seventy-one.[9]

The Liberals were still very much divided at this time; indeed, one might better speak of the Liberal "parties" than of the Liberals as a whole, for there were a number of more or less independent groups, each adhering to some favorite leader. Zayas had the most numerous following, but not a majority. Ernesto Asbert ranked next, and was by no means reconciled to an inactive place in party politics, despite the Riva incident. General Gerardo Machado and Colonel Carlos Mendieta directed a so-called Unionist wing of the Liberal party.[10] And there were smaller groups headed by José Miguel Gómez, Alberto Barreras, "Pino" Guerra, and Eusebio Hernández. While most of these men had some aspirations for the presidency, the names of Zayas and Gómez were the most often mentioned, with that of Zayas more prominently to the fore; the evil fame of José Miguel was not yet sufficiently far back in the past for him to have re-

[8] Cabrera, 37.
[9] Merino and Ibarzábal, 27.

[10] Curiously enough, Machado and Mendieta were to be rivals for the Liberal nomination in 1924.

covered his popularity. So Zayas, the "perpetual candidate," or "Bryan of Cuba" (as he was often called), who had been publicly disparaged by José Miguel, Orestes Ferrara, and other prominent Liberals, was the only logical figure for the nomination. In due time he won it in the Liberal assembly of March 20, 1916, gaining the support of the Machado-Mendieta and "Pino" Guerra factions. Nevertheless, it was almost hopeless for him to go to the polls unless he could obtain the backing of the former Liberal chieftain.[11]

With the nomination of Zayas the campaign entered a vigorous stage, based more on arguments about reëlectionism than on the merits of the candidates themselves. Every act of the Menocal government was criticized as tending toward the retention of power through the use of power, or, as a pro-Menocal writing has expressed it, not because of any violation of the laws, but on account of "the probability that he might some day intend to commit crimes against the law of elections." [12] These charges had their logical conclusion in a bill brought in by Menocal's Conservative opponent, Senator Maza, to the effect that a President who was a candidate for reëlection should step down from his office during the electoral period. This bill, known as the "Maza law," passed both houses of Congress in May.[13] Menocal vetoed it in a message to Congress of July 1916, basing his action on the Constitution, which permitted of a two-term presidency and called for the exercise of executive power by the President in a way that was at variance with the provisions of the Maza law.[14] One writer claims that the Maza plan

[11] For a discussion of events leading to the nomination of Zayas, see Merino and Ibarzábal: 18; 31-36.

[12] Ibid., 37.

[13] Ibid., 38. The principal paragraph of the law is also in Pardo Suárez, 177.

[14] In Mensajes presidenciales, I, 695-697.

was favored by the majority of the Conservatives themselves, but it was not possible to get a two-thirds vote in
Congress to overcome the President's veto.[15] Meanwhile,
affairs had taken a turn for the better in the Liberal camp.
Gómez and Zayas buried the hatchet in June, and the former
agreed to support Zayas's candidacy and even to direct the
campaign, though under an agreement which Dolz said left
Zayas a "prisoner" of Gómez.[16] It appears that the latter
was to be allowed to name certain of the party's candidates
for congressional and municipal posts.   Early in October,
although the Hernández group of Liberals passed over to
the Conservatives, the much more important Asbertist faction made a pact with the Liberals.[17] This virtually assured Zayas of victory in the province of Havana.   The
Conservatives had, previous to this time, tried to effect a
trade whereby they were to get the votes of that province
for Menocal in exchange for letting a Liberal, Eugenio
Azpiazu, become mayor of the capital.   This was denounced
by Varona as "a lack of respect for the public conscience," [18]
and eventually it came to naught.

The campaign was one of violence on both sides, dupli-
cating the scenes of 1905.   The eventual greater crime of
the Conservatives in "stealing" the election has tended to
obscure the fact that the Liberals were also entitled to little credit for their conduct.   From the first, they cried out
"Either Zayas or revolution!"   This their newspapers and
orators did not hesitate to say in so many words, but it
might have been implied, too, from their other acts and
statements.   Mendieta uttered something like a threat in a
speech at the Liberal assembly in March, when he said

[15] Pardo Suárez, 179.
[16] Dolz, 7.
[17] Merino and Ibarzábal: 43-44; 53.
[18] Interview in *Nación*, July 24, 1916.

that the Liberals would compel the Conservatives to respect their rights, "as they counted on sufficient forces for
that purpose." [19] Gómez later made similar veiled threats,[20]
and on one occasion, so it is claimed, even went with a
party of friends and shot up the house of a Conservative
leader in the province of Santa Clara.[21]   However that may
have been, the whole country was soon almost in a state
of war. On August 6 at a Conservative meeting in Marianao,
near Havana, there was an affray with a Liberal policeman
in which six persons were wounded. Similar incidents occurred in numerous towns of the republic: at Manguito on
August 13, when three were killed and two wounded; at
Cienfuegos on August 19, with one dead and three wounded;
at Güines on September 17, when an Asbertist candidate
for mayor killed his Conservative rival; at Camajuaní,
where twenty-eight were wounded in a battle of Liberals
and Conservatives; at Camagüey on October 7, with one
killed and thirteen wounded; at Güira de Melena in October,
when a political riot was settled by a charge of government
cavalry, with a number of men wounded; in Havana itself
on October 18, when several persons were wounded in a
collision at the corner of Belascoín and Zanja streets; and,
indeed, at various other places, when men were killed or
wounded or even when they got off without harm, or when
buildings were burned or other deeds of violence were performed. Naturally, each party claimed that the other was
to blame, and probably with truth, in that both parties
were at fault, but the Conservatives point out that the Liberals had only seven men killed in the preëlection campaign,
while the Conservatives lost forty-two, arguing from this
that the Liberals were more often the aggressors.[22]

[19] Merino and Ibarzábal, 35.
[20] *Ibid.*, 46.
[21] Dolz, 13.
[22] Merino and Ibarzábal, 45-60.

The frequency with which these incidents occurred led the government to appoint military supervisors in a number of towns, and this gave rise to a fresh controversy. Zayas later charged that these officials destroyed the liberties of the municipalities and brought influence to bear in favor of the Conservatives. But there was a mixed commission created by Menocal that intervened in matters affecting the supervisors, the Conservatives claimed, and this body was, if anything, more Liberal than Conservative; it was composed of Dolz and Carlos Fonts Ster'ling for the Conservatives and Ferrara and José Manuel Cortina for the Liberals, with Sanguily, who had often acted with the Liberals, as the neutral member. And eight of the supervisors eventually joined in the revolution against Menocal.[23] Certainly, too, the appointment of military supervisors has been the normal procedure in Cuba at times of a presidential election, both before this time and since,—even when Zayas was President. It is probable that they did do something to affect the elections, Conservatives for the Conservatives, and Liberals for the Liberals, for political partisanship in Cuba is too intense for one to expect abstention from the use of influence and authority by anybody in a position to employ them. In the light of other evidence, however, it is doubtful whether their conduct had any substantial effect on the result.

The elections were held on November 1, 1916. There were a number of riots and shooting affrays, in course of which three Conservative presidents of electoral boards were killed. There were also charges by each party that the other had hindered the voting of opponents and committed innumerable frauds. With respect to the last-named charge, certainly, both sides were right. It is said that there were over

[23] Dolz, 9-12.

a million names on the voting lists and that about eight hundred thousand votes were cast. Yet, three years later the census was to show that there were only 477,786 eligible voters in Cuba. And the election was close! That speaks for itself,—and for both parties.[24] Disorder and violence on this day can hardly have been the rule, however. One Liberal partisan has said that the elections were "serene" and "tranquil," "with an appearance of impartiality and legality."[25] And the Liberal newspapers of November 2, at which time it was popularly believed that the Liberals had won, praised Menocal for his conduct of the elections.[26] This was also done by the directorate of the Liberal party that same day in a formal communication to the President.[27] In the light of such evidence as this, it seems likely that the government must have been reasonably fair,—or at least no worse than the Liberals,—up to and including election day itself. The real complaint of the Liberals concerns what happened after that date.

The story is often told in Cuba that Menocal was ready to concede defeat the night of the 1st, but some of the women of his family were not willing to accept that outcome. So when a suggestion was made of a way to falsify the result it was seized upon by "feminine passion," and Menocal was persuaded to adopt it.[28] It may be that the

[24] Varona, who was as nearly impartial as any Cuban could be, said that both sides committed "illegalities" in the election. "Everybody knows that in that respect all were equal." Varona, *Declaraciones*, in *Prensa*, Jan. 29, 1917.

[25] Cabrera, 41.

[26] Quotations from *Heraldo de Cuba, Triunfo,* and *Nación*, all Liberal organs, are given in Dolz, 16-18.

[27] See on this score an open letter of Menocal to the Liberal directorate of Nov. 5, 1916, and a letter of the Conservative directorate to the Liberal organization on Nov. 7, 1916, in Merino and Ibarzábal, respectively at pp. 63-65 and 65-66; also in another communication of the Conservatives to the Liberals of Feb. 4, 1917, and of Menocal to Gómez of Feb. 5, 1917, in Cabrera, respectively at pp. 342-344, at 343, and 378-381, at 380, and in Merino and Ibarzábal, pp. 82-83, at 83, and 84-85, at 85.

[28] See, for example, in Cabrera, 19-20.

story is not true, but it can hardly be doubted that action was taken which robbed the Liberals of a victory. An intimation of what was coming was given when the government announced on the 3d that later returns seemed likely to upset what had at first appeared to be a Conservative defeat. A peculiar thing happened with telegraphic notices about the election. It had been arranged that telegrams with preliminary reports should be sent from each voting precinct to the Central Electoral Board in Havana. These came in regularly until noon of the 2d, when they stopped. On the 3d they began to be received again, but from the Secretary of Government instead of from the telegraph office as was required by law. The Board protested about this on the 4th, and from that time forward it received no more telegrams at all. It seems also that the originals of those that had been sent were removed from the telegraph files, so as to leave no trace.[29] It is said, too, that the packages containing the electoral documents, which were to be forwarded to Havana for final scrutiny, were opened and falsified by government agents in the post-office. The work was done very slowly, and it was not until late in December that the supposed "results" were published.[30] Some evidence appearing to connect the President himself with this procedure turned up in a telegram by his secretary, Eusebio Azpiazu, to Conservative followers in Trinidad. This telegram, under date of November 2, the day after the elections, read as follows: "The general bids me to felicitate you and to tell you to make every effort and omit no act that may bring about victory." Azpiazu did not deny the telegram, but claimed to have sent it on his own initiative.[31] The Liberal contention that the returns had been tampered

[29] Cabrera, 48-49, n. 2.
[30] Pardo Suárez, 180.

[31] Cabrera, 67-68; Merino and Ibarzábal, 65; Trelles, *Biblioteca*, II, 121.

with was sustained, first by the Central Electoral Board, and then on final appeal by the Supreme Court on January 12, 1917. The result was left in doubt, however, as the elections in a few precincts in Santa Clara and Oriente were required to be held again, since the packages with the original vote of these districts had mysteriously "disappeared." [32]

Meanwhile, charges and counter-charges had been hurled back and forth, while the country drifted toward civil war. The Liberals called attention to numerous removals of their partisans from government service, especially in the Department of Communications (including the post and telegraph offices) since the elections. Menocal admitted that there had been some dismissals, but claimed they had been few in number and for just cause.[33] The Liberals were even more concerned about the movements of troops that were ordered by the government. Whatever the leaders may have had in mind, Liberal partisans were certainly talking revolution as early as the first week in November, and it was only natural that dispositions should be made to meet such a contingency. Especially did the Liberals protest against the sending of troops to Santa Clara and Oriente, where the supplementary elections were to be held, insisting that the government intended to use them to prevent Liberals from voting. And, indeed, the Liberals did have a normal expectation of victory if the elections, which had been set for February 14 in Santa Clara and February 20 in Oriente, should be conducted fairly. They had already been awarded the electoral vote of the provinces of Havana and Camagüey, with Pinar del Río and Matanzas given to the Conservatives. The addition of either Santa Clara or

[32] Cabrera: 18; 51; 55; 63-64; 392-394; Merino and Ibarzábal, 79-80.
[33] Letter to Gómez of Feb. 5, 1917, in Cabrera, 378-381, at 380, and Merino and Ibarzábal, 84-85, at 85.

Oriente would decide the issue in favor of the Liberals. In Santa Clara they had a majority of 1164, except for the six precincts where the new elections were to be held, and these could muster a total of only 2,401 names on the voting lists, a number that was probably far in excess of the actual voters in that district, which, incidentally, had ordinarily been a Liberal stronghold. And even if there had been no fraud in the voting lists it was doubtful whether as many as two-thirds of the eligible voters would go to the polls. The situation in the several precincts of Oriente where another election was required was much the same.[34] On this account, as early as December 1916 one of the Liberal leaders, General Eduardo Guzmán, had proposed that the United States should be invited to supervise any additional elections that might be necessary, but his suggestion was formally rejected by Liberals and Conservatives alike.[35] Later, some Liberals thought it would have been well to have adopted that plan,[36] but it had no chance of acceptance at any time; it would have meant defeat for the Conservatives, which was reason enough for them to oppose it, and it was a bad political maneuver for the Liberals to "bring in the foreigner." No doubt some of their leaders already had in mind the methods of 1906, in case the government should not yield the issue of its own accord.

Meanwhile, the Liberals were convinced that the Conservatives intended to go to the supplementary elections with "blood and fire." They charged them with distributing arms and munitions in the districts where the partial elections were to be held,—with the pardon of criminals who

---

[34] For one reference out of many, see letter of Ferrara and Cabrera to President Wilson, Feb. 10, 1917, in Cabrera, 104-109, at 105-106.

[35] Merino and Ibarzábal, 78.

[36] Cabrera, 81.

were sent there to spread terror among the inhabitants,—with the transfer of employes of the post-office and telegraph stations and the substitution of Conservative agents,—with the despatch of troops under the command of men notoriously in favor of the reëlection,—with the location of voting-booths out in the woods, far from the towns,—with putting hindrances upon Liberals who wished to approach them, even including the vice-presidential candidate, Carlos Mendieta, on one occasion,—and, in general, with taking violent means to impress upon Liberal voters that they were not under any circumstances going to be allowed to win.[37] Some remarks of the Conservative party leader, Ricardo Dolz, served in no small measure to contribute to this view. In course of a talk with an editor of La Discusión, a Conservative daily, Dolz denounced the decisions of the Central Electoral Board and the Supreme Court, claiming that hundreds of fraudulent votes had been awarded to the Liberals, while the Conservatives had been deprived even of those that most clearly belonged to them,[38] and he then went on as follows about the way the Conservatives intended to battle for victory in the partial elections:

"The Conservative party is full of ardor and ready for the struggle. . . . It will fight with such courage as will surely leave a profound mark on our electoral history. Our presidents of electoral boards will not be killed,[39] and if the case requires it that will happen to those of the opposite band."[40]

Many prominent Conservatives were far from agreeing with Dolz, notably Varona, González Lanuza, Freyre, Maza,

[37] Cabrera, 68-69; also in letter of Ferrara and Cabrera to President Wilson, Feb. 10, 1917, in *Ibid.*, 104-109, at 107-108.

[38] A detailed account of Conservative assertions on this score is given in Dolz, 16-18.

[39] This has reference to the murder of three Conservative presidents on election day.

[40] Cabrera, 67, n. 1, quoting from *Discusión* of Jan. 23, 1917.

and Cosme de la Torriente, all of whom wished to concede the victory to the Liberals. In an interview published in Heraldo de Cuba on January 24, 1917, Varona deplored the Conservative attacks on the Supreme Court decision.[41] Five days later he gave out another interview in which he called upon all Cubans to put aside domestic strife. Both sides were equally guilty of committing electoral crimes in the general elections, he said, but (alluding to Dolz's remarks) "never have I known a chief of a government party to declare that one should go to an election to obtain a victory at all costs." [42] Torriente was quoted as saying that it was almost impossible for the Conservatives to win the partial elections in the face of the advantage that the Liberals possessed. Indeed, he held that the Liberals had in fact won on November 1st.[43] Freyre said that the Liberal victory was indisputable. "Dr. Zayas is the President of Cuba. The Conservatives ought to take a stand against the manifest reëlectionist intentions of the government." [44] Several days later, unable on account of ill health to attend a meeting of Conservative leaders, Freyre wrote to Dolz that "our triumph appears impossible if we try to obtain it in a peaceful contest between citizens." [45] Maza endeavored to oppose the Dolz current at that same meeting, but according to Cabrera "Violence imposed silence upon him, and some of the less impassioned of his coreligionists saved his life by getting him out of the place." [46] Maza's long letter to Menocal calling on him to recognize the victory of Zayas has already been quoted in part.[47] In addition he went

[41] Quoted in Cabrera, 355-356.
[42] Varona, *Declaraciones*, in *Prensa* of Jan. 29, 1917.
[43] Cabrera, 388-391, quoting from *Nación* of Jan. 27, 1917.
[44] Cabrera, 71, quoting *Heraldo de Cuba* of Jan. 30, 1917.
[45] Freyre to Dolz, Feb. 4, 1917, in Cabrera, 345-347, at 346.
[46] Cabrera, 75.
[47] *Supra,* pp. 322-323.

frankly into the whole situation, remarking upon Menocal's pledges against a second term and on the various improprieties associated with his attempt to win a reëlection, nevertheless.[48]

The attitude of these men was well known to the Liberals long before the publication of their opinions mentioned above. Indeed, Varona and others had been holding meetings of leaders of both parties, in hopes of settling the issue without strife. On one of these occasions the Conservatives offered to withdraw Menocal, if the Liberals would do the same with Zayas, and hold a new election for somebody else.[49] It was said that Menocal objected especially to Zayas, whom he considered "unworthy" of the presidency.[50] If he was reflecting on the private character of his opponent there was nobody in Cuba but could furnish confirmatory evidence,—but this same Menocal was to boost Zayas into the presidency four years later! At any rate, the Liberals would not agree to the compromise suggested. Instead, the directorate of that party formally declared its views on January 26, to the effect that the Santa Clara elections were unnecessary, but suggesting, in case the government insisted on holding them, that they be supervised by a committee of six men. The men were specifically named by them, but, though four were Conservatives, two of the four were Varona and Torriente.[51] Naturally, since this would have assured a Liberal victory and since the Conservatives had determined to win for themselves, these proposals were rejected.[52] Meanwhile, on February 3, Gómez had directed a letter to Menocal about the situa-

[48] Maza to Menocal (date not given), in Cabrera, 357-367.

[49] Dolz, 32.

[50] Comment of Ferrara, quoted in Cabrera, 80.

[51] Quoted in Cabrera, 338-341. Also in Merino and Ibarzábal, 82.

[52] The Conservative reply, under date of Feb. 4, 1917, is in Cabrera, 342-344. Also in Merino and Ibarzábal, 82-83.

tion. This letter, which had in fact been prepared by Zayas, stated the Liberal case, and called on Menocal out of "patriotism" and "duty" to make such dispositions in Santa Clara as would give the Liberals a fair chance.[53] Menocal answered, on the 5th, that "If it were not for the deference I owe you as my predecessor in the presidency of the republic and as a former companion in arms in the Army of Liberation I would perhaps abstain from any reply." He then went on to say that the elections would be conducted lawfully,—but did not agree to the specific requests of Gómez.[54] The latter wrote again, on the 6th, objecting to Menocal's aspersions, "a bit monarchical in flavor," on his previous communication, and calling attention to the fact that Menocal himself had sent a similar letter to Gómez in connection with the elections of 1912.[55] This marked the end of the negotiations. And, indeed, the revolution had already been decided upon.[56]

[53] Quoted in Cabrera, 348-354.
[54] Quoted in Cabrera, 278-381. Also in Merino and Ibarzábal, 84-85.
[55] Quoted in Cabrera, 382-384.
[56] For some comment on authorities, see the note at the end of chapter XVI.

CHAPTER XVI

THE REVOLUTION OF FEBRUARY

SPEAKING of the situation as it was at the beginning of February 1917, the Menocal historians of this period have this to say:

"The Liberals were already talking of revolution, without the least caution. The Liberal directorate was meeting daily to treat of the elections. But in truth they talked only of something else: they were making up a list of the friends they had in the army; they were sending orders to their coreligionists in the provinces to be ready for the great 'jamboree' (*chambelona*) that they were going to start; different revolutionary projects were discussed; plans for some of them were made; they studied what would be the most suitable movements; they enquired into the means for combat of which they could dispose; and discussed the place, day, and hour it would be convenient for them to begin the revolution. Some preferred to await the elections in Villas,[1] but most of them did not wish to wait even a moment. There were also those who favored making the revolution in Havana, and others who thought it more practical to go at once to the country. Of the triumph of the revolution they were sure, superlatively sure; their victory was going to be absolutely certain. They counted upon large forces of the army in Havana, on the troops that were garrisoning Santiago de Cuba and Camagüey, and on some scattered detachments throughout the island; all those troops were commanded by chiefs and officials who inclined to the Liberal party. Liberals who had been veterans of the War of Independence were disposed anew to lead a following, but this time, as in the Revolution of August, against the Cuban government. They were sure of winning, for even without fighting they knew the way to cause the government to fall. The country was in the midst of the sugar harvesting season; sugar, on account of the European War, was

[1] Villas, otherwise Cuatro (Four) Villas, is the old Spanish name for Santa Clara province, and is still employed quite as much as the present-day official name.

362

selling very dear, and at the first burning of a cane-field the planters would clamor for the immediate intervention of the United States, and that country, as at the time of the Revolution of August, would decide in favor of the revolutionists. There was not even a probability of losing. The hours of the Menocal government were already numbered." [2]

This represents the situation substantially as it was. At least as early as February 4, 1917, the revolution was decided upon, and the plans, already drawn up, must have been discussed for some time beforehand. Ferrara approached Raimundo Cabrera on the 4th, asking him to accompany him on a mission to the United States. He later told Cabrera that all arrangements for an insurrection had been made prior to his departure from Cuba on the 5th, and expressed surprise that Gómez had not acquainted Cabrera with the facts.[3] Down to February 1917 the Liberals had had rather the better of the moral issue between them and the Conservatives, especially as concerned post-election happenings. Now, however, they threw all that to the winds by going out in revolution. It would have been preferable, as Cabrera said, to have proposed "conspiracy and war, for after May 20, when all violences would have been committed and every legal recourse and protest exhausted uselessly." [4] Hispanic Americans have a peculiar outlook on such a state of affairs as then existed in Cuba, however, that Anglo-Americans find hard to understand. When convinced that they are not going to get fair treatment they withdraw from any attempt at victory by legal methods, holding that it would be of no avail and would unnecessarily risk the lives of their partisans. And then they risk a great many more lives in a civil war, with its attendant damage

[2] Merino and Ibarzábal, 86. The supreme confidence of the Liberals appears also from Cabrera's account, notably in opinions expressed to Cabrera by Ferrara, e.g., in Cabrera: 118; 125. Also cf. Cabrera, 400.
[3] Cf. Cabrera: 118; 124.
[4] *Ibid.,* 125.

to property and dangers of outside interference, and concede the legal victory to their opponents! This was what happened in Cuba.

The plan was for Gómez to put himself at the head of the insurrectionists in Santa Clara, and then entrain for Havana and in three or four days compel Menocal to abdicate, so that the partial elections could be held without illegal interference.[5] Matters did not turn out that way, however, for, whatever his political shortcomings, Menocal showed that he had greater talent for a military campaign than his opponents. Moreover, the action of the United States government was to follow a different course from what it had been in 1906, contributing substantially to the Liberal defeat. The definitive decision for the revolution was made at a meeting in Gómez's home, at which Zayas, Asbert, Ferrara, Machado, Cortina, Agustín García Osuna, and Dámaso Pasalodos were also present. At first it was set for February 14, the day of the partial elections in Santa Clara, but at the suggestion of Zayas this arrangement was changed so that Zayas was to give the signal, after first making a visit to the electoral districts in Santa Clara. Meanwhile, preparations were to go ahead, with precise fields of operation assigned to the different generals. Gómez left Havana in his yacht "Julito" on February 8, announcing that he was going fishing in the Caribbean. Instead, he made a landing on the 10th in the Bay of Juan Hernández, Camagüey, near Tunas de Zaza, Santa Clara, and put himself at the head of the revolution. Zayas that same day gave the expected signal. Not being allowed to approach one of the electoral districts, he held a meeting in the city of Santa Clara, attended also by Machado, Mendieta,

[5] Statement of Ferrara, referred to in Cabrera, 124-125.

Guzmán, and several others, and as a result orders were given to begin the conflict.[6]

During all the time that had elapsed since the elections of November and the outbreak of the revolution in February the United States had by no means been an indifferent spectator. Indeed, the Washington authorities were more than usually interested in the maintenance of peace in Cuba, for it was becoming increasingly clear that the United States must enter the war against Germany, and the Cuban sugar crop was an indispensable item in the plans of the American officials; they did not propose to allow it to be destroyed in a civil war if that could be avoided. There was a hint of the Washington attitude as early as November 1916. The United States minister at this time was Mr. William Elliott Gonzales, son of a Cuban who had been wounded at Cárdenas when López assaulted that place in 1850. A brother of this man, too, had fought with Máximo Gómez in 1898. Gonzales himself was thoroughly American,—so much so, so it is said, that he spoke Spanish with difficulty. He was in the United States late in November when he received an enquiry from a friend asking his views on the situation. Gonzales sent a cablegram in which he expressed an opinion that peace in Cuba depended on the wisdom and patriotism of the Cubans themselves. He expected that Menocal would act justly, but was also convinced that any improprieties could be corrected in a permanent and satisfactory fashion only by the employment of the methods provided by the law. In the excited state of Cuban opinion this was taken by some Liberals to mean

[6] Cabrera, 190-193, n.1; also 275; also statement of Giménez Lanier, in Cabrera, 246-252, at 249; and *Relato . . . del coronel Roberto Méndez Peñate*, in Cabrera, 399-419, at 400. Cabrera and Giménez (who was present at the meeting) make it appear that the conference in Santa Clara was held on Feb. 10, but Méndez Peñate, who was also in attendance, says it was the 9th.

that the United States would back Menocal in his endeavors to win the election by fraud, and so Manuel Márquez Sterling, editor of La Nación, a prominent Liberal organ, wrote to Gonzales on November 30 asking for a fuller statement of his ideas. Gonzales, presumably after communicating with his superiors, replied on December 3, making it plain that his basic idea was that all should respect the law, with a special responsibility attaching to those in high place.[7]

If they had not been blinded by the vision of 1906 the Liberals might have gathered from this that the United States opposed the idea of a revolution. With the outbreak of hostilities in February 1917 this attitude became more and more insistent. On February 11 Gonzales gave out to the press a long note of Secretary of State Lansing that he had delivered to the Cuban government the day before, with reference to the new elections in Santa Clara. Lansing urged both parties to arrange their differences through the methods that the law established, calling attention to a similar controversy in the history of the United States, the Hayes-Tilden election, which had been settled peacefully, even though the decision favored the candidate that received a minority of the vote. This note, described by Cabrera as having a paternalistic tone, and by Merino and Ibarzábal as somewhat nebulous in character, was at first not fully understood. The language was clear enough, but Cubans wanted to know what the United States proposed *to do*. The Menocal government itself was doubtful about it for a time, and replied a bit sharply that "some erroneous information" must have been given to the President of the United States if the note intended to imply that any

[7] The letter (in Spanish) is printed in full in Merino and Ibarzábal, 75- 77, and Cabrera, 333-337.

departure from legal methods was being contemplated. Rather, the Cuban authorities intended to proceed vigorously against all law-breakers. In this connection there was a peculiar feature of the Cuban note,—something of an oddity for a diplomatic communication,—in the shape of an envenomed assertion that a plot against President Menocal's life had just been discovered.[8] Several men were arrested for their complicity in the alleged plot, although many Liberals have insisted that no such project had ever entered into their plans.[9]

The Lansing note was several days too late for the achievement of its intended purpose, for the Liberals had already gone out in revolution by the time it was published on the 13th. Cabrera thought that the civil war might have been avoided if the note had come six days sooner,[10] but that is doubtful, as the Liberals expected a repetition of the Revolution of August, eleven years before. In any event the United States was not long in clearing up the meaning of the first note. In a communication of February 14, which Minister Gonzales gave out to the press that same day, the Washington authorities expressed apprehension over the news of the revolution in Cuba, and went on to say that the United States gave its "confidence and support" only to constitutional governments. There was also a somewhat vague statement to the effect that the United States would oppose such governments as came to power through the medium of revolution or other illegal means.[11] Five days later, on the 19th, Gonzales gave out a third note, de-

[8] For the Lansing note (in Spanish) and the Cuban reply, with comments thereon, see Cabrera, 116-117, n.1, also 116-122, and Merino and Ibarzábal, 94-96. Both appear, also, in Havana newspapers of Feb. 13, 1917.

[9] Cf. Cabrera: 121; 124; 190-196, n. 1, at 192.
[10] Ibid., 121.
[11] Ibid., 124, n. 1; Merino and Ibarzábal, 98; Havana newspapers of Feb. 14, 1917.

scribed by Cabrera as "autocratic" in tone, "explicit and harsh," condemning the revolution to inevitable defeat. The United States announced that it supported the government and that the insurrection, which was characterized as "lawless and unconstitutional," would "not be countenanced." The United States would hold the leaders of the revolt responsible for damage to the persons and property of foreigners and would study what attitude should be adopted toward those who were participating in the disturbances.[12] Yet stronger expressions were employed in several later communications, written, no doubt, with an eye rather more to the forthcoming war with Germany than to a consideration of United States-Cuban relations in themselves. Answering a request of the Santiago Chamber of Commerce for an intervention, the Washington authorities cabled on February 25 that the United States would attribute any damage to crops to those who were in rebellion, insisting, also, that the latter must lay down their arms, as the United States would support only constitutional methods for reaching a settlement of difficulties.[13] Two days later Gonzales gave out another note to the press. An American had been killed by insurrectionists at the Carlota mine near Cienfuegos. Some Menocal troops had pursued the men implicated in the act, and the United States now asked the Cuban government to continue its efforts to capture and punish all of them, and so too with other rebels who "should dare" to make any attack on the lives or property of Americans. Indeed, the United States would oppose a pardon or amnesty for them.[14]

The strong tone of the "Gonzales notes," as these com-

[12] Cabrera, 154-155, n.1; Merino and Ibarzábal, 108-109; and Havana newspapers of Feb. 19, 1917.
[13] In Discusión, Feb. 25, 1917.
[14] In Merino and Ibarzábal, 141; also Havana newspapers of Feb. 27, 1917.

munications are called in Cuba, is explained not merely by the approach of war between the United States and Germany, but also by the fact that American public opinion favored Menocal. Much had been written about the corruption of the Gómez administration and the uprightness of the government of Menocal, besides which the latter had an especial claim on the good-will of Americans as one who had been educated in the United States and had intimate relations with the business men of the country. Furthermore, the Liberals were regarded as rather more hostile to the United States than the Conservatives were, and their action in going out in revolution at a time when the United States was about to declare war on Germany was looked upon as something like a pro-German maneuver.[15] At any rate, the Gonzales notes virtually settled the issue in Cuba, leaving the military campaigns as a mere detail, for the Liberals could not expect to win in the face of the opposition of the United States. Their hopes had been so great that the disillusionment was all the more bitter, and one still hears vigorous denunciations of Gonzales and President Wilson for the part they played in the Revolution of February, as the insurrection of 1917 is called. For this, Ferrara is largely responsible. As head of the revolutionary delegation in the United States his experiences were anything but happy.[16] But as proprietor of the influential Heraldo de Cuba and the Reforma Social he was in a position to express his views and "put them over" among the people of Cuba. Gonzales has been condemned in particular for giving out the American notes to the press, an act amounting to "contempt of the Cuban Secretary of State," as

[15] For evidence concerning American public opinion, see Cabrera, 135-136, and *passim*. Cf. also articles in American periodicals at that time.
[16] Cf. Cabrera, *passim*.

Varona called it.[17]   Although the American attitude made the Liberal defeat inevitable, the other phases of the revolution may not be lightly dismissed, for the events of February were to be in the background of all that happened in the remaining years of Menocal's term, with some influence, too, beyond that time, even to the present day.

Gómez may be said to have put himself at the head of the revolution the day he landed on the southern shores of Santa Clara on February 10.   On the 10th, too, Baldomero Acosta, Liberal mayor of Marianao,[18] and "Pino" Guerra went out in revolt in the west.   It is said that they were involved in the alleged plot against Menocal, and when that failed left for the country the night of the 9th.[19] The first overt act of the campaign took place, however, at Camp Columbia, near Havana, on the 11th.   It appears that the plan was to rouse the whole garrison for the Liberal cause and then join with the police of Havana in a night attack to overthrow the government.   At two o'clock in the morning of the 11th two shots were fired as a signal, and immediately the camp was in an uproar, but only a small portion of the garrison joined in the revolt.   So, instead of marching on Havana the rebels were obliged to flee to the country.[20]   That same day Colonel Enrique Quiñones rose in Camagüey, taking possession of the capital of the province.   The next day Major Rigoberto Fernández, with virtually the entire garrison at his back, declared against the Menocal government in Santiago, and occupied the city. And on the 13th the troops in Guantánamo took over that

[17] Varona, Enrique José, *Discurso leído . . . la noche del 22 de diciembre de 1921,* in *Academia nacional de artes y letras,* v. VI, pp. 239-246, at 241.

[18] The name "Baldomero Acosta" is quite well known in the United States as that of a ball-player formerly with Washington in the American League and more recently with Louisville of the American Association. The ball-player is a son of the former mayor.

[19] Merino and Ibarzábal, 89-91.

[20] *Ibid.,* 91-93.

place in the name of the revolution. Word came presently that Guerra was at the head of a band in Pinar del Río, that Acosta, Loinaz del Castillo, and Carlos Guas were "out" in Havana, and that Machado, Mendieta, and others had risen in Santa Clara. Meanwhile, Gómez was marching north in Santa Clara, with the idea of seizing the railway and entraining for Havana. At this moment, when the prospects of the Liberals seemed to have a roseate hue, there occurred an event that gave an entirely new turn to the campaign. Not able yet to compete with the Liberals in the field, the Menocal government destroyed the railway bridge at Jatibonico, Camagüey, on the 13th, and Gómez's plan for a quick descent on Havana was nipped in the bud. Menocal now had time to prepare his forces, and he certainly made good use of his opportunity.

It is often asserted that the Liberals hoped to "blackmail" Menocal to an acceptance of their views as the only means of avoiding the entry of the United States, which had been fatal to the government party in a similar situation in 1906. Menocal failed to respond in the way expected, however, or to follow the course Estrada Palma had taken. He announced that there was no need of intervention,—that he would be able to put down the revolution without help. He also gave out that he had just purchased ten thousand rifles and five million rounds of ammunition from the United States government,[21] and he issued a call for volunteers. Menocal did, indeed, have a nucleus of military strength that Estrada Palma had lacked, although a considerable body of the army had gone out with the other side. A number of other steps, since greatly criticized

[21] Merino and Ibarzábal, 98; the sale of munitions by the United States government to the constituted authorities in Cuba is also mentioned in *Civil war in Cuba*, in *Independent*, v. LXXXIX, p. 344, Feb. 26, 1917.

by the Liberals as savoring of high-handed methods, were taken by him, all of them in the background of military affairs, but calculated to strengthen his position. Leading journals of the Liberal party were at once suppressed, on the ground that they were contributing to promote disorder. Heraldo de Cuba was obliged to suspend publication on February 12, La Nación on the 13th, and El Triunfo and La Prensa on the 14th. La Prensa later "rectified" its political opinions, and reappeared in April. This left in the field only journals that were backing the government or that had a safely neutral tinge.[22] Men were arrested by the hundreds, too, not only captives in battle, but also those suspected of conspiracy. Among the latter was the famous ex-governor of Havana, Ernesto Asbert.[23] It had been intended for him to serve as one of the insurrectionist generals in Havana province.[24]

Meanwhile the supplementary elections in Santa Clara were held on February 14. The Liberals made no effort to participate in them, although it is probably true that any action on their part would have had no effect on the result, because the government had its own views about counting the vote. In a normally Liberal district the Conservatives polled 2,427 votes to thirty-three for the Liberals. As there were only 2,401 voters on a presumably padded list, it must be admitted that the Conservatives were *extraordinarily* successful.[25] The elections in Oriente, scheduled for the 24th, had to be postponed, because of the military situation in that province. Later they were set for April 9. There seem to have been some irregularities in

[22] Merino and Ibarzábal: 96-97; 273-282.

[23] *Ibid.*, 117.

[24] Statement of Dámaso Pasalodos, in Cabrera, 190-196, n. 1, at 192.

[25] Statement of Alfredo Zayas, Mar., 1917, quoted in Pardo Suárez, 166-167; also see Cabrera, 296-297, n. 2, and *La protesta Liberal*, in Cabrera, 395-398, at 396-397, and in Pardo Suárez, 163-168, at 164-165.

the methods employed in choosing the date; for example, the call was issued on March 18 and became official by publication in the Gazette *the day before!* The result of the elections was quite as *extraordinary* as in the case of Santa Clara. To quote from a formal Liberal protest of May 7, 1917:

"The special elections of Oriente do not differ from those of Santa Clara as concerns the supposed and unlikely enthusiasm of the voters; and the same phenomenon is to be observed in them with respect to the desertion of Liberal voters and their conversion into Conservatives. There, as in Santa Clara, there were no voters in arms, or in prison, or absent, or dead. All voted, as is to be deduced from the electoral documents, even those who gave their suffrages in a district that was food for flames the day of the election." [26]

Menocal early took steps to bring all the resources of the state into his own hands by a law suspending constitutional guarantees. In a message of March 5, 1917, he asked Congress for such a law, including a provision for him to dispose of the funds of the treasury as he saw fit in attending to the expenses occasioned by the insurrection.[27] By an enactment of March 5 in the House and March 6 in the Senate, Congress granted his request. That is the simple story. Back of it, however, there was not a little violence. It was not possible to have a quorum in the House without the Liberal members, only a few of whom were present, but a quorum was nevertheless declared and the measure voted. All manner of pressure and threats was brought to bear on the Liberal representatives, and one of them, Alberto Barreras, who was also governor-elect of Havana, was arrested as he left the House and not released for several

---

[26] *La protesta Liberal,* in Cabrera, 395-398, at 397-398, and in Pardo Suárez, 163-168, at 166.

[27] In *Mensajes presidenciales,* I, 731-732; also in Merino and Ibarzábal, 117-119.

months. In that case, certainly, his right as a congressman to immunity did not protect him.[28]

The Liberals expected to win the campaign in the field, however, and then settle with Menocal at their pleasure. Meanwhile, Ferrara endeavored to make what seemed to him a satisfactory arrangement to avoid bloodshed. On February 12, despite the disapproval of his associate, Raimundo Cabrera, he sent a fire-eating cablegram to Menocal calling upon him to resign. Menocal replied next day that he was surprised at Ferrara's "unheard-of audacity," at the same time asserting his intention of putting down the revolt "with a firm hand" instead of resigning. Later, on March 1st, Ferrara cabled Wifredo Fernández, offering "the retirement from public life of all the chiefs of the existing armed movement" if Menocal would agree to "a solution that may save independence and liberty." Fernández replied that there was no likelihood of a loss of independence, as Menocal was about to suppress the insurrection. He added that the greatest danger to liberty was the employment of military rebellion such as was being espoused by Ferrara, whom many considered a "disturbing element of the republic." The Ferrara notes certainly did not help the Liberal cause, for they gave the Conservatives the last word and a chance to ridicule the author,—a fatal thing in Hispanic American opinion. An organization of Menocal supporters telegraphed the New York Herald that the greatest benefit Ferrara could confer on Cuba would be not to return, adding, with an allusion to his Italian birth, that "he who did not know how to be a patriot in his own land cannot be so in that of another." And Dolz called attention to Fer-

[28] Statements of Ignacio Remírez and Alberto Barreras, in Cabrera, 200-   205, n. 1, at 200-202, and 274-277, n. 1.

rara's "lordship" over the revolution, as evidenced by his offer to dispose of the future of its chiefs.[29]

Menocal's principal attention, however, was given to the enemy in the field. It has been said that he personally "directed every military movement of the Federal forces during the revolution."[30] However that may be, the government troops were so quickly and so uniformly successful that one writer has been led to say "there never was any fighting worthy of the name."[31] This is hardly correct. There were at least a score of battles, in which losses were not great, because of the comparatively small numbers engaged, but it was decidedly "unpleasant" for those who took part in them. The revolt was quickly crushed in the west; indeed, there was very little fighting in Pinar del Río, Havana, and Matanzas. So Menocal was soon able to turn to Santa Clara. After several minor encounters a government column under Colonel Rosendo Collazo caught Gómez in a trap at Caicaje on March 7, and captured him and almost his entire command. This battle was decisive of the war,—in so far as it had not already been determined by the attitude of the United States. There remained a great deal to do in Camagüey and especially in Oriente, however.

In Camagüey, the Liberal senator-elect Gustavo Caballero took charge of the revolution, and by Conservative account inaugurated a reign of terror. But his rule was brief. Government troops under Colonel Eduardo Pujol swept all before them in that province, and on February 26 recovered the capital. The fighting went on for a time, and received an impulse after Caicaje through the appearance of Mendieta

[29] The entire correspondence appears in Merino and Ibarzábal: 101-103; 115-117. Only the cablegrams between Ferrara and Menocal are given in Cabrera, at 139-140, n. 1.

[30] Marvin, George, *Keeping Cuba libre*, in *World's work*, v. XXXIV, pp. 553-567, at 565; Sept., 1917. Cf. also Merino and Ibarzábal, 149-150.

[31] Marvin, *Op. cit.*, at 563.

and others who had escaped from Santa Clara, but it all
came to an end with the defeat and capture of Caballero
on April 21. Some of the leaders, including Mendieta, got
away by taking ship to foreign parts. There is quite a
story in connection with Caballero. According to the government account he was wounded in the battle in which he
was captured, and died on the train en route to the city of
Camagüey,[32] but the Liberals assert, quite probably with
truth, that he "died" because he was executed.[33] In consequence, Caballero has taken rank in Liberal pronouncements as the martyr of the Revolution of February, as was
Villuendas in the elections of 1905.[34]

As might have been expected from the traditions of the
country the war was at its worst and was most long continued in Oriente. When Rigoberto Fernández took the lead
in the revolt by seizing Santiago on February 12 the entire
military garrison of the province, somewhat less than a thousand men, followed him, except for a few of the officers.
After Caicaje the Liberals were still hopeful that Fernández
might save the situation for them and bring about honest
elections by carrying on the war until the United States
should intervene. Fernández disappointed them, however.
As Cabrera put it, "The Odyssey of Caicaje terminated in

[32] Merino and Ibarzábal: 171; 178.
[33] Cabrera, 280.
[34] The following story, which may or
may not be true, is a sample of what
one hears in Cuba. This was told to
the writer by a man of some distinction who is not a politician.

"Pujol telegraphed to Menocal
about the surrender, and got back a
telegram to take Caballero's corpse
to Camagüey. Pujol then sent word
that Caballero was alive, but was
again told to take the body to Camagüey. So Caballero was put into a
separate car from the other prisoners,
and when the train reached Camagüey he was brought out dead. The
authenticity of the telegrams has
been vouched for in a story given
out by *Heraldo*, and the Zayas
government claims to have found
some state papers bearing upon the
incident. The only answer the Menocal people have made is to suggest
that the authorities investigate further and find out the truth about
the death of Lavastida under a Liberal régime in 1909—thus replying
merely with a *tu quoque*."

a combat and a defeat. That of Santiago ended, without resistance, in flight." [35] There is a legend, based on statements of Fernández, that the United States naval officers deceived the Liberal commander with promises of support for the revolution, thus accounting for the lack of distinction with which the latter handled the campaign in Oriente. The facts alleged in this connection are utterly at variance with the whole course of the United States policies at this time, but as the story is often insisted upon by the Liberals it may well be repeated here, as told by Fernández himself.

On the very day that he took possession of Santiago, Fernández planned to obstruct the channel leading up to the bay, so as to defend the city from any Conservative attempt to retake it, but the American naval authorities (at first Commodore Knox and then his successor, Commodore Belknap) objected, engaging to prevent the entry of any Menocal vessel, according to Fernández. Nevertheless, the government boat "Cuba" was later permitted to come in and disembark troops. Fernández himself presently abandoned Santiago at the request of Commodore Belknap, so he said, doing so in order to avoid the destruction of the city in a battle between the Menocal forces and his own; he took this course on Belknap's promise to keep the government troops out, but the latter were, notwithstanding, allowed afterward to enter the city. Belknap furthermore agreed that President Wilson would see to it that the partial elections in Oriente should be conducted honestly. All of these matters were bolstered up in an ample correspondence which Fernández retained in his possession, but when he went to Haiti, after the revolution broke down, he was seized by American officials, and these papers were taken from him. He was also deprived of some $194,000. This was

[35] Cabrera, 211-216, especially at 213.

government money, but Fernández, not recognizing the Menocal régime, felt it to be his "duty" to distribute this fund among the officers of the revolution who had been obliged to take refuge in the United States! [36] The tales of Fernández appear to have impressed Cabrera,[37] but they were vigorously denied by the United States. A communication from Washington to the American minster referred to the "insistence" with which the story was being told that the United States was considering taking sides with the insurrectionists. It was incomprehensible how any such erroneous impression could have gotten out, the note went on, and to correct it the United States reasserted that it would consider the rebels as outside the protection of the law until they should lay down their arms and submit to the constitutional government. This message was received on March 24 by the consular office in Guantánamo, which was instructed to deliver it to the consul at Santiago and cause it to be published throughout Cuba.[38]

The Cuban government account of this affair, which in this instance at least would seem to be reasonably accurate, is as follows. When Fernández heard that troops were coming to attack him he appealed to the commander of the American naval squadron to prevent bloodshed and destruction in Santiago, and the latter agreed to take possession of the city if Fernández and his men would leave it. A formal invitation was issued in a letter of March 8 to Commodore Belknap by José García Muñoz, whom Fernández had appointed temporary civil governor of Oriente. In this document García Muñoz recited that Fernández could not protect the city, as he was obliged to employ all his forces in operations in the field, and so he requested the landing

[36] Fernández, Rigoberto, *Exposición al presidente de los Estados Unidos,* quoted in Cabrera, 420-430.
[37] Cabrera: 212; 280.
[38] Quoted (in Spanish) in *Ibid.,* 280-281, n. 1.

of some five hundred men from the American vessels.[39]
That same day a body of United States marines was landed,
and Fernández was told to withdraw his troops within
twenty-four hours. By midnight the last insurrectionist
soldier had departed from the city; indeed, most of them
had gone the day before. They were informed that they
would not be allowed to return, unless they should deliver
their arms to American outposts before entering the city.
But the Americans did not interfere in any way with civilian
functionaries in the pursuit of their duties.[40]   Later, some
American forces occupied Guantánamo, Manzanillo, and
Nuevitas, and a body was also sent inland to protect the
mines of El Cobre.[41]

The Menocal government turned to military affairs in
Oriente shortly after the Gómez debacle at Caicaje. Colonel
Miguel Varona landed at Nuevitas on the north coast of
Camagüey with nine hundred men, and proceeded to Santiago, which he entered on March 26. Next day, after some
little fighting, he took both Caimanera and Guantánamo.
Colonels Matías Betancourt and Julio Sanguily joined with
Varona in the work of pacification in Oriente, and by May
the revolution had descended to the stage of "glorified
vagrancy," on the basis of "loot, license, and laziness." Indeed, it was continued that long only because the leaders
were afraid of what might happen to them if they surrendered.[42]   There was not a little destruction of railway
properties and sugar estates, but there was no longer the
slightest doubt about the issue of the war.[43]

[39] This letter is published in Merino and Ibarzábal, 194-196.
[40] *Ibid:* 192; 194-198.
[41] Cabrera, 257, n. 1.
[42] Marvin, *Op. cit.*, at 564.
[43] For an amusing account of the later stages of the conflict in Oriente, see Marvin, *Op. cit.*, at 553-561. Marvin points out how the fear of a Liberal attack on Guantánamo caused the American commander of the naval station at Caimanera to occupy the first-named city, thus bringing to pass the "third intervention" in Cuba.

The closing days of the revolt were inextricably involved in the larger question of the World War. Opinion in Allied countries was convinced that the insurrection was in reality a German maneuver, designed to bring about the destruction of the sugar crop and to divert the attention of the United States. Especially in the United States was this view taken. In the excited "spy fever" days of 1917 it was pointed out that the revolution began at just about the time when the United States broke relations with Germany, and sensational "evidence" was published to prove the Cuban Liberal-Germanic plot. There is no doubt but that an occasional irresponsible Liberal general, piqued at United States support of the government, made assertions and threats of a pro-German character, but there is no reason whatever to connect the revolution as a whole or the Liberal party with German designs.[44] Menocal was shrewd enough to take advantage of the situation, however, and to further the belief of the United States government and the American public in the German connection. It is probable, too, that Cuba's prompt declaration of war against Germany on April 7, just one day after that of the United States, had "two thoughts" in it for the state of affairs in Cuba to "one" of hostility to Germany.[45] It is noteworthy, however, that the Liberal members attended the meeting of Congress which authorized the declaration, and José Manuel

[44] Apart from Liberal denials and the lack of specific evidence, there is the supporting statement of the pro-Menocal historians of the Revolution of February. Referring to the Liberal position after the Cuban declaration of war against Germany, they go on as follows: "Against the revolutionists there now weighed a new and grave accusation: that of being anti-patriots, that of working against the country in aid of the foreign enemy. We confess that in all the in- vestigations we made we could not find any definite proof which would authorize so grave a charge." Merino and Ibarzábal, 249.

[45] Ferrara and Cabrera had a very uncomfortable time in the United States in consequence of the alleged pro-German character of the Cuban revolt, and the latter frequently comments on this factor, quoting also from American newspapers. See, for example, Cabrera: 164-168, n. 1-3; 216, n. 2; 229-230, n. 1; and 296.

Cortina made an eloquent speech, in course of which he praised the United States for the noble and generous help it had always given to the people of Cuba.[46] Now that both Cuba and the United States had entered the world conflict the latter was in no mood to let local difficulties in the island interfere with the larger plans for the war. So, vigorous messages were sent to Cuba pointing out that any alteration of public order tending to obstruct the output of the sugar crop would be considered a hostile act by the United States, and the insurrectionists were advised that if they did not submit to the Cuban government at once the United States would consider them and treat them as enemies of its own.[47]

Right from the first, many Liberals, discouraged by the attitude of the United States, had refrained from taking part in the revolt, and numbers of others surrendered, or at any rate withdrew from the conflict, after the defeat at Caicaje. Among those who proceeded early to get into the good graces of the government was Zayas. Generally considered a timid person, with a careful regard for his own skin, the Liberal candidate's conduct was certainly very disappointing to the Liberals.[48] After authorizing the outbreak of hostilities he himself disappeared, but turned up later in the capital, where he was not molested. As one writer has put it, "Zayas came into Havana and lived quite harmlessly out at the castle of Madame Abreu, who also maintained there the only chimpanzee born in captivity." [49] This is expressive of a certain disapproval with which his action was viewed by all parties. It killed Zayas with the Liberals, and was largely responsible for his flop to the Conservatives

[46] Merino and Ibarzábal, 247-248.   in Cabrera, 281-282, n. 1.
[47] One Lansing message to this ef-   [48] Cf. Cabrera, 275-276.
fect (in Spanish and undated) is given   [49] Marvin, *Op. cit.*, at 563.

in 1920. In this connection the story is often told that Gómez was not fighting for Zayas in 1917, but for himself.[50] The claim is made that he hoped to play the leading part in winning the war, then declare himself dictator, and afterward take over the presidency. In the absence of specific evidence it must be regarded as doubtful that he had any such idea in mind at the outset of the campaign, but in the light of Zayas's conduct the thing itself might have happened in case the Liberals had defeated Menocal.

Gómez, indeed, recovered and even enhanced his former prestige. It can hardly be said that he distinguished himself as a general, but the Cuban mind does not enquire too closely into matters of military technique. He did risk his life and his fortune, which was in direct contrast to Zayas's action. From this time forward the popularity of José Miguel grew until it attained to very nearly Olympian heights. For a while, however, his supporters were alarmed lest the Menocal government might execute him. He was interned in the castle of El Príncipe in Havana, which was usually employed as a prison for those guilty of felony. One day a rumor reached Ferrara and Cabrera in New York that caused chills to run up and down their spine: that the Conservatives claimed to have discovered a Liberal plot to rescue Gómez. What his friends feared was an "official assassination, based on flight," an old trick which the Cubans had learned from the traditions of the colony.[51] No doubt Ferrara and Cabrera recalled the "flight" of Lavastida in the time of Gómez's presidency. An attachment of some six million dollars is said to have been placed upon José Miguel's estates, on the basis of liabilities he had incurred

[50] This tale was repeated to the writer by responsible persons. It is also given currency in Merino and Ibarzábal, 103, and Johnson, IV, 332-335.
[51] Cabrera, 200.

in damages to property as a result of his seditious acts,[52] although it is probable that no collection was ever made. Gómez remained in prison until September 24, 1917, when he was allowed to depart to his "América" estate.

The Conservative historians of the events of 1917 make a great parade of the clemency displayed by the Menocal government in liquidating the revolution. Elsewhere in Hispanic America, they said, "all military men in rebellion would have been shot, without exception . . . and almost without asking their names . . . All would have 'tried to escape, so that it would be necessary to kill them by shooting them from behind' . . . The Cuban people had the satisfaction of knowing that nobody was shot." [53] This is true. A number were condemned to death, and others subjected to penalties of varying degree, but Menocal reduced all penalties through use of his pardoning power, and on March 18, 1918, an ample amnesty bill was passed. The Liberals were not wholly satisfied with it, since it did not restore all office-holders to their jobs, but it did open the jails, and allowed those who had left the country to return, without fear of punishment.[54] It is not necessary to belittle this meritorious achievement of the Menocal administration, but there is another story behind it. It is almost certain that the United States insisted on such a policy; Cabrera speaks vaguely of the success that Ferrara had in getting the United States to guarantee protection for the lives of Liberals, and says that Minister Gonzales assured other members of the diplomatic corps in Havana that the penalty of death would not be applied to any of the insurrectionist prisoners.[55] This accords with general

[52] Cabrera, 267, n. 3.   [54] Cf. infra, p. 533.
[53] Merino and Ibarzábal, 283-287.   [55] Cabrera: 201-205; 205, n. 1.
See also Dolz, 35.

opinion in Cuba. The following statement made to the writer on October 20, 1924, is representative of what one usually hears:

"Recently the Conservatives have had a great deal to say about the magnanimity of Menocal in 1917, and, indeed, there was general leniency at that time, but only under compulsion of Secretary Lansing. Menocal wanted to execute Gómez and some of the others concerned in the insurrection, but Lansing insisted to Pablo Desvernine that there was to be 'no blood.' Desvernine was at that time Secretary of State, but was in Washington on a visit." [56]

There is no clear evidence, however, that United States pressure was required, and therefore it is only fair to give the Menocal government credit on the basis of what it did.

On May 8, 1917, Congress met to proclaim the victorious candidates, and Menocal and Núñez were declared the winners by eighty-six electoral votes to thirty-six. The Liberals had drawn up a formal protest, the day before, against the validity of the elections, and this document was presented at the meeting, but was rejected.[57] More to the point, however, was that some forty Liberal congressmen, at the suggestion of Zayas, so it is said,[58] attended the session, when without their presence there would have been no quorum. At least one Liberal, who had risked his life in the field, was disgusted at this easy acquiescence of the politicians of his party in the victory of Menocal.[59] On May 9 there was a fresh attempt to assassinate Menocal, or, at least, so government reports of the 10th alleged,[60] although Cabrera called it "a tragic farce . . . to heap discredit before the powerful ally against the defeated Liberals." [61] On May

[56] This whole subject was discussed in an anti-Menocal article in *Heraldo de Cuba*, Oct. 29, 1924.

[57] The Liberal protest is in Cabrera, 395-398, and Pardo Suárez, 163-168.

[58] Merino and Ibarzábal, 250.

[59] Méndez Peñate, Roberto, *Relato*, quoted in Cabrera, 399-419, at 413.

[60] Merino and Ibarzábal, 251-255, give a detailed account of this affair.

[61] Cabrera, 297-298.

20 Menocal went through the ceremony of inaugural for a second term, taking the oath to "respect the law and the institutions of the country." Thus were the elections of 1917 brought to their "logical" conclusion! [62]

[62] The elections of 1916 and more particularly their sequel the Revolution of February have a vast body of materials comparable in quantity with the parallel period of 1905-1906. Trelles mentions a number of items, but there are two that stand out. One of these is the volume by Cabrera, which is an engaging literary work as well as a valuable source-book for the events of 1916-1917. This is a narrative of Cabrera's own experiences as a Liberal emissary in the United States, but in writing it, says Cabrera, "I present the picture of what surrounds me: the medium of my struggles and sufferings, the individuals, the collectivity, the complete scene of my own legend." Cabrera writes as a Liberal partisan, not as a historian, but there is a note of sincerity that is impossible to escape, and the volume (especially the second edition, which the writer used) is so well bolstered with documents in appendices and footnotes that it takes rank as one of the leading works in the field of Cuban historiography. On the other hand, one finds a presentation from the Conser- vative point of view in the Merino and Ibarzábal history. This makes a pretence of impartiality, though it is in fact a rather crudely partisan Menocal pamphlet. But it is the only work that covers these exciting years as a whole, and it introduces documentary evidence and a point of view which serve as a check on Liberal accounts. The greater part of this volume (pages 89 to 287 of the second edition) is devoted to the period of the war, with a detailed story of the campaigns. All other books and pamphlets referring to these years are of a highly specialized character, such as personal reminiscences, legal briefs, arguments, and the like.

Naturally, with a disputed election and a civil war to deal with, there are many articles on Cuban affairs at this time. Among the most important in American periodicals is the one by Marvin, cited here, while there were a number of other formal articles or editorial utterances worthy of at least some attention. Johnson, IV, 328-345, has a chapter on this subject, but it is not too well informed.

CHAPTER XVII

GOING DOWN: MENOCAL'S SECOND TERM, 1917-1921

THE inauguration of Menocal for a second term on May 20, 1917, in a sense marked a new turn in the history of the republic. Down to this time, although matters had been getting steadily worse, there had been something commendable in each administration and not a few reputable men, greatly outnumbered to be sure, in the field of politics. But from 1917 on, at least to May 20, 1925, it is hard to find anything good to say about anybody or anything in the conduct of the Cuban state. If some honest and capable citizens still held important government posts, they were without influence and almost without voice to check the rapidly growing evils in Cuban affairs. Menocal himself seems to have changed from the man of high purposes who took over the presidential toga in 1913, or at least to have become reconciled to a corrupt ambient which he had at first decried.

At the outset of Menocal's new term Cuba found herself in the midst of the great World War. It would hardly be claimed by anybody that Cuba "won the war" or that she contributed very substantially to the result, but her achievement was respectable. In his message of April 6 Menocal took the same position as that already announced by President Wilson against unrestricted submarine warfare, but he also made a special point of the republic's close ties with the United States, holding that Cuba could not, "without loss of dignity and decorum, show indifference to

386

the noble attitude assumed by the United States." He went on to explain that Cuba could not remain neutral, as that would compel her to treat all belligerents alike, which should not be done as against the United States, her "friend and ally." [1] Four German steamers in Havana and two more at other ports were at once seized by the Cuban government and turned over to the United States. On the score of the "conduct of the war" in Cuba, matters were handled very much as they were in the neighboring republic to the north, minus a great deal of the excitement. Under the leadership of the President's wife, Red Cross work was organized. Cuba contributed generously to the United States Liberty loans. There were the various meatless and wheatless days. Some Cuban officers went to United States training camps, while several camps were also established in Cuba. A hospital unit of a hundred doctors and nurses was despatched to France. The American, French, and Belgian national holidays (July 4, 14, and 21) were observed in Cuba. The United States declaration of war against Austria was followed by a Cuban declaration of December 16, 1917, specifically because of the United States action. There were numerous resounding pronouncements of Cuban accord with the United States. And finally, first among the nations of the world, Cuba in 1923 paid her war debt to the United States; it amounted to less than seven million dollars, but payment was in full.[2]

The one really important achievement of Cuba in the war was in vastly increasing the output of sugar, which was an indispensable product for the allies. To be sure, a very

[1] The Menocal message is in Merino and Ibarzábal, 244-247. A portion of it in an English translation is in Johnson, IV, 346-348.
[2] For an account of Cuba's participation in the war, see an article by Menocal, *Cuba's part in the World War*, in *Current history*, v. IX, pt. I, pp. 315-318; Nov., 1918. There is also a highly laudatory chapter in Johnson, IV, 346-354.

good price was obtained, though not so high as it might have been, without government intervention. There was some talk of sending an army of twenty-five thousand men to France, but transports were lacking, and the question was raised whether Cubans would be adapted to the rigorous winter climate of northern France. There was no overwhelming enthusiasm for the idea, anyway. At least one man in public life wished to do something, however. This was Fernando Ortiz, among the most notable scholars that the republic has produced [3] and at that time one of the few really estimable men in the House. Ortiz wanted to send at least a small Cuban force to Europe, if only as a symbol of an active participation in the conflict, and brought in a bill to that effect. Congress voted the bill, but the troops were never sent. A universal military service law was enacted in the summer of 1918, but the war was over before any practical result came of it.

The truth is, most of the "war measures" in Cuba were primarily concerned with local affairs. It was not at all improbable that there might have been another uprising, and there was always the possibility of damage to the sugar crop. In 1917 Menocal asked the Washington government to send some troops to Cuba, and in consequence about sixteen hundred men were landed in Oriente and a thousand in Camagüey. Not until 1922 were these men withdrawn.[4] In like manner it is often asserted that the military law of 1918 was in fact a protective measure against the Liberals, but a complete farce so far as the World War was concerned. Furthermore, Menocal retained the extraordinary powers that were granted to him in consequence of the Revolution of February and the declaration of war against Germany, and was a virtual dictator to the end of his rule,

[3] Cf. *infra,* p. 636.   [4] Trelles, *Biblioteca,* II, 125.

legislating by decree and otherwise conducting himself as an all-powerful, irresponsible head of the state.[5] Nothing was more irksome to the Cubans than this phase of his government, and the President was bitterly condemned for it by his opponents, both during his administration and afterward. Early in 1919, for example, Carlos Mendieta wrote a celebrated editorial for Heraldo de Cuba entitled "Good-bye, dictatorship!" (¡Adios, dictadura!), basing it on the rumor that the United States had "turned her eyes toward Cuba," with the idea of having fair elections in 1920. Mendieta's article was a most sweeping, if also extravagant, denunciation of the Menocal government, and got him into trouble with the authorities. He was haled into court and fined five hundred dollars for insulting the President. Immediately a popular subscription was started to reimburse Mendieta, with contributions limited to a penny apiece.[6]

Mendieta called the Menocal rule a "classic and vulgar dictatorship," with nothing of positive achievement in its favor such as had served in some measure to excuse the despotism of a Porfirio Díaz of Mexico. He charged Menocal with responsibility for "the almost complete abandonment of public services, without excepting education and the highways, the greater part of which are impassable, just as if we might be in the primitive days of neighborhood roads." This assertion is supported in the writings of men like Carlos Trelles, who cannot be accused of violent partisanship. Trelles pointed out that education in Cuba had steadily declined since the beginning of the century,

[5] Cf. Ibid., II, 122.
[6] The Mendieta article first appeared in Heraldo de Cuba on Jan. 29, 1919, and was republished, with comments, on May 19, 1919. The story of the trial was given in an extra of Feb. 3, 1919, and the regular issue of the following day.

reaching its lowest state under Menocal. In the time of General Wood seventy-five persons per thousand attended school, but in 1920 this had fallen away to fifty, while the ratio of pupils in school to the entire population was approximately only a third of what it was in the United States. On the other hand the number of teachers had nearly doubled, but this was because the *botella* (bottle), or graft, had entered the school system. In marked contrast with the decline in education was the increase in the numbers and the expense of the army. From the 1,700 soldiers of General Wood and three thousand rural guards of Don Tomás, the army had grown to over ten thousand men under Gómez, more than fifteen thousand in 1916, and about eighteen thousand in 1919.[7] As for roads, Menocal did indeed build 456 kilometres of them in eight years, but this was the poorest record that had been made since the inauguration of the republic. Nevertheless, he had spent on highway construction almost as much as his three predecessors combined and about seven times as much per kilometre as had been expended by Estrada Palma. All this was without taking into account the rapid deterioration of roads through lack of needed repairs.[8]

Of course, other agencies of the government must share in the responsibility that attaches to the name of Menocal for the administration of the country's affairs. Congress,

[7] Trelles, *El progreso (1902 a 1905) y el retroceso (1906 a 1922) de la república de Cuba*, 11-13.   [8] *Ibid.*, 18-19. The following table, based on Trelles, gives some idea of the situation:

Rule	Years	Kilo-metres	Aver-age	Cost	Aver-age
Estrada Palma...	4	328	82	$ 2,058,000	$ 6,275
Magoon	2	608	304	11,154,000	18,345
Gómez	4	500	125	6,309,000	12,618
Menocal	8	456	57	19,435,000	42,620

To be sure, a great many other factors were involved, chief among which was the greatly increased cost of materials in later years.

for example, either failed to enact really needed legislation or else voted laws that were bad. In Menocal's second term, however, Congress was less of a factor than it had been before, because of the President's employment of executive decrees in many cases or his corruption of congressmen through lavish use of collectorships in the lottery and other financial lures when he wanted an appearance of legislative sanction. There were a number of laws of "economic defence" and the like, growing out of the World War situation, some of them dating back to Menocal's first term. While these may have been unobjectionable in the main, it is frequently asserted that they were administered in an improper fashion. For example, no rice could be imported or sugar exported without a permit, but it is claimed that Menocal's associates found no difficulty in obtaining permits, and others could get them if they "paid the price." Another much criticized bit of legislation was the tourist law of August 15, 1919, which authorized certain games of skill where patrons were wont to bet on the result. Under this law jai-alai made its legal reëntry into the capital, and gambling at the Casino and horse-racing were permitted in the suburbs of Havana at Marianao. It was such a bill as those which Gómez and Menocal had both vetoed. Menocal had different views in 1919, and so too other members of his family, who fought for the measure in Congress and, so it is said, obtained the jai-alai concession when the bill became a law. Another Menocal supporter received his reward in connection with horse-racing. This was Ricardo Dolz, who became president of the company organized to promote that sport. August 15, 1919, too, is the date of a law as a result of which the La Osa estate, belonging to the government, was turned over on surprisingly generous terms to a private company which was constructing a bridge over the Almendares River. As the reputation of some of the grantees was none too clean,[9] the affair was looked upon as a scandalous graft deal. Yet another matter of this sort also goes back to that period: a concession granted to a company, made up exclusively of politicians, for a public market monopoly in the city of Havana. This occasioned an advance in the price of agricultural products, in part because the sellers, who were obliged to dispose of their goods in the market or not at all, were required to pay exorbitant prices for their stands there.

Despite the rise of prices in these years and the heavy expense occasioned by the Revolution of February, the government was increasingly prosperous. Foreign trade grew until it amounted to well over a billion dollars' worth with the United States alone in 1920, although it is true that the value of money had declined so greatly that it can hardly be taken as a correct index. Revenues advanced from the thirty-seven to fifty-two millions of Menocal's first term to some seventy millions in 1918 and $108,000,000 in 1920. The budget for a while lagged slightly behind, but jumped to $136,000,000 for the fiscal year 1920-1921, equal to forty-five dollars per inhabitant. But in point of fact Menocal spent $182,000,000 that year. Things had changed since the days of Don Tomás! Then, with approximately fifteen millions a year, or eight dollars per inhabitant, much more was accomplished for education and other useful public services than in the extravagant days of Menocal. Altogether, in eight years of rule, the latter spent some six hundred million dollars, and that without taking into account the enormous floating debt he left behind or the expenditures of the various municipal and provincial governments.

[9] One member of the company was the notorious "Pote." Cf. *infra,* pp. 398-399.

If these were added, the total might reach a billion dollars.[10]

Prosperous as it was, the government did not feel able to finance all its needs without a resort to loans. There were two issues in 1917. One was for seven millions, and was employed in making a final settlement of the Ports Company case. The other was a "war loan" for thirty millions. Menocal is alleged to have tried to provide for this by decree, but the United States insisted on a law of Congress. Half of the money was applied to debts of the government, but the other fifteen millions were supposed to be for military purposes. It is said that ten millions were spent in Cuba and had so little to do with the war that payment of the remaining five millions was stopped. A considerable fraction of this "war debt" was employed in the purchase of a presidential mansion.

It will be recalled that José Miguel had left a great skeleton palace in the Villanueva tract which he acquired in exchange for the Arsenal lands. During his first term Menocal tried, without success, to get a grant from Congress that might enable him to finish this building.[11] Meanwhile an elaborately expensive palace, far better than any government edifice in the capital, had been undertaken by Governor Asbert for the province of Havana. Early in his second term Menocal purchased this for the nation. According to one account he thereby relieved the province of an embarrassing burden of debt, while another story has it that he virtually compelled the provincial authorities to sell the building. In any event it came to $3,750,000, or more than double the cost of the White House in Washing-

[10] Trelles, *El progreso (1902 a 1905) y el retroceso (1906 a 1922) de la república de Cuba*, 20-21; also Trelles, *Biblioteca*, II, 127.

[11] For example, see Menocal's messages of Nov. 3, 1913, and Mar. 18, 1914, in *Mensajes presidenciales*, I: 459-474, at 469; and 496.

ton, to say nothing of the million that had already been wasted on the Villanueva structure.[12]   But this was not all. It was necessary to furnish this splendid palace in fitting style.   It is said that a hundred thousand dollars was spent for linen alone, and a commission of sixty thousand was paid to a cousin of the President for an excellent but somewhat fantastic painting of the battle of Victoria de las Tunas, the scene of Menocal's greatest glory in the War of Independence.[13]   And, incidentally, the authorized budget of the presidency had now advanced from the $62,390 a year that Estrada Palma got in 1905 to $226,000 for Menocal in 1919,[14] which of course did not include the expenditures on the palace or, indeed, various other items that were in fact under the President's control.

These incidents give a hint of financial improprieties on the part of Menocal himself, but there are two opinions, even among those who disapprove of Menocal, as to whether he actually should be called a grafter.   The following are some statements on this score, all from men whose views are worthy of attention:

(1) "Menocal did not take anything, but let his relatives and friends help themselves."

(2) "Menocal was a very wealthy man, and may not have grafted himself, but he certainly let others do it under him."

(3) "I can excuse Gómez, though he was a grafter, but not Menocal, even though he personally may not have taken a cent.   He was a man of education and training, and is therefore all the more to be censured for letting the political affairs of the country sink to the corrupt level they reached in his administration."

(4) "Menocal profited, perhaps, but less than Gómez or Zayas.   For

[12] Trelles, *El progreso (1902 a 1905) y el retroceso (1906 a 1922) de la república de Cuba:* 23; also 23, n. 1.

[13] This is based on statements of reputable persons to the writer.   Similar but more extreme charges have been made frequently in the newspapers.   One of the writer's inform-

ants claimed that Menocal even went so far as to remove the linen of the palace to his own home at the end of his term.

[14] Trelles, *El progreso (1902 a 1905) y el retroceso (1906 a 1922) de la república de Cuba,* 23.

example, the government deposited its money with the National Bank of Cuba, and the bank loaned Menocal large sums for his sugar-mills on favorable terms,—so favorable, indeed, that he never paid them back. But, then, no politician would have done so."

(5) "It is not true that Menocal did not take graft for himself. The War of Independence ruined him. To be sure, he got a large salary as manager of the Chaparra estates, but not wealth, and now he is a multi-millionaire. And his friends and relatives also feathered their nests."

(6) "Menocal was a white glove grafter on a large scale. He was worth about a million when he became President, but left office with thirty or forty millions. And he let his relatives have anything they wanted. He made a lot by taking over the rice import monopoly for himself and associates, and something more through the private sale of sugar export permits."

The following is an interesting comment in an article that appeared recently in an American periodical:

"Menocal—unapproachable, dignified, lavish—led the third administration, which began with a necessary breathing space after the ruin accomplished by Gomez. But, eventually, it improved on these methods and introduced one or two tricks that even Gomez had not thought of. There was great activity and small accomplishment by the Department of Public Works, where plans and estimates were prepared and payments made for imaginary roads and fictitious bridges over non-existent rivers. More than a score of banks were looted by their directors while the government stood passively by. With the rise in price of sugar, incident to the Great War, business began to boom and fortunes to pile up on every hand. Naturally, the governmental revenues, reflecting the growing prosperity of the country, doubled and tripled in amount. Soon the country, individually and as a whole, became money mad. Several of the Cabinet secretaries and a large number of other public officials, tempted by the overnight fortunes amassed by business men, started businesses of their own, utilizing as capital their positions of confidence and trust in the government. Menocal himself has never been proven a participant in the graft; not so, however, three members of his Cabinet and a large following of personal friends to whose venality he was always obstinately blind. Speculation was Menocal's failing, but due to good judgment and luck, his life since office has been on a scale that might tax the resources of a prince. Half a billion in taxes was collected while he was President, but the only signs of progress in his day that remain are the presidential mansion and a bronze and marble statue of Antonio Maceo." [15]

That there was a lot of grafting under Menocal would hardly be denied by anybody. Sebastián Gelabert, who was for a time Secretary of the Treasury under Zayas, declared in June 1921 that Cuba had been paying fifteen millions a year to holders of *botellas,* or false employes.[16] And the state of the Department of Public Works, as revealed when Zayas succeeded to the presidency in 1921, showed that fraudulent contracts had been made on a vast scale. On one other matter, too, there is virtual unanimity, and that is that Menocal's friends and relatives were allowed to enrich themselves. Indeed, as a nepotist Menocal far surpassed José Miguel, though hardly rivalling his successor in the presidency,—"because his family was not so large," as one man put it to the writer. Three of his brothers were in Congress, and other relatives and friends had good government jobs, while it is said that all members of the family, even including the women, had collectorships in the lottery. All in all, the following denunciation by Mendieta may not have been too severe:

"Menocal has converted Cuba into a factory that is a theatre of caprices, dilapidations, and madness. He has usurped the power, and has wronged his compatriots. His work of decomposition is almost impossible to repair. He has relaxed public customs, with a governmental régime contrary to every precept of economy, and has enthroned the desire for lucre in official circles." [17]

For a while a good many elements in Cuba were willing to excuse the shortcomings of the Menocal administration, for the country was indeed enjoying such prosperity as it had never before known. It was the same sort of war and

[15] *Cuba, an American ward again?,* in *Independent,* v. CXIII, pp. 35-38; July 19, 1924.

[16] Trelles, *Biblioteca,* II, 121.

[17] Mendieta, *Op. cit.*

post-war inflation boom as was experienced at that time in the United States, but in Cuba it was more pronounced; as a one-product country the island republic ranges farther in either direction than its great northern neighbor, one moment climbing the empyrean heights, and the next touching the depths of degradation and despair. With exceptionally large crops of sugar and a high price that got even higher when restrictions were withdrawn at the close of the war the island was flooded with money. Where sugar had brought an average of three cents a pound in the past, it rose to five and a half cents during the war, and to twenty-two and a half cents in 1920. Everything else went up in proportion. According to a statement of Menocal early in 1920, deposits in banks and savings institutions had increased a thousand per cent in the preceding six years, and land values had advanced five hundred per cent.[18] The most characteristic note of the day, however, and more in keeping with the pleasure-loving instincts of the Cuban people, was the wild orgy of extravagance that broke out in the island, such that this period has come to be called "the dance of the millions." Much of this self-indulgent happiness overflowed in trips to other parts of the world, to the accompaniment of "good times" of a very exciting variety.

The dance of the millions was a mere false bubble of prosperity, and when it burst there was nothing left. Overproduction of sugar in different parts of the world caused the market to break, during the summer of 1920, and the price crashed down until it was only some three and five-eighths cents in 1921. All business fell with it. The banks had made heavy loans to finance the sugar crop on the basis of the prevailing high prices of the product, but when

[18] De Bekker, Leander J   , *Cuba*   pp. 230-231; Feb. 21, 1920.
and her president, in *Nation*, v. CX,

the market collapsed their security was wiped out. The borrowers could not repay, and the banks could not meet their other obligations. In order to tide over the situation the government on October 10, 1920, declared a moratorium, or suspension, in the payment of debts until December 1st, and presently extended the time to January 1st, and then to February 1st. At the same time, Cuban firms which had ordered goods in the United States and elsewhere at high prices now refused to take them. To be sure, prices generally had fallen not only for Cuban sugar but also for most other materials all over the world, but it is doubtful if the goods could have been paid for, even at the new prices. As early as July 1920 the congestion at the Havana docks was so great that an American commission visited Cuba to see what could be done to relieve the situation.

Early in January 1921, General Crowder came to Cuba to assist the republic in solving its electoral dispute (of which presently), and as part of his duties he also made suggestions concerning the economic crisis. As a result the moratorium was continued on a sliding scale, with a provision for a series of gradual payments. The ultimate date for merchants was fixed at May 15, and for the banks at June 15. These steps partially averted financial disaster, but eventually, owing to "spineless execution" of the bank liquidating act of January 31, 1921, most of the banks failed, nevertheless. The most notorious case was that of the National Bank of Cuba itself. The affairs of this institution had been conducted in an outrageously improper manner, especially by one of its officers, a Spaniard named José López, or "Pote" as he was generally called in Cuba. The bank had never been "National" except in name, for "Pote" controlled more than fifty per cent of the shares, bought with money that had been loaned to him by the bank. "Pote," one of the most notorious characters in the republican era, was originally a bookseller, who accumulated a fortune through graft in supplying books and other materials for the schools, and added to it by famous deals in public works and sanitation contracts with the state. When the affairs of his "National" bank began to be revealed "Pote" committed suicide. An enquiry developed that he was at that time in debt to the bank in some nine million dollars. There were numerous officials both of the National and of other banks who also had a guilty record, such that they were criminally indicted, but they were later included in an amnesty law of the Zayas period.[19] While the Cuban banks and branches of European banks were quite generally failing, two great institutions, the National City Bank of New York and the Royal Bank of Canada, met every obligation. They lost heavily, but probably made money in the end, through the improvement of their relative place in the Cuban financial world and through later advances in the value of the security they took over from their debtors.

The least becoming thing in Menocal's eight year rule was the manner of his passing,—his handling of the elections of 1920, which were even more scandalously stolen than were those of 1916. He might yet have saved his name by holding honest elections at this time, but he chose to go from bad to worse, even turning "traitor to his party," as Pérez puts it, by thrusting his former opponent Zayas into the presidency, in order at all costs to beat Gómez.[20] After the Revolution of February there was a revival of the split in Liberal ranks as between Zayas and Gómez, but this time it was Gómez that had the upper hand. Indeed, Zayas was no longer recognized as a member of the

[19] Cf. *infra*, pp. 534-535.   [20] Cf. Pérez, 13.

party by most of the Liberals, and so in 1919 he took his group and formed a new organization which he called the Popular party. It announced a noisy program of "non-interference of other nations in Cuba's affairs," or virtually the familiar old anti-Platt Amendment platform, but in point of fact it was a mere "pirate party," ready to jump in any direction that might prove to its advantage. The opportunity soon came. Whatever his promises to General Emilio Núñez may have been in 1916, Menocal appears to have had different views as 1920 approached. At first he hit upon General Rafael Montalvo, a veteran of '95, former Cabinet official under Estrada Palma, and more recently prominent in the sugar industry, but presently consideration of Montalvo was dropped. According to one account Menocal was convinced that Montalvo could not win, but another story has it that there was a violent personal controversy between the two men. It was then that an arrangement was made for Zayas to become the joint candidate of the Conservative and Popular parties, or virtually of the former, which represented ninety per cent of the strength in this alliance. In other words, Zayas made a complete flop, and, in a sense, so too Menocal. Núñez jumped in the other direction, passing over to the Liberal camp.[21]

Long before the formation of the "National League," as the Conservative-Popular union was called, there had been rumblings and murmurs about the forthcoming election. The Liberals wanted assurances this time that they would not be robbed, and the idea developed that some sort of help from the United States was necessary. Menocal himself, as early as 1917, advocated the taking of a new census as the basis for a purification of the voting lists.[22] Eventually both the

[21] General Francisco Carrillo was the vice-presidential nominee for the Conservatives.

[22] Message to Congress of Apr. 2, 1917, quoted in Merino and Ibarzábal, 234-243, at 240.

Conservatives and Liberals concurred in the issue of an invitation to General Crowder to come to Cuba and assist in drawing up a new election law. This was the same officer who had had such marked success in handling electoral problems in the Magoon era. In addition to his well-known integrity, tirelessness as a worker, and legal and administrative ability, he now had back of him a great prestige which he had gained for his achievements in American military councils in the World War. So, early in 1919 the invitation was extended, and on February 15 Minister Gonzales announced that Crowder had accepted. About a month later, on March 18, Crowder came over from Florida in an airplane. He at once went to work on his task. A census was duly taken, and studies were made of all elections since 1909, so as to know the different varieties of fraud that had been practiced, with the idea of providing against them in the future. In the end, the number and character of the guarantees in the new law against fraud, all based on previous Cuban experience, were such as to constitute an indictment of the nation. Greater reliance was placed on the judiciary than had been the case under the old law,—so much so that it was virtually impossible for a man lawfully to become President of Cuba without the acquiescence of the Supreme Court. The law was just as strong or as weak as the judiciary, and it is said that Crowder told Menocal that any failure to obtain a prompt result under it would be fraught with grave consequences for Cuba.[23]

Despite the seeming cordiality of his original invitation, Menocal in fact paid little attention to the requirements of the Crowder law. One provision, against the union of parties, was done away with by amendment so as to permit of the Conservative-Popular alliance, and other "safeguards" were

[23] For something more on the Crowder law, see *infra*, pp. 574-577.

flagrantly disregarded. Speaking generally of Cuban elections and of the election of 1920 in particular, Doctor Herbert J. Spinden, an official observer, has this to say:

"The ancient psychology of Spanish politics flares up luridly in Cuba . . . In their long wars for independence Cubans exhibited a willingness to die for their country . . . But since securing independence they have not shown an ability to live for their country . . . Many of the things complained of in Cuban politics could be matched . . . in the United States. But . . . We have never suffered from a President who went into office a poor man and came out a multi-millionaire. We have never suffered from the coercive action of an army or from other grave evils which exist in the politics of Cuba . . . we have never had at the head of our nation a man like Menocal, who over his own signature pardoned 335 criminals during the electoral period, of which 44 were murderers . . . The story of the last election is sordid and cynical to a degree. All mayors of liberal towns were shorn of their executive rights and military supervisors · responsible to the Secretary of the Interior and having at their beck and call the intimidating forces of the army were put in charge throughout Cuba. These men were armed and they shot to kill in ill-starred Sagua. In addition, then, to all petty trickery in counting ballots and juggling figures, there were forces abroad in the last election which were sinister in the extreme. There can be little doubt but that this was stolen." [24]

As early as August 1920, the Liberals, who had nominated Gómez for the presidency (with Miguel Arango for Vice-President), threatened to withdraw from the elections, which was virtually as much as to say that they would provoke United States intervention or start an insurrection unless they were given a fair chance for victory. The Washington government did not want another Revolution of August or February, and took steps at once to adjust the situation. In a note of August 30 it was made clear that the Liberals had better go to the polls; the United States would not favor

[24] Spinden, Herbert Joseph, *America and her duty in Cuba,* in Boston *Transcript,* Aug. 7, 1923. The author, who is an official of the Peabody Museum of Cambridge, Massachusetts, is one of the leading anthropologists in the United States.

either party, but would have official observers on hand, with the idea of avoiding intimidation or fraud.[25] This was very like intervention, but it is said that Menocal was prevailed upon to request the observers, although the suggestion came from Washington.[26] So the observers "came," and "saw," but could not prevent the evil methods of other years to win the election. What were these methods? For one thing the Department of the Interior was combined with that of War under one Secretary, Charles [27] Hernández. This meant that the man who was responsible for the conduct of the elections might also make use of the regular soldiery and the rural guards in such ways as he saw fit. As Secretary of the Interior, Hernández suspended or supplanted mayors and police chiefs in Liberal towns, and as Secretary of War appointed military supervisors in their places, picking the officers he wanted. It was all done on a pretence of maintaining order, but was in fact a political maneuver. Out of 112 municipalities, there were seventy-three, mainly in Liberal territory, that were put under military supervisors. Most of the higher officers of the army dared to refuse to do political work, to their credit be it said, but enough lesser officials were found to supply the need, often mere sergeants or corporals, and some of them instituted a veritable reign of terror. Between March 1st and October 6, 1920, too, as already stated, Menocal pardoned 335 criminals, including forty-four murderers, in order to use them as gunmen and bullies and to get the value of their "family influence." [28]

Spinden tells of one case in Santo Domingo that illustrates

[25] Spinden, Herbert Joseph, *Shall the United States intervene in Cuba?*, in *World's work*, v. XLI, pp. 465-483, Mar., 1921, is the best available account of the elections of 1920, and is the principal basis of the story given here.

[26] López, Jacinto, *El fracaso del*

general *Crowder en Cuba*, in *Reforma social*, v. XX, pp. 99-112, at 99; June, 1921.

[27] Not Carlos, as usually in Spanish, but Charles.

[28] Cf. *supra*, pp. 319-320, and *infra*, pp. 565-566.

how these methods worked out. Santo Domingo was then, as it usually is, one of the "crucial" electoral points in the "crucial" province of Santa Clara. On September 13, 1920, it seems that Congressman Adolfo Núñez wrote Menocal a letter about conditions there. He asked for the transfer to that town of three specifically named military officers, "to counteract Troadio Pérez, who has ranged himself with José Miguel"; he reported that the Conservative mayor was doing nothing to further the campaign, and asked that he be "called to order"; and he insisted on the pardon of a certain criminal, José de Jesús Fundora, because "his family, friends, and fellow party members . . . are many and of great importance in that district." No evidence is at hand as to what may have happened to the mayor, but Fundora was pardoned on September 29. He had already served two years and a half of a sentence of nearly fifteen years for murder, but the court that sentenced him refused to recommend a pardon, which was the usual procedure in such cases. So Menocal went over their heads and pardoned him anyway. Various steps are alleged to have been taken, too, to "counteract" Sergeant Pérez,—among them, several attempts to murder him, but Pérez escaped.

While the Conservatives were ready to use violence, if necessary, in order to win the election, they also employed other measures to poll as large an actual vote as they could. In particular, they endeavored to split the negro vote, which was normally Liberal, and for this purpose gave an impulse to passions that were, to say the least, improper. In Cuba, as elsewhere in the Americas, the negroes retained some traces of their ancient African superstitions, and were wont to give vent to them in the ceremonial of their secret societies, or *ñañigos,* as they were called. Formerly they had observed many weird rites, such, for example, as that of initiation when they drank the blood of a freshly killed rooster, perhaps mixing the potion with alcohol. In particular they indulged in certain dances called *congas* that were described as shameful. Attempts had been made under Spanish and United States rule to suppress these organizations, but they lived on in secret, to some extent. The societies themselves were bitterly hostile to one another, and it had so happened that the head of one of them had murdered the head of another. Menocal now stepped in, and pardoned the murderer, thus reviving the old feud between the two organizations and their followers. There were a number of shooting affrays, but presumably Menocal gained Zayas some votes. Also, parades of negroes favoring the National League candidates were allowed, to the accompaniment of *congas* in the public streets.

Election day came on November 1st, one day ahead of that in the United States. The voters turned out in great numbers, where they could, especially in Santa Clara, which was literally the "battle-ground" of the election, for fourteen men were killed there that day. There were many who did not vote, however, especially in the rural districts, where there were evidences of intimidation. In the outskirts of Santo Domingo, for example, the Conservatives voted 96.5 per cent of their enrollment, as against 10.7 per cent for the Liberals. And yet the majority for Zayas in the rural districts of Santa Clara was only 1195, despite the fact that bands of armed men were riding about and other means were being employed to keep down the Liberal vote. At Guaracabulla, where Gómez had an enrollment of eighty-six votes more than Zayas, the voting-place was not allowed to open. At Hernando 151 Liberals were enrolled, but only seventeen voted, and at Nazareno just eight voted out of 108. Even the larger towns had to encounter something in the way of armed intimidation. At Sagua la Grande the sergeant in charge ordered his men to fire into a body of Liberals, and several were killed. At Cienfuegos a number of criminals were appointed policemen! Strong-arm methods were not, however, the usual means employed to get a favorable vote. There were other simpler and more vulgar devices. At Guaso the polls were closed before the regular hour; indeed, this was done in various places as soon as the Conservatives had voted. At Salamanca the voting was delayed, with some thirty an hour being admitted to the polling-place, and in consequence about eighty Liberals did not get a chance to vote. At Colón, Matanzas, the military supervisor, a sergeant, burned the returns when they indicated a Liberal majority. And yet the Conservatives carried Santa Clara by only 2325 votes in a total of 86,411, and all of Cuba by 10,585 in 312,765. Naturally, the Liberals were no mere innocent lambs themselves in the course of this election. These affairs in Cuba are all a matter of opportunity, and the greater blame attaches to the Conservatives merely because they were in a position to be more frequently unlawful and because they could not have won in a fair election. As matters were, Zayas "lost" only the province of Havana, and was declared elected.

In the midst of an excitement and bitterness that paralleled the days of 1916, appeals were now taken in in accord with the provisions of the electoral law, but the end of the year came without a decision being reached, due in part to the introduction of technicalities into the preliminary hearings, to promote delay. It began to look as if the issue might be postponed to the very day of the next inaugural, and the country seemed drifting again toward civil war. In this emergency the United States decided to act. On January 6, 1921, without formal prior notice to the

Cuban authorities, General Crowder turned up in Havana, as the special representative of President Wilson. His arrival was viewed with mixed feelings. On the whole, the Liberals welcomed him, for they were convinced that Menocal would yield the election only through force, and as the United States would not permit of a revolution its intervention was necessary. Indeed, as early as November 7, 1920, the Liberals had suggested a United States provisional government for the holding of new elections. The Conservatives were not at all pleased over the coming of Crowder. It is said that Menocal resented it, and announced while Crowder was en route to Cuba that he would not receive him. He did not go to any such length, however, when Crowder arrived. Some others, less partisan than Menocal, were also disturbed, and among them the veteran political theorist Enrique José Varona, ever suspicious of the United States and hopeful that Cuba, left to herself, might evolve out of the ills that afflicted her life. He referred ominously to this appointment "for functions as extensive as they are obscure." [29]

Crowder went to work in his usual efficient manner. On January 10 he addressed a long communication to Menocal, objecting to the delays in the decision of disputed cases, and pointing out how matters might be expedited. He called attention to the fact that many municipal governments were already *ad interim* administrations, that the provincial governments would become so in February, and, of course, the national government on May 20, unless an adjustment might in the meantime be reached. The situation was therefore "one of great gravity," which when considered with the existing financial crisis "constitutes a menace to the National life,

[29] Varona, Enrique José, *Discurso de artes y letras*, v. VI, pp. 239-246, leído . . . la noche del 22 de diciembre de 1921, in *Academia nacional* at 241.

calling for extraordinary remedial measures." It is not surprising that Crowder's suggestions were adopted, and presently the dockets were cleared sufficiently for the Supreme Court to render the final decisions. This body acted creditably, just as it had in 1916, and on the whole favored the contentions of the Liberals. The elections in some two hundred and fifty voting districts, about twenty per cent of the total, were annulled, and new partial elections were called for, to be held simultaneously in March,—a proposal of Crowder. Crowder now did everything he could to make these a success. He personally visited and inspected all the storm centres. He got Menocal, Gómez, and Zayas together on February 26, and a "pact of honor" was arranged. Menocal agreed not to use military supervisors, but to have inspectors present representing the Central Electoral Board, and the date was set for March 15. Everything now seemed to have been made ready either for an honest election or else a just cause for complaint on which the United States might act, when suddenly all was upset again, and Crowder's efforts went for naught.

Attention has already been called to that odd quirk of character which makes Hispanic Americans withdraw from an electoral contest when they think they cannot win, whether from lack of votes or because of the employment of violent methods by the other side. Gómez and the Liberals got it into their heads that they were not going to receive fair play. It was true, indeed, that the Conservatives were quite as determined that Gómez should not become President as the Liberals were that Zayas should not. Neither side was going to concede the victory, short of compulsion by the United States. The Liberals failed to realize that their only chance of success was to go through with the elections and rely on the United States to see that justice was done. As the date for the partial elections approached, however, the usual suspicions of governmental improprieties developed, and bitterness cropped out to such an extent that in Colón, Matanzas, there was a veritable battle of Liberals and Conservatives on March 9. Hundreds of shots were fired, and some casualties sustained. So the Liberals refused to go to the polls on March 15, and, of course, Zayas won!

The action of Gómez and his partisans, which appears stupid to the Anglo-American mind, can be excused only on the ground that it was typically Hispanic American. If they could have been a little more patient and gone to the elections it is probable that they would have had the support of the United States in a review of the affair that would have placed the Liberal candidate in the presidential chair on May 20. The writer has it on good authority that Crowder himself stated privately that in his opinion Gómez would have been proclaimed President instead of Zayas if he had coöperated in the attempt to solve the electoral dispute instead of withdrawing. But the Liberals felt, mistakenly, that they had taken the right course to *win*. Gómez went to Washington to lay his case before the State Department and to appeal for a United States provisional government to supervise new elections. He entered a formal petition to this effect on April 5, which, to say the least, showed confidence in the United States.[30] Meanwhile, in Cuba, the Liberals refused to make a quorum in Congress, expecting in this way to prevent a formal proclamation of victory for Zayas. The United States had no basis for an intervention, however. It had not been invited to take that action by

[30] There were, of course, a number of Cubans who did not share this confidence. Carbonell, Miguel Ángel, *El peligro del águila* (Habana, 1922), is a volume of somewhat airy persi- flage reflecting this view. Carbonell first ran this material as a series in a Havana daily paper, *Nación*, from Apr. 8 to Apr. 26, 1921, at the time José Miguel was in Washington.

the constituted authorities as in 1906, and it could not do anything on a mere possibility, or even a probability, that the Conservatives would have stolen the elections of March 15 if the Liberals had gone to the polls. In other words, there was no case under the Permanent Treaty. So Gómez's petition was denied, and on April 17 the United States formally recognized the election of Zayas, at the same time intimating that there might indeed be an intervention if a legal government were not in office on May 20. Gómez accepted the decision, and announced that he had given up the contest, but the excitement in Cuba continued for a time. The Liberal candidate for governor of the province of Havana was murdered, and Zayas's private secretary also fell by an assassin's hand. Threats were freely made that Zayas would be "dead" before he became President. Gradually, however, the atmosphere cleared, for the Liberals could not but recognize the futility of further opposition in the face of the attitude of the United States. So at length the Liberals went to Congress, and Zayas was duly inaugurated on May 20.

And what of Gómez? The outcome of the election was an overwhelming blow to him. He went to New York, where he was taken sick, and died there on June 13. Although it may be considered small satisfaction by some, there was nothing that could more surely enthrone him in the hearts of the Cuban people than his death at this time. He became the newest and greatest of the Liberal martyrs. He was the "patriot" who had yielded his own "just claims" in the face of the Washington decision, so as to save his country from civil war. And he died of a "broken heart." An always likeable figure during his life, he became popular almost to the point of deification in death. Not even the name of a Martí, Máximo Gómez, or Maceo can to this day rouse the Cuban masses to such enthusiasm as can that of José Miguel. His remains were taken to Havana, and on June 19 a great funeral was held. There was a procession two miles long, and the streets were strewn with flowers. In course of the march there was a riot, in which scores were hurt and one man killed, but it was based on devotion to Gómez more than opposition to the authorities. Eager to render one more last service to their chief, his admirers broke through the police, in an effort to carry the coffin. So passed José Miguel, a man who had his faults, but who should not be judged too harshly in a final review of his character.

And what then of Menocal? To many he will appear a more pathetic figure than Gómez. A man of wonderful gifts and good intentions, he had failed by the very victories he had won, for in gaining them he had outdone his predecessors in political iniquities of a sort that he himself had denounced. To be sure, he was to some extent a victim of bad luck, in that he went out of office at the time of a grave economic depression following on the heels of unparalleled prosperity. Governments and rulers are always blamed for such moments as this, however little they may have been responsible for them. In the case of Menocal, however, his political shortcomings were to live in Cuban memory when complaints about the depression had been forgotten. As Pérez has said, he did not "respect liberties," and failed, therefore, to "gain the esteem of his people." Fortunately for Menocal's ultimate place in Cuban history he was again to play a prominent part in the politics of the country, and this time was to conduct himself more in keeping with the reputation he had before he first became President.[31]

[31] There is not even a third-rate book available on Menocal's second term. One must therefore depend upon periodical articles, newspaper items, and other somewhat superficial evidences until such time as a student comes along who is able to make the several years of intensive study of

government documents and other evidences that such a period requires before its history can be written satisfactorily. Fortunately, however, there is an exceptionally valuable brief study by Trelles (the *El progreso* pamphlet) that touches prominently on this period and an unusually worth-while article, by Spinden, on the elections of 1920. Furthermore, of course, numerous witnesses are still alive, and the period is sufficiently far back in the past so that at least some of the venom and partisanship have disappeared. The writer believes that later investigations will indeed add much material and correct some statements contained here, but will make very little substantial change in the narrative of these years.

CHAPTER XVIII

ZAYAS AND CROWDER, 1921-1923

FEW men ever had a better chance than Zayas to make a distinguished record, and none more dismally failed. The depths of degradation to which Cuba sank under Menocal had developed an aroused public opinion in the island among the better elements of the educated classes, and the emergencies of the financial situation had brought about the direct assistance of the United States, as represented by the mission of General Crowder. This gave Zayas what might have been a favorable opening for a praiseworthy administration. United States Secretary of State Hughes is said to have told him that he had an opportunity to make his name the greatest of any President in Hispanic American history, if he would carry through the reforms that came to be known as the "moralization program." Zayas agreed to do it, but lacked the character and, indeed, the sincere desire necessary to obtain results, and, one by one, promises and reforms alike fell by the wayside. In the end a "new low" in shameless political depravity was attained, farther down than the worst stages of the Menocal régime. For two years, however, the evils were held in check and something in the way of reform momentarily accomplished, through the presence of Crowder, who had the backing of the United States. These two men, Zayas and Crowder, who might almost be symbolized as "Evil" and "Good," dominated the years 1921-1923. For a while, "Good" was almost more influential than "Evil," but at length the latter won. All that remained of Crowder's work was the record of what he had attempted to do for Cuba, together with his revelations of conditions that needed to be corrected, but doubtless that was of value as a stimulus to public opinion and as a basis for action in the future.

The people of Cuba had no illusions about Zayas when he became President. They had long regarded him as a brilliantly clever man, of considerable intellectual attainments, but with the common failings of the politician and exceptionally low moral standards. Of an old Cuban family, Zayas himself had fallen upon evil days financially, and despite his reputed shrewdness both as a politician and lawyer he had never succeeded in repairing the family fortunes. This was not because he was not willing to engage in any scandalous affair that would yield him a sure return. Indeed, he was ready to pick up "easy money" in such small quantities that people were calling him a "*peseta*-stealer" as early as the electoral campaign of 1908.[1] Possibly one reason for his ill-success was that he was a notoriously timid man, who shunned danger in a land where physical courage is one of the most highly admired traits. As one volume has set forth on this score,

"This peculiar man, who is very tenacious in his desires, is at the same time a timid character . . . Doctor Zayas did not take a direct part in any of the revolutions,—to be sure, on account of his conviction as an evolutionist, but undoubtedly, also, because of the timidity of his character."[2]

All accounts agree that Zayas possessed an almost oriental patience and immobility of countenance such that he was

[1] This was in part due to the fact that Zayas carried a Spanish *peseta* as a souvenir of the days he had spent in prison at Ceuta at the time he was deported from Cuba during the War of Independence. Cf. Martínez Ortiz, II, 820. The *peseta* had a normal value of about twenty cents.

[2] Merino and Ibarzábal, 18.

often called "El Chino" (The Chinaman).[3] A story is told of him that is usually regarded as having a representative value beyond the incident. At the time when he and a number of other Cubans were being deported to a Spanish prison in Africa, during the War of Independence, Zayas developed a severe toothache. Noticing that Zayas's face bore no evidences of pain, González Lanuza asked how he endured his trouble so easily. Thereupon, Zayas replied: "It does not hurt. Nothing ever hurts me much." By extension this remark has been taken to mean that Zayas had a kind of permanent anæsthetic, both physically and in the realm of morals. So far as his morals were concerned, neither friend nor foe defends Zayas from grave charges. It is a question just how far one should proceed with evidence on this score, especially since other persons than Zayas who are still alive and who may be "more sinned against than sinning" would also be involved. Perhaps it is well to let the matter rest with the following brief generalization out of a rather long statement by a distinguished Cuban:

"Zayas himself comes of a good family, but he is to a certain extent a degenerate, with especially morbid sensual proclivities."

Few will deny that Zayas was what might be termed a "slippery" individual. His word was of no value, but whatever stand he might take it was always hard, if not impossible, to pin him down to an admission of error. The following statement is illustrative of this phase of the peculiar psychology of Zayas:

"At the time of the Constitutional Assembly he declared himself an atheist, but while he was President he stood sponsor at the baptism into the Catholic faith of one of his grandchildren. As one has to swear that he believes in the Catholic religion in order to be a sponsor,

[3] It is sometimes said that this is because Zayas had Chinese blood in him, but there seems to be no basis in fact for the assertion.

we might have here a case of conversion, were it not that it was merely part of a constant farce, the same before the Constitutional Assembly as before the Catholic priest."

Zayas had already dipped his hands in the public treasury before his elevation to the presidency, though not as deeply as some others. The best known instance of this sort is in connection with his famous "history of Cuba." On April 12, 1913, a little over a month before the inauguration of Menocal, Gómez published a decree appointing Zayas to write a history of Cuba at a salary of six thousand dollars a year and authorizing him to go to Spain whenever he thought best, to get copies of documents from the Spanish archives. This created a storm of disapproval within the Academy of History, of which Zayas was a member, because it put that body in a ridiculous position, as it had been founded by the government for just such purposes as now seemed to be involved in the decree on behalf of Zayas. At a meeting on April 24, at which Zayas was not present, although he knew that this matter was to be taken up, it was decided to cite Zayas to appear and explain his connection with the affair. In course of the debate Manuel Sanguily remarked that if the idea were merely to give Zayas a generously paying government job, some other means of doing it should be found. Zayas attended the following meeting, on May 1st, and defended the decree, but every other member present held that its execution would not be consistent with the objects of the society. A committee, headed by Sanguily, was appointed to wait upon the President to see whether the decree might be modified or annulled, and this body reported back to the Academy in the meeting of May 14. Sanguily explained that Gómez told them the decree had been issued at Zayas's own request, in order to provide him with a means of living after his retirement from the vice-presidency on May 20. Gómez even showed them the original of the decree, which was written in Zayas's own hand. He agreed, however, to modify it so as to allow Zayas, in conjunction with the Academy, to gather materials for an eventually to be written history,—still at six thousand a year for Zayas. Since the Academy had gained its point, this solution of the difficulty was accepted, and in the meeting of May 14 Zayas expressed his satisfaction, saying further that he proposed to work very hard in order to collect for the Academy "a veritable treasure of historical documents."

The above is from the formal account in the minutes of the meetings of the Academy.[4] It may be supplemented by the following statement, which comes direct from a person who had an intimate knowledge of the whole affair:

"When the matter first came before the Academy, Zayas pretended that the publication of the decree in the Gazette was the first he knew of the affair, but later was obliged to admit that the story told by Gómez to the Sanguily committee was true, although he made a 'saving-face' excuse to account for his earlier statement to the contrary. Menocal allowed Zayas to hold his job until just before the elections of 1916, when Zayas was again the candidate as against Menocal. Then Menocal sent an enquiry to the Academy, asking what Zayas had turned in so far in the way of materials. The Academy could give but one answer, and that answer was 'Nothing!'"

It is often asserted in print that Zayas held this post eight years, and collected something like fifty thousand dollars. In view of the above statement,—unless, indeed, the "soft job" was restored after the Revolution of February (which would be quite possible, as *botellas* are often given to uncomfortable opponents),—it would seem that Zayas "earned" only some twenty thousand dollars out of his "history," but what other "historian" was ever paid at an equally generous

[4] Academia de la historia, *Anales,* v. VI, pp. 48-58; Jan.-Feb., 1924.

rate? !! [5] To be sure, Zayas *did* begin a history in 1916,—
very likely as an election maneuver. It concerned events of
the years 1867-1868, but was wholly lacking in five-hundred-
dollars-a-month historical technique.[6] Of a piece with this
"history" affair is another pre-presidential incident in Zayas's
career. It seems that he borrowed five thousand dollars at
the National Bank, but when that institution got into difficulties and an attempt was made to collect the debt Zayas
denied his own signature. No doubt, he had never intended
to pay it anyway, for it was merely a "political loan," of a
type that had become fashionable in governmental circles
before Zayas gathered in his bit.

A number of other estimates bearing on the career and
character of this strange individual should be given, but they
involve a discussion of his administration, and may therefore be taken up more suitably in the next chapter. One
such opinion may be given here, by way of a preliminary
estimate of his rule:

"Cuba is a country of *vice versas*. The case of Doctor Zayas is proof
of that assertion, for when he won he did not collect, and when he lost
he did . . . It would have been an act of ingratitude on the part of
the Cubans not to have consented to his elevation to the supreme
bureaucratic throne, for in an interval of four years,—long for politicians
who are waiting, but short in the infinite course of ungrateful time,—
he could realize the maximum work of prostituting public customs in a
proportion superior to anything that had gone before, and, as a consequence of that, private customs, too; and he was able to elevate his
endless and insatiable relatives to the category of Sotomayor of the
table . . . He was a traitor to his party and political creed, throwing
down his twenty years of Liberalism as if they were a castle of cards.
Thus he went to the executive power, with the hatred of his friends of
other years and the scorn of his one-time coreligionists . . . Of his

[5] Merino and Ibarzábal, 37, say that
Zayas collected "more than twenty
thousand dollars" for his history. It
is to be noted, however, that the
Merino and Ibarzábal volume was
written in 1917.

[6] The Zayas "history," entitled *Un
capítulo de la historia general de
Cuba*, is in *Cuba contemporánea*, v.
XI, pp. 14-47; May, 1916.

government, not the least eulogy can be made, unless it may be for his impassiveness in supporting everything, his leniency in combating enemies, and the serenity with which he has confronted difficult situations that have presented themselves, always resolving them to his own satisfaction." [7]

Back in the 1912 campaign Heraldo de Cuba, a Liberal organ, had said that "the election of Doctor Zayas would be a disgrace to the country." [8]   This was prophetic of what was actually to come to pass.

General Crowder is too well known as a man of high character and extraordinary executive ability to require extended comment for the present generation of readers.   His meritorious work at the time of the Magoon rule has already been described.   Two other yet greater services had fallen to his lot to perform.   It was Crowder who was responsible for the difficult and involved task of organizing civil government in the Philippines.   And, as everybody knows, he raised the American army for the World War under the terms of the Selective Service Law.   In the performance of this duty he had under him 193,117 subordinates, with whose aid he registered nearly twenty-four million men, classified industrially as well as in a military way some seventeen million, physically examined about eight million, selected and entrained nearly four million, and had two million more ready on Armistice Day to respond to demands for man-power in case they should be needed.   The problem that confronted him in Cuba was in many respects the hardest of all, because it did not carry with it any authority to act.   As already set forth, however, Zayas was compelled by the exigencies of the situation to take a goodly portion of American advice during the first two years of his administration,—or at least

[7] Pérez, 15-16.
[8] Quoted in Merino and Ibarzábal, **19.**

to appear so to do,—and so Crowder's investigations and suggestions had at times an almost decisive influence on the course of governmental action. Some comments upon him from this purely Cuban angle of his career may therefore be worth while, though his place in public esteem was already assured before this latest association of his with the island's affairs.

It would be easy to accumulate a volume of laudatory comment on Crowder's work in Cuba, including printed statements as well as oral. They would boil down to something like the following: beyond anything else Crowder is honest; he is also a man of vast legal knowledge and a tremendous, dynamic activity, with executive ability that is uncommon; he is sincerely desirous of the welfare of Cuba, feeling assured that what is best for Cuba is likewise best for the United States; he has a more detailed knowledge of Cuban affairs than any man in the island, whether native or foreigner; and except for General Wood there is no American among those who have served in Cuba who rivals him in the greatness and unselfishness of his achievements. There is no particular advantage in adding up columns of praise of this tenor. Rather, in the case of a man with such an impregnably good record it is preferable to seek serious statements that reflect some criticism, the better to explain the position Crowder has occupied in Cuba and to hint at the difficulties he has had to encounter. It will be noticed, however, that in all the statements that follow there is rather more on the constructive than on the destructive side with respect to his character and work.

(1) "Crowder is so honest he leans backward, and some day he may injure his spine. He does not speak Spanish, and perhaps on that account is not fully acquainted with Spanish American character. As a result he is a little too impatient for immediate results, and too insistent in his pressure on Cuban officials."

(2) "It may be said to General Crowder's credit that he is possibly the most unpopular man in Cuba. A lot of Americans don't like him because he will not use his office as a collection agency for their contracts,[9] and the politicians are against him because he represents a possible check on their pocket-filling propensities."

(3) "General Crowder is the only man in Cuba who has a detailed statistical knowledge of affairs in the island, and he uses the data he compiles as the basis for suggestions about desirable legislation. He is perhaps a little too confident that the laws he proposes would solve the ills of Cuban life."

(4) "General Crowder is unmarried, and therefore has no distractions of a family nature, but is wedded to his work. He is burningly desirous of bringing about an improvement in Cuban affairs, and is impatient over the slowness with which things move. One would not know that he had been Provost-General of the American army during the war, for he never mentions it, but he will talk for hours about Cuba. A tremendous worker himself, he drives his office staff wild; there is none of the usual 'social secretary' dilly-dallying in the American embassy of Havana, such as one finds in the embassies elsewhere, for Crowder is hungry for data on a variety of subjects,—so much so, that the office can't keep up with him. He has a certain pride in his record, but feels that he is failing in Cuba, because matters are going just the opposite to what he desires. The one criticism that might be made of him is that he has not fully caught the spirit of these people, not quite grasping to the full the undisciplined, individualistic traits they have, and expecting them to act too much as Anglo-Saxons would. So he has not learned that all the laws in the world mean nothing to a Hispanic-blooded person, if it does not fit his convenience. In consequence, the General is often over-hopeful of some good result,—only to be cast down when high-class men act just about as disgracefully as their more lowly fellows."

These remarks may be allowed to stand without comment, except in one particular. Crowder's reliance on legislation is probably overemphasized. Two things must be remembered in this connection. One is, that Cuba is a country that lacks organic laws of a political code, except in so far as Crowder himself was able to put his own suggestions on the statute-books during the intervention of 1906-1909. There

[9] Cf. *infra*, pp. 544-545.

is a real value in getting correct principles into a code, whatever the immediate action may be that is taken upon them. In the second place, Crowder has never had administrative power in Cuba, and cannot be held responsible for the failure to execute the laws. Even in the years of his greatest influence, 1921-1923, his "power" (which, after all, amounted to nothing more than the Washington authorities were willing to do in backing up his suggestions) was not nearly as great as some people have supposed. Witness, for example, the utter failure of the bank liquidating acts of January 1921, through Crowder's inability to get ordinarily honest, courageous action on an admittedly good law. Other similar instances will appear in the sequel.

Even before Zayas became President it was apparent that United States help would be necessary to save the country from bankruptcy and the possibility of intervention. Menocal was about to leave office, with nothing in the treasury and an unknown though certainly enormous floating debt, but a seriously impaired government income, to say nothing of the heavy requirements on Cuban bonds. It was clear that the administration would find it difficult to obtain money enough for running expenses, without any of the usual opportunities for graft on a large scale. So Zayas was ready to be friendly and attentive to Crowder, who was at that time the personal representative of President Harding, as formerly he had been of President Wilson, but not yet ambassador to Cuba. Trying to carry water on each shoulder, however, Zayas endeavored to conceal his momentary subserviency to Crowder, but when confronted with both angles of his pretence, he came to the fore in his usual clever manner and reconciled them. He wrote a letter to Heraldo de Cuba, under date of May 12, 1921, as follows:

"In the letter published this morning I asserted that I had no knowledge of a cablegram which it was said had been sent to the Cuban minister at Washington requesting him to ask of that government that General Crowder, in his character as special envoy and personal representative, should remain with us. That statement is strictly correct. I had no knowledge of such a cablegram, but it was natural that I should not have, because General Crowder is accredited to the government of my very respected friend President Mario G. Menocal. Had I been consulted regarding the sending of such a cablegram I should have given it my unqualified approval, because I esteem at its full value the aid which he has already given to Cuba, and in case his government should permit him to remain among us, I shall not hesitate, upon assuming the government of Cuba, to utilize the valuable and disinterested services he is capable of rendering in resolving many difficult problems which confront us. This attitude I announced at the time of the arrival of General Crowder in Cuba, indicating in a newspaper his great knowledge of our affairs, his clear intelligence, and his good intentions." [10]

In view of the way Zayas later kicked over the traces, this letter has a peculiar interest beyond that of the moment when it was written.

Zayas had already drawn up his first message to Congress by the time he entered office, and it was read in the joint session of May 21, 1921. Some of its main features were undoubtedly the suggestions of Crowder, easily recognizable as such, and were in the nature of a preliminary announcement of the reforms that would be necessary if Cuba were to set her house in order. Zayas began by promising to keep to his own functions, "without invading or usurping your powers in the least." Next came recommendations for changes in the electoral code,—all in line with Crowder's ideas.[11] A number of constitutional reforms were proposed: for executive Secretaries to appear before Congress; limiting congressional immunity; changing the two-thirds quorum rule to a majority or less; for direct vote of the people for

[10] Quoted in *Heraldo de Cuba*, May   [11] Cf. *infra*, pp. 574-579.
13, 1921.

President and Vice-President, "prohibiting that of the first in two successive terms"; and for a thorough revision of the paragraphs concerning municipal and provincial government. Almost certainly this portion of the message was first suggested by Crowder. The budget for 1921-1922 had already been made out for over $104,000,000. Zayas asked for a cut in this to a sum between fifty and sixty millions. This clearly was a Crowder measure. Zayas referred to the difficulties of the banks and the sugar industry, and proposed the founding of a new national bank. In dealing with public works he laid stress on his plan to build the much talked of central highway from end to end of the island. As a program and a promise this message was admirable, but as a sincere exemplification of Zayas's desires it was an arrant farce, not worth the paper it was written upon. After Zayas got matters into his own hands in 1923, he legislated by decree frequently, in typical Menocal fashion. Electoral reforms were never undertaken, except to make matters worse than they were before.[12] There were long congressional discussions about the proposed constitutional changes, but nothing was ever done.[13] National bank projects were indeed taken up, but, as will appear, with corrupt motives in mind. Even the budget was not acted upon for the fiscal year 1921-1922, but was reduced the following year as a result of the insistence of the United States.

The finances of the country were in a very bad way when Zayas assumed the presidency. In the fiscal year 1920-1921 the receipts of the government amounted to nearly $108,-000,000, the greatest in the history of the republic. The budget for that year (actually the budget of 1918-1919, which

[12] Cf. *infra*, pp. 577-578.
[13] For some of these discussions, see Pardo Suárez, 260-296. Naturally, they appear in more ample form in the *Diarios de sesiones* volumes of the two houses of Congress.

was the most recent one that Congress had approved) called for an expenditure of some sixty-four millions, but the government in fact spent about $182,000,000. It was already clear, in May 1921, that there would be a considerable falling-off in revenue for 1921-1922, and, indeed, only some fifty-seven millions were eventually collected. In the face of that was the budget for $104,000,000 and an overwhelming burden of current and funded debt. Congress, to be sure (for the ninth time since 1905), did not act on the budget, which legally put into effect the sixty-four million budget of 1918-1919. Cuba had already, earlier in 1921, defaulted for the first time in her history on her bonded debt, both domestic and foreign; indeed, it was in expectation of this event that President Wilson was induced in large measure to send Crowder to Cuba as his special agent, as the relations of the countries under the Permanent Treaty were seriously involved in the financial debacle. Through the good offices of the United States an emergency loan of five million dollars was effected with J. P. Morgan and Company, which enabled the republic to resume payments on the funded debt. This left the handling of the floating debt as the most pressing immediate problem, and at once raised the point that was the basis of Crowder's influence during the next two years: the necessity for a loan if these debts were to be paid and the credit of the republic maintained.

The worst situation of all with respect to the floating debt was that of the left-over contracts of the Menocal régime in the Department of Public Works. Enormous sums were owing under contracts with this branch of the government, and it was known that many of the agreements were tainted with fraud. Crowder told Zayas that this condition would have to be cleared up before Cuba could get a loan. Zayas at first resisted an investigation, but when he became convinced that he must permit one or get no loan he yielded to Crowder's demands. On August 13, 1921, he issued a decree covering contracts on which work had not been completed. All illegal contracts were to be annulled, and on legal contracts there was to be a readjustment in unit prices or else a cancellation of the contract. This necessitated an investigation, and it was undertaken under the direction of Major Albert Lyman, the United States military attaché. He found that there was more than forty-nine million dollars' worth of work that had been contracted for, of which some thirty-seven millions' worth was as yet unexecuted. The prices charged were far in excess of those prevailing for private work at the time the contracts were made, and the amounts of money involved were much greater than those which had been authorized by Congress. Some contracts had never had congressional sanction at all. There was a total of 354 contracts, assuming obligations far beyond Cuba's ability to pay. Crowder now brought pressure upon Zayas to correct the evils that had been laid bare, but the work of the latter was half-hearted and imperfect. In some cases he annulled contracts, but gave the contractors a bonus, and in various ways there continued to be a "goat" in the department's affairs.[14] Of course, too, there were many other debts, besides those originating in the Department of Public Works.

Crowder spent most of his time during 1921 in acquiring information about every phase of Cuban affairs, and it was not until 1922, with a vast array of facts and figures at his command, that he proceeded more actively than before to

[14] Conn, Edward L   , *The crisis in Cuba:* III, *The goat in the treasury*, in (Philadelphia *Public ledger*, reprinted in) Berkeley (California) *Gazette*, Nov. 21, 1923. In various Hispanic American countries the word *"chivo,"* or goat, is used as a synonym for graft,—possibly on the analogy of a goat's giving milk.

make suggestions for the renovation of public life. His ideas were embodied in a series of communications that he sent directly to Zayas which have come to be known as the "fifteen memoranda," for they were numbered consecutively from one to fifteen. Only one of the memoranda, number thirteen, has ever been published in full, but enough information about all of them has reached the hands of other persons so that a great deal may be said about them, although the originals are not as yet available. The series appears to have begun in February or March 1922. The first on which the writer has a note is number three, of March 10, 1922. This made suggestions for needed constitutional amendments,—the same as those already proposed in Zayas's opening message to Congress. Number five, of April 3, 1922, asked what had been done about the revision of contracts in the Department of Public Works and what to find out the actual indebtedness of the government. Presumably, not much had been accomplished. Number six, of April 12, 1922, urged Zayas to get Congress to pass a budget, instead of neglecting it as it had done since 1918, and suggested the terms that the budget ought to contain. Number seven, also on April 12, stated that the maximum of the budget should be fifty-five million dollars, and pointed out where savings could be effected. Number eight, of May 5, 1922, charged that graft and corruption were still rampant in the various administrative departments, thus undermining Cuban credit and making it necessary for the government to act. Number nine, of May 10, 1922, appears to have been an important communication with respect to the national audit that had been undertaken by Secretary Gelabert of the Treasury Department. It seems that a rather careless estimate had figured the total floating debt, as of May 20, 1921, to be some forty-six millions. No attempt had been made to ascertain any additional floating indebtedness up to June 30, 1921, or for the fiscal year 1921-1922, although it was known that expenditures for the latter period would probably exceed receipts by fifteen million dollars. These additional sums since May 20, 1921, ought therefore to have been added to the previous total, since they had not been paid. Crowder pointed out that this indebtedness could be met only by a drastic reduction in the cost of government such that the revenues would produce a surplus over expenditures (an unlikely event), or else by a loan. A really accurate audit would be necessary, however, before a loan could be discussed, but at any rate something must be done, as creditors with just claims, not merely those with fraudulent contracts in the Public Works Department, were pressing for the payments due them. Numbers ten and eleven, of May 15 and June 26, 1922, discussed needed reforms of the lottery, a matter which the bankers with whom negotiations for a loan were being undertaken considered of especial importance as a preliminary to an agreement.[15]

This is a good point to pause to mention some of the precise evils on which Crowder's charges of corruption in public office were based. The newspapers of that period are teeming with assertions on this score, but one need not rely upon them, for the pronouncements of some of the most responsible bodies in Cuban life, such, for example, as the Rotary Club of Havana and various economic associations, are replete with condemnations of the immorality in public administration. One case was that of a contract to provide food supplies for the army at such an exorbitant rate that it accounted for one-fourth of the entire military expense. The contract was awarded without any resort to public

[15] The subject of lottery reform at   chapter XXIII.
this time is considered more fully in

bidding as the law required. The matter came to public attention in April 1922 when Zayas was about to re-award the contract to the same firm. It is said that Crowder protested, though with what success the writer is not in- formed. Undoubtedly there was a tidbit of graft in the deal for Cuba's "first citizen," as also for various others. Graft continued at a normal pace in the administration of the custom-house, one of the outstanding rivals of the lottery and the Department of Public Works in the sum total of its pilferings. Conservative estimates calculated a loss of fifteen per cent through graft in the collection of revenues and another twenty-five per cent in disbursements, while other estimates were even higher. One notorious instance of this sort was brought to light in the Bureau of Communications, of the Department of Government, in April 1922. The officers of the telegraph operators' union were claiming that the budget discriminated against the men whose affairs they handled, and so sent a petition to Zayas in which they made direct charges about the number of "imaginary" jobs in the bureau, holding that if these were suppressed there would be enough for the just needs of the telegraphers. An investigation revealed the existence of some sixty or seventy sinecures, given to the holders by order of the Secretary of Government, Francisco Martínez. It was charged that the salaries were paid indirectly to Martínez himself and that he was also turning an "honest penny" by tolerating gambling in Marianao and prostitution in Havana. Both he and his brother-in-law, who had become his private secretary, were poor when he went into office, and now they were rich. Even the notoriety over the illegalities in the Department of Public Works was not sufficient to banish graft there. New contracts were still made on much the same basis as before, without advertising or public bidding or an award to the lowest responsible bidder; indeed, most of the awards went to political friends totally unqualified to do the work called for and at ridiculously high prices. No doubt the sum total of the amounts stolen from the government was not so great as it had been under Menocal or as it was to be later under Zayas, but graft as an institution was more widespread than ever, with virtual immunity from punishment for the grafters, and the President was not making a sincere effort to stop it. Obviously this was not a healthy background for a loan.

One of the first problems Crowder had to face upon his arrival in Cuba in January 1921 was the banking situation. Something has already been said about this in connection with the moratorium, but there were other matters to consider. There was the question of the punishment to be meted out for crimes of the bank officials and that of the rehabilitation of the National Bank. By and with the advice of Crowder some banking legislation was enacted as early as January 31, 1921, and a Bank Liquidation Committee was constituted. As already mentioned, however, the execution of this law was worse than futile. The bankers were protected from criminal liability, in part because Zayas and a number of other leading politicians were likely to be compromised, because of the large "loans" that had been made to them without an observance of the requirements of the law. And presently, when the National Bank failed, it carried down with it some twenty millions of government funds that had been on deposit there. Meanwhile, Congress took no action on Zayas's request for a new law, as set forth in his message of May 21, 1921, and repeated on November 7, 1921. Seeking an expert opinion, Crowder had caused an invitation to be extended to William P. Harding, a member of the Federal Reserve Board of the United States, to come to Cuba and make an investigation of the financial situation. Harding was in Cuba for about two months during 1921, and at length reported that it would take a large staff of experts several years to make an accounting, such was the disorder in which he found affairs. He suggested that a fresh start be made, with a good accounting system. Asked to propose a national banking law, he eventually drew up a plan, and gave it to Crowder while the latter was in Washington in January 1922.

One of the features of the Harding plan was a proposed National Reserve Bank, which should be the only Cuban bank of issue and should be so constituted as to keep Cuban money on a parity with the dollar. Harding suggested that it should have a capital of twenty million dollars, of which five millions should be subscribed, half by United States citizens and half by the Cuban treasury. The President of Cuba was to name four directors, and the American stockholders four more, while a ninth was to be chosen by the other eight members of the board. In case of disagreement the Federal Reserve Board of the United States was to indicate a preference as between the two receiving the highest vote. There was to be a gold reserve to redeem the proposed issue of Cuban money (to replace American paper, current in the island), half of it on deposit in Havana and half in New York. This, of course, meant a virtual United States control, but Harding felt that Americans would not invest in the bank on any other basis, believing also that the stabilizing influence of American participation was necessary to the success of the bank. With the Harding report before it, a Cuban committee drew up a substitute plan. This was framed cleverly to resemble the much praised Federal Reserve Act of the United States,—but for conditions that were utterly different. The greater part of the capital was to be subscribed in Cuba, and a majority of the board of directors was to be appointed by the Cuban President. There was to be a gold reserve, but redemption of paper was to take place in Cuba alone. A somewhat extraordinary National Banking Commission was provided for, with the Secretary of the Treasury as chairman, and five others, appointed by the President at a salary of ten thousand a year. There were to be three technical advisers, too, with salaries of nine thousand each. The "work" assigned to this committee was of such a character that, as Harding said, it could be done just as well and far more inexpensively in the Treasury Department, as most of it was mere routine. Some such central committee was necessary in the United States to produce uniformity, he said, as there were twelve federal reserve banks, but in Cuba there was to be but a single bank. Secretary Mellon of the United States Treasury Department is said to have stated that he agreed with Harding. As for the latter, he would have nothing further to do with the matter, not being interested in any system that would not certainly keep Cuban money at par with the dollar. No doubt, too, he could see,—as who could not?,—that the Cuban plan would have projected the bank into politics, making it a perquisite of the President. Crowder made the reserve bank project the subject of his memorandum number twelve, of July 10, 1922, suggesting that the republic get back to the Harding plan, but nothing was accomplished along this line. He was successful in warding off the substitute measure, however, although later in Zayas's term new and yet more extreme Cuban "plans" were to be devised.

It will be obvious from the foregoing that something more than mere suggestions of reform was going to be necessary if any positive results were to be attained. The men in power were not fit instruments of a moralization program, and

Crowder was eager to replace them with officials who would be incorruptible. So, taking advantage of the popular clamor against certain members of the existing Cabinet, and with the back-log of the necessity for the loan, he brought pressure to bear to cause the dismissal of the Zayas Secretaries and the appointment of upright men in their place.[16] The old Cabinet resigned on June 15, 1922, and a new one, made up of men whose names were probably approved by Crowder, was inducted into office four days later. This was the origin of the so-called "Honest Cabinet." Zayas consented, for the country had not yet negotiated the loan of which it stood in need, and the bankers were vitally interested in obtaining an honest administration of Cuba's affairs.

The Honest Cabinet went to work with a will, and rendered a really meritorious service. The budget was reduced some fifty per cent. Many unnecessary employes were separated from the rolls, and bonuses to others were abolished. They did especially well in untangling the contract situation in the Public Works Department. Responding unwillingly to pressure Zayas had annulled ninety-eight out of the 354 contracts in that department, though often to the accompaniment of improprieties, as already stated. By the time that the Honest Cabinet came into office the amount of Public Works contracts had jumped to nearly eighty millions, of which sixty were involved in the remaining 256 contracts still hanging fire from the Menocal period, while there was nearly thirty millions of work still unexecuted. In some nine months the Honest Cabinet was able to dispose of all but ninety-five contracts, of which fourteen more would certainly

[16] Machado, 19-20, n. 1, says that Crowder "exerted no pressure whatsoever" in this affair, but Trelles, *Biblioteca*, II, 128, enters the following under date of June 12, 1922: "General Crowder exacts the immediate renovation of the Cabinet, due to the fact that public opinion was accusing certain Secretaries of having realized acts that were improper for honest functionaries." The Trelles statement is probably the correct version.

have been cancelled if the Honest Cabinet had remained in power, as they were illegal. It was discovered that numerous frauds were being committed in the new contracts of the Zayas period, as well as in those from the time of Menocal. A paving contract for Cienfuegos went to a company in which a son of Zayas and a son of one of his intimate friends (who had been appointed to an important post in the Public Works Department) were among the heavy stockholders. A brother of the president of the Senate held a contract for repairing a road in the province of Camagüey. A dredging contract for the port of Havana was given to an American company of a somewhat unsavory history; this company was a client of the law firm of which Zayas was a member, and it is said that it paid eight per cent of all its contract amounts to Zayas's law partner. The president of the Senate and an ex-Secretary of Public Works acquired the paving contract for the city of Camagüey, although another was put forward as the holder who was in fact a mere dummy for the two men.[17]

The appointment of the Honest Cabinet was a most important step as a preliminary to the loan, and marked the influence of Crowder at its height. The need for a loan had already been discussed *pro* and *con* for many months. Most of the politicians had very little financial knowledge, and since the sum to be obtained was to be applied chiefly in payment of the country's floating debt and not on "succulent affairs" that would be profitable to themselves they opposed the loan altogether or else wanted to cut down the amount. To them the value of the nation's credit meant nothing. They thought the golden flow would continue just the same, credit or no credit. Not a few respectable elements of the

[17] Conn, Edward L   , *The*   *ger,* reprinted in) Berkeley (Califor-
crisis in Cuba: III, *The goat in the*   nia) *Gazette,* Nov. 21, 1923.
treasury, in (Philadelphia *Public led-*

non-political class felt the same way, for a high regard for
national credit cannot be said to be a notable trait in Hispanic American character.[18]   It was Crowder himself who
suggested that fifty million dollars would be needed.   The
politicians objected that the floating debt could not possibly
be more than half as much, but some others claim that Crowder and the Morgan experts underestimated the amount,
asserting that it was at least seventy millions.   At length,
in 1925, the Debt Commission fixed the amount due as $43,-
540,983.40, or considerably more than the thirty-five millions which were eventually applied on the floating debt
out of the proceeds of the loan.[19]   Whatever some of the
other politicians may have thought, Zayas fully appreciated
the importance of the loan.   Nobody has ever called him a
fool; at any rate, he realized that the reëstablishment of
Cuban credit meant the difference between "dividends" and
a "deficit" for the remaining years of his administration.[20]
So, now that the Honest Cabinet had been appointed, he
asked Crowder what more would be required before the
United States would approve the fifty million dollar loan.
This drew forth a reply from Crowder in the shape of the
famous memorandum number thirteen of July 21, 1922.

[18] Cf. Machado, 82-83, especially n.
23-24.   Machado was not enthusiastic
about paying debts "whose legitimacy
is doubtful," feeling sure, too, that
the total of the floating debt could
not be more than thirty million.

[19] The Debt Commission, created by
a law of September 13, 1922, held its
first meeting on the following October 13, and its last on February 19,
1925, at which time it finished its
work.   In all, it received 28,201 claims
totaling $45,777,629.20, and ordered
payment of $32,047,192.27, in addition
to $8,596,174.55 for salaries and pen-
sions of government employes and
$2,897,616.58 for veterans' pensions.

[20] The writer recognizes how difficult it is for even the educated person
with a non-financial mind to grasp
the value of a loan that does not contribute directly to a yield in revenue.
A recent statement by an American
railway president referred to a huge
loan his company had effected for
the purchase and improvement of
railway equipment.   Going on, he
said that the amount borrowed was
now yielding the company twenty per
cent.   Cuba was in just such a position as that, except that the indirect
value of a restoration of credit was
perhaps worth far more than twenty
per cent.

Memorandum number thirteen was perhaps not nearly
so interesting a document in itself as some of the other communications of Crowder to Zayas, but it attained to a peculiar notoriety because it was the only one that was ever
published and was the first of which the public had heard.
Heraldo de Cuba procured a copy in some fashion as yet unknown, and brought it out in translation on August 5, 1922.
Unlike the exhaustive discussions that it is said were a
marked feature of its twelve predecessors, number thirteen
appeared to be an informal letter, just as if it might have
been dictated off-hand; indeed, in his opening paragraph
Crowder remarked that everything he was saying was subject to revision. First he called attention to the financial
situation. Resumption of payments on the bonded debt had
taken place, not out of ordinary revenues, but from proceeds of the Morgan emergency loan of five millions, while
the domestic loan of 1917 was still some three millions in
arrears. The floating debt was embarrassingly large; Manuel
Despaigne, the new Secretary of the Treasury, had said that
it was about equal to the total expected annual receipts.
So Cuba was in unusual danger, and extraordinary measures
were needed to save her credit. On account of her rights
under the Permanent Treaty the United States needed to
have an assurance that the Cuban government would take
adequate steps to secure prompt payment of interest and
sinking fund charges on its bonds. Congress should therefore pass laws providing for the loan, assigning permanent
revenues for service upon it, and making certain reforms.
The economies of the new budget must be realized, and the
graft alluded to in memorandum number eight done away
with, in part through the removal of certain officials from
office, under a suspension of the civil service law. Charges
were persistently being made about extensive frauds in the

custom-house and internal revenue bureau, and these must be proved false or the evils corrected, as a condition precedent to a loan. Corrupt conditions in the judiciary were specifically alluded to by Crowder,[21] and he also mentioned the improper conditions that still surrounded the award of government contracts, such as the failure to call for competitive bids or to insist on reasonable unit prices. While not demanding any radical immediate reform in these branches, Crowder felt that some steps ought at least to be undertaken.[22]

The publication of memorandum number thirteen roused a double-barreled storm of disapproval in Cuba. By many, the action of the United States, through Crowder, was looked upon as an unwarranted interference in Cuban affairs, at the same time that the evils in the political life of the republic which had caused it were unsparingly denounced. In an editorial entitled 'Worse than the Platt Amendment," Heraldo de Cuba viewed the loan project with concern, fearing that it might put Cuba "in the position of Haiti," but went on to say that the country deserved no better fate for having endured the corrupt rule of Menocal and Zayas, together with the improprieties of other administrative officials, of Congress, and of the judiciary, as well as for maintaining the lottery. Cuba might not have so much to fear from Crowder, but his successor could be another Magoon.[23] In a news item of the same day Heraldo de Cuba said that Crowder had insisted that the laws of the moralization program must be approved by August 15. Secretary Despaigne urged that this course should be taken, as the republic needed the loan, and Secretary of State Carlos Manuel de Céspedes

---

[21] See *infra*, pp. 539-546.

[22] Memorandum number thirteen was first published in Spanish in *Heraldo de Cuba* of Aug. 5, 1922. It was later republished in other newspapers,—for example, in *Tarde* of Nov. 13, 1924.

[23] *Heraldo de Cuba*, Aug. 5, 1922.

was quoted as calling on the patriotism of the people to help in reëstablishing Cuban credit and thereby the security of the country, for the reforms demanded were only such as every good government should wish to have.[24]

Whether or not there ever was any such thing as a Crowder ultimatum, the desired legislation was enacted by August 30. A little while later, on October 10, 1922, Crowder left Cuba on a visit to Washington. In this connection Diario de la Marina came out with an editorial on what he had accomplished in the twenty-two months since he came to the island in January 1921. According to this influential newspaper the following achievements were to be credited to Crowder:

He was responsible for relieving the congestion at the docks of Havana in 1921, causing eighty million dollars' worth of merchandise to be placed in warehouses.

He had saved the country from civil war over the Zayas-Gómez issue.

It was on his initiative that the budget had been reduced from $130,000,000 to fifty-five millions.

Due to him, there had been a partial administrative reorganization, with the elimination of about fifteen thousand unnecessary employes.

He had brought about a change in Zayas's first Cabinet, resulting in the resignation of seven of its nine members.

The lottery had been reformed, and in consequence the illegal collection of ten million dollars had been brought to an end and a "sentence of death" imposed upon "the subsidized press."

He had promulgated a legislative, financial, and moralization program which included: a law for a fifty million loan, to take care of the floating debt; a law for a new accounting system of the republic, although Zayas intended to veto it;

[24] *Heraldo de Cuba,* Aug. 5, 1922.

a law for cancelling illegal contracts and classifying the others that went to make up the floating debt; a law eliminating venal judges; and a law suspending certain portions of the Civil Service Code, so that the new Secretaries might reorganize their departments with an honest personnel.

In attaining these ends Crowder had had to contend with the lukewarm help of the Zayas government and the "almost seditious" attacks of opponents of reform. He had succeeded, however. His object in all his work had been the same as that embodied in the language of President Mc-Kinley in his instructions to the Philippine Commission in 1900:

> "In all the forms of government and administrative provision . . . bear in mind that the government . . . is designed not for our satisfaction, . . . but for the happiness, peace, and prosperity of the people . . . and the measures adopted should be made to conform to their customs, their habits, and even their prejudices, to the fullest extent consistent with the accomplishment of the indispensable requisites of just and effective government."[25]

So it was, that Crowder wanted his reforms in Cuba to be in the hands of Cubans themselves. Referring to the purification of the lottery (which, to be sure, was to be of very short duration), Diario de la Marina mentioned its sequel of indictments, which had even reached out to include Zayas's own son, and quoted another Havana paper to the effect that if everybody who had participated in graft in Cuba were treated as he deserved "the whole island of Cuba would have to be converted into an immense prison to hold them all." In conclusion, Diario de la Marina defended Crowder against the charge that he was an "intervention despot," asserting that impartial observers held that public sentiment was really in his favor, because he was friendly to Cuba and

[25] This document, though signed by McKinley, was the work of Elihu   Root.

wanted to take steps to avoid civil wars and the necessity for interventions.[26]

Matters now moved rapidly toward an agreement for a loan. To be sure, there was a notoriously corrupt mid-term election in 1922,[27] but there was no political disturbance as a sequel. The Morgan house is said to have asked that further and drastic changes be made to mitigate the evils of the lottery and that assurances be given that the Honest Cabinet would be kept in office as some guarantee that other reforms already in effect would be maintained. Zayas promised to accede to both requests, and on that basis the final steps were taken, and the loan agreement signed early in 1923. The loan was issued at 96.77, with a five and a half per cent coupon rate and 1953 as the date of maturity, yielding over forty-eight millions to the Cuban treasury. About seven million was devoted to payment of the war debt to the United States, and six million more was turned over to the Department of Public Works for use in connection with sanitation only. The rest was to be applied on the floating debt, and not be available for anything else, which was a great disappointment to the politicians, who in consequence have since expressed their feeling about the loan that was "forced" on Cuba. It was already clear that there would not be enough to pay all claims. So it was decided to make a beginning by paying seventy per cent of the debts due in the Department of Public Works, after scaling down or annulling many of the contracts, and thirty per cent of all other debts. Whether or not these payments were actually made, it is certain that most of the other obligations were compelled to wait and had not been met by the end of Zayas's term. And meanwhile the government boasted of

[26] *Resultados de la intervención de la marina, unipersonal: . . . la actuación del general Crowder en Cuba*, in *Diario*   Oct. 10, 1922.   [27] See *infra*, pp. 575-577.

the vast sums it was accumulating in the treasury,—really, to a great extent, the unexpended surplus of the loan.[28]

Zayas now had the loan, and, furthermore, the economic prospects of the country had taken a decided turn for the better. The 1922-1923 sugar crop was large, and brought a a very good price. This was, of course, reflected in government receipts, which eventually proved to be nearly seventy-three millions for 1922-1923, with a likelihood of yet better returns for the following year. There was no longer any reasonable doubt but that Cuba could meet her financial obligations with an ample margin to spare. So Zayas felt that the time had come for him to break with Crowder, especially since it was now virtually certain that there would be ample funds in the treasury to enrich the "patriots" who could get their hands on them if the Crowder reforms were out of the way. Other politicians as well as Zayas had long been restive under the restraints that had been put upon them, and the newspapers which were subordinate to their interests had subjected the American representative to a constant fire of attack. On one ocasion there was a resolution of Congress asking for more information about the nature of his mission.[29] On another, following the appointment of the Honest Cabinet, Congress called upon the United States government to adjust itself to the spirit of the Platt Amendment as embodied in the letter of Secretary Root to General Wood of April 3, 1901, in which it was stated that the rights of the United States were not to be interpreted as amounting to a privilege of interfering in the affairs of Cuba.[30] On the same order was a strangely worded preface

[28] On this score, note the following editorial: *A just petition of the merchants,* in *Diario de la marina,* translated in Havana *Post,* Nov. 24, 1925.

[29] *Reforms under Cuba's new president,* in *Current history,* v. XIV, pp. 715-716, at 715; July, 1921.

[30] Machado, 20-22, n. 2, quotes this resolution. The date of the letter to General Wood is given mistakenly as Apr. 2.

to an amnesty bill which passed the Senate on October 9, 1922. This claimed that graft should not be prosecuted as a crime, alleging that it had been "introduced" under the American administration of Governor Magoon and had developed naturally out of that. The resolution went on to recite the various forms of corruption in Cuban political life and to argue that graft had become customary and therefore permissive. So the bill proposed a blanket immunity for all grafters. The United States objected to the resolution, and that part of the bill was killed in the House.[31] Not a few respectable men of the non-political class, too, were opposed to the Crowder mission, even though they approved of his measures, for they were afraid it might possibly result in a loss of independence. To them "the worst Cuban government is better than the best foreign government," although they would have modified that statement with an expression of confidence that in course of time Cuba would evolve to satisfactory political conditions by her own efforts alone. Zayas was clever enough to take advantage of this feeling and also to profit by certain features of President Harding's policy, to shake off the ties that had bound him to Crowder and declare for himself.

Zayas had at least three reasons why he wanted to steer his own course, but all of them may be summed up in the one word "graft." In the first place, he wanted to get rid of the Honest Cabinet. He had had a number of collisions with his Secretaries, especially Manuel Despaigne of the Treasury and Demetrio Castillo of Public Works. He objected to some of their dismissals of employees, and they also blocked him by refusing to countersign a number of his appointments. As early as January 1923 there were rumors

[31] Conn, Edward L   , Cuba   lic ledger, reprinted in) Berkeley
not free but enslaved: VII, Surgery (California) Gazette, Nov. 26, 1923.
for sore spots, in (Philadelphia Pub-

that Zayas was going to dismiss the Honest Cabinet, where-upon the United States sent a message of enquiry, for the loan had been approved on the basis of its retention. Zayas did not yet have the proceeds of the loan; so it behooved him to tread softly. Therefore he replied, so it is said, with a promise to keep his Secretaries "indefinitely," and so got his money. About this time, "reason number two" was developing in his mind. A magnificent deal had been rigged up for the purchase by the state of the Santa Clara Convent of Havana, at a great profit to Zayas and associated politicians. In the back of the President's head, too, was his "third reason,"—the "reform" of the lottery, which he proposed to undertake in a very different manner from what the bankers and the United States government had expected,—a way that promised millions to Cuba's "hard-working" executive. The Santa Clara project came up first, but Despaigne refused to authorize it, and was backed up in his course by the other honest members of the Cabinet. Thereupon Zayas subjected them to all manner of indignities in hopes of getting them to resign, but they would not do so. Early in April, affairs had come to such a pass that it was common talk that Zayas intended to dismiss his Cabinet, despite the promises he had made.[32] Presently he hit upon a campaign cry that gave him his opening, raising the issue of "nationalism." He pictured his Cabinet as representative of the United States rather than of Cuba. So on April 3, 1923, he dismissed four of his Secretaries (Arístides Agramonte, Demetrio Castillo, Manuel Despaigne, and Ricardo Lancís) for "high reasons of state," as he put it, and brought back the old corrupt crowd in their place. Naturally this met with disapproval on the part of the United States

[32] It is said that the dismissal of these men was foreshadowed, several days before it occurred, by a toast which the President's wife offered at a dinner, in which she drank to the fall of the Cabinet.

government, which reminded Zayas of his promise to keep his ministers "indefinitely." Zayas is said to have replied,—and certainly such an answer would have been characteristic of the man,—that he had indeed made such a promise, but that the word "indefinitely" might imply a short time as well as a long one, holding therefore that he had kept his word. And no doubt he had, for *his* word was a variable and slippery thing.[33]

For a few months, now, Cuba was rampant with "nationalism." It may be taken as a general rule, with few exceptions, that all politicians and their henchmen are anti-United States, not at all because of any fear of American "imperialism," but because Washington tends to be a check on their accumulating illegal profits. Indeed, nothing could be more absurd than the "nationalism" issue in Cuba, for if there is one country in Hispanic America where the ghost of American aggression has been bottled up that country is Cuba.[34] Heraldo de Cuba, which has always been nationalistic in a very real sense, could not follow the "nationalism" of Zayas. In its issue of April 3, 1923, the day of the dismissal of the Honest Cabinet, it refuted the state-

[33] Conn, Edward L   , *The crisis in Cuba:* II, *A presidential Aladdin,* in (Philadelphia *Public ledger,* reprinted in) Berkeley (California) *Gazette,* Nov. 20, 1923.

[34] It would, no doubt, be possible to cite thousands of expressions to this effect in Cuban writings, even in the great majority of the newspapers which at various times, for corrupt reasons, lend their columns to attacks on the United States. The following is a sample statement of Orestes Ferrara, a man who was always a fire-eating but sincere nationalist, though recognizing in 1923, as he had in 1909, that there was no real danger of an annexation to the United States unless the Cubans provoked it themselves: "The truth is, that the only danger to our independence is in annexation, and not in that as the product of a violent act by our neighbors from the north, for they would never do any such thing, but as a consequence of a work that is daily being realized in Cuban territory itself." Speech of Ferrara, quoted in Cámara de representantes, *Diario de sesiones,* Feb. 16, 1910, v. XII, no. 42, p. 3. A similar statement is the following: "Those who insult the American people by constantly declaring that they want to take over Cuba must be fiends or idiots." *The faith of an American president,* in *Comercio* (Cienfuegos), translated in Havana *Post,* May 14, 1924. Cf., also, *infra,* pp. 646-648.

ment of Wifredo Fernández that the Secretaries were in rebellion against the President, asserting that they were being separated from their posts because they would not countenance repellant and immoral deals. Heraldo de Cuba went on to say that Zayas was resolved, if the United States should put any difficulties in his way, to lay his case before the Pan-American Congress, which was about to meet in Santiago, Chile. It was pointed out, too, that not all the Secretaries of the Honest Cabinet were to go.[35] In that same issue of Heraldo de Cuba, Ferrara replied to Wifredo Fernández, who had accused him of saying that the five Secretaries (really four), about to be dismissed, were the only ones who knew how to serve Cuba, and of defending them in their influence in Cuban affairs. Denying that he had made the statement attributed to him, Ferrara went on to the effect that the cry of rebellion was not on the part of the Secretaries, but rather of their opponents, whom they had prevented from committing nefarious crimes against the state for nearly a year. The dismissed Secretaries were worthy of admiration, for they represented respect for law and honesty as against shameless frauds. It was not a question of there being just five honest Cubans or of their interference with the President's constitutional rights, but rather one of national decorum and sovereignty. To save Cuba, it was necessary to have an honest administration. The Secretaries ought not to defend a President who was doing bad things, and they were under no obligation to resign; rather, it was better for them to stay in office, no matter how unpleasant, in order to save Cuba.[36] This probably represented the opinion of the majority of the

[35] *El doctor A. Zayas . . . ha dirigido a todos los secretarios una carta circular en la que les pide la renuncia,* in *Heraldo de Cuba,* Apr. 3, 1923.

[36] Ferrara, Orestes, *Lo que dije y pienso,* in *Heraldo de Cuba,* Apr. 3, 1923.

decent element among the educated classes in Cuba. Certainly there was a lot more smoke than fire to the nationalism of Zayas.

There were no thunderbolts from the direction of Washington. Crowder, who had given up his former category as special agent of President Harding to become, in January 1923, the first American ambassador to Cuba,—such was the importance of this post,—was thoroughly muzzled, except as Secretary Hughes might permit him to speak. That appeared to mean that he could not say anything at all. Thus encouraged, the Cuban politicians proceeded gaily to the enactment of the Santa Clara purchase and the "reform" of the lottery. As for the lottery, its evil features were either sanctioned or else made worse than ever, and the bill was passed by a great majority.[37] Zayas vetoed it, thus again "complying" with his promise, but he did so in a "come on, boys!" message that praised Congress for its noble sentiments and implied approval. Congress then passed the measure over his veto, by ninety-six to three in the House on July 23 and unanimously in the Senate next day, and Zayas affixed his signature on August 4. Not satisfied with having the fleshpots in their own hands again, and a little restive under the criticism of those who had not been swept off their feet by the cry of nationalism, Congress prefixed a resolution to explain why it had voted the bill the first time and then ratified it again. Principal among the reasons assigned was the necessity, so it would appear, of putting the United States government in its proper place. In the language of the resolution,

"Because there has been scattered through the country the version that there have been official intimations on the part of the government of the United States, if Congress should not ratify the law it would

[37] For a discussion of the lottery bill itself, see *infra*, pp. 558-561.

abandon the full exercise of its constitutional powers to resolve in domestic affairs."

Going on then to speak of the restoration of credit and the generally happy financial situation of the republic, the resolution maintained that there was not the slightest cause for any interference with the prerogatives of Congress, and censured those who had attacked its members for enacting the law. In conclusion, it said with respect to the attitude of their opponents that it was

"A political maneuver that ought not to have been initiated and that will have a dangerous amplitude for our nationality itself unless all factors of Cuban society unite to bear to the government and Congress of the United States the firm impression that the people of Cuba would feel profoundly wounded in their sentiments if there should be any intent to exercise that interference, which is improper, because our republic is fulfilling its international obligations with all exactitude; which is unlawful, as the treaties that define their relations with other states do not authorize it; and which is disquieting, because it would end definitively in breaking morally the solid ties of historic association that unite us to the great American nation." [38]

This resolution, which outraged all precedents of diplomatic intercourse between countries that intended to remain at peace, was none too well received in the United States. The Outlook commented upon it editorially in an article entitled "Independence or impudence?", implying the latter.[39] During the summer of 1923 Crowder had written two more memoranda (the fourteenth and fifteenth) protesting against the terms of the lottery law, but scant attention was paid to him. And why not?,—for there was not even a whisper from Washington. One Cuban newspaper has suggested that American meekness in 1923 is to be interpreted, not that Zayas defeated the United States, but, rather, that

[38] *Gaceta*, Aug. 4, 1923.   655; Aug. 29, 1923.
[39] In *Outlook*, v. CXXXIV, pp. 654-

the Republican party wanted to avoid giving any chance for people to call it imperialistic in the uncertain pre-presidential campaign situation of that time.[40]   A more likely reason for the American attitude, however, is the one that Zayas had had in mind in dismissing the Honest Cabinet,— the fear of Washington that a strong stand might hurt the United States before the Pan-American Congress and in its general Hispanic American policy.   On this score the following is a statement concerning Secretary of State Hughes and his policy that was made by a man of long experience in Hispanic America, to whose opinions the writer is inclined to subscribe:

"Hughes is so afraid that somebody may say that the United States acted improperly or in an imperialistic manner that he leans backwards, and in so doing does a lot of harm, here in Cuba at any rate. He does not realize that Hispanic American peoples respect strong actions, however much they may shout against them at the time, and that in any event their momentary outbursts pass away very quickly. In fact, no amount of gentle methods will do away with Hispanic American criticism, and it won't stop 'nationalistic' politicians, whose patriotism has a very definite relation to their own personal fortunes. In Cuba, Hughes did not back up Crowder when Zayas kicked over the traces in 1923. So Zayas has not only been enabled to pose as the savior of Cuban liberties, but has also been virtually defended in the most stupendous campaign of graft I have ever witnessed, because Hughes will not let the Cubans have a revolution or will not take the responsibility of stopping these evils himself. As I see it, he ought to do one or the other, even at the cost of a revolution, which would indeed be a terrible calamity. Better still, no doubt, would be for him to have the moral courage to undertake and see through a program of reform such as all decent Cubans want, irrespective of what anybody might say, Cubans, Hispanic Americans, or Democrats in the United States, since there is no real danger in such a policy and since it is based on right principles." [41]

[40] *Did Zayas save the country from the stamp of Uncle Sam's hoof?*, in *Avisador comercial*, translated in Havana *Post*, Dec. 6, 1924.

[41] This statement was made to the writer in May 1924, just after the abortive revolution against Zayas, which was doomed to failure when the United States followed its recently developed policy of backing the government in power.

Zayas did indeed make all the political capital he could out of having "saved" the country, and kept singing the same tune to the end of his administration. To be sure, to the understanding ear it was in a weird key. Some go so far as to assert that the cry of Cuban "nationalism" was first suggested *in New York,*—by American financial interests which hoped to enhance their own profits through lining Zayas's pockets with American dollars in return for improper concessions, if Crowder were out of the way. It is doubtful whether there was any such precise arrangement, but it would have been conceivable with a man like Zayas. A generalization by Spinden so aptly covers his case that the subject may be dismissed by quoting it:

"Patriotism is the last resort of scoundrels. We may rest assured that the vociferous spoilers in Cuba will not neglect the proper phrases to hide their evil designs. The ordinary man in the streets . . . will grin and bear it, and national pride will be invoked to make him turn against the United States as somehow deeply to blame. That is part of the price we must pay to achieve real leadership in moral things." [42]

One more statement may be quoted, this time with respect to the other of the two most prominent actors in this period, General Crowder.

"You can't help feeling proud of the general for what he tried to do in Cuba, but he may have made a mistake in insisting on the loan. There would have been chaos without it, but that might have hastened some effective reform that would help to eradicate the graft that is eating at the heart of the republic now."

Was it a mistake? Who can say? If it was, who can deny that it was an honest and generous one? And was there any good reason why his achievements should have been surrendered so easily? [43]

[42] Spinden, Herbert Joseph, *America and her duty in Cuba,* in Boston *Transcript,* Aug. 7, 1923.

[43] For some comment on authorities for the Zayas period, see note at the end of chapter XX.

CHAPTER XIX

CORRUPTION AND REMONSTRANCE

1923-1924

With United States help, offered through the medium of General Crowder's services, Cuba had had a chance to become the model republic of Hispanic America, *if* the pace could have been maintained. Zayas gave the moralization program such a setback, however, that except as an example all of the work was lost. Indeed, the last two years of the Zayas rule were so utterly depraved that a beginning would have to be made from a point farther back than at the time he took office in 1921. To be sure, in some respects the situation was better in 1925. The country was not nearly in such a bad way financially, though the prospects of sugar were none too flattering. And there was a peaceful succession to the presidency. In neither case, however, was Zayas entitled to any particular credit. As has already been pointed out, Cuban prosperity is dependent on factors quite outside of government, which may hinder progress but cannot produce it. And Zayas gave up the presidency only when it was clear to him that he could not reëlect himself, not even with the employment of the methods of 1916 and 1920. The one merit accruing to him is that he recognized this fact, and yielded to the inevitable. It may be interesting at this point to give some opinions of Zayas, set forth in the light of his conduct down to the summer of 1924. The following are a few sample statements, including one that is ultra-favorable, but not altogether out of line with the others:

(1) "People do not understand Zayas, who is really a great man. To be sure, he has not been perfect. You can't defend the Santa Clara purchase or his nepotism. And everything they say about . . . ! ! . . . is true. All else about Zayas is good. He is an idealist, and admires Lincoln above any man in history, possessing an unusually rich library on his life. Everybody knows he is no fool, and, above all, he has remark-able patience. He has a perfect passion for freedom of speech, and in the face of insult he calmly bides his time. He has often been urged to suspend certain newspapers that attack him or to exile a vociferous opponent, but he refuses to do so, insisting that the way to get rid of license in expression is to let it run its course. He believes in Cuba for the Cubans, and in time to come will be regarded as the greatest man the country has produced."

(2) "If it is true that Zayas has made a study of the life of Lincoln it was only to learn how to do the opposite!"

(3) "Zayas has been Cuba's worst ruler since the separation from Spain. He has been the worst nepotist and the worst grafter. He has made many improvements on paper,—almost none at all in fact. He will get a bill put through for a road, have some engineer relative draw up a plan, pay him half a million, and nothing more will be done,— except for the division of the spoil. The more than thirty millions he has accumulated in the treasury are all a false appearance. He has them, through not paying the floating debt, but he himself is far more likely to get a lot of this money than ever the creditors are to receive a cent."

(4) "Zayas is not ashamed to rake in *pesetas* if he can't get *pesos*.[1] Worse than his own graft, however, is the way he lets his relatives ride. Worse yet is that his wife's relatives are feeding at the public crib, too."

(5) "Zayas's 'nationalism' is only a farce. Of course, it is a useful cry in practical politics, but at the very time that he was shouting loudest about 'Cuba for the Cubans' he was making deals with great corporations so as to give excessive privileges in Cuba to foreigners. Some people praise him for stepping down from the presidency, instead of reëlecting himself by force, but he knew perfectly well that there would be a real revolution if he intended to inflict himself on Cuba again and that the army would be on the other side. So he made the best arrangement he could, to keep himself and his relatives out of jail."

[1] The *peseta* has a normal value of   dollar.
twenty cents, and the *peso* of a

It would be easy to accumulate thousands of Zayas items from newspapers and other Cuban sources, but they would not differ appreciably from the above. A few such statements are referred to later, in connection with the events of these years. It happens, too, that several carefully thought-out articles have appeared in United States periodicals dealing with Zayas. In September 1925 there was a series of articles by Albert Whiting Fox in the Washington Post about the evil conditions that were causing what seemed almost like a national uprising against Zayas at that time. In November 1923 Edward L. Conn had a similar series of articles in the Philadelphia Public Ledger, with an even more detailed survey of Zayas's conduct and other iniquities in Cuban political life. More recently other estimates of the Zayas government have appeared. The following recites one characteristic instance of the President's procedure:

"On taking over the presidency, Dr. Zayas found that in the budget he was allowed about three hundred thousand dollars annually for the Executive Department of the government. Repeatedly he appealed to Congress to increase this amount by $180,000, threatening, if his wishes were not respected, to close the palace and return to his home at Morro No. 3. Congress . . . turned a deaf ear to his distress. He then appealed for aid to his Cabinet, . . . and one of them, Capt. Castillo Pokorny, an honor graduate of West Point, . . . suggested that, if Dr. Zayas found himself unable to live within his allotment, it would be a fitting recognition of the straits in which the country found itself if the President were to close the palace and discharge the hordes of servants who were proving so costly. Current bills for supplies at the palace were unpaid, and eventually came before the debt commission, together with thousands of unpaid accounts left over from Menocal's administration. Among these bills were some for hundreds of dollars' worth of perfume, one for eight hundred dollars' worth of eggs,—one month's consumption of the presidential family,—others of ten and twenty thousand dollars for pheasants and roses. Balked by both Congress and the Cabinet, Dr. Zayas pondered deeply and shortly evolved a wonderful new scheme. With the help of Erasmos Regue

Feros, Secretary of Justice, he issued a decree *ordering* the payment to himself of the funds he so much coveted."

Various other instances of presidential misconduct are mentioned in the same article.[2] The following is another interesting characterization of Zayas and his government:

"Proceeding cautiously at first, he obtained a loan of $50,000,000 in this country. This done, he threw off the 'vicious intermeddling of Washington,' placed fourteen members of his family in strategic positions in the administration, and, his forces thus distributed, laid siege to the public treasury. The loan offered the first chance . . . Not only the available portion of the loan but also the annual revenue, amounting to $81,000,000, was exhausted before public employees could be paid, before overdue coupons on the public debt could be taken up, before some $400,000 due the United States on postal money order account could be turned over. Public works appropriations were also closely scrutinized. Great interest was shown in the cleaning of streets and the repair of highways and bridges, and large appropriations were obtained for these purposes. The money was promptly withdrawn from the Treasury, but the cleaning and the repairs are still to be done. A foreign engineer, interested in comparative costs on bridge-repairing, took a list of seven bridges that the records showed had been recently repaired at a cost of $367,000. He found not only that the repairs had not been made, but that not one of the bridges had ever existed! The Cuban politicians did not overlook the more usual forms of graft. Gambling places and houses of prostitution paid heavily for exemption from police molestation. Contracts for food and supplies in the jails and other public institutions were fully exploited. A peculiarity of the Cuban fiscal system was also made to yield its due. Each municipality must submit its annual budget to the Department of the Interior for its approval. These budgets being largely false, it was worth money to approve them. And the money was forthcoming. Large sums were paid to the officials of the department for approval and included in the amounts for which the local public was mulcted."[3]

---

[2] *Cuba, an American ward again?*, in *Independent*, v. CXIII, pp. 35-38, at 36; July 19, 1924. Among other things, this article asserts that Zayas held his history-writing job for eight years, receiving "almost fifty thousand dollars." Cf. *supra*, pp. 416-418.

[3] Norton, Henry Kittredge, *Self-determination in the West Indies*, in *World's work*, v. LI, pp. 77-84, at 81-82; Nov., 1925. This is the first of a series of three articles under this title.

The orgy of graft alluded to in these statements was made possible by an era of prosperity that filled the treasury. For 1923-1924 government receipts were about ninety-one millions and a half, and about ninety-three and a half for 1924-1925,—this, of course, in addition to the sums that were misappropriated before ever they got into the record. Since the government was not paying off the floating debt, this left an ample amount for political rewards.[4] Indeed, for a time it seemed as if there was almost more than Zayas and his cohorts could spend. Over a twelve-month, from the spring of 1923 to the spring of 1924, the so-called "surplus" in the treasury advanced from some three millions to about thirty-four. Meanwhile, the creditors, to whom much more than this sum was due, were obliged to wait. Late in 1924 Zayas issued a decree to the effect that twenty per cent of the back salary due government employes would now be paid to them; he tried to make capital out of it, as if it were a Christmas gift. There were hints, however, that even this belated and moderate regard for one group of the nation's creditors was being displayed because a few presidential favorites were to obtain special advantages from the measure.[5] This was a mere bagatelle in the sum total of the floating debt, and caused no particular strain on the government's resources. For other reasons, however,—presently to be discussed,—the surplus did turn downward in 1924, and people were alarmed lest the new President would

[4] The money order account between the United States and Cuba is one sample of the way in which the latter allowed debts to run, while revenues were accumulating. As part of the postal agreement between the two countries, Cuba was required to keep four hundred thousand dollars on deposit in Washington, but, instead of doing so, actually permitted a deficit to develop. So, on money orders drawn in Cuba and payable in the United States, the latter was paying out money without reimbursement, although the Cuban post-office had received the full amount. This was a mild theft inflicted on the American people.

[5] See, for example, *A ridiculous twenty per cent,* in *Discusión,* translated in Havana *Post,* Nov. 25, 1924.

be left with nothing but debts, and no cash at all for current needs. Pressure was brought to bear on Zayas, and in December 1924 he announced that he would leave twenty-five million in the treasury for the next government. This was as much as to say: "I won't take it all, but will leave a little for you." In point of fact, however, the "surplus" on May 20, 1925, was variously estimated from a mere two hundred thousand dollars, at the highest, all the way down to a deficit of two millions, while in any event the floating debt was still *floating!*

Inevitably, an account of the last two years of Zayas's administration must deal mainly with political corruption. It should be remembered, too, that Zayas was not alone in the picture. By this time the overwhelming presumption with regard to any politician, national or local, was that he was a grafter and perhaps a criminal.[6] The man who was most nearly responsible for this condition, however, was the President himself, and so attention may be directed primarily to those deals in which he was concerned. The first of the ultra-notorious graft projects was the purchase of the Santa Clara Convent, to serve as a government office building. In 1920, when Havana real estate prices were skyrocketing, this was sold by the church authorities to a private syndicate for a mere fraction of the figure Zayas agreed upon in the low-priced real estate era of 1923, and the 1920 purchase was also on very easy terms.[7] This seems to have been part of a deal that was arranged before Zayas became President. At any rate, on February 6, 1922, the company offered the building to the government at an ex-

[6] Cf. *infra*, p. 573.

[7] Norton, Henry Kittredge, *Op. cit.*, 82, gives the price as six hundred thousand, while Conn, Edward L   , *The crisis in Cuba: II, A presidential Aladdin,* in (Philadelphia *Public ledger,* republished in) Berkeley (California) *Gazette,* Nov. 20, 1923, says it was a million. There is also some mention of this deal in the *Gaceta,* Mar. 13, 1923, but without any reference to the price.

aggerated price. The administration did not act at that
time, so Zayas said, because of other "transcendental problems,"—which might have been rendered "because of Crowder." On August 9, 1922, a new offer was made at a lower
price: $2,350,000! The "transcendental problems" were
still operating, but on March 10, 1923, Zayas issued a decree
for the purchase that was countersigned by Erasmo Regüeiferos, Secretary of Justice.[8]

Immediately there was a storm of protest. The opposition
of the Honest Cabinet has been alluded to already. Congress, too, addressed a number of unpleasant enquiries to
the President. Presumably the congressmen had not been
declared "in" on the deal; in this connection it is interesting to note that a petition of the House to the President
for information concerning the purchase was fathered by
Representative Sagaró, who played an unsavory part, later,
in the Cárdenas Bay affair. Zayas had stated that the
Cabinet approved the purchase, although everybody knew
that the refusal of four Secretaries to countenance it was
what cost them their places in the following April. He
was asked to explain his statement, and also to account for
his failure to get legislative sanction for the deal or the signature of his Secretary of the Treasury to the decree. On
April 2, 1923, the same day he dismissed the four honest
Secretaries, Zayas sent his answer to the House.

It was a long and mystifying document, full of legal
terminology. The House had requested a copy of the agreement of the Cabinet for the purchase. This, Zayas did
not give, for the simple reason that there had never been
any such agreement. It seems that Zayas and Regüeiferos
were handling this affair, but on February 3, 1923, the other

[8] For the decree, which gives a presidential view of the antecedents of
the sale, see the *Gaceta*, Mar. 13,
1923.

Secretaries addressed them an enquiry about the legal title to the convent and the contract price. This amounted to an agreement of the Secretaries, Zayas claimed, "for without a desire for its acquisition there would be no order for the said study." Later, however, they "ratified" it, he said, for there was a Cabinet meeting at which they entered no objections. He had had Regüeiferos countersign the decree instead of the Secretary of the Treasury (who at that time was the incorruptible Manuel Despaigne), because the former had done all the preliminary work and it was a matter that concerned various departments, not merely the Treasury alone. He admitted that the Secretary of the Treasury would eventually have to approve it,—and well might he admit it, for he intended very soon to have a Secretary who would be more amenable to his wishes than Despaigne. He denied that he needed a law in order to make the agreement, claiming that he had authority so to do under article sixty-eight of the Constitution, which gave the President a right to issue decrees for the execution of the laws,—a very "elastic" interpretation of that paragraph, it would appear. In this connection he cited various precedents of similar actions by other Presidents. In that, certainly, he was right! In commenting upon it, Heraldo de Cuba pointed out that most of the precedents were from the Menocal era, but even then at no such "monstrous price" as Zayas wanted to pay for Santa Clara. Zayas did admit that he would have to get congressional sanction before he could expend the money called for by the decree. Congressmen must have taken particular notice of this admission, for it meant that their "interests" would eventually have to be considered. In defence of the price, Zayas named other pieces of Havana real estate that had been sold at an even higher figure, and claimed anyway that the amount was of scant importance, as it was to be paid on easy terms over a period of years.[9] It was more than a year, however, before Congress sanctioned the deal, but in June 1924 a bill was enacted, which Zayas signed and the Secretary of the Treasury countersigned, but the latter was now, not Manuel Despaigne, but Carlos Portela.[10] Just how much Zayas made out of this deal, and how much more was distributed to other officials and congressmen, is uncertain, but the total of the graft involved was probably considerably more than a million.

Another major grafting deal, though later in making its appearance in public, was enacted into law with much more facility and at an earlier date than the Santa Clara purchase, for Zayas now knew better how to proceed. This was the famous Tarafa Law, a piece of legislation so replete with complications that it is difficult to describe in the brief space that can be allotted to it.[11] As originally presented, the bill seemed to be a national service law of a distinctly "patriotic" flavor, but it eventually developed that the whole affair was largely a battle of American interests, especially of those connected with the Cuba Railway on the one hand and some of the sugar companies on the other. Each side, indeed, had an arguable case, though not without defects, but the main interest here is the connection of the government, whose course seems to have been dictated by the amount of personal profit that the politicians were able to derive from the controversy.

In an island with such a plethora of good harbors as Cuba possesses, it was a simple matter for many of the

[9] The Zayas answer and an article commenting upon it (*El ejecutivo y el "affaire" del convento de Santa Clara*) are in *Heraldo de Cuba,* Apr. 3, 1923.

[10] The law is in the *Gaceta,* June 13, 1924.

[11] The writer possesses data enough for a monograph on this law, though it would have many lacunæ, especially as concerns placing the responsibility for the graft involved.

sugar companies to develop ports of their own, with private railway lines connecting them with their near-by estates. Approximately thirty-one per cent of the 1922-1923 crop was shipped without being hauled over public service railways, and of that amount eighty-five per cent was the product of American companies. Altogether, there were forty-seven private ports in operation, all of them in the eastern provinces. The government had acquiesced in the employment of these ports, but it was a question whether anything that could be called more than a revocable license had ever been given, but in many cases they had been used for twenty years, and in some for thirty. Naturally, the eastern railways were deprived of an opportunity to earn freight from companies with private ports, and the situation was aggravated for them by events growing out of the depression of 1921. The banks, it will be remembered, had loaned vast sums on sugar estates, and were eventually obliged to foreclose and take over the properties which had served as security. Among others, the National City Bank of New York found itself with a number of plantations on its hands in Camagüey. These were incorporated as a subsidiary of the bank, as the General Sugar Company, and the proposal was made to make use of the private port of Santa María. At the same time, the American Sugar Company planned to adopt the private port method of shipping from its estates in Camagüey. This was a serious matter to at least one railway, the Cuba Northern, in northern Camagüey, commonly called the "Tarafa Line," because it was very largely the creation of Colonel José Miguel Tarafa, its chief stockholder and president. He is credited with devising the bill which came to be known by his name, though he himself was not in politics and therefore not its official sponsor.

As originally drafted, the bill applied to all sugar estates using private ports, which especially affected Camagüey and Oriente. The private ports were to be closed, and the sugar companies required to use the public service railways in sending their products to an authorized port. This was what it amounted to in fact, but very few persons, not even most members of Congress, knew the precise terms of the bill, for Tarafa and his co-workers kept them shrouded in mystery. No secret was made, however, about there being some sort of bill that they earnestly wanted to have passed, and no expense was spared, while, furthermore, the Cuban "flag" was waved vigorously about this "thoroughly Cuban measure." Tarafa gave the members of Congress an excursion over his line, but this was not all that he, or somebody, gave them. It is conservatively estimated that he spent at least half a million to assure the approval of Zayas and Congress. Indeed, at the height of Zayas's controversy with the Veterans and Patriots Association in the fall of 1923 the latter gave out a public statement in which it was asserted that a minimum of six thousand dollars was paid to representatives, twenty thousand to senators, and five hundred thousand to the President. At length, on August 10, 1923, the bill was passed by the House in a typically Cuban fashion. At two o'clock in the morning, without prior notice, it was introduced, and it passed three hours later by eighty-eight to nine. As one newspaper remarked of this action:

"When the measure was read, its terms became known to the representatives for the first time. And no copies of it were distributed beforehand or even after it had been approved." [12]

It might be mentioned, too, that the bill was a long and complicated document that would have been difficult for an

[12] *Aprobación por sorpresa de la ley Tarafa,* in *Mercurio,* Aug. 11, 1923.

expert lawyer to understand after hours of study. It purported to be a measure for consolidating the railways of the country, or some of them, under a Cuban charter, but at this stage of the controversy people's minds were directed to the fact that it seemed to levy a kind of tribute on the sugar companies and associated industries.

Immediately there was an outcry against the law, and not least of all in Cuba, especially by the powerful association of landowners and planters (*hacendados* and *colonos*), which included in its membership some of the wealthiest men in the island among those whose income was not derived from politics. In this connection it is to be observed that the great sugar companies procure a large proportion of their commodity from neighboring landowners and from planters to whom the company rents lands of its own.[13] So it was not merely the companies that would suffer, but also a great many Cubans. These men, individually, and through the press and their organizations, came out against the bill, calling it confiscatory and censuring the secrecy and graft that had been employed to procure its enactment. Indeed, Cuban business interests generally were opposed to the measure. Naturally, too, the sugar companies protested, and carried their case to Washington. Newspapers and magazines in the United States gave columns of space to the affair, and with few exceptions, whether Republican or Democratic, denounced it as confiscatory. Secretary Hughes is said to have requested a delay before the bill should be carried any farther.[14] Meanwhile, the sugar companies pleaded their cause before the State Department, employing no less a figure than Elihu Root to present their claims. It was at this stage that other Ameri-

---

[13] Cf. *infra*, p. 614.
[14] New York *Journal of commerce*, Aug. 14, 1923.

can interests began to appear on the opposite side, especially those which were interested in the affairs of the Cuba Railway, and they too had their representatives in Washington. It is generally regarded that the companies had what amounted to at least a prescriptive right to use the private ports and that the original draft of the Tarafa bill involved a virtual, if indirect, confiscation of their properties, which would have been in contravention of article three of the Permanent Treaty, but the ever-cautious Mr. Hughes was not convinced that they had proved their case sufficiently for him to take any decisive action. According to some accounts he regarded the railway consolidation as a purely Cuban measure, but objected to the confiscatory features with reference to the sugar interests, while others claim he maintained that the sugar companies had not proved their case at all. At any rate, the sugar men seem to have decided that it would be best for them to deal directly with the railway interests. Meanwhile, too, General Sugar had dropped out of the fight,—whether because its port of Santa María had been validated by the government or for other reasons cannot be asserted with certainty. Several conferences were now held in New York between officials of the different interests, with Tarafa present, and as a result a new bill was drawn up, to the effect that the private ports in use prior to 1923 were not to be disturbed, but that there were to be no new ones; in other words, the public service railways were to get the benefit of any further development of the sugar industry. This compromise satisfied most Cuban sugar men, and some, but not all, of the foreigners. It did not satisfy a great many other people in Cuba, however. Attention now began to be directed to the railway features of the bill, which permitted of the consolidation into one system of any three interconnecting

roads, of which two must be Cuban. It was generally understood that this law was to serve as the basis for the
merger of the Cuba Railway (an American corporation)
with two Cuban lines, the Camagüey and Nuevitas (all of
whose stock was owned by the Cuba Railway) and the
Cuba Northern. This amounted to an expansion of the
Cuba Railway, which would inevitably have by far the
greater amount of stock in the new consolidated railway.
On September 21, 1923, the Senate passed the bill, amended
in accord with the changes made in New York, by fifteen
to four, and on the 25th the House passed the amended
bill by ninety-two to seven. The sugar interests which
had intended to create private ports, but were now barred
from doing so, still hoped to defeat it, and prevailed
upon Hughes to get Zayas to hear their arguments before
signing it. The latter overruled their objections, however,
and signed the bill on October 9, 1923. This marked the
departure from his official family of another member of the
one-time Honest Cabinet. Enrique Hernández Cartaya, a
hold-over from that body, who had been serving as Secretary of the Treasury, refused to countenance the deal, and
so sent in his resignation.

Apart from the matter of graft, it seems probable that
some of the features of the Tarafa Law were of doubtful
advisability. For example, it permits of rebates in freight
bills. And it is uneconomic in that it is cheaper to ship
from near-by private ports. On the other hand, many
argue the advantages of a single great railway system, on
the analogy of the mergers at present being advocated in
the United States. It is believed that the consolidated line
may eventually acquire the United Railways and other companies in Cuba. To many Cubans, however, it seems that
the formation of the much boasted national company has

in fact resulted in turning over a Cuban line to a foreign corporation, which may in time monopolize the railway facilities of the island. And for this they blame the "nationalistic" Zayas! As for the graft in the deal, it is generally believed that Colonel Tarafa could tell whence it came and how it was distributed. In November 1924 La Discusión had a series of articles denouncing him for "ditching" the minority stockholders of the Cuba Northern in bringing about the consolidation. The inference was that Tarafa himself got a large retainer, part of which he used to win the "sympathy" of Zayas and Congress. Whatever the truth may be as to the source of the graft and the moral obliquity involved in offering it, it is generally admitted that the law was bought.[15]

However much Zayas may have profited by the Santa Clara and Tarafa deals, he had not confined himself to them, but had various "sources of income." Not a man of considerable means before he became President, he was able after two years, at a salary of twenty-five thousand a year, to acquire a three hundred thousand dollar estate of some six hundred acres, just outside of Havana. To be sure, this fine property, which he named after his wife "Villa María," may not have involved him in as much expense as it might some other man, for it is said that he used soldiers and convicts in work on the place and took quantities of stone from the government quarries,—all, of course, without paying any money. As for the national palace in Havana, that became a residence for whole bevies of the Zayas family. One month the presidential expense account showed an item of ten thousand dollars for "chickens," to say nothing of a comparatively small amount for rouge and hair-

---

[15] The law is in the *Gaceta*, Oct. 9, ed. by Juan de Dios Tejada, Habana 1923. For an English version, see [1923]. *Cuban railway consolidation law,* tr.

pins.[16]   There was something more than mere board and room, however luxurious, for the relatives of the President and his wife.   At least fourteen were provided with good positions in the government service.   The President's son, Alfredo Zayas, Jr., became director-general of the lottery.[17] A brother, Francisco Zayas, was once at the head of the Department of Public Instruction, and later minister to France.   A stepson, "Willie" Gómez Conlon, was major-domo of the palace; for a while he had a perfumery stand there, and it behooved the politicians to patronize his business, but presently it was ridiculed out of existence.   Andrés Pereira, a son-in-law, was comptroller-general of the republic.   Another son-in-law, Celso Cuellar del Río, held a notarial post worth fifty thousand a year; he is now a senator.   Carlos Portela, a cousin, was Under-Secretary of the Treasury,—later becoming Secretary.   A nephew, José María Zayas, held an important post in the customs service. And similarly with the others among the fourteen favorites of fortune, one of whom is described as "probably a nephew." [18]

It must not be imagined that the Cuban people resigned themselves to these evils without registering an objection. To be sure, the decent elements of Cuba always labor under grave and almost insuperable handicaps in governmental matters, but this was one of the times when there was an aroused public opinion.   Crowder's fifteen memoranda had taught them to speak their mind.   It began to be expressed vigorously while Zayas was maneuvering with a view to ridding himself of the Honest Cabinet.   Just a day ahead of Zayas's letter dismissing four of his Secretaries, Gonzalo

[16] Cf. *supra*, p. 166.
[17] Cf. *infra*, pp. 535-537.
[18] Conn, Edward L   , *The* *crisis* *in* *Cuba:* II, *A* *presidential*

Aladdin, in (Philadelphia *Public ledger,* reprinted in) Berkeley (California) *Gazette,* Nov. 20, 1923.

Freyre de Andrade, a prominent and respected Conservative among the better class of the old school, wrote an open letter, announcing his withdrawal from the Conservative party. He arraigned it for the evils that had developed under Menocal and Zayas, and asserted that there was no hope of betterment, because leadership among the Conservatives must fall inevitably to one or other of these same two men, to whom the other members of the party organization were wholly subservient.[19]   This letter was merely a symptom of the times.   The very next day, on April 2, 1923, an organization, called the Cuban Committee of National and Civic Renovation, got out a *manifiesto*, or public statement, denouncing the corruption in governmental circles.   The real author of the document was the president of the organization, Fernando Ortiz, a former member of the House and one of the most brilliant scholars in the era of the republic. Among the hundreds of other signers were, as Heraldo de Cuba put it,

"Cubans of the greatest distinction, many of them eminent figures in science and the realm of intellectuality, and, almost all, men who live outside of political parties, without connections or bonds that tie them to their assemblies."

One of the signers was Mario Macbeath, president of the Rotary Club of Havana, one of the most respected organizations in Cuba, and presidents or officials of scores of other non-political associations also affixed their names.   In fine, the *manifiesto* was in no sense of the word a political document, but represented men who were desirous of the regeneration of Cuba, without thought of any direct advantage to themselves.   The document itself went into detail about numerous evils, including the following: tax frauds that were

[19] Freyre   de   Andrade,   Gonzalo,   *Conservador,* Apr. 1, 1923, in *Heraldo Carta . . . separándose del partido   de Cuba,* Apr. 2, 1923.

forced on people by government officials for the benefit of the latter; the graft in customs collections; the state of abandonment, as well as the corruption, in the affairs of the Public Works Department; lack of attention to sanitation and public charity; the exploitation of lewd women by the higher politicians; the decline in education, and its accompaniment of a rapid increase in illiteracy; the corruption of the judiciary; the use of the army in politics; the glaring remissness of Congress in failing to enact needed laws, and its startling activity in fostering every conceivable form of governmental impropriety; the unconstitutional acts of the President in legislating by decree; and electoral manipulations that tended to keep the power in the hands of those least worthy of possessing it, as, for example, in the election of 1922, when more than a fifth of the candidates had at one time or another been adjudged guilty of crime.   In closing, the *manifiesto* called upon the people to save Cuba.   The present administration was not the only one that had been to blame, for, indeed, these evils had their roots in Spanish colonial customs, but they had developed into a "political parasitism" that was

"inefficient from lack of culture, rotten in character, ready to compromise with every sort of delinquency, hand in glove with all kinds of fraud, an unbridled pilferer from the public treasury, and incapable . . . of submitting human selfishness to the limits which . . . civilization and the interdependence of modern world relations impose."

The document ended with an exhortation to the politicians to make the necessary sacrifices to bring about the complete renovation of Cuban life, for otherwise "Tomorrow we shall ask it of the people!" [20]

From this time forward there was a growing impatience

[20] Junta cubana de renovación nacional-cívica, *Manifiesto del 2 de abril* *de 1923,* in *Heraldo de Cuba,* Apr. 4, 1923.

with the Zayas government that was enhanced by the practical certainty that Zayas would reëlect himself if given a chance. Among numerous organizations that began to make themselves heard was the Veterans Association, which had kept out of politics since its brush with Gómez and had taken its place as perhaps the most highly revered group in the country, standing in a sense for a thoroughgoing Cuban patriotism. This body felt aggrieved, because in the midst of an orgy of political extravagance the pensions of the veterans of '95 were not being paid. As many of the men were now quite old and dependent for a living on their pensions, the Association took up their cause, and issued a call for veterans all over Cuba to send delegates to Havana to join in a resounding protest. Prominent among the leaders of the Veterans at this time was General Carlos García Vélez, a son of the famous Calixto García. García Vélez was a man whose own past history had its political shadows. He had long been a leading figure in the Cuban diplomatic service, and was at that very moment minister to England, but he had shown a disposition to spend more money than his own resources permitted. It is said that the government had once paid his private debts while he was minister to Mexico and that he had recently demanded forty thousand dollars to settle his accounts, holding out a threat of trouble unless this sum should be given to him.[21] Apparently the request, if made, must have been denied, for now García Vélez came out furiously for reform, and in one of the meetings of the Association pushed through a resolution condemning the Tarafa Law. Later, the directorate of the Association repudiated this action, on grounds that the organization did not wish to appear in a political matter that had no direct bearing on its own functions. So García Vélez

[21] "A Sage," in Havana *Post,* May 8, 1924.

decided to found a new society which might serve as a medium for an expression of the public will against the government. Thus it was that the Veterans and Patriots Association was established, and from this time forward for over half a year it held the centre of the stage in the demonstrations against the existing order.

The first meeting of the new Association was held on August 12, 1923, in the Maxim Theatre, Havana. The building was not large enough to hold all who wished to attend, but places were reserved for a number of high officers who had fought in the Army of Liberation. At the outset some of the speakers hoped to confine the activities of the body to the pension question, but, while that was being discussed, in came García Vélez and strode to the platform to the accompaniment of an ovation. He at once asked for permission to speak, and delivered an ultra-patriotic address in which he declared that the republic was in danger and could be saved only by attacking such evils as the lottery and Tarafa laws represented. Others followed with equally or even more fiery addresses, some of them so violent that Heraldo de Cuba felt it could not print them.[22] García Vélez kept jumping to his feet to send the meeting into a paroxysm of enthusiasm. In the end an agreement was taken for a permanent assembly until the present grave problems were resolved, and a committee was appointed to ask Congress to repeal the lottery and Tarafa laws and to regularize the pay of veterans' pensions. Then, after a final speech of García Vélez, in which he bade the veterans to be ready for any contingency, the meeting adjourned.[23] On August 31, 1923, another great meeting was held, this

[22] One such suggestion that Heraldo de Cuba did mention was for the veterans to go to the legislative halls and throw the furniture out of the window!

[23] The meeting is described in detail in Heraldo de Cuba, Aug. 13, 1923.

time at the Martí Theatre, Havana, at which it was decided to make twelve specific recommendations to Congress. These amounted to an adoption of the Crowder moralization program, although not set forth as such. In addition to the three points agreed upon in the August 12 meeting, Congress was asked: to pass laws to guarantee the independence of the courts; to derogate those portions of the electoral code that gave practical control of party assemblies to congressmen and politicians; to vote a law of accounting to fix responsibility for disbursements; to limit congressional immunity so that it could not protect men guilty of common crimes; to abolish presidential reëlection, by constitutional amendment; to provide against amnesties for common crimes. One other recommendation concerned a law of merely passing interest, having to do with customs tariff favors for the Cuba Northern Railway, and two others seem merely to have been reaching out for popular approval: one about giving preferential rights to Cuban laborers; and one advocating woman's suffrage.[24]

For several months, now, there was something of the stir of impending revolution, which the Veterans and Patriots had openly threatened. Talk of an uprising could be heard on every street corner. Interest spread to the United States, where the press gave generous space to the news from Cuba. The already-mentioned articles of Fox and Conn attracted great attention both in the United States and Cuba. Fox's account ran serially in five numbers of the Washington Post during September. To him it seemed that either revolution or intervention was inevitable. In a sense Crowder was the axis of the controversy, he said,—in that the issue was between his policies and those of Zayas. The nationalistic

[24] *Asamblea magna de Veteranos y   aldo de Cuba,* Sept. 1, 1923.
Patriotas: proclama al país, in *Her-*

movement was really a form of hostility to the United States, serving as a shield behind which the politicians were engaging in graft. Zayas himself was very clever in his use of the patriotic appeal, hoping to go to the very limit of United States patience before stopping short. In illustration of this, Fox told how Zayas had enquired of Hughes whether he did not have a right to make changes in his Cabinet. Obviously the American Secretary could not very well say "No," and so Zayas claimed that this admission justified him in dismissing the Honest Cabinet. Fox felt that all the best elements in Cuba, including business men, were on the side of the Veterans and Patriots, and he had what proved to be an unduly exalted idea of the leadership of García Vélez, pointing out that he still held his post of minister to London, though in open opposition to Zayas, for the latter was too discreet to risk precipitating a conflict through relieving him. Both sides were opposed to intervention, Fox noted, but the Veterans and Patriots would like the approval of the United States, and Zayas had gone to some pains, during August, to get the Washington authorities to say that they would not support a revolutionary movement, but Hughes had not given him an answer, one way or the other. Zayas and his followers could not be in accord with the United States, because that would mean an end to their graft, but all recognized that the American government held the key to the situation in case it desired to use it. Fox held that a continuance of corruption would mean an eventual intervention, insisting that it was the duty of the United States under article three of the Platt Amendment to correct the situation, as a régime like that of Zayas did not give adequate protection to life, liberty, and property. In commenting on these articles, Heraldo de Cuba expressed an opinion that they probably represented the views of

Crowder, Hughes, and Coolidge (who had just become President of the United States, following Harding's death), as well as Fox. Though denying the applicability of the Platt Amendment, Heraldo de Cuba said Fox had shown that Cuba was in danger from the United States, and therefore urged the two Cuban factions to effect a compromise.[25]

There was no disposition in Cuba to follow Heraldo de Cuba's advice, however. The controversy continued. Crowder was indeed injected into it, though maintaining a discreet silence himself. Leaders of the Veterans and Patriots openly praised him. One of them, Carlos Mendieta, Liberal candidate for Vice-President in 1916 and now regarded as a strong probability for the Liberal nomination for the presidency in 1924, came out in a public statement to the effect that Crowder was a better friend of Cuba than Zayas. He denounced the dismissal of the Honest Cabinet as an act of "theatrical patriotism," holding that Zayas's nationalism was synonymous with corruption. According to Mendieta, Zayas claimed that any interference with corruption would provoke intervention, but Mendieta felt, on the contrary, that corruption itself would surely bring it on.[26] Zayas, meanwhile, was a little worried, as witness his enquiry of the United States government, mentioned by Fox. On September 20, 1923, orders were given for the arrest of the Veterans and Patriots' leaders, and twenty of them were taken, but García Vélez, Manuel Despaigne, and Oscar Soto, respectively president, treasurer, and secretary of the organization, escaped. On the 22d Zayas announced that they would not be molested if they would return to Havana,

[25] The Fox articles (used by the writer only in Spanish translation) and the comment of Heraldo de Cuba appear in issues of the latter of Sept. 11, 12, 13, 14, and 19, 1923. They were published in the Washington Post from the 10th to the 14th.

[26] Conn, Edward L , The crisis in Cuba: I, Reform or revolution, in (Philadelphia Public ledger, republished in) Berkeley (California) Gazette, Nov. 19, 1923.

but García Vélez refused to accept the proffered immunity. The other twenty men were released.[27]   Despaigne and Soto soon put in an appearance again.

It is probable that the original order for the arrest of these men was not altogether a Zayas measure, for the President usually preferred to temporize, in hopes that delay might eventually turn matters to his advantage. More in line with his customary procedure was a long letter he wrote to General Alfredo Rego on October 10, 1923, which was given to the press several days later. It was a typical Zayas document. He welcomed the Veterans and Patriots' program, for its aims were the same as his own! He defended the lottery and Tarafa laws, but was ready to sign bills for most of the other features requested by the Veterans and Patriots, "if Congress would enact a law." He opposed an accounting law, for the law as it was, was adequate "for the purposes of an honest administration." He had twice asked Congress to enact a law against the reëlection of a President, though unwilling to admit that reëlection necessarily involved disorder, "for that depends on the personal characteristics of the chief of the state." He claimed to have undertaken all manner of reforms, many of them with marked success, and of course denied any improprieties by his government. Throughout, he endeavored to give a false impression, as, for example, mentioning reforms that were really due to the pressure from Crowder and failing to state how they had since been abandoned. Naturally, he did not expect to deceive the leaders of the Veterans and Patriots, but he hoped, no doubt, to go over their heads to make an impression on the people. In line with this were several gentle thrusts at the Veterans and Patriots. It

[27] *Ibid.*

was not to be wondered at, he said, that foreigners should seek the protection of their governments, but he was surprised that any Cubans should have gone abroad to make complaints against their own country's authorities, thus intimating that his opponents were in favor of an intervention that Zayas's own great "patriotism" was desirous of avoiding.[28]

Just a few days later, on October 14, 1923, the supreme council of the Veterans and Patriots, with delegates from every part of Cuba, held a great meeting in Havana at the Fausto Theatre. About a thousand persons were present. The final details in organization were settled, in which connection it is to be noted that such respected figures as Sanguily, Mendieta, Maza y Artola, and Hernández Cartaya were included among the honorary presidents and Enrique José Varona was first of the six active vice-presidents. A new *manifiesto*, or statement to the public, was read and approved that for straight speaking surpassed anything of the sort that had ever been known in Cuba, according to Heraldo de Cuba, even including "concrete accusations against the President." The announced occasion for the document was the resistance of Congress and the President to meeting the demands set forth by the Veterans and Patriots in their earlier petitions to the government. The illicit profits of congressmen and the President on such acts as the lottery and Tarafa laws were alluded to, specifically and without reserve, as typical of the evils which were leading the country along the road to bankruptcy and intervention. The program of August 29 was again recited (though with the omission of the woman's suffrage clause), and the underlying reason was given why it had been decided upon: in effect, so that the President and most senators

[28] The Zayas letter is in *Mundo,* Oct. 13, 1923.

and representatives, who "arrived poor to the posts they hold and have rapidly enriched themselves in them," might be restrained from further acts of lawlessness. The subsidized press was excoriated in no uncertain fashion for its "calumnies" against the Association and its leaders; just three Havana papers were exempted from this sweeping condemnation. Some further agreements were taken, suggesting the need of additional reforms not mentioned in the program of August 29, and authority was given to the supreme council to "decide what it may think necessary for the good of the country," implying even revolution if deemed best. Throughout the meeting there was a great deal of violent oratory, much of which found its way into the formal agreements that were drawn up. When one member suggested that the language of the *manifiesto* should be toned down, there was an angry remonstrance, in course of which Soto declared that there was no necessity for any change, as this was a "revolutionary assembly"; indeed, according to him, they had been in revolution for forty-eight days, during which they had done everything except actually engage in battle.[29]

It is hardly necessary to give a detailed story of the next half year in the controversy between the government and the Veterans and Patriots. The issue was already joined by October 1923, and it was merely a question of time when it should be settled one way or the other, as neither side

[29] The *manifiesto* and agreements, together with comment thereon, are to be found in *El manifiesto redactado por Veteranos y Patriotas,* in *Heraldo de Cuba,* Oct. 15, 1923. *Heraldo de Cuba,* which had supported the Tarafa Law, was deeply offended because it was not included in the list of papers that were described as having backed the ideas for which the Veterans and Patriots stood. This act of "injustice" was not to be wondered at, said *Heraldo de Cuba,* as some of the leaders of the Association were until recently holders of *botellas* (easy jobs) and collectorships in the lottery and organizers of *chivos* (graft deals). In point of fact, said *Heraldo de Cuba,* it had been sustaining this moralization campaign for ten years.

would yield. There were charges and counter-charges in Cuba; in the United States the Conn articles followed those of Fox, and there was considerable uneasiness in business and governmental circles. No outbreak took place during the fall and winter, however. The elements back of the Veterans and Patriots most certainly wanted no revolution in the cane-cutting season, and when that should be finished in the spring it would be nearly time for a presidential election, at which matters might conceivably be settled by the ballot; or if the elections should be conducted unfairly there would then be an undeniable basis for a protest, perhaps even in arms. On the other hand the cane-cutting season would loom up again as an anti-revolution argument. The United States, if willing to take a hand, could have resolved the issue, but Washington, though thoroughly disapproving the Zayas régime and although it might be said to have been defeated in a diplomatic encounter with Zayas, seemed altogether unwilling to undertake a campaign on behalf of the principles it had urged so insistently down to the spring of 1923. So it behooved the Veterans and Patriots to settle this matter alone, and at length the more ardent spirits of the Association could contain themselves no longer.

On April 30, 1924, a revolt broke out near Cienfuegos under the leadership of Colonel Federico Laredo Brú. García Vélez, then in New York, was believed to have given the order for the uprising and to have departed for Cuba to take command himself. Reports of revolutionary activity came in from thirty or forty towns of Santa Clara, although the government insisted that the outbreak was of no consequence, being limited to twenty-three soldiers who had deserted from the army. Later it appeared that somewhat more than that number, admittedly as many as five hundred, arose in arms, but the official reports were substantially correct, just the same. The revolution proved a ridiculous failure, and was virtually at an end inside of a week, with hardly a battle, if indeed any fighting at all. Then followed a series of explanations and recriminations which tended to throw light on the whole movement. García Vélez, who for a moment had been a national idol, was now unqualifiedly denounced. His own bad political past was recited against him, and his leadership of the Veterans and Patriots was described as cowardly, treasonable, or incompetent. Some accused him of spending the Association's funds on his own pleasures in New York cabarets, and one of his associates in that city complained that he had led the other members of the committee to believe that he had left for Cuba, when in fact he had remained in New York.[30] Insinuations against other leaders of the Veterans and Patriots were also freely indulged in, and it was claimed that "The organization was never intended to accomplish any of the reforms that it enunciated," but was designed to attract a following "so that its leaders could control a large part of the federal patronage and mayhaps prove a deciding factor in the presidential election." [31]   Some advanced the idea that Zayas himself had staged the revolution, so that he could gain prestige by putting it down.[32] After all, however, the determining factor in the conflict was the attitude of

[30] For a particularly scathing denunciation of García Vélez, insisting that he was either a coward or a traitor, see ¿Cobarde o traidor?, in Sol, May 15, 1924. Another paper, which, like Sol, had strongly supported the Veterans and Patriots' cause, declared that García Vélez was merely "incapable of leading an armed movement, and much less one based on the regeneration of the country." Neither a coward nor a traitor, in Heraldo, translated in Havana Post, May 19, 1924.

[31] "A Sage," in Havana Post, May 27, 1924. In an earlier editorial, May 8, 1924, the same writer said of the Veterans and Patriots' leaders that "only Colonel Manuel Despaigne can be absolved from 'crookedness.'"

[32] This is suggested, though not positively asserted, by Ramón Vasconcelos, in Heraldo de Cuba, May 8, 1924.

the United States. The Washington authorities as thoroughly approved of the Veterans and Patriots' program as they disapproved of Zayas, and probably believed in the sincerity of the reform movement, but from the first news of the outbreak they came out on the side of the constituted power. An embargo was placed on the sale of munitions to the insurrectionists, while Zayas was allowed to purchase needed equipment from the United States government itself. More than anything else, this probably accounts for the failure of the movement to gather headway. In keeping with its policy in dealing with other Caribbean countries as well as Cuba, Washington seemed to be putting a veto on revolution, whatever the cause. So it was useless to proceed, and the expected uprisings in the eastern provinces did not materialize.

It is probable that many of the criticisms of the Veterans and Patriots' movement, after the dismal failure of the Laredo Brú uprising, were overdrawn. The leadership was faulty, but not so insincere as was frequently alleged. Not only Despaigne, but also Carlos Alzugaray and a number of others were at least honest, whatever may be said for their judgment. Back of them were the best elements in Cuba, who were undoubtedly inspired by a desire for thoroughgoing reform, and not by any idea of personal profit. As for García Vélez, the writer is impressed by the opinion of those who say that his real motive in the campaign of the Veterans and Patriots was not, indeed, reform and not revenge or blackmail against Zayas, but ambition for the presidency. He prated about revolution, but did not want it, hoping, however, to get the backing of the Association at some favorable turn in the political situation that might carry him to the first magistracy of the republic,—and perhaps a chance then to reap his profits. It was a mistake for the Veterans and Patriots to have entered the political arena at all, and certainly for them to have engaged in an armed revolt. As a protesting body they could have kept alive the moralization movement, but their defeat in such a fiasco as the so-called revolution of 1924 gave Cuba to the politicians, who felt henceforth that there was no further need for them to restrain themselves in the pursuit of private fortune at the expense of the state.

Almost surely Zayas had *not* staged the Laredo Brú revolt, for he was frightened; it was impossible to say how far it might go, in a country that disapproved of Zayas, even though it may not have wanted revolution. For a while Zayas put aside his much vaunted "patience," and acted as Menocal might have done. He provided for a strict watch over communications by telegraph or telephone, forbade radio broadcasting, suspended El Sol and El Heraldo (not Heraldo de Cuba), exiled some of his opponents, and arrested Alzugaray, Soto, and other leaders of the Veterans and Patriots. Incidentally, too, he decreed himself a million dollars for war purposes, and bought military supplies in the United States.[33] With the crisis past, however, he soon restored matters to the *status quo,* making no effort (be it said to his credit) to wreak vengeance upon his opponents.[34] And, indeed, there was no longer any reason

[33] The Cuban Senate, somewhat unexpectedly, approved the million dollar decree. In commenting upon this, one writer said: "It makes very little difference whether the lower house concurs or not since the million dollars have already been spent." "A Sage," in Havana *Post,* May 15, 1924.

[34] While the issue of the revolution was still uncertain, Zayas initiated a famous case against a number of highly respected citizens, members of the Good Government Association, who had given out a public statement alleging that Zayas was a poor man when he became President and had used his office to make himself rich. These men were accused of insulting the President, and a penalty of six months' imprisonment was asked for them. In their *manifiesto* they had referred to Zayas's having overdrawn his account at the National Bank and his denial of his own signature on that occasion, prior to his inauguration as President, and to his lavish

to be afraid of them, for the Veterans and Patriots were "very dead."[35]

expenditures more recently on his newly acquired Villa María estate. The judge in the case, Enrique Almagro, sought to get documents that might throw light on the affair, but the court emissaries were refused access to the papers in the keeping of the Bank Liquidation Committee, as also to the files of Villa María. The case came up for trial on May 8. The defendants asserted that there was no insult to the President, as they had merely told the truth. Presently Almagro rendered a somewhat unique decision, holding that there was no necessary reason for believing that the defendants' charges were correct and that therefore there was no insult. It was conceivable, he said, that Zayas might have been an avaricious man who was really wealthy but wished to make himself appear poor. Then lately he might have changed his mind, and that could account for the difference between the National Bank incident and the expenditures on Villa María. And as for Zayas's having overdrawn his account, why Almagro had once overdrawn his,—for eight dollars! So with this "defence" of Zayas, Almagro dismissed the case. (*Heraldo de Cuba,* May 9, 1924). Commenting upon the Almagro decision one paper said: "We do not know of whom he reminded us more, whether of Machiavelli or Anatole France. But we can indeed affirm that the irony of Eca de Queiroz had this morning . . . a terrible competitor." (*País,* May 8, 1924). José María Eça (or Eza) de Queiroz (1843-1900) was a Portuguese novelist, celebrated for an ironical humor which he employed in satirizing his own times.

[35] For some comment on authorities, see note at the end of chapter XX.

CHAPTER XX

EXIT ZAYAS, 1924-1925

ONE immediate result of the defeat of the Veterans and Patriots was the resumption of corruption, with scarcely any further need for attention to public opinion. The Santa Clara purchase at length became a law, early in June 1924, and the most notorious amnesty bill in the history of the republic was enacted in that same month.[1] To be sure, there were other ways of making money outside of the great "deals," as by picking it up in small amounts in transactions that were engaged in frequently over a long period of time. There was an enormous graft, for example, in the importation of laborers for work on sugar plantations. This mainly concerned negroes from Haiti and Jamaica, but applied also to the Chinese. As for the last-named, Cuba had a Chinese exclusion law that was operating very rigidly, according to the official reports of Zayas. In his message to Congress of April 7, 1924, Zayas said that three persons of Chinese race were admitted to Cuba in 1922 and seven in 1923, and a year later (April 6, 1925) he said that none at all came in during 1924. Yet it was common knowledge that they were entering every year by the thousands. One paper claimed that there were 150,000 in Cuba, most of whom had arrived since the census of 1919; a shipload of five hundred had been landed just a few days before.[2] Another writer asserted that a Cuban consular representative in

[1] For a discussion of the amnesty bill, see *infra*, pp. 534-538.

[2] *La invasión amarilla*, in *Mundo*, May 10, 1924.

Canton, China, was said to have cleared two hundred thousand dollars in three years for his visés of passports.[3] In the light of Zayas's exceedingly meagre estimates it is not hard to believe the charges to the effect that he was profiting from this traffic.[4] On the other hand, the government now ceased to do much of anything of a really useful constructive character. From this time forward, to the end of Zayas's rule, hardly a day passed but that some newspaper complained of congressional inaction. For weeks there would be no meetings of either house, unless to pass upon some notorious bit of legislation. Even the most imperatively needed laws, such as the sanction of the budget and of further payments on the floating debt (to say nothing of reforms), were left without study or even to fail because of congressional inertia. The same phenomenon was to be observed in administrative circles. Practically nothing was done to get rid of the illegal contracts in the Public Works Department after the dismissal of the Honest Cabinet, and various of the national services were sadly neglected.[5] This is not to say that no money was being expended. By no means! Furthermore, Zayas was now planning to employ a large portion of his thirty-three million surplus on a "program" of public works, ostensibly for such things as the long discussed central highway and other roads as well as on aqueducts, schools, and hospitals.[6] There was little or no enthusiasm for the Zayas projects, however, as it was pretty generally understood that the politicians would get

[3] "A Sage," in Havana *Post*, May 14, 1924.

[4] *La inmigración china*, in *Diario de la marina*, May 15, 1924, gives a good brief summary of Chinese immigration from 1847 to 1924.

[5] *The streets of Havana*, in *Heraldo de Cuba*, translated in Havana *Post*, May 10, 1924, is one among scores of articles calling attention to the failure of the government to perform its ordinary administrative duties, even in the care of such well known thoroughfares as Obispo and O'Reilly streets.

[6] From an interview with the President's son-in-law, Celso Cuellar del Río, in *Discusión*, May 10, 1924.

the money, and it was suspected that the real object was to assist Zayas to win a reëlection through gifts to various persons and at least a promise of gold to many others.[7]

Zayas was indeed looking ahead to the elections in November. He had gone into office on a one-term platform, and had frequently expressed himself as opposed to reëlection, but nobody, least of all Zayas, believed that he would not run if he had a reasonable chance of success. When asked by a reporter, in the fall of 1923, whether he would be a candidate, Zayas is said to have replied: "I am not a candidate, but if I should be . . . I would not employ any censurable means." [8] Eventually, in May 1924, with the campaign of the Veterans and Patriots now dead, Zayas came out in the open, and announced that he would run again, presumably as in 1920, as the candidate of a Conservative-Popular coalition. He was still "opposed to reëlection," but Congress had "five times" neglected his requests to take action on the matter; so apparently there was no help for it but that he must run! Presently he received the Popular nomination, which amounted to passing over to his right hand what he already held in his left.

The campaign within the Liberal party was the one that commanded perhaps the major share of attention during the summer of 1924. It developed into a battle between General Machado and Colonel Mendieta, the one-time allies of 1916. The latter was commonly regarded at the choice of the rank and file of the party, and he was favored, too, by the regeneration element, for he had taken part in the demonstrations against Zayas and was believed to be a man

[7] Among editorials to this effect are one in *Pais* of May 13, 1924, and another in *Sol* of May 16.

[8] Conn, Edward L   , *Cuba not free but enslaved:* VIII, *Zayas defends his acts,* in (Philadelphia *Public ledger,* republished in) Berkeley (California) *Gazette,* Nov. 27, 1923.

of unimpeachable honesty. Machado, who had been out of politics since 1917, was not nearly so well known, although he had been prominent both as a soldier and in the higher ranks of the Liberal councils prior to his withdrawal of seven years before. Furthermore, whether justly or not, he was regarded by many as seeking office in order to increase his already considerable fortune. Machado, however, proved himself far better able than his opponent to meet the exigencies of a Cuban political situation. Mendieta remained at home, insisting that he would win if the delegates to the assembly voted as the people wanted them to do. He even had the moral courage to give out an interview in which he asserted that Cuba's future lay in her going hand in hand with the United States.[9] That was no secret to the intelligent people of the republic, but it was a brave thing to say, for a few diatribes on the Platt Amendment would have been more productive of votes. Mendieta also came out emphatically for honest government. On the other hand, Machado adapted himself to conditions as they were, went to the Liberal assembly or wherever else it was desirable to go in order to further his cause, perhaps made a number of promises, and certainly won many friends through the medium of his admittedly agreeable personality. So, when the votes were counted, Machado had won. There was some talk of a contest or of a separate ticket, but Mendieta declined to go back of the action of the assembly, although he did refuse to take any part in the coming campaign, releasing his followers to vote as they pleased.

The nomination of Machado was not unexpected, but an unlooked for event took place at the Conservative assembly. Zayas failed of nomination! Menocal proved to have a majority, with Méndez Capote as his running-mate. Of

[9] From an interview in *Heraldo de Cuba*, May 19, 1924.

course, the Zayas adherents claimed that the nomination was stolen, but the fact was that Zayas now had the formal backing of the insignificant Popular party alone. There followed a number of conferences between Machado and Zayas about a Liberal-Popular alliance, and there was a quite general belief that a new ticket of the two men would emerge, with Zayas at the head of it. So Cuban opinion was considerably surprised when on August 23 Zayas withdrew his own candidacy in favor of Machado, with Carlos De la Rosa of the Popular party as the vice-presidential nominee. At the same time, the public was informed that Zayas was to have the right to name three Cabinet Secretaries in case Machado should prove successful at the polls. The only real surprise over this line-up is that anybody should have expected a different result. As between Zayas and Machado, the advantage was with the latter. He could offer votes as against Zayas's rather dubious government control. Only the strongest of strong-hand measures could win for the Populars, and such a victory would be an all too obvious absurdity. Furthermore, Zayas was not in the same position that Menocal had been to employ force, for the officers of the army were for the most part strong supporters of the Conservative party or at any rate hostile to Zayas. Indeed, so great was the opposition to the scantily esteemed occupant of the presidential chair that it is highly probable that his election on any basis would have provoked a revolution beside which not only that of 1924 but even those of 1917 and 1906 might have paled into insignificance. This was freely predicted in newspaper editorials, and was also stated privately to the writer by more than one responsible and disinterested person. And Zayas, who had never been either a fool or a fighter, could see the handwriting on the wall. It is probable that he thought more of saving his neck, in his conversations with Machado, than of retaining his power, and possibly his right to name three Secretaries was merely a blind, back of which the real agreement was that the President and his relatives and friends were not to be prosecuted for any crimes they might have committed while Zayas was in power.

In view of the reputed unpopularity of Machado's victory over Mendieta, it may be wondered why the latter could hope to command an especially large vote. Any Liberal, however, whether Machado or somebody else, had at least two reasons for an expectation of victory. One was, that Cuba is normally Liberal,—not that there is the slightest difference in principle between the two great parties in Cuba; indeed, except for the non-reëlection promise, very few persons in Cuba could have recited any of the forty tenets in the Machado "platform," which (as is customary in Cuba) was prepared and published by him *after* his nomination. Only once in five elections had the Liberals triumphed since the party was formed in 1905, but they had in fact represented a majority every time, although a split in their ranks in 1912 gave the Conservatives the only victory to which they were entitled. The word "Liberal" had an appeal that gave the party its start, and the habit of voting that ticket had passed on from father to son. The unfair treatment the Liberals had received in 1916 and 1920 had also added to their numbers, and strengthened them in loyalty to the organization.

The second reason why Machado could count on a large vote was because of the reputation of his opponent. Menocal was the strongest man in the inner councils of the Conservative party, and possibly the only one who could have beaten Zayas for the nomination, but he was hated more than any man in Cuba. Even Zayas might have had a chance for the popular vote ahead of Menocal, although if restricted to a choice between these two it is quite possible that a double assassination would have been called in to settle the issue. The character of Menocal's eight year rule, coupled with the fact that he was a man of the classes, a gentleman, and an aristocrat, was enough to make him an utterly unpopular candidate. People were sure to cast their ballots for Machado, in order to vote *against* Menocal. And yet there were unusual circumstances that might have given the Conservatives cause for hope. In 1922, when no government pressure was exercised, they had carried Pinar del Río, and lost Santa Clara and Oriente by slender majorities. These three provinces would give them the victory if they could take them in 1924. Several things now gave them a seeming advantage in Oriente, chief among which was the accession of the one-time Liberal spellbinder, the immensely popular and influential colored politician, Juan Gualberto Gómez. In addition, the moralization program had been adopted at the time of the assembly,—a novelty in Cuba,—as a party platform, and this, together with Mendieta's withdrawal from the conflict, which was interpreted as a virtual condemnation of Machado, appeared likely to attract many Liberals. It was stated privately, too, —and believed by many reputable men,—that this was a new Menocal who was going to the polls, a man who was eager to redeem both Cuba and his own good name. Naturally, there were many who were far from convinced of the sudden reformation of the Conservative chief, however.

Feeling that they could count on Pinar del Río and Oriente, the Conservatives concentrated on Santa Clara, which again became the battleground of the campaign. For a brief moment it looked as if there might be an "old-time" election, punctuated with strife. On October 5 there

was a collision between Menocal's own *entourage* and the
police of Camagüey, in which several men were killed and
more than two score wounded. It seems that 1917 had not
been forgotten, for the Liberal papers were full of "Remember Caballero!" stories and warnings for Menocal not
to visit Camagüey. Predictions were freely made that if
he included that city in his tour he would never leave it
alive. Each side promptly blamed the other for the affair,
but there was no denying *the fight*. Almost on the eve
of the election, on October 29, there was another affray,
at Jicotea, in Santa Clara, when several persons were
wounded in a fracas that took place while Menocal's train
was leaving the station. The Conservatives were daily
making charges, too, of undue favoritism on the part of the
government in aid of Machado's candidacy. Strong hints
were given by them that they might go out in revolution if
they were "robbed" of victory, which they insisted they
could not lose unless it were stolen from them. They tried
to create an impression that the United States would intervene if Menocal were "deprived of the election," but this
was a maneuver that not only had no basis in fact but
was also without effect, for nobody believed it. While
there was some truth in Conservative charges that the government was assisting Machado, the handling of the elections, on the whole, was at least "reasonably fair." Only
crass stupidity could have induced the authorities to employ
such measures as Menocal had once used, because for days
before the election it was evident to everybody not blinded
by partisanship that on an honest vote Machado was sure
to win. All that the government had to do was to safeguard the interests of the Liberals as against any possible
aggressions of the other side, but without any necessity
for manufacturing votes. It is probably true that arms

were distributed at various points, to be used if the Conservatives should endeavor to upset the election, and the military supervisors appointed to various electoral districts were almost certainly not favorable to Menocal. Undoubtedly, too, there was a great deal of vote-buying, but by both sides, for that is so inherently a part of every Cuban election that is not considered overly corrupt.[10] Still other steps were taken by the government. Many employes in the national service were relieved of their positions because they were known to favor Menocal. With a view to counteracting Menocal's influence with the officers of the army, Zayas issued a decree promoting sergeants to the rank of lieutenants in case they had served a stipulated long period of years. Other charges might be mentioned, too, but whatever it may have intended to do in case there should develop any danger of defeat, the actual conduct of the government was such that it did not materially affect the result. To Zayas, therefore, goes some credit, not as for an honest election, but for not being so stupid as to take steps which were unnecessary, to produce a Machado victory.[11]

The one disturbing factor was whether the Conservatives might start a revolution following their defeat. Preëlection maneuvers had plainly carried such a threat, but the thing did not seem to "go over." It was "not in the air."

[10] One Conservative paper out in the provinces later bewailed the party's handling of the election in its district because it was so niggardly in the buying of votes. The Liberals, on the other hand, had given a dollar and a piece of a lottery ticket (at a cost of perhaps twenty-five cents, with a possible yield of a thousand dollars) to all who had cared to apply.

[11] The writer was in Sancti Spíritus, a supposedly "crucial point," on the day of the election. There was certainly no interference there, though both Liberals and Conservatives told him about the intimidations in the rural districts by armed men of "the other side." There was, indeed, an air of tenseness, as of something that might take place, and the great crowd in the plaza that night experienced several scares. Once a shot was fired. This seemed ominous,—but it was succeeded almost immediately by a great cheer and an impromptu parade, in the midst of which could be seen a figure on horseback. It proved to be none other than "the candidate" himself, General Machado.

The only real excitement was of a wholesome type, in an outburst of joy in victory that swept the country. Night and day, with or without bibulous incentive, the Liberals shouted their cries and sang their songs, to the accompaniment of cruel gibes at the defeated party and especially its candidate.[12] It was quite some time before the returns were complete, but it was fairly evident from the first that Machado had an immense majority. On the final count he carried every province except Pinar del Río. It was now Menocal's turn, in customary Hispanic American fashion, to dispute the election and then keep the country in a turmoil for several months until a revolution or the intervention of the United States should come along to settle matters. For a while he seemed likely to run to form. On November 2, the day after the election, he and Méndez Capote issued a statement claiming that the election had been illegal and "declining responsibility for the future." The more hot-headed of the Conservatives would, indeed, have welcomed a revolution, but Menocal stopped short of that, although at first he appears to have contemplated taking all the legal steps available for lodging a protest. Several days later, however, he did something that has happened rarely, if at all, anywhere else in Hispanic America: he acknowledged defeat! It is said on good authority that he decided to do so after a long conference

[12] The principal Liberal cry was "A pié" (Ah pee-ay), meaning "Afoot," in contradistinction to the term "A caballo," or "On horseback," by which the Liberals characterized the Conservatives. The latter developed from the fact that Menocal rode a magnificent white charger while conducting his campaign, and it seemed also to carry the figurative idea of Conservative aristocracy as opposed to Liberal democracy. One of the songs heard by the writer ran as follows:

"Menocal se reventó
Que esta vez fué diferente:
Gonzales no era ministro,
Ni era Wilson presidente."

Freely translated, this might be rendered: "Menocal went 'bust,' for this time it was different: Gonzales wasn't minister, nor Wilson President." The reference to Gonzales and Wilson is illustrative of the ineradicable Liberal belief that these two men were responsible for the victory of Menocal in 1916-1917.

with Crowder, who persuaded him to take this course. The big thing, however, is that Menocal *did it*. He even wrote a letter of felicitation to his victorious opponent,—a letter, indeed, which might have been somewhat more cordially phrased,—a courtesy which is part of the normal aftermath of an election in the United States, but is almost unheard of in Hispanic America. This act of Menocal should go far to redeem his reputation, for he furnished his country an example of greatness in defeat. In any event his campaign had not been an utter failure. He alone prevented the nomination and a possible victory for Zayas. And the adoption of a platform announcing a real issue,—whether or not Menocal was responsible for it, and even if it were not sincere,—marked a step forward in the evolution of Cuban politics.[13]

The election was now over, with six months to go before the end of the Zayas orgy. It had so far been an "orgy," indeed, but yet the Cuban chief of state might well have claimed that he had never been entirely free to act. First there was Crowder, then the Veterans and Patriots, and more recently the possibility of a Conservative revolution. All these annoyances were now out of his way, however, and in addition he had virtual assurance of immunity from prosecution at the end of his term. So for the first time he had an opportunity to give broad expression to his natural instincts. A brief term to characterize this period might almost be written: "Zayas becomes himself!" Not quite, however,—for Machado and the law were in the offing if the administration got too far out of hand. And Machado was obliged to speak out loud on at least one occasion, al-

[13] The material here on the election of 1924 is taken from an article by the writer entitled *The election of* *Machado in Cuba*, in Oakland (California) *Tribune*, Mar. 29 and Apr. 5, 1925.

though he appears in the main to have let matters take their course until Zayas should step down from power. So the latter was able *almost* to "become himself," even though he lacked a little of being so. It is hardly necessary, under the circumstances, to say what was to be the nature of the Zayas rule henceforth. And yet, some of the graft deals of this era were so utterly bald and shameless as to cause "admiration," making other notorious affairs appear almost honest by comparison. One of the earliest transactions of this sort was the expropriation by the government, at a phenomenal price, of some lands that were designed (at least in theory) to be utilized as a westerly continuation of the Malecón drive along the ocean front of Havana. While it is always difficult to obtain precise information about events of this type, the following is substantially what happened.

According to old Spanish laws which had never been derogated, the government owned the coast-line of Cuba for a distance of twenty meters from the shore. Nevertheless, whether as a result of special favors or otherwise, many Spaniards in colonial days had been allowed to squat upon these lands and use them as if they were their own. That was what happened in the case of the lot involved in the famous deal of 1924, which was a strip of coast from G to O streets in the Vedado district, or eight blocks of very nearly solid rock that was often completely under water. The heirs of the two Spaniards who had occupied this territory had it taken away from them when Spain went to war with the United States, as the government wished to set up fortifications there. They entered a claim on this account during the Magoon era, and were awarded a large sum of money (which would seem to raise some question as to the applicability of the old Spanish laws), but were never paid.

Early in the ensuing Gómez administration the scheme that was to culminate in the deal of 1924 had its inception. Zayas has not definitely been connected with it at that stage, although there are many who believe that he had a hand, since it is quite generally alleged that his "precious" cousin, Carlos Portela, was one of the moving spirits. At any rate, a rather shadowy group of Cubans made a bargain for some outlying lands of an estate other than that of the two Spaniards already mentioned, paying an amount variously estimated at from eleven thousand to forty-five thousand dollars for them. In the deed it was stated that the seller was not certain that the lands in question belonged to his estate, but the buyer was to take all the risk. The lands, indeed, were of indefinite location, and had to be indicated precisely before they could be recorded under the names of the purchasers. So presently the already described lot in Vedado was selected as the region intended to be covered in the terms of the deed. Not much more seems to have been accomplished while Gómez was in power. Late in 1913 the men who were managing this affair organized as an American corporation under the name North Havana Land Company, to which ostensibly the promoters ceded their rights,—a familiar device of throwing up a smoke screen, so as to conceal the identity of those who were in fact to reap the financial benefits to be obtained. Then there was a long delay, until after the dismissal of the Honest Cabinet in 1923. Early in May of that year an underofficial of the Public Works Department began an action to expropriate the lands of the company for the Malecón continuation, and appraisers were named who fixed a valuation of approximately $2,300,000! When the case was brought to trial one of the prosecuting attorneys in the Department of Justice was on the point of entering an appeal from the decision of the judge condemning the property for the amount brought in by the appraisers, whereupon Secretary Aurelio Sandoval of the Department of Public Works wrote to Secretary Regüeiferos of the Department of Justice, on May 30, 1924, asking that no such action be taken. So when the maneuvering was over, including an estimated expenditure of a good many thousands of dollars among officials of the courts, the decision of the tribunal was allowed to stand. The Secretary of the Treasury, who, oddly enough, happened to be Carlos Portela, now recommended that the monies be paid, and so Zayas stepped in with a decree ordering the payment to the company's agent of $2,247,075.65. This took place late in October, and without any "undue delay" and without waiting for the sanction of Congress the moneys were withdrawn from the treasury. One may be pardoned for considering this a very flattering deal for the company, since the sum it received was some five thousand to twenty thousand per cent more than originally was expended for these lands. Of course, however, a great deal had to be given away. Even El Mundo, ordinarily a fawning administration journal, estimated that more than half of the amount obtained was paid out in "commissions." [14]

Normally Congress might have been expected to raise some such protest as it had made over the Santa Clara purchase, for its consent had not been procured, but its interests were being taken care of in another direction in a deal that was perhaps the most startlingly "raw" among the many of the Zayas era. This was the Cárdenas Bay affair. On November 23, 1924, Heraldo de Cuba came out with an editorial

[14] *The Malecón land affair*, in *Mundo*, translated in Havana *Post*, Oct. 28, 1924. The fullest and most outspoken accounts of this incident are to be found in *Heraldo de Cuba*. The press pretty generally condemned it, and numerous citations might be given. There is an assertion in *Heraldo de Cuba*, Dec. 1, 1924, that Zayas himself "received a million dollars."

asserting that a number of immoral laws had already been passed that month, although the Senate had met but once, and the House not at all, but the latter was believed to have passed the bills in a secret meeting at the close of the previous session in June. One of these was an appropriation of $2,700,000 for dredging and other improvements in the harbor of Cárdenas, Matanzas.[15] On ensuing days, presumably as a result of investigations made by the editor of the paper, Gustavo González Beauville, who was himself a member of the House, the details of the plan and its passage through the House were made known for the first time. It seems that an illegal meeting of the House had been held on June 10, 1924, when none of the officers and fewer than twenty-five of the 116 representatives were present, or very many less than the two-thirds required for a quorum. Three men, named as Oscar del Pino, Bartolomé Sagaró, and Matías Rubio, organized the meeting, however, and in five minutes, according to Heraldo de Cuba, they passed twenty-nine bills, dispensing with readings and the other formalities called for by the rules of the House. The Cárdenas Bay bill must have been very nearly the worst of the lot, for it was put through in a way calculated to deceive even the members of the June 10 meeting. As it reached the Senate it was the third article in a bill of which the first appropriated seventy thousand dollars for a road between Bahía Honda and Consolación del Norte, in another part of the country, west of Havana. Yet the records of the House showed the Bahía Honda road project as a three article bill in itself, with no mention of the Cárdenas Bay appropriation at all. Heraldo de Cuba concluded that the bill which reached the Senate had never in fact been voted on, but had been substituted for the one

[15] *Un grupo de leyes inmorales,* in *Heraldo de Cuba,* Nov. 23, 1924.

passed in the rump meeting of the House. The Senate approved it almost in secret in the sole meeting it held during November.

Naturally, the bill itself had some very remarkable features. The concession was to be awarded under such peculiar circumstances that it was obvious that only an already determined group, or "company," could fulfil the requirements; for example, the contract was to be signed within *five days* after the bill became a law, which would not have been time enough for an honest concern even to make soundings in the bay of Cárdenas. Seven hundred thousand dollars was to be paid to the company in advance! To be sure, it had to give a million dollar bond for fulfilment of its contract,—but with a firm that was bonded to the government for only twenty-five thousand dollars. The other two million of the appropriation was to be paid in three equal amounts over a period of three years. In addition, the company was to receive a *fifty year concession* authorizing it to collect charges on goods using the Cárdenas docks, at prices that were at least double those generally prevailing at the time in other cities; it was to be allowed to condemn lands, without limitations as to amount or quality, for its docks and warehouses; it was to have the exclusive warehouse privilege at that port; and it was to be allowed the use of all government dredging materials and bring in anything else it needed free of duty. These provisions were bad enough in themselves, and the fifty year term of the special privileges might have been worse, except that there was the familiar provision allowing the government to cancel the contract,—on payment of an indemnity of a million in cash to the company. No doubt, it was intended that this clause of the contract should at no very distant date become operative.

The revelations of Heraldo de Cuba were taken up by other journals, and the famous Cárdenas Bay bill became the topic of the hour. All eyes were now turned upon Zayas, who had not yet attached his signature, although as Heraldo de Cuba put it he had been offered "three hundred thousand reasons" for signing it.[16] Some strong representations were made to get Zayas to veto the bill, but he is said to have replied that he had no reason to doubt the genuineness of the document itself, since the president of the House (then absent in the Isle of Pines) had not asked to have it returned, and he thought the bill itself was good. So he proposed to allow it to become a law, though without his signature, through permitting the ten day period in which he might have vetoed it to pass,—a course he had followed a number of times before, as for example with the lottery law and the Santa Clara purchase act. On December 1, 1924, therefore, the final legislative step was taken, with the publication of the act in the Gaceta. And it is possible that Zayas got his "three hundred thousand reasons" with something to spare, for in an editorial of that same day Heraldo de Cuba set his profit at $350,000.[17]

The Malecón and Cárdenas Bay affairs were not by any means the only graft deals of this period and not even the largest in amounts involved among those that were planned. And Heraldo de Cuba was not alone in condemning them. Even the papers that were ordinarily Zayas apologists permitted themselves to refer generally to graft or to denounce some Secretary, while endeavoring to defend Zayas. Over a period of less than three weeks, from November 15 to

[16] In a later editorial entitled *El país de las viceversas*, in *Heraldo de Cuba*, Dec. 1, 1924, it was said that Zayas had been offered "three hundred thousand *weighty* reasons," but the term *"de peso,"* or "weighty," may also mean "dollar."

[17] González Beauville, Gustavo, *Estatua de cieno*, in *Heraldo de Cuba*, Dec. 1, 1924.

December 4, the writer noted criticisms on this score in El Comercio, Diario de la Marina, La Discusión, El Heraldo, Heraldo de Cuba, El Mundo, La Noche, El País, Havana Post, El Sol, La Tarde, and El Triunfo. Undoubtedly, too, there were similar accusations in other papers. The following were among the things complained of, aside from those already described: graft in the custom-house, by arrangement between shippers and government officials; a municipal loan graft; graft in Haitian and Jamaican immigration, growing out of the importation of these laborers on authorization by presidential decree; a proposed European "tour of investigation" for a committee of congressmen,—a bill that Zayas vetoed when it got too prominently in the news; the Palatino fire-company graft; the Güines aqueduct contract; the attempt to dispossess the Caujeri Indians of their lands; the $2,500,000 purchase of the Matadero lands; the preparations for a fraudulent grab of the Christmas lottery prizes, as in 1923; [18] graft in the Public Works Department in the alleged building or repair of roads and in other functions of this branch of the service, notably the central highway project; the proposed rehabilitation of the National Bank; the graft from the protection of gambling-houses; and numerous pardons and other small transactions. Many of these deals never got beyond the project stage, indeed, but it was in the air that no reasonable opportunity to turn an illegal profit was being missed. Quite as objectionable as the deals themselves was the way in which Zayas was carrying through his measures, acting like Menocal, as Heraldo de Cuba put it, in considering the treasury his own,[19] and conducting himself as a financial dictator in expending moneys by decree, on the ground that there was

[18] Cf. *infra*, pp. 561-562.
[19] *Pobre país*, in *Heraldo de Cuba*, Nov. 18, 1924.

no law to prevent him, since Congress was failing to pass budgets or other needed legislation.[20]

There was a great deal of frank speaking in connection with these charges. Heraldo de Cuba had many a dart for Celso Cuellar del Río, the President's son-in-law, characterizing him as the most voracious of the gang. On one occasion it gave the street number and a detailed description of a gambling place which it claimed was being protected by Cuellar for seven hundred dollars a day.[21] And Zayas was not spared. González Beauville alluded to a time, a short while before, when Zayas went to Zulueta Street at midnight to get his percentage in a gambling-house graft.[22] Indeed, the President represented "a new and a tragic dance of the millions," [23] for "In the inconceivable sacking of the treasury of the Cuban people Zayas is leaving Menocal very far behind"; [24] he had

"the sad honor of having been the first President to quote a market price on his signature, at times very low,—pardons, small transactions, etc.,—at other times a little dear, as in the case of the Malecón affair." [25]

In a similar vein Heraldo de Cuba later remarked that Zayas was not an aspirant for glory, popularity, or the affection of the people, but aspired only to gold, in pursuit of which he had disposed of everything he could sell,—decrees, laws, resolutions, and pardons.[26]

The greatest deals of the closing months of the Zayas rule were two that failed for the time being, the National Bank scheme, involving some thirty-one millions, and the central

[20] El congreso responsable de la bancarrota de la hacienda, in Discusión, Nov. 20, 1924.
[21] News item in Heraldo de Cuba, Nov. 15, 1924.
[22] González Beauville, Gustavo, Estatua de cieno, in Heraldo de Cuba, Dec. 1, 1924.

[23] Pobre país, in Heraldo de Cuba, Nov. 18, 1924.
[24] Zayas se lleva la república, in Heraldo de Cuba, Dec. 1, 1924.
[25] Editorial inset, in Heraldo de Cuba, Dec. 1, 1924.
[26] Zayas, idólatra del oro, in Heraldo de Cuba, Dec 3, 1924.

highway project, at a cost of more than $390,000,000. The rehabilitation of the National Bank had been suggested in August 1924 by the Bank Liquidation Committee, an administrative body that had been functioning ever since the crash of 1921. The government was to lend the new institution ten million dollars and deposit all government funds with it, national, provincial, and municipal, paying two per cent to the bank to reimburse it for handling them. A particularly bad feature was the injection of the bank into politics through the inclusion of the Secretary of the Treasury, *ex-officio,* on the board of directors, and another was the provision that the new law could not be changed for thirty years without the bank's consent. The central highway deal was, of course, a more pretentious affair. While nobody denied that Cuba needed roads, the cost of this bill seemed likely to be out of all proportion to its worth and to involve considerable rewards for certain Conservatives who had been associated with Zayas and must now step down from their positions of influence. Some claimed that the graft in the deal ran as high as $340,000,000, and, naturally, there was to be the usual heavy initial payment feature. Finally, in February 1925, Machado himself came out against the bill, calling attention to the fact that the financial prospects of the republic were none too favorable for supporting such a law, owing to the drop in the price of sugar. This had its effect. It was the master's voice! At any rate no action was taken prior to the end of Zayas's term.

The corrupt deals that have been mentioned here were only a few out of the many. For example, the early part of 1925 saw the central highway project rivalled by a bill that was to put immigration in the hands of José Manuel Govín for thirty years. This, too, failed of passage. Zayas meanwhile issued more decrees than ever, and was even sustained in his procedure by a decision, late in January, of the Supreme Court. To be sure, Congress still neglected its duties, rarely meeting. For a time it was interested in "constitutional reform,"—but it soon developed that the most desired reform was one increasing the number of representatives and lengthening the terms of members to six years for representatives and twelve for senators! The movement, however, did not get very far. Another matter of interest in these days was the already discussed ratification by the United States of the Isle of Pines treaty.[27]

In one particular, at least, it would seem that Heraldo de Cuba was wrong, when it remarked that Zayas did not aspire to glory, for the President devoted himself, heart and soul, to a measure designed to perpetuate his name. That was the erection of a monument to himself *before he went out of office.* Popular subscriptions were called for, and the politicians and a few others put down their names. Late in November, Zayas issued a decree appropriating thirty-six thousand dollars for a new park in front of the presidential palace where it was proposed to erect the statue. Naturally, the whole project met with disapproval, and even more with ridicule. It had been suggested that the monument carry the legend "Restorer of the liberties of his country," alluding to his "nationalism" of 1923. Various proposals were now made for other legends, on the analogy of names of battles placed on great generals' tombs, but in the case of Zayas to read: "Santa Clara Convent deal"; "Malecón affair"; and "Cárdenas Bay contract." One writer, after remarking that Zayas's desire for the monument was indicative of senility, went on to say that the statue "cannot be equestrian, because the only animal Zayas could be por-

[27] See *supra,* pp. 157-159.

trayed as riding would be a goat." [28]   When it is remembered that the word "chivo," or "goat," is synonymous with "graft," the inference is inescapable.   According to another critic:

> "The statue ought to be made, not of marble, but of slime . . . In that way his memory will be perpetuated, not in imperishable bronze as befits his frauds, but in the . . . mud that is so congenial to the chief of the state." [29]

Early in the new year the students of the University and other schools of Havana staged a demonstration against the erection of the monument, threatening to destroy it if it ever were put up.   Zayas had his monument, nevertheless.   As one writer has put it:

> "Another project was completed with éclat, a project which shows better than anything else the utter shamelessness of the Cuban politician and the embryonic state of Cuban democracy.   In the center of the public square facing the presidential palace, Zayas erected his statue in enduring stone.   And on its base is a tablet which informs the reader that this monument was erected by a 'grateful people' to the 'restorer of the liberties of his country!' " [30]

In a sense the monument just got "under the gun," for the statue was not received in Havana until May 16, four days before the end of Zayas's term, but it was mounted on its pedestal that same day.

The greatest title to fame that Zayas himself has claimed lies in his assertion of "nationalism."   In his final long message to Congress at the opening of the session in April 1925, he put special emphasis upon it, saying that this had amounted to a "cult" with him.   As he set it forth, in referring to Cuban relations with the United States:

[28] Editorial in *Heraldo*, translated in Havana *Post*, Nov. 22, 1924.

[29] González Beauville, Gustavo, *Estatua de cieno*, in *Heraldo de Cuba*, Dec. 1, 1924.

[30] Norton, Henry Kittredge, *Self-determination in the West Indies*, in *World's work*, v. LI, pp. 77-84 at 83; Nov., 1925.

"Perhaps my greatest reward on leaving the duties which I discharge is in having the full consciousness of having brought about a rectification of an erroneous concept about our capacity for the life of an independent nation and of our qualities as citizens, and, in consequence, of having caused a change from a status of an annoying and belittling tutelage to that of a correct, adequate, and reciprocal conduct where our dignity does not suffer."

In this same message Zayas alluded to a book that he proposed to publish, to be entitled *Four years of government,* and intimated that in this volume

"I shall have to put in clear relief my conduct with respect to the interference of the American government in Cuba." [31]

It would perhaps be too cruel a judgment to say that the man who was willing to risk intervention in 1906, who besought it in 1917, and who publicly expressed approval of the Crowder mission in 1921 should set up as his principal achievement what was, after all, little more than the tolerance of Secretary Hughes for a Zayas political maneuver designed to bring about, not "freedom," but "freedom for grafters," in Cuba. Zayas, indeed, made some other claims for himself at different times, most of which, however,— such as those about prosperity, the "surplus," and reform, —must be discounted or rejected altogether. Liberal organs that opposed Zayas personally have praised him for his conduct of elections, but there they were thinking more of the victory of their party than of any specially meritorious conduct, although, as already pointed out, he was entitled at least to some negative praise. He certainly has a right to consideration on another score. It is said, probably with truth, that apart from matters involving corruption Zayas could be counted upon to take a sound, conservative, and generally correct stand. Business interests were not par-

[31] Zayas to Congress, Apr. 6, 1925,   8901, especially at 8849, 8851, and in *Gaceta,* Apr. 20, 1925, pp. 8849-   8852.

ticularly hostile to him.   Indeed, along economic lines he may have rendered something of real service, though at a tremendous cost.   There will be two opinions about his methods of handling strikes, with which Cuba continued to be infested during his administration.   Zayas pretty generally turned up on the side of the employer, even including —decidedly so!—the foreign capitalist, not hesitating at times to exile union leaders or in other ways to use force. In defence of this procedure it must be admitted that it is hard to be patient with the extreme radicalism that manifests itself in the councils of Cuban labor.   In conclusion, however, making all due allowance for anything that may redound to the credit of Zayas, it is difficult to escape the conviction that he had been by far the worst President of Cuba and one of the most corrupt rulers any nation in history has ever had.[32]

[32] There is not even a fifth-rate book covering the Zayas period, and Zayas's own volume, if it ever is to appear, has not been available to the writer. So, aside from a few pamphlets, one is forced to rely on published documents, periodical literature, and the evidences of living witnesses.   There are some rather better than usual articles in English, notably those of Conn, Fox, Norton, and Spinden, but they need the backlog of the support and "atmosphere" of Cuban materials.   For the details of the story one will go inevitably to the newspapers.   *Heraldo de Cuba,* a frank and independent, if also outspoken, journal has been most employed here, but it is always possible to reach virtually the same result through the medium of other Cuban papers.   The Havana *Post,* with its translations of important editorials from the Cuban press and its capable "A Sage" column, is especially helpful.   Much of this material could not have been used with even moderate safety, however, if the writer had not been able to supplement it by his experience of Cuban life, including conversations with well-informed persons, during his two visits of 1924 in the island of Cuba.

CHAPTER XXI

THE CONSTITUTION AND CONGRESS

THE Constitution of Cuba has many excellences. Some features have, indeed, proved to be bad in the way they have worked out, but the evil is not apparent at first reading, and is due rather to the way they have been interpreted than to anything inherently wrong in them. A Constitution such as Cuba has might have been equally satisfactory to the people of the United States as the one they possess, while the Cubans would have had no better fortune with the fundamental document of the northern republic than they have had with their own. The difference in the degree of success the two Constitutions have had is due wholly to the difference in the two peoples. The Cubans, handicapped by evil political traditions which put the personal advantage of office-holders far above any consideration of public service, have debauched their own Constitution, so that it appears to be seriously defective in many particulars. No document could have been devised, however, that would have been able to avoid the evils in Cuban political life, for it could not possibly rise superior to the level of the people.

In general, the Constitution resembles that of the United States, with a number of improvements in the light of American experience and in accord with Cuban conditions. It is a much longer and far more detailed document, with a total of 115 "articles," distributed through fourteen "titles."

In addition, there is a preamble, some transitory provisions in unnumbered paragraphs (no longer important), the Platt Amendment "appendix," and the Permanent Treaty with the United States in the same terms as the appendix. The two last-named features belong rather to the field of relations with the United States than to the subject under discussion here, and so may be omitted from consideration. The following is a brief summary of the fourteen titles:

Title I proclaims an independent republic for Cuba and adjacent islands, and divides the territory into the six already existing provinces.

Title II defines who are Cubans, including the native-born and naturalized foreigners.

Title III provides that foreigners are entitled to the same protection and civil rights and subject to the same civil obligations as Cubans.

Title IV is the Cuban "Bill of Rights." It is more complete than that of the United States. One article announces freedom of worship and the separation of church and state. Another makes primary education compulsory and free. Universal man-suffrage is provided for, and a paragraph is included "to assure the intervention of minorities in the preparation of the census of voters and other electoral matters and in their representation in the House of Representatives, the Provincial Councils, and Municipal Boards." In all, there are thirty-two articles in this title.

Title V vests sovereignty in the Cuban people.

Title VI, in twenty-one articles, deals with the legislative power. In the main this follows the Constitution of the United States. Congress is made up of two chambers, the Senate, and the House of Representatives. There are four senators from each of the six provinces, elected for eight years, with the body renewable by half, every four years. Thirty-five years is the minimum age for senators. They are elected indirectly, with the selection to some extent influenced by wealth; the choice is made by the members of the Provincial Councils and twice their number of additional electors, who are chosen by the voters of the provinces, except that half of them are to be among the largest tax-payers. The Senate has the exclusive right to try impeachments, confirm nominations, and approve treaties, like the Senate of the United States. The minimum age for a representative is twenty-five years, with one representative for every twenty-five thousand inhabitants, chosen by direct election every four years. The House is renewable by half, every two years. This branch alone has the power to impeach government officers. Each chamber is judge of elections to its own body, and neither may expel a member, except by two-thirds vote. Congress as a whole has much the same sort of powers as the Congress of the United States, such as the right to participate in all legislation, which includes the passing of an annual budget. A presidential veto may be overcome by a two-thirds vote. Notable in the light of later events is this provision: "Senators and representatives shall be arrested or indicted only upon permission of the body to which they belong . . . except in case they are caught in the act in the commission of some crime." Another important paragraph requires that they shall not "commence their sessions without two-thirds of the total number of their members being present, or continue them without an absolute majority of them."

Title VII concerns the executive branch. To be President one must be at least forty years old, and Cuban-born. The method of election is by presidential electors, as in the United States, and the term of office is four years. The powers of the President are virtually the same as those of a President of the United States.

Title VIII provides for a Vice-President.

Title IX makes provision for Cabinet officers,—something that was not done directly in the Constitution of the United States. One noteworthy paragraph calls for the appropriate secretaries to countersign all presidential documents. In effect, this has meant no more than that a President must control his Cabinet.

Title X concerns the judiciary. The Supreme Court alone is specifically provided for.

Title XI has to do with provincial government. Here a departure is made from the system of the United States, in that the provinces are distinctly subordinate to the national government. Instead of leaving it to the provinces to set up their own government, the Constitution settles it that there shall be a governor and a single-chamber legislative body, the Provincial Council. Either the national or the provincial government may take the initiative in impeachments, but in any event the Senate is the court of trial.

Title XII, concerning municipalities, is a section that has no counterpart in the United States Constitution, and like the preceding title emphasizes the centralized character of the Cuban state. Government by a mayor (*alcalde*) and Board of Aldermen (*ayuntamiento*) is provided for, and in other respects the superior position of the national authorities is asserted.

Title XIII declares that all lands in Cuban territory not belonging to a province, a municipality, or private individuals is part of the national estate.

Title XIV sets forth the method of amending the Constitution, making it so difficult that no amendments have so far been adopted. Two-thirds of the members of each house must concur in proposing an amendment, after which a constitutional convention is to be called which may accept or reject it, but not do anything else.

But "What is the Constitution among friends?" A pessimist might be pardoned for holding that the Cuban Constitution has been used primarily to promote evil rather than check it. Government everywhere, in the United States as well as in Cuba, is to a great extent incompetent and bad. There are degrees of difference, however. As one Cuban writer recently remarked, after a visit to the United States, there were grafters in the northern republic, but there were also good roads and excellent schools; the politicians had to accomplish some good for the community they served, not merely provide sinecures for themselves and their friends.[1] There is, indeed, some service rendered by the government in the United States. If, for example, a road is built, it will be a good road. In Cuba, however, it will be paid for at a generous rate, but not built, or at best only half built, so that in a few years it will be worth nothing. The typical Cuban politician is a grafter, if not a criminal; in the elections of 1922, as already stated, more than one-fifth of the candidates had penal antecedents.[2] Not only do they accept graft; they solicit it. As one man expressed it (and the present writer has ample evidence to the same effect):

"Taxpayers are not permitted to be honest if they want to. Inspectors invariably suggest a false return and a division with them of the saving thus effected. To refuse is to invite endless interference, petty annoyance, and an excessive levy. The courts afford no adequate protection. The Supreme Court has recently held that the courts cannot take jurisdiction of a criminal charge against an official unless he has first been

[1] *Impressions,* in *Diario de la marina,* translated in Havana *Post,* May 16, 1924.

[2] Trelles, *El progreso (1902 a 1905) y el retroceso (1906 a 1922) de la república de Cuba,* 25.

found guilty in an 'administrative trial' on charges preferred by the chief of his department!"[3]

This is not to say that all government employes are bad. The great majority of them, the rank and file, are not. Most of them may owe their positions to some sort of influence, but they derive merely a living from them, and not a very luxurious one, either. The only work that is ever done in government circles is done by them, and few people are more frank than they in expressing themselves about the bad character of Cuban politics. One should distinguish between these men and the politicians, including among the latter those employes who are in positions that enable them to get the money. As for the latter,

"No power has yet been able to curb the appetite of the Cuban politicians for pelf. Because of the 'accursed intermeddling of the Colossus of the North,' they have been forced to develop a new technique of public pilfering, but the despotic tradition of Spanish maladministration persists in all its pristine vigor."[4]

Few factors of Cuban history illustrate the evils of politics more clearly than the workings of Congress.

As already noted, the Constitution calls for the intervention of minorities in various legislative bodies of the republic. To carry this into effect it was at first provided in the case of representatives that individuals could vote for candidates for two-thirds of the offices to be filled. It developed, however, that a very small minority might elect one-third of the representatives under this law,—a minority that might conceivably be a mere fraction of a third of the total vote. On the other hand, skilful politicians virtually nullified the act through a device called *"el copo,"* by putting two tickets

---

[3] Norton, Henry Kittredge, *Self-determination in the West Indies,* in   *World's work,* v. LI, pp. 77-84, at 83; Nov., 1925.   [4] *Ibid.,* 81.

in the field which were really the same.[5] So the law was changed at the time of the United States intervention of 1906 to 1909 in favor of proportional representation. According to the new arrangement, individuals vote for the full number of representatives to which the province is entitled, and then each party gets its proportion according to the total of its vote. A theoretically bad feature of this law is that it might make it hard for a President to get a working majority, but in point of fact no Cuban President has encountered any difficulty on this score, because it has always been possible through corrupt methods, mainly in connection with the lottery, to get as large a vote as may be needed. The politicians have succeeded in defeating the new law, however, at least in a measure, through the medium of a practice called the *"refuerzo"* (reinforcement), the practical effect of which is to assure the victory of the more corrupt candidates in a party list.[6]

The United States Constitution provides that a majority of either house of Congress constitutes a quorum, whereas two-thirds of the membership is required in Cuba. It is doubtful whether it would be correct to say that the quorum evil that has developed in Cuba is wholly, or even mainly, due to the difference in the number who must be present, for the writer has confidence in the ability of Cuban politicians to get around any constitutional provision ever made, but in practice a third of the members, plus one (thirty-nine Representatives in the present House of 115 or nine Senators of the twenty-four in the Senate), can block all legislation, merely by absenting themselves. Members of the legislative bodies have availed themselves of this power to such an extent that for weeks at a time there may not be

[5] For an explanation of *"el copo,"* cf. *supra,* p. 170, n. 26.   [6] This is taken up in detail *infra,* pp. 569-572.

a single meeting of either house while Congress is "in session." Nothing was done by the early Cuban government to compel attendance by absent members, but some action was taken during the United States intervention. On January 2, 1909, Governor Magoon issued a decree to the following effect:

Henceforth, no member of Congress was to absent himself without the consent of the house to which he belonged.

No house was to grant leaves of absence to more than a sixth of its membership.

Any five senators or fifteen representatives could form a quorum for the sake of issuing process to compel absent members to attend, with a right to order them arrested and brought to the meeting of their house.

Members absent without leave were to receive no pay. In that same month the intervention came to an end, and the law was a dead letter in the ensuing administration of President Gómez. Toward the end of the Gómez administration the Magoon decree was repealed. Since that time there has been no compulsory attendance of members, and many make a practice of going only when it is to their financial interest to do so. The President is usually able to get a quorum, however, no matter what the political complexion of Congress may be, for he may make it "worth their while" to attend.

The paragraph about immunity from arrest is not strikingly different from the provision in the Constitution of the United States that congressmen shall be "privileged from Arrest during their Attendance at the Session of their respective Houses, and in going to and returning from the same." Congress passed a bill on the score of immunity in 1903, covering all the offences in the penal code, and providing that a congressman could be tried for a crime only after solicitation by the Supreme Court of the house to which the man belonged, together with the consent of that body; without such consent there could be no trial. President Estrada Palma, the only executive of high principles the Cuban Republic has ever had, vetoed this in a message of December 31, 1903, that deserves special mention. In part he wrote as follows:

"The project in this case removes them [the senators and representatives] from the jurisdiction of the regular courts, and creates for them an exclusive privilege which is not contained either in the letter or in the spirit of the Constitution. This, on the contrary, does so . . . only for the opinions and votes issued in the exercise of their duties. And if it demands that they may not be indicted for common crimes . . . without the prior authorization of the respective legislative body, it does not do so with the intention of establishing a personal privilege, but in order to protect the senator or representative against any plot which may be hatched as the result of their actions in the discharge of their functions . . . These, consequently, are fully included within the terms of article 11, which declares that all Cubans are equal under the laws, adding that the Republic does not recognize prerogatives or personal privileges."

The President also condemned a transient feature releasing certain congressmen already tried or sentenced by judicial bodies, saying that it struck at the judiciary, making it subordinate to the legislative branch. If any of the three branches of government, legislative, judicial, or executive, "is worthy of a higher respect," he said, "it would be the judicial power alone."

Upon receipt of this message the House passed a resolution regretting the "unseemly and improper language used." The bill became a law over the President's veto. It is not too much to say that, as a result, Congress has become a haven of criminals and grafters. Newspapers have taken advantage of congressional immunity by employing congressmen on their editorial staffs as a buffer against suits for libel. Indeed, many defamatory articles are published for the sole purpose of exacting tribute or graft. A careful examination of Supreme Court requests for the right to try representatives on charges of crime shows that three such requests were granted down to 1923, and 709 were denied. Fifty-four more were pending, many of which have since been denied, and none (so far as the writer knows) granted. And not only this, but it is also worthy of note that the immunity evil grows progressively worse.[7] In the case of the Senate, complete data are not at hand, but in about a hundred requests, a single one has been granted. It may be added that precise information on this and other scores involving corruption is difficult to obtain, because they are dealt with in secret sessions. Furthermore, it is regarded as a grave breach of loyalty to the group for one congressman to reveal anything concerning the misdeeds or crimes of another, whatever the political affiliation of the offender. Some newspapers might even go so far as to denounce such revelations as "treason." One must remember, too, that congressmen are often permitted to commit crimes without being arrested, because of the known futility of any effort to punish them and the danger involved for the person who would make such an attempt.[8] If in rare instances a congressman is delivered over to the courts for trial, or some other member of the political class, not a congressman, is charged with a crime, it does not mean that he will suffer the normal penalty, even if he is declared guilty. A prac-

[7] Ortiz, 16. Ortiz says there were forty-two such cases in the Estrada Palma era, thirty-five in that of Gómez, 279 under Menocal, and 356 (!) during the first two years of Zayas.

[8] This is expressed by one writer as follows: "By Cuban law, a Congressman is immune from process-serving . . . He can drive his motor car over the speed limits or his neighbor's live-stock, or shoot the lights out of lampposts, without getting arrested. In each instance the remonstrating policeman gets arrested." Marvin, George, *Keeping Cuba libre*, in *World's work*, v. XXXIV, pp. 553-567, at 566; Sept., 1917.

tice has sprung up of introducing amnesty laws covering ordinary crimes, and one must indeed be lacking in influence or wealth if he cannot get himself included in an amnesty. This applies to private citizens and politicians both. Of course, somebody has to be "paid," if there is not otherwise some strong practical reason for a grant of this favor. Amnesties are in addition to the wholesale issue of pardons, but the former are preferred by the average criminal, since they wipe the slate clean, leaving it as if no crime had been committed at all.[9]

A study of congressional legislation in the era of the republic shows very little constructive work and a great deal that is evil. The overthrow of Spain necessitated a new political system dissociated from the monarchical and colonial organization of earlier times. Much was done by the United States military government to provide Cuba with organic laws. Indeed, something of the sort was an absolute prerequisite to the establishment of the new government at all. There were fifteen such laws enacted by orders of the military governors.[10] The Cuban Constitution called

[9] For data concerning amnesties, pardons, and the bad state of the law courts see chapter XXII.

[10] The following is a list of the legal contributions of the military government:

1. Postal code	Order	115	July 21, 1899.
2. School law	"	226	Dec. 6, 1899.
3. Customs tariff	"	198	May 12, 1900.
4. Creation of correctional courts	"	213	May 25, 1900.
5. Due process of law,—against unlawful seizure and disturbance of property	"	362	Sept. 17, 1900.
6. Writ of habeas corpus	"	427	Oct. 15, 1900.
7. Organization of rural guards	"	114	Apr. 5, 1901.
8. Organization and regulation of police force	"	156	June 11, 1901.
9. Customs ordinances	"	173	June 22, 1901.
10. Vaccination law	"	165	June 24, 1901.
11. Railroad law	"	34	Feb. 7, 1902.
12. Railway tariffs	"	117	Apr. 28, 1902.
13. Quarantine laws and regulations	"	122	Apr. 29, 1902.
14. Revenue cutter service	"	154	May 14, 1902.
15. Immigration law and regulations	"	155	May 15, 1902.

for at least twenty-eight more. During the Estrada Palma administration only four were passed, together with a modification of General Wood's rural guards law. The four new laws were by no means the most urgently needed. They covered the following subjects:

1. Diplomatic and Consular Service. This has since been repealed.

2. Provincial government. This did little more than repeat the Constitution, and its futility was amply proved in the electoral disturbances of the Estrada Palma era.

3. Parliamentary procedure in relations between the House and Senate.

4. Procedure in cases of unconstitutionality. All of these were enacted in 1903, except the third, which dates from July 22, 1902. The main interest of Congress in these years was the securing of the Speyer loan of thirty-five million dollars (February 27, 1903) and the internal loan of $11,500,000, both applicable to the bonus for the soldiers of the Cuban War of Independence.

Possibly the greatest constructive work of the Magoon administration in the 1906-1909 intervention was the enactment of a political code. Some of the laws passed at that time have since been revised fundamentally, but the following twelve are still substantially in effect, though several of them have been amended:

1. Organic law of the executive power.
2. Organic law of the judiciary.
3. Organic law of the provinces.
4. Organic law of the municipalities.
5. Municipal accounting law.
6. Municipal tax law.
7. Civil service law.
8. Electoral law.
9. Military penal law.

10. Law of military procedure.
11. Law of expropriations or condemnations of property.
12. Law for demarcation of estates in common.

At least eleven more organic laws were still needed at the time of the restoration of Cuban government in 1909. The following is a list of them:

1. Revision of the civil code and law of civil procedure.
2. Revision of the penal code and law of criminal procedure.
3. Revision of the code of commerce.
4. Revision of the law of public instruction.
5. Revision of the law governing the railway commission.
6. Revision of the law of eminent domain.
7. Revision of the law of public works.
8. Revision of the law of administrative contracts.
9. Forestry law.
10. Law of mines and mining.
11. Patent law.

Yet, virtually nothing has been done since 1909, although the legal provisions covering these subjects date back for the most part to the Spanish régime, and far back in that. For example, under the existing civil and commercial codes it is difficult to collect debts or to obtain proper security. The penal code still contains slavery precepts. These matters have been adjusted in Porto Rico and the Philippine Islands, which were acquired from Spain by the United States in 1898, but not in Cuba, although an equal length of time has elapsed. Governor Magoon (January 6, 1908) appointed some Cuban lawyers to draft a new penal code and law of criminal procedure, but nothing came of it. A law for a new committee was enacted on March 11, 1923, but nothing was done.

During the administration of Gómez, Congress passed only two important organic acts, the Territorial Bank of Cuba law of June 20, 1910, and the suspension of payments law of June 29, 1911.[11]   On the other hand, this period marked the inauguration of notorious graft bills on a large scale, such as the lottery law of July 8, 1909, the Ports (or Dredging) Company concession of February 23, 1911, and the law for the exchange of the Arsenal property for Villanueva of July 23, 1911.   The story of legislation in the Gómez period has been repeated in the administrations of Menocal and Zayas, except that matters have become progressively worse.   Legislation has been personal, not constructive.   There is not even a law of public order, to regulate the suspension of constitutional guarantees, as called for by Article 41 of the Constitution.   The only law applicable therefore is that of the Spanish colony!   Indeed, Congress rarely performs its constitutional duty of approving the budget.   Nine times in the history of the republic Congress has not acted at all.   Even when it does act, it takes the budget the President submits.   On the other hand, down to the summer of 1923 there had been sixteen amnesty bills (with another, the worst of the lot, in 1924), 349 pension acts, and fifty special private donations, usually to individuals.   Between 1915 and 1920 there were six general retirement laws affecting employes on the civil list.   The pensions they were to receive were made *inheritable!*   A three per cent deduction is indeed made from the salaries of these employes,—but the amount secured by that means is far from covering the cost of the plan.   On June 30, 1913, a general retirement law for land and sea forces was enacted, and on April 11, 1918 (modified June 11, 1922), a pension law for members of the Army of Liberation and the Civil Auxiliary Corps, or civilians who aided in the winning of

[11] There were indeed some further minor laws at this time, including an amendment to General Wood's school law, the organization of a permanent army, a modification of a hunting and game law of the Magoon era, and a nautical school law.

independence, was put on the statute-books. This last would seem to be a particularly objectionable raid on the treasury, as the beneficiaries had already had the proceeds of the above-mentioned loans of the Estrada Palma era, besides a three million dollar gift from the United States. The cost of this bill is over three millions a year, and constantly becoming greater.

This functional inefficiency of Congress is aggravated by the notoriously well known fact that a considerable proportion of legislation is based upon motives of fraud or graft. Often there is secrecy about pending legislation when there can be no possible reason for it except fraud. Indeed, it is hard to get copies of a bill before it is published in the Gazette (Gaceta) as a law. When the iniquitous lottery law of the Zayas government was being considered, a certain congressman who was opposed to it was able only with difficulty to get a copy. At the time of the Santa Clara Convent deal one newspaper published the following frank statement:

"We are not going to defend this much discussed question, simply because we have not been given money to defend it. Everybody knows here that when lances are broken in favor of or against a transaction of that class it is because money has been given, or else that the newspapers and newspapermen have not been considered in the division." [12]

Indeed, it is generally admitted that the attention of Congress is almost exclusively devoted to the consideration of measures that will redound to the private benefit of the congressmen themselves, whatever the merits of the bill. The great work of revising the codes and enacting important constructive laws is hardly taken up at all; when there is "nothing in it" for congressmen, there are likely to be no sessions. On the other hand, the lottery law of 1923 received

[12] *Lucha,* May 18, 1923.

a very nearly unanimous vote in both houses, without any division along party lines. Even if there were not plenty of evidence of bribery on other scores, the character of this vote would be indicative of corruption.

A few only out of the many evils of congressional life have been taken up here,[13] but the most disheartening feature is that the legislative body, together with all other branches of government activities, has gone from bad to worse. The failures of Congress to pass the budget, for example, have all occurred in the past twelve years. In the early days of the republic there were a number of men of high character taking part in political life. Each new administration saw fewer of them, until at present there are hardly any left. This is no irresponsible assertion. It is vouched for by the most highly respected men in the republic. Carlos Trelles delivered a noteworthy address on April 14, 1923, showing how the affairs of the nation had become worse with each succeeding administration.[14] In a brilliant essay as long ago as 1914 Mario Guiral Moreno pointed out that the politicians had abandoned issues that might have made for a wholesome atmosphere and adopted all the evils of personalism, with its "ignoble intrigues and bastard ambitions," easy shifts from one party to another and inter-party transactions,—in fine, a system of "I—ism" (*yoismo*). Budgets were being voted in those days, but Guiral Moreno showed how they meant nothing at all, for expenditures were always far greater than budgets, owing to the passing of special laws, often for purely electoral purposes, chargeable generally "against funds not devoted to other objects." He also asserted that the politicians were

[13] Many specific instances of corruption are treated elsewhere. [14] Trelles, *Op. cit.*

responsible for stirring up the race war of 1912 and other evils.

"To prove the sincerity of their preachings some of those 'politicians' have taken off their shoes and stockings on the very platform to convince their hearers that they do not disdain to imitate those who from necessity or habit go barefooted; they have put up with the practices of the negro secret societies (*ñañiguismo*),[15] permitting the production in the streets of this capital of spectacles appropriate to African regions, to the lessening of our good name and culture."[16]

The social evil alluded to by Guiral Moreno can hardly be considered serious now, but corrupt political practices have become more general, if not worse. Enrique José Varona has frequently lamented the growing degradation of political life. In 1921, for example, he pointed out that many of the dangers besetting the country were due to personalism in politics, instead of principle. In the War of Independence, he said, men fought for liberty, and not for Máximo Gómez or Antonio Maceo. Now, things were different, become a chaos of personalities amounting to republican feudalism. Politicians spoke the word "country," but had it only on their lips.[17] To quote another distinguished student of Cuban affairs, "Instead of carrying to public power a proportional representation of wealth, we are carrying wealth to the hands of the representatives of the public power."[18]

Yet more to the point was an open letter of Gonzalo Freyre de Andrade, April 1, 1923, withdrawing from the

[15] The practices of the *ñañigos*, or negro secret societies, are said to be notoriously lewd and superstitious.

[16] Guiral Moreno, *Nuestros problemas políticos, económicos y sociales*, in *Cuba contemporánea*, v. V, pp. 401-424, at 422; Aug., 1914. The author gives a table (at 416-417) covering the years 1899 to 1915, showing the estimate of receipts and budget amounts for each year, together with the actual (and in every case greater) receipts and expenditures of those years. The figures are complete only for the years 1902-1913.

[17] Varona, Enrique José, *Discurso leído . . . la noche del 22 de diciembre de 1921*, in *Academia nacional de artes y letras*, v. VI, pp. 239-246, at 242; 1921.

[18] Carrión, Miguel de, *El desenvolvimiento social de Cuba en los últimos veinte años*, in *Cuba contemporánea*, v. XXVII, pp. 6-27, at 20; Sept., 1921.

Conservative party. Freyre is quite generally recognized by respectable elements in Cuban society as an honorable man. He had just served eight years as a representative in Congress, during which time, according to Heraldo de Cuba, his work had always been "high-minded, noble, well-intentioned, and of a sincere and pure patriotism." In this letter, directed to the president of the party in his district, he remarked that his term was ending that day, and requested that his name be erased from the Conservative rolls. He had been obliged constantly to break with his party in Congress, because the new men had shown themselves too eager to undertake abominable crusades against liberty and the public treasury. He then made a detailed series of charges concerning the misconduct of the Conservatives during the ten years they had been in power, and asked where were the doctrines, example, and virtues of the founders of the party, of men like González Lanuza and Varona, answering his own question by the assertion that nothing but the name Conservative remained. He himself had no plans for entering a new party, but would follow any that would put up for the presidency "a virtuous and energetic Cuban, capable of restoring to Cuba its lost credit and of reconquering its eclipsed independence." [19]

Next day, on April 2, 1923, a *manifiesto,* or public statement, was given out by an organization called the Junta Cubana de Renovación Nacional-Cívica (Cuban Committee for National and Civic Renovation). This is important, not merely for what it says, but especially because of the high character of the hundreds of men who signed it. According to Heraldo de Cuba, they were "Cubans of the greatest distinction, many of them eminent figures in science and

[19] Freyre de Andrade, Gonzalo, *Conservador,* in *Heraldo de Cuba, Carta . . . separándose del partido* Apr. 2, 1923.

the realm of intellectuality, and almost all men who live outside of political parties, without connections or bonds that tie them to their assemblies." The document was prepared by Fernando Ortiz, a distinguished lawyer, sociologist, and historian, the president of the Junta.[20]   Ortiz, long a member of Congress, had voluntarily withdrawn from that body, because he could not countenance its corrupt practices.   Among the signers was Mario Macbeath, president of the Rotary Club of Havana, possibly the most respected organization in Cuba.   Presidents or officials of scores of other non-political organizations also affixed their names. In fine, the *manifiesto* was in no sense of the word a political document, for the signers represented loose affiliations with different parties, or, more properly, were men who were desirous of the regeneration of Cuba, without any thought of personal advantage to themselves.

The document itself was a denunciation of all branches of the Cuban government, making many specific charges. While no one branch of government was singled out for attack, the executive was perhaps considered the most culpable, but the corruption and inefficiency of Congress inevitably found a place in the *manifiesto*.   After reciting numerous evils in Cuban political life, the *manifiesto* charged Congress with being asleep, calling attention to its delinquency in failing to provide the complementary laws called for by the Constitution and its negligence with respect to the budget, while it displayed "an unbridled legislative activity in the grant of fabulous credits."   Many important reforms were named that the President had recently requested of Congress, but that body had either done nothing, or else passed a bill that made the situation worse than before,—

[20] For something further about Ortiz, cf. *supra,* p. 388, and *infra,* p. 636.

and the President had not made use of the veto![21]   On the other hand, during the history of the republic Congress had passed over four hundred laws for pensions or gifts, and over two hundred and fifty public works laws, enough for roads, schools, and fine buildings all over Cuba if the funds had been honestly applied.   Furthermore, it had enacted sixteen amnesty bills, which might have brought about a few just releases, but the majority of those who received the favor of these laws were the worst sort of criminals, who for political reasons (to assist congressmen in retaining their posts) were allowed to escape the penalties they had incurred.[22]   The *manifiesto* then went on to refer to the protection afforded by Congress to members of its own body committing crimes, through the interpretation given to congressional immunity.   As a result, there was no law which congressmen and their friends need obey.   For them the Constitution was a mere formality, to be scorned if it molested them.[23]

It is hardly necessary to go on reciting evidence concerning the failure of Congress to fulfil its constitutional duties. Any number of other documents might be adduced.   Charges such as those referred to above have been made by the most responsible associations in Cuba, such, for example, as the Congress of Economic Corporations, the Association for Good Government, the National Assembly of Veterans, and the Rotary Club of Havana.   In a six months period from

[21] The seeming inconsistency of President Zayas is explained by the fact that his requests for legislation were made in response to pressure from the United States, without any sincere desire on his part for political reform; indeed, as is pointed out elsewhere, his requests were mainly for the sake of appearances, with the idea of temporizing until a changed situation might allow him to escape altogether from his promises of reform.   In this he was to prove successful.

[22] The figures of the *manifiesto*, it will be noted, differ slightly from those of the writer, though substantially the same.

[23] Junta cubana de renovación nacional-cívica, *Manifiesto del 2 de abril de 1923*, in *Heraldo de Cuba*, Apr. 4, 1923.

November 1921 to April 1922 there were eighty-four complaints in the press of Havana concerning political graft and corruption, many of them involving congressmen. And that was a comparatively "pure" era, owing to the influence of Crowder and the financial stringency of those times. The last two years of the Zayas administration would easily have yielded eighty-four charges a month.

What is the meaning of all this? In a word, that the evils of the colonial era live on. For a little while the ideals engendered by the struggle for independence held the politicians in check, but the Latin memory is short, and soon afterward the old materialism and personalism of Spanish days reasserted themselves. By the close of the Zayas administration they had probably outdistanced their colonial prototype. A number of important reforms might be suggested for the correction of existing evils, but it would probably be a waste of ink to set them down. Even if adopted, they would not change things one iota, for the trouble is not in the laws or the Constitution but in the men who are at the helm in political affairs. Instead of disinterested statesmen, the republic has developed a governmental class which is an incubus upon the life of the island. It is to be hoped that this reign of political parasitism marks only a transitional stage,—the storm before the calm,—but it cannot be allowed to grow much worse, or the Cuban Republic will be past saving.[24]

[24] A copy of the Cuban Constitution in both Spanish and English appears in International bureau of the American republics, *American constitutions*, II, 109-154. There is also an English translation in Johnson, IV, 204-240. As for the character of Congress it would easily be possible to accumulate a great volume of items, what with government documents, articles in periodicals and newspapers, pamphlets, and passages in books which are primarily devoted to other subjects. The articles of Carrión, Guiral Moreno, Ortiz, Trelles, and Varona, cited here, are among the more noteworthy items, as also are the *manifiestos* of various Cuban societies that have concerned themselves with political practices in the era of the republic.

CHAPTER XXII

THE FUTILITY OF THE LAW IN CUBA

CUBA has a Congress that has never passed the constructive legislation called for by the Constitution of 1902, while at the same time displaying a ready alacrity in enacting bills which are beneficial to politicians alone. The executive has coöperated with Congress in promoting major grafting bills and in maintaining the government lottery, and it has struck out on its own account to engage in transactions for the enrichment of the President and other members of the administration. And the judiciary has joined with the legislative and executive branches to make the law a mockery in Cuba, all for the sake of the political class, at the expense of the republic. Amnesties, pardons, and the corruption of the courts are among the means employed in bringing about this condition of affairs.

As amnesties have to be passed into law through the normal processes of legislative enactment, involving publication of the record, it is possible to obtain a wealth of incontrovertible material on this subject. Nevertheless, it is usually necessary to go behind the language of the laws or even of debates, because it is so often the custom to use broad general terms to fit what is really an individual case. From 1899 to 1924 twenty-nine amnesties were enacted in Cuba. The record is not so bad as it might appear, for prior to 1909 there were eighteen amnesties which were a natural aftermath of the disturbed times following the establishment of independence. There were nine orders for an amnesty during the military intervention by the United States, and three more (one by Taft and two by Magoon) at the outset of the intervention following the revolution of 1906. Only one of these has ever been criticized to any great extent. On October 10, 1906, Mr. Taft proclaimed an amnesty for those who had taken part in the insurrection, on account of their political acts, but not for ordinary non-political crimes. The trouble was, that he exempted those who had seized property for military purposes. This is the famous "horse-thief paragraph" of the Taft proclamation, as a result of which the insurrectionist soldiers were virtually authorized to keep the horses they had picked up in course of the campaign. Mr. Taft also recommended to the solicitude of the provincial governors those who had committed ordinary crimes before the dissolution of the insurrectionist forces. Governor Magoon's order of April 23, 1907, extended the terms of the Taft proclamation to the government troops for the period of the revolution of 1906.

Very little objection has been made, either, to the six amnesties during the rule of Estrada Palma. The first of these was introduced on May 21, 1902, the day after the surrender of the island to Cuban authorities by the United States military government. The bill called for an amnesty for crimes committed by American citizens during the period of the intervention. An amendment provided for the liberation of soldiers of the Cuban army on account of any penalty they might then be undergoing. Some objection was made to this, because a number of them were men who had committed fresh crimes after having been pardoned by General Wood, who had not granted any such favor to American criminals. No doubt, too, it was the wish of the promoters of this bill not to associate a Cuban matter with what was intended to be a symbol of gratitude to the United States.

As the bill went through, June 9, 1902, it did not include the amendment. The other five amnesties of the Estrada Palma period were as follows:

October 3, 1902, for all municipal employes on account of crimes committed in their official capacity prior to May 20, 1902 (the birth-date of the republic), and for all who had committed crimes in connection with the previous election.

November 10, 1902, for all public crimes of the press, but to include crimes against individuals only if the person damaged should consent. An amendment proposed to include non-political crimes of the press, but this was dropped.

June 10, 1903, for crimes growing out of the strike of Havana laborers in November 1902. On the night of November 23-24, as already mentioned,[1] the laborers had attacked the police. A sanguinary battle followed, in which twenty laborers were killed and over a hundred wounded. In the discussion of the bill the question was again raised whether any but political crimes could be fit subjects of an amnesty and therefore whether there should be an amnesty for a strike. While this issue was not definitely settled, the enactment of the bill as a law must be considered a step toward the ultimate pernicious principle that there is no limit to the scope of an amnesty in Cuba.

January 30, 1906, for crimes of all public functionaries except municipal officials (included in the law of October 3, 1902) to May 20, 1902, and for all officials, municipal or otherwise, to December 31, 1905. This bill grew out of the disturbances in connection with the elections of 1905.

May 19, 1906, for crimes of rebellion, conspiracy, disobedience, and attacks on constituted authorities, between September 23 and December 1, 1905. This was a supplement to the preceding, covering group acts, while the other

[1] Cf. *supra*, pp. 178-179.

concerned misdeeds of individuals. Leaders of the Moderate party held that the amnesty principle should be confined to group acts, but they were overruled.

The black period in the history of Cuban amnesties begins with the administration of President Gómez. Four laws were enacted at that time, as follows:

March 6, 1909, a sweeping, jail-delivery law for crimes to January 28, 1909, when the United States intervention came to an end. The bill was requested by President Gómez himself in a message of February 1st, in which he expressed a desire that it should be "the most extensive of all the amnesties granted up to now." Gómez went on to say that this would be the only such act he would suggest, and "indeed, I propose to close forever the series of pardons." The law was introduced by Orestes Ferrara, one of the most brilliant and respected of Cuban politicians in the post-intervention period of the republic's history. The Liberal Party got behind the bill, holding that it should be the biggest ever, as an act of patriotism, to register the joy of Cubans in getting back the republic. The Conservatives endeavored to narrow the bill. As González Lanuza remarked, in order to celebrate the birth of a child one need not loose his "tigers." The Liberals had the whip-hand, however, and there was a succession of "patriotism" and "happiness of homes" speeches, to the accompaniment of amendments amplifying the terms of the bill. The old objection that an amnesty should be considered as covering only political crimes was "snowed under" in the bill as it became a law, except as this might be considered a special act of grace. About the only thing that can be said in favor of this bill is that amnestied criminals were not released from civil responsibility for their crimes. Not to go into detail, it may be said that nearly all crimes, public or private, that could be remembered at the

time were included, except those involving the death penalty
and crimes of moral turpitude, such as rape or "youthful
corruption." Even second-offence criminals were not excluded, and the President was empowered to reduce the
penalty of those under sentence of death to the next lower
penalty and the sentences of the few others not included
in the terms of the bill by one-fourth. Thus was this somewhat strange means of exemplifying Cuban "patriotism"
consummated.

February 22, 1910, for crimes of the press to February
15, 1910. Press crimes had been included in the law of 1909,
but this was a more ample bill, besides extending the period
of time.

June 7, 1910, a law amplifying the law of 1909, for crimes
committed before January 28, 1909. The growing group
consciousness of the political class was manifested by a
provision amnestying public officials for "any crime." Such
crimes as attack on constituted authority, firing a gun or
pistol (*disparo de arma de fuego*), public disorder, and in-
fraction of the railway law were also added. The reason
for this law was that the Supreme Court had interpreted
the earlier law in a way to restrict it as much as possible.
The "patriots" in Congress would have none of that.

June 29, 1911, for crimes in connection with the election
of November 1, 1910. This bill was opposed by the Conservatives and some Liberals, among whom was Ferrara
(who had voted for earlier bills), on the ground that there
had been too many amnesty laws already.

The Conservatives had made a commendable record in
opposing amnesty laws during the Gómez administration,
but were to add some chapters to amnesty history themselves, once they got into power under Menocal and Zayas.
It is to be noted, too, that many of the laws of this period

were couched in terms none too easy to understand, with frequent references to paragraphs of a code, rather than a specific mention of a crime. At the outset of this period, however, there were several amnesty bills that failed. The most celebrated of these was a bill of 1913, which is nevertheless worthy of mention because most of its paragraphs were eventually enacted into law. Among a number of categories provided for were laborers in strikes, the rebels in the race war of 1912, and (most in the limelight of all) the murderers of General Riva, chief of police of Havana. As already set forth, three prominent politicians had been responsible for the death of Riva, under circumstances that left them small title to considerations of clemency.[2] It was generally agreed that Congressman Arias had begun the shooting, but it was on account of a quarrel of his political chief, General Asbert, who also took part in the affray. The bill referred obscurely to the Asbert and Arias affair, aiming to include the former in a paragraph about "crimes of governors of provinces" and the latter in one about "shooting off a firearm at a definitely determined person." Ferrara was one of those who opposed the bill, and was the only one who alluded to Asbert in the debate, and then without mentioning him by name. "I do not believe that such ample measures should be dictated for one man alone," he said, "however respectable he may be." As for the labor paragraph, concerning which a number of members availed themselves of the opportunity to make "noble" speeches, he called it a bit of *"populacheria,"* or playing to the gallery, to get votes. The bill was passed, but need not be considered, because it was vetoed by Menocal, primarily, it is believed, because of the objections of Secretary of State Bryan on behalf of the United States. The ostensible reason

---

[2] This incident is described in detail *supra* at pp. 339-345.

given by the President for vetoing the bill was that amnesties should concern political crimes only.

The Asbert bill was presently enacted into law on February 2, 1915. The phraseology was most obscure, but it was understood that this was meant for Asbert alone, without any other of the usual features of amnesty bills. Even Arias was excluded, for those who had declared themselves authors of the crimes mentioned in the bill were not to receive the benefit of the law, and Arias had confessed, while Asbert had not. Ferrara voted for the bill, though declaring himself opposed to the general idea of amnesties.

"We have seen liberty given to the worst types of delinquents," he said, "without any other merit or reason than the support of some politician-friend or the blind clemency of our first citizen."

Ferrara went on to say it would therefore be unjust to oppose this amnesty, "which refers in a specific manner to General Asbert," who committed a crime, but at the bottom of his heart is "an honorable man." The fact that Asbert had already been in prison more than a year also had some weight with him. Menocal vetoed this bill, too. Amnesties in other lands, he said, had been given only for political, electoral, or press crimes, and almost never for common crimes, which were subject for pardon, and not amnesty. Amnesties for a single person were even less fitting, even though that person might not be named in the bill, as at present. Furthermore, Asbert had been condemned by the Supreme Court, and it was not wise to overthrow the decisions of that august tribunal. This excellent statement was nothing more than a gesture, however. Menocal had previously informed his henchmen that they were free to vote against his veto. By a vote of four to sixty-four the veto was not sustained by the House, and similar action followed in the Senate. This time, too, the United States government raised no objection, taking the view that Arias was the more culpable. Quite aside from the question whether the United States government should have concerned itself in the first place, it is difficult in the light of the facts in the Riva murder to consider this change of front as anything but a moral quibble.

The paragraphs of the 1913 bill referring to crimes of the insurrectionists in the race war of 1912 were presently embodied in a separate amnesty by a law of March 10, 1915. In vetoing the earlier bill President Menocal had stated that this matter was a fit subject for an amnesty if it should appear in a bill by itself. In like manner a bill for election crimes and misdemeanors to April 30, 1915, for the preceding election, met with no objection, and became a law on July 7, 1915. While the revolution of 1917 was in progress a law of February 27 promised an amnesty to insurrectionists who should surrender within ten days. Little if any fault could be found with these three laws. A bill of 1918, covering the 1916-1917 elections and the revolution of 1917, developed into a political battle between the Conservatives (then in power) and the Liberals, who had felt that they had been robbed of victory in the elections and had therefore taken up arms against the government. The Liberals insisted that government officials and military officers involved in the insurrection should be restored to their jobs and freed from civil responsibility for their acts. But as the bill became law, on March 18, 1918, it excluded army officers, though suggesting that the President might pardon them, without however restoring them to their military posts. It was also provided that politicians would not get back their positions through the amnesty, though they were permitted to have recourse to legal proceedings in the matter. This was supplemented by a law of August 22, 1919, for election crimes since November 1, 1916. A paragraph amnestying crimes in connection with the formation or renewal of political parties, to May 1, 1919, had a bearing on the political deal that was presently to result in Menocal's backing Zayas, his earlier opponent on the Liberal ticket, as the *Conservative* candidate for the presidency.

Up to the summer of 1924 but one amnesty bill had been passed during the administration of President Zayas,—the law of June 5, 1924,—but this was a measure that for utter indefensibility surpassed all its predecessors combined. The Gómez law of 1909 was possibly more sweeping, but had the shadow of an excuse, and was not so clearly on behalf of "distinguished" criminals as the Zayas bill. These, of course, were provided for in general paragraphs intended to cover their specific case. No better comment on this bill can be made than that given in the editorial columns of the Havana Post by "A. Sage." His remarks follow:

"Contrary to the opinion generally held, the amnesty law will not open the prison doors to all delinquents. The ordinary garden variety of crooks will get very little from it, as it was specially drafted to give relief to 'members of the best families,' and only the influential authors of misdemeanors and crimes will be washed clean of criminal 'antecedents.' Those Cubans of less distinguished families will remain in durance vile.

"Heading the list of those favored by the amnesty is Representative Joseph R. Cano, who shot and killed one of his fellow Representatives, Rafael Martinez Alonso, about two years ago, in the Hotel Luz. Cano fled from Cuba after the House had granted the judiciary permission to bring proceedings against him for his crime. He long has been anxious to return to Cuba and resume his seat in the lower house and to carry on his candidacy for Governor of Havana province, to which he aspired at the time Alonso was murdered.

"Ex-Mayor Marcelino Diaz de Villegas, with the president of the city council, the councilmen, and other high officials of the last Havana city administration also are among those included in the whitewashing applied by the amnesty law. The accusations brought against them for malversion of public funds and a long list of other crimes now will be dropped.

"Ex-Governor Vigo of Matanzas province, and ex-Governor Lora of Oriente province, along with Provincial Treasurer Socias of the latter province, who were facing trials for dissipation of public funds, have nothing further to fear and no longer can it be officially written that they have 'criminal antecedents.'

"The ex-mayor, with several aldermen and municipal employes of Perico, who attempted to blackmail Manager Caldwell of Central Tinguaro, will enjoy the full benefits of the amnesty law.

"The assassins of Florencio Guerra, mayor of Cienfuegos, also are saved from punishment by the amnesty law.

"Lorenzo Vizquiera, who shot Policeman Juan Viola, and Angel Lopez Urquizo, who killed a policeman in Vibora, also are set free by virtue of the law, as well as Ramon Navarro, who killed his landlord, Dr. Gonzalez Nokey, in the courtroom.

"Juan Cobos, who murdered his wife on the Prado, in front of the offices of Representative Herrera Sotolongo, the champion in the lower house of the law, will regain his liberty.

"Last, but not least, the son of President Zayas, Alfredo Zayas Jr., now director of the lottery, who was implicated with Norberto Alfonso, the director of the lottery at the time, in malversion of funds and in other frauds, has his slate wiped clean. Alfonso, who was an humble druggist in Jesus del Monte at the time he was named lottery director, soon developed a genius for trading in valuable real estate and made the fullest use of rights he assumed by virtue of his office over automobiles and other Government properties, naturally, together with other lottery officials, profits greatly by the signing of the amnesty law by the President.

"The amnesty could not have been more pious and far-reaching for influential delinquents. It even absolves the unknown authors of the robbery of the $100,000 in Liberty bonds which had been deposited in the national treasury by an American insurance company as a bond for its operations in Cuba; and also all the customs administrators, fiscal-zone employes, and municipal, provincial, and Government treasurers who have misapplied or stolen public funds.

"It will be consoling to the depositors and creditors of the defunct banks to know that the liquidating commissions and their employes have not been overlooked in this masterpiece of legislation, and that they are fully exonerated for anything they may have done since the bank crash of 1920 in the handling of the properties and funds of these institutions." [3]

[3] Havana *Post,* June 6, 1924.

The Martínez Alonso murder had developed from the ambition of Representative José Ramón Cano to become governor of the province of Havana. It seems that Cano, a wealthy mulatto, had paid Martínez Alonso a sum of money to assist him in his campaign against Alberto Barreras, a man of good reputation. It is said that Martínez Alonso took the money, but helped Barreras, who won the election. Later, when Cano sat across the table from Martínez Alonso at the Hotel Luz, he drew a revolver and shot his vis-a-vis under the table. According to common report, a Cabinet officer concealed Cano in his house, whence he made his way to the United States, returning just before the amnesty bill was passed. Following the enactment of the bill he ran for reëlection to the House, and was successful! He was accused of buying votes and bribing electoral officials, wherefore his certificate of reëlection was denied by the Supreme Court in February 1925. On May 14, 1925, some "unknown persons" murdered Cano as he was leaving the jai-alai court of Havana.

There were thirty or forty officials of the city of Havana freed by the amnesty who had been under indictment since 1921. In the meantime they had adopted an ingenious device to postpone paying the penalty of their crimes. The Cuban law allows three continuances of a trial, without assignment of reasons, for such duration as the judges may decide. The men were indicted together. They then began to ask continuances in turn, and the judge in the case sustained them! As a result they had not yet been brought to trial. The case of the President's son was in some respects even worse. He was Assistant Director General of the Lottery at the time he was indicted, but in the meantime his august father had promoted him to be Director

General! No doubt he had displayed the type of ability that was most desired.

The following were some of the categories of crimes affected by the law of 1924: crimes punishable by sentences of not more than six years or by fine; crimes against persons in certain stipulated cases; crimes committed by those who got three votes on a conviction by the Supreme Court; crimes having to do with the press, perjury, and duelling; administrative and judicial infractions of the law; crimes of public functionaries in connection with their duties and of others who were condemned with them; crimes of those who were members of an elective body; crimes in connection with strikes; and political crimes prior to January 1, 1915. In all other instances the law covered crimes to April 1, 1924. Those who were guilty of robbery, forgery, counterfeiting, and banking crimes were specially excepted from the amnesty, and it was also stipulated that receipt of the privileges of this law did not include a restoration to the office held at the time of the crime.

On ensuing days the newspapers had stories concerning those who had availed themselves of the amnesty. On June 6, for example, one paper named forty-two persons, describing their crimes. One was the private secretary of the chief engineer of Havana; there were a number who had been guilty of infringement of the postal code, attempted theft, wounding, shooting, and acts against constituted authority; one was the man who had killed his wife; another had wounded his concubine; some laborers had thrown dynamite in the Havana-Madrid Inn; and Representative Cano was an early arrival.[4] Next day there were various others. One was the former treasurer of the province of Oriente who had been guilty of embezzlement, in company with Ex-Gover-

[4] *Mundo*, June 7, 1924.

nor Lora and others; a number had committed rape; and one had been charged with "homicide through imprudence."[5] The despicable character of some of these crimes may lead one to wonder at the oft-recurring desire of Congress for an amnesty. According to Enrique José Varona it is "sometimes in order to serve the interests of brokers in this traffic; at others, to repay what are improperly called political 'services'; and at still others from a badly directed sense of commiseration."[6] The "political services" of these criminals are usually rendered in connection with elections, more particularly in elections about to take place than as a reward for past favors. Some mention of this is made elsewhere.[7] Family influence has been suggested as another factor behind these bills.[8]

The grafting phase of the jail-delivery evil, alluded to by Varona, comes up more frequently in the case of executive pardons. "There is not a meeting of the secretaries of state," says Varona, "but that on the following day there is published the interminable list of pardons."[9] If that were true in 1915, when Varona made his pronouncement, it is even more notably the case in recent years. It has been openly and publicly asserted, for example, that there was a regular traffic in pardons at more or less definitely established rates during the Zayas administration.[10] Certainly, an abnormally great number of pardons was granted. The

[5] *Mundo*, June 8, 1924.

[6] Varona, Enrique José, *Recepción en la Academia nacional de artes y letras: discurso leído el día 11 de enero de 1915*, in Varona, *Por Cuba: discursos*, 315-342, at 328.

[7] E. g., *supra*, pp. 403-404, and *infra*, p. 573.

[8] Junta cubana de renovación nacional-cívica, *Manifiesto del 2 de abril de 1923*, in *Heraldo de Cuba*, Apr. 4, 1923. The importance of "family influence" in Cuban politics is mentioned *supra*, pp. 319-320, and *infra*, pp. 565-566.

[9] Varona, *Op. cit.*, at 328.

[10] While it would be difficult to cite a concrete case, the newspapers have repeatedly made assertions to this effect.

following table gives some idea of the growth of this evil: [11]

President.	Months in office.	Pardons per month.	Murderers pardoned.	Average per month.
Estrada Palma	54	6	6	.11
Gómez	52	29	15	.56
Menocal	96	30	50	.52
Zayas	25	33	55	2.20

From this it will appear that in his first twenty-five months of rule (beyond which point the writer does not have the figures) Zayas was issuing five and a half times as many pardons as Estrada Palma had given, including twenty times as many for murderers. Indeed, in the race between murderers to kill and the President to show them clemency the latter was winning out, as more murderers were pardoned by him in those months than were convicted. The affinity between pardons and elections is borne out by the records. Thus, Menocal issued 231 pardons in October 1916, and in September 1920 gave seventy-five, of which nineteen were for murderers. In October 1922 Zayas pardoned sixty-three persons, or about double his usual monthly quota.[12]

The amnesty and pardon evils are accentuated by the bad state of the judiciary. There are less than twenty-seven convictions in every hundred trials for murder, and only fourteen convictions in every hundred crimes of all sorts. In consequence there is a growing public consciousness of impunity and therefore a startling advance in the commission of crimes. The population of Cuba increases about three and five-tenths per cent each year, but cases of manslaughter are increasing at the rate of twenty per cent and killings of all kinds fifteen per cent. From July 1, 1922, to June

[11] For the record (none too good) of the intervening Magoon era, see *supra*, pp. 254-255.

[12] The *data* on pardons given here are from Ortiz, 15-16.

30, 1923, there were 833 murders, or an average of 269 to the million. The United States is notoriously bad in the number of murders, but the record of the northern republic is only eighty-five to the million, or less than a third of the average for Cuba. In a presidential election year the Cuban average is likely to jump; for example, it was 339 to the million in 1920-1921. Other crimes are also advancing more rapidly than the rate of population, notably robbery, which is increasing ten per cent a year. In other words, not only is crime increasing, but also, as Ortiz expresses it,

"Our delinquency is losing its culture, is retrograding, becoming more violent and primitive instead of more astute and progressive as in other countries of the world of normal cultivation."

In like manner other social evils have been advancing in intensity and in amount. This is true of gambling in its many and varied forms, also prostitution, corruption of minors, rape, abduction, and suicide.[13]

Not only are the courts ineffective in handling criminal cases, but they are also corrupt or inefficient in the performance of all their duties. Although the Supreme Court at times comes in for denunciations,[14] it is usually given a good reputation for rectitude and ability, but is the only court in the island that is relatively free from scandal. In any event the Supreme Court is helpless, as most of the iniquities can be perpetrated by a resort to courts lower down. Judges are political appointees, and resemble in bad character the men from whom they receive their posts. Many of them do little more than draw their pay, absenting themselves from their duties or going on "vacation," while secretaries are left to do the work. The President has the power

[13] The *data* given here on crime and public morals are from Ortiz, 17-23.

[14] For example, in Junta cubana de renovación nacional-cívica, *Op. cit.*

to remove judges, but, for reasons best known to himself, rarely avails himself of the opportunity. It is said that reputable lawyers will take a case to court only as a last resort, and then they prefer to lose in the lower court, in order to escape graft, hoping they may win on an appeal to the Supreme Court.[15] The following are brief statements about the courts, chosen at random from a number in the writer's possession:

(1) "The courts are notoriously corrupt. Money will decide almost any case. Foreigners usually prefer either to write off unfulfilled contracts or else make an adjustment out of court. Their main remedies are a greater preliminary watchfulness and increased prices to cover the extra hazard of the business."

(2) "I was born in Spain, but became an American citizen. A few years ago I returned to my former allegiance to Spain. Why? Because I was living in Cuba, where my American citizenship never did me any good. The Cuban government owed me thirty-five thousand dollars, and I wanted the State Department to give a hint to the Cuban government to pay. But the policy of the United States is not to make a fuss, if possible to avoid it. I was told to go to the Cuban courts for my remedy. And this in Cuba! So I am once again a Spaniard."

Usually men in business will deny that they have ever paid graft, but admit that the practice is general on the part of nearly everybody else. Now and then a man will tell you frankly that he has given his bit to political job-holders, though insisting, and very likely with truth, that he was obliged to do so. One such instance is involved in the following statement:

"Graft is constantly being thrust at you. I don't like it, but I have paid it, and taken my profit, rather than suffer the annoyance that would surely follow if I refused. On one occasion I had a case in the courts. An underling of the judge came to see me, and said he could

[15] Conn, Edward L_____, *The crisis in Cuba: V, Courts of infrequent justice*, in (Philadelphia *Public ledger*, reprinted in) Berkeley (California) *Gazette*, Nov. 23, 1923. Scores of Cuban references could be added to substantiate Conn's remarks.

get a decision for me if I would give him fifty dollars; otherwise, it looked as if I would lose. I told him I would make him a present of fifty dollars, if I won. He was satisfied,—and I won! There was another case involving several hundred dollars' worth of valuables. I won, but the judge has kept the valuables. He is probably waiting for fifty dollars, and I'll have to pay it. If you decline to enter a graft deal with them, they do not attribute it to honesty. They think you are afraid you may get caught, and are at great pains to explain how safe it is."

A number of specific instances of judicial corruption are referred to elsewhere by the writer in connection with notable cases of administrative graft. The major thefts are perhaps not such a hindrance to ordinary business dealing, however, as the constant, comparatively petty graft indulged in by the judges whenever occasion therefor presents itself or can be made. The following is a typical case, within the writer's knowledge; the names used are all fictitious. Several prominent Americans and Englishmen, including Colonel Roe, his son Richard, and the brothers Colonel and Major Coe, purchased T. Island, and organized the T. Development Company. Colonel Roe was a retired officer in the American army; the Coes were officers of the British army. Richard Roe was made manager of the company, holding a general power of attorney. On several occasions, this company employed the services of a lawyer named Ladrón to draw up certain papers and do other bits of legal routine work. When they wished to pay him he wanted seven thousand dollars!! The company offered to settle for six hundred dollars, which was in itself a considerable amount for the services performed, but the lawyer refused, and brought suit for the seven thousand. The case dragged along for some time, with at length a decision in favor of the lawyer and an appeal. While the case was still before the court of first instance, two things happened: Richard Roe left for the United States, giving a power-of-attorney to the company's new lawyer, Bueno; and the judges learned that the company had about four thousand dollars in the bank at Moreno! The judge of the court of first instance went on a vacation, leaving the municipal judge in charge of the court, while a young lawyer was designated to take the latter's place in the municipal court. Acting now in the higher court, the former municipal judge affirmed a decision he himself had given in the lower court, and ordered the money seized. Then he, too, went on vacation, leaving the young lawyer in charge of both courts, with instructions to seize the money. Bueno objected, but his objection was set aside by the second judge before he left, on the ground that Richard Roe had not left any evidence that he could give a power-of-attorney for the company, although this same judge had, in the first place, accepted the suit against Richard Roe in the company's name and all the papers had been served on him. The young temporary judge drew the money out of the bank *after banking hours* on a Saturday afternoon. He happened to be a good friend of Mercante, the leading business man of Moreno, who supplied the company with provisions. When he mentioned the affair to Mercante that afternoon, Mercante made him promise to have nothing further to do with it and to hold the money. That night Major Coe arrived in Moreno, and Mercante told him about it. Major Coe was a man of no little private influence, and he went into action at once. He was therefore able to get a decision the following Monday for the return of the money to the bank. At last accounts, it was there yet, but still in litigation. The two judges were theoretically "removed" by a *promotion* to better posts in another part of the country!

Numerous responsible associations or individuals could be

quoted in support of the charges against the judiciary. It will perhaps be sufficient, however, to quote the American ambassador, General Enoch H. Crowder, on this score, making use of memorandum thirteen, the only one of the "fifteen memoranda" that has so far appeared in print. As already stated, it concerned the conditions precedent to an approval of the fifty million dollar loan, presently secured in 1923. The memorandum was dated July 21, 1922. One paragraph of this document discussed the judiciary. General Crowder asserted that charges still persisted as to the malfeasance in office of subordinate members of the judicial branch, including the secretaries of courts. He also noted the failure of the courts to be prompt in trying the crimes of bankers connected with the institutions undergoing liquidation and those of politicians involved in graft deals. There was no reason for the delay in the proceedings against the officials of Havana for frauds and other misdeeds, he said. He complained, too, because the bank defaulters had not been extradited. While not making judicial reform an absolute prerequisite to the loan, the ambassador felt that an investigation and proper proceedings should be instituted to improve the situation.[16]

And so on, *ad infinitum*. The charge quoted to the Spaniard about United States policy is true. There is a statement by Secretary of State Seward on this score in 1866 which would seem to have been adopted as the normal practice of the United States in Hispanic American affairs. The case arose in a controversy involving an American in Colombia, but is certainly applicable to the procedure of the United States in Cuba:

[16] Crowder, Enoch Herbert, *El memorandum no. 13*, translated to Spanish in *Heraldo de Cuba*, Aug. 5, 1922; republished in *Tarde*, Nov. 13, 1924.

"We are unfortunately too familiar with complaints of the delay and inefficiency of the courts in the South American republics. We must, however, continue to repose confidence in their independence and integrity, or we must take the broad ground that those States are like those of Oriental semi-civilized countries—outside the pale within which the law of nations, as generally accepted by christendom, is understood to govern. The people who go to these regions and encounter great risks in the hope of great rewards, must be regarded as taking all the circumstances into consideration, and cannot with reason ask their government to complain that they stand on a common footing with native subjects in respect to the alleged wants of an able, prompt, and conscientious judiciary. We cannot undertake to supervise the arrangements of the whole world for litigation, because American citizens voluntarily expose themselves to be concerned in their deficiencies." [17]

This stand is a handicap in the submission of claims in Cuba for denial of justice, although it is probably true that Americans and other foreigners receive as much consideration from the iniquitous workings of the courts as do the Cubans themselves. The Permanent Treaty between the United States and Cuba does, indeed, give the former a right to insist on better treatment, on grounds that the Cuban government, through the delinquency of its law courts, is not furnishing the adequate protection to property that Cuba has agreed to give. Nevertheless, the United States is not at all likely to act in any other way toward Cuba than it would toward Colombia, except in case of an intervention on other scores, when it is probable that a reorganization of legal procedure and practice might be attempted, along with other reforms. It is not with any idea of holding a brief for the foreigner that this is being written. Most foreigners adapt themselves to the situation as they find it. It is Cuba that has

[17] Seward, William Henry, to Allan A Burton (minister to Colombia), no. 137, Apr. 27, 1866, Dip. Cor. 1866, III, 522-523, quoted in *A digest of international law,* ed. by John Bassett Moore (8 vols. Washington. 1906), v. VI, p. 660.

to pay; for the cost of supporting her parasite class is eventually passed on to the people as a whole.[18]

[18] This chapter is based on a study of Cuban government documents and the published statements of various organizations and individuals, supplemented by material in the newspapers and the oral comments of a number of men interviewed by the writer. Of special note in connection with amnesties is the following *Relación de antecedentes con motivo de indultos y leyes de amnistía promulgadas a partir del año 1899,* coll. by Lorenzo Pérez. The collection by Señor Pérez, who is Assistant Director of the Library of the House of Representatives, was based principally on the *Diarios de sesiones* volumes of the proceedings of the House. The collection was never published, but exists in bound form in the Library of the House. An outstandingly important item on all matters considered here is the Ortiz pamphlet entitled *La decadencia cubana.*

CHAPTER XXIII

THE CUBAN GOVERNMENT LOTTERY

THE history of the government lottery in Cuba constitutes one of the darkest chapters in the story of the republic, and, like most other things in the political life of the country, represents a steadily growing evil that would seem to have reached its climax in the administration of President Zayas. Cuba had long been accustomed to the Spanish lottery, but the United States military government of 1898-1902 made short shrift of that. There were stirrings for a lottery law during the Estrada Palma administration, but the President was able to head them off.[1] Just as in the case of so many other iniquities in Cuban politics, the starting-point,—or perhaps better, the revival of the colonial norm,—was the administration of President Gómez. The bill was introduced in the House on February 17, 1909, by Rafael Martínez Ortiz, who was opposed to the idea of a lottery, and said so in the preamble, but recognized that there was a popular demand for it, and felt that his bill was less harmful than any other that might be proposed. The revenues were to be devoted to the building of bridges and roads. It soon developed, however, that the mild bill of Martínez Ortiz was not at all to the liking of the majority. They wanted the lottery, but one with a "punch," like the old Spanish lottery. So a new bill was substituted, and Martínez Ortiz went over to the opposition. The Conservatives were taking a party stand against the bill, but

[1] Cf. *supra*, pp. 168-169.

when it came to a vote many of their members joined with the Liberals in passing it. The vote in the House was fifty-three to twenty, and in the Senate seventeen to two. Senators Cristóbal Laguardia and Salvador Cisneros Betancourt opposed it in the Senate.

"Laughable and ridiculous is the reasoning which our leading men uphold in justifying the repugnant game of the lottery," said Cisneros Betancourt. "It is said: 'The people wish it, and we their representatives ought to temporize with it and please them in whatever they propose.'" He then went on to draw a parallel in connection with the game of jai-alai,[2] which the people wanted, but the concession was to expire in another year. (But jai-alai came back with the "tourist" law of the Menocal era). It was true that Cubans liked all kinds of gambling, said Cisneros, and there were those who were planning to have a Cuban Monte Carlo. Should that be reason enough for giving it to them? (However that may be, the Casino was also established in the epoch of Menocal). There were even those who believed in protection for prostitution, said Cisneros. (And certainly in 1925 it was notorious that government officials were sharing in this traffic. The exploitation of "margaritas" by high politicans was one of the express charges of the distinguished gentlemen who signed the manifiesto of the Cuban Committee of National and Civic Renovation).[3] According to Cisneros the lottery was introduced in part to give more political jobs. (In this, certainly, he was prophetic.) He held that the people were wrong in wanting the lottery and that their representatives ought therefore not to give it to them.

Senator Gonzalo Pérez was one of the principal speakers on behalf of the bill. His arguments sound like those

[2] Described infra, p. 606, n. 25.
[3] Heraldo de Cuba, Apr. 4, 1923. Cf. supra, pp. 522-524.

of a man who knows the thing he is speaking for has scant public reason for existence, but who wants to make a showing on behalf of a program that has already been decided upon. The lottery was immoral, he said, but there were worse things (not naming them) which were sanctioned by the government. In a sense, too, the lottery was not so very bad, for it gave hope of wealth to the poor man, sustaining and animating him. Anyway, the people wanted it, and would spend their money on foreign lotteries if they did not have one of their own. It was better to keep the money in Cuba; indeed, it was necessary, so that the country might have roads, public buildings, hospitals, schools, and houses for workmen, and as a result of these improvements the morals of the people would be so built up that the lottery would no longer be necessary, for Cuba would be happy, thanks to the lottery.[4] Called on for a speech in the House, González Lanuza spoke rather pessimistically, feeling certain that the bill would pass, although lotteries in all times had been condemned by writers on government economy. He came out convincingly, however, against two of the arguments of the proponents of the bill, showing that the installation of the lottery would not prevent the purchase of the tickets of foreign lotteries or gambling in other forms, and insisting that the mere wish of the people for the lottery was not sufficient reason for giving it to them; on this latter point he asked whether the Chinese should be allowed to have their opium simply because they wanted it.[5]

The government lottery has been in existence since 1909, but the material and "moral" results predicted by Senator

[4] The speech of Cisneros and press clippings referring to those of Laguardia and Pérez, together with comments of the newspapers, appear in a pamphlet published by Cisneros Betancourt.

[5] Speech of May 12, 1909, in González Lanuza, 837-841.

Pérez have as yet failed to put in an appearance. Indeed, the current has been the other way, with the lottery no small contributor. The bill of 1909 was signed by Gómez on July 7. It was a long document of nine "titles" and forty-nine articles, supplemented by a *reglamento,* or set of regulations, in nineteen "chapters" of seventy-one articles. The following is a brief summary of the more notable articles:

1. The institution was to be styled The National Lottery of Cuba.

2. It was to have a General Directorate, annexed to the Department of the Treasury. The Director General was to be nominated by the President, with the approval of the Senate.

3. No other lottery tickets were to be allowed in Cuba.

7. Unsold tickets were to be taken for the account of the Department of the Treasury. A list of these was to be published before the drawing.

10. Seventy per cent of the total of the tickets was to be given in prizes.

20. Two globes, with little balls in them, were to be used in drawings for the prizes. The first was to contain all the numbers of the lottery, one for each ball, and the second all the prizes. One was to be taken from each at the same time, and the process continued until all the prizes were drawn.

21. The drawings were to be made by children nine to fourteen years of age from two designated orphan institutions.

31. There were to be not more than three drawings a month or more than two extraordinary drawings (i.e. for unusually large prizes) a year.

33. Foreign lotteries were prohibited.

34. The revenues derived from the lottery were to go into the treasury.

35. As many "collectors" were to be appointed to facilitate sale of the tickets as might be necessary.

36. The Secretary of the Treasury was to appoint them.

38. The collectors were to be allowed three per cent of the face value of the tickets they should acquire and sell.

39. They could authorize others to sell the tickets directly to the public, but the crying of tickets was "absolutely prohibited."

40. They were to turn in their unsold tickets or telegraph their numbers before noon of the day before the drawing.

42. People might have a right to subscribe regularly for one or more precise numbers.

43. The cost of handling was not to be over five per cent of the value of the tickets.

49. All of the personnel of the lottery must be Cubans.

The law authorized the President to draw up a supplementary regulation concerning the operation of the lottery bureau. The republic has been in existence nearly a quarter of a century without the enactment of the supplementary laws called for by the Cuban Constitution, but the decree for the regulation was issued the same day the bill was signed, on July 7, 1909. It went into detail about drawings and the functions of the various officials. The Director was required to give bond for ten thousand dollars, and the Assistant Director for five thousand. In the light of the opportunities for graft on a colossal scale that these positions were eventually to afford, these amounts were a mere bagatelle. A provision was made for keeping books, but nothing was said about publicity of accounts. Among regulations that were not in fact observed when the bill became a law were the following: no collector was to charge more than the legal price for a ticket "on any pretext whatsoever"; no minors were to be employed in selling tickets; no re-seller was to raise the price or to cry his wares; the office of the collector was not to be used for any other business.

Assuming compliance with the law, it will be observed that the public paid $588,000[6] to produce a net revenue to the government of $123,200.[7]   At five per cent, the operating cost was twenty-eight thousand dollars.   To men like Martínez Ortiz, Cisneros Betancourt, and Laguardia this seemed like a bad law, but by comparison with later laws it was lily-white.   By 1912 the politicians knew more clearly what they wanted, and an amendment became a law on July 9, 1912, which made changes, among others, in the following articles of the earlier law:

2. The Director General was not to be removable, except by formal process.   (The intent of this was to strengthen this officer as against his former superior, the Secretary of the Treasury.)

30. The determination of the plan of drawings was to be in the hands of the Director General, instead of the Secretary of the Treasury as in the law of 1909.

31. The number of annual extraordinary drawings was reduced to the one at Christmas.

35. The number of "collectors" was fixed at one to each three thousand inhabitants.

36. Collectors were to be appointed by the Secretary of the Treasury on nomination of the Director General.   All

---

[6] The face value, $560,000, plus the legal five per cent profit to the re-sellers.

[7] That is, one hundred per cent, less three per cent profit to the collectors, less seventy per cent for prizes, and less the five per cent operating cost, or twenty-two per cent.

were to be Cubans, and a complete list of their names was to be published in the official Gazette. They were not to be removed from their collectorships, except for justifiable cause in a formal process to be instituted by the Director General. Something was said about new appointees and those already on the list "who may be ratified" in their posts. (The old law had said nothing about dismissal. Apparently the new law was intended to allow of as clean a sweep of the old collectors as might be desired).

37. "Collectors will not be obliged to give bond for the performance of their duties." (The old law had required bond). The allotment of tickets was to be equal to each collector, who was to pay for them at the time he got them.

38. If a collector failed to call for his tickets his collectorship might be cancelled.

39. Anybody might be employed to resell tickets, but crying them or charging more than five per cent beyond the face value was made punishable by a fine of three dollars the first time and ten thereafter. (The fine was twenty-five dollars in the first law, and there were various limitations upon reselling).

42. No private subscription to numbers was henceforth to be allowed, as all the tickets were to be allotted to the collectors.

43. The operating allowance of the lottery bureau was raised from five per cent to twelve. The Director General was to appoint all lesser officials of the bureau, and was to nominate men for the higher posts, for appointment by the Secretary of the Treasury.

49. Funds accruing from prize-winning tickets that had not been collected and from fines against collectors were to be paid into the lottery bureau.

The virtual effect of this law was to make the lottery bureau an autonomous department, instead of a mere branch of the Department of the Treasury, as before. The new percentage assigned to the bureau for operating costs was so extravagant that it was amended by presidential decree of the same date as the bill to nine per cent, and still further to eight per cent by a law of October 29, 1914. On this basis the financial result for a single drawing remained the same as before, except that the operating cost was increased from twenty-eight thousand dollars to $44,800, and the net revenue decreased from $123,200 to $106,400, or nineteen per cent of the face value of the tickets. This was the only apparent change, but an entering wedge for corruption was established, especially through the provisions that removed the bureau from the control of the Secretary of the Treasury. In point of fact it has existed since 1912 as a virtually independent branch of government, subject only to the President. In consequence a number of evil practices came into existence, as follows:

There was no audit of the bureau's accounts by the Auditor General and no inspection of its work by the Secretary of the Treasury. If books were kept, they were merely for the private information of the bureau officials and the President. The full eight per cent expense was always drawn, and as this was far beyond the actual expenses of the bureau the greater part was employed in political patronage.

A figure quite outside the intent of the law appeared in the wholesale dealers (*acaparadores*), who bought up the tickets at an advance in price from the collectors and sold them at a still higher price to the resellers. As one result the collectorship (*colecturía*) became a valuable privilege involving no risk and no labor, and was eagerly sought by those having personal or political influence. Furthermore, the extra profit to the collector and the profit to the whole-sale dealer were added to the cost of the tickets in violation of the law, so that the price now ranged from perhaps a minimum of twenty-four dollars to a maximum that might be as high as forty, instead of the legal twenty-one; out in the rural districts the price is said to have reached fifty dollars, at times. Perhaps thirty dollars would be a fair average for the cost of a ticket during the operation of this law.

It became the practice to cede the three per cent, formerly allowed as the profit of the collectors, to the officials of the bureau as a reward for their coöperation in enabling the collectors and wholesalers to get their illegal profit.

No attempt was made to comply with the law with re-gard to collectorships. Instead of a legal five or six hun-dred, there were as many as two thousand in 1922. Ap-pointments, which were supposed to be permanent during good behavior, were in fact revocable at the will of the Director General. The names appearing in the register of collectors were fictitious, back of which the real holders hid their identity.

On this basis the actual financial result in violation of the law showed a startlingly increased cost to the public, although the net to the treasury was not disturbed. This is most vividly represented if one takes, not merely the figures for a single drawing, but the sum total for the drawings of an entire year. With the inclusion of the proceeds of the Christmas lottery the government's nine-teen per cent net amounted to about four million dollars. Meanwhile the people paid $31,579,000 (one hundred and fifty per cent) for at least a theoretical opportunity to win $14,737,100 (seventy per cent) in prizes. The collectors, wholesalers, and resellers between them took in an illegal $9,473,400, to say nothing of the above-mentioned three per cent graft of $631,600 or the excess over actual costs from the $1,684,300 (eight per cent) allowed for the administrative needs of the bureau. From this it appears that the Cuban people were paying some ten dollars a head for lottery tickets each year, of which more than three dollars, or a total of some nine millions and a half, was mulcted from them in defiance of law, for corrupt purposes. As Cuban revenues in the Zayas period varied from some fifty-five millions to seventy-five millions, it will be seen that the graft bill of the lottery alone has ranged from thirteen to eighteen per cent of the total government receipts from all sources, while the cost to the public has been from forty to sixty per cent of that amount, to produce a net yield of only five to seven per cent. The biggest part of the illegal profit went to the collectors, who averaged about $273 a month for each of the approximately two thousand collectorships, or $3,276 a year. In point of fact, however, there were not two thousand *collectors!* Many individuals held more than one collectorship. A careful investigation revealed the following corrupt situation during the Zayas period:

Some eight or nine hundred collectorships were reserved by the Director General himself for direct sale to wholesalers. This yielded from two hundred thousand dollars to $250,000 a month, or $2,400,000 to three millions a year, for the personal or political uses of the President and the Director General. According to one writer [8] President Zayas took over a million a year from this sum, and the Director

---

[3] Conn, Edward L   , *Cuba Public ledger,* reprinted in) Berkeley *not free but enslaved:* VI, *Huge* (California) *Gazette,* Nov. 24, 1923. *graft in the lottery,* in (Philadelphia

General (who by an extraordinary coincidence happened to be the President's own son!) a sum almost as large. The remainder was used as a "slush fund," especially for distribution among the newspapers.

Some two hundred collectorships were distributed among senators, and two hundred and fifty to three hundred more to members of the House. The average number of collectorships held by senators was about eight, but one senator was known to have sixteen and another fourteen. Not more than two senators had no collectorships at all. The average for representatives was between two and three, but several were known to have six, while there were not more than ten at the outside without any.

The remaining six or eight hundred were distributed to various members of the political class. Curiously enough, Cabinet officers held a comparatively small number, but this is not to be wondered at, for they had remarkable opportunities for graft in other ways. Officers of the police, army officers, political leaders other than congressmen (and of all parties!), newspaper men, judges, and men or women who were prominent for other reasons were among the holders. *A very few* were given to crippled or aged veterans or to the widows of distinguished Cuban patriots.

These facts about the lottery, which were notorious, were particularly in the public eye in 1921 and 1922, when the republic was in need of a loan. As already mentioned, the depression of 1920-1921 had caused Cuba to default on the interest and sinking fund requirements of the bonded debt, while there was a floating debt that was believed to be about fifty million dollars. One of the stumbling-blocks in the way of negotiating a fresh loan was the well-known corruption of the lottery bureau. Various suggestions by prominent individuals and civic institutions were made, most of which amounted to little more than a call for an enforcement of the law, and at length President Zayas agreed to do something. On June 26, 1922, he issued an executive decree for the reform of the lottery. This was a clever document, like the man who wrote it, but it was not sincere. The decree pretended to reëstablish the lottery on a lawful basis, but it did not clearly do away with the wholesale dealers, or deprive the collectors of their sinecure, or require the bureau to be held accountable before the courts for violations of law, and no steps were taken to remove the corrupt officials of the lottery. As was natural, the former illegal practices continued. The President is said to have promised, however, to amend these details, or even to bring about the abolition of the lottery altogether. The bankers had been particularly concerned over this matter, but eventually seem to have been satisfied that something would be done, and loaned Cuba fifty million dollars. Meanwhile, too, there had been a favorable turn in the sugar market, and government receipts began to pick up.

Zayas now had the loan, and there was every indication that the depression was past. He was therefore ready and eager to repudiate his promises, though skilful, as always, in "saving face" and appearing to act as he had agreed. It was at this time that he raised the "nationalism" cry against the interference of the United States in Cuban affairs. The retention of the lottery was but a single factor in this campaign, but was an important one. So the expected bill for the suppression of the lottery turned out to be quite something else! It is the general belief in Cuba, by friend and foe of Zayas alike, that the new lottery law, which was eventually put on the statute-books under date of August 4, 1923, was prepared in the presidential palace. It was then put through the Senate and House by one of those surprise votes for which the Cuban Congress is quite too famous. The first time the general public knew that such a bill was pending was when the papers of April 28, 1923, carried news items that the bill had been reported out and passed unanimously by the Senate on the day before. The House did not act until July 10, when it held an all-night session and passed the bill in the early morning of the 11th by ninety-five to five. The substantial unanimity of these votes is noteworthy. The press charged that it was because the congressmen had been promised a number of additional collectorships.

The lottery law of 1909 is sometimes referred to as the "bad" law, while the law of 1912 is styled "worse," leaving to the law of 1923 the popular credit of being the "worst." In effect, it legalized the former unlawful practices. The bill itself masqueraded as a pension law on behalf of veterans and as a bonus to government employes; the bonus had been promised by a law of 1920, to take care of the increased cost of living, but had never been paid. The lottery on its new basis was merely "an incident" in this bill, to provide the funds for these admittedly worthy purposes. There was also a long "nationalistic" preamble, insulting the United States, but this has been discussed already; no doubt, it was intended to account for the virtually unanimous vote the bill was designed to have. President Zayas vetoed it, knowing full well that he would not be "sustained." There was no fire in the President's veto. On the contrary, he praised Congress for the "noble" sentiments it had expressed,—in the preamble. With this preliminary "clap-trap" out of the way, attention may now be given to the really fundamental thing,—the terms of the new law. The following noteworthy changes were made in articles of the previous law:

2. The bureau was made autonomous. (This was a fresh step away from the Secretary of the Treasury, leaving the lottery management entirely a matter between the President and the Director General).

31. The maximum number of tickets was set at thirty-five thousand, except for the Christmas lottery, the number for which was to be decided by the Director General, in agreement with the President.

35. There were to be two thousand collectorships, established wherever the Director General might deem best, and the law was so ambiguously worded that it was now made to appear that more than one collectorship could be held by a single person. (This not only greatly increased the legal number of collectorships and endorsed the plural holding evil, but also removed former restrictions on territorial distribution in accord with population).

36. Collectors were to be appointed by the Director General, with the approval of the President. They were to hold their posts for life, being irremovable, except on voluntary retirement, failure to make the payments for their tickets as required by law, imprisonment for crime, loss of citizenship, or mental incapacity. (This again strengthened the Director General, in conjunction with the President. And the former requirement for publication of the names of collectors was omitted! A seemingly inconsistent feature declared that these "life" collectorships were assignable. One might wonder whose "life" was involved).

39. The prohibition against increasing the price of a ticket more than five per cent beyond its face value was omitted!

All existing collectorships were cancelled! The new collectors were to be appointed within thirty days after the bill should become a law. In overcoming the President's veto, the House prefixed a resolution explaining why it had voted for the law. The principal play was made on "nationalism," in an attack on the United States, but one of the other reasons assigned was to do away with the "immorality" of the unstable tenure of the collectors, who were menaced with a possible loss of their collectorships under the old law. Nevertheless, as will be observed, the solicitude of the House for the collectors was most tenderly expressed in the bill itself by depriving *all of them* of their posts,—very likely so that congressmen might get more collectorships for themselves. Now that his "veto" had been overcome, President Zayas sanctioned the law. When it was published in the Gazette, a composite of the entire law as it then stood was inserted. No doubt, this may have served to keep some people from looking up the former derogated provisions, thus concealing the all too obvious iniquity of the law of 1923.

The financial result of the new law would normally be similar to that of the illegal operation of the old law, except that thirty-five thousand tickets are now issued for each drawing, but, for reasons that are not altogether clear, the profit on the tickets has not been so great as before. A decline in Cuban prosperity has, doubtless, had much to do with it. It may be due in part to a loss of confidence in the honesty of the lottery from the standpoint of drawings for prizes. On this score a somewhat celebrated incident is alleged to have taken place in connection with the Christmas lottery of 1923. The President's wife won the second prize, which amounted to two hundred thousand dollars. Quite a story is told about this affair,—one that has been repeated in perhaps every newspaper of the island. It is said that a certain man had long been in the habit of buying the full ticket[9] for number 4,444. The 1909 law gave

[9] Each ticket is divided into a hundred pieces, and each piece shares proportionately in any prize that may be won.

individuals a right to do this, and, although that provision was not retained in later laws, it was customary to permit it. Putting in his bid, as usual, for number 4,444, the man was told he could not have it, because the wife of the President had asked for it. When the story came out, after the number had won its huge prize, the fame of "*los cuatro cuatros*" (the four fours) reached to the farthest village, and not a few protests were voiced. At one place, for example, a parade was staged in which a goat with four fours painted on him was the central figure. As the word "*chivo*," which means "goat," is the Cuban equivalent of "graft," the implication was clear.[10]

This is by no means the only story of its kind concerning dishonest manipulation of the lottery since it has been under the control of the President and his son, following the law of 1923. It is said that the first prize of three hundred thousand dollars, in the Christmas lottery of 1923, was also won in the palace, though no one person held the full ticket. Some newspapers charged that a new deal was being arranged, prior to the Christmas lottery of 1924. The names of the winners of large prizes are not given out, and it is believed that much fraud develops from this fact. It is said, for example, that the Director General collects all the prizes on unsold numbers that are returned to the bureau before the drawing. As the books of the lottery have never been audited, this certainly would be possible. There may be no truth in these rumors, but the record of the President and his son (the latter of whom was indicted for malfeasance in office when he was Assistant Director General of the lottery in 1921) leads one to believe that if these things can

[10] Many insist that such a fraud as the one alleged in the case of the four fours is impossible, with the publicity of drawings, but it has been explained to the writer just how it might be worked for one number. It cannot be asserted, however, that that method was employed.

be done they have done them. Certainly, one would have to be an optimist to believe that he had his full lawful percentage of chance for a prize when he bought a ticket. And yet, though the excess of cost above the face value has declined, the lottery is far from a moribund institution. People buy tickets, perhaps, in hopes that the lottery officials will let a few prizes slip through their hands. Possibly even they are too optimistic.[11]

[11] The lottery laws are to be found in various sections of the published documents of the republic,—for example, in the following: the *Gaceta,* or official Gazette; República de Cuba, *Leyes y decretos de la república;* and *Diarios de sesiones,* or journals of Congress, with each house having its own set. The last-named item is particularly interesting for the earlier period, as it gives a detailed account of the debates. Lately, the "surprise vote" method of legislation has cut down the record of speeches. Important laws are often published separately in pamphlet form, and a number of publications of lottery laws have appeared. It would not be difficult to accumulate a volume of items dealing with discussions of the lottery. The very great majority contain denunciations on the score of its corruption, while a much smaller number object to the institution itself.

CHAPTER XXIV

CUBAN ELECTION EVILS

THE legislative, executive, and judicial branches of the Cuban government are notoriously corrupt or inefficient, usually both, and this is a condition of affairs that is generally recognized and deplored, except by the political class, which profits from it. If this is so, why then do not the people make a clean sweep of their rulers through use of the ballot? This is a question that might be asked seriously outside of Cuba, but hardly in that republic itself. The people do not overturn the politicians, because the latter will give them no chance to do so. All the people may do, at the best, is to choose among candidates that are perhaps equally bad, and sometimes not even this much of a privilege is accorded them.

Social and economic conditions in Cuba make political life very different from what it is in the United States.[1] As in most Hispanic lands, so too in Cuba, the native-born "better class" elements have had but indifferent success in competing with foreigners in business, although, indeed, there are some noteworthy exceptions. So the great majority of the educated Cubans feel that they have no alternative but to go into one of the professions (law, medicine, teaching, arms, literature, journalism, engineering, architecture) or into politics. Often, indeed, they combine the two, the better to make both ends meet. To some extent this springs

[1] A moderately extensive survey of social and economic conditions is given *infra* in chapters XXV and XXVI.

564

from necessity, as the pickings in the professions are not great enough to enable all who are in them to live on a moderately good scale. It is a "necessity," for there is a wide separation of classes in Cuba, with very little of the middle-class element that is the backbone of a country like the United States. The well-born Cuban would on no account engage in manual labor. He has reached a stage where he will consider a good business position but even that has not yet attained to a very high place in the social scale. Certainly, the humdrum life in the lower ranks of business, with its slow progress toward a remotely possible affluence, has nothing in it for the Cuban to compare with politics, not even with the light-paying, but highly respected small government job. The game of politics, with all its risks,—even risk of death in troubled times,—appeals to the Hispanic love of adventure. And for the more fortunate it points the royal road to wealth, a wealth that may run far into the millions, on a financial capital of less than a "shoestring." To be sure, riches can be obtained only through utilizing one's opportunities for corruption, but so firmly rooted is the Spanish colonial practice of "government for the sake of the office-holders" that almost no social stigma is involved in graft, and there is hardly any need for concealment. It is the traditionally expected thing, and merely evidences the fact that the man who engages in it is "not a fool."

The successful politician has more than himself and his own immediate family to look out for, however. He must do what he can to see that all his relatives and his wife's relatives get jobs that will at least yield them a living wage, or better than that, if possible. This comes about through the curse of family influence, an evil of Hispanic life that is comparatively unknown in the United States. In Cuba it has frequently happened that a President has appointed, not one, but several of his relatives to some of the highest posts of government. Zayas was especially notorious for this. Other politicians do what they can in proportion to their opportunities. And father, brother, son, uncle, nephew, cousin to the nth degree, and various "in-laws" are all members of "the family" in Cuba. Besides, one may also help a friend by feeding him at the public crib. The thing is criticized, but it is doubtful if those who object the loudest would do anything else themselves. Thousands upon thousands of government employes make nothing more than a bare living out of their positions, but there are other thousands from all ranks of society who want similar posts. In consequence there is a constant tendency to multiply jobs, while the competition for the more profitable places is lessened momentarily only as these, too, are increased in number. In fine, there has developed a "political class," which, as one writer has put it, takes the place of the middle class (non-existent in Cuba) that a republic needs to have. It is, indeed, a parasite class, which has made "politics our only industry and administrative fraud the only open road to fortune for our compatriots." This writer went on to describe it as an industry stronger than sugar, more lucrative than railways, and surer than banking, shipping, and commerce. It brought many ills in its train, such as upsets of public order, lowering of social and moral standards, and a retarding of individual betterment, but was inevitable under the peculiar social conditions of Cuba.[2]

A detailed story of the different Cuban elections has already been given. So far as presidential elections go, the following comment hits the mark:

[2] Carrión, Miguel de, *El desenvolvimiento social de Cuba en los últimos veinte años*, in *Cuba contemporánea*, v. XXVII, pp. 6-27, 19-20; Sept., 1921.

"In the history of Cuba no Candidate for the presidency has ever lost an election who was backed by the government. [Estrada] Palma reëlected himself to be ousted by a revolution; Gomez, leader of the revolution, who was favored by the intervention government, became president; Menocal was supported by Gomez with the rural guard and defeated Zayas, and four years later he reëlected himself, and in the following election threw the support of the government to Zayas who was declared president by a decision of the supreme court." [3]

In like manner Zayas supported Machado, who was elected in 1924. The evil is one that has grown progressively worse. A first period of increasingly bad conditions reached its culmination in 1905, resulting in the revolution of 1906, followed by the United States intervention of 1906-1909. During the intervention a law of elections was promulgated which was primarily the work of the then Colonel Crowder, as head of the Advisory Law Commission. This was an outgrowth of a careful taking of the census, and contained a number of excellent features, including the following: public registration of voters; the holding of elections on a single day; district electoral boards containing representatives of all parties; official tickets; proportional representation in the House and in provincial and municipal councils; the secret ballot; a first scrutiny of the vote by the officials of the district electoral board; municipal, provincial, and national electoral boards for the hearing of cases on infractions of the law; and an appeal from them to the law courts. No objection could be found with the elections of 1908, and those of 1910, 1912, and 1914 were in the main not badly conducted. In 1916 fraud on a great scale made its appearance, however, and it became worse in ensuing years. As the present writer set forth on another occasion:

"The buying of votes and voting of dead men are within an American's ken, but in Cuba the latter, at least, is indulged in to a degree that

[3] "A Sage," in Havana *Post,* July 15, 1924

would hardly pass muster in twentieth-century United States. The number of votes at a presidential election has been known to be about double the total number of voters in Cuba, and this in spite of every conceivable device to keep adherents of the opposite party from voting at all. Soldiers have patrolled the polls or ridden through the country to intimidate the opposition. Clocks are moved forward or backward as the exigencies of the voting hours demand. There are innumerable tricks to delay the voting so that the opposition voters never get to the booths. Criminals have been pardoned to serve as hoodlums and to get the votes their 'family influence' represents. And if the vote of a particular precinct is still adverse, one may burn the polling place and destroy the record. A President, in control of the army and the political machinery, must have a veritable national uprising against him to lose an election, if he takes advantage of his powers. The precedents are generally to the effect that he would be an unusual President who would not do so."[4]

The writer might have added that a national uprising would probably be ineffective, because of the recent policy of the United States in lending support to a government in power in the event of a revolution. A much clearer idea of the meaning of some of the practices referred to will be obtained if a few of them, at least, are discussed somewhat more in detail.

"*Forros*" is a term used for false voters, recruited from many sources. There have been many falsifications of the census and the voting lists, to get names upon them that could be voted. An examination of these lists reveals such names as Cristóbal Colón (Spanish for Christopher Columbus), Diego Velázquez (the Spanish conqueror of Cuba), Valeriano Weyler (the famous "Butcher" of War of Independence notoriety), and the names of all the other numerous captain-generals of Cuba. It would seem that no very great amount of imagination was used in these cases by the falsifiers of the lists. There were so many *forros*, however,

[4] Chapman, Charles Edward, *The Cuban election problem,* in *American review of reviews,* v. LXX, pp. 413-419; Oct., 1924.

that it was indeed difficult to get names enough to serve, for prior to 1919 there were more *forros* than actual voters! This has been an abuse practiced by both parties. In a hard-fought presidential election, the number of *forros* would be kept down, through challenges from both sides, except in cases where the government was exerting special pressure. In that case the government *forros* would be counted, and the others not. The evil has been more notice-able, however, in the partial elections in between elections for the presidency. At such times political interest has not been nearly so intense, and in consequence the number of *forros* might well decide an election. The *forros* grew out of corrections of the voting lists as established by the census and electoral law of 1908. Down to that time there had been special registrations for each election, as in the United States. In 1908 it was provided that the register of voters should be permanent, plus those who should subsequently gain the right to vote, and minus those who from death or other cause should lose it. The addition or removal of names was intended to be merely a clerical task in the keeping of the municipal electoral boards. The latter seem to have been much better at addition than subtraction, for by 1919, in a man-suffrage country, the voters represented the im-possible number of 44.2 per cent of the population. A strik-ing case was that of Candelaria in Pinar del Río. This town, with a total of 9,234 inhabitants, was able to muster 25,820 voters!

Another evil is the *"refuerzo."* This has applied especially in the case of elections to Congress and the provincial and municipal councils, growing out of the fact that one voted for the full number of representatives or councillors to the province or municipality, instead of for just one from a limited district, as in the United States. Thus, if a province were entitled to twenty-five representatives in Congress, one might vote twenty-five names. In such an event a man might vote for some of his party's candidates, and not for others, thus giving a *"refuerzo,"* or reinforcement, to those whom he favored. So far, the proceeding was quite within the law; indeed, it was just what had been contemplated, on the theory that it would bring about the election of the best candidates. In practice, however, there developed the peculiar anomaly of a candidate in opposition to other candidates of his own party, as well as against those of the other party. The situation was still further complicated by the fact that Cuba had adopted the system of proportional representation, by an enactment of the Magoon era, as the means for securing the influence of minorities that is called for by the Constitution. To get around the possible confusion that might result from a "straight ticket" vote it was further enacted that in case of a tie those names coming nearest the top of the ballot should receive first consideration. So, quite apart from the maneuvers in the nominating assemblies to get a place at the top of the ticket, there has been a considerable competition among members of the same party to get a *refuerzo* at the time of the vote. It will be seen, therefore, that the straight party vote, for which a politician in the United States might normally strive, was one of the last things to be desired by a candidate of either party whose name was toward the lower end of the list. The voters were therefore bribed or otherwise influenced to vote only for one name in the party list, and not vote at all for other names, or even to vote all the candidates but one of another party! And since those candidates whose names were far down on the ballot needed to get a greater vote than those at the top, the latter engaged in the *refuerzo* as well as the former, in order to safeguard their own candidacies.

The *refuerzo* has not stopped there. Politicians of the two parties might get together and arrange fraudulent trades, —say of votes for a senator of one party as against votes for the presidential candidate of another. Cases have even occurred where one entire set of party officials would be bought up, in which case they would throw their influence to a *refuerzo* all along the line in favor of the candidates of the other party. Frequently, members of opposite parties have gotten together and appointed an "administrator" to handle the purchase of the vote for all members of the group. There would still be a chance to win the election, after an adverse vote had been turned in, through a falsification at the time of the count or during transmission of the vote to the capital. Many of the practices employed are also included in current definitions of the *refuerzo*. For example, it has often been arranged by officials of both parties to mutilate enough straight tickets or vote a sufficient number of partially blank ballots to secure a result other than that in the vote as cast. This has been done in collusion with the municipal electoral board, at the time it counted the vote. It was not so difficult to arrange as might seem likely. Municipal boards were made up of an equal number from the two parties, together with a municipal judge, who determined the result in case of a difference between the party representatives. So, if officials of the opposite parties agreed, their representatives in the boards could control the situation. If it were deemed desirable to secure the coöperation of the judge, that was a simple affair, for municipal judges were, and still are, political appointees who do not even have to be lawyers. They are therefore menaced with being relieved of their post or transferred, while their appointment in the first place, together with promotions or other favors, is purely a matter of political favor. This was a factor that assisted not only in the illegal *refuerzo,* but also in presidential control of elections! There was plenty of opportunity in which to complete the fraud, even if it had not been accomplished by the time of the first scrutiny of the vote. The votes were left in the hands of the judge of the electoral board, with no guaranties whatsoever. So he might open the package and change the vote, or it could be done afterward by postal officials before its delivery at the capital. Meanwhile, it went through a further scrutiny on the part of higher electoral boards. Falsification in these later stages has been indulged in only in case the opposite parties could not agree, being especially employed by the government party in a presidential election. According to common report, there was a great deal of this in the election of 1916.

These dishonest practices have been the more easily engaged in because of other evils in Cuban political life that make escape from the legal consequences easy and reward for success alluring. As already stated, there was an appeal under the law of 1908 from the findings of the lower electoral boards to those higher in the scale, and from them to the courts, but the appeal to the higher boards may be said to have involved a distinction without a difference, and the courts were notoriously corrupt. At best the courts were given to the adoption of legal devices to avoid rendering a decision. As most of the appeals against frauds in the electoral boards have come at times of a presidential election, and as the government party has been more likely to have perpetrated them, the judges did not wish to take the responsibility for upsetting the vote and thus risk losing their posts. Even a conviction for electoral frauds has held few terrors, for pardons and amnesties have followed crime in rapid succession in Cuba, and election crimes have always been forgiven. On the other hand, there has been that "compensation for fraud to the political servant" known in Cuba as the *"botella"* (bottle), which has been defined as "pretended employment, without any work to do,"—the "soft" government job.[5] All this has been without taking into account the factor of intimidation of the voter, already alluded to. That has been accomplished not merely by use of the army, the rural guards, and the police, but also by employment of thugs called *"matones,"* or "killers."

Yet another evil has also existed to assist the politicians in their control of the vote. Political parties have been recognized by the law, but have had an extra-legal position, without any provision for regulation of their internal management, in imitation of the system in the United States. This has worked out very badly in Cuba, and is a matter the importance of which cannot be overemphasized. The Cuban electorate has had a choice of voting only as between the men whose names appear on the official ballots. Some attempts have been made to bring the methods of nomination under the law, so as to get lists of candidates more nearly responsive to the wishes of the people, but the politicians of all parties have joined in resistance to this innovation, as it threatened their "ownership" of the government. In consequence, the voters have had little to pick from; usually it has been a case of one "crook" or another, as witness the case of the elections of 1922, when more than a fifth of the candidates on the official ballots had criminal antecedents. Indeed, within any given party the worst man is likely to win the nomination and gain the position

[5] Ortiz, Fernando, *La reforma electoral de Crowder en Cuba,* in *Reforma social,* v. XX, pp. 214-225, at 222; July, 1921.

at the top of the ballot, for all sorts of frauds have been perpetrated, without any criminal liability attaching. When, for example, President Menocal found that the majority in his party assembly (as the conventions are called) would be against him, he caused his Cabinet Secretaries to be included as members of the assembly *ex-officio,* and thus dominated the vote. There was no law to stop him, and he had the supreme argument of force on his side. The dominant position of the President in the party assembly is one of the principal causes for the formation of fractional groups. Unable to get what they want within their own party, some men get out, form an organization of their own, and make headway as a "pirate" party, to which favors must be granted to keep them from swinging the balance in the opposite direction. The most famous instance in recent years was the formation of the Popular party by Alfredo Zayas in 1919, a maneuver which carried him to the presidency.

The law of 1908 was not responsible for these evils, but was associated with them in the popular mind, and when the bitterly criticized election of 1916 was followed by fraudulent elections in 1918 there was an insistent demand in many quarters for a new law, although the reputed author of the old law, the former Colonel Crowder, was held in great respect,—all the more so, perhaps, in the light of the reputation he had won in organizing the American army in the World War. So in 1919 President Menocal issued an invitation to this famous officer, now become a general, to come to Cuba and give his advice for drawing up a new law of elections. Both the Conservatives and Liberals announced their willingness to coöperate in the plan, although the latter (then out of power) set forth through a committee of their members in the House that the trouble was not in the laws, but in the failure to observe them. According to these men, no reform could avoid an improper conduct of the elections, unless accompanied by a preventive action on the part of the United States, for "the evil was in the men in the government, not in the precepts of the law." This assertion was so eminently in accord with the facts that it is hardly worth while to devote much space to the Crowder election law of 1919. There was, indeed, a most valuable preliminary work accomplished in the form of a new census, taken that same year. The ratio of voters turned out to be 17.2 per cent of the population, instead of the 44.2 per cent previously on the registration lists. The law itself was a bulky document, making a fat volume. Past elections were studied, and an attempt was made to meet all improprieties that had developed. The law is primarily interesting, however, in the light of the way it was *not* carried out. For example, it was provided that where the voting ratio in any voting district (*barrio,* or ward) was one per cent higher than at the preceding election it was presumptively fraudulent, and if over three per cent, conclusively so. On this basis the following result was obtained in the elections of 1922:

Total voting districts.	Number with less than one per cent increase.	Number with over one per cent increase but less than three.	Number with over three per cent.
1193	387	512	294
100%	32.4%	42.9%	24.7%

Thus only 32.4 per cent of the vote was presumptively legal under the terms of the law, and 67.6 per cent was fraudulent. This would seem to imply that the *forros* still live.

General Crowder attempted to overcome the "pirate

party" evil by a provision forbidding different parties from carrying the same names as candidates for office. As already mentioned, these groups, called "parties," were merely for the purpose of traffic in votes. They were not confined to national politics, but existed also within provinces and even within municipalities, so the leader could get one or two places in a trade whereby his group would support the larger party in its other candidacies. This paragraph of the Crowder law did not suit President Menocal, and he had it amended, after which he formed the Conservative-Popular alliance for the elections of 1920. In that year these two parties had identical lists of candidates. The same thing happened in 1924, but this time the Popular party joined with the Liberals.

The "repeating" evil had been so prominent prior to 1919,—that is to say, plural voting by individuals, who, of course, had but a single legal vote,—that the new law called for each man to have a certificate (*cédula*) of a right to vote. The idea was that this could be checked off and repeating avoided, since no one without a certificate was to be allowed to vote. The only effect of this paragraph was to add a new commodity to the Cuban market. The certificates were sold freely to the highest bidder. In 1922 the market price in Havana was fifty dollars, while from ten to fifteen dollars was the normal range in the country districts. And, despite efforts of the new law to overcome it, the *refuerzo* in its worst forms continued unchecked. In the elections of 1922 *refuerzos* were quite generally sold by political chiefs to candidates for municipal and provincial office, as well as for those who were running for election to the national House. In Madruga, province of Havana, seven Liberal, five Conservative, and two Popular candidates for representative, together with several aspirants for provincial and municipal posts, formed a coalition to buy up the electoral board. Each candidate for representative contributed fifteen hundred dollars, and nine others gave five hundred apiece, while the rest got on the ticket free, for personal reasons. In all, the sum of $22,500 was paid, of which each of nine "college," or voting district, boards got five hundred dollars, while the municipal electoral board got eighteen thousand. The work was done by substituting false ballots for the real ones. The case was by no means unique; such things probably happen in every election in each voting district, being notorious in the elections of 1922.[6] Indeed, what with *forros*, the *refuerzo*, and the sale of voting certificates, those elections were possibly the most fraudulent ever held in Cuba.

Another feature of the law, supplemented by a law of June 11, 1921, had led to the hope that the evil political machine could be overthrown through a free reorganization of each party, prior to an election. The politicians found an easy way to get around that, by a law of January 2, 1922, against the reorganization of political parties. President Zayas allowed the bill to become a law without his signature,—a procedure often followed by him in the case of bad legislation that should have been vetoed. According to this law, the men comprising the existing executive committee of each party (so framed as to include the Liberal, Conservative, and Popular parties only) were to nominate all municipal, provincial, and national candidates for the elections of 1922. Great care was taken to see that these committees should be composed of the "right men." For example, provincial executive committees were to designate municipal executive committees in localities that did not

[6] The writer has personal knowledge of what happened at one of the sugar-mills. Just two men went to the polls, but when the announcement was given out it seems that three hundred had "voted."

have them, and all vacancies on existing committees were to be supplied by members of the committees themselves. The lists of candidates selected by these committees were to be printed on the official ballot. Thus the discredited politicians were enabled to retain control of party management, to assure the constant reëlection of themselves. And yet the elections of 1922 are often styled "good," because there was no presidential interference with armed forces. That was because the outcome of the election was a matter of indifference to the President. The Liberals were successful, but the pseudo-Popular-Conservative occupant of the executive chair later found no difficulty in getting an almost unanimous vote in Congress whenever he wanted it. That, however, does not directly concern elections, although it may help in a measure to explain them.

The fraudulent character of the elections of 1920 and 1922 caused General Crowder (who had become United States ambassador to Cuba in 1923) and a number of leading Cubans to think about a new law, to meet some of the evils that had persisted, or developed, despite the law of 1919. To overcome the *forros* evil, it was proposed to require frequent meetings of municipal electoral boards to get the voting lists ready before January 1, 1924, because by the law of 1919 nobody could vote at an election unless he were a registered voter. In addition to being excluded from the elections of 1924, those who should register and did not do so were to be fined. The article that Menocal had derogated, to the effect that no man could appear as a candidate on two party lists, was to be restored. The voting certificate was to be done away with, and in its place a requirement was to be inserted that officials of a voting district electoral board were to reside in the district, so that they might know the voters personally. Other safeguards against "repeating" were also proposed. To guard against the *refuerzo* it was suggested that individuals be required to vote a straight ticket; the adoption of the "single member district" plan in use in the United States was considered, but dropped, as it would have required an amendment to the Constitution, a virtual impossibility under the circumstances. The law was introduced in the House on February 22, 1923, by Fernando Ortiz and Santiago Rey. The latter, who was president of the Conservative party, was to have charge of the bill. Just at that time President Zayas raised his "nationalism" issue against the United States, and Rey went over to his side. Zayas did promise to call a congressional committee "later" to discuss the matter of a new election law, but a precise date was never set, and nothing was done.

The elections of 1924 have been heralded abroad as "fair," but they were that only in so far as they represented the preference of the people for Machado over Menocal. The same evils manifested themselves as before, and if, indeed, there was comparatively little violence, it was probably because the victory of Machado was so overwhelmingly sure that it was unnecessary. In conclusion it may be said that there is probably no law that would serve any better than the election law of 1919. That, indeed, has not checked fraud. Furthermore, it has some features that are distinctly bad. As one keen-minded Cuban gentleman of Santiago told the writer,

"The Crowder law is based on party conventions, beginning with the election of ward delegates, then municipal, then provincial, and finally national. No decent man has a chance to get far in politics by this course. It is too democratic for Cuba. The Spanish system, based on property-holding, payment of a poll-tax, or the literacy test, was much better."

There is probably no way to bring about honesty in Cuban elections, except by evolution toward better standards, or unless there is an upheaval that will overwhelm the present political class. Until one or other happens, election laws are likely to be just so much waste paper. There is nothing in sight at present, however, to make one expectant of either eventuality for many years.[7]

[7] This chapter is based in part on the various election laws, which may be found in the official Gazette, or *Gaceta,* at the appropriate date. Nearly every volume or article dealing with political happenings in Cuba has something to say about election evils. The volumes of Barbarrosa, Cabrera, Collazo, Dolz, Martínez Ortiz, Merino and Ibarzábal, and Pardo Suárez are particularly noteworthy, and among scores of articles those of Marvin, Ortiz, Scott, and Spinden are perhaps outstanding.

CHAPTER XXV

SOCIAL FACTORS IN CUBAN LIFE [1]

Cuba has a population of more than three millions; at the close of 1922 it was estimated that there were 3,123,040 persons in the island, of whom 2,193,936, or almost exactly seventy per cent, were white, while most of the rest were black. The presence of two such dissimilar races in the island is only one factor, however, in the numerous problems of Cuban society. Foreigners make up a goodly proportion of the whites, and they do not become Cuban. The colored people are patriotic, but retain many of their ancestral traits. There are no organized classes. The white laborer is to be distinguished from the colored, and the Spanish capitalist from the Cuban. In fine, there is no real national unity, or, as one writer has put it, the Cuban state is "an almost hypothetical entity," because there is no "Cuban society."[2]

A discriminating census, taken by a group of men from Mississippi, would probably cut down the white man's pro-

[1] As originally planned it was intended to include separate chapters on the Cuban social inheritance, race problems, women, and education. When eventually it was decided to deal primarily with political conditions since 1902, it seemed desirable to include at least some hint of these other matters, in addition to what appears, incidentally, elsewhere in the narrative. This chapter is not to be considered as in any sense a summary, however, but rather as a suggestion that might work out in formulation into quite different proportions.

[2] Carrión, Miguel de, *El desenvolvimiento social de Cuba en los últimos veinte años*, in *Cuba contemporánea*, v. XXVII, pp. 6-27, at 24; Sept., 1921.

portion very materially from the now generally estimated seventy per cent. The difference is that in the United States a man is "colored" unless he is all white, while in Cuba one may "pass for white," notwithstanding a few kinky hairs and a shadowy complexion. Certainly, many of the "white" Cubans of the rural districts, or *"guajiros,"* as they are called, have some negro blood in them. Even on this basis the whites were once so greatly in the minority that they were in terror lest Cuba become "another Haiti." That danger seems now to be too remote for serious consideration, as the whites, already in the majority, are gaining a greater and greater preponderance every year. This is due to immigration, which is for the most part white. Thousands of negro laborers come in each year from Haiti and Jamaica during cane-cutting season, but most of them are shipped out again as soon as the crop is gathered. Those who remain do not multiply to any extent, as they are rarely accompanied by wives. In 1919 the census showed 44,609 persons in Cuba born in other islands of the West Indies, of whom 8,318 were women.

As already pointed out, the Cuban negro differs from his racial brother in the United States,[3] and many observers claim that the Cuban is the better of the two. He has the courteous Spanish manner and personal dignity; his features have little of the thickness so characteristic of the American negro; he dresses neatly and in reasonably good taste; and he is not domineering or loud-mouthed. He makes a good laborer in the fields, and can be used with success in some of the lighter forms of manufacturing. His faults are those of the race wherever it is found. He lacks morality, as measured by Anglo-Saxon standards, but he confines his amours to people of his own color, and has not

[3] Cf. *supra,* p. 22.

been guilty of attacks on white women. He is inclined to idleness, and somewhat addicted to petty dishonesty. He retains a little more superstition, perhaps, than does the negro of the United States, and is reputed to find some medium for its expression in his *ñañigos,* or secret societies. While it could hardly be said that he is on a plane of social and political equality with the whites, there is a real toleration that allows him to aspire to distinction in any field. Two negroes have been among the leading figures in the political life of the republic, Martín Morúa Delgado (once president of the Senate and later Secretary of Agriculture) and Juan Gualberto Gómez (senator and spellbinder from Oriente), while there been many others who have attained to high place not only in politics but also in journalism and literature.

There is a considerable number of Chinese who help to make up the thirty per cent of Cuba's colored population. They began to be imported into the country to serve as laborers during the latter half of the nineteenth century, but as their coming has always represented almost wholly an immigration of men, there were few of them left at the outset of the republican era. According to the census of 1919 there were 16,146 persons of the yellow race in the island, of whom 15,518 were men. Only 10,300, however, were definitely entered as Chinese, though doubtless there were many more in the group styled "unknown." Mention has already been made of their entry by the thousands in recent years,[4] despite the existence of anti-Mongolian immigration laws. They serve mainly as laborers in the fields, although a few are merchants or truck gardeners. As in other parts of the world, they keep to themselves, and since there are not many women among them they appear

[4] Cf. *supra,* pp. 481-482.

to be a mere passing factor in the social history of the island.[5]

By all odds the most important element numerically
among the foreigners are the Spaniards. Thousands come
into Cuba every year, most of them from Galicia and As-
turias or other parts of northern Spain; in 1923, for example, the official records showed 46,439 immigrants from
Spain. Most of them intend to return to their native country as soon as they have accumulated wealth enough to live
comfortably thenceforward in the towns where they were
born; so there is a heavy outgoing flow of the Spanish population. For the same reason the great majority of Spanish
immigrants are men. The census of 1919 shows that out
of a total of 272,030 foreigners, 245,644 were Spaniards, or
about eight and a half per cent of the entire population of
the island, but only 58,472 were women, as against 187,172
men.

However Spaniards may have lacked perfection in political
matters, they have usually enjoyed a high rating in the
business world. Certainly this is true of them in Cuba.
They occupy a prominent place in the sugar and tobacco
industries, but in the main they are not so much a land-
holding as they are a commercial, money-lending class. They
are the principal retail merchants in the island, in big business and in little. While many of them remain in Havana,—
there were 76,390 in the capital and 97,539 in Havana province as a whole in 1919,—they dominate the mercantile life
of the rural districts almost as outstandingly as that of the

[5] It must be borne in mind that
the racial situation indicated by the
census of 1919 may have been
changed considerably by the activity of the Zayas government in encouraging "the public and clandes-
tine immigration of the worst and
most uncivil elements of population,"
or, in other words, "uncivilized
Ethiopians and unabsorbable Asiatics,
with their smallpox, malaria, fe-
tiches, opium, and misery." Ortiz,
29.

cities. The Spanish-owned *bodega,* or general store, is not merely the retail emporium, but also the place of resort for a loan (perhaps at usurious interest) or as an exchange where one may dispose of his crop. The Spaniard is in every sense of the word a good worker and a good business man. He has vigor, energy, endurance, and determination; he will work long hours effectively and without complaint; and his word, once pledged, is "as good as his bond." Any hostility the Cubans may have felt toward the Spaniards has long since passed. Now, there is at times an agitation for a more permanent form of Spanish immigration,—for Spaniards who will come *with their families* and take out naturalization papers,—but the canny Iberian still prefers to look upon Cuba as the royal road to an eventual life of ease in Spain,—a wealth to be obtained, not now in politics, but in a game he plays much better, in business.

There is a paternalistic flavor to the life of most Spaniards in Cuba that is more akin to the practices of a medieval guild than it is to society as it exists in the United States. Thousands of Spaniards come as apprentices, or "dependents," as they are called, to an already established business, recommended to some friend or relative by their fathers in Spain. They receive a salary, but a large portion is put to their credit toward an eventual partnership in the business. When the senior partner betakes himself to Spain, the others below him "move up a notch." The "dependent" in the business has very little personal freedom in the initial stages of his career. The senior partner is at one and the same time his business superior and in the place of a father, —an autocratic, though usually kindly, father if he wills. The young man will hardly leave the shop, day or night, except for his "night off," once a month, or when he may have been given permission to go to night-school or to his club. "To his club,"—for nearly all the Spaniards in Cuba belong to some club named for the region whence they came. In January 1926, for example, the Galician Club of Havana had a membership of 67,712 members, the Asturian Club 60,-351, and two others respectively 44,243 and 16,859. Obviously, many of the members do not reside in Havana. These great institutions are for the common benefit of members, a kind of insurance against sickness or other misfortune, as well as for pleasurable associations. The dues are comparatively light, but the "turnover" in collections is so great that the organizations themselves are very wealthy, with club-houses that are the wonder of every visitor to Havana. If one seeks for faults in the Spanish population he finds it in the normal characteristics of the race,—more particularly in a weakness for women. The well-to-do among them also like a game of chance. These are matters of no very great concern, however. The real Spanish problem, as the Cubans see it, is how to get more Spaniards who will come and *take root* as citizens of the republic.

Although there are some considerable colonies from various European and Hispanic American countries, the United States ranks next to Spain among white countries in the number of its citizens who live in Cuba, while the business interests of Americans surpass those of any other foreign people. Unlike the Spaniards, most American residents of Cuba have their families with them, it would seem, for in a total of 9,555 Americans in 1919, there were 5,278 men and 4,277 women. Nevertheless, the great majority expect to return to the United States, although there is no inconsiderable proportion of them who are satisfied to stay in Cuba for the rest of their days. Other considerable white colonies in 1919 were those from Mexico (3,469), France (2,340), and Great Britain (1,089), with about eleven thousand more scattering, and possibly a number of others from the islands of the West Indies whose immigrants in Cuba are mainly negro.

The Cubans themselves may be divided into three social groups, depending very largely on their position in the economic life of the country. At one extreme are the laborers, many of them negro or negroid. At the other are the land-holding class, made up of people of white blood. In between are the men in the professions and the politicians, mostly white in the upper ranks, but containing a considerable proportion of negroid elements, notably among the holders of government soft jobs, or *botellas*. The laborers of the cities do not differ sufficiently from laborers in the United States to call for comment here, although mention may be made of their radicalism on the one hand and of a lower standard of living they have on the other. The *guajiro*, however, has no parallel in the United States. He is a rural wanderer. Now and then he will work for somebody else, and at other times will "squat" in any locality he likes, build himself a hovel, raise a crop, and remain there until ordered to move on. He is able to do this because there are many vast estates in Cuban hands that are not worked by their owners, since taxes are collected only on developed lands. The recent phenomenal growth of the sugar industry has very greatly reduced the opportunities available to the *guajiro* squatter, however.

Contrary to a pretty generally diffused opinion, Cuba is not "owned" by foreigners, but belongs in greatest part to the Cubans themselves, especially those of the great land-owning class. To be sure, they are in a sense subordinated to the foreign-owned sugar companies (except as they themselves have large holdings in these corporations) and to other business interests in the hands of Americans, Englishmen, and Spaniards. Their position is impregnable, however, so long as they hold the land. Unquestionably these people are the "best" in Cuban society, educated as well as wealthy, genteel, honorable, and delightful. They live apart from politics, unless forced to take a hand indirectly in defence of their properties. Naturally, they are conservative in tendency and not sympathetic to the government that has developed in Cuba under the republic. That is not to say they are not patriotic, although it would be difficult to determine just what stand they might take with regard to the ultimate political destiny of Cuba.

The professional and political class is made up of widely varying elements, but they are alike in origin in that they are the heirs of the workers for independence. Many of those in the professions, including most doctors, some teachers, and a few lawyers, lean rather to the ideals of the landholding class, but the others depend frankly on political connections as their principal support in the battle for existence. The Spaniards may be the merchants, American and Cuban proprietors between them control the great agricultural resources of the island, but the leaders in the Army of Liberation have taken their reward in the "ownership" of the government. If financially successful they may make a place for themselves or their descendants in the ranks of the landed aristocracy. Meanwhile, they cling to "the government," both as a living and as a hope. They are the nearest thing to a native-born middle class that Cuba possesses, but their destiny is to go up to the Cuban "four hundred," or down to the hopeless mass, or else to remain as they are, a parasite, a detriment, and a danger.

There are of course numerous cross-cuts in Cuban society along other lines than those treated here. One of these involves a distinction between people who live in Havana and those who dwell elsewhere in the republic. The wealth and power of the country tends to concentrate in the capital. Especially is this true of the native-born element among the land-holding and political classes. A study of Parker, *Cubans of to-day*, shows not only that the great majority of those named in that volume reside in the city of Havana, but also that most of them were born in the province. While Parker concerned himself primarily with officials, writers, physicians, and teachers, the same result undoubtedly would be obtained for wealthy Cubans not coming within the above categories. Indeed, a composite Cuban leader, on the basis of the comparative numbers of those included in *Cubans of to-day*, would not only be a native of Havana province and a resident of the capital, but he would also be a graduate of the University of Havana (the majority), although he would have spent some time abroad (over half of those listed,—mostly in the United States, with about a third receiving part of their education in a foreign country). He might be a veteran of the War of Independence (about a third), and would most likely be an official, with perhaps some other profession, too, notably journalism. A comparison with *Who's who in America* shows a much wider distribution of leadership in the United States, both in territory and in profession. To be sure, there may be a difference in the character of the two volumes mentioned, but the generalization as to the overwhelming predominance of the capital in the social life of Cuba holds true.

From the foregoing it will be seen that Cuban society is indeed a conglomerate of many diverse elements. The only thing that brings unity into the whole is the underlying factor of an American-tinctured Hispanic character. On this basis the Cubans of all classes will be found to have much in common, though in varying proportions. They have not yet emancipated themselves from the evils of their Hispanic heritage. They frankly put family, friends, and self ahead of the welfare of the country. They indulge themselves in whatever appeals to their material ego. Thus, illicit unions with women play a large part in the life of men, and are no bar sinister to social prestige or even the highest political office. This is a factor which is productive not only of offences involving moral turpitude but also of crimes of violence and physical and mental disease. One manifestation is in a certain fondness for the perusal of pornographic literature, the sale of which is virtually unrestricted.[6] Indeed, most of the ills which afflict the people of Cuba might be traced to that Hispanic self-indulgence which is one of the foundation stones of Cuban character and which has in some respects become worse than it was at the source on account of a greater New World lack of discipline than existed in the mother country Spain.[7] The native-born Cuban is likely to be improvident and addicted

[6] Among allusions to the pornographic literature evil may be noted the comments in Barbarrosa: 49; 121; and Wright, 97.

[7] For a rather pessimistic discussion of Cuba's evil Hispanic heritage, see Carrión, *Op. cit.*, at pp. 12-13. Enrique José Varona, in a comparatively mild and subdued fashion, has frequently lectured the Cubans about their faults. In his *Nuestra indisciplina* (*Cuba contemporánea*, v. IV [Jan., 1914], pp. 12-16) he called particular attention to the Cuban lack of discipline, which had become more pronounced since the winning of independence. In an address of 1915 (*Recepción en la Academia nacional de artes y letras: discurso leído el día 11 de enero de 1915*, in Varona, *Por Cuba: discursos* [Habana. 1918], pp. 315-342) he gave a general denunciation of the vices in Cuban life, reaching the conclusion that "Republican Cuba seems to be a twin sister of Cuba of colonial times," to the accompaniment of "incompetence, favoritism, nepotism, and corruption," with "justice . . . in hands that ignorance makes stupid, when interest does not twist them," and politics of the same dishonest mould as in the pre-independence era. "Only in this have we progressed: our parasites are not foreign, but indigenous." In a similar vein is an address by him in 1921 (*Discurso leído . . . la noche del 22 de diciembre de 1921*, in *Academia nacional de artes y letras*, v. VI [Habana. 1921], pp. 239-246. The most scathing denunciation of the ills of Cuban life, however, is to be found in Ortiz, *La decadencia cubana*, a remarkable pamphlet of 1924, in which the assertions of its author are backed up by an array of statistical data that is startling in its reach.

to gambling. There is very little ambition for fame, very little altruism that reaches beyond one's immediate circle, and therefore very little real work or achievement. It is probable that no man in Cuba has such a detailed knowledge of his own country as has the American ambassador, General Crowder. There are not even any government statistics worthy of the name. If there is personal pride, it is too often merely in a display of wealth. Thus one will find good automobiles—the modern "baronial escutcheon" in Hispanic America—in a country that lacks highways and even in cities that do not possess a single hundred-yard stretch of ordinarily decent road.[8] Even the usually praiseworthy factor of family love has its dark side, for it leads not only to nepotism in politics,[9] but also to extravagance and to over-indulgence of the whims of children. If a man's son cheats at school, commits rape, robs, or does a murder he may be sure that he will be defended by his father to the best of his ability against the "injustice" of punishment. The sole unpardonable fault is infidelity of one's own wife. These are generalizations, to be sure, and subject to qualification. One such would be that the women, as in all lands, are very much better than the men,—certainly so, from the standpoint of conduct.[10]

[8] Due to bad road conditions, the reckless Hispanic mode of driving, and lack of care, automobiles in Cuba do not last long. In Manzanillo, for example (as a sales agent told the writer), there were some four hundred good machines in 1924, but not a single repair shop! There is a market, however, as anybody who happens to have made some money is likely to buy an expensive automobile, whether he can use it or not.

[9] Cf. *supra*, p. 465.

[10] It is, of course, difficult to find a non-partisan discussion of Cuban women by Cuban writers. There is much of value, however, in Cuban novels, such, for example, as those of Raimundo Cabrera. A somewhat unsympathetic, but searching and useful account, is to be found in the chapter entitled *Home life* in Wright, 98-133. As the author says of Cuban parents: "Their love for their offspring is not the less sincere because it is tempered by neither wisdom nor foresight." *Ibid.*, 102. There is a brief and unfavorable characterization of Cuban women in Franck, 45-48, which, however, has something of interest in it.

In the light of these evils in Cuban character the already described iniquities of Cuban politics become reasonably explicable. Among a people accustomed to self-indulgence, with personal profit at state expense a tradition of the land, most individuals work frankly and whole-heartedly for themselves. To struggle for reputation, glory, or achievement for such an abstraction as the nation, at the risk of sacrificing one's own comfort, would be to play the part of a fool. And advancement comes, not through merit, but through influence. It is far more worth while to be able to say "I have the backing of Senator So-and-So" than to have the greatest ability, broadest information, or best product when one is seeking a favor. It is often said that the "better people" in the United States do not go in for politics, but that is far more accurately the case in Cuba. If only the politicians were a little more moderate in their graft deals, so that there might be no appreciable danger of their ruining the country, decent persons would hardly give the government a thought, except perhaps to refer contemptuously to "those canaille!", as if to people of a different world. In other words, the atmosphere is favorable to political shortcomings in Cuba. Many of the evils incidental to the activities of government have already been recounted. Some of them which have a direct bearing on social conditions are worth mentioning here.

Education in the republican era has been going backwards instead of forward. Cuba is now fifty-three per cent illiterate, and sixty-eight per cent of the Cuban children do not enter school. In 1900 fifty per cent more children attended school (seventy-five each thousand) than do so now (fifty a thousand in 1920). Only one child in each hundred gets as far as the fifth grade. Seventy-one pupils out of 234,000 attending school in 1919 finished their studies, or less than a third of one per cent, and only one out of every 215 goes through the primary schools. Just one schoolhouse has been built in a Cuban city since independence, and only eighty in the country.[11] It is hardly necessary to add that these conditions are *not* due to any lack of expenditures! It is also unnecessary to say that the above figures do not agree with the so-called "statistics" of the Cuban government; in Zayas's message to Congress of April 7, 1924, for example, it was made to appear that Cuba was only 27.1 per cent illiterate, a record that was better than that of any other country in Hispanic America.

Conditions are particularly bad in the primary schools. In 1922 Ramiro Guerra, vice-president of the University Pedagogical Association, published a pamphlet in which he made eighteen recommendations for an improvement of the system, which, however, might better be described as eighteen revelations of existing evils along the lines mentioned above. He found the root of the trouble in politics, even though the Secretary of Public Instruction might happen to be a man of understanding and good character, for he would have to struggle "against vested interests, established habits, and professional politicians accustomed to avail themselves of the secretariat to satisfy the needs of their local politics." In Guerra's opinion, "All the electoral, political, banking, and financial reforms will be ephemeral and inefficacious if based on a population the majority of which is made up of illiterates."[12] In 1924 Alfredo María Aguayo, president of the above-named association and a professor of pedagogy in the University, made a similar arraignment of conditions, going a little farther, in that he asserted that

[11] Ortiz, 10-13.
[12] Guerra y Sánchez, Ramiro, *Un programa nacional de acción peda-* *gógica* (Habana. 1922. 15pp.), especially at pp. 13-15.

not one Secretary of Public Instruction since 1902 had been anything more than a dilettante in educational affairs. He denounced the government in this connection for its lack of idealism, its incompetence, and its lack of loyalty to the cause of the school, claiming that the system had already taken on the characteristics of colonial times, and holding that it must be removed from direct governmental control if anything worth while was to be accomplished.[13]   Other equally searching criticisms of the workings of Cuban primary education might also be quoted to the same effect.[14]

Higher education, in the six high schools of Cuba (one for each province) and the University of Havana, also suffers from various ills, though not nearly so many as in the institutions lower down. The University is in the main a typical Hispanic American professional school, with the usual four colleges of law, medicine, engineering, and arts and sciences, the last-named primarily devoted to the training of teachers. By way of illustration it is worthy of note that there is just one professor of history and no course in the history of Cuba; Cuban history is taught in infantile fashion in the primary schools, and there only. Students are in the University to work, however, and have few "activities" outside the classroom. As in other Hispanic countries, much of their spare time is devoted to a somewhat extraordinary interest in politics.[15]

[13] Aguayo, Alfredo María, *Factores cualitativos de nuestra decadencia escolar*, in *Revista bimestre cubana*, v. XIX, pp. 81-95; Mar.-Apr., 1924.

[14] Two in particular are worthy of note on account of the high character and scholarship of the men who wrote them: the already cited pamphlet of Ortiz and another by Carlos Trelles, entitled *La instrucción primaria de Cuba comparada con la de algunos otros países*, in *Cuba contemporánea*, v. XXXIII, pp. 325-382; Dec., 1923.

[15] The following is a rather vivid description of the University as it was in 1910 and as, to a great extent, it still is today:

"It seems strange, yet is a fact, that the University has always been co-educational . . . for it was so far from the thought of its founders that women would attend that they forgot to bar them, and now perhaps one

The propensity of the students to mingle in political affairs seems at first thought commendable, but the Cuban youth, although he has the merit of good intentions, flies off the handle too readily in radical demonstrations that are far more indicative of lack of discipline than they are of righteousness and good judgment. On questions touching the University itself he may have something more of wisdom. Late in 1923, for example, conditions at the University were suffering from dry rot as of a government bureau. Many of the professors were little better than holders of a *botella,* doing nothing at all for their pay. The situation was corrected in a manner that certainly knows no parallel in the history of universities in the United States. The students, disgusted with the "cutting" of their professors, rose in *armed rebellion,* drove the faculty off the campus, and for two days held possession of the University. The government hesitated to do anything, fearful lest it might incur the unpopularity that the Spanish government suffered in the famous case of the student martyrs. So, presently, what

sixth or even a fifth of the students are girls; most of these are enrolled in the school of pedagogics . . . Of what Americans know as 'college life' there is none at all in this University. When I investigated I found that the student body was not organized; there were no elections . . . I found no rushes, rows, and rivalries between the 'years.' In fact, the courses are so arranged that no recognition of classes is practicable. There were no flourishing athletic organizations . . . There is no gymnasium . . . There is no campus daily paper, no comic weekly, no literary monthly . . . In short, the student here never goes to college; he merely attends school. He goes to classes and he comes home again,—not to a dormitory or a club or a friendly 'frat house,' but to a *bordin* . . . What, besides 'beating' his boarding house, is the young man doing with his leisure time? The question had better pass uninvestigated. They are a solemn set, these Cuban students, pale, emaciated, and sunken eyed. I'd like to think it is consumption of too much midnight oil ails all of them. Some, certainly, are seriousminded and well-informed, and they take a surprising, and, to an American, inexplicable, interest in matters one might imagine would concern them not at all. They frequently lead in demonstrations for or against the government . . . There is perhaps no body in this community any single man or institution desires less to antagonize, nor any body that, once antagonized, or, *vice versa,* pleased, can make its opinions quite so obvious to all concerned, as can the students of Havana University." Wright, 35-37.

amounted to a surrender to the students was arranged, with the dismissal of more than a hundred professors. Also, a new method was adopted for choosing a president of the University. He was to be *elected* every two years by the alumni, faculty, and *students,* each of which groups was to have an equal vote! The University is located on an eminence in the Vedado district, commanding a fine view of the city, bay, and ocean. Formerly it was the site of a Spanish powder factory, and it still has several one-time military *patios,* or open courts, now attractively planted to flowers and trees. Some of the buildings are excellent, though more are needed. American influences are beginning to make themselves felt, even to the point of the possession of a stadium (in course of erection in 1924) where various games are played, including baseball and, oddly enough, American football. This apparently marks a conscious effort toward the development of a University spirit among the students, as distinguished from the purely professional spirit of the typical Hispanic American institution of higher learning. In 1926 there were 4499 students at the University, of whom 2928 were in daily attendance and 1571 doing part-time work. The government does not interfere in the management of the University, if indeed it also neglects it.

Another matter, which, like education, is at least akin to the realm of letters, may perhaps be discussed more appropriately under the heading of social factors: the newspapers. In Hispanic America the newspaper ordinarily performs the same function as the newspapers and moderately serious popular magazines perform jointly in the United States, for no vast body of magazine readers *per se* has as yet been built up. While less true in Cuba than in most of the southern republics, it is nevertheless a fact that newspapers are still the principal resort of the people, not merely for news, but also for more or less serious articles. Editorials, too, have an importance in the public mind that they appear to have lost in the United States. The press of Cuba is almost solely the press of Havana. Each considerable town will have its daily, or two or three of them, or perhaps only a weekly, but they contain local items, in the main, and have little of general interest except the national and foreign news, which is given in far more ample detail by the papers of Havana. Indeed, the latter are the chief reliance of the people in all parts of the island; even the great and relatively distant city of Santiago depends more on the journals from the capital than it does on the local sheets. One thing of note *does* appear in the provincial papers. They bring out that Havana, with its politicians, is a parasite on the rest of the country, and bitterly resent the favoritism for the capital in national services and the neglect of the other districts of the island. In some respects the papers of Havana are a part of the United States news' system,—certainly more so than elsewhere in Hispanic America. Events in the northern republic vie with those in Cuba in allotment of space, and sports in particular, notably major league ball-games, are followed with quite as keen an interest and understanding as they are in the United States. European news is treated in about the same fashion as in the American papers, except that some of the Havana dailies pay special attention to Spain, thus recognizing the natural demand of the great Spanish population of Cuba. Nevertheless, the Havana papers display the Hispanic American characteristics already mentioned, as well as some others, such as a freedom of speech that is a never-ending marvel to the Anglo-American reader and a financial reason for existence that is all too obviously based on political graft.

The number of newspapers in Havana is a constantly varying quantity, but it is always astonishingly large. In 1917, for example, there were thirty-seven dailies in Havana of presumably general circulation, or more than twice as many as there were in New York City.[16] Taking into account the difference in population, that would have meant a ratio of forty or fifty to one in favor of Havana, in a country where more than half the people were illiterate and most of the rest too poor to part lightly with the five-cent piece which is the normal price of a paper. It cannot be the advertising that pays the expense of printing, for circulation is limited. There remains one further source of revenue, which is asserted on every hand and frankly admitted by journalists themselves: the illegal government subsidy for political purposes. "Freedom of speech," too, takes no account of libel, and at times is employed, beyond a doubt, as the basis of blackmail. Naturally, one expects to find politics somehow responsible, and, if so, is sure not to be disappointed. There is a normally greater latitude in speech in Hispanic countries than in English-speaking lands, but in its extreme forms in Cuba this practice springs from the congressional immunity evil. Most of the newspapers of Havana are controlled by congressmen, or else have congressmen as editorial writers on their staffs. These men can say anything, and as the laws are interpreted in Cuba incur no responsibility. By extension, the newspapers for which they write,—or at least to which they lend their names, —seem also to be immune from punishment, unless the national executive may happen to suspend them during some

[16] Marvin, George, *Keeping Cuba libre*, in *World's work*, v. XXXIV, pp. 553-567, at 566; Sept., 1917. The reference to New York newspapers must have been merely to those in English, of general circulation.

emergency at a time when they have taken sides against the administration.[17]

This is not to say that there are no good newspapers in Havana. Several are excellent from every standpoint. A few others have merits, if also their conduct is not wholly to be commended. The dean of the Havana press is Diario de la Marina, founded in 1830. This is the organ of the Spanish colony, and therefore attached to no political party, but in general it is conservative in tendency. Whatever Diario de la Marina has to say is worthy of consideration, as it is perhaps the most nearly independent journal in the capital and is a reputable publication. Naturally, Spanish news gets a lot of space in this paper. El Mercurio is one of several commercial papers, and is excellent of its kind. It is devoted to the interests of the Cuban sugar men, and avoids politics, except as that affects business. For news concerning sugar, tobacco, custom-house regulations, and the various markets this is probably the best paper in Cuba. Perhaps the most influential daily is Heraldo de Cuba, about which one may hear many stories *pro* and *con*. Founded by Orestes Ferrara and edited later by Carlos Mendieta, both men of extraordinary prestige in Cuba, this paper is now in the hands of Gustavo González Beauville, a member of the House of Representatives. If there were but one paper in Havana capable of existing without a political subsidy, this surely would be that one, as it has the largest circulation in the island. And if it does get a subsidy it can hardly be from the national executive, as no paper has more violently and unrestrainedly attacked the Cuban Presidents

[17] These evils are discussed freely by the newspapers themselves,—with regard to *other newspapers,* which are sometimes referred to generally, but not infrequently mentioned specifically. One such editorial,—out of many,—is *Impressions,* in *Diario de la marina,* translated in Havana *Post,* July 12, 1924. This objects to the practice of employing congressmen as newspaper men.

than has Heraldo de Cuba. Some refer to it as a "yellow journal," but the writer is inclined to believe that it is one of the most valuable sources of information about Cuba among Cuban periodicals. To be sure, it is destructive in its comment, but it provides something more than rhetoric, as it has the financial resources to enable it to get at the facts.

One group of papers, commonly regarded as belonging to the Govín family, contains three prominent dailies, El Mundo (a morning paper, edited for many years by Rafael María Govín), La Prensa (which comes out in the afternoon), and the Havana Post (the leading English-language paper). El Mundo perhaps ranks second in the island in circulation, and it has enormous resources behind it, but there its resemblance to Heraldo de Cuba stops. If El Mundo does not get a government subsidy, then all the writer's informants in Cuba are mistaken. It is difficult to escape the impression that the Govín family is in business for the money and makes "policies" subservient to the pocket-book. El Mundo adopts the attitude of an intensely "nationalistic" sheet, and so is always looking for a chance to attack "Yankee imperialism," not only in Cuba but also in other parts of the Americas,—or the Philippines, for that matter. The writer is not familiar with a certain New York paper, said to be another property of the Govín family, but doubts whether it is as anti-American as El Mundo.[18] El Mundo poses as an independent journal in politics and in other respects, but its "courtesy" to Cuban Presidents,— any of them,—is in marked contrast to the straight speaking

[18] The writer has it on good authority that one member of the family is reputed to have sought to ingratiate himself in the favor of the king of Spain, with a view to obtaining a decoration, by discussing methods with Alfonso XIII of making Spanish propaganda in Hispanic America to defeat United States influence there.

of Heraldo de Cuba. In its editorial tone El Mundo has an air of being the watch-dog and saviour of Cuba, but its protests against administrative evils are usually mild to the point of politeness.

La Prensa is too much like El Mundo to merit consideration, but the Havana Post demands attention. The writer doubts the supposed connection between this paper and the Govín family, not so much because it has a radically different policy, as because it openly charges El Mundo with being a subsidized sheet and is able to attack such pet projects of the proprietors of El Mundo as the Govín immigration bill of 1925.[19] The Havana Post is an excellent newspaper, the best English-language paper with which the writer is acquainted in Hispanic America. It is a patriotic American journal, devoted to the interests of the American colony, but takes a great interest in the "passing show" of Cuban life, political and otherwise. Three of its features are especially noteworthy. One is its weekly summary of Cuban news,— a convenient medium of information. Another its two columns of translations, daily, of leading editorials in other Cuban papers. And third the comments of "A Sage," presumably Mr. John Thomas Wilford, the very capable editor of the paper, who has been connected with the Post since 1909, though not as editor until 1919. In his somewhat more restrained American style, "A Sage" lacks only a little of being as frank as Heraldo de Cuba in condemning existing evils. His manner, however, is rather that of a man who is laughing a bit cynically at a people whom he cannot take seriously, certainly in so far as their politics are concerned. Nevertheless, what he says is worth while, because the "Sage" brings real intellectual power to his task, fortified by detailed information, the perspective of a foreigner, and an

[19] Cf. *supra*, p. 500.

intimate acquaintance with Cuban character. There is another American publication, not a newspaper, which is deserving of mention: the Times of Cuba, a monthly review. Under the able editorship of Mr. Edward O'Brien this periodical has acquired a vast circulation. It is one of the best condensed sources of information about Cuba, especially along economic lines, that there is in the island.

Certain papers of Havana are ordinarily classed as Liberal, while others are Conservative, with El Triunfo and La Discusión as the two leaders, respectively.[20] Heraldo de Cuba is often called Liberal, but, while it is anti-Conservative, it is quite as likely to attack members and policies of the Liberal party. The life of the party journal is in direct ratio to the success of the party in politics, now on the highroad of affluence, now falling to the level of infrequent publication or even suspension. El Sol and El Heraldo[21] are papers without definite political tendency, though more Liberal than Conservative. They are like Heraldo de Cuba in their propensity to criticize, but do not have the financial resources to be equally independent and above suspicion. La Lucha is one of a group of three, including also La Noche and El Imparcial, which are the property of a man named José Hernández Guzmán. These papers are a complaisant lot, backing opposite policies with great facility. It is said that the owner supported the three leading candidates for the presidency in the early stages of the campaign of 1924, lending Imparcial to Menocal, Noche to Machado, and Lucha to Zayas. La Lucha was once the property of a Spaniard named San Miguel who had fought the independence movement, but remained in Cuba to publish a news-

[20] *Nación* was once a prominent Liberal paper, and *Día* and *Nuevo país* were Conservative dailies. *Día* was revived in 1924 at the time of the Menocal campaign.

[21] *Heraldo* has lately ceased publication.

paper under the republic. When asked why he had done so, he is said to have replied, with a sweeping gesture: "I remain—to attend the funeral of this." He therefore used his paper primarily to enhance his own fortune by fair means or foul, but also to stir up discord, urging all sides on "to every possible calamity." [22]   Another prominent daily in Havana is El País, which, like Diario de la Marina, caters a great deal to the Spanish colony. La Política Cómica is a humorous weekly, which, nevertheless, has a certain importance in the political field. There are yet other papers, and there is much more that could be said about those named here, some of it in their favor, and some (with perhaps added details about subsidies) that is not so good. Taken together they are an incomparable source of information about Cuban affairs, for they tend to check one another, and from the standpoint of their value as newspapers they are at least vigorously and attractively written, and reasonably well supplied with information on the events of the day.[23]

Something has already been said about the startling increase in crime in Cuba, due to amnesties, pardons, congressional immunity, and the inept and dishonest administration of justice. In like manner gambling, forbidden by law but protected by government officials, who are partners or proprietors in these enterprises, flourishes to such a degree that Cuba is often called the "Monte Carlo of America." The lottery, the cock-fight, jai-alai, horse-racing, and the Casino are merely better known instruments of a habit that reaches beyond them into every nook and cranny of the nation. Prostitution, too, is a running-mate of gambling.

---

[22] Wright, 146.

[23] For a brief statement about Cuban newspapers as of any given time, one may consult the *American newspaper annual and directory*, edited by N. W. Ayer and Sons, which includes Havana papers, as well as those of the United States and Canada.

Over a period of ten years cases of abduction doubled and corruption of minors quadrupled. Suicides increased seven times over, between 1899 and 1923; in comparison with the United States the people of Cuba have a violent desire to kill themselves that is eight times greater than that of their neighbors.[24] In some countries religion might serve as a disciplinary factor to hold the people in check, but in Cuba the church seems to have lost its grip; a writer who wishes to win applause can do so easily by lashing at the church, which surely is very different from conditions as they are in the United States.

Social evils are always more easy to discern than excellences, but it must not be imagined for a moment that the Cubans lack their normal share of good traits offsetting the bad. They are generous to a fault, and except as they may have reached the point of luxury are industrious, eager to learn, and quick in doing so. Above all, however, they possess, along with others of the Hispanic race, that delightful quality of friendliness and likeableness that is embodied in the Spanish word *"simpatía"* (literally, but not accurately, "sympathy"), a word that has no exact rendering in English, since the thing itself does not too clearly exist among Anglo-American peoples. For example, despite a greater class separation than in the United States, there is a democracy of manner that the northern republic never knows. A man at the top of the social scale will converse familiarly, and not condescendingly, with one of the opposite category. On the other hand, a waiter may pick up your newspaper and stand by your table and read it, if you are not using it. Withal, there is no passing of the boundaries of real courtesy and respect. The very characteristics which are productive of so much evil have also their attractive side. If a man

[24] Ortiz, 21-23.

will unblushingly violate the proprieties on his own account, he at least is willing to let others conduct their lives in the way they see fit, provided they occasion no trouble to himself. In consequence there is an atmosphere of personal freedom that is almost unknown in the United States, where all one's activities are subordinated to "what people may say." Americans ordinarily cannot grasp the full flavor of this freedom unless they have lived for long periods of time in Hispanic countries, and when they do comprehend it, it is the thing that most often decides them to abandon their native land and remain where one is free to be himself. In other words, the Cubans are individualists, and, whatever there may be against such an ideal on many scores, it also carries with it a zest of life that conformity to "the group" can never yield. The very politicians, whose shortcomings the writer has so freely described, are far more likeable as human beings than the most puritanically God-fearing, "good" Americans have ever been. Furthermore, there is *nothing* that is hopelessly bad in Cuban character. The evils can be met and overcome, without destroying the praiseworthy features. There has already been something of "improvement" in a quarter century of republican life. Cubans live better than they did,—more hygienically, more comfortably, with better clothing, and more of the concomitants of a high social order, in the way of municipal services, theatres, good shops, and what not. There is less of social stigma attached to work, higher educational ideals (despite governmental practices), even a somewhat lessening tolerance of children's faults, and very much greater freedom for women. In other words, underneath an all too easily visible surface of badness there is a deep current flowing that moves on to better things.

Thus far in this recital the writer has discussed the social order in terms of "evil" and "good," as those words are ordinarily understood in English. If, however, he were writing more as a philosopher than as a historian he might banish these terms, especially the former, altogether. It is open to question whether *life* may not be better in Cuba than it is in the United States. For example, the moralist may find it necessary to condemn jai-alai[25] as it is played in Havana, or even baseball, because of the attendant gambling,[26] but individuals enjoy them, quite apart from any

[25] Jai-alai, called *"pelota"* (ball) in Spain and *"frontón"* (from the word for the "court" in which it is played) in Mexico, and usually translated as "Basque ball" in English, is a beautiful and attractive game belonging to the same "family" as tennis and hand-ball. It may even have been the ancestor of the two last-named sports. At any rate, it is of an ancient vintage in the history of the Basque provinces of northern Spain. The court is a rectangle 210 feet long and sixteen wide, paved with cement, and bounded by a front, rear, and one long side wall of smooth-surfaced granite. On the other long side, beyond a narrow space of open ground, are the seats for the public. The ball is like an enlarged golf ball, solid and very fast. It is handled by the players through the medium of a curve-shaped *cesta*, or basket, which is two or three feet long and just wide enough to admit of receiving the ball. There are various games, but the one most often played is between two-men teams of "whites" and "blues." The ball is served against the front wall, and then is to be played on the fly or first bound by a member of the other side. It may bound against the side or rear walls without its counting against the player, as only the bound on the floor is considered. The play goes back and forth, first one side handling the ball and then the other, until a player misses or hits out of bounds. That scores a point for the other side. The game may last any stipulated number of points, but it is usually twenty-five or thirty in Havana. It calls for a dexterity, skill, gracefulness, and speed that have to be seen to be appreciated. Gambling on the result, however, is an all too apparent accompaniment,—indeed, an "audible" one, for blocks away. A Cuban crowd,—or a Spanish one, for that matter, as many of those in attendance are Spaniards and so too most of the players,—is not satisfied with a single beforehand bet on the result, but wagers are made mostly during the process of the play, and at surprising odds. A team leading thirteen to nine may be held as high as five to one,—and a few minutes later a rally may cause the odds to veer in the opposite direction. Withal, there is a din that never stops until the game is finished. The popular term "Palace of Shouts" (*Gritos*) for the court in Havana is well deserved, but the actual amount of noise is almost greater to the cubic inch than it would be to the cubic foot in any athletic contest in the United States. It must be remembered, too, that the betting is heavy, reaching into hundreds or even thousands of dollars, though the individual with the "roll" may look as if he didn't know where his next cent was coming from.

[26] Franck, 25-29, has an interesting description of baseball as it is played in Cuba. In this case, however, the

false notions they may have as to their prospects of gaining sudden wealth. It makes for not a little human happiness. Undoubtedly, also, it is productive of a great deal of misery, —for a kind of corruptly diverted perspective that may serve in a measure to check social "progress." Is there not some mean between the extremes of prohibition on the one hand and unbridled license on the other? This, of course, is not a question for the historian to answer, but he would leave a false idea of the facts in the minds of his readers if he did not at least present a suggestion of the *spirit* in things as they are, as well as the mere external appearance in a language that might well be misinterpreted in another direction.[27]

story of the gambling is somewhat overdrawn; at any rate, in several games that the present writer saw, the great majority of the grand-stand crowd seemed to take no part in the betting. Nevertheless, there was a great deal of gambling, if, indeed, less than in jai-alai, and the enthusiasm of the crowd surpassed even that of a World's Series ball-game in the United States. The Cubans play real baseball, and several of their athletes have distinguished themselves in the great leagues of the United States. Adolfo Luque, playing with Cincinnati, was the champion pitcher of America in 1923 and 1925, and Miguel Gonzales has for years rated as one of the best catchers in baseball. The Cuban papers give a lot of space to the game, and the accounts have a Hispanic freedom and spiritedness that make them far more vivid than the average "story" in the American newspaper. The Cincinnati team of the National League,—"our beloved Cincy," as they call it,—is the favorite "big league" club of the Cuban people, for Cuban players have more often been given a chance by that team than by any other.

[27] While there is little that could be characterized as a serious social study concerning Cuba, there is, of course, a vast body of materials that might be utilized. There are a great many books of description and travel by Americans dealing with Cuba and scores of articles, most of them rather superficial. One volume, however, is especially worthy of comment, *Cuba*, by Irene Aloha Wright. This is a remarkable book for an American to have written, not only because of its information and its insight, but also because of its almost Hispanic independence and freedom of expression. Miss Wright based her impressions on a number of years' residence in Cuba, during which time she took an active part in the every-day life of the country serving for a while as a reporter on *Diario de la marina*. She outspokenly decried many of the conditions in the social atmosphere of the country,—although it may be observed, incidentally, that Miss Wright has continued to reside either in Cuba or Spain ever since, in preference to her own America. Though written as far back as 1910 Miss Wright's book is still worth reading, because of its grasp on some of the underlying factors in Cuban life. Cuban

writers, while they lack the perspective of the foreigner in discussing social conditions, have a far more detailed and accurate knowledge of particular institutions. The articles and pamphlets of Aguayo, Carrión, Guerra, Ortiz, Trelles, and Varona on education and other matters, cited in this chapter, are valuable samples of this type of literature. The volume on the census of 1919 (*Censo de la república de Cuba: año de 1919*) is a treasure-house of information, as also are its predecessors of 1899 and 1907. All three were prepared under American auspices, with great care. Parker, *Cubans of to-day*, is a useful volume. Any number of other references might be given. Indeed, there are few fields of Cuban history more prolifically rich in materials and less carefully worked out in well formulated studies. And hardly any subject is nearly so interesting.

CHAPTER XXVI

MATERIAL AND INTELLECTUAL CONDITIONS [1]

THE phenomenal wealth of Cuba is due in part to its natural resources and in part to the virtual underwriting of the republic by the United States through the Permanent Treaty, or Platt Amendment. Sugar is easily Cuba's chief product. The climate and soil of the island are so well adapted to the growth of the sugar-cane that Cuba has come to be recognized as the "sugar-bowl of the world." The sugar crop, which in 1911 amounted to 1,379,609 tons, was about 5,100,-000 in 1925, or nearly a fourth of the world's total production. Between 1909 and 1925 the annual crop was generally larger than in the preceding year, but there were wide fluctuations in price. Sugar rose from a normal level of around three cents a pound, to as much as five and a half cents during the World War, and then to an inflated level of twenty-two and a half cents in 1920. In that same year the market broke, and the price fell to three and five-eighths cents, rising again in 1923 to an average level of four and nine-tenths cents. Heavy production in different parts of the world caused a fall in price to less than three cents in 1925. The greater part of Cuban sugar estates is under the control of American companies. In 1924 over sixty per cent of the industry was in American hands. Altogether, the American investment in Cuba sugar is worth approxi-

[1] The writer at first proposed to have separate chapters on the sugar industry, the railways, financial history, general economic problems, and intellectual productivity, but decided at length to reduce this material to the comparatively short space given here. Cf. p. 581, n. 1.

mately a billion dollars, or more than all the sugar properties combined in lands under the American flag. Normally the United States takes from ninety to ninety-five per cent of the entire Cuban crop.

Cuban tobacco products are among the most highly regarded in the world, but the industry though second in importance in the island, does not compare with that of sugar. All other Cuban industries are insignificant by comparison with sugar or tobacco. In recent years the market for molasses, a by-product of sugar, has assumed considerable proportions. The island is adapted to fruit culture, notably citrus fruits, bananas, pineapples, and cocoanuts, but the full possibilities of this industry have not yet been realized. The grazing industry has attained to some prominence. There are iron, manganese, copper, and asphalt mines in the island, especially in Oriente. The henequen industry of Matanzas and sponge industry of Batabanó are locally important. In Cuban industries as a whole the United States has a total investment of nearly a billion and a half. This compares with eighty millions in 1901, which at that time was considered large. While most of the American money is in sugar, there are also vast sums in tobacco, mining, fruit, railways, street car companies, docks, warehouses, electric light and power companies, telephone companies, banks, hotels, steamship lines, and Cuban bonds sold in the northern republic. In 1923 American holdings in Cuba were estimated as twenty-seven per cent of the entire sum invested in the twenty republics to the south of the United States! Mexico, in which the American investment reached an amount second only to that of Cuba, had but seventeen per cent.

Cuba is an intensely commercial country, exporting all but a little of what it produces and importing nearly everything it consumes, even including food products, which constitute some thirty-five to forty per cent of the total. Sugar makes up eighty-five per cent or more of the exports in value, with tobacco eight or ten per cent, and other products scattering. The increase in the value of Cuban trade has been little less than phenomenal. At the beginning of the century (1900 to 1904) Cuba had an average annual volume of trade of about $136,000,000. This had reached a total of slightly more than three hundred million in 1914 and approximately $725,000,000 in 1924, the highest figure up to that time in Cuban history, except for the inflation period of 1919-1920. In 1920 the volume of trade with the United States alone was $1,125,000,000, but value in dollars was hardly a correct index then. Cuban products enjoy a preferential tariff of twenty per cent in the United States, while those from the United States get a concession of from twenty to forty per cent in Cuba. This is one of the reasons for the dominant position of the United States in Cuban trade. At the opening of the century (1900 to 1904) the normal value of the United States trade was only some $101,000,000. Disregarding the abnormal figures for 1920, American commerce with Cuba had reached $553,510,261 in 1924, or about seventy-six per cent of the total. The importance of this trade to the United States is illustrated by figures for 1923 showing that Cuba with $367,345,910 stood second in the world in exports to the United States, and with $181,717,272 was sixth in imports from that country! This far surpassed the value of American trade with any other part of Hispanic America. On account of the decline in the price of sugar the value of Cuban trade with the United States was over fifty millions smaller in 1925 than it was in 1924.

There are two principal railway systems in Cuba, which also control several lesser lines. The United Railways of Havana is an English company which is the dominant factor in the west, while the Cuba Railroad, an American company, is equally powerful in the east. The latter has greatly extended its sphere of influence through acquiring virtual ownership of the Cuba Northern in 1924. While the island is, on the whole, well served by railways, with some 3250 miles in operation, the same cannot be said for the roads. Vast sums have been expended in road-building, but with little or no benefit to the republic, because of graft or lack of care. Naturally enough, government figures on this score are unreliable. Direct steamship connection exists with numerous European and American ports, with frequent sailings, and there is train service to the United States, availing itself of a ferry from Havana to Key West.

Cuba had no currency of its own until 1915, using a variety of Spanish, American, and other foreign coins. Since 1915 there has been a Cuban coinage system paralleling that of the United States, but American money is also legal tender and is in fact in general use. The revenues of the government, which were some forty-one millions in 1910, rose to about double that figure in 1919, and still further to nearly $110,000,000 in 1921, but fell away to about fifty-seven million the next year as a result of the depression of 1920-1921. But in 1924 they were more than ninety-one million, and nearly ninety-three million in 1925. Expenditures ordinarily keep pace with revenues. In 1925 Cuba had a foreign debt of about eighty-seven million and a domestic debt just under twelve million. In addition there is a floating debt of perhaps fourteen million.[2]

So much for the story in brief. Something further should be said, however, to bring the situation more clearly into view. Unquestionably the sugar industry is in the back-

[2] The *data* given here were obtained from a study of the many admirable publications of the Bureau of Foreign and Domestic Commerce at Washington.

ground of every important phase of Cuban life. As virtually
a one-product country Cuba is an economic football. When
prosperity gives it a kick it soars high, but when depression
boots it, it drives at the enemy's line and is batted back.
The last years of Menocal's rule were eloquent of that.
Sugar is produced in every province in Cuba, but especially
in Camagüey and Oriente, with Santa Clara and Matanzas
also making a good showing. In Spanish days the two first-
named provinces were not greatly utilized for sugar estates,
but the growing demand for Cuba's chief product and the
development of railway facilities have contributed to make
this region preëminent. Forests have been burned to give
room for cane, and the ashes and stumps left in the fields
to serve as fertilizer. Occasionally the more valuable species
of timber are first cut down and hauled away, but perhaps
more often they are not. Thus, woods that are highly prized
in the north,—mahogany, for example,—are sacrificed to
make room for sugar. The method of planting is very
simple. Men with sharp-pointed sticks make holes in the
ground about four feet apart, and others follow them bearing
short lengths of cane, each containing one or two joints.
These are thrust, one at a time, in the holes that have just
been made, and then made firm by pressing the earth around
them through stamping with the bare feet. The cane sprouts
quickly from the eyes of the sections, and in eighteen months
is ready for cutting. The original stalk lasts without re-
planting, however, for from five to twenty-five years; indeed,
it is said that some of the cane-fields of Oriente have still
produced good crops after sixty years. The cane responds
readily to fertilizing processes, but without some assistance
of that sort the soil becomes exhausted much earlier than
otherwise. Fire is one of the grave threats of the cane-field,
as there are few growing things that are easier to ignite and

more difficult to stop. Public opinion has been educated to an appreciation of the importance of the sugar crop to all in the community; so nearly everybody turns out to help check a blaze that has started, and woe betide any man suspected of having set fire to a field deliberately! There would be no waiting for the decision of a law court.

Perhaps not more than a tenth of the sugar produced in Cuba comes from "administration cane," or that which is grown under the direct management of the great companies in control of the sugar-mills, or "*centrales,*" as they are called. Instead, the "*colono*" (colonist) system is in almost general use, although in a variety of forms. In many cases a man will be a proprietor of his own lands, but will sell his cane to a near-by mill. The more generally accepted meaning for this system, however, concerns the men who get lands from the central company on a peculiar rental basis whereby they receive in *sugar,* or its market price, a certain percentage on every hundred pounds of *cane* delivered. It may range from four to eight per cent, though perhaps more often somewhere between those limits. Thus, if it were six per cent, the *colono* would get six pounds of sugar, or more likely the price of six pounds, for every hundred pounds of cane, leaving the company whatever amount of sugar above six pounds it could get out of that amount of cane. As sugar averages only a little more than eleven pounds to each hundred of cane, the administration ordinarily has less than half the total amount, out of which to pay its expenses and provide dividends. Such scientific methods have been employed by the great sugar companies, however, that profits begin at a moderately low cost per pound. At the present time it is said that sugar is profitable at a price of three cents, although there are undoubtedly some concerns that can make money under the three cent level.

As one travels in Cuba he passes miles and miles of growing cane, and presently sees a tall chimney, perhaps two
hundred feet high, which marks the location of a mill.   The
cutting season, though varying with different estates, runs
ordinarily from December to June, in the dry season.   No
labor-saving devices have yet been able to supersede the
traditional workman in the fields, who takes his *machete,*
or harvesting knife, and goes from stalk to stalk, cutting it
near the ground.   Several more strokes, and he has stripped
it of its leaves, shaved off the top, and divided what is left
into two pieces about three feet long.   These are gathered
by men driving two-wheeled ox-carts, and taken directly
to the mill, or, more often, to the nearest station of the nar-
row-gauge railway that winds here and there through the
estate.   The mill itself has an enormously expensive but
highly efficient equipment for extracting the juice from the
cane and then reducing it to raw sugar, although the refining
process is usually completed after shipment to the United
States.   Good wages are paid,—enough for the Cuban *guajiro*
to work from four to six months, and then "loaf and buy
lottery tickets the rest of the year"; [3] at least, so some of
the writers say, although there are other factors in Cuban
life (to be mentioned presently) which keep the laborer in
a state that is far from one of affluence.   There are not
enough laborers in Cuba to meet the demand, and so thousands of others are brought in,—Spaniards, Haitians, Ja-
maicans, and Chinese,—most of whom return to their native
country (except the Chinese) at the end of the cutting season.   Then ensues the "dead" season, from June to December, when the cane may be left to itself, with very little
supervision, and without any need, therefore, for a considerable labor supply.   Thus Cuba, which is a bee-hive in winter,

[3] Franck, 82.

becomes "dead" in the summer,—though very much alive in the ways of pleasurable recreation.

During the latter part of the dead season in sugar, the tobacco industry is at its most active stage, from October to January, although various other processes are necessary, before the finished product reaches the market, that consume most of the year. Tobacco may be grown in every province of Cuba, but Pinar del Río is by all odds the greatest producer. There, in the famous Vuelta Abajo district, of which the city of Pinar del Río is approximately the centre, is grown the best tobacco leaf in the world. Vuelta Abajo is only some thirty miles long from west to east and ten miles wide, and not all of its fields yield the finest grade of tobacco, but, in those that do, it is not unusual for the net to run as high as two thousand dollars an acre. Most of the lands of Pinar del Río, however, in Vuelta Abajo or out of it, are far less profitable than that. The industry itself is highly complicated, involving seeding, transplanting, an expensive process of cultivation, cutting and curing of the leaf, and its shipment to Havana. The project is usually handled on shares between a landholder, who also provides capital, and a *veguero,* or planter, who carries on all the work. The modern tobacco field looks, in the distance, like a series of great snow-banks,—an effect produced by wide-spreading canopies of cheese-cloth, to protect the plants from a persistent and dangerous insect pest. There is an enormous consumption of tobacco in Cuba,—perhaps forty per cent of the total crop. About two-thirds of the portion that is exported goes out in the form of leaf, and most of the remaining third in cigars.

The other industries of Cuba may be passed over here, except for some further comment on the railroads. Cuba's first railway was built at Güines, province of Havana, in

1837,—before even a mile had been built anywhere else under the Spanish Flag. This formed the nucleus for the later development of the powerful United Railways of Havana, an English company which today occupies a dominant position among the public service railways in the three western provinces of Cuba. There was not a great deal of railway building under Spain, however; at the close of Spanish rule there were perhaps a thousand miles of track in the island, or less than a third of what Cuba possesses now; in 1900 it had increased to 1135 miles, nine-tenths of which radiated from Havana, with but a little over a hundred miles in the three eastern provinces, constituting about three-fourths of the territory of the island. In that same year an enterprise got under way that was to open up eastern Cuba and immeasurably increase the wealth and resources of the country. This was the building of the Cuba Railway, the story of which reads more like a romance than a drab recital of a business transaction.

Early in 1900 Sir William Van Horne, famous as the builder of the Canadian Pacific Railway, was in Cuba, on his way to British Guiana. He never went any farther. Seeing great possibilities for a railway in eastern Cuba, he resolved to put his ideas to the test. Under the handicap of the Foraker Law,[4] he not only could expect no government subsidy, but also could not even obtain a government charter. There was nothing in the law that prevented one from building a railway as a private undertaking, however, and he was able to gain assurances of approval from the United States military government. Van Horne then went to New York, interested a number of American and Canadian capitalists, and in April 1900 incorporated with his associates

[4] Cf. *supra,* pp: 105; 123.

under a New Jersey charter as the Cuba Company, which was to develop the resources of Cuba "in all practicable ways." This was rather an aristocrat among stock companies, for there were only 160 shares, each with a par value of fifty thousand dollars. In recent years the shares have been split up. In 1902 the Cuba Railroad Company was incorporated as a subsidiary of this organization. Meanwhile, Van Horne had proceeded with tremendous energy in the building of his line, which was to run eastward from the city of Santa Clara to Santiago in the south of Oriente and to Antilla, on Nipe Bay, on the northern shore of the same province. Owners had to be induced to part with strips of their land, either as a free gift or on their own terms. Eventually some assistance was obtained from the Wood government, though mainly in quieting the title of the company to the lands it had acquired and in the grant of a revocable license for it to cross streams, roads, or other public property. As early as December 1, 1902, the road was completed and ready for traffic! Thus, Santiago was brought within one day's ride of Havana, where formerly it had taken ten days, and a new Cuba, since become the richest part of the island, was opened to productive development.

There are several other comparatively unimportant public service railways in addition to the United and Cuba lines, but of perhaps more interest are the numerous private railways of the great sugar companies. These not only assist in getting the cane to the mill, but also carry the raw sugar to a near-by port or else to a station of some public service railway. In the latter event the private lines may have a standard gauge track, although narrow gauge lines are usually employed. The private lines are wholly subordinated to the industry they represent, doing very little business on other scores, and ordinarily they shut down altogether during the dead season of the sugar estates.

The phenomenal wealth of Cuba is based very largely on the existence of the Permanent Treaty with the United States, as none acknowledge more readily than the more serious-minded of the Cuban writers.[5] A great many, however, wonder whether the vast influx of foreign capital into the island has been of any benefit to the Cubans themselves. Varona has called attention to this factor in numerous essays, pointing out that Cuba's best lands are foreign-owned, growing sugar (and to a less extent tobacco) for export, at the same time that the Cubans import from abroad almost everything they consume, even including food and other articles that might be produced at home. He felt that care should be taken to assist the Cubans in retaining possession of their own soil.[6] Much the same position has been taken by other Cuban writers. Ortiz has asserted that two-thirds of the sugar industry is under American control (not to mention other industries that are more or less completely American), although admitting that ninety-five per cent of the plantations, on the *"colono"* basis, are in Hispano-Cuban hands and that American ownership of Cuban soil does not amount to more than 16.72 per cent. He feared some political consequences, remarking that the Americans, however altruistic, would be more likely to think of their estates than of Cuba; they certainly would never destroy

[5] For example, Pérez, Luis Marino, *Cuba and the United States*, in *Inter-America* (Eng. ed.), v. V, pp. 358-361, at 360; Aug., 1922.

[6] Varona, Enrique José, *Discurso sobre el capital extranjero . . . el 8 de junio de 1911*, in *De la colonia a la república*, 257-261, is one item out of many in Varona's writings to this effect. His attitude, as usual in his works, was less that of anti-foreign propaganda than of lecturing the Cuban people to get them to mend their ways. "Our tendency is to live from the budget, and not from the land," he once said. *Mirando adelante* (May 14, 1915), in *De la colonia a la república*, 267-268, at 268.

them voluntarily, as many Cubans of the independence era had done.[7]

There can be little quarrel with these statements, especially in the form that men like Varona and Ortiz put them, as a Cuban matter rather than as an aggressive foreign evil. Popular opinion, however, is inclined to exaggerate the amount of the resources already in foreign hands. As one writer has put it, the Cubans won their independence from Spain only to turn the country over to alien business interests, except that the Cubans retained the taxes, the national hymn, and the flag,—and also politics.[8] The American investment in Cuba is certainly great, but the Cubans still "own" their own country; indeed, many of the "American" corporations operating in the islands are owned in part by Cubans holding securities of these companies. Aside from that, one of the more reputable Havana papers recently pointed out that Americans owned only some fifteen per cent of Cuban wealth, or about $1,250,000,000 in a total of eight billions. A great deal more, however, was in other foreign hands.[9] It cannot be denied that foreign capital, particularly American, *does* dominate the economic life of Cuba and consequently has a very great influence on social and political conditions. Whether this is a situation that is good or bad is something that may be argued *pro* and *con*. One thing ought to be said, nevertheless, and that is that the United States government, except in times of an emergency, does not render any considerable aid to the American companies in Cuba. The State Department has consistently taken the stand that it is not a claims agency, and American

[7] Ortiz, 24-27.
[8] Roa, Jorge, *Del ambiente actual*, in *Diario de la marina*, May 13, 1924.
[9] *Foreign capital is greatly respon-* sible for Cuba's welfare, in *Diario de la marina*, translated in Havana *Post*, Feb. 11, 1925.

business concerns have usually adapted themselves to conditions as they found them.[10]

Popular opinion concerning the aggrandizement of foreign corporations occasionally finds expression in Congress. Soon after the installation of the Gómez government, for example, Emilio Arteaga introduced a bill in the House, on February 19, 1909, prohibiting the purchase of real estate in Cuba by foreigners; in the preliminary discussions it had even been suggested that foreigners already owning lands should be required to become Cuban citizens, but that feature was not included in the bill as presented. For a time it seemed to have a chance of passing, as it was backed by El Triunfo, the principal Liberal organ of that period, generally regarded as the mouthpiece of President Gómez. Almost at once it became apparent, however, that the existence of foreign capital was the lesser of two evils. Business interests were frightened, various enterprises were halted, and Cuban values showed a tendency to drop "through the bottom." So the bill was reported unfavorably, and beaten decisively, forty-nine to eleven, in a vote taken March 8, 1909.[11] Among those who opposed the measure was the eminent and respected González Lanuza, who said that the trouble was, not that the Cubans were selling their lands to the foreigners, but that they were placed in such a position that they could not do anything else. Furthermore, if immigrants were to be attracted who would take root in Cuba it was necessary to give them a chance to acquire land.[12]

[10] Incidentally, it may be remarked that American capital in no sense acts as a unit. One of the principal concerns of most American companies is competition, not with Cubans or with European corporations, but with other Americans. In any controversy involving American capital there are usually American companies on both sides. Witness, for example, the battle over the Tarafa Law. Cf. *supra*, pp. 458-464.

[11] Havana *Post* for Feb. 19, 20, 26, and Mar. 4, 5, 9.

[12] Speech in the session of Mar. 8, 1909, in *Prohibición a los extranjeros de adquirir tierras*, in González Lanuza, 797-803.

That Cuba as a whole profits from the presence of foreign capital is impossible to deny; without it Cuba would sink from being relatively the richest country in Hispanic America to a level certainly very much farther down. The question that interests the Cuban people, however, is whether they themselves gain from it. To the writer it seems that beyond a doubt they do. Small as Cuba is, it supports a considerable *Cuban* population, rather greater per square mile than in most parts of Hispanic America. And it must be that a very notable individual opportunity is offered, for there is an extraordinary number of wealthy Cubans in the island,—certainly rather more *per capita* than almost anywhere else in Hispanic America. Furthermore, not only indirectly, but also in many direct ways the foreign companies do much to benefit both Cuba and the Cubans. They employ vast numbers of Cubans,—virtually all that are willing to work; they help local cane-farmers with loans and in other ways to keep up their cultivation; some of the best schools in Cuba are provided by them, free of charge; a number of trades are taught to Cubans through their agency, such as those of mechanics, locomotive engineers, and carpenters; large amounts are expended by them in sanitation; hospitals are furnished which are available for people generally in their district as well as for their own employes; near-by towns often receive aid from them in municipal improvements, such as the installation of sewage systems and the building of slaughter-houses; many of the roads in their district are kept in repair by them; and housing conditions on the foreign-owned estates are usually better than in those under Cuban control. These are but a few incidental ways in which Cubans are benefited by foreign capital. The greatest single item, however, is in the amount of revenue it pays to the Cuban state. If most of it is wasted, it is hardly the fault of the foreign companies. All this is *not* to say that Cuba is better off with her wealth in foreign hands than she would be if the same wealth were Cuban-owned. It seems to the writer that Cuba is merely going through an inevitable preliminary process. All countries in their economic youth, the United States included, turn to foreign capital for the initial stages of their development. Eventually they may win over the foreign enterprises to themselves if they deserve to have them. Cubans may feel a dislike for foreign capital now, just as the American hated the "bloated British bondholder" a century ago, but they may just as surely regain their country as the people of the United States have won back theirs, if they will do what Varona and Ortiz recommend: do the best they can with the capital they already possess, and meanwhile correct the defects, notably corrupt government, that keep them from improving their condition beyond what it is today.[13]

To be sure, there are a number of evils that grow out of the presence of foreign capital in Cuba. Indirectly, of course, the greatest springs from the vast revenues collected by the state, without which the now colossal graft in Cuba would sink perhaps to a Honduranian scale. It is often asked whether the companies themselves do not also engage directly in graft, with the idea of influencing politics for purposes of their own. The question in fact resolves itself

[13] A phase of the unpopularity of foreign capital is to be found in attacks on the National City Bank of New York, one of the most important banking houses doing business in Cuba. As a prominent Spaniard said to the writer: "The unpopularity of the National City Bank amounts to nothing. It is because debtors hate their creditors when they find it difficult to pay, and the National City insists upon payment on the due date, and not several days later. The Royal Bank of Canada does the same thing, but does not have such a large loan business as the City Bank." Both the National City and the Royal Bank met all their obligations in the crash of 1920, but have probably made things up to some extent since, as they no longer face the competition of Cuban and continental European institutions which closed their doors at that time. People know their money is safe with the above-named banks.

into two distinct parts. The companies *do* indulge in graft, almost all of them. Usually, however, it is not because they are meddling in politics, but because the politicians are meddling with them. Rather than suffer annoyance most of the foreign corporations will do such things as provide Cuban officials with houses free of charge, or employ politicians and their friends as "lawyers," without any work to do. Ordinarily, the greater corporations do not have to go beyond this stage, as they are indirectly too valuable to the politicians in Havana through the revenues they provide. It is probable that some of the foreign companies do seek special favors by means of improprieties on a great scale, but that would not seem to apply to the sugar interests, which want primarily to be let alone.

There are, indeed, a number of bad corporate practices which are indulged in by Cuban companies as well as foreign and are a fraud on stockholders, usually foreigners, rather than on the Cubans themselves. Quite often, so it is said, a stock company will be formed to engage in the sugar business. The promoters will keep control, and will give themselves good high-paying jobs as officers of the company. Presently a few large dividends will be paid, enabling the promoters to unload their stock at a high price,—and then dividends will be passed, and the stock come smashing down. Reacquiring control, the officers,—that is to say, the promoters,—will suggest a bond issue, and when this is put through will keep fifty-one per cent of the bonds, and again unload the stock. Next the company is forced into receivership, and given to the bondholders, the original promoters. If in fact they have a good sugar property they may at this point carry on the business in a more reputable manner; otherwise they may look for a new crop of "easy marks," and go through the same operation as before. Even when corporate iniquities are not indulged in on the scale just described, there are many improprieties of a lesser order. Aside from the high-paying office graft,—for such it often is,—men in control of a company may organize several other companies for themselves, using their position with the larger concern in order to make unfair profits for the ones in which they have full ownership. One such case came to the writer's notice, where a coal company, organized by officers of a great corporation, was given the sole right to sell coal to the latter,—and did so at more than the market price. Practices of this sort are, of course, a form of robbing the small stockholder such as is engaged in everywhere, but in Cuba the law is less likely to impose a check on these operations than in countries where government is on a somewhat more respectable basis.

Quite apart from foreign capital in itself, there are a number of other problems in the economic life of Cuba. One is a bad system of taxation. Taxes on real estate are very light, and on unimproved lands nothing at all. One writer says that during the Magoon era the only time all the Cuban members of the Advisory Law Commission agreed was in opposing a tax on unimproved land. They asserted that it would cause a revolution, although they were really afraid lest those who were thus taxed might demand a greater representation in government, which the politicians wanted to keep to themselves.[14] Other sources of revenue had therefore to be tapped. Something has been obtained from industrial taxes:

"Every shop, factory, office, here, pays for the privilege of bidding for trade; wagons and carriages, automobiles and carts; peddlers, funerals, and public amusements,—every form of activity and energy, in short, is taxed." [15]

[14] Wright, 196.   [15] *Ibid.,* 197.

The total of these contributions, however, is not very heavy, and the addition of the lottery revenue leaves the government still far short of its needs. As already pointed out, it is the custom-house that accounts for the great bulk of the national income. And the tax is high. In 1909 Cuba was paying $12.10 *per capita* in customs duties alone, as compared with the following sums at that time in countries with a high protective tariff: United States $3.55; France $2.22; Italy $1.72; Germany $1.22; and Austria $.51.[16] Later, Cuba collected still more. In Menocal's best year for customs receipts, he took in over thirty dollars per inhabitant, though averaging about seventeen for the entire period of his rule, while Zayas averaged about twenty-three dollars. The evil, however, is not so much in the amount as in the character of the goods that pay the duties, for the system is frankly one of "extortion for revenue only,"— taxes, not so much on luxuries or on products for which Cuba has an "infant industry," but on necessities, with the burden falling heaviest on those least able to pay, on the mass of the Cuban people.[17]

This brings up a question, often discussed in Cuba, that would be worthy of consideration if there were the slightest chance that it would be treated seriously by the politicians. That is, the desirability of legislation to promote economic diversity, especially along the lines of protection for Cuban industries that might produce some of the necessities at present purchased abroad. There is frequently a great deal of talk along these lines, but nothing of importance is ever accomplished, as the Cuban government is "in business" for

[16] Wright, 198.
[17] *Ibid:* 194; 198. Many Cuban writers have called attention to this same evil. Varona did so frequently, e. g. in *A los Conservadores,* no. 4 in *Siete circulares: 1910 a 1913,* in *De la colonia a la república,* 247-250, at 247-248.

"revenue only," and not for Cuba.[18]   To be sure, some industries have sprung up in Cuba as a result of the high tariff,—
those producing beer, soap, and cement, for example,—but
they occupy a very insignificant position in the sum total of
Cuban wealth.

Certainly one problem in Cuba about which volumes
could be written is that concerning labor.   The greater part
of the labor supply is floating and without steady employment, due to the peculiarities of the sugar industry.   From
December to June, labor is at a premium, and from June
until near December is a drug on the market.   In most other
industries there is work the year around, but they do not
compare in importance with sugar.   And if technical skill
is required it is more often a foreigner who is engaged than
a Cuban, as the latter rarely has the type of ability demanded, though a good workman at tasks he understands.
One of the most annoying conditions, however,—wherever
the fault may lie,—is the prevalence of strikes.   The situation is not the same as in the United States.   Labor is not
in the least degree conservative, but is ignorant and oppor-
tunist, at the beck and call of leaders, frequently Spanish
radicals, who do not command respect; many of them use
their power to blackmail proprietors into paying them graft
in order to avoid a strike.   Most of the newspapers condemn
the propensity of the laborers to strike, and they speak out
on this score with a freedom that no journal in the United
States would display.   The government, as a rule, does noth-

[18] *Las entidades económicas y la
reforma arancelaria,* in *Diario de la
marina,* May 14, 1924, is one such
article, out of many.   This stated
that the Association of Havana Merchants had joined with the National
Association of Industry in approving
the proposed tariff reform to protect
Cuban infant industries.   *An important problem,* in *Prensa,* translated in
Havana *Post,* May 14, 1924, advocated protection for the poultry industry, asserting that Cuba was paying fifteen millions for poultry and
eggs, with eggs at from four to ten
cents apiece.

ing, although congressmen will make radical labor speeches and will at times promote amnesty bills in favor of strikers who have broken the laws. If the government *does* move, it will almost always take the side of the employers. This is easy to comprehend. Profits for employers mean also a large volume of foreign trade, which means revenue for the government, which means the politicians. The laborers, even if they are right, must not be allowed to cut down the funds in the treasury. If popular opinion as represented by the newspapers is correct, however, the laborers of Cuba are more often wrong than right. They strike if they think they can win, irrespective of the merits of their case. And if one group wins, another strikes; and then the first group, which may have made a binding agreement to accept certain terms, will blithely forget its contract, and go out again.[19]

In the fall of 1924 something new in strikes made its appearance in Cuba, this being a series of outbreaks at the sugar mills. Owing to the migratory character of labor, and especially the wholesale departure of workmen during the dead season, there had never been any unions at the mills. A number of labor leaders, in great part Spaniards, now proposed to organize the workers, and instituted various de-

---

[19] The following are some sample comments to this effect in connection with a strike that broke out on the United Railways in May 1924. "When the railroaders win a strike, then another union decrees a strike, believing that it also can triumph in its demands, regardless of whether they are justified or not." *Again a strike*, in *Sol*, translated in Havana *Post*, May 27, 1924. Speaking of the demands of the railway employes, "A Sage" had this to say: "The railway could stand the additional burden if by so doing an end to the striking proclivities of its employes could be reached . . . It is certain, however, as the past experience has shown, that every time a concession is made to the workers by the railway, or by any other company, it encourages the workers to make further demands." Havana *Post*, May 27, 1924. While the strike was going on, a laborer named Emilio Marichal attempted to murder General Archibald Jack, the manager of the railway, wounding him severely. The laborer was given a light sentence, and an amnesty bill was soon introduced on his behalf, though in this instance without success. Marichal's sentence expires during 1926.

mands, just on the eve of the cane-cutting season. They insisted on such things as recognition of the union, the closed shop, an eight-hour day, higher wages, equal pay at all seasons of the year, and a right for the walking delegates of the union to have a place in the mills and to participate in their administration. This caused general consternation in Cuba, owing to the menace to the very life of the island through a possible failure of the sugar crop. Almost without exception the newspapers condemned the movement, and called on the government to act. Some were fearful of strong hand methods, however, as witness the following:

"The mill strike cannot be ended through force. If violence is employed there will be no sugar crop this year. Have the mill owners and the sugar planters forgotten that one man with a box of matches can destroy all the cane plantations of a mill without being seen or caught? Do they ignore that there is nothing so easy to 'sabotage' as a sugar-cane field?"[20]

Presently there was talk of the railway laborers going out in sympathy with the sugar workers and even of a general strike. This drew forth the following comment in one newspaper:

"Our laborers do not suffer the sting of cold or the pangs of hunger . . . Many of the locomotive-drivers and engineers in Cuba, without exaggeration, earn more money than . . . men who work with their heads. No real reasons exist in Cuba for the workingmen to become desperate. On the contrary there is always an ample field for work in town and country. To talk, therefore, of 'shaking off the chains of oppression' is not only absurd but insincere."[21]

The national authorities at length decided to act. On November 12, 1924, Zayas demanded that the mill-owners and their employes come to an agreement, or otherwise the gov-

[20] *With violence there will be no crop,* in *Heraldo,* translated Havana *Post,* Nov. 15, 1924.

[21] *The mill strike,* in *Lucha,* translated in Havana *Post,* Nov. 28, 1924.

ernment would take a hand. When he denied the right of strikers to dictate conditions for the acceptance of workmen at the mills and expressed an intention of deporting the "pernicious foreigners" who, he asserted, were largely responsible for the strikes, he intimated plainly enough which side of the controversy he was likely to adopt. A few days later he began deporting Spanish labor leaders, and meanwhile gave such aid to the mill-men as he could in protecting their cane. A number of fields were burned, however; on November 25, for example, it is said that twenty-five thousand *arrobas* of sugar (625,000 pounds) were destroyed. In December the strikes were on their last legs. Late rains played into the hands of the owners, making early grinding unnecessary, and the long duration of the dispute had pretty well depleted the financial resources of the strikers. So much for the sugar strike of 1924. But what of the future?

These comments will give a false view of the situation, however, if they are interpreted as implying that the laborers have no cause for complaint. They do have cause, but the complaint is misdirected. The fact that the newspapers and non-union people are generally against them is accounted for not merely by the mistakes of the workmen and their radicalism but also because the public opinion that the former reflect is that of capital and politics. It is probable that capital is far less at fault than politics. That brings up the familiar bugaboo of Cuban life,—the extreme cost of a parasite government. Here is the way one writer states the case:

"Cuba's population numbers approximately three million. These pay to the government through the custom-house alone $30,000,000 to $45,000,000 per annum, or $10 to $15 per capita, three or four times the figure for the highly protective United States. Nor are the Cuban duties paid by the rich on luxuries alone. The bulk of Cuba's imports consists of food and clothing for her common people. The import duties are paid from the sweat of the laborer's brow. In addition to this the Cuban pays in internal taxes another $10 per capita. He contributes, albeit voluntarily, nearly $12,000,000 more to a corrupt lottery from which the government receives only $4,000,000 or $5,000,000. To the official cost of, say, $25 per capita which the Cuban pays for government must be added, besides the lottery burden, first, all those little extortions and petty tributes which he must pay every time he comes in contact with an official but which never show in the accounts; and second, the uncalculated and incalculable losses which he suffers from the kind of government he gets. Is it to be wondered at that occasionally he looks wistfully at the Porto Rican, his former fellow-sufferer under the yoke of Spain, who now enjoys all the blessings of good government, protection of life and property, schools, roads, libraries, and many other things of which the Cuban does not even dream, all at a cost of $11 per capita, and wonders if 'Cuba Libre' is not a snare and a delusion? And when he sees that Porto Rican safe within the tariff wall of the United States, making money out of his sugar while Cuba counts her deficits on hers, and thinks of the additional $105,000,000 which Cuba loses each year because she is outside that wall—$35 for every man, woman, and child in the island—more than enough to pay for the decent government he would have if he were within it—who shall blame him if he indulges in some mental calculations as to the price of liberty which it would be treason for him to utter?" [22]

At least one writer goes beyond the Cuban politicians to place responsibility upon the United States for "betraying" the Cuban people by making them independent politically and thus utterly *dependent* economically on the whim of the great neighbor to the north. Asking what Cuba really wants, this writer answers the question as follows:

"Assuredly it is not that parasites be permitted to speak in her name any longer; to parade in the trappings of a fictitious independence; to bleed her for their support, in the name of a liberty she does not possess; but, instead, nothing more or less than opportunity to produce her crops in quietude, to sell them for what they are worth, and to buy from the proceeds what she must have at a fair price for it. Closer

[22] Norton, Henry Kittredge, *Self-determination in the West Indies*, in *World's work*, v. LI, pp. 77-84, at 84; Nov., 1925.

economic relation to the United States! To obtain that she'd actually be willing to continue to tolerate this republic of hers, if Washington which erected will not permit her to abolish it; could she but have altered tariffs to enable her to sell what she might then grow . . . she'd be well able to support her politicians, if their keep is the penalty laid upon her for Washington's erroneous snap judgment of her needs."[23]

There is more than a little truth in this. Cuba *is* utterly at the mercy of the United States economically. She is a one-crop country, dependent upon the American market, and subordinated in that to the interests of sugar men whose estates are under the American flag. All goes well when the price of sugar is high, but the pinch comes when it is low. At the time of the phenomenal drop in 1920-1921, for example, the United States clapped on an emergency tariff of two cents a pound (subsequently withdrawn), to protect the companies in continental United States, Porto Rico, Hawaii, and the Philippines. Cuba still had her twenty per cent advantage over other countries, but it availed her little. It is not to be wondered at, therefore, that Cuban writers and Cuban politicians are constantly agitating for a revision of the reciprocity treaty, so as to put Cuban sugar on a still more favorable basis in the American market.[24] It must be admitted that the plea has merit, for Cuba and the United States economically are one, Cuba pays well for American goods, and the United States has certain special political advantages under the Permanent Treaty, but the island republic has so far not been too successful in its quest of a more favorable treaty. The sugar interests of the United

[23] Wright, 206. The quotation is from an admirable chapter entitled *Wanted: a market!*, 194-206.

[24] For an excellent argument to this effect, see Pérez, Luis Marino, *Op. cit. A ray of hope*, in *Mercurio*, translated in Havana *Post*, May 15, 1924, is a sample editorial, out of hundreds, to the same effect. This also was the basic idea in an address delivered by Cosme de la Torriente, Cuban ambassador to the United States, at a banquet in the Biltmore Hotel, New York City, Apr. 23, 1924, on the occasion of the inauguration of the Cuban Chamber of Commerce at New York.

States are opposed to any change, but it is doubtful if that is solely accountable for Cuba's failure to gain a lower tariff, and it may not be even the principal obstacle in Cuba's way. The fact is, that the tariff on sugar is, next to the Permanent Treaty, the most important medium of pressure the United States can use in dealings with Cuba, and while graft continues to be the norm of political procedure in that country it is not likely that the United States will grant any privileges which, after all, would probably be utilized primarily to the advantage of the corrupt, parasitic, and anti-American political class.

Cuban literature since the winning of independence has lost what was once almost its sole *raison d'être*, that of being a weapon in the struggle for liberty against Spain. Both in poetry and in prose the nineteenth century furnished many names worthy of the best in Hispanic American letters, among which those of Heredia, Varela, Saco, Luz y Caballero, and Martí perhaps stand out from the rest. These men were Cuban patriots above all else, using their writings primarily for purposes of attack against the "oppressor," Spain. With liberty attained, however, there has been very little in the life of the republic to inspire a new band of intellectuals. Protests against the political corruption of one's own countrymen are no such ringing theme as a battle for freedom against the outlander.

There are few names that must needs be mentioned in a review of intellectual life in the period of the republic. By general consent Enrique José Varona is given first rank among the literary figures of the period. It is a question, however, whether his best work may not have belonged to the pre-independence era. He was in the front rank of the workers for separation from Spain, and, indeed, since his literary début in 1879 he has been associated with almost every important intellectual movement in Cuba. A philosopher of the school of Herbert Spencer, he taught the gospel of freedom, finding a medium especially in the *Revista cubana* (Cuban review) and later in *La patria* (The fatherland), of both of which magazines he was the editor. After the winning of independence he served as Secretary of Public Instruction under General Wood, and was later president of the Conservative party for a while and Vice-President of the republic from 1913 to 1917, but in the main he has not been active in politics. He has continued to write on social, political, and economic subjects, but while greatly respected he has not been followed in his counsels. His essays might have been penned by a Puritan of colonial New England, in so far as their unimpeachable moral judgments are concerned, and, indeed, they read very much like a Protestant tract lecturing the people for their sins, though simply and logically presented. Like nearly all of the patriots of pre-independence days, Varona is slightly anti-American and still seems to feel the suspicions of 1898. Nevertheless, there is a world of sound advice in his preachings, and the day might well come when the Cubans should make some attempt to profit by them.

A number of others might also be named who, like Varona, belong to two ages in Cuban literature, with possibly their best work in the earlier of the two. Manuel Sanguily, another of the literary battlers for independence, is one. He was famous primarily as an orator. Under the republic he participated actively in politics until 1913, and did comparatively little writing. A rather more notable literary figure in republican times is Raimundo Cabrera, a leading Cuban novelist and descriptive writer, some of whose best works were published during the era of the republic. His

Mis malos tiempos, one of the principal authorities for the exciting events around the Revolution of February, is also a delightful literary product, and his novels are a faithful portrait of Cuban life since 1900.

One of the more important literary developments of the republican period has been the founding of a number of excellent magazines, which is all the more noteworthy in that journals of this class do not often flourish in Hispanic American countries.   The following is one writer's rather enthusiastic judgment of them:

"At present the periodicals published in the island equal if they do not surpass in literary qualities those of any other nation. Take, for example, the beautifully illustrated *Figaro*, long conducted by the poet Manuel S. Pichardo; *Cuba y America*, whose purpose is 'the regeneration of Cuban culture,' and whose editor, Salvador Salazar, is an enthusiastic student of literature; or the scholarly monthly *Cuba Contemporánea*, directed by Carlos de Velasco, which is doing an unsurpassed service for the study of Cuban literature.   The famous organ of the ancient society, Los Amigos del Pais, entitled *La Revista bimestre cubana*, has also been revived." [25]

Reforma Social, one of the best monthly reviews in Hispanic America, ought also to be included in this list.

There are several writers of note who belong wholly to the republic.   One of these is Rafael Martínez Ortiz, whose two-volume history, entitled *Cuba: los primeros años de independencia* (Cuba: the first years of independence) is in every sense a meritorious study.   The author was a prominent Liberal in the political life of the republic, but was able to subordinate partisanship in writing history and to employ the technique of the historian.   His history is also in a most

[25] Coester, Alfred, *The literary history of Spanish America* (New York. 1919), pp. 428-429.   Coester has an entire chapter on Cuba (pp. 373-430), but only a mere fragment touches the republic. The reference to Salazar is inaccurate, for Raimundo Cabrera, who founded *Cuba y América* in 1897, was its editor until it suspended publication in 1920.

attractive style. Another outstanding figure is Carlos Trelles, the Cuban Medina, whose bibliographical output has been phenomenal in amount and value on every phase of Cuban history. Except for the great Chilean just alluded to, there is perhaps no bibliographer in the world who outranks Trelles,—certainly none in the two Americas. Trelles occasionally turns aside for a searching analysis and denunciation of existing social and political conditions. Possibly the man of the most varied intellectual attainments in contemporary Cuban letters is Fernando Ortiz, lawyer, criminologist, historian, one-time professor in the University, for a while a representative in Congress, now president of the Academy of History, president of the Sociedad Económica de los Amigos del País (Economic Society of the Friends of the Country), editor of *Revista bimestre cubana* (Bi-monthly Cuban review), and also editor of *Archivos del folklore cubano* (Archives of Cuban folklore). He is the author of several historical studies on social aspects of colonial times, especially concerning the negroes, and is a prolific writer on contemporary social and political problems, dealing one moment with education, another with judicial questions, and at all times standing for a thoroughgoing correction of present-day evils. With that manysidedness that has characterized a number of the great Hispanic scholars of the past, he also has the highmindedness of the true Cuban patriot. Several other men would be deserving of notice in a more extensive survey of Cuban intellectual productivity, such as the already mentioned editors of Cuba's leading periodicals or Alfredo Aguayo for his writtings on education.[26] In addition, one might well name the

[26] *Cubans of to-day*, the Cuban "Who's Who," includes a number of men who have attained to distinction in literature, education, and art. Ninety-five were authors or journalists; ninety-seven, educators; and eleven, artists or musicians. These figures would be reduced to perhaps

following: in literary criticism José María Chacón, Jorge Mañach, Enrique Hernández Miyares, Manuel Márquez Sterling; the poets Agustín Acosta, Bonifacio Byrne, Gustavo Sánchez Galarraga, Juan Marinello, Rubén Martínez Villena; among novelists Miguel de Carrión, Carlos Loveira; the historians Emilio Bacardí, Domingo Figarola, Fernando Figueredo, Francisco González del Valle, and Antonio Valverde; in law Mariano Aramburo, Antonio Sánchez de Bustamante; in science Israel Castellanos, Carlos De la Torre, Jorge Le-Roy, Emilio Roig; and in art the painter Leopoldo Romañach.[27]

Something has already been said about education and the newspapers,[28] both of which subjects might ordinarily be considered under the heading of intellectual life. In Cuba, however, it would seem that they belong rather more in the realm of social problems.[29]

thirty-five, twenty-seven, and seven, respectively, if the men were considered merely from the standpoint of the profession in which they were most prominent.

[27] An outstandingly important discussion of recent tendencies in the history of Cuban culture is Mañach, Jorge, *La crisis de la alta cultura en Cuba*, Habana, 1925, an address which was published in a pamphlet of forty-four pages.

[28] *Supra*, pp. 592-603.

[29] One cannot complain of lack of material on the score of economic conditions, for there is an abundance of it in Cuban and United States government documents, articles in periodicals, news items and editorials, and in a number of books. Probably the best continuing material along statistical lines is that provided in the frequent Bulletins of the Bureau of Foreign and Domestic Commerce, in the Department of Commerce at Washington. Concerning intellectual productivity there is as yet little but the works of the men themselves, with nothing of great account in the way of formulated studies concerning them. Comments in the Cuban reviews are undoubtedly the nearest thing to critical appreciations that have yet appeared.

CHAPTER XXVII

THE FUTURE OF CUBA: A QUESTION

WHAT does the future hold forth for Cuba? What for the relations of the United States and Cuba? What ought to be done in Cuba, and what, if any, are the obligations of the United States? An answer to these questions is not easy,— all the less so, since it is difficult to say what is the precise character of Cuban-American relations now. The basis for the relationships between Cuba and the United States is, of course, the Permanent Treaty, growing out of the Platt Amendment.[1] According to one's attitude toward Cuban affairs the famous "appendix" means much or little. At the one extreme are those who hold it means a right for the United States to intervene in Cuba at any time, since it is always possible to find instances where there has not been an adequate "protection of life, property, and individual liberty." Indeed, one would not need to hunt very hard for such cases in the notoriously bad Cuban governments of recent years. At the other extreme are those who deny that the Platt Amendment imposes any limitation on Cuban sovereignty or who reject it altogether. Among the more interesting writings of Cubans are volumes by Ambrosio Valentín López Hidalgo, a veteran of the War of Independence, and Luis Machado, a prominent young lawyer of Havana.

López Hidalgo held that the Platt Amendment and the subsequent treaty did limit Cuban sovereignty, and, in so much, represented a non-fulfilment of the promise of inde-

[1] See *supra,* chapter VI, *passim,* especially at pp. 135-137.

pendence in the Joint Resolution of April 20, 1898. In this connection he drew an interesting parallel between the language of the Joint Resolution and that of the American Declaration of Independence.[2] After indulging himself in a few denunciations of American bad faith López Hidalgo went on to say that most of the articles of the Platt Amendment contained political principles that any good Cuban government might well have adopted. The worst feature of the document, he said, was because it was *imposed* upon Cuba. Even article three, about intervention, would not be objectionable if it were confined to an action "for preserving the independence of Cuba." Article eight about the Permanent Treaty, López Hidalgo insisted was bad in every way, on the ground that the political and civil conditions of nations are not permanent, wherefore no permanent treaty should ever be made. Cubans ought to form a political party to bring about the abrogation of the treaty, he thought, but the preliminary work should be the political regeneration of Cuba, so as to prove to the United States that the Permanent Treaty is unnecessary. He then proceeded to denounce some of the various evils with which Cuba is afflicted.

The volume of Machado, though exhibiting all the fiery impatience of a young man,—so much so, that the writer of the foreword, Rafael Montoro, former Cuban Secretary of State, said he could not agree with the author in all his conclusions,—is, nevertheless, more directly to the point than the work of López Hidalgo. Like López Hidalgo, Machado held that the Platt Amendment contradicted the

[2] A well-known American statesman, in remarking on this to the writer, said it was indicative of the paucity of words and ideas of the congressmen who subscribed to the Joint Resolution rather than of any intended parallelism in the case of the United States in 1776 and that of Cuba in 1898.

Joint Resolution, and he remarked further that the Permanent Treaty which grew out of it was a unilateral contract, with Cuba having all of the obligations and none of the rights. Nevertheless, it *was* a treaty, but, as such, was quite as open to Cuban interpretation as to that of the United States. In practice, only the American interpretation had been employed, and that had developed into a form of meddling in Cuban affairs that was not warranted by any of the terms of the document. Machado then set forth his own views.

According to Machado some of the paragraphs of the Platt Amendment and the treaty were temporary, since become obsolete, while others concerning Cuban territory were in part fulfilled and in part awaiting the action of the United States, and still others were those that were actively in effect. In the first group he included articles four (for validation of the acts of the United States military government), five (about sanitation), and eight (calling for the permanent treaty). The inclusion of the sanitation article in this group is not in accord with the usual view on that subject. Machado worked it out on the basis of his understanding of the words "the plans already devised," holding that it referred only to the specific projects of the period of General Wood. Articles six (about the Isle of Pines) and seven (concerning coaling stations) were referred to as "the most grievous" for Cubans of any in the treaty. Article six has since become obsolete with the ratification in 1925 of the treaty which recognizes Cuban sovereignty over the Isle of Pines, and the vicissitudes of the coaling station clause have already been discussed.[3] About the only objection Machado had to article one (against making treaties that might impair the independence

[3] *Supra*, pp. 156-159.

of Cuba) was the popular myth that had grown up, not only abroad but even in Cuba, that Cuba could make no treaties without the consent of the United States. Obviously, Machado was right on this score. The right of Cuba to make treaties has never been questioned, and probably will not be, as it is unlikely that Cuba would offer voluntarily to "impair the independence" of the country. As to article two (about public debts), however, there are few who would follow Machado, who seems to have suggested, though in vague terms, that Cuba need not consult the United States before negotiating a foreign loan.

Like most other commentators on the Permanent Treaty, Machado found article three (about intervention) the "nerve" and "axis" of the whole document. Intervention, he pointed out, was a normal right in international law, though to be exercised only in extraordinary emergencies. The American experiment of putting it in a treaty with Cuba had been adopted in later treaties of other nations, as witness in the case of the defeated Central Powers in the World War. That did not mean, however, that they were no longer independent, sovereign countries, and there was no such implication in the case of Cuba. He held that the "preservation of Cuban independence" meant no more than such a guarantee as that of the neutrality of Belgium in the agreements of European powers, and the right of intervention was to accrue only in case of a direct foreign attack; in other words, it was nothing more than a defensive alliance between the United States and Cuba. As for the "maintenance of a government adequate for the protection of life, property, and individual liberty," he quoted a remark which he alleged Elihu Root had made to Méndez Capote in 1901, to the effect that an intervention on that score would take place "only in case Cuba should reach such a state of anarchy as to signify the absence of any government at all." Machado denied the right of the United States to intervene to prevent bad government or even revolution, and also took the position that an intervention ought normally to be preceded by an express invitation of the Cuban authorities.

A competent English student, Sydney Brooks, wrote a series of articles from 1910 to 1914 in which he presented some interesting points of view concerning the Permanent Treaty.[4] He saw in it a "dormant suzerainty" of the United States. According to him it meant that Cuba could not go to war without United States consent or indulge in "financial caprices" that had earned a "noxious immortality" for Nicaragua and Venezuela. Indeed, he felt that it was a great advantage to Cuba. "It would seem as though the experiment of self-government were being tried under more promising conditions in Cuba than obtain anywhere else in or around the southern hemisphere." Capital was almost as safe in Cuba, he thought, as in a state of the United States. Some evils had, indeed, developed to bring the "Platt Amendment," as he preferred to call it, into the limelight, for government was "expensive," with politicians "feathering their own nests," wherefore some elements advocated a more direct and stronger United States control, and even the anti-American politicians did not really want any lessening of the bond. They did show a tendency to go just to the edge of intervention, however, as they had in 1906, in order to achieve their own ends. Thus the Platt

[4] Brooks, Sydney, *Cuba*, in *Fortnightly review*, v. XCIV, pp. 796-808, Nov., 1910; repub. in *Living age*, v. CCLXVII, pp. 653-661, Dec. 10, 1910; *An English view of Cuba*, in *Forum*, v. XLVI, pp. 461-470, Oct., 1911; *The truth about Cuba*, in *Independent*, v. LXXI, pp. 1193-1197, Nov. 30, 1911; *Cuba and the Cuban question*, in *North American*, v. CXCVI, pp. 52-62, July, 1912; *Some impressions of Cuba* in *North American*, v. CXCIX, pp. 734-735, May, 1914. For references to a number of other articles on Cuba by the same author one may look in the *Readers' guide*.

Amendment to some extent put a premium on revolutionary violence, in order to blackmail a party in power through the threat of a United States intervention. On this account a kind of corollary to the Amendment had developed in the shape of "meddling" by the United States to ward off threatened dangers, wherefore the United States ambassador acted as a virtual supervisor or censor of Cuban affairs.

The best American opinion is not unlike that of the Cuban Machado in its main implications. Machado, indeed, quoted writings of Elihu Root, Senator Platt, and James Brown Scott (president of the American Institute of International Law) to the effect that the Platt Amendment, or (to cite what should be considered the superior document) the Permanent Treaty, in no way limited the sovereignty of Cuba and setting forth the same interpretation of the article on intervention. On this score a distinguished American statesman recently took the same position in a conversation with the writer. *A propos* of bad political conditions in the southern republic he remarked that "Cuba has an indefeasible right to stew in her own juice." López Hidalgo and Machado were alike in representing that the Platt Amendment and the treaty were inconsistent with the Joint Resolution, despite Machado's somewhat illogical conclusion that it did not limit Cuban independence at all. The American point of view has been well expressed by John Bassett Moore, an expert in international law and prominent in American national counsels during McKinley's administrations. His statement follows:

"The question whether the Platt Amendment was justified is one upon which, so far as I recall, I have never before been asked to express an opinion. As Assistant Secretary of State during the war with Spain, and as legal adviser to the Peace Commission at Paris, I do not think

I ever heard the question mooted as to whether the United States would be precluded, by the Teller resolution, from taking any measures whatsoever to safeguard the maintenance of peace and order in Cuba after our intervention should have secured for the island its independence of Spain. There was, indeed, nothing to raise this precise question at that juncture. Prior to the negotiations at Paris there existed, as I distinctly recall, a widespread skepticism in the United States as to the feasibility of eventually giving effect to the Teller resolution. Possibly the Spanish Commissioners were not wholly unadvised of this feeling when, early in the negotiations, they proposed to cede Cuba to the United States; and I think they were surprised as well as chagrined when President McKinley declined to entertain the proposal. President McKinley, as you no doubt are aware, in effect compelled the omission from the resolution of intervention, in April 1898, of a clause recognizing the insurgent organization called the Republic of Cuba; and the fact is well known that his reason for so doing was his belief that the United States, in intervening to expel by force the government of Spain, should, in the interest of all concerned, preserve its freedom to deal as might seem best, during the war and at its close, with conditions as they might then be found to exist. This was not conceived to be incompatible with the Teller resolution. Among the grounds on which the intervention of the United States was justified, abroad as well as at home, that which was most generally accepted was the need of putting an end to the disorders that had more or less prevailed in the island during the preceding thirty years. It is a very common thing, as the events of even the past few years have shown, for the period succeeding the establishment, by war, of the independence of a new state, to be characterized by tumults, by disregard of life and property, and by revolutionary activities, growing out of inexperience in government and the personal rivalries of political or military chieftains. It is equally notorious that such conditions have repeatedly given rise to foreign intervention, armed as well as unarmed, without other justification than that which international practice affords. It was considerations such as these that inspired the Platt Amendment; and they were reinforced by the further consideration that the United States would, in conformity with declarations repeatedly made in the course of the preceding hundred years, stand ready to protect the island's independence against attack. In mentioning these declarations, I do not intend to imply that they were wholly altruistic. They were made in the interest of the United States as well as in that of Cuba. This mutuality of interest was fully understood by all those by whom the armed intervention of the United States in behalf of Cuba was urged; they relied upon it for the fruition of their efforts. Mutuality of interest is the principle on which the Platt Amendment is founded.

In making these explanations, I do not intend to enter into the discussion of any of the particular questions of interpretation that have arisen concerning the amendment. I have always believed that the amendment is capable of being interpreted in a sense compatible with the maintenance of Cuban independence and self-government, in substance as well as in form; and I have always acted upon the belief that it should be so interpreted. This was, in my opinion, the intention of the United States." [5]

In fine, stripping the discussions of the treaty of all complaints about the manner in which it was put through, there is very little difference between American and Cuban interpretations. Machado's insistence that the United States has no right under article five to be concerned over Cuban sanitation, however, has a very weak basis to rest upon. The United States authorities were interested in this as a permanent question, to protect the ports of the southern states. On this score General Wood wrote to Secretary Root, on February 19, 1901, as follows:

"There is another phase of this Cuban situation which seems to be of vital importance; that is the sanitary conditions which will probably exist in Havana and other large cities under a Cuban government. As I understand it the purpose of the war was not only to assist the Cubans, but, in a general sense, to abate a nuisance. It is probable that if we leave the island of Cuba without a definite agreement with the government to come in reference to the maintenance of good sanitary conditions, that we shall soon find Havana and all other large cities in practically the same condition of sanitation as during the Spanish War and a menace to our Southern seaports and the consequent interference with commerce will continue . . . It is highly probable that after the withdrawal of the Americans this work will be carried out in anything but a complete and perfect manner. This question of control of sanitation of Cuban ports is, in my opinion, of vital importance to the United States." [6]

[5] Moore to the writer, Mar. 15, 1925.   [6] Quoted in Root, 187.

It was this letter that decided the Washington authorities to write article five into the Platt Amendment.

So, from a strictly legal standpoint, Cuba is independent, despite the Permanent Treaty. Her complete freedom of action is limited, but so is that of any country that makes any treaties at all, or at times even without treaties, when a nation's acts run contrary to the principles of international law. The kinds of things that are required of Cuba have also appeared in the treaties of other countries. The objection on the basis of United States "meddling" has no valid basis, for it is the habit of all ambassadors to take up matters that affect their own country's interests. Is it not true, however, that the interests of the United States in Cuba are so great as in fact to establish a peculiar relationship between them, different from that which ordinarily exists between two sovereign and independent nations? The writer believes that this is so. As Machado put it,

"Cuba is now not merely the key of the Gulf of Mexico; Cuba today is the key of the United States."

And again,

"For the United States the independence of Cuba is a vital subject. Given our privileged geographical situation, equidistant between the two Americas, closing the passage which puts the waters of two worlds and two civilizations into communication, one hour away from American territory, we have the most important strategic position of the whole continent, and the security of the south of the United States is in our hands."

Under these circumstances, are there not some limitations on allowing Cuba to "stew in her own juice?" Is there not some point where the United States might step in, short of actual anarchy or foreign invasion? If so, does not that constitute a virtual protectorate, at least from the standpoint of a moral obligation to help the Cubans help themselves? There are a great many Cubans who feel that this is the case; Machado seemed to believe that they were far more numerous than those who adopted his own view of the Permanent Treaty. Indeed, a general acceptance of the idea of American trusteeship in Cuba has undoubtedly contributed to the economic well-being of that country, and is the sole reason why the bonds of Cuba should sell in the market at a better price than those of Argentina, Brazil, Chile, France, and most other countries. Even so, unless the United States is willing to render Cuba yet more assistance, the island republic is not likely for many years to be anything but the plaything and football of the political class, which represents little more than itself, and not the best interests of the country. So far as the United States is concerned, the matter is not greatly material. With the Permanent Treaty in effect, this country is amply protected from the standpoint of Cuba. The people in Cuba are not satisfied with the way things are going in the island, however, and they look to the future for a change. Opinions range all the way from maintenance of the *status quo,* to annexation to the United States on the one hand, or to an independence divorced from the Permanent Treaty, on the other. It may be well to consider these varying points of view.

Annexation to the United States would be utterly unthinkable except through the admission of Cuba to the Union as a state. That, however, is a contingency that is too remote to merit extended discussion. It could not come until Cuba had attained to a satisfactory domestic situation, as American political practice does not permit of federal intervention in the affairs of the states. Furthermore, many elements in the United States would be opposed to the inclusion of Cuba in the Union. Aside from those who might object on racial or religious grounds, there are powerful business interests, some of them doing business in Cuba and others in the United States, which are immensely better off with things as they are than they would be with Cuba brought within the purview of American law, tariff and otherwise. Some would object, too, on general political grounds, through opposition to "imperialism" or a fear that annexation might have a bad effect on American relations with the other Hispanic American republics. So, while the admission of Cuba as a state may be considered in the realm of possibility, it is perhaps also true that the initiative must come, if at all, from Cuba. Before Cuba would be accepted, however, her own domestic affairs would have to be in such a satisfactory condition that, no doubt, she would then prefer to go her own way as a republic.

Seemingly at the opposite pole from annexation as a state, but really not far away, would be a divorce from the Permanent Treaty. Not until Cuba had attained to such a condition as might entitle her to ask admission to the Union would the United States be likely to give up the treaty, and even then the clause guaranteeing Cuban independence would probably be the basis of some new agreement. The surest way for Cuba to rid herself of the Permanent Treaty, if she so desires, would be to do away with the evils of her political life, including the self-styled "nationalistic" politicians, who shout the loudest against the treaty, though knowing full well that their own pernicious activities are a certain bar to its abrogation.

A great many believe that there should be a more active American supervision of Cuban affairs, especially in the way of financial control, with perhaps also some responsibility for the general course of politics. Foreign business men quite often favor such a change as this, though, curiously enough, that is far more the case with Europeans than with Americans. Not a few Cubans, too, would like to see something of the sort as a temporary measure. It is difficult to see how it could be brought about, however, except as the result of a fresh intervention. Certainly, no Cuban government made up of the present political class would consent to this, and any better element should find it difficult or impossible to get into power, without the backing of the United States; and if it did get into power the need for an increased American control might be unnecessary.

There are some who claim that the next move should be in the direction of a diminished American authority, with the Permanent Treaty retained, but tucked away in a "pigeon-hole," to be used only in an emergency, and with the American ambassador no longer "meddling," but limiting himself to the same sorts of activities as other foreign representatives engage in. This idea results from a misunderstanding of the meaning and implications of the Permanent Treaty. If the treaty is retained it cannot be "used" any less than it is already. The United States ambassador "meddles" more than other ministers because American interests are vastly more important than those of other countries. The next step in the direction of greater freedom of action for Cuba cannot be less than an abrogation of the treaty itself, in whole or in part. As things are, Cuba does as she pleases, and is held in check, if at all, only by the fear of an American intervention,—an intervention which the suggestions (or "meddlings") of the American ambassador are calculated to avoid.

With admission to the American Union as a state or divorce from the Permanent Treaty left out of the reckoning as too remote for present consideration, three possibilities for the immediate future are left for Cuba: a continuance of existing evils, provided they do not get too far out of hand; intervention; or moral backing of the regeneration element by the United States. That the United States is extremely unwilling to intervene in Cuban affairs, the history of the republic has furnished ample proof. Nevertheless, the attitude of the United States is not only permissive of political evils in Cuba, it is charged, but also is virtually responsible for them. Especially is this so in view of the recent American policy of supporting existing governments in Cuba and other Caribbean countries, irrespective of their character. This does, indeed, discourage revolution, which cannot hope to succeed in the face of American aid to the government party, but it also enthrones the political class beyond the possibility of dislodgement. The following comment of a keen-minded, reputable Cuban is interesting:

"The worst thing about the present situation is its utter hopelessness. The politicians are a bad lot,—necessarily so, for democracy in Cuba is a farce. The United States is to blame, for she will not allow revolutions against the government and also will take no responsibility for its conduct. If the United States will not let the Cubans save themselves, she ought at least to take responsibility by selecting a President. The Washington authorities are too indifferent or too timid to do this, however, although it might temporarily solve our ills. There is plenty of reason for an intervention, if the United States cared to go that far, as sanitation is not being kept up and financial matters are handled in such a way as to run contrary to the provisions of the Platt Amendment. If the United States will not take some such step, then she ought to let Cuba entirely alone. That would be better than an uncertainty, although it would mean that the republic would become another Haiti or Honduras. Eventually, Cuba will probably join the United States as a state. That is her real destiny. But what will happen in the meantime?"

From the standpoint of her own interests, it may be no

concern of the United States that Cuba is in the grip of a corrupt political class, but it is conceivable that a continuance of present evils might arouse the Cubans to such a pitch of opposition to the politicians that they would confront both the home government and the United States in an effort to gain real freedom for themselves. A situation might well develop in such an event that would bring a call for United States intervention. In this connection the ease with which millions of dollars' worth of property can be destroyed in the cane-fields of Cuba is worth bearing in mind. In such a contingency there would probably be no prolonged delay to speculate over the meaning of article three of the treaty. The United States would act! Intervention by the United States would be wholly undesirable from the standpoint of the advantage of the northern republic. It cannot be asserted too strongly that American interests do not call for direct control of Cuba; indeed, they are best served when the Cubans can take care of themselves. Nevertheless, no matter what the circumstances leading to an intervention might be, it would be viewed with suspicion in all parts of the world, especially in Hispanic America. And it is true that it is far easier to go into a country than it is to get out of it, afterward. Assuming an intervention, however, what ought to be accomplished? It is possible to name many things,—among others, the following:

I. The lottery should be reformed, but not done away with, since the people would then patronize the Mexican and Spanish lotteries. Provisions should be made for an open audit and for doing away with the enormous profits of middlemen. Politicians should not be allowed to hold collectorships; these should be reserved as a kind of pension for deserving public servants who had retired.

II. Provision should be made for an audit of all municipal and provincial accounts. This has never been done, and in consequence there has been no check on bad practices.

III. A hierarchy of courts should be set up to try offences against public revenues. That would be a step toward the elimination of graft.

IV. Immunity of congressmen from punishment for crime should be done away with.

V. The two-thirds quorum rule of Congress should be abrogated, and process established to compel the attendance of absentees. A Magoon law of "no work, no pay," might be reënacted.

VI. The much needed codes and other forms of constructive legislation already referred to[7] should be prepared and put into operation.

VII. There should be a complete reorganization of education. Many Cubans regard this as the most fundamentally needed reform of all.

Even if these things were done, what permanent benefit would come? Unless the intervention lasted long enough to establish these reforms, as has been the case with the codes provided for Porto Rico and the Philippines, there would be an early, if not an immediate, return to normal Cuban methods, following the departure of the American governor. One cannot change traditions and customs by a few laws. The lifetime of a full generation would be required if the reforms were to become part and parcel of Cuban practices. But of all things, from the standpoint of United States interests, a long intervention is one of the least to be desired. All of the features of the above-mentioned platform would have a much better chance of permanence if they might come as a result of Cuban action

[7] E.g., see *supra*, p. 517.

under Cuban leadership. There are many worthy men who sincerely desire to do all these things for Cuba, but they are helpless, as matters are. They might, indeed, face the Cuban politicians who "own" the government, supported to a considerable extent (as it would be) by the United States, and they might win in the conflict, but Cuba would be ruined. So, naturally, they draw back. If, however, they might have the moral backing of the United States, at least to the extent of the northern republic's not giving direct aid to the politician-owned government of Cuba, then victory might be easy and not too expensive. The present situation does, indeed, offer a curious anomaly of the anti-American political class being kept in power to prey upon their country by the government of the United States. And yet the writer does not go so far as to complain of United States policy. There is much to be said in its favor. Certainly it makes things easier for the United States,—always provided she can depend on the Cuban regenerationists not to risk the economic ruin of their country in a desperate civil war and can keep Cuban governments up to a respectable performance of their international obligations. The United States can well say that it is not in the business of neighborhood reform, and it is an unanswerable argument. Nevertheless, many Cubans feel that the great republic of the north has some special obligations toward the island which differentiate the case of Cuba from that of other countries.

There is, indeed, one final possibility,—a bit improbable, perhaps, but undeniably the best solution of Cuban affairs,—and that is that in some way, through the normal processes of Cuban political machinery, a clean government may come to the fore, without intervention, revolution, or kindred ills. The only possible manner in which a start in this direction can be made is by the election of a President who is at once honest and able. Such a man would probably fail, as Estrada Palma did,—or his work would be without effect, unless he might be succeeded by several more Presidents of the same stamp,—but he would at least have a remote chance for success, and this by the very best method in which it could be attained. It may be observed that this seems to treat the solution of Cuban ills as to a great extent an executive problem. The writer believes that for the immediate future this is true. The time has not yet come for any honest, reasonably well informed man to talk of reform through an early development of Cuban democracy. Eventually that must take place, if the republic is to mean anything, but the start will have to be made in the traditional manner *from above*. The reforms, indeed, must reach into all other branches,—Congress, the judiciary, provincial and municipal government, and the conduct of elections,—but the President must lead the way.

This volume takes the story of Cuba to May 20, 1925. On that day the new President, General Gerardo Machado, went into office. No man could have made any stronger promises than Machado on the score of inaugurating an honest administration. His record in the past had been such that there seemed to be at least a possibility that he was sincere. Though formerly a member of the political class, he belonged to it in a period when it still had some claims to respectability. Leaving it voluntarily, he displayed an ability to make a living and even considerable wealth outside of politics. Not being under any such "necessity" for graft as his immediate predecessor, he may choose to avoid it, and indeed, has stated that he is going to leave the presidency with less money than he had when he went into it, besides initiating reforms to bring about honest government.[8]   Too much reliance should not be placed on expressions of good intention, even granting they are sincere, but an honest and capable executive is Cuba's greatest hope. The best elements in Cuban society would get behind such a man as Machado has promised to be, and when that occurs, whether the man be Machado or some later President, Cuba will have a chance to escape the virtual bondage in which she is now held by the corrupt politicians and to become "Cuba Libre" indeed. It is in the interest of the United States, as well as in that of Cuba, that this should come to pass.

[8] This is not the place to deal with the administration of President Machado, who has been in office less than a year, as this is being written. Some rumors about him have come to the writer's notice that are, in the main, favorable. He seems disposed to maintain good relations with the United States. Prior to his inauguration he made a trip north, visiting President Coolidge in Washington, and since becoming President he has taken some steps along the lines of the moralization program. In particular, he has done some noteworthy things in connection with the problems of the judiciary. Three committees have been appointed to undertake the following code revisions: revision of the civil codes and codes of procedure; revision of the commercial code; and revision of the criminal code. Furthermore, he has started to purify the courts, filing cases against a number of judges on grounds of crime or inefficiency. If Machado carries through these reforms successfully he will have done enough, without more, to make his name famous in the annals of Cuba. Withal, while vigorously attacking evils in his own administration, so it is said, he has avoided any revelation of the scandals of his predecessors, which may in part account for the fact that Congress has supported him. On the other hand, if rumor is correct, he has conducted himself like a typical Hispanic American dictator in certain other matters. He has deported labor agitators by the hundreds. There have been several incidents of the "Lavastida affair" type. Some claim that he has completed the work, begun by Menocal and Zayas, of destroying the democratic character of internal party management, as called for by the electoral law of 1919,—this, in preparation for victory in the elections of 1928. The writer presents these comments about Machado without insisting that they are true or false. One thing, however, he does believe: Machado has a chance to make his name the greatest in the history of the republic. He has ability enough to meet the demands of the situation. But will he avoid the corrupt practices of most of his predecessors? Will he say "No!" to family and friends? Will he carry through the reforms that he has begun? And will he hold an honest election in 1928? If he will do these things, then not Zayas, Menocal, Gómez, or even honest old Don Tomás will have made so good a record. This writer wishes that he may accomplish these things,—or, at least, make an effort to do so.

ESSAY ON AUTHORITIES

The amount of material on the republic of Cuba already reduced to writing is, of course, more than one man could read in ten thousand years. Furthermore, there is an extraordinary lack of well formulated studies that might otherwise save the investigator's time and lead more surely to a well rounded volume of history. Even the preliminary stage of the collection and editing of materials has hardly been reached as yet, except for the bibliographical work of Carlos Trelles. The field is wide open, therefore, for the writer of monographs, who must make his own estimate of the documents, but it is difficult for the general historian. The items listed below are intended to portray this state of affairs. Nearly all of them (and many more, besides) have also been cited in the text. No attempt has been made to attain to adequate proportions in the individual descriptions, since with respect to the more important works the greater part of the comment already appears in the bibliographical footnotes at the end of the various chapters. The following chart shows how the material has been classified for presentation:

I. PRINTED MATERIAL

BIBLIOGRAPHIES

GOVERNMENT DOCUMENTS

A. *Cuban*
B. *United States*

PERIODICALS

A. *Cuban magazines*
B. *United States and other foreign magazines*
C. *Newspapers*
D. *Some noteworthy articles*

BOOKS

II. OTHER EVIDENCE

MANUSCRIPTS

STATEMENTS OF LIVING WITNESSES

I. PRINTED MATERIAL

BIBLIOGRAPHIES

1. Trelles, Carlos Manuel. *Biblioteca histórica cubana* 2v. Matanzas, Cuba. I: 1922; II: 1924. A third volume, not available to the writer, has recently been published.

There are many volumes of bibliography with at least some bearing on the Cuban republic, and, of course, many other books that contain lists of materials on Cuba. It is not necessary, however, to mention more than the single item given here, as an intelligent use of the Trelles *Biblioteca* will take one as far as he may wish to go. This is but one of many bibliographical works on Cuba by the same author,[1] but is the most generally useful of all. Volume one treats more particularly of the colonial epoch, with volume two devoted to the republic. Pages 1 to 129 in this volume deal chronologically with Cuban history since 1898, and 129 to 487 are concerned with special phases of Cuban affairs, such as the Senate, the House, diplomatic history, and the history of provinces, cities, and towns, to name only a few of the topics included. While most of the items are of Cuban origin, the author has made every effort to cite American and other publications as well. Important government documents, periodical articles, and pamphlets are entered as well as books. One novelty in a bibliography is Trelles's own running historical comments interspersed between the items,—a valuable source of information in itself. While it would be possible to pick out some technical inaccuracies in the methods of entry, the substantial character of the work and the facility with which it may be used are such that Trelles deserves to rank second only to Medina, the great Chilean, among the bibliographers of the western world. Certainly his volumes are a treasure-house for the student of Cuban affairs.

GOVERNMENT DOCUMENTS

While one may find scattered documents here and there of the sort often called "primary," other than those emanating

---

[1] Cf. Jones, Cecil Knight, *Hispanic* works of bibliography by Trelles, all *American bibliographies,* Baltimore, published prior to the *Biblioteca.* 1922. This lists no fewer than ten

from government sources,—such as printed letters, diaries, handbills, and public statements,—the number of those at present known and accessible is not very great, and their importance for the general subject of Cuban history since 1902 is not outstanding. Unquestionably much useful material will be found in government publications of such countries as Spain, England, and Cuba's neighbors in the Caribbean, but the documents of the republic of Cuba will, of course, be the most noteworthy, and those of the United States will undoubtedly rank next.

A. *Cuban*

In addition to the publications named below, the Cuban government gets out many others emanating from the different secretariats and various commissions, to say nothing of the haphazard printings of local bodies. Those given here are perhaps the more important among the government publications. Except where place and date of publication are given, all are published at Havana in continuing sets.

2. Academia de artes y letras. *Anales.*
    Published irregularly, since 1916.
3. Academia de la historia. *Anales.*
    Issued as a quarterly, but in fact published irregularly, since 1922.
4. Cámara de representantes. *Diario de sesiones.*
    This has been published since the establishment of the republic. It is concerned with the debates in the House.

5. Cámara de representantes. *Memoria de los trabajos realizados.*
    This covers the transactions of the House, including matter about the organization of the House, proposals for legislation, laws promulgated, and messages from the President. Each volume covers a legislative period of two years, and the set is complete to date.

6. Cámara de representantes. *Mensajes presidenciales remitidos al Congreso.*
    While the messages of the Presidents contained here may also be found in other publications, and while this set includes only selected messages, it is nevertheless an exceedingly convenient medium for the use of the more important presidential communications. Only one volume, taking to March 5, 1917, has so far been published.

7. *Coleccion legislativa: leyes, decretos y resoluciones.*

This contains the laws, decrees, and treaties of the republic. The fifty-three volumes already published are complete to 1916.

8. Cuban census office. *Report on the census of Cuba, 1899.* Washington. 1900. Also published in Spanish at Washington in 1899.

Although issued under the auspices of the United States War Department, this may properly be considered a Cuban government publication. It is the first of three very important volumes embodying the results of the censuses of 1899, 1907, and 1919. Taken together they represent one of the most useful sources of information that can be found. All three were carefully and capably prepared. See items 9 and 13 below.

9. Dirección general del censo. *Census of the republic of Cuba, 1919.* Havana. 1920. An edition in Spanish was published at Havana in 1921.

See comment at item 8 *supra;* also *supra,* p. 608, n. 27.

10. *Gaceta oficial de la república.*

Issued daily except Sundays and holidays, and complete from 1902 to date. It contains all laws, decrees, and regulations of the republic, besides decisions of the Supreme Court and other important matter.

11. *Jurisprudencia del tribunal supremo.*

This has to do with cases before the Supreme Court. Thirty-eight volumes have thus far been issued, covering the period to 1907.

12. *Memoria de la administración del presidente de la república.*

Following the practice adopted by Governor Magoon, the Cuban government in 1909 inaugurated this set of annual reports of the President. Each volume covers the political year, from July 1st to the following June 30. The set embraces a digest of all administration activities, and is complete to date.

13. Oficina del censo. *Cuba: population, history and resources . . . census of Cuba, taken in the year 1907.*

Washington. 1909. First issued in Spanish, at Washington in 1908.

See comment at item 8, *supra.*

14. *Report of provisional administration.* 2v. Havana. 1908-1909. Also published in Spanish at Havana in the same years.

The two volumes cover respectively from October 13, 1906, to December 1, 1907, and from the last-named date to December 1, 1908. These record the activities of the United States provisional government under Governor Magoon.

15. Senado. *Diario de sesiones.*

This is the Senate publication paralleling that mentioned *supra* in item 4 for the House.

16. Senado. *Memoria de los trabajos realizados.*

In like manner this parallels the similar publication for the House noted *supra* in item 5.

B. *United States*

There is a vast wealth of material about Cuba in United States government publications. A moderately careful survey covering the period from May 20, 1902, to 1923 revealed some 825 sets of papers totaling 11,544 closely printed pages, and it is noteworthy that the amount of material published about Cuba is increasing in volume. That is particularly true of matter having to do with trade and investment conditions, although political documents, notably those involving claims, especially Spanish claims, also bulk large. The Taft and Bacon *Report,* drawn upon very heavily for the data in chapters VIII and IX, is one important single item. There is scant point in reciting here the various sets of United States government publications,[2] but some mention ought to be made of the very important work being done in recent years by the Bureau of Foreign and Domestic Commerce, of the Department of Commerce. This gets out daily consular and trade reports, occasional reports of special agents and commercial attachés, and frequently appearing trade information bul-

[2] They are set forth in ample detail in the well-known *Guide to the study of American history* by Edward Channing, Albert Bushnell Hart, and Frederick Jackson Turner (first published in 1896, and in various editions since then).

letins. While Cuba is only one country out of many dealt with by the Bureau, there is no better source of information concerning economic affairs in the island republic than in these publications. The bulletins issued by the Pan-American Union are also noteworthy, as much of their information is derived from consular reports. On the other hand, some of the material in this set is in the nature of pleasant propaganda. Of special note among its publications is the set entitled *American constitutions,* in which (in v. II, pp. 109-154) one may find the Cuban Constitution in both Spanish and English.

Periodicals

A. *Cuban magazines*

Items 2 and 3 *supra* might well have been considered here. Among the other reviews and quarterlies those named below are undoubtedly the most serious and worthwhile for the purposes of the student of Cuban history. All of them are of exceptionally high calibre. Cf. *supra,* p. 635.

17. *Cuba contemporánea.* Issued monthly at Havana since 1913.

Under the able editorship of Carlos de Velasco (cf. *infra,* p. 673) and, more recently, Mario Guiral Moreno, this has won a name for itself as one of the leading magazines in all Hispanic America. While covering a wide range in subject-matter, it has a number of articles that are very important as materials for Cuban history.

18. *Cuba y América.* A weekly magazine, published since 1897, at first for two years in New York, and afterward in Havana, to 1917, when it ceased publication.

Broad in subject-matter, like the preceding. Long edited by Raimundo Cabrera. Cf. *supra,* pp. 634-635, and *infra,* p. 667.

19. *Reforma social.* A monthly review, published in New York from 1914 to 1921, and since then in Havana.

A publication of the influential Orestes Ferrara, devoted to "social, economic, political, parliamentary, statistical, and sanitation questions."

20. *Revista bimestre cubana.* Founded originally in 1831 as the organ of the Sociedad Económica de los Amigos

del País (Economic Society of the Friends of the Country), established in 1793, it lived three years, being edited by the famous José Antonio Saco. Revived in 1911, and published bi-monthly ever since, under the editorship of the distinguished Cuban scholar, Fernando Ortiz.

This important review is one of the leading sources of information about Cuban affairs, especially those having a broad social and economic scope.

B. *United States and other foreign magazines*

Naturally, the material about Cuba appears only incidentally in the magazines of other countries, but there is an especially great number of articles in periodicals published in the United States. A survey of the well-known indices of American periodical literature, *Poole's index*, and the *Readers' guide* for the years from May 20, 1902, to 1925 revealed approximately two thousand articles about Cuba, to which must be added those in periodicals not listed in the above-named volumes and others in newspapers. By far the most important magazine for the historical scholar is the *Hispanic American historical review*, now published by Duke University. Under the able editorship of Doctor James Alexander Robertson, this periodical is the one indispensable tool of the Hispanic American field, and is as useful for Cuba as for the other republics south of the United States. Occasional articles also appear in other serious periodicals. The material in popular magazines is rarely of a high quality, consisting mainly of digests from the New York newspapers or else of uninformed or partisan surveys. Now and then one gets useful data from them, however, and they are always helpful as an indication of the trend of American opinion. The best current sources of information among them are the *American review of reviews* and *Current history*, which give brief summaries of Cuban events, while some of the other magazines, notably *World's work*, occasionally publish longer articles of much interest and value. In the periodicals of other countries the articles about Cuba are fewer in number and usually of less importance.

C. *Newspapers*

The newspapers unquestionably are one of the most important forms of contemporary material for events in Cuba and opinions about them. The Cuban papers have already

been discussed in detail *supra*, pp. 596-603. Except for an
occasional formal article, the newspapers of the United
States and other foreign countries are, of course, much
less important, although they do reflect the outsider's attitude with respect to Cuban affairs.

D. *Some noteworthy articles*

The articles named below are only a few of those cited
in this volume. Another list equally long and possibly
equally important (including a number of articles that
the writer saw but did not have occasion to use) might
easily be drawn up. Of those referred to here, however,
the following would appear to be outstandingly worth
while:

21. Aguayo, Alfredo Miguel. *Factores cualitativos de nues-
    tra decadencia escolar*, in *Revista bimestre cubana*, v.
    XIX, pp. 81-95; Mar.-Apr., 1924.

22. Brooks, Sydney. *Cuba*, in *Fortnightly review*, v. XCIV,
    pp. 796-806; Nov., 1910.

    For a number of other articles on Cuba by the same
    author, see *supra*, p. 319, n. 1, and p. 642, n. 4.

23. Carrión, Miguel de. *El desenvolvimiento social de Cuba
    en los últimos veinte años*, in *Cuba contemporánea*,
    v. XXVII, pp. 6-27; Sept., 1921.

24. Conn, Edward L   . *The crisis in Cuba*, in (Phila-
    delphia *Public ledger*, republished in) Berkeley (Cali-
    fornia) *Gazette*, Nov. 19-24, 26-29, 1923.

    A series of ten articles, with the title for the last
    five changing to *Cuba not free but enslaved*.

25. Crowder, Enoch Herbert. *El memorandum no. 13*, tr.
    Sp. in *Heraldo de Cuba*, Aug. 5, 1922.

26. *Cuba, an American ward again?*, in *Independent*, v.
    CXIII, pp. 35-38; July 19, 1924.

27. Fox, Albert Whiting. [*Articles on the state of affairs
    in Cuba at the time of the Veterans and Patriots'
    movement*], in (Washington *Post*, Sept. 10-14, 1923,
    tr. Sp. in) *Heraldo de Cuba*, Sept. 11-14, 19, 1923.

28. Guiral Moreno, Mario. *Nuestros problemas políticos,
    económicos y sociales*, in *Cuba contemporánea*, v. V,
    pp. 401-424; Aug., 1914.

29. La inmigración china, in Diario de la marina, May 15, 1924.

30. Johnston, Sir Harry. An Englishman's impressions of American rule in Cuba, in McClure, v. XXXIII, pp. 496-504; Sept., 1909.

31. Junta cubana de renovación nacional-cívica. Manifiesto del 2 de abril de 1923, in Heraldo de Cuba, Apr. 4, 1923.

32. Kennedy, W   M. The revolution in Cuba, in Living age, v. CCLXXVI, pp. 463-468; Feb. 22, 1923.

33. Marvin, George. Keeping Cuba libre, in World's work, v. XXXIV, pp. 553-567; Sept., 1917.

34. Menocal, Mario García. Cuba's part in the World War, in Current history, v. IX, pt. 1, pp. 315-318; Nov., 1918.

35. Norton, Henry Kittredge. Self-determination in the West Indies, in World's work, v. LI, pp. 77-84; Nov., 1925.

36. Ortiz, Fernando. La reforma electoral de Crowder en Cuba, in Reforma social, v. XX, pp. 214-225; July, 1921.

37. Pérez, Luis Marino. Cuba and the United States, in Inter-America (Eng. ed.), v. V, pp. 358-361; Aug., 1922.

38. Resultados de la intervención unipersonal: . . . la actuación del general Crowder en Cuba, in Diario de la marina, Oct. 10, 1922.

39. Scott, James Brown. The Attitude of the United States toward political disturbances in Cuba, in American journal of international law, v. XI, pp. 419-423; Apr., 1917.

40. Spinden, Herbert Joseph. America and her duty in Cuba, in Boston Transcript, Aug. 7, 1923.

41. Spinden, Herbert Joseph. Shall the United States intervene in Cuba?, in World's work, v. XLI, pp. 465-483; Mar., 1921.

42. Varona, Enrique José. Discurso leído . . . en la sesión extraordinaria celebrada la noche del 22 de diciembre de 1921, in Academia nacional de artes y letras, v. VI (Habana. 1921), pp. 239-246.

43. Varona, Enrique José. *Nuestra indisciplina,* in *Cuba contemporánea,* v. IV, pp. 12-16; Jan., 1914.
44. Varona, Enrique José. *El talón de Aquiles,* in *Fígaro,* v. XXII, p. 490; Sept. 30, 1906.
45. Watterson, Henry. *Again 'Cuba libre',* in Havana *Post,* Jan. 29, 1909.
46. Whittlesey, D   S. *Geographic factors in the relations of the United States and Cuba,* in *Geographic review,* v. XII, p. 241-256; Apr., 1922.
47. Wigdil, Walter. *Addition without division = revolution,* in *Independent,* v. LXXII, pp. 1352-1356; June 20, 1912.

Books

Obviously, as used here, the word "Books" is meant to include printed volumes not embraced in the other categories already discussed. The list given below does not contain all of the books on Cuba in the era of the republic, as a glance at the invaluable Trelles will readily show. Probably the most important works are named, however, together with some of less consequence to which the writer had occasion to refer. A number of other useful volumes might be mentioned, especially of a general descriptive or economic character, but they are not essential in a broad list. Much valuable material may often be found, too, in volumes only partly devoted to Cuba, but few, if any, are indispensable in a study of the republic. If the books were classified they might fall into the following groups: important histories of broad periods (with the Martínez Ortiz work the sole item!); historical monographs (with Cabrera and Velasco alone deserving inclusion); discussions of particular phases or events of Cuban history; collections of articles and addresses; partisan works on special fields; eulogies; works of description and travel; and important pamphlets. Taken together, they do not constitute a very satisfactory set of materials. The historian must go beyond them to other sources of information. Many of these items have already been described in footnotes in the body of this volume, and in that case a reference is made to the appropriate page. The list follows:

48. Barbarrosa, Enrique. *El proceso de la república.* Habana. 1911.

This is a collection of editorials written by the author during the Estrada Palma and Magoon eras and the first part of the Gómez administration. Somewhat given to extravagance and excessive fault-finding, the volume is nevertheless a useful aid for the period it covers. Cf. p. 225, n. 42.

49. Cabrera, Raimundo. *Mis malos tiempos*. 2 ed. Habana. 1920. The first edition was also published at Habana in 1920.

Although intended primarily as a relation of the author's personal experiences at the time of the Revolution of February, this volume is in fact so well documented and so admirably well done that it is virtually a historical monograph of great merit. For something further about the author, a principal figure in the literary history of Cuba, see *supra*, pp. 634-635. This volume is commented upon in some detail at p. 385, n. 62.

50. Cisneros Betancourt, Salvador. *Voto particular . . . contra el proyecto de lotería nacional*. Habana. 1909.

A thirty-two page pamphlet recording the author's opposition to the lottery bill of 1909, together with some comments of the press.

51. Collazo, Enrique. *Cuba intervenida*. Habana. 1910.

A violent and partisan pro-Liberal volume blaming the Moderates for the intervention of the United States in Cuba in 1906. Cf. p. 225, n. 42.

52. *Cubans of to-day*, ed. by William Belmont Parker. New York and London. 1919.

One of several "Who's who" volumes on Hispanic American countries published under the auspices of the Hispanic Society of America. This has the defects of all such works, which was expressed by a reviewer of the volume for Chile, with a play on the two Spanish words for the verb "to be": "No están todos los que son, ni son todos los que están" (All the really important persons are not included, nor are all those who are included really important). It is nevertheless a very useful compendium as of the date compiled. For some further comment see *supra*, p. 589.

53. Dollero, Adolfo. *Cultura cubana*. Habana. 1916.

A volume of 480 pages, by an Italian. It contains much of historical and contemporary interest, not only on social and economic aspects of Cuban life, but also on literary and scientific matters. Furthermore, there is something about Cubans who have distinguished themselves abroad and concerning foreigners who have made a name for themselves in Cuba. This is supplemented by two later volumes of the same author: *Cultura cubana: Matanzas* (Habana. 1919. 438 pages); and *Cultura cubana: Pinar del Río* (Habana. 1921. 436 pages).

54. Dolz, Ricardo. *El proceso electoral de 1916.* Habana. 1917.

A forty page pamphlet presenting the Conservative argument in justification of the party's conduct in the elections of 1916.

55. Forbes-Lindsay, Charles Harcourt Ainslie. *Cuba and her people of to-day.* Boston. 1911.

This is typical of the better class descriptive works of Hispanic American countries. After a brief historical account, it enters upon a general discussion of the geographical, social, political, and economic characteristics of Cuba, with particular emphasis on economic factors. Although in a sense now out of date, it still has some value as material for history. Among other volumes of this character that have appeared in recent years are those of Charles Berchon (1910), John Brooks Henderson (1916), Alpheus Hyatt Verrill (1920), and those of Franck and Wright entered below at items 56 and 84.

56. Franck, Harry Alverson. *Roaming through the West Indies.* New York. 1920.

This is representative of a large group of descriptive works which include Cuba as part of a wider field. Only some eighty pages are devoted to Cuba. Franck "hits off" Cuban life in an interesting, clever manner, but does not go into it very deeply.

57. González Lanuza, José. *Discursos y trabajos.* Habana. 1921.

While this might be entered in the group of government documents, since it was issued at state expense as a publication of the House, it would seem to be more appropriate to discuss it here as a volume of Gonzáles Lanuza himself. It consists of selections from the *Diarios de sesiones* volumes of the House of

those portions that include speeches of González
Lanuza during the period of his membership, from
1909 to 1915. His speeches on fifty-one different bills
(representing considerably more than that number of
times when González Lanuza spoke) are included,
making a volume of 975 pages covering every variety
of subject-matter before the House in those years.
The work is particularly noteworthy because of the
intellectual attainments and high character of González
Lanuza.

58. Guerra y Sánchez, Ramiro. *Un cuarto de siglo de evolu-
ción cubana*. Habana. 1924.

A "quarter of a century of progress" eulogy, reciting the achievements of the republic from 1899 to
1924. Devoted mainly to a study of economic advance, it nevertheless points out errors in political
life and the lack of attention to education.

59. Guerra y Sánchez, Ramiro. *Historia de Cuba*. Habana.
1922.

A text-book of Cuban history for use in the Cuban
schools. It is interesting as indicative of what Cubans
learn with respect to their own history. Only a
small portion of the volume touches the republic. Cf.
supra, p. 231, and p. 231, n. 10. There are several
other volumes of this same character; for example,
one by Isidro Pérez Martínez (2 ed. 1925), and another by Carlos Valdés Codina (1905).

60. Johnson, Willis Fletcher. *The history of Cuba*. 5 v.
New York. 1920.

This is pleasingly written, but it might better have
ended at 1902, as the part devoted to the republic
(a little over a hundred pages of volume four) is
filled with inaccuracies, and reads like an off-hand
dictation by a Menocal adherent. Volume five is a
descriptive account of Cuban resources. So far as
the republic is concerned, this is the most valuable part
of Johnson's work.

61. López Hidalgo, Ambrosio Valentín. *Cuba y la enmienda
Platt*. Habana. 1921.

A useful discussion of the Platt Amendment and
Permanent Treaty. Taken up *supra*, pp. 638-639.

62. Lozano Casado, Miguel. *La personalidad del general José Miguel Gómez.* Habana. 1913.

   A eulogy of Gómez, especially interesting for its presentation of the personal traits of the likeable José Miguel. Cf. p. 317, n. 61.

63. Machado y Ortega, Luis. *La enmienda Platt.* Habana. 1922.

   Another useful discussion of the Platt Amendment and Permanent Treaty. Taken up in detail *supra,* pp. 639-642.

64. Martí, Carlos. *Forjando patria.* Habana. 1917.

   A eulogy of Menocal, covering his first administration. Superficial. Cf. p. 345, n. 37.

65. Martínez Ortiz, Rafael. *Cuba: los primeros años de independencia,* 2 v. 2 ed. Paris. 1921. The first edition, consisting only of volume one, was published in 1911 at Habana.

   This excellent work, covering the years 1899 to 1909 (though in less detail after 1906), easily takes first rank in the field of historical writings with reference to the era of the republic. Indeed, it stands alone, for there is nothing else that merits being called a first-rate volume of history. That, however, does not in any way reflect upon Martínez Ortiz, whose work would be well to the front if it had fifty competitors instead of none. For further comments, see: p. 124, n. 19; p. 175, n. 27; p. 225, n. 42; and p. 269, n. 26.

66. Merino, Bernardo, and Federico de Ibarzábal. *La revolución de febrero,* 2 ed. Habana. 1918. The first edition was published in Habana in 1917.

   A pro-Menocal account of the Revolution of February. A work of considerable utility, despite its partisanship. Cf. *supra,* p. 385, n. 62.

67. *Military notes on Cuba. 1909.* Washington. 1909.

   Published under the auspices of the United States War Department, this belongs in the category of official descriptive works, but emphasizes military geography.

68. Ortiz, Fernando. *La decadencia cubana.* Habana. 1924.

   Only thirty-two pages long, this pamphlet, because of its amazing collection of data and the distinction of the author, is one of the indispensable items that must be used by the student of Cuban history. It takes the same point of view as the Trelles pamphlet, given below at item 79, that under the corrupt and inefficient management of the politicians the affairs of the republic have been going from bad to worse. Dealing with education, justice, public morals, collective wealth, and public finances, Ortiz marshals a startling array of facts that make his conclusions inevitable. Cf. also: p. 525, n. 24; p. 546, n. 18; and p. 608, n. 27.

69. Pardo Suárez, Vicente. *La elección presidencial en Cuba.* Habana. 1923.

This is a useful volume, presenting an argument against presidential reëlection. From that standpoint the various elections in the era of the republic are discussed, and a number of valuable documents are embodied in the text in substantiation of the position taken by the author.

70. Pérez, Juan de Dios. *Figuras nacionales.* Ranchuelo, Cuba. 1924.

This brief pamphlet (twenty-eight pages long) characterizing the different Cuban Presidents is useful because of the frankness and impartiality of the author, who appears also to have been more than usually well informed.

71. Quesada, Gonzalo de. *Cuba.* Washington. 1905.

Published by the International Bureau of American Republics (otherwise Pan-American Union), this has the usual merits and defects of an exhaustive but official presentation of information. Obviously, because of the early date of its appearance, it is a mere starting-point, so far as the history of the republic is concerned.

72. Rodríguez, Francisco de Paula. *Sociología cubana.* Habana. 1919.

An eighty-three page pamphlet of addresses by the author before Masonic lodges. It contains some worthwhile appreciations of contemporary Cuban psychology and social life.

73. Roig, Enrique. *La ley del dragado.* Habana. 1915.

A legal brief, presented to the Judiciary Committee of the House of Representatives, objecting to the proposed cancellation of the contract of the government with the Ports Company.

74. Root, Elihu. *The military and colonial policy of the United States,* ed. by Robert Bacon and James Brown Scott. Cambridge, Massachusetts. 1916.

Although but forty pages of this volume are devoted to Cuba, that portion is of great importance as concerns the Platt Amendment and United States relations with Cuba, because of the tremendous influence of Elihu Root in these matters. The Cuban section is made up almost wholly of extracts from Root's reports while he was United States Secretary of War.

75. Rousset, Ricardo. *Historial de Cuba.* 3 v. Habana. 1918.

This has to do with local history and description, taking up the six provinces of Cuba in turn, from west to east.

76. Sanguily, Manuel. *Discursos y conferencias.* 2 v. Habana. 1918-1919.

A collection of addresses by a man often pronounced to be the leading orator of his time. Only the second half of volume two, from 1902 to 1916, relates to the republic. This includes twelve addresses, which are of some general interest in connection with questions of the day.

77. Sanjenís, Avelino. *Tiburón.* Habana. 1915.

An attack on Gómez by a man who served as one of his private secretaries during his administration. With all due allowance for the grievance of the author against his former chief, it may nevertheless be characterized as a work of some value for the period it covers. Cf. p. 317, n. 61.

78. *Los sucesos del Prado.* Habana. 1914.

A compilation by various writers dealing with the murder of General Armando de la Riva. Cf. p. 345, n. 37.

79. Trelles, Carlos Manuel. *El progreso (1902 a 1905) y el retroceso (1906 a 1922) de la república de Cuba.* Habana. 1923.

Though a mere thirty page pamphlet, this publication of its distinguished author has an importance out of all proportion to its length. Trelles has accumulated a wealth of data to show that the republic, after making noteworthy progress to 1905, retrograded steadily thereafter. Education, the army, immigration, sanitation, roads, national expenditures, the lottery, and criminality are some of the headings under which he discusses this topic. The Trelles pamphlet is a good companion-piece to the one by Ortiz, mentioned *supra* at item 68. Also cf: p. 412, n. 31; p. 525, n. 24; and p. 546, n. 27.

80. Varona, Enrique José. *De la colonia a la república.* Habana. 1919.

This is a collection of articles and addresses by a man generally regarded as one of the greatest intellectual figures that Cuba has produced. Cf. *supra,* p. 633. Less than a fifth of the volume relates to the era of the republic, but that much is a valuable commentary on the social, economic, and political phases of Cuban history, especially from 1906 to 1915.

81. Varona, Enrique José. *Por Cuba: discursos.* Habana. 1918.

Also a collection of Varona addresses. Particularly notable for its frank discussion of Cuban political ills is the one entitled *Recepción en la academia nacional de artes y letras: discurso leído el día 11 de enero de 1915,* at pp. 315-342.

82. Vasconcelos, Ramón. *El general Gómez y la sedición de mayo.* 2 ed. Habana. 1916. The first edition was also published in Habana in 1916.

This is a brief pamphlet (twenty-nine pages long), by a negro of recognized ability as a journalist, dealing with the race war of 1912 and charging Gómez with responsibility therefor.

83. Velasco, Carlos de. *Estrada Palma: contribución histórica.* Habana. 1911.

This volume, prepared by one of the leading scholars of the republican era, is made up of articles and addresses by Velasco and others which for the most part had previously been published elsewhere. Much of the value of the book is due, however, to the ample data provided by Velasco in footnotes. Taken as a whole the work ranks with that of Cabrera as one of the leading examples of Cuban historical literature dealing with the republic. See also p. 225, n. 42.

84. Wright, Irene Aloha. *Cuba*. New York. 1910.

This volume, which is more fully described *supra* at p. 607, n. 27, is a really remarkable work, not only the best of its class among those on Cuba, but also outstanding in the entire field of Hispanic American description and travel. The author knew the subject with which she dealt, and had no hesitancy in speaking her mind. The book makes a fascinating social study, and is valuable also for economic data as well as for its general descriptive account. It is the kind of volume that never gets wholly "out of date."

II. OTHER EVIDENCE

MANUSCRIPTS

The enormous body of manuscript material touching upon the republic is not yet available, except as one may stumble in haphazard fashion on particular documents here and there. Government files of Cuban and United States bureaus are not open to the investigator, and presumably that would also be true of other countries whose unpublished official papers might happen to have valuable material. As for private correspondence, hardly anybody, if indeed anyone at all, has given a thought to accumulating a collection. Nevertheless, the writer has been able to use important manuscripts, some of which have been cited in the account. A number of others could not be quoted to their source, however.

STATEMENTS OF LIVING WITNESSES

In a subject like the present, where innumerable witnesses have lived in Cuba during the time of the events described,— some of them for the entire period of the republic,—one must inevitably turn to living witnesses for information, or more particularly for opinions. There is, indeed, scant difference between an oral statement judicially made and carefully taken and a printed document, which, after all, is merely the statement written down. To be sure, most statements, even if "carefully taken," are not so "judicially made" as they would be if the author were to publish his responsibility to the world. This defect is to some extent cured, however, where the investigator gathers a number of statements on different sides of the same question, as they tend to check one another. The writer procured hundreds of such statements, but has used them sparingly and only when they represented a widespread opinion of a considerable group or some particularly striking view. While many of those who gave them would have consented to the use of their names, many others would not, and so the writer has followed a consistent policy of not mentioning any of them. At all events the statements do little more than lend color to an account which rests fundamentally on more substantial evidence.

INDEX

677